THE HISTORY OF THE
REFORMATION

THE HISTORY OF THE REFORMATION

by

JAMES POUNDER WHITNEY, D.D.

SOMETIME DIXIE PROFESSOR OF ECCLESIASTICAL HISTORY IN THE
UNIVERSITY OF CAMBRIDGE

Published for the
Church Historical Society

LONDON

S · P · C · K

1958

First published in 1907
New edition . . 1940
Reprinted . . . 1958

MADE AND PRINTED BY OFFSET IN GREAT BRITAIN BY
WILLIAM CLOWES AND SONS, LIMITED, LONDON AND BECCLES

CONTENTS

MEMOIR OF DR. WHITNEY

JAMES POUNDER WHITNEY was born on St. Andrew's Day 1857. His father was vicar of Marsden near Huddersfield, and Yorkshire remained a strong loyalty in Whitney's life. He came up to King's College, Cambridge, as a Foundation Scholar in 1877, having received his earlier education at King James' School, Almondbury, and Owens College, Manchester, under A. W. Ward. His original training was in Mathematics, and he was placed 24th Wrangler in the Mathematical Tripos in January 1881. In those days of undivided Triposes a good man was accustomed to read two subjects concurrently, and Whitney had always spent much time on History. In December 1881 he took the Historical Tripos and was placed at the top of the First Class, bracketed with his friend and contemporary at King's, J. K. Stephen.[1] His Cambridge career was crowned by his election in the summer of 1882 as Lightfoot Scholar and Whewell Scholar.

On leaving Cambridge, Whitney was ordained by Bishop Fraser of Manchester at Trinity 1883, and spent four years (1883–87) as curate of St. James, Birch-in-Rusholme, combining this with an assistant lectureship at Owens College. He was subsequently curate at All Saints, Battersea Park (1887–88) and at St. Mary, Scarborough (1888–90), when he met his wife, Roberta F. A. Champley, whom he married in 1891. In 1890 he became rector of Hempstead with Lessingham, Norfolk, and in 1895 his connection with Cambridge was renewed when his College appointed him to the living of Milton. From 1900 to 1905 he was in Canada as Principal of Bishop's College, Len-

---

[1] To-day, when there are over 200 candidates in either Part of the Historical Tripos, it is interesting to see that then the class list consisted of eight names, including for the first time two women.

noxville, and Canon of Quebec Cathedral, but in 1906 he again returned to Cambridge as Hulsean Lecturer and Chaplain of St. Edward's. In 1908 he was chosen Professor of Ecclesiastical History at King's College, London, where he spent ten useful and happy years in his house at Hampstead. He resigned his professorship in 1918 and accepted the living of Wicken Bonhunt in Essex; but after a few months returned to academic life on his election in 1919 to the Dixie Professorship of Ecclesiastical History at Cambridge, which had been vacant since the death of Dr. Gwatkin in 1916.

The Dixie Professorship had been founded by Emmanuel College in 1882 out of money from the trusts of Sir Wolstan Dixie, who died in 1594. Whitney was the third holder, in succession to Creighton and Gwatkin. His election brought him a Fellowship at Emmanuel. Always a most loyal Kingsman, he rejoiced in this new connection with Cambridge, not least because it symbolised the breadth of his religious sympathy. In his Inaugural Lecture he wrote :

" I pass from King's, founded by the misunderstood King Henry VI as a check upon Lollardy, to Emmanuel, founded to foster Puritanism, and, as I need not say, I do so with hardly any sense of change. Yet, on the other hand, King's was also the home of the great Evangelical Charles Simeon, where he dwelt during his magnificent ministry at Holy Trinity: it was also the home of George Williams, who brought to Cambridge the influence of the Oxford Movement, and it was further the home of Rowland Williams, who wrote in *Essays and Reviews*. And now from King's I pass to Sir Walter Mildmay's College of Emmanuel, founded to support Puritanism, and yet it was the College where Sancroft, afterwards the Non-juring Archbishop of Canterbury, was Master. It was also the home of William Law, the famous Non-juror whose writings so deeply influenced John Wesley, and at a later date John Keble, so that Methodism and Tractarianism own a common father in one commemorated in our chapel windows. I know of no more significant blending of diverse influences and varied thoughts."

He settled in a house in St. Peter's Terrace, which had formerly been occupied by Dr. Hort, where his hospitable table was always open to his friends and pupils, and his library, covering all branches of ecclesiastical history, always available to those who sought it. Living perhaps somewhat aloof from the current life of the place, he was nevertheless assiduous in his attendance at College meetings and at the Boards of the Historical and Theological Faculties.

His comments (on the History Board at least) could be caustic and penetrating; a Parthian shot delivered unexpectedly from an apparently somnolent form often enlivened the proceedings. I shall never forget one occasion, after a long and fruitless debate on some unimportant point, when Whitney rose from his chair to leave the room while business was still proceeding, but before doing so, walked round the table and remarked in a stage whisper: "I should like to alter the whole system." On another occasion when the Board was discussing, perhaps too indulgently, a somewhat impracticable scheme propounded by a middle-aged colleague, Whitney began his speech with the words: "And I also, when I was in London, was much troubled by young men with broad views."

Whitney possessed an astonishing range of historical knowledge. He used to say with pride that he had lectured on every period but one of ecclesiastical history—I forget which the missing period was, but it was short and unimportant. Medieval history was perhaps his chief interest, but he was equally at home in the Early Church and in the Reformation. His mind was extraordinarily retentive of facts, and he had a marvellous bibliographical memory. He wrote comparatively little, but everything he wrote is packed with learning. A few chapters in the Cambridge Histories, two collected volumes of Essays and an excellent text-book on the Reformation, give an inadequate idea of his contribution to knowledge.[1] The catholicity of his sympathies may be seen in the fact that his own work was equally divided between Hildebrand and Wyclif, between Erasmus and Luther. The many-sidedness of history and the inter-relation of diverse influences were leading ideas with him, and he was always attempting to express this in his brief summaries of an epoch.

One reason for the smallness of his published work is that his learning was ceaselessly expended on his pupils and friends

---

[1] With H. M. Gwatkin he edited the early volumes of the *Cambridge Medieval History*, and after Gwatkin's death he formed the link during the difficult period of reconstruction after the War.

—the words are interchangeable. He did not instruct so much as inspire and stimulate, for he spoke as to an equal and his knowledge was largely conveyed in the form of comments upon books. He never confused education with research, though he knew the importance of both. No one believed more than he in the value of original authorities, but he did not overestimate the unpublished or neglect secondary works. His Inaugural Lecture contains an earnest plea for the publication of original texts—both new editions of standard collections and cheap reprints for training students—and at the same time for the better study of secondary writers.

"It is sometimes thought enough to say that History must be written from original authorities. But we should add the rider that it cannot be written solely from them. There must also be a knowledge of secondary authorities. We cannot afford to neglect our predecessors, and we learn even from their mistakes. But that is a slight consideration compared with others. Very often from a secondary writer we get a clue or a suggestion, which, as we think it over along with our original authorities, illuminates a tangled period or a darkened corner. . . . History is its own interpreter. Each successive generation sees some aspect of the original evidence which it alone is able to understand. Of course, in doing this, it runs some risk of reading into the past something of its own modes of thought. But this risk is lessened if there is a continuous school of interpretation going steadily on from age to age and growing as it goes. There will, of necessity, be something in past discussions which each generation must discard, but there is much more from which it can learn."

When choosing special subjects he always prescribed texts with a view to future work, and he always added references to one or two suggestive modern books, and when recommending further reading he knew the just place to be held by old and new, by large and small. At first one was inclined to doubt the wisdom of some of his recommendations—books almost forgotten, like Neander's *Ecclesiastical History*, Greenwood's *Cathedra Petri* or Kington Oliphant's *Frederic II*—but he taught one that good books do not grow old: these books gave a wider vision or a point of view that could not be found elsewhere, and if they were a bit out of date, he knew where they needed correction and where the latest information was to be found. He always encouraged his pupils to continue their

x

studies in later life and kept up a correspondence with them: it would be impossible to calculate the number of lives (especially among the parish clergy) which he must have supplied with intellectual interests and the amount of scholarly work which he inspired.

His ideals in the study of history were those of Ranke and his school—a concrete narration of events, based on documents and leaving no room for the historian's own views to appear. He always regretted the large element of Political Science in the Historical Tripos at Cambridge, and spoke often of the opposition in early years between the views of Seeley and of Ward. He was distrustful of anything approximating to a philosophy of history, which inevitably introduced the historian's personality and general views: men differed in their interpretation of the historical process, but they could agree to get on with the historian's proper job of investigating the evidence.

In appearance an old-fashioned country clergyman, Whitney preserved all his life a simple personal faith and a devout piety. His churchmanship was of the Tractarian tradition, but he fully appreciated the strength and value of the Evangelical and Broad Church schools,[1] though, conservative in Church and State, it is probable that he never felt much sympathy for the newer developments in any of the three parties. His piety was essentially Anglican, deep-rooted, taken for granted, unpolemical. His convictions were strong, but he made little attempt to convert others to them. His belief in the historic episcopate led him to condemn unequivocally the doctrines of Ultramontanism and Presbyterianism, but for Roman Catholicism and for Nonconformity he had respect and appreciation. His friends were drawn from all the churches, and in the realm of scholarship he could work with men of any religion or of none. His religious convictions, his scientific detachment, and his sympathy with all sincerely held opinions reveals itself in all his work.

[1] It is worth putting on record that the books to which he most often referred as giving a just view of nineteenth century religion were Connop Thirlwall's *Charges* and Hort's *Life and Letters*.

Whitney was a great *raconteur*. His recollections, wholly without malice, were extremely racy and amusing. He could bring to life the figures of the past, whether they were his historical teachers at Manchester and Cambridge, A. W. Ward and J. R. Seeley, the great theologian-historians, Stubbs, Lightfoot, Hort, his contemporaries at King's, such as G. W. Prothero, J. E. C. Welldon, A. J. Maclean, J. R. Harmer, J. K. Stephen, and W. R. Inge, his early vicars, Archdeacons Anson and Blunt, or his later colleagues, Acton and Bury, J. N. Figgis and R. V. Lawrence, A. C. Headlam and Kirshbaum Knight.

Retaining full vigour of mind and body till his eightieth year, he determined to collect together the more important of his periodical contributions. After the publication of his *Hildebrandine Essays* in 1932, he turned to his other favourite period, working simultaneously on a collection of *Reformation Essays* and a new edition of his admirable textbook on *The Reformation*. The former was published a few weeks before his death, and the latter, largely prepared in proof, has been completed by the care of Miss M. T. Stead. His work finished, he was taken ill in January 1939 and died on June 17th.

By the generosity of his widow, his desire has been fulfilled that his library should remain available to undergraduates, and about 4,000 volumes will be added to the Seeley Historical Library, where they will form the Whitney Collection on Ecclesiastical History.

R. E. BALFOUR

(*The substance of this Memoir appeared in "The Cambridge Review."*)

BIBLIOGRAPHY OF DR. WHITNEY'S WORKS

The Helvetic Reformation. Ch. X of *Cambridge Modern History*, vol. 2, 1904.

The Reformation, being an outline of the history of the Church from A.D. 1503 to A.D. 1648. Vol. 6 of "The Church Universal" Series. Rivingtons, 1907.

Religious Movements in the Fourteenth Century. Richard Rolle. Wyclif. The Lollards. Ch. 2 of *Cambridge History of English Literature*, vol. 2, 1908.

Reformation Literature in England. Ch. 2, *ibid.*, vol. 3, 1909.

Pope Gregory VII and the Hildebrandine Ideal. Church Quarterly Review, July 1910.

The Historic Episcopate in Relation to the Visible Unity of the Christian Church, paper in the Official Report of the Church Congress held at Cambridge, 1910.

The Jesuits and the Council of Trent. English Church Review, Oct. 1910.

Continuity throughout the Reformation. Essay 6 in *London Theological Studies.* University of London Press, 1911.

The Elizabethan Settlement. Quarterly Review, January 1912.

Conversion of the Teutons. Ch. 16 (b) of *Cambridge Medieval History*, vol. 2, 1913.

The Episcopate and the Reformation. Four articles in the *English Church Review*, December 1915–March 1916.

The Medieval Church in the West and *The Papacy and the Reformation.* Two lectures in *Our Place in Christendom.* Longmans, 1916.

The Episcopate and the Reformation. Our Outlook. Hulsean Lectures, 1906–07. Handbooks of Catholic Faith and Practice. Robert Scott, 1917.

The Second Century, being a series of readings in Church History for Lent and other times. S.P.C.K., 1919.

Gregory VII. English Historical Review. April 1919.

The Study of Ecclesiastical History Today. An Inaugural address . . . given at Emmanuel College, Monday 26 May, 1919. C.U.P., 1919.

Five Short Instructions on the Teaching of the Church about Marriage. S.P.C.K., 1919.

Erasmus. *English Historical Review*, Jan. 1920.

Introduction to Vol. 3 of the *Cambridge Medieval History*, 1921.

Bibliography of Church History. Historical Association Leaflet, No. 55, 1923. (Reprinted by S.P.C.K.)

Constantine and the Empire. Theology, June 1925.

Peter Damiani and Humbert. Cambridge Historical Journal, 1925.

The Reform of the Church. Ch. 1 of *Cambridge Medieval History*, vol. 5, 1926.

A Note on the Work of the Wyclif Society. No. 6 in *Essays in history presented to Reginald Lane Poole*. Ed. H. W. C. Davis. Oxford, 1927.

The late Professor Bury, an Impression. Cambridge Historical Journal, 1927.

Some Notes on the Roman Controversy. Theology, October 1927.

The Council of Nicaea in Relation to Medieval Thought and the Synodical Principle, being the Nicaean Lecture: 1927. Faith Press, 1928.

The National Church and the Papacy. Paper in *The Anglican Communion, Past, Present and Future*, Edited by H. A. Wilson, being the Report of the Church Congress at Cheltenham, 1928.

The Reformation Settlement. Issued for the Education of the Church Electorate Committee by the Press and Publication Board of the Church Assembly. London, 1929.

The Meaning of the Historic Episcopate. Theology, June 1930.

Hildebrandine Essays. C.U.P., 1932.

The Earlier Growth of Papal Jurisdiction in *Cambridge Historical Journal*, 1932.

The Lightfoot Scholarships in Ecclesiastical History. Chapter in *Lightfoot of Durham*, edited by G. R. Eden and F. C. Macdonald. C.U.P., 1932.

Reformation Essays. Published for the Church Historical Society. S.P.C.K., 1939.

R. E. B.

PREFATORY NOTE

I HAD been working for some years with Dr. Whitney on his *Reformation Essays* (S.P.C.K. 1939) and on this new edition of his *History of the Reformation*, and, when he fell ill in the end of 1938, the ' Essays ' being already in the press, I was asked by Mrs. Whitney to prepare the ' History ' for publication. Dr. Whitney had completed the work to the end of the Council of Trent (Ch. XIII), and those thirteen chapters stand as he wrote them. He had discussed the treatment of the Netherlands and of England very fully with me, and had made numerous notes of topics to be included and authorities to be consulted. One or two paragraphs, *e.g.*, that on John à Lasco, he had already written ; but for the form of these two chapters (XIV and XV) I must take entire responsibility. The latter part of the chapter on England (XV), dealing with the Stuart period, I did not venture to rewrite, as, apart from the completed paragraph on Hooker, there was little material among Dr. Whitney's papers.

The two final chapters, on Poland and on the Papacy after Trent, had been revised and the emendations and additions, of which I had Dr. Whitney's notes, have been incorporated in them. It is tragic that he did not live to see the book through the press himself.

In dealing with Dr. Whitney's papers and in clearing up difficult points, I had the invaluable help of Dr. Whitney's most distinguished pupil, Mr. R. E. Balfour of King's, to whom I cannot adequately express my gratitude. He has put all Dr. Whitney's friends under an obligation by the ' Memoir ' and the Bibliography of his works he has contributed to this Edition.

The accuracy of the references throughout the ' History ' is my responsibility.

M. T. STEAD.

INTRODUCTION

The great work of the medieval Church had been to evangelise the nations of the West. In the East it had to maintain itself against Mahomedanism: in the West it succeeded in gaining young and growing nations and moulded them to new ideals of life. The power of the medieval world lay partly in the loftiness of its ideals, and partly in the strength of its institutions. No age ever showed in individual lives a keener sense of duty, a greater readiness for self-sacrifice; the ideals of the monastic life, of the Mendicant Friars, of the greater bishops and of the simpler parish priests, can hardly be surpassed. No age ever threw greater strength into its institutions, as we see even more in religious than in political or social life. The conception of the great Christian society, with its common brotherhood and common life, appealed to the very best side of medieval nature. Under the leadership of the great Roman See, with its apostolic traditions, its missionary zeal, its practical ability, and its advantages inherited from the Empire, the younger nations of the West formed a real Christian commonwealth, expressed in the Church and, on a smaller and less enduring scale, in the Holy Roman Empire. As these nations developed a more vigorous life of their own, the importance of the Empire grew less, and there were even signs, in legislation, in literature, and in diversified tendencies, that it might be hard to combine the vigour of the separate lives with the common unity of the Church. But the Middle Ages, never surprised at contradictions between ideals and facts, had scarcely felt this difficulty.

Medieval ideals and institutions.

The great medieval Popes had been, as a rule, the assertors of moral force, the guardians of ecclesiastical unity. If sometimes they laid more stress on the organisation of the moral force than on the principles underlying it; if they did not always discriminate between ecclesiastical unity and their own control (which was the readiest means

The Papacy.

of enforcing it), these tendencies were natural to the time. For the Middle Ages turned naturally to organising and forming institutions, and the genius of Rome was at its best in practical order and detail. The medieval mind, always quick to seize an idea, had grasped with fervent faith the idea of ecclesiastical unity; it was not given to criticising the forms in which ideas were expressed unless some practical difficulty arose. Broadly speaking, the unity of the Western Church at the close of the Middle Ages meant to most minds the power of the Papacy. The separation of the Eastern Church was indeed a difficulty, but it stood remote from Western life, and at the Council of Florence had reached a temporary union with its brethren, though not a union of hearts. But other issues had brought a greater difficulty closer; the contests of Popes and Emperors, the abasement of the sojourn at Avignon, the scandal of the Schism, the discussions of the Conciliar movement, the many questions raised between Popes and kings, and even inside the hierarchy itself: all these had left behind a mass of thought and literature, undigested by the generations who inherited it, remote for the most part from their lives and need, yet awaiting examination and certain to be examined. But Papal obedience and ecclesiastical unity had been so long practically identical that to question the former might easily seem to impair the latter. Far-sighted critics like Sir Thomas More could see that here lay the problem of the coming time, which men would solve in different ways.

The later Popes had indeed forced on this problem. The connection between Italy and Germany—the legacy of the Empire—had entangled the Papacy in politics. Italy had a nicely balanced State-system of its own, while Germany, with its lack of central power and its sharp local divisions, was politically the least stable State of Europe. This relation, therefore, led to many complications and disturbances, intensified by other causes. The appearance of the French in Italy opened up new possibilities to the Papacy after it had safely brought its power, increased rather than diminished, through the storms of the Councils of the West. By a process of growth comparable to that of the Prince-Bishoprics of Germany, the Papacy had gained possession of its Temporal States, and these now needed reconquest and consolidation. Sixtus IV (†1484), like other Italian princes, had pursued dynastic schemes for the benefit of his family; Alexander VI (1492–1503), with the help of his son, Cesare Borgia, aimed further at a re-establishment of the temporal power. Henceforth the Papacy had its own territorial interests to consider, and Italian politics brought it into rivalry with France, Germany and Spain. At a time when the great nations were becoming strong and separate powers, with objects of their own, a great strain was thus put on the old ties of ecclesiastical unity. Forces of disunion were at work which the Middle Ages had developed but not brought to their fullest strength; the task of maintaining Christian unity was harder because the Papacy, hitherto its great and often unselfish guardian, had now territorial and dynastic interests of its own to which more sacred interests were often sacrificed. These interests weighed strongly with Popes, secular rather than spiritual in tone, Italian in their diplomacy and state-craft.

The problem of the relations between the Papacy and the monarchies of Europe had already presented itself to the Middle Ages, and was for them identical with the The relations of Church and State. But the great Papacy Councils of the West had brought into greater and the clearness a conception of an ecclesiastical unity European distinct from Papal supremacy, a distinction which increased States. historical knowledge and study of primitive times was bound to emphasise. Each nation, moreover, had its own peculiar features. Germany had Prince-Bishops, sometimes laymen in all but name, sprung almost as a matter of course from noble families, often involved in the dynastic and local feuds that abounded there, independent in many respects of Emperor or Pope. In Spain the Church was noted for the rigid and spiritual lives of its bishops, and had become closely bound up with the royal power, itself deeply religious in tone. In France the bishops were practically dependent upon the

Crown; liberty from external interference meant subjection to internal control. In England strongly expressed anti-Papal legislation was often ineffective in action: theoretical anomalies in royal and Papal relations were disregarded: ecclesiastical appointments, especially to bishoprics, were matters of bargain between King and Pope. If the Papal jurisdiction was exercised in much the same way throughout Europe, these lesser differences ought not to be overlooked, and it should be borne in mind that the restraints placed by France and England upon Papal taxation over the clergy had led to increased demands upon Germany. That country had, therefore, a special interest in administrative reform. Many such questions of reform had been raised in the great Councils; but the Papacy, by its diplomacy, had evaded the demands and emerged from the struggle stronger than before. The Councils had failed to do what was needed and expected: men looked to the Papacy—the power which had overcome the Councils—to succeed where they had failed. But the Papacy had special objects of its own: the very Concordats [1] with England and Germany by which it had gained its victory, and the unsettled controversy on Gallican liberties, not only tied its hands, but also recognised the existence of national interests and divisions that worked against unity. The unity of the Western Church was threatened with inevitable dangers, made more acute by the condition of the Papacy itself. For the Papacy might indeed as before represent Western unity; but it did little to strengthen or even preserve it.

And there was a further cause of danger. The Middle Ages, strong in their institutions, regarding man as a member of a guild, a community, or a church, had tended to repress the individual. But now in politics and in trade, in life generally, individual character was asserting itself. The change in art was typical. The great artistic works had been up to now, and for the most

Growth of Individual- ism.

[1] See Creighton, *History of the Popes during the Reformation* (large edn.), I. pp. 406–7, and *Appendix*, pp. 450–51; for the German Concordat see Geiseler, IV. p. 302. The English Concordat in Wilkins, *Concilia*, III. p. 391: see Makower, *Constitutional History of the Church of England* (English trans.), p. 45.

part, buildings, expressions of a corporate life in which the artist's name and individuality were sunk; art now threw itself into channels where individual force and individual names were to be joined for ever. The founder, for instance, of a new order, the teacher in a university had been less than his order, less than his system. St. Dominic is for us the first of his order; St. Thomas Aquinas, the writer of the *Summa* ; Wyclif, the almost impersonal head of a movement. In the newer age that was coming St. Ignatius Loyola is a personality that inspires his order; Erasmus and Luther are personalities above all else. The contrast carried itself into remoter corners; it was certain the life of the Church would be richer because more varied in its individual parts, but it would not be easy to balance claims of authority and individual freedom which the older world had hardly felt to conflict.

Much is often said of the moral disorders and licence, partly due to growing riches and changing tastes, that marked the fifteenth century. It was as easy to see the ecclesiastical abuses; tardy or even corrupt courts at Rome and elsewhere; excessive fees and corruption; vows made but disregarded; duties unperformed. The older monastic orders—themselves products of earlier reformations—did little to mend matters. The evidence for their widespread corruption is inconclusive, especially in England, but they no longer served their original purposes: extreme poverty or too great wealth brought each its own perils. The average monastic life was not indeed impure but it was no longer strenuous, and new foundations were therefore few. The Mendicant Orders—Franciscans and Dominicans—had also, although to a smaller degree, grown cold from their first enthusiasm. It was felt that the exemptions from episcopal control (a departure from primitive rule), given so freely to monasteries and generally to the Friars, had been unwise, and fresh powers of visitation were widely sought. Archbishop Warham in England (1511) and Cardinal Ximenes in Spain had exercised large powers of monastic visitation intended to quicken and reform religious life.

But the Church has never, even at its worst, rested content in face of moral or administrative evils: the quickening of life—always a strain and an effort—has always been marked by the bringing out from its treasuries things new and old; sometimes it puts new life into old forms and institutions; sometimes it develops new organisations or new forms of devotion. All these features we can see in the years just before the sixteenth century; apart from "the Reformation in Head and Members" urged by the great Councils, mysticism, a deeper religious learning, new discipline of life, new forms of devotion, all bore witness to the reviving strength of the Church, and the new demands new needs made upon her. Pilgrimages, shrines, relics, had never been more highly regarded: some special cults (such as that of St. Anne)[1] developed rapidly at the end of the fifteenth century; whatever is thought of their virtue in themselves, their popularity is a sign of devotional feeling. As significant, too, is the growth of religious literature in the popular tongues, the increased influence of popular preaching. Nor was biblical study neglected; Gerson, the great theologian of France, wished to simplify theology upon this basis: in Germany theologians like John Wessel (1420–89) took the same line; the University of Erfurt (founded in 1392) was noted for its modern spirit and its biblical exegesis illustrated by Matthias Döring [2] (†1469); translations of the Bible into High German had appeared before the days of Luther, but they were made from the Vulgate, while Luther used the original versions.

These attempts to remedy evils in life and to place theology in a fresh light both for study and teaching showed them-

Monastic Revivals.

selves in many ways in Germany; in the monastic and semi-monastic orders they led to a return to original rules and a stricter visitation of evils. Among

---

[1] *Der Cultus der heiligen Anna am Ausgange des Mittelalters:* G. Schaumkell (Freiburg im B.), 1893.

[2] *Matthias Döring, ein deutscher Minorit des 15 Jahrhunderts:* P. Albert (Stuttgart: 1892). Döring also had plans for organising his Order and opposed those of his superiors. For the Bible: Acton's *Lectures on Modern History*, pp. 102–3.

the Benedictines John Busch, a monk near Bursfeld, organised the Lower Saxon convents and set up a type which was
largely followed over a larger area; seventy-five foundations
joined the Bursfeld congregation. Among the Franciscans
a lapse from original ideals had brought on the struggle
between the Conventuals (who had already adopted laxer
rules and more settled homes) and the Observants (who
desired a stricter observance of the Founder's life of poverty
and alms): here, again, a reform took place. Diedrech
Coelde, writer of a simple catechetical exposition of belief
and duty, *The Mirror of the Christian*, and a well-known
itinerant preacher, reorganised his order in North Holland,
Belgium and the Rhine district. The movement spread to
the Augustinian Friars, first organised by Zolter (under
Pius II in 1438) and later by Andreas Proles, their Vicar-
General (1473–1503). John von Staupitz, the teacher of
Luther, carried on and extended the work. All these were
monastic reformers—hating existing evils, inspired by the
old monastic ideals, spending themselves in education and
preaching, freely able to use the new ally of instruction, the
printing-press—animated by a deep love of their Saviour
often most touchingly expressed.

It was by an Italian continuation of this movement that
(1504) the Italian Benedictines also were reorganised; that
among the Camaldolites a separate and strictly ascetic congregation was formed; that Matteo de Bassi (1526) gathered the
Capuchins—a strict section of Franciscans marked by their
more Franciscan life and their pointed hood (*cappucino*).
The last—a genuine revival of their order, both in their
preaching and in their popular sympathies—did much for
the Church, and became a separate order in 1619. Among
some members of "The Oratory of Divine Love," formed
among the more religious Humanists at Rome (1523), arose
the Order of Theatines (1524), named from the See (Theate)
of its leading member, Caraffa, afterwards Paul IV. Caraffa's
sojourn in Spain and his tastes brought him into touch with
the strictest Spanish theology and the stricter clerical life of
the seculars; this element, combined with the better impulses

of the Renaissance, was seen in the Theatines, who, as secular priests under monastic vows, devoted themselves mainly to preaching, care of the sick, pastoral duties generally, and the training of the clergy. Somewhat similar was the Order of the Barnabites (1530). But the rapid growth and great influence of the Jesuits—themselves a part of this widespread movement—was to overshadow these earlier and lesser branches of it.

The work of the learned Cardinal Nicholas (Krebs), of Cusa, as Papal Legate in Germany (1451), was similar. A former advocate of the Conciliar theory, he now worked for the Papacy, whose power for reform was, in his opinion, not exhausted, as was the Council's; from Salzburg to the Netherlands he journeyed, preaching with great effect, holding Synods (which were more frequent now, as in all days of reform), and visiting the monasteries. "He," says Trithemius (himself a worker of the same class), "appeared in Germany as an angel of light appears in the midst of darkness and confusion; he re-established the unity of the Church, strengthening the authority of the visible head, scattering abundant seeds of new life. . . . God was the starting-point of all his knowledge—the glory of God and the bettering of mankind the object of all his wisdom."[1] We are too apt to consider the work of ecclesiastical and monastic discipline as purely technical, but this new and firmer discipline enforced a high ideal where it was most needed, on the priests and teachers of all; the restoration of monastic discipline meant not only the removal of scandals, but the increased efficiency of what were at once schools, religious communities and the medieval counterparts of our religious societies.

Amid general tendencies and broad results isolated currents of thought can often be noticed. One such had existed in

Mysticism. Brethren of the Common Life.

Germany in the School of Mystics, necessarily more absorbed in the personal than the social side of religion. But even such influence joined with others to keep alive the ideal and the practice of the Church; they were in no sense heretical in doctrine, they

[1] I owe this reference to Janssen, *Geschichte*, I. p. 4 (German edn.).

were not even anti-Papal in politics. Many of these influences were grouped around centres of that remarkable society the Brethren of the Common Life.

Founded at Deventer by Gerhard Groot (about A.D. 1380) [1] with a simple and practical aim—the improvement of life and the work of education—the Brethren were afterwards organised upon a semi-monastic model. Their spread was rapid, and they soon became the leading influence in the Netherlands and North-West Germany. Copying of MSS., and later on the printing of books, were among their practical works; the love of classics and a sound religious tone were the chief marks of the education they gave. Not only the Bible, but the Fathers also, were the objects of their study: if some of their pupils equalled Italians in their learning, most of them surpassed the Italians in the purity of their lives. Germany, and not Italy, was the earlier field of the popular Renaissance; from 1456–1506 no less than nine universities were founded, and the movement there had an ethical and practical tone lacking in Italy. Of this German Renaissance the Brethren of the Common Life were, above all, the forerunners and the authors. Their history belongs to the century before the Reformation, but their importance is greatest in the Reformation period itself, for their labours began a movement sometimes called the Catholic Reformation, sometimes the Counter-Reformation, a movement too often regarded as a mere reaction against the Protestant Reformation, beginning only when that had spent its force. But a truer conception is to see the origin of both Protestant Reformation and Catholic Reformation (or Counter-Reformation) in an impulse earlier and wider spread than either, and containing the germs of both. In that earlier movement the Brethren of the Common Life played a leading part.

The Revival of Learning—a phrase often used to imply more ignorance on the part of the Middle Ages than they possessed—covers to a large extent separate movements in

---

[1] See Ullmann, *Reformers before the Reformation* (T. and T. Clark, 1855), Vol. II. pp. 59 *seq.*; Groot's Letters in Mulder, *Epistolæ Gerardi Magni* (Utrecht, 1933).

Italy and Germany.[1] In the former it was classical, artistic and sometimes even pagan; in the latter it was practical and educational, allied to theology. In England, under Grocyn, Colet and More, it was more akin to the German type. Under Nicholas V the Renaissance captured the Papacy itself. The Curia—that group of officials, who often bought their posts and lived on their fees, whose interest lay in opposing reform—was now deeply tinged with the classical spirit, somewhat indeed with the pagan. Absorbed in its politics, affected mainly by the Italian side of the Renaissance, the Papacy was out of touch with the better side of ecclesiastical life. It was a problem whether the energy and power of this great movement could ·be controlled and guided by the Church. Julius II saw the problem, and so far as art and architecture went, he solved it. But other Popes hardly saw the difficulty or the chance, and the merits of Leo X have often been exaggerated in this direction. The failure of the Conciliar movement had left the Papacy the guardian of the Church's unity, the official leader of any possible reform. But it was not until well into the sixteenth century that it rose to the height of its work. Hence it was that a man like Erasmus, the product of the early German movement for reform, was in imperfect sympathy with the Papacy itself while an advocate of all that the Papacy originally stood for.

The Revival of Learning.

In Spain no less than in Germany the Church had passed through a critical time. The constant presence of the Moors, the seeming need of a crusade against these tangible enemies of the Cross, had given Spanish Christianity a character of its own—serene, lofty, enthusiastic on the one hand, but self-absorbed and intolerant on the other. Circumstances had led to a closer union of Church and State than was found

[1] For Italy, Jacob Burckhardt, *The Civilisation of the Renaissance in Italy* (trans. by S. G. C. Middlemore). For France, A. A. Tilley, *The Literature of the French Renaissance* (2 vols., Cambridge, 1904) and *From Montaigne to Molière* (London, 1908); R. C. Christie, *Etienne Dolet* (London, 1899), Imbart de la Tour, *Les Origines de la Réforme* (3 vols., Paris, 1914). Generally, *The Cambridge Modern History*, Vol. I. Chaps. VII, IX, XI, XIII, XIV, XVI–XIX.

elsewhere. The relations with the Papacy were regulated by the Concordat of 1482, by which the Crown gained the nomination to bishoprics, converted under Adrian VI into the right of presentation. The royal right of "Placet," together with the anti-Papal enactments of the Cortes, had limited (much as in England) Papal jurisdiction and taxation. The Inquisition, after a long medieval history, had been revived: in Aragon by Ferdinand (1483) and in Castile, with more hesitation, by Isabella in 1480. Twenty years later the right of appeal from it to the Pope was done away with, and henceforth it was an instrument of civil government at times too strong for the power controlling it. The Papacy was ready to restrain its powers, as desired to do by the Cortes of Aragon under Charles V, had not the King protested. Where the royal power was so great many rulers would have used the Church purely for their own political ends. It was the peculiarity of "the Catholic sovereigns," as they well deserved to be called, to place before themselves a high religious ideal. Queen Isabella found a Cardinal strenuous fellow-worker in Cardinal Ximenes, Ximenes. a strict Franciscan and after 1492 her confessor. In 1495 he was raised to the rich and important archbishopric of Toledo, although he was less aristocratic than his predecessors. He carried on both among regulars and seculars a work of reform. Strict monastic visitations and the appointment to high offices and bishoprics of men of only the highest character changed the ecclesiastical tone of the country. And with him learning as well as piety was essential. His national feeling led him to revive the old Spanish Liturgy of the so-called Mozarabic Rite. This had grown up in earlier centuries and had been approved by Pope Alexander II (1065), but Gregory VII tried to replace it by the Roman Use. Before the days of Ximenes it had disappeared: he, however, restored it at Toledo and reprinted it (1502). But this part of his ideal had less success than his wider scheme of a vigorous, learned and purified Spanish Church. His own foundation, the University of Alcala (1498), produced the Complutensian Polyglot, and its biblical studies were as famous as the scholastic attainments of its older rival, Salamanca. At the latter university the influence of Aquinas was supreme, and hence Spanish theologians gained a reputation for depth and conservatism, joined to a high level of life. It should be set against the frequent cruelty of the Inquisition that under Ximenes it was used to enforce upon the clergy a rigorous purity and zeal.

If, then, the evils from which the Church suffered were great, it was something that they were admitted and that their removal had been attempted. Means of reform—local movements of reform in varied directions—were at hand to help a general movement. Higher ideals of life, new heights of learning, had been held up to, or indeed by, the expiring Middle Ages. It was important for the world, when political causes and jealousies—national and dynastic—were rending it, to realise its ecclesiastical and spiritual unity. But new forms of life, new currents of thought, are hard to control. And the future of Europe, at any rate, depended upon the spirit and vigour in which the Church approached her task. Signs of danger and of promise were strangely mingled. Would the leaders of the Church have the sagacity to see them both? Would they have the power and the courage to seize the one and escape the other?

II

THE PAPACY AND THE LATERAN COUNCIL

ON August 18, 1503, Alexander VI (Borgia) died, as it was said, to the unspeakable joy of all Rome. Even he had acknowledged, somewhat tardily, the need for reform in discipline, although his great aim had been to consolidate the States of the Church. A commission had been appointed to consider what was needed, and it had reported (1497)—sales of benefices were to be prohibited, pluralities, even if held by Cardinals, to be restricted. This impulse to better things, however, soon passed away under the stress of politics and dynastic projects. The Conclave that followed his death—divided into French, Italian and Spanish parties—compromised by the election of Pius III (Cardinal Piccolomini, a nephew of Pius II), worthy in character but aged and sickly. Wide reform and a council were promised. The Archbishop of Mayence formulated the needs of Germany, which, repeated in 1457, 1510 and 1522, may be summarised mainly as reforms in Papal relations, ecclesiastical finance and patronage. But these hopes were ended by the new Pope's death (October 18). On All Saints' Day Guiliano della Rovere succeeded and became Julius II. His Papacy (1503–13) was filled by Italian wars, in which as a patriot and even as a soldier the Pope played a leading part. By the League of Cambrai, formed against Venice (1508), he gained for the Papacy Ravenna (that old rival of Rome), Rimini and Faenza; by the Holy League, formed against France by him with Venice, Spain and England (1511), he further gained Parma and Piacenza. Thus he consolidated the temporal power. Criticism, both then and since, has dealt severely with the warfare and diplomacy that gained his end. That end was frankly secular; indeed, the only approach to spirituality in Julius was his grand and deliberate employment of art at its best. But without the Papal States the Pope would have been undoubtedly weaker; the absence of possessions does not always imply freedom from cares, nor

Julius II, 1503.

13

the lack of temporalities a gain of spirituality. For influence in Italian politics the Papal States were a necessity to the Popes; their existence caused no more scandal (except to idealists) than the possession by a bishop of lands or fiefs. Claims to these territories, variously founded and not always enforced, had been acquired by a process centuries long. But when gained, the territories had been ruled more as estates or fiefs than as an ordered State; vassals inside and outside had held the real power, and it was not until the days of Julius II that the Papacy really ruled in its own territory. When churchmen elsewhere were striving at high moral aims, the secure acquisition, or even the peaceful ordering of territory seemed a poor ideal by comparison. But this policy gave the Papacy a sure footing in Italy, without which its influence at this time would have been small; and the wealth of the Popes, especially their affluence in ready money, made them desirable allies. Italian sympathy went with Julius; his policy was manly and respectable, even if his warfare (like his notorious evil life), was unsuited to a Pope. At any rate, it made the Papacy a power to be reckoned with in politics, and in Italian politics it was of the first importance.

There was here nothing very lofty, such could hardly be looked for from Julius' character, but his edict against simony in Papal elections, published on his accession and further recommended to the Cardinals on his death-bed, was a slight sign of better days.

Lewis XII of France, "the eldest son of the Church," when annoyed by Papal policy could retaliate upon the Pope **Anti-Papal Policy of Lewis XII.** by exchanging spheres of action. Attacked by the Pope in politics he could reply in spiritual matters. A French Synod called (September 14, 1510) at Tours[1] urged reform, condemned the Pope's action, affirmed the King's right to defend himself even by withdrawing his obedience, and appealed for justice to a General

[1] *Le Concile Gallican de Pise-Milan*, A. Renaudet (Paris, 1922), founded on Florentine MSS. with a good short Introduction. *Histoire des Conciles* of Hefele continued by Hergenröther, revised by Leclercq, Vol. VIII, Pt. I, pp. 275–84 (Tours) and pp. 323 *seq.* (Pisa Milan).

Council. Next year, in the midst of these political difficulties and of a campaign where Julius commanded in person, five discontented Cardinals, headed by the Spaniard Carvajal, called a Council at Pisa for September 1, 1511. The Pope's reply was to fulfil tardily his earlier promise by summoning a General Council to meet at the Lateran on April 19, 1512.

Its objects were to extinguish schism, reform the Church, and arrange a crusade against the Turks, who were a constant danger to Europe. But taken as a reply to Lewis this summons lost much of its grace and power. The obedience of other sovereigns was not too sure. Maximilian in Germany had not only assumed the title of Emperor, although not crowned by the Pope, but amid his countless plans had even dreamt of becoming Pope as well as Emperor. And Diet after Diet had long placed ecclesiastical reform among the first necessities of the Empire.

Maximilian sought advice at this time from the great Heidelberg scholar Wimpheling. The Emperor had thought of introducing a Pragmatic Sanction as in France (by which his jurisdiction and right of nomination to offices would be secured), of appropriating the annates (here following Spanish precedents), and, lastly, of obtaining practical independence for the Church in Germany under the guidance of a permanent Legate with the fullest power. Wimpheling's advice was to proceed by reforming the financial and judicial relations between Germany and the Curia rather than by such radical changes as suggested. The evils he named had been complained of in 1457, and were to appear in German *gravamina* again and again before their final appearance at Trent in 1561. The greater freedom of France and England had increased the Papal demands upon Germany, and the failure of all reforms in her politics threw stress upon the needed ecclesiastical reforms.

The Emperor Maximilian.

The attempted Council at Pisa fell somewhat flat, in spite of lukewarm support from France. The Council called by Julius, on the other hand, slightly postponed by some French successes, at length was opened on May 3 (1512) with an eloquent sermon by Ægidius of Viterbo on the need of reform and of a Turkish crusade. After declaring its rival at Pisa schismatic it was prorogued to November 3. By that time Maximilian had given his adhesion to the Lateran assembly, and sent Duke George of Saxony to urge reform. The delicate question of the French Pragmatic Sanction had also been opened, but affairs moved slowly. On February 20, 1513, Julius died.

The new Pope, Leo X—Giovanni de' Medici, son of Lorenzo the Magnificent—was an Italian, skilled in politics, but lacking the restless energy and force of Julius

Leo X, 1513. II; in himself he was a child of the Renaissance with all its love of ease and beauty, but his official patronage of art and literature was slight and ineffective.[1] For a time the wars of the Allies against France lingered on, but if the aims of Julius, now the aims of Leo also, were to be reached, and a schism to be avoided, peace had to be made. The schismatic cardinals were pardoned and (December 19, 1513) the submission of France to the Council received. The easy schism thus easily reconciled, questions of doctrine came up for discussion, and the philosophic crudities of Italian philosophers led to a decree against deniers of the soul's immortality. The committee appointed to prepare a scheme of reform reported, but mainly in general terms; there were no adequate attempts to meet the reasonable complaints of Germany and France; the restrictions now placed on pluralities could be easily evaded (May 1514). Next year a decree limited exemptions from episcopal control; yearly visitations of convents so exempted were to be made by the diocesan.

Another decree ordered that all cases concerning benefices (except those reserved by the Pope) should, in the first instance, come before the bishop. Yet another decree

Censorship of the Press. placed the control of all printing-presses in the hands of the bishops. Everybody felt that some guidance and restraint was needed, but there were differing views as to the proper authorities to exercise it. Many held that the Church, specially bound to teach in the sphere of religion, was the proper body: others held that the

[1] See *Camb. Mod. Hist.*, II, c. 1 (F. X. Kraus).

Universities, teachers in all branches of learning, could do the work better. Much was to be said on either side: with the printing press a new force had come into the world, and it would be the better for guidance. There was much in Milton's later argument that truth would prevail in the end and should therefore be left free, but not every writer was inspired by motives solely good: some men might pour forth mischief-making pages with bad ends in view. For such writers a check was needed, as we indeed with more experience must feel to-day. Only experiment could find the best plan to follow. So we come to indexes of varying value put out by varying bodies with different motives and different skill. The plan adopted by the Council was to place the control of all printing-presses in the hands of the bishops.

The idea of the assembly was not any new legislation but the enforcing of old rules, much as Colet urged on the English Southern Convention in 1512: one most-needed decree insisted once again on the frequent meeting of Synods, a feature of Church life which had shown itself in every time of reform and also of late specially in Spain and Germany. More, however, had been looked for from the Council, and had it not been for the friction, hardly restrained by the Pope, between cardinals and bishops, more might have been gained. Against the Curia the bishops were almost powerless, but against their old foes, monks and Regulars, they had some success.[1] Controversy between them lasted for four years, and Ægidius of Viterbo, Vicar-General of the Augustinians, has left us a lively account of it all. We have the demands of the Bishops, clearly dissatisfied with the administration of the College of Cardinals, and we have the criticisms of the Regulars, who made a skilful appeal to the ever-growing power of the Pope. The Bishops took up the plan of a close association among themselves with executive officers and assemblies when needed: in this way their rights, especially against the Regulars, might be defended. But such an organisation

Results of the Council. The Curia and the Bishops.

[1] See Hefele-Leclercq, *Les Conciles*, Vol. VIII, Pt. I, pp. 451 *seq.*

might easily bring danger to the powers both of the Pope and of the College of Cardinals: it would certainly be inconvenient to them: so it was opposed and came to nothing. For a time the Regulars had great anxiety but, in the end, it was decided that the already existing administration by Pope and Cardinals would suffice. The bishops had hoped for more from Leo X than they had been able to get from Julius II, for it was not in pure irony that he had spoken of trying to please everybody: to do so would ensure his own ease, which he always greatly desired, and in the end the bishops did gain a little more control both over monastic houses internally and over the preaching of their members outside. It was a somewhat scanty result, but the suggestion and the spirit of the bishops was significant. Papal centralisation, on the one hand, and monastic exemptions on the other, had made large inroads upon the primitive powers and independence of bishops. These difficulties were to find more vigorous expression and to become more critical later on at Trent. Leo, following the way of ease, favoured the Regulars, who could be very insistent: in the end existing things were but little disturbed. The apology of Pallavicini, that every monarch must have his provincial subalterns and that the Pope found his in the Regulars, does little to justify the slight legislative result, and, in reality, only states what was the position.

The negotiations between the Popes and France turned mainly on the Pragmatic Sanction of Bourges, due to Charles **The Pragmatic Sanction of Bourges (1438).** VII (1438). This document, which regulated procedure in the French Church, looked back to the Conciliar struggles, in which the University of Paris with its great theologians had played such a leading part. But its form and its regulations were due to the growing absolute power of the Crown. One clause expressed the old Gallican spirit of the French Church: it declared that a General Council had a supremacy even above the Papacy. Then it went on to abolish expectative grants of benefices and also annates, which were no longer to be paid. Bishops and abbots were henceforth to be elected by the Chapters. Popes had protested against such a change in practices which had grown up, and Louis XI had been ready to give way. But Charles VIII and Louis XII maintained their rights, and the French clergy were with them. In 1515, however, Francis I, who like Charles VIII had Italian wars and schemes of Italian power, began negotiating with Leo X: French power had now to be reckoned with in Italy, since after his victory at Marignano (September 1515), Francis had regained Milan. He and Leo X soon came to terms at Bologna, Francis intent on power and the Pope on his Papal and dynastic interests; the final ratification came about at Rome (August 1516) and this new Concordat was approved by the Council of the Lateran (December 19, 1516): the Pragmatic Concordat of Bologna, August 1516. Sanction of Bourges was annulled by the bull *Pastor Eternus* (December 19, 1516). This Concordat of Bologna (1516),[1] as it was called, had somewhat neglected the interests of the French Church, and it was not well received in France: it regulated ecclesiastical appointments; archbishoprics, bishoprics and abbeys were to be filled by royal nomination: the King was to present a graduate in divinity for Papal institution within six months, but this stipulation for learning was not to hold for clerks of high birth. Thus all the higher offices of the French Church fell to the King, and this laid the foundation of much royal despotism in the future.

The clause regulating appointments left in most cases of bishoprics and abbeys nomination to the King, to be followed by institution by the Pope. This applied to the "consistorial" offices so called because, being greater, they were given by the Pope in Consistory. A few exempted abbeys kept their old right of election. All lesser benefices (cures and prebends), which were filled through collation by the patrons, remained as before, but patrons with ten to fifty benefices had to yield one presentation to the Pope: those

---

[1] *See* Lavisse, *Histoire de France illustrée*, V. 1, pp. 252 *seq.*; the Bull. *Pastor Æternus* in Mirbt; *Quellen zur Geschichte des Papsttums und des Römische Katholizismus* (4th edn., Tübingen, 1924), p. 252; Pastor, *Geschichte des Päpste*, IV, pp. 91 *seq.* (English translation VII, pp. 140 *seq.*).

with more than fifty yielded two. Appointments of successors to clerics who died at Rome were kept by the Pope. Patrons lost while the Pope and the King gained. As for jurisdiction, greater causes were reserved for Papal decision either at Rome or by commissioners: ordinary causes were to come before the ordinary local courts in due gradation. In April 1517 the Papal ambassador, the Bishop of Bayeux, presented to the King the two bulls of the year before, one confirming the Concordat of Bologna, and the other annulling the Pragmatic Sanction of Bourges.

The Parliament of Paris, followed by those of other places, refused to register the Concordat when ordered to do so (May 1517) and a struggle followed which showed the feeling of the country: a census of benefices heightened the fear of a revival of annates. The Parliament of Paris also objected to the reservation of causes to the Pope, and to the abolition of elections by Chapters, which it asserted to be against the liberties of the Church. The University of Paris, which did not as a rule see eye to eye with the Parliament, took the same line of opposition. It was not until 1527 that the King by a Bed of Justice forced the Parliament to give way and register his edict. For a time the struggle was ended, but the Estates protested against the Concordat in 1560, 1579 and 1583, and they had solid grounds for their actions.

When the Council, which had never numbered much more than one hundred cardinals and bishops, was dissolved (March 16, 1517) its actual accomplishments were smaller than its significance.[1] It had been the outcome of the two leading factors in the Church politics of the time—a wide and deep wish for reform, and the more secular needs of the Papacy. The Papacy had for many years gathered to itself nearly all ecclesiastical power; it had directed nearly all ecclesiastical work; men looked to it now to undertake the pressing need of reform, but this if not beyond its power was outside its wish. The Council was ready to undertake the work, but it split on the rock of

The
Lateran
Council.

[1] Hefele-Leclercq, *Les Conciles*, Vol. VIII, Pt. I, pp. 339 *seq.*, and pp. 396 *seq.* For Bishops and Regulars, pp. 451 *seq.*

opposition between the Curia and the Bishops—an opposition that was to grow even stronger by the Council of Trent. The one fact that did come out more clearly than ever was the power of the Pope. He was "as a second God upon earth," said one bishop. The high Papal theory had never been more boldly stated than by the learned Thomas de Vio (Cardinal Cajetan), General of the Dominicans, in a sermon at the second Session (May 1512). But as yet the Papacy had not risen to the call made upon it, and was led rather by minor considerations than by religious impulse or principle. There was a divergence, more marked as the century went on, between this exaltation of Papal power and this demand for reform which the Papacy had so far failed to meet. While the Western Church, however, had thus shown its needs and wishes, its ruling theory and its lack of power, political combinations and new social developments were changing everything. The rulers of the West—like the Popes themselves —found motives more inspiring than their unity or religious faith. The Turk, who had crushed the Christianity of the East, was thundering at the gate of the West; ecclesiastical revolution, to gather force from political anarchy and social change, was at hand. Germany, more than all States bound up with Italy and with Rome, more open than all States to the disorders of Church life, was to be its seat. Many countries were to be changed by that revolution: the Church of the West was to be rent into more than two: new opinions were to be preached and new religious bodies formed. Particular parts of it were to move towards different goals, and an age of doctrinal Confessions was to begin. We have to follow separate histories, sometimes entangled, sometimes apart. Even the fabric of States was to change, although this did not happen everywhere. In Italy, for instance, the story of the Reformation belongs more to that of thought than of churches and creeds. But that special turn of national history is peculiar.

III

GERMANY AND THE REFORMATION UP TO
1529

CHURCH life in Germany early in the sixteenth century had marked features of its own; nowhere were the higher offices

Germany at the Beginning of the Sixteenth Century. of more political importance and more secular in administration. At a date little later a Bavarian prince was Archbishop of Cologne and held four other sees without being in priest's orders. Less striking cases of the same aristocratic abuse were common. The princes to whose families this abuse was due were, moreover, drawing all power into their own hands, and this influence was specially strong in the Cathedral Chapters, many of which, like that of Augsburg, were the special booty of the local aristocracy. Beneath all this there lay, however, both the revival of learning with its great schools at Deventer, Schletstadt, and elsewhere, and also the deep movement towards a higher life among the Brethren of the Common Life, the Benedictines, Augustinian Friars, and others. Under better political circumstances, and with effective national institutions, these movements would have been more effective; in the tangled fight of emperor, princes, cities, and peasants they lost much of their force. A more efficient Church unity—such as a strong and unselfish Papacy, had it existed, might have directed—could have saved them; but it was here—in the relations of Papacy and the German Church—that most faults had been already laid bare.

The Humanist movement in Germany was (as said before) mainly Christian in tone and, above all, educational. The

Humanism. Renaissance in general has often been described as the Revival, almost accidental, of Classical, and especially of Greek, learning. But this was a symptom, a result, of it rather than its cause. That deeper cause was a vivid interest in human nature, closely bound up with the new prevalence of individualism. This interest showed itself in many ways, in society, in art, and in the political institutions of the day. Everywhere men launched out into new seas of life and thought because new springs of individual life sprang forth. And the quickened individual life brought with it a wider sympathy for human nature and human thought in whatever forms it could be seen. In ancient literature, as in the world around them, men searched for and found Humanity. In it they found, just as they did in themselves and others, ideas and impulses which they had not felt before. A wide and general interest in ancient life and thought led to the Revival of Letters, but this revival was, in reality, only one form of a more general and a wider impulse. Intercourse with Italian Humanists could not fail to bring in other and even more pagan elements, and a fresh cause of discord between the Humanists and some leading churchmen had just arisen.

Johann Reuchlin, the greatest of German Humanists, often reminding us in his varied career of Gregory of Heimburg, was born at Pforzheim (December 28, 1455). When fifteen he went to the University of Freiburg-im- Reuchlin, 1455–1522. Breisgau: three years later he became a chorister (for he had musical tastes) at the court of Baden-Durlach, and was sent by the Margrave to Paris as tutor to one of his sons. At Paris he learnt more Greek, a language towards which John Wessel had already turned him: his name of Capnio, by which he was so commonly known, is the Greek translation of his surname and, as it were, told his allegiance to his study. Then followed an interval at Basle (1474), where he again met Wessel, and became himself a missionary for Greek: he was friendly with the Amerbachs, with their circle of "readers," and he began a Greek lexicon: his reputation as a rising scholar soon brought him both fame and jealousy. He revisited Paris (1477) and this time turned to Hebrew, taught there by Hermonymus: afterwards passing to Law at Orleans and Poitiers, thus preparing himself for public life. Back in Germany he then entered the service of Eberhard "with the Beard," whom Maximilian made (1495) the first Duke of Würtemberg.

In 1492 he again went to Italy, visiting Rome and Florence; and he there caught from Pico della Mirandola the idea that the key to all philosophy, Christian and Neoplatonic, lay in

23

the Jewish Cabbala: so now he devoted himself to Hebrew, "the divine language" and therefore the first of studies: he wrote (1495) his work *de Verbo mirifico*, a dialogue between a Christian and a Jewish Rabbi, followed (1517) by *De Arte Cabalistica*.[1] As a help to students he wrote a Hebrew grammar and a lexicon. But not only in the world of letters was he renowned, but in that of politics too: the Emperor Frederick III enobled him and made him an Imperial Councillor. On the death of the Duke (1495) he went to Heidelberg in the service of the Count Palatine and his Chancellor, Dalberg, Bishop of Worms. But when the disturbed politics of Würtemberg allowed he went back to Stuttgart, and for some years was a member and then president of the court of the Swabian League. But he returned to life in a university, lecturing at Ingolstadt, and then reading at Tübingen until his death at Stuttgart (1522).

The incident and the trial which is most widely known and which disturbed the German Church so greatly had to do with the Hebrew studies Reuchlin loved so deeply. A converted Jew, Pfefferkorn, wished to destroy all Jewish books, and the Dominicans of Cologne, especially the Inquisitor-General, Jacob Hochstraten, agreed with him. Reuchlin took the wiser side of learning and tolerance; the strife soon became of literary, theological, and even of political importance. From a summons to appear before the Inquisition at Mayence, Reuchlin appealed to Leo X (1513). A Papal commission (July 1516) sympathised with the new learning, and acquitted him of heresy; but Leo, preferring personal peace to action, put off his own decision.

In Germany, however, the whole strength of learning had been thrown on the side of Reuchlin; his opponents, the reactionary party—which in ecclesiastical matters so often claims to represent traditions greater and better than its own principles —had been consolidated; parties were strongly marked. When Leo (June 1520) gave his decision, condemning Reuchlin's

[1] *A Short Survey of the Literature of Rabbinical and Medieval Judaism:* W. O. S. Oesterley and G. H. Box (S.P.C.K., 1920), pp. 235 *seq.*, especially p. 253.

book, the *Augenspiegel*, the theological significance of the struggle was exhausted; but its literary and scholastic significance remained. Ulrich von Hutten, a knight who shared the national enthusiasm of his class and was a scholar with a patriotism enriched by classical models, mocked the ignorant obscurantists of Cologne in the *Epistolæ Obscurorum Virorum*,[1] written by him and Crotus Rubianus: Reuchlin had published a collection of letters *Epistolæ Clarorum Virorum* addressed to him by sympathetic scholars. This suggested to Crotus Rubianus, the leading humorist of the Erfurt circle, a satire on the men whose chief fanaticism was the hatred of "the poets" as they called the Humanists. A collection of letters supposed to be written by these men to each other was made a revelation of ignorance, unconscious and unashamed, and of profligacy unashamed. The delineation was artistically perfect: "the artifice of ridicule was almost impossible to detect." It has been rightly called "the most cruel and most natural of satires." In 1515 the first Part, written by Crotus Rubianus, was published, and in 1517 a second Part by Ulrich von Hutten was added: other slight additions, possibly by other hands, were added later. To be laughed at is always more annoying than to be out-argued, and so, while the intellectual Humanists entered on their triumph, the Obscurantists became bitterer. But for the historian this perfect satire has its side of sadness, for no one doubted at the time that the evil life of the monks and friars here depicted was largely true to fact. But the literary history of the *Epistolæ* is amusing. An edition came out in England in 1710 and was reprinted in 1742: it was reviewed by Steele in the *Tatler*, and like the editor he took the collection to be letters really written by real men. He thought the writers blockheads and wondered that they could so far lack sense as to write such incoherent

---

[1] The classical edition is that by Edward Böcking: *Ulrichi Hutteni Eq. Operum Supplementum: Epistolæ Obscurorum Virorum* (Leipzig, 1864–9). See also *Epp. Obs. Vir.: Latin Text with an English Rendering, Notes and Historical Introduction:* Francis Griffin Stokes (London, 1900): this is an excellent work. In the *Quarterly Review*, January 1912, there is a masterly article on the *Epistolæ* by Sir A. W. Ward, whose knowledge of the period was almost unrivalled.

conceptions with gravity. This is a great testimony to the writers of the satire and helps us to understand its immense effect at the time.

The greatest name in Germany and far beyond was that of Desiderius Erasmus.[1] Born at Rotterdam about 1466,

Erasmus, 1466–1536.

he was educated partly at Deventer, partly at Hertogenbusch, in schools taught by Brethren of the Common Life. Here he had the best teaching which the Middle Ages could give, tinged by classical learning and directed especially to the study of the Fathers and of the Bible. Thus his youth was passed under the reforming and creative influences noted before. But his birth gave him little happiness of home: his mother was unmarried and his father, misled by report of her death, had become a monk. Thus his schools meant more for him than did his home. From his father he inherited a gaiety of disposition, which with him became humour of a quite modern type: he also inherited from him a love for manuscripts which his father had largely copied. At an early date a companion inspired him with an impulse towards the study of St. Jerome, who was his model, both for Theology and Latinity, throughout his life, just as he was the favourite Father of the Brethren. In 1487 he made his profession and entered in the Augustinian house at Steyn: his somewhat unscrupulous guardians urged him to take what was a natural step for a scholar of pious tastes, if with no strong vocation. In a monastery he might expect a chance of quiet study to add to his store; already he knew all Horace and Terence by heart. So at the time he had inducement enough for what he did, although afterwards his monastic life disappointed him. But his mind was really too detached and too independent for such a home: in later years, when he had left

---

[1] For Erasmus see an article I wrote in the *English Historical Review*, January 1920; it gave an account of the literature on him, and in my volume of Reformation Essays, 1939, this has been brought up to date. The late Dr. Allen's most excellent edition of the Epistles, Vols. I–VII, is the greatest work of all, and comes down to December 1528. Dr. Nichols' English translation in three volumes comes down to December 1518. The notes and Introductions in these, especially in Dr. Allen's great work, are full of information: the dates are not certain, see Allen I, 584.

it and all Europe knew his name, his superiors urged him to return and it cost him some trouble to keep the freedom of travel and dress which he desired. But there was nothing either in his life or his aims which went against religion.

By another usual change he entered the service of the Bishop of Cambrai: he was ordained priest (1492) and in 1495 we find him at the University of Paris, where Greek had been taught for nearly forty years. Thus he had begun his new life, emphatically that of a cosmopolitan scholar, at home wherever learning was to be found, and in his own case, owing to his birthplace amid the shifting politics of the Netherlands, with slender patriotism to counteract the wider tastes.

He visited England first in 1499–1500, and here he found "a thick crop of ancient learning": he had been invited by Thomas Grocyn, and a speedy friendship with John Colet and Thomas More formed a brotherhood delightful and fruitful, based upon a love of religion and the "sound letters" needed for its growth. Erasmus had already settled tastes: Colet had already at Oxford lectured with novel freshness and power on the Pauline Epistles, and so friendship had a strong foundation in interests that were alike. But there is no ground for making Colet the spiritual father of his friends: the tie was rather that of brothers. Then for some years Erasmus moved from one place to another, with longer halts at Paris and Louvain, but in 1506 he came again to England, where he added Tunstall and Warham to his patrons, both generous and kindly for years to come. At last (1506) his scholar's dream came true and he was able to visit Italy. Rome was, he thought, the common fatherland of learned men, and the sun of the Renaissance was still in the sky. Moreover, he had the practical aim of adding to his Greek although his gain here was perhaps not so very great. At Turin he received his Doctor's degree, but Italy he found was more for Classics than for Theology. At Rome, where he delighted in the libraries and the learned scholars, he might have stayed, and there was some talk of a Bishopric in Sicily. But if Italy were the land of promises, England, so far as patrons went, was the land of deeds. He was troubled, too, by the care of the pupils with whom he travelled. At Venice he expressed his surprise that the great Aldine Press, which had done so much for secular scholarship, had not brought out a Greek New Testament. The criticism reveals differing aims in letters, and when (1509) he came once more to England, where learning was basking in the early dawn of Henry VIII, he was probably more at home. He had already printed at Venice an enlarged edition of his *Adages* which sold so largely and opened paths of new learning to many youthful students. On his journey thither he planned and wrote his *Praise of Folly* (*Encomium Moriæ*), and already he was preparing his *Novum Instrumentum* (*New Testament*), although it only came out later (1516).

His theological devotion was deepening and with it came an inclination to teaching, no longer with private and profitable pupils but on a larger scale. Through the influence of Fisher he was made Lady Margaret Reader (or Professor) at Cambridge: this foundation of the Lady Margaret, mother of Henry VII, was meant to quicken pastoral work by sacred learning. The semi-paganism of some Italian scholars had only made him more devoted to Scriptural study, and the zeal for it which for some years afterwards marked Cambridge was doubtless due to his work there, even if the University had to appeal to his old pupil Lord Mountjoy to help towards his salary. And probably too what he had seen of a great printing-press at Venice had shown him a new field of influence. For in those days a master-printer gathered round him scholars to read manuscripts, who afterwards corrected the "proofs," but he himself chose the works and so really directed public tastes. A great Press was thus an ally, even a possible rival, of the Universities in the world of scholarship and teaching. His later association with Froben and Amorbach at Basle (where his beloved friend, the gentle Beatus Phenanus, was a reader) was to make Erasmus greater in the world than he had been before. The Press was a power even then.

He left England for the Continent in July 1514, and although he moved about much, Basle was henceforth the real centre of his work. His *Novum Instrumentum* and his editions of many Fathers were splendid gifts to Christian scholarship: his critical work would not be highly rated in these later days, but it gave a foundation and his exegesis was always reverent and often fresh. Some novelties in it were seized upon and exaggerated by men who had not his regard for the authority of the Church. So it came about that he was hailed by one side in the Reformation struggles as their guide into new fields of thought or doctrine, and by others as the pillar of a learning which could not but help the Church. The many abuses in the Church life of his day he condemned and even ridiculed, but he joined a deep regard for authority and tradition (which really means a continuous life) with a scholar's dislike of un-balanced and turbulent thought. And this is seen clearly in his view of Luther and the Lutheran controversy: with much that Luther said and with many of his denunciations he agreed, but his extreme expressions and his violence he disliked. The Christian life could not flourish in a world of anger and noise.

Until 1521 he was mainly at Louvain, which was his more settled home from July 1517 until 1521, when he left it for Basle. At Louvain the academic atmosphere was strangely mixed. It was a home of conservative learning and scholasti-cism was cultivated. But on the other side the foundation of the Professorships of the Three Languages, Hebrew, Greek and Latin, drew many to the newer studies and brought thither the breath of a newer spirit. Much was due to the great human-ist Bustaiden, who as a Councillor of State dwelt at Malines.[1] But if he laid the foundation, the arrival of Erasmus threw a flood of light upon the edifice and shone throughout Europe. It was hoped that Greek and Latin should be taught as living languages, not mere dead tongues, and ancient humanism revived. This use of Latin kept touch with the old medieval world of learning, and in it Erasmus, as we see from his interest in Colet's reformation (for it was not a new foundation) of St. Paul's School, was pre-eminently at home. So too was Melanchthon in another realm. But in Germany theological disputes, centred in the Augsburg Confession, broke up the harmony. The Jesuit teachers, inspired as much by the great

---

[1] For Louvain see *L'Université de Louvain* (lectures given at the Col-lege of France in 1915) by Paul Delannoy. (Paris, 1915.)

learning of Laynez as by the almost mystic piety of St. Ignatius, kept for some two or three generations to the same medieval type. But then harmony changed to discord. In England the harmonising influence lasted a little longer, and the Caroline divines, who were inspired by it, were, because of their tastes, sometimes called reactionary. The change, on the one side a desire of the common Latin speech, on the other a new growth of national languages, created almost a new world. Christian Thomasius, one of the founders of the University at Halle (†1728), was the first Professor to lecture in German instead of Latin, and the change (coming to a climax in the deplorable ignorance of Latin in many places to-day) was disastrous for the sound learning which Erasmus loved; for later Western civilisation had its roots in the ancient Latin world.

It was not surprising that at Louvain, academic disputes became too dominant, as they so often do, and Erasmus left it Œcolam-   in 1521 for Basle. But after some years of happy padius.   work there he found his peace disturbed by the disputes and even riots of the Reformation: for Œcolampadius, a corrector of Froben's press, he had a very deep love, but Farel, whom he called "an ignorant ranter," was a different type of man. The climate grew too disturbed for a scholar's calm, and so (1529) he moved to Freiburg in the Breisgau. The charm of that lovely city might well have been inducement enough, but Erasmus had further a wish to stay in the lands of the Emperor, one of whose Councillors he was. But even here he could not for ever gain the longed-for "beata tranquillitas." In 1535 he left Freiburg for Basle, where (July 12, 1536) he died. It is hardly too much to say that although many great scholars have founded schools and ardent disciples in many lands have treasured their names in many fields of learning or of thought, none has ever filled the vacant place of Erasmus. It was a place fit for a scholar shaped by the past and yet able to reach the highest levels of his day. It was unique and uniquely filled.

The Reformation in Germany centres round Martin Luther.[1]

---

[1] The Life by Melanchthon in *Vitæ Quattuor Reformatorum*, edited by Neander (Berlin, 1841): Julius Köstlin *Martin Luther Sein Leben und seine*

While alive he drew to himself the sympathy of his fellow-countrymen and made his name the banner of the new movement: after his death regard for his memory and his theology became so strong as even to obscure much of the real history. Only in our own days have historical research and criticism made it possible to pass behind long-standing legends and controversies and depict him as he really was. But the mass of literature is so vast as to make a true estimate, whether of his personality or his true place in history, difficult if not impossible. A great national hero, a religious leader, patriots and partisans on different sides have woven round him veils of veneration or detraction which it is hard for calmer criticism to unravel.

Martin Luther, Nov. 10. 1483–Feb. 18. 1546.

He was born (St. Martin's Eve, November 10, probably 1483) at Eisleben in the county of Mansfeld: so naturally he was christened Martin. His parents were peasants with property of their own: his father Hans had come from Mohra in the west of Thuringia: his mother Margaret belonged to Eisenach. From Eisleben they soon moved to Mansfeld, and here Hans became a prosperous copper-miner. From his simple pious home and after a school at Mansfeld, Martin went to one at Magdeburg (1497) and a year later to Eisenach. Then for seven years (1501–8) he studied at the University of Erfurt. Here he came into wider currents of thought: a vivid patriotism, seen in the historical writings of the day, was everywhere moulding younger Germans: national politics with their sharp criticism of Papal pressure, the stirring life of the Renaissance with its new studies (although these were not prominent at Erfurt), were then both of them influencing youth. The University, noted for its Biblical studies, was known as Modernist, that is,

---

Werke (2 vols., Berlin, 1903); Dr. James Mackinnon, *Luther and the Reformation* (London, 1925); H. Böhmer, *Luther and the Reformation in the Light of Modern Research* (trans. by S. S. G. Potter: London, 1930); *The Cambridge Modern History*, Vol. II, chap. iv, by Dr. T. M. Linsday; J. M. Reu, *Thirty-five Years of Luther Research* (Chicago, 1917) is a very full Bibliography. The Life in six vols. by Hartmann Grisar, S.J. (1913–17) is on a large scale. In my volume *Reformation Essays* is one on Luther. There are many Lives; among them *Martin Luther: the Man and his Work*, by A. C. McGiffert (London, 1911), may be mentioned.

mainly given to the later Nominalism: Occam and above all
Gabriel Biel were read rather than Aquinas and the more
orthodox schoolmen. From Erfurt he passed to Wittenberg
(1508), the new University founded (1502) by the Elector
Frederick, the leading prince of the day, pious, prudent and
popular, who wished to have a University in his own part of
Saxony. But before Luther went there he had already come
under influences and passed through changes, which affected
his whole later life.

Like some other Reformers, notably Calvin and Beza, he
had been meant for the Law, but that suited him little, and,
under an impulse variously ascribed to the death of a friend or
to dread of a thunderstorm, he vowed himself to a religious
life, as many another young man might have done: he entered
(May 1505) the convent of Augustinian Friars at Erfurt and a
year later made his profession: then he took to the study of
Theology with an eye to teaching, and was ordained priest
(1507). After about a year at Wittenberg, where he lectured
on Ethics, he returned to his convent at Erfurt and remained
there for some two years, probably teaching Theology.
Evidence and opinions about his earlier life are conflicting, and
his own accounts given in later years are not always consistent
with one another, while his Table-talk, once supposed to
describe him as he really was, is a later collection, largely edited
and not altogether trustworthy. It is probably safest to sup-
pose him more of a normal monastic than later narratives and
legends depict him. In later years his spiritual struggles seemed
to him (as so often happens) darker and more intense than they
had seemed at the time and as he had described them. He had
an impulsive, vigorous nature: conflicts, temptations and
depressions he certainly knew: the spiritual was very near to
him: the sense of God's presence and the load of sin were very
real: he was quick to receive impressions, interested in all he
read, pious in life, and eager to know the truth as it seemed at
that day. He was most certainly not the evil-natured man his
enemies have painted: neither was he the martyr to monastic
system which his followers have assumed him to have
been.

He was never a real theologian or an accurate scholar; he was a great preacher, earnest and effective; a copious and fluent writer with a power of rapid work and an instinct for the popular understanding. Besides the Nominalist Scholastics he continuously studied St. Augustine, probably after 1509, and that Father's influence on him was most marked: the Augustinian doctrines of grace were indeed the real foundation of his whole theology: he exaggerates one side of St. Augustine's doctrine just as St. Augustine treated St. Paul's. To the German mystics with their individual sense of God he was much indebted, especially to Tauler, whose sermons he recommended to his friend Spalatin, the Elector's Chancellor, and to whom he at first ascribed the *Deutsche Theologie*, which he reprinted (his first edition being in 1516) with great commendation. He was thus turned by his reading, apart from the traditions of his Order and his own inclinations, to a close study of the Scriptures and above all of St. Paul.

Luther's Personality and Studies.

The Order of Friars to which he belonged had, like others, been reformed. Zolter had organised the German Congregation, and later on Andreas Proles, towards the end of the fifteenth century, brought about a reform which led to the separation of some thirty houses in the Saxon Province with a stricter Observance: to this group the Erfurt convent belonged. These Observants were placed directly under the General of the Order at Rome, who appointed a Vicar over them. This post was since 1503 held by John von Staupitz, an evangelical theologian of a type commoner then than is sometimes supposed: we have an illustration of this in the picture drawn by Erasmus of Vitrarius, a companion sketch to that he drew of Colet. Staupitz was such another; he had deep spiritual insight and great knowledge of the Bible, and with loving care for individuals he kept up the spiritual earnestness which Proles had restored: to him and also to one or two of the older brethren Luther was much indebted. Their rules of discipline were not oppressively stringent, the religious and moral atmosphere was good: study of the Scriptures was encouraged and enforced: each brother

The Augustinian Friars.

on his profession was given a copy of them for his own use, and Luther when he left Erfurt for Wittenberg greatly lamented the loss of his "copy bound in red" which he had to return to the house.

Staupitz was a valued adviser of the Elector and was made Dean and Professor of Biblical Theology at Wittenberg: he knew Luther's ability and therefore called him (1508) to lecture on Ethics; after this date the friendship of the two men became closer. Then came Luther's speedy return to Erfurt, and while there he was sent in the autumn of 1510 with a comrade to Rome on the business of the Order. As already said, the Convents under Staupitz were strict Observants and stood apart from the other German Augustinians, the Conventuals, who formed part of the larger organisation. Staupitz wished to bring about a union under himself of all the Saxon convents: twenty-two of them agreed, but seven, including Erfurt and Nuremberg, objected. It is not certain whether the question of strictness as against laxity caused the objection or not: it may have been merely a matter of politics within the Order. Attempts had lately been made at Rome to stop or at any rate restrict the too great multiplicity of monastic divisions. The General at Rome favoured the plan formed by Staupitz and there was indeed much for it: through it reform could have been extended to all the Saxon houses. A Papal bull (September 30, 1510) had approved the scheme and Staupitz was already styled Provincial for Thuringia and Saxony. The Observants at Erfurt sent Luther, along with Nathin, one of his teachers, to Halle to interest on their side Prince Adolf of Nassau, the Cathedral Provost, for a petition to the Archbishop of Mayence against the change. Then in the autumn of 1510 he was sent along with a senior comrade to Rome to plead against it. Staupitz himself saw the difficulties in the way of his arrangement and agreed to a compromise which, while leaving him control of all the houses, allowed the old Observant convents their independent Chapter (July 1511). But the seven opponent houses would not even accept this, although a minority of their members, probably including Luther, were willing to agree. Staupitz therefore dropped the matter (1512) and we hear no more of it: there is no reason to think that it greatly affected Luther himself, but his life at Erfurt would naturally, however, be now less comfortable, and it must have been a relief when in the spring of 1512 he was called once more to Wittenberg, this time to succeed Staupitz as Professor of Biblical Theology. Nor was the effect upon Luther of his Roman visit as great at the time as in his own eyes and those of others it seemed later: he saw Rome as any ordinary Catholic might and there was at the time no sign of hostility to the Papacy on his part.[1]

Wittenberg was henceforth to be the scene of Luther's life and work: at the Cologne Chapter (May 1512) he was named Sub-prior of the Wittenberg Augustinians with the duty of directing their studies: he himself read for his Doctorate which he soon took (October 1512). Besides lecturing as Professor he preached at times in the city church near his convent and (1515) was appointed one of the regular preachers there. Wittenberg, although a new University, was not, when Luther went there, much affected by the Humanist movement: the Professors were most of them at the time and after rather of other schools; it was only when Melanchthon came thither as Professor (1518) that Humanism took root there. At Wittenberg Luther carried on his reading much on his former Erfurt lines: more and more St. Augustine was his guide. As Doctor of Divinity he could now speak with more authority. His hearers included many Augustinians, and thus, as well as from his official position among them, his influence in the Order was great. But others were changing and thinking much as he did. Hence it was that so many of his Order followed him, and became pastors in his newly-organised Church, often at the invitation of the civil authorities.

He was now greatly affected by his work as preacher to mixed congregations: he learnt to speak simply and with force in language that all could understand: in closer touch with his hearers he came to know more of the human soul. Thus his outward activities and his inner experiences combined to make him a strong leader of men. He still went on with his

---

[1] H. Böhmer: *Luthers Romfahrt*, Leipsic, 1914.

study of St. Augustine and it was not mere accident that the literary contest between him and Erasmus arose on the question of free-will; it was a deeply rooted difference between the two mên. He lectured on the Psalms soon after his Doctorate and again in 1519: on the Romans (1516), followed by Galatians (1516–17). There has been much discussion as to the date when his distinctive doctrines first appeared, but probably his lectures on the Romans mark a turning-point. As to his writings we have little of them before 1513: then onwards to 1519 we have more, and after that date a continuous stream, largely booklets and sermons, all of them effectively written, for Luther, like Zwingli, was something of a journalist with the appropriate gifts, and he had ready means of spreading his views through the printing-press and the book fairs, such as the great fair at Leipzig.

Finally, it is probably in these Wittenberg years that we may place his most rapid growth. His old Augustinianism and his Nominalism, tinged by his vivid sense of God's presence and a simple individualism found in the Mystics, all worked together to build up the later Luther. But he was never a very deep or consistent theologian: he was more of the ready lecturer and the popular preacher, able through his own strong personality to arouse and lead rather than to teach. And it was a matter which touched both popular religion and the standpoint which he had already reached that caused his entrance upon a larger scene and a greater strife.

In the Middle Ages, as at all times, popular theology had on many points outrun authorised theology: the fifteenth century was overladen both in bold speculations and prac-

Popular Theology. tical details by the results of past generations. There were many matters in which a large and fluctuating body of fluid opinions and varying practices had gathered round a small nucleus of admitted doctrine. This was notably the case with the theory of Indulgences. The Church as a body, with a discipline of its own, had the power of imposing external penalties for sin, but to ensure forgiveness contrition was needed in addition to this penalty: furthermore, since the Church was a divine body the performance or the

36

neglect of any duty prescribed by it had a real bearing upon the spiritual life. The custom had grown up—purely as a matter of practice—of granting an indulgence or remission of these external penalties on account of some special act of faith or charity duly performed. In the Ely Registers of John de Fordham (1388–1426), for instance, there are numerous entries of Indulgences mainly for works of charity: repairs of roads, support of the blind, of hermits, and of pilgrims, maintenance of chapels, making good losses by fire, release of captives, prayers for the success of the King in the Welsh war (1405), prayers for the dead, and so on. The tendency in later years was for the granting of these Indulgences to pass more and more into the hands of the Pope, in this respect as in others episcopal power being weakened. But in any case the process meant the substitution by some authority representing the Church of a general act of penance for a number of varied acts prescribed in separate cases by an inferior authority.

All this, however, related solely to the outward act of penance. As public penance had become rarer, and sacramental confession laid stress on its other elements—the confession and absolution—the act of penance had become more and more nominal, more like the ordinary fines of civil life as tabulated in medieval codes. The conception of fines in short, devoted to religious or ecclesiastical objects grew up, and was extended by the system of Indulgences, reckoned for so many years in proportion to the amount. But with the vivid medieval notion of Purgatory, the expression (say) of an Indulgence for a hundred years (originally only a measure of scale) was open to misconstruction, and in the hands of ecclesiastical rulers not specially spiritual in mind the system itself was open to abuse. From a war against the Turks the objects multiplied until (1509) Julius II issued an Indulgence for the rebuilding of St. Peter's.

But this simpler aspect of Indulgences—which, however, open to abuse, did yet emphasise both the idea of sin and also the fact that no sin is merely a private matter, but concerns the Church—was complicated by another doctrine, that of the Treasure of the Church, its accumulation of prayers and

Indulgences.

blessings: upon this medieval thinkers had speculated widely though not wisely. More and more the control of Indulgences, the assumed power to use the Treasure of the Church, had passed from the Episcopate to the Popes. Indulgences were a form of Papal income, and as such at times opposed by jealous sovereigns: like other branches of Papal income, they were often condemned both by isolated thinkers and popular opinion; the "questers," or preachers of Indulgences, were often hated and despised, even where freely encouraged in their trade.

This doctrine and practice of Indulgence is specially hard for us to estimate fairly; speculation and discussion were still at work upon it; both its scientific and its popular expression were tinged by the ecclesiastical, legal, and social ideas of the day. In practice it touched on the one side the power and finances of the Curia: on the other, the defective clerical discipline and the lax moral sense of the day. Indulgences had caused discussion both on the scholastic and the practical side: doctrinally they needed definition, practically they needed reform. Efforts after a stricter monastic and clerical discipline, the study of theology on a more biblical basis, would make these needs more apparent; both these elements were found in the Saxon Augustinians under Staupitz; a keen personal sense of sin, and the apprehension of a living Saviour, would deepen the sense of abuse: both these feelings were found in Luther.

The charge of the Indulgence issued by Leo X for the rebuilding of St. Peter's was given along with half the proceeds in his provinces of Mayence and Magdeburg to Archbishop Albert of the Brandenburg line; he could thus recoup himself for a payment to Leo which had gained him, although already, at twenty-four, Archbishop of Magdeburg and Administrator of Halberstadt, the See of Mayence. For political reasons the Elector of Saxony did not allow Tetzel the Commissioner to preach it in his land, but he visited the neighbouring places. Already a visitation of the Augustinian convents (in May 1515 Luther had been elected District-Vicar for the ten—later eleven—convents of

Luther's theses.

Meissen and Thuringia) had convinced him as to the need of a reform of discipline: already he had studied the Pauline epistles with their insistence upon justification by faith, and lectured upon them. From this standpoint, and also as a teacher and preacher who dealt with practical questions and knew the views of the common man, Luther was bound to oppose this development of Indulgences. But the method of his opposition was academic and medieval; he fastened ninety-five theses, or topics for argument, to the door of the Castle Church. While he laid stress upon the spiritual process of repentance, Luther proposed, by the medieval process of disputation, to discuss the kernel of accepted doctrine apart from accretions of opinion or unhealthy practice: he wished to ascertain the true teaching of the Church: from the Bishop of Brandenburg, his Ordinary, to whom he wrote, he received a reply approving his views, but advising silence.[1] Luther had no doubt but that the Pope would be on his side. The Indulgence was a discreditable business, bordering on simony, one of many by which the Fuggers, the great banking house of Augsburg, had grown rich. More than all this, however, the doctrine itself needed discussion.

The area of the discussion widened: University opinion had then more interest for princes and populace than it has often had since. Political causes intensified its tone, and it ceased to be a mere search after truth. The Elector Frederick, from jealousy of the House of Brandenburg, would naturally defend Luther: others from interested motives would attack him. Public and academic opinion was already excited not only by the Reuchlin discussion, but by the demands for Church reform, in Germany a question of politics. Tetzel, naturally concerned, took up the opposition; his fellow Dominicans, still sore from the Reuchlin incident, sided with him. Against Luther's theological grounds stress was laid upon the power of the Pope and ecclesiastical order. Not only Hochstraten the

---

[1] For the ninety-five theses see W. Köhler, *Luther's 95 Thesen samt seine Resolutionen* (including the controversial writings of Tetzel, Eck, Prierias, and Luther's reply to them (Leipzig, 1903). Also in Wace and Buchheim, *Luther's Primary Works* (London, 1883).

Inquisitor, but a Dominican in higher place—Silvester Mazzo-lini (Prierias), Master of the Palace to the Pope, and a learned commentator upon Aquinas—issued a reply. The Universal Church was in practice the Roman Church: the Roman Church was in practice the Pope: the custom of the Church was as binding as law, and any doubt upon it was heresy. Such was his argument. Ground was thus deliberately chosen upon which no distinction of doctrines, customs, or authority could be admitted. In his replies (some of which were, like other pamphlets of the day, coarse in tone), Luther was led on to draw distinctions as to Papal power, and the doctrine of the Church and of St. Thomas Aquinas. But he was still ready to submit to the decision of the Pope, and he had no doubt that must be.

Although he was called to Rome[1] (July 1518), it was finally arranged, through the stand taken by the Elector Frederick, **Luther and Cajetan, 1518.** that Luther should appear instead before the Legate, Cardinal Cajetan, at the Augsburg Diet (September). Thomas de Vio (Cajetan) was the Dominican whose sermon at the Lateran Council had so strongly set forth the Curialist ideal of the Papal power. His learning was undoubted; he was far from accepting the vulgar view of Indulgences, but his first anxiety was to silence the controversy that had arisen. He and Luther, although neither thought well of the other, went some way towards meeting each other, but they started from opposite points: it was hard to reconcile authority stretched to cover existing customs, and views stretched to cover insubordination. The interview ended in Luther's appeal to the Pope "better informed," afterwards enlarged to an appeal from the Pope to a Council.

The question had now grown larger. Luther had in his favour his own personal vigour and force, backed by the growing school of Wittenberg, by the reaction against the Thomist theology, by the national feeling of Germans against the Papacy. But the Embassy of Miltitz, wisely chosen by the Pope as both a diplomatist and a Saxon, seemed likely to compose the strife even at this later stage (December 1518). Luther

[1] P. Kalkoff, *Forschungen zu Luther's Römischen Prozess* (Rome, 1905).

was ready to admit the use, within limits, of Indulgences, and the need of unity along with respect for Papal commands: he would keep silence if his antagonists did the same. From Miltitz he gathered that the abuses he had attacked were not likely to be maintained by the Papal Court. It mattered little that the decretal of Leo X, borne by Miltitz, stated as a minimum the doctrine of St. Thomas, although not exactly the doctrine of Tetzel (who was now, indeed, in disgrace): by the power of the keys the sacrament of penance removed the guilt of sin, and the Indulgence, by using the Treasure of the Church, could remove its temporal punishment: the Pope could, by the means of prayer (*per modum suffragii*), transfer an Indulgence to souls in Purgatory. Silence upon these lines was certainly possible, had not the Leipzig disputation (June 1519) raised wider issues.

John of Eck (Maier), of Ingolstadt, had grown from a youthful prodigy into a scholastic gladiator, and was eager for distinction: Carlstadt, a former colleague of Luther's, a scholar but ill-balanced in mind, and in the end a preacher of revolution, was equally eager to state his views. A literary dispute between the two arose (May 1518), and Luther, who arranged a personal discussion between them at Leipzig (June 27, 1519), was in the end drawn into it himself. Directly challenged upon the primacy of the Pope and the Roman See, he was led on to express views of it labelled by his opponents as Hussite, and later on owned as such by himself. It is hard to give blame to either party for breaking the truce, but Luther, as the leader and as personally pledged, had to bear the most of it: the negotiations, complicated and unsatisfactory, were at an end: Luther had taken up a new position, and the quarrel had passed into its second stage. His language was not at all times consistent, and the point had been raised more by his adversaries than by himself. But it was to be the controversy of the time, and Luther—a man of impulse and instinct rather than reflection and insight —now threw himself into it heart and soul. He had not faced the question previously, but when he did so, he found that unexpected logical results followed from his position.

Other theologians or writers—Wyclif in England and Gregory of Heimburg, in Germany, for instance—had reached

Influences in favour of Luther. the same position, but nothing of importance had come from their assertions. Luther's fate differed from theirs, mainly because of the altered times and the political circumstances of Germany. There was an admitted need of reform, political and ecclesiastical, there were difficult and strained relations between Emperor, Pope, and Princes; above all, there was a ferment of thought which led parties readily to crystallise around a nucleus of definite assertion. The Papal Nuncio Aleander said (1521) that the priests joined in Luther's revolt, not for his sake, but from hatred of Rome; five years before this he had heard from many Germans that they were only waiting for some foolish man to give the signal by opening his mouth against Rome. Luther also drew to himself some of the Hussite feeling, never wholly dead: something, too, of the old Conciliar sympathies went out towards him, at any rate in the earlier stages of his influence. The doctrine of Wyclif, carried to the young University of Prague, had become the watchword of the Bohemian nationalists eager to oppose the encroaching German influence. The death of Hus—whose leading works were bare literal copies of Wyclif's—had been followed by long wars, settled in outward form by the Council of Basle. The compromise by which Communion in both kinds was allowed to the Bohemians had never been sanctioned by the Popes, but this outward mark of difference still continued, and its more extended use was urged later at Trent both by the Emperor Ferdinand and the French ambassadors. Thus the memory of a revolt against Papal authority joined to doctrinal heresy was still kept alive; the printing-press, by publishing some of Hus's works about this time, brought his views forward still more. At Erfurt, too, where Luther had been trained, the Conciliar theory of Church politics survived. In many ways, then, a movement which was anti-Papal could depend upon a sympathy more widely spread than could one which was purely doctrinal or reforming.

But it was more important that he also gathered around himself the growing national feeling: a typical German in virtues as in failings, in his hearty sincerity as in his frequent coarseness and blunt independence, he now stood as a representative of his nation in a struggle where more than academic and clerical interests were involved. **German National Feeling.**

His great writings of 1520—his *Address to the Nobility of the German Nation* and his *Babylonian Captivity*—showed him to be every inch a popular leader; the knights led by Ulrich von Hutten and Franz von Sickingen, freelances, one in letters and the other in the field, took up his cause; in the tangled state of politics he was a useful ally for some who did not share his opinions; the Bull of condemnation (June 15, 1520) brought to Germany by Eck met a cool reception: it was easy for a territorial prince to shelter a subject in even greater dangers, and Frederick the Wise was not likely to give up a Professor of his favoured University. He urged further consideration upon the Pope, while Luther himself grew bolder and bolder, until at the end of 1520 he burnt the Papal Bull.

The first of Luther's so-called Primary Works[1] was that: *To the Christian Nobility of the German Nation respecting the Reformation of the Christian Estate* (August 1520), and by the end of the month 4,000 copies had been sold, largely owing to its vigorous, homely, German style. It was dedicated to Nicholas von Ams- **The Primary Works: To the Christian Nobility.** dorf, a colleague of his at Wittenberg, and his helper in the changes there, then afterwards a preacher at Magdeburg; he was also an intermediary in Luther's marriage to Catherine von Bora (June 1525): in 1542 he was made Protestant Bishop of Naumburg by the Elector (1532–54) of Saxony, John Frederick, nephew of Frederick the Wise, in defiance of the Chapter, through his supposed prerogative as *summus episcopus*. There was also an address to the Emperor Charles, urging him to undertake a reformation. The short work itself depicted three walls which the "Romanists" (the term usually applied to the Papal party up to the Recess of Ratisbon (1542) when the term "Catholic" was used) had built about themselves and which

[1] Wace and Buchheim, *Martin Luther's Primary Works and the ninety-five Theses* (London, 1883). Ludwig Lemme, *Die drei grossen Reformationsschriften vom Jahre 1920* (Gotha, 1884).

must be broken down. The first wall was the claim to free-dom from temporal jurisdiction and the consequent exaltation of Papal power. All Christians belonged to the Spiritual Estate: "Baptism, Gospel, and Faith alone make Christian people and all are one in priesthood and privilege. Any baptised person has been consecrated priest, bishop, and pope, although it does not become everyone to exercise these offices. A priest should be nothing in Christendom but a functionary:" if deposed for abuse of his office he is "a peasant and a citizen like the rest," all power being derived from the community: there was no such thing as "an indelible character," which was only a human invention. "The temporal power has been ordained of God for the punishment of the bad," and so it must do its duty "whether it strikes popes, bishops, priests, monks or nuns." It was the arch-devil himself who had said in the ecclesiastical law that no pope could be deposed. So it is for the temporal power, that is all Christian people, to break down this wall.

The second wall was the claim that no one save the Pope could interpret the Scriptures. A common man might have true understanding and Luther asked if the Pope had not often erred. The keys were not given to Peter alone but to the whole community. To alter "I believe in the Holy Christian Church" into "I believe in the Pope of Rome" was a devilish and damn-able. heresy. All Christians were priests: every Christian should understand and defend the faith and condemn all errors.

So we come to the third wall: that no one save the Pope may call a Council. So much do they tremble for themselves before a true free Council that they overawe Kings and Princes by fear of offending God if they do not obey them. Not only did the Emperor Constantine call the Council of Nicæa, but later Emperors had done the same. Since need requires and the Pope is a cause of offence, all faithful members of the body should strive for a true free Council. There being no authority in the Church save for reformation, if the Pope wrongly hinders a Council he should be treated as a raving madman and excommunicated. Finally, he hopes that he has laid the spectre with which Romanists have terrified their conscience.

If they hinder a Council they are of the fellowship of Antichrist and the Devil.

He then passes on to sketch the subjects for a Council to discuss. The pomp of the Pope, the College of Cardinals with their riches, have sucked Italy dry and are now attacking Germany. The wealth of Germany flows to Rome. There should be fewer cardinals or else the Pope should support them. There was at Rome a swarm of vermin, the Papal officials. Annates and the fees for the pallium (the Indulgence for St. Peter's at Rome, and the pluralities of Albert of Brandenburg are glanced at). Hindrance of reforms as at Strassbourg, and grants in *commendam* are spoken of. The simony, debauchery, and villainy found at Rome are denounced.

Luther concludes with a list of twenty-seven articles for the Council to discuss. Here he follows in places the medieval *Centum Gravamena* repeatedly made by German Diets. Papal jurisdiction, confirmation of bishops and gifts of the pallium must be abolished by Imperial law. Everything should be left to the jurisdiction of temporal authorities. So he would sweep away "the wretched, heathen, unchristian misrule of the Pope." The terrible oaths sworn by bishops to the Pope must be abolished. And the Pope should have no power over the Emperor except to crown him as a bishop crowns a king. That the Pope was the rightful heir to the Empire according to the lying Donation of Constantine was a puerile reason. To the temporal States of the Pope he gives strong condemnation. Pilgrimages, building of new mendicant monasteries, preachings by and confessions to mendicant Friars, institutions of new Orders (the Papacy, we may note, had moved in this direction) were condemned: clerical celibacy was discussed at length and denounced: the oath of chastity in this sense was a devilish tyranny. Masses for the dead, church wakes, and enforced fasting should be swept away. These and other abuses proved that the Pope was Antichrist. The Bohemians should be befriended, not oppressed: the administration of the Communion in both kinds was not heretical. Scholasticism should be given up, but the retaining of Aristotle's Logic, Rhetoric and Poetic was advised: Canon Law he would abolish utterly.

Luxurious living, drunkenness, buying on credit, and the abuse of banking as by the Fuggers at Augsburg were to be condemned.

Luther's devotion to the Empire, his strong German patriotism, his repetition of complaints long felt and voiced come out again and again: he writes, too, so as to be understood by common men. This helps us to understand how he came to be a national leader and hero. His placing of all power in the community, his insistence on the right of every man to give his own interpretation of Scripture, were largely carried out in the Lutheran Reformation in Germany. Cities and even rural parishes chose what they would have and elected pastors for themselves. Hence the whole movement became chaotic; there was little coherence in institution and even variety in doctrine. Zwingli might exalt the place of the scholar, Calvin might place all control in the hands of the consistory of ministers, but in the Lutheran ideal the individuality of the common man was left comparatively supreme. Hence came the sweeping away of what might have been reformed and kept, and over all was the power, unquestioned and left, of the Emperor and the Princes. The Prince as *summus episcopus*, the power of each city to order Church worship and Church matters as it liked, brought in a new state of Christianity, which needed all the influence and energy of Luther to control it even in some small degree. Melanchthon saw and lamented this result.

There may be noted in the main arguments of this work a resemblance to the doctrines of Wyclif: at the Leipzig Disputation a printed copy of the *De Ecclesia* by Hus was put in his hands, and as it largely repeated Wyclif, the duty of lay Princes to carry out reform, and the responsibility of all Christian laymen were emphasised. Luther, indeed, came to feel and acknowledge his kinship with the Hussites, and through them he had an indirect debt to Wyclif.

The Babylonian Captivity of the Church, in the form of a letter to Hermann Tulichius (early in October 1520), was written in Latin, being meant for scholars, but was translated into German rather against the author's wish.

The Babylonian Captivity.

46

He begins by saying that Eck and Emser, instructing him on the primacy of the Pope, had done more than they meant. He had denied any divine right to the Papacy while still admitting that it had a human right, but after hearing them he was sure that the Papacy was the kingdom of Babylon and the power of the mighty hunter Nimrod; for the Papacy is the mighty hunting of the Bishop of Rome. The very name of the work recalls the days of Avignon, and so much of history, discreditable to the Papacy, was, as it were, its background.

Here Luther deals with the Eucharist and its doctrine. He had thought, foolishly he thinks, that administration in two kinds should well be determined by a General Council. But he was told that the Church had settled it, and must be obeyed. This he now disputes.

There are only three Sacraments, Baptism, Penance, and the Communion, not seven. Then he deals at length with "the sacrament of the bread." He will not have it that the sixth chapter of St. John deals with the matter at all. Both kinds were originally given to the laity, and to withhold one from them is impious and against the institution of Christ. Thus there is a bondage put on Christians in the denial of the Cup. The second bondage arose from accepting the Pope's decrees. His conscience here revolts: he will be called a Wyclifite and six hundred other names, but this he little cares for. He then discusses Transubstantiation, touching on "substance" and "accidents." For himself, trusting in the words of Christ, he will believe "not only that the body of Christ is in the bread, but that the bread is the body of Christ." But no man need consider he is a heretic if he believes that real bread and real wine remain on the altar. But that the Mass is a good work (by this he means a work of righteousness conducive to salvation) or that it is a sacrifice he denies. It is "the Testament of Christ," a promise of the remission of sins, confirmed to us by the death of Christ. The great misery is that few recognise the richness of this promise.

Incidentally he speaks of details. It was deplorable that no layman should hear the words of institution, and he condemns (with reason) the custom which had grown up of saying them

47

secretly. As for the recipients, there is no worthy preparation for the Mass or rightful use of it except through faith. Its whole virtue lies in the words of Christ. He gave a sign, His own Body and His own Blood, in the bread and wine. The word of promise is the testament, and the sign is the sacrament.

There are two difficulties which are wont to beset us: the sense of our unworthiness, and the other is the greatness of the blessing.

The institution of suffrages, anniversaries, and masses offered for gain he condemns. He holds that the prayers we say in the Mass are good works, if true prayers, but the Mass itself is not such. Thus priests attribute to the Mass what really belongs to the prayers. It is easy for the worshippers to be deceived by the many ceremonies which have grown up around the Mass: showy pomp hides its simplicity.

But what is to be said to the Canon of the Mass and the authority of the Fathers? He would rather deny their authority than hold the Mass a work or a sacrifice. The words "sacrifice" and "oblations" he refers to the collects and prayers, not to anything in the Mass. The elevation of the Host is a remnant of the Hebrew rite by which any offering to God was held up towards heaven. When the priest says Mass publicly let him remember that he is only receiving and giving to others the communion in the Mass; in a private Mass he is giving it to himself. Votive masses said for fees are condemned. The worthy partakers, for whom the Mass was intended, are those whose consciences are troubled: any man harassed by remorse or temptation to sin may come to it to receive remission of his sins by faith.

On Holy Baptism, he starts with a defence of Infant Baptism, and he relies on the divine promise: "He who believes and is baptised shall be saved:" this promise is far above all works, vows, religious orders, inventions of man. No Christian can lose his salvation by any sins except by unbelief. It is wrong to hold that the virtue of Baptism can be lost by sin, leaving penitence as a second plank of refuge after sin. Human traditions wrong the promise of God and man's own faith. We must look more to the word than to the sign. Baptism is a symbol of death and resurrection and he could wish for total immersion. He denounces the authority of Pope, bishop or anybody over a Christian man unless he gives his consent. And there are now so many ordinances, rites, and works that Christians forget their baptism. All vows, of religious orders or pilgrimages or aught else, he would do away with, and this would well be done by a general edict: of this he writes at length, and he attacks the Papal dispensations, such as from vows or marriage.

Next comes the sacrament of Penance. This sacrament consists (as the two foregoing) of the divine word and the believer's faith. But the powers of the Church have overlaid it. Contrition has been put before faith and made a merit. So faith has suffered. Secret confession as practised, although it has no Scriptural warrant, is highly satisfactory and even necessary: so far from wishing it done away with he rejoices that it does exist. It is well to unbosom our conscience to a brother and then get from him the word of consolation so as to quicken faith by a sense of God's mercy. But confession has been made into a tyranny, with its reserved cases. But any brother is able to absolve, for Christ has given all believers this power. Satisfaction (which he had treated of with Indulgences) is really a change of life: it is so strongly urged as necessary that no room is left for faith. With these he passes on from the three Sacraments which he accepts to speak of the four others which he rejects.

Confirmation he does not hold to be of divine institution: laying on of hands was practised for various things, but Confirmation has been invented so that bishops may have some work in the Church. But Christ said no word about Confirmation, so that something necessary to a Sacrament is wanting.

Matrimony fails to be a sacrament in much the same way: it has no word of promise. The tyrants of Rome at one time annul marriages and at another enforce them. But if the Pope or any bishop or official dissolves a marriage as contrary to his laws he is an Antichrist, going contrary to God's laws in nature. Spiritual affinities should be done away with. Idler

E
49

still is the doctrine of legal relationship and impediments: annulment of a betrothal by intercourse with a third party he discards. He touches on the impediment of Holy Orders, but is clearly against clerical celibacy. Divorce he detests, and would prefer bigamy, but its lawfulness or not he dare not define. Dissolution of marriage for the cause of desertion he does not pronounce upon. He would care little for any rule on this point laid down by Pope or bishops, but he would value the opinion of any two good and learned men decidedly in the spirit of Christ.

The Sacrament of Orders is unknown to the Church of Christ: it is invented by the Church of the Pope: it has no promise of grace, no place in Scripture. But he does not think that a rule practised for so many ages should be condemned. The Church has no power to establish any divine promise of grace as is involved in the assumption that it is governed by the Holy Spirit. Hence Orders are not a sacrament. He speaks of the pseudo-Dionysian rulings, for which he cares little. And finally he holds that all the baptised are equally priests with those ordained. He who does not preach the word of God, being called to this very office by the Church, is not a priest. A young man must not be deceived by the tonsure, vestments, and ceremonies into thinking that he is a priest.

Finally, he comes to Extreme Unction, which has been made a sacrament and kept for the extremity of life. As for its mention in St. James, many think that it was probably not written by the Apostle and is not worthy of the Apostolic spirit, although it has the sanction of usage. What the Epistle enjoins agrees not in form, practice or efficacy with that practised to-day.

At the very end he says that it might seem fitting to include as Sacraments all those things to which a divine promise is attached, such as prayer, the word, and the cross. Speaking of Confirmation he had asked why, if everything the Apostles did is to be reckoned as a sacrament, preaching should not be. It seemed best to hold as Sacraments only those promises which have signs annexed to them. So, to speak with perfect accuracy, only Baptism and Communion would be such. Penitence (or penance) is without any visible or appointed sign, and is nothing but a way of return to Baptism. But the absence in it of a sign should force the schoolmen to deny it a place among Sacraments.

He hears that fresh Bulls and Papal curses are being prepared against him and that he is to be forced to recant. If this is true he would like "this little book" to be part of his recantation. But if he had recanted, which he had declared he never would, the work would have been a curious appendix.

Looking at the work as a whole, it enables us to see the nature and scope of Luther's powers. He was not a systematic theologian himself and no rival would have been convinced by him. He referred to St. Cyprian, St. Augustine, the Pseudo-Dionysians, and St. Thomas Aquinas; to Aristotle at greater length. But, in reality, these excursions into scholarship have no essential link with his argument, which depends entirely on two fundamental doctrines, justification by faith and the priesthood of each individual Christian. These meet us at every turn. As a result, it is easy to see how Lutheranism, as taught by the great leader, tended to bring about anarchy in Church order and constitution, and a purely individual conception of religion. Hence might come licence in thought and action, but in the end this might cause an instinctive appeal to the powers which could enforce order, to the princes and the municipal authorities.

But although the *Babylonian Captivity* has little or nothing of the fiery force of the *Appeal to the Nobility*, or even of the *Christian Liberty*, and was written to convince scholars (which it was not very likely to do), it shows the experience which Luther had gained by his parochial ministry at Wittenberg. No man who had not had such experience could have written it: the writer knew the common man, his needs and his habits of mind, so that a work written by Luther as a scholar shows us more of Luther as a pastor than we see in either of the companion Primary Works.

The third work, *Concerning Christian Liberty* (also in November 1520), was dedicated to Leo X himself. He said

that he might have spoken strongly against the Pope's predecessors, but of him he asserted that he had said nothing
Christian   dishonourable although he had found fault with
Liberty.   his partisans. Eck he speaks of as "a notorious
adversary of Christ": Cardinal Cajetan as "an imprudent
and unfaithful, nay unfaithful legate." Carl Miltitz
had been more successful and had arranged a conference when Eck by his Disputation threw them all into confusion. But it was not conciliatory when Luther spoke of the
Church of Rome as "formerly the most holy of all churches,"
but now "become the most lawless den of thieves, the most
shameless of all brothels, the very kingdom of sin, death, and
hell: so that not even Antichrist, if he were to come, could
devise any addition to its wickedness." Luther had no intention of recanting: he had "no rage against Leo" and assumes
respect for him. But it was oddly mixed with other things.

His Erfurt friend, John Lang, had not liked the *Appeal to
the Nobility*, which he saw rightly would raise conflict, and
had urged him to recall it. But it was too late for this, and
Luther wrote (August 18, 1520) to Lang, telling him that he
held the Pope to be Antichrist, and that therefore he owed
him no obedience unless he also owed it to Antichrist. There
was therefore something unreal in addressing Pope Leo at all.
The distinction between a man himself and his office, familiar
in Italy where many ecclesiastics took things as they were,
was out of place in such fundamental matters.

After the Epistle comes the tractate itself, which has not the
striking force of the Address to the Nobility, and is more of a
theological tract.

It starts from two propositions: "A Christian man is the
freest Lord of all, and subject to none: he is, at the same time,
the most dutiful servant of all and subject to everyone." No
outward things can help to produce a state of justification and
Christian liberty, nor an unjustified state and one of slavery.
These statements are opened out at length and with much
repetition.

One thing, and one alone, is needful for life—justification
and Christian liberty, and that is the Gospel of Christ. Faith

has nothing to do with works: a Christian should put aside all trust on works and strengthen his faith. Faith alone, without works, justifies, sets free, and saves. If you wish to fulfil the law, believe in Christ. Christian liberty, our faith, has for its effect, not a bad or careless life: no one should need the law or works for justification and salvation. The believing soul, by its faith in Christ, becomes free from all sin and endowed with the righteousness and the life of Christ.

He passes on to discuss what character belongs to those now called "priests" as distinct from the laity. By the use of the words "priest," "clergy," "ecclesiastic," an injustice has been done to the rest of Christians, and the customary use of these terms is hurtful. It has led to pomp, power, tyranny, and degradation of the laity.

Works are to be done, not with any hope of justification by them, but only to bring the body into subjection and purify it. A Christian, consecrated by his faith, does good works but is not made more of a Christian by them. "Good works do not make a good man, but a good man does good works." So an unworthy and condemned man gains all the riches of salvation in Christ, and needs nothing but to believe that this is so.

Every man will be able to judge and discriminate between laws, to know the blind and foolish pastors, and the true and good. As for works, anything not directed to keeping the body under or helping our neighbour is no good or Christian work. The faith of Christ does not set us free from works but from the belief in them. As for ceremonies, the Christian man will meet men whom he must resist, hardened ceremonialists who will urge their ceremonies on him as if they could save. He may also come across simple men unable to understand the liberty of faith. These should be spared for fear of offence. The laws, such as those of tradition, should be denounced, and yet observed for the sake of the weak until they become able to understand their liberty. Ceremonies and works are unavoidable, but faith has to be taught. Often the ordinances of men have been taught, "the pestilent, impious, soul-destroying traditions of pontiffs and opinions of theologians." As poverty is imperilled by riches, honesty amid business, purity among pleasures, so faith is imperilled by ceremonies. Hypocrites who follow works never learn the faith for which such exist. The Christian must learn of God.

In teaching justification by faith Luther was on ground which he often trod. But expounded as it is by him here he seems to make the individual a judge of everything. This would result in anarchy of Church worship and of Church order. This would inevitably happen unless some power, stronger than the individual conscience or taste, stepped in to set up some order and secure it. This was, in truth, what took place. Princes in States, Councils in the cities, ordered the churches and the Church's ways as they pleased. Hence the power of the Princes, the control of the civic magistrates supplied ordinances and forms to replace what they were pleased to sweep away. And beneath all this the sovereignty of individual faith often grew into licence. And Luther himself, still more Melanchthon and others like him, saw religious anarchy and social evil grow, rather than the pious life and worship they had hoped to see.

But the force of habit, and the conservatism of worshippers, had still much power. Hence it was that many Lutheran local churches kept, for instance, the old Eucharistic vestments. Calvinists discarded them, but in many Lutheran churches, notably in Scandinavian countries, they were kept. The same thing happened with many of the olden Church furniture and ornaments, so that outwardly there might be less change than Luther's teaching might have been expected to bring about. But uniformity there was not, and indeed it was not held necessary.

In January 1521 the Diet of Worms [1] met under the new Emperor Charles V in person: his election (June 28, 1519) had been carried against the French party and had not been welcome to the Pope. As the ruler of Spain and the Netherlands he had other interests than those of Germany alone to consider. The Spanish influences of his youth (although he was brought up in the Netherlands) had given him an ideal of a church reformed after the Spanish model—righteous and disciplined, but under the

The Diet of Worms, 1521.

[1] Kidd, *Documents*, pp. 79 *seq.*

control of the State, and at times not shrinking from an anti-Papal policy. His religious principles were the real guide of his life, but the needs of his scattered and discordant realms and the constant poverty of his means made him less effective for good than with more power he would have been. Leo, dreading lest Charles, master of Naples as he was, should become too powerful an Emperor, had supported the election of Francis I of France. Remembering this, Charles's advisers were willing to favour Luther in order to embarrass the Pope: not only they, but Aleander also saw Luther's importance. But, to begin with, many high ecclesiastics, both in Germany and at Rome, had thought it a mere quarrel between Augustinians and Dominicans. They had often had such before, and did not understand that a more critical case had now to be dealt with.

In April Luther appeared before the Diet, and was asked whether he were willing to withdraw his works: after a day's consideration he refused unless convinced from Scripture of their falsehood. This was a formal defiance of the Church, for to neither Pope nor Council would he now submit: the fallibility of Councils he indeed expressly asserted. Negotiations, with little result, delayed the climax until (May 1521) by the authority of the Emperor, though against the wish of some Electors, Luther was put under the ban of the Empire: his teaching was to be suppressed, and his books destroyed (Edict of Worms). It was significant that this condemnation was generally held more really important than that by the Pope. This very Diet, however, had presented to the Emperor Wimpheling's old list of complaints against the Curia, dealing mainly with fees, patronage, and conflicts of jurisdiction; at its close the Archbishop of Mayence wrote to the Pope that the number of Lutherans was increased, few laymen sided with the clergy, the majority even of priests were ashamed to support the Roman Church, "so hateful was the name of the Roman Curia and the Papal decrees."

Thus a movement, not more formidable at first than others of no permanent effect, had by the circumstances of its origin and the manner in which it was met, become of the greatest moment. The incident could not, as

Its results.

55

Leo, blind to its gravity, had hoped, be speedily closed. The Emperor, a good Catholic, as he truthfully asserted, devout and orthodox in doctrine as were his Spanish subjects, might have small sympathy with Luther, although his advisers saw possible political uses for this bold heretic. But in religion the Emperor and Pope were drawn together: politics had also thrown them together, and Milan (November 19, 1521) had just been seized by their allied armies. England, too, rising now to a greater position in Europe, was in their alliance. At this very time, however, Leo died (December 1, 1521), though not before he had heard the reward of his alliance—the recovery of Parma and Piacenza for his dominions. But the crisis in Germany, quieted only for a time, outweighed this purely territorial gain.

On January 9, 1522, Adrian of Utrecht, formerly tutor to the Emperor and now his Viceroy in Spain, was elected Pope, since neither French nor Spanish could carry their candidates. In the Conclave Imperial and French parties (preparing the way for the later right of exclusion claimed by the great Powers and later on admitted) were formed: there was also a small neutral party headed by Cardinal Colonna. In some ways the obvious choice was Cardinal Giulio de Medici, son of the Giuliano de Medici who had been murdered in the Pazzi conspiracy: of his mother nothing was known, but he had been dispensed from his bar of illegitimacy. He had been made a Cardinal the year of his cousin's accession, and after two or three years became his leading man of affairs, so that he held all the tangled threads of Papal diplomacy: it may be noted that he followed other Italians in holding the see of Worcester. But there was a natural objection to making the Papacy something of a family inheritance, and there was an even stronger objection to another Florentine Pope. Francis I announced that if Medici were elected no one in France would obey the Pope.

Adrian VI., Jan. 9, 1522– Sept. 14(?), 1523.

Henry VIII, too, entered hopefully as a diplomatist into the Italian atmosphere: both Francis I and Charles V had promised to help Wolsey's ascent, but Charles was wishful for de Medici's success, and, failing that, had mentioned the name of his old tutor Adrian, Bishop of Tortosa. But Wolsey was so hopeful

56

that he even offered to finance a Spanish army for a march towards Rome to overawe the Cardinals.

The Conclave of thirty-nine Cardinals began on December 27, 1521, and many scrutinies only ended in smoke. The election was a very secular matter flavoured with finance and the closure was only nominal. Despairing of his hopes and faced by many rivals, de Medici said that it seemed best to choose an absent Cardinal, and at the eleventh scrutiny named the Cardinal of Tortosa, a saintly man and also elderly, being sixty-three. Cardinal Cajetan made an enthusiastic speech on his spiritual merits, and so (January 9, 1522) Adrian VI was elected. It was strange that so secular a process should have ended in the choice of a really spiritually minded man, intent upon righteousness and fit to compare in character with the best of his forerunners.[1]

Adrian was a Cardinal of four years' standing, but with few Roman interests: his origin was lowly: but teachers at Zwolle, Deventer, and Louvain had formed his mind by the excellent methods of the Brethren of the Common Life. He became a Professor at Louvain, and was Chancellor and Rector there. Others had formed his mind, but his piety was all his own. He became tutor to Charles, and a member of the Council for the Netherlands. Then he passed to Spain, where he worked with Ximenes: when he was made Bishop of Tortosa he gave up the benefices he held, and after the death of Ximenes (November 8, 1517) he became chief Minister to Charles, not only in civil politics, but as Inquisitor-General for Castile and Leon (the Inquisition being almost a Crown department): the difficulties he had to face were great, complicated, and varied; if he did not reach effectual success, his character and simple piety were known to all: public life had not made him secular or self-seeking.

In the fourteenth century there had grown up a custom for

[1] The Conclaves for the whole period are well treated by Pastor. Two smaller works by J. B. Sägmüller are most useful: *Die Papstwahlen und die Staaten von* 1447 *bis* 1555 (Tübingen, 1890) and *Die Papstwahlbullen und das staatliche Recht der Exclusive* (Tübingen, 1892). For earlier times: R. Zoepffel: *Die Papstwahlen* (Göttingen, 1871), which describes the Ceremonies, is also of use.

the Cardinals, like the Electors to the Empire, to draw up
Capitulation binding the new Pope, whether one of themselves
or another to be elected. It was connected with the *Professio
Fidei*, customary for all Bishops, and it had grown into a
method of strengthening the control of the College over Papal
power and action. There was now little hesitation in saying
what the future Pope was to do: he was to extirpate heresy,
bring about peace in the west, drive out the Turks, and reform
the Church. This was a large programme, somewhat indefinite
and hard to fulfil. But the conditions for their own advantage
were easier and more definite: the number of Cardinals was to
be reduced to twenty-four, with permission for two of the
Papal kindred. Cardinals whose income fell below the six
thousand ducats held necessary were to receive pensions from
the Pope, and their incomes were secured on the taxes of the
subject cities.[1] The Inquisition in Spain had become an organ
of royal influence and Church reform; if it had no sympathy
with the newer thought of the day, it had a keen interest in
clerical discipline. The same might be looked for from the
new Pope. His treatment of Luther might probably be stricter
than Leo's had been; theology was to him a matter of vital
importance.

One of his first acts was significant.[2] Erasmus—the type of
a reformer bent on divine learning, eager to repress evil in high
The Pope and and low, broad in sympathy but orthodox in theol-
Erasmus.   ogy, with a zeal for unity as fervent as that of S. Paul
himself—was asked to Rome. It is characteristic of the way in
which parties overlapped and yet were distinctly forming that
Erasmus was suspected by some of writing Henry VIII's attack
upon Luther and by others of being the author of Luther's
reply. The immediate result of "the Lutheran tragedy" was
that those who put unity before reform began to dread reform
itself: that many of those who hoped for reform began to think

[1] For the history of the Capitulations see: Jean Lulvès: *Papstliche
Wahlkapitulationen* (Rome, 1909) and *Die Machtbestrebungen des Kar-
dinalats bis zur Aufstellung der ersten Papstlichen Wahlkapitulationen*
(Rome, 1910)—two excellent studies.

[2] For his Papacy: Pastor: IV. 2, pp. 1–157 (*German*), IX. 34–250
(*English*); C. Höfler: *Adrian VI.* (Vienna, 1880).

it incompatible with unity. The cause of unity was thus weighted by mistaken advocates with that of abuses: the cause of reform was equally wrongly weighted with that of revolution. It is easy for mistaken men either of thought or action to prejudice great issues in such a way. But Erasmus was one who kept his head clear amid strife and discord: the accession of Adrian seemed to promise a reform furthered by the guardian of Western unity, the Pope himself. He refused Adrian's invitation to Rome, but stated his views of what was needed. A Council must meet: everyone must give up something for the common good. The evil had gone too far for burning or amputation. To consider these questions there should be called from every country men of unsullied integrity, grave, mild, gracious and without passion, whose opinions—and here the letter breaks off, a tempting field for conjecture. But such a council Erasmus had long desired.

Two elements of opposition very near the Papacy had, however, to be reckoned with—the officials of the Curia dependent upon offices bought, in many cases, for large sums, and the extreme conservative theologians alarmed at the spread of a new learning with which they did not sympathise and a criticism which they held dangerous. The one deprecated change in the central administration, the other needed but to see a doctrine or practice attacked to become convinced of its necessity to guard more fundamental points. The former party naturally had its stronghold at Rome; the latter in the Sorbonne, at Louvain, Ingoldstadt and Cologne. In theological matters they could also depend upon Spanish ecclesiastics, but in matters of discipline the Spaniards, themselves trained up under a strict system, wished to see the same everywhere enforced.

The new Pope declared Luther's opinions insipid and unreasonable; he saw, however, how much support they had gained from unchecked abuses and from political interests involved. He at once addressed himself, therefore, to the most urgent questions of practice and manners. First he took up the question of Indulgences and the administration of the Curia.

He desired a return to a more primitive discipline of penance, which would restore Indulgences to their former place, and lay stress upon two elements—the inward feeling of the penitent, and the service done to the Church by the deed of penance or the money equivalent paid for the Indulgences. But an objection was made by some of the Curia that any regulation of the subject might be regarded as a confession of error in the face of criticism, and so both the unregulated opinions and the practical abuses were finally left undealt with. The officials, however, were charged to be more sparing and cautious in their issue of indulgences. Unsuccessful here, Adrian next turned to dispensations, especially in cases of marriage. Here, again, the interests of officials who had bought their offices and depended upon the fees were concerned. This influence was powerful enough to stay reform, but the Pope insisted upon care in the issue of dispensations, and also by a decree made void all reservations to benefices and dignities granted since 1484. At home among theologians and in the ecclesiastical atmosphere of Spain—although even there he had not been very successful in his dealings with men and worldly forces—Adrian was out of sympathy with the Roman Court, and failed to understand its delicate politics. The interests of Italy, he was told, made the action he suggested unwise, but in one respect he and his advisers, Spanish theologians and Italian men of affairs, were agreed—heresy in Germany must be suppressed by strong measures, and at once. The plea of Erasmus for unselfish reform and abstinence from repression was disregarded. But this was not the fault of Adrian himself: he desired reform, but had not the confidence of Roman officials absorbed in their duties; nor was he in accord with the high view of Papal prerogative held at the Curia: he had said in his book on the Sacraments that many Popes had been heretics,[1] and that so the Pope was liable to err in matters of faith. This meant that he for himself would be careful in his actions, but it also meant that he did not fully share the view of the Papacy common at Rome.

[1] "Plures enim fuerunt pontifices Romani haeretici." Quoted by Fr. Puller in *The Primitive Saints and the See of Rome* (London, 1900), p. 498. Adrian's work was reprinted when he was Pope.

In Germany the dread of the Turks and the religious ferment were the leading features projected upon a background
of political anarchy. The Emperor had returned Confusion in
(1521) to Spain, leaving behind him a Council of Germany.
Regency, in which his brother Ferdinand and Frederick
of Saxony were the leading figures. For some years a very
open state of things existed. Plans for appropriating the
annates to the Turkish War and heavily taxing the monasteries were proposed. Luther's temporary captivity in the
Wartburg—his "Patmos," in reality his refuge from all
dangers—left Melanchthon, the gentle scholar, Reuchlin's
nephew and now the leader of thought at Wittenberg, where
(1518) he had become Professor, and Carlstadt, the reckless
and outspoken innovator, to be leaders of the ecclesiastical
opposition. The Diet at Nüremberg (1522) listened to Adrian's
sincere promises of reform, qualified by assertions of its difficulty, but refused to carry out the Decree of Worms. To many
Germans the suppression of Luther appeared to mean the sanction of felt abuses. Let the Pope call a free Council in Germany to settle everything. Until that met the Gospel was to
be preached "in the true Christian sense." The utmost Germany would promise was a vague regulation of preachers and
a censorship of the Press. But the execution of these measures
depended upon the local Princes, and was therefore ineffective.
Meanwhile the Lutherans had declared monastic vows mistaken. Everywhere, especially among the Augustinians, monks
were leaving their monasteries. Some, like Luther himself a
little later, were taking wives. Changes in the Mass were
demanded and sometimes made, not only the restoration of
the chalice to the laity, but more radical alterations. But these
ecclesiastical questions were overshadowed by politics—externally, the rivalry of France and Spain, with England thrown
in as a deciding weight: internally, the warfare between Franz
von Sickingen with his knights against some princes.

In the spring of 1522 Franz von Sickingen, the best known
of the knights and their elected leader, attacked his old enemy
the Archbishop of Trier (Treves); on the surface it was
"a private war" of the common type, and the pretext for it

was slight. But in reality it was something more: it was a bid for power by the knights. Against the Council of Regency which was trying to enforce some central rule they had a special grudge: they would have liked to restore the most anarchic days of feudalism so as to be left free to pillage and oppress at their pleasure. But some of the Princes took the field against them, and the war ended in the destruction by the new artillery of Sickingen's castle supposed to be impregnable, and his fatal injury in its ruins.

The Knights' War.
Sept. 1522–April 1523.

Sickingen's schemes were not merely political: he had joined the yet unconsolidated Lutherans, and had offered Luther himself a shelter which Bucer had afterwards gladly accepted; another of his chaplains was married as was Bucer; Sickingen and his friends insisted upon Communion in both kinds and made other changes. In the Middle Ages mercenaries and other men of violence had shown regard for religious services and even for doctrines, although piety might seem oddly joined to their life. It was the same now with some on the reformed side, although Sickingen was a strange religious leader. In neither case can we assume insincerity or a wish to utilise religious interests for base purposes. In days of speedy change the characters of men are more strangely compounded and moved than in times of quiet. And when social, political and religious movements are all causing unrest, motives and actions are curiously mixed. It was to be so now: Hutten had held up Ziska as a model for his friend Sickingen, and so the Hussite tradition was revived on the political as already on the ecclesiastical side. Bucer travelled as ambassador for Sickingen, and as such visited Luther to ask his help. But his mission failed, and as yet Luther, to his credit, refused to enter the paths of secular politics.

The Lutheran movement had now passed into its third stage; it was thus bound up with German politics. Adrian was no politician, in spite of his political experience. "Let a man be never so good, how much depends upon the times in which he is born," he said once, and his times and his responsibilities were hard indeed. He represented some of the freshest currents of religious thought and represented them at the centre of Christianity, but the theologian of simple life (he lived on a ducat a day) was not strong enough for his task. The new currents of thought had not yet lifted the Papacy from its medieval moorings. And it had as yet no great organisation for clerical reform (such as the Inquisition had been in Spain) ready to its hand. When the Papacy had been moved, and the organisation had been found, Adrian's reform and cleansing of the Church might be accomplished. Until then political complications and the German tragedy were rending the Church's life.

Adrian's pathetic Papacy closed in 1523 (September 14). His successor was Cardinal Giulio de Medici (Clement VII), a clever Italian diplomatist and politician, a thorough man of affairs, as popular in Rome as Adrian had been unpopular. Critical politics made a speedy election desirable. As before, French and Imperial parties were formed, but there was also a cross-division between the older Cardinals and those created by Leo X. The Conclave began (October 1, 1523) a fortnight after Adrian's death. De Medici, even more determined than before to become Pope, was favoured by Charles V, but disliked by the French ecclesiastics. Thirty-five members of the college were in Rome, and three French Cardinals arrived, booted and spurred from their journey, in time for the first scrutiny. Farnese was hopeful for himself, and Colonna had a chance: other names were tossed about. Wolsey was again most eager, and the Emperor was induced to write a letter in his favour, but the messenger was unhappily delayed until the election was over. Some French lay diplomatists on their arrival fancied that de Medici was after all too wary and politic to be strongly fixed in his imperialist sympathy, and so their first strong antipathy to him was lessened.

Restlessness among the citizens, even fears of a possible schism, and pressure of politics signified by threats of a reduced diet, soothed the electors into acquiescence, and de Medici's persistence was rewarded when (November 19, 1523) he was elected with an unanimity of votes rather than of convictions.

Clement VII., 1523.

He did a generous and politic act, thoughtfully foreshadowed in the capitulations, by dividing his numerous benefices among his electors. There was now a political Pope, having all the useful arts and knowledge which Adrian VI had lacked, but without his sincere and pervading piety. It may be noted that when a formal right of excluding beforehand a candidate by name was allowed to the monarchs of Germany and France, the closure was more strictly observed in the elections. So far it had become something more formal than real.

Germany first of all called for the Pope's attention. A Diet was to meet at Nuremberg (January 1524), and there Cardinal Campeggio appeared as legate. His reception was bad, and the utmost he could gain was an assurance that the Edict of Worms should be carried out as far as possible. Once more a Council was demanded: until it met, a national assembly for the consideration of grievances was suggested. Meanwhile the Word of God was to be preached according to the Doctors of the Church. The Emperor was as displeased as the Pope at the disregard of the Edict so peculiarly his work. A Council, however, he wished for, and urged upon the Pope: Trent was even suggested as its seat. Clement felt his difficulty and sought help from Henry VIII, Luther's royal antagonist. Pressure on German merchants, applied by Henry, might be transmitted to German princes, and at any rate a protest might be raised against Germany alone considering and settling doctrines for Western Christendom.

Hostile camps—even in the Council of Regency itself—were by this time clearly formed. Upon the Pope's instruc-*Divisions* tions the legate himself at Regensburg (Ratisbon) *in Germany.* organised the Catholic party (June 1524). Ferdi-*Regensburg* nand, the Emperor's brother, who held the Aus-*League,* *1524.* trian lands, and the two Dukes of Bavaria took the lead. In Bavaria the University of Ingolstadt, where the controversialist Eck was a teacher, had been reorganised in a Catholic sense, the Duke's Chancellor, Leonard von Eck, strongly supporting the work.

A commission, independent of the Bishops, whose zeal did

not satisfy the Duke, was appointed to degrade unworthy clerks; in return for the support given to the Church the Duke was granted a fifth of the ecclesiastical incomes in his territory, a grant renewed from time to time. Catholic Bavaria, long hesitating in its policy, now Reaction. definitely took its stand on the Catholic side, but the impulse to this step had come from the State, inspired by the active influence of Eck. The religious tone of Austria, where the ducal support was secured in a like way, was the same, and these two States formed the nucleus of a strong Catholic league. If North Germany was the home of the Protestant revolt, South Germany was thus the home of the reaction against it. Around Bavaria and Austria gathered a group of princes, mainly ecclesiastical: from Salzburg, Basle (where the Bishop Christopher von Uttenheim, a friend of Erasmus, had greatly raised the tone of life), Augsburg, Strassbourg, Passau, Brixen, Freising, and Trent. Some of these, especially Basle and Augsburg, had already begun reform and revival. The Conference of Regensburg formed three commissions, for the quarrels of clergy and laity, reform and doctrine respectively. Preachers were to be licensed and ordered to abide by the old Doctors of the Church: excessive fees were to be reduced: the number of holidays to be lessened: preachers were to be more earnest and priests more holy: the too free and trivial use of excommunication and interdicts, the abuses of Indulgences, were forbidden: the clergy were to be more restrained in life and dress: a commission of competent theologians in every diocese were to enforce these decisions; at the same time all Lutherans were to be expelled. Even thus early it was found that where the chances of Catholic reform were strongest, tenderness towards the Lutherans and a wish for reconciliation were the weakest. Thus the hostile camps were formed; there was a party of ecclesiastical reformers in sharp doctrinal opposition to Luther, but their relations to the Papacy were affected by political considerations, and especially by the attitude of the Pope and Emperor to each other. For the present, however, this party had enough influence with Charles to bring to nothing the proposed National Council. At a much later date Charles was inclined to adopt this suggestion, fearing it was his only way of securing reform.

Inside the Lutheran movement itself varying tendencies were seen. While in the Wartburg, Luther began his New Testament (1522), followed by the Old Testament (to be finished only in 1534). Apart from its inestimable value to the nation, its influence upon the language was comparable to that of the English Bible upon England, and it placed Luther even more in touch with the national feeling. Already his boldness and his loud cry for reforms, long ago and repeatedly demanded by the nation, had given him a national position: now he popularised the scriptural movement begun on a large scale first by Erasmus. But if in some ways typically German, Luther was also typically scholastic; he never departed from the standpoint of his master Staupitz, as did other leaders of the revolt—unlike the Calvinists, he kept the crucifix and the Catholic vestments: unlike the Zwinglians he never denied the Real and Bodily presence of Christ in the Holy Eucharist: the iconoclasm of men like Carlstadt met with no sympathy from him: his sacramental doctrine—often called Consubstantiation, a term he did not use himself—was an illogical attempt to keep what he regarded as essential in the Catholic doctrine, and at the same time to deny the form—Transubstantiation—in which that doctrine was generally and often crudely explained. The one part of Church life for which he felt no concern was that of government; a fact which may be accounted for: Church polity had been weakened by the stress laid upon Papal power, lowering the historic importance of Episcopate and priesthood: the monastic system instead of supplementing too often weakened Church order: in Germany, owing to the inroads of the princely families upon the sees and chapters, the Episcopate was weaker than elsewhere and Luther had once dissuaded Staupitz from accepting a See. Luther lived under these conditions, and—even if he disregarded his vows—was a monk at heart, although technically a friar. This was his doctrinal position, but he had been led on, much as Wyclif had been before him, to repudiate the Papacy as anti-Christian. Looking

And in the Lutheran Movement itself.

too exclusively upon the prevalent corruptions, he was absolutely free from any scruples as to a breach of unity or from any regard for the Church polity that secured it. It was here even more than in doctrine that he differed from Erasmus, to whom unity of organisation was an essential, the framework of Christian charity and the bond that formed it. Luther was fitted by his strong personality and his national enthusiasm to lead a great movement: he was conservative in many respects, but his conservatism lacked a sense of proportion: hence any movement led by him was likely to become even more revolutionary than he and his followers meant. Had the movement been treated otherwise than it was, had the sense of proportion been supplied from outside, Luther might have led a great revival inside the Church—an upheaval akin to that wrought by the old monastic orders or the friars—instead of a separation from it. The manner in which he was met, his own lack of regard for unity, and the political state of Germany, combined to make his movement a schism.

Luther's comrade, Melanchthon—more learned and more of a theologian—was doctrinally, although not personally, more capable of leading a schism. He was born in Baden at Bretten: his father was an armourer related to Reuchlin, and his mother, a very sensible woman, was of good family. He went to school at Pforzheim, and came to his great kinsman. He took his Bachelor's degree at Heidelberg (1511) and became a Master at Tübingen: in 1518 the Elector Frederick made him Professor of Greek at Wittenberg: there he became Luther's close and beloved friend, although he was fourteen years younger. His renown as a scholar and a lecturer was widespread and well-founded, so much that attempts were made to attract him into the opposite camp, in the University of Ingolstadt. His earlier Humanism was never lost: he lectured on the classics as on the Bible, and with the same success. Education on sound lines he furthered by many editions of classics and by text-books. So many-sided was his work that he was called *Preceptor Germaniae*. He was of a refined and gentle nature, and his love of peace and tolerance of mind made him, after Luther's death, suspect

Melanchthon, 1497–1560.

by more violent Lutherans.[1] But his deep-rooted Christianity intensified his real beauty of soul. His *Loci Communes*—first produced in 1521 and revised in later editions—has been rightly called the first Protestant system of theology. From this book—said by Luther to be worthy of a place in the Canon—was afterwards derived a school of Protestant scholastics—building upon the Bible alone, interpreting it through a doctrinal system purely personal and subjective; independent to begin with, this school became later on more traditional, more fettered by great names than even medieval scholasticism itself. Broadly speaking, this system disregarded the whole outward life of the Church, laid small stress upon the Sacraments, and developed all theology from the kernal of justification by faith, which gradually became more prominent. Too much stress is often laid upon this the leading positive doctrine of Luther, and it is forgotten that his negations were as important in their effect. On the positive side many in high office held views approaching his, but they did not share his negations—his disregard of the Episcopate and general Church order. This central doctrine led to much controversy—of the most unprofitable because most subjective kind—among Protestants themselves; it was afterwards blamed as the cause of much religious anarchy and moral licence. It was very significant that Erasmus, when urged to write against Luther, chose as his ground of attack the Free Will of man (the point upon which the Leipzig Disputation turned); through the stress laid upon original sin and the Divine grace man's responsibility and his dependence upon the means of grace were held too lightly: this Erasmus felt, and hence his choice of topic.

The extreme doctrines of some preachers, such as Carlstadt, and of others more fanatic and less educated, joined to **Extreme** the social pressure upon the lower classes, produced **Doctrines.** the Peasants' Revolt (1524–5) and the Anabaptist Rising; the latter an attempt to set up a kingdom of God

---

[1] His life was written by his friend Camerarius: *De Vita P. M. Narratio* (Leipzig, 1566) and reprinted often since, as by G. T. Frobelius (Halle, 1777) and by Neander in his *Vitae Quattuor Reformatorum* (Berlin, 1841).

with community of goods and licence of life. Both in Germany and Switzerland there grew up an extreme wing of Reformers, carrying some of the Lutheran and Zwinglian doctrines further than their authors did, and in some cases combining religious innovation with social discontent. Thomas Münzer, at Zwickau (1521), and others, had not only declaimed against the existing system, and advocated change; they went further, and claimed direct inspiration; a new society —based on this new life and new power—was to be constructed; personal consecration and illumination was demanded from its members, hence infants were excluded and infant baptism denied; it was one of the many attempts to form a holy and elect society; Taborite (Hussite) influence helped in the earlier stages; not all the leaders were extreme or dangerous men; some were peaceful if ignorant followers of the earlier mystics; Luther, and even still more Zwingli, had earlier stood in close relations with them. At Zürich the Anabaptist leaders were among Zwingli's earliest disciples, and felt disappointed when he would not join their separatist conventicles; he, for his part, was hurt at the discredit they brought upon his principles and his movement, and hence his measures against them were as harsh as their speech against him. But they could fairly claim that his principles could be stretched to cover their acts. Something of this same connection existed between the earlier Anabaptist movement and the Reformation in other places. It would be unjust to put down to all the Anabaptists the views of the extreme men, but historically and politically the movement was led by these.

While Luther was in the Wartburg these teachers of spiritual exaltation, hostile to learning, partly broke up the University at Wittenberg; only Luther's sudden reappearance and exercise of strong personal influence and common sense checked the movement there (March 1522). Yet under Carlstadt and Münzer it broke out again at Mühlhausen, marked this time by fiercer iconoclasm and attacks upon the monasteries (1524). But the Peasants' Revolt soon swallowed up this other movement. Like the English Peasants' Revolt in 1381, this was a complicated movement; in

Their Practical Results.

69

some places, as at Waldshut, an Austrian town, north-west of Zürich, and at Gröningen (south of Zürich), social and religious causes worked together, in others the two were distinct; as the social movement grew, it emphasised the democratic spirit of the religious revolution, objecting to tithes, and claiming the appointment of the parish priests. Early in 1525 the war broke out, and resulted in the suppression of the peasants by the Princes. Luther, dreading the anarchy that might result from the rising, and not much in sympathy with its social causes (here he differed from Zwingli), had exhorted the Princes to act with firmness and strength. This they did, and although the fanatic rising at Münster (1534) was a later form of the movement, an extreme attempt to realise a free kingdom on earth, Social Revolution and aggressive Anabaptism perished together. The result was that the Princes—already the foremost element of the nation—had increased their power. Luther had lost much of his popularity among the democracy, and his movement was discredited in the eyes of many in the upper classes by its association with Anabaptism. Many who had worked for reform, and looked to Lutheranism as likely to hasten it, now drew away from any connection with it.

Before 1524 the Humanist current had split itself into many diverse streams. Renaissance, Reformation, Counter-Reforma-

Humanism and the German Reformers. tion were all parts of one great movement aiming at improvement; different elements were mingled in different proportions in them, but the general problem before the world was to reject the evil elements and preserve the good. To do this should have been the special object of the Church. The Papacy, except on the artistic side, had not so far shown itself alive to this great need; and had it not been for a few great scholars like Erasmus, the Revival of Learning would not have been utilised for the service of the Church. Humanism had at first on the whole sympathised rather with Luther than with his opponents. But a few years made a great difference. Ulrich von Hutten, discredited by his alliance with von Sickingen in his private war, noted for the licence of his life and the power of his pen, represented one division of the Humanists; Melanchthon, with all a scholar's enthusiasm and much of a scholar's timidity, stood for another; Erasmus, through many years firm in his principles and continuous in his work when all around were changing, stood for another. And these took different sides in the religious struggle. But there were others—Johann Faber (Vicar-General of Constanz, an early friend of Zwingli's, but after a visit to Rome in 1522 an opponent of his), Pirkheimer, of Nuremberg, Cochlœus, and other scholars besides, who now definitely took up their stand on the anti-Lutheran side. The Catholic gathering at Regensburg (June 1524) had expressed the same tendency. The forces of defence were drawing closer together against the forces of attack. But from this time onward the main weight of the purely literary Humanist movement was thrown upon the Catholic side; reform itself— much as it was desired—seemed to many of less importance than unity and the maintenance of faith. The Anabaptist movement and the Peasants' War had helped to bring about this result. The death of Ulrich von Hutten (end of August 1523), one of the more revolutionary Humanists, may be taken as the water-shed between the Renaissance and the Reformation. Refused—and with some reason—the friendship of Erasmus at Basle, he found a resting-place at Zürich, where Zwingli— himself the product of Humanism, and with little regard for authority and tradition—befriended him. From this time Zwingli stood apart, not only from his former "master," Erasmus, but from his old friend Glareanus (Löriti), "the shadow of Erasmus," as he was called. In September, 1524, the treatise of Erasmus on Free-will marked his definite opposition to the new movement. Luther he had considered, so he said, a kind of necessary evil in the corrupt state of the Church. From such a violent remedy he had hoped for a return of health to the Christian body. But now a new, rude, and intractable generation was growing up; the ranters who had arisen would ruin both the Gospel and good letters. If he must be a slave, he had rather be a slave to Pope and Bishops than to these newly risen tyrants. It was for the sake of good letters in the sacred sense understood by him that Erasmus—much as he loathed gladiatorial contests—stepped into the hated arena.

In 1526 a Diet was to meet at Speier (Spires), but much had happened before it met. The victory of Pavia (February

The Diet of Speier (Spires), 1526.

25, 1525) had made Francis I of France a captive to Charles, and had thus given the Papacy reason to dread the Emperor: the possessor of Naples could not be allowed to grow too powerful in Italy. At the very time the Diet met the Papal troops and those of France and Milan, with England as a cool ally, were fighting against the Emperor. Francis had been set free by a treaty (January 14, 1526), in which, among other things, he promised help against heresy. But Clement, for political reasons, released Francis from the obligation of his oath, which, indeed, sat only too lightly upon him, and the anti-Spanish League of Cognac followed (May 22, 1526). The Allies, however, met with small success. In Germany too the Princes were considering alliances; in July 1525, Duke George of Saxony, the Elector of Brandenburg, the Archbishop of Mayence, and others met at Dessau to discuss a Catholic league; in October the Landgrave, Philip of Hesse—the ablest and least conventional of the Protestant leaders—tried to form a Protestant alliance to hinder the pro-

Opposed Leagues.

posed enforcement of the Edict of Worms and arrest the persecution, already begun, of Protestant preachers. At Gotha (February 1526) Hesse and Saxony (where the Elector Frederick had been succeeded by his brother John (May 1525)) formed such a league, enlarged (June 1526) by the adhesion of three Brunswick Princes, Anhalt, and the city of Magdeburg. It was not likely, therefore, that the ecclesiastical unity of Germany could be maintained. The Emperor, keenly alive to the danger of heresy and specially anxious to carry out his own Edict of Worms, was not, however, likely to concede too much to the Pope. The old complaints against the Curia and the Church were renewed when the Diet met at Speier (June 25, 1526); a majority of the Princes decided in favour of the marriage of priests, communion in both kinds, the reduction of holidays, the abolition of private Masses, and a restricted use of German in the Mass and Holy Baptism; the appointment of Bishops—practically in the hands of the Pope with Emperor or Princes—was freely criticised. But Ferdinand, who in the Emperor's absence took his place, forbade in his name all innovations, and, pending a General Council(a national German Assembly Charles would not at present hear of), urged the execution of the Edict of Worms. But the Princes, knowing that Charles's relations with the Pope were now altered, deemed him unlikely to press an Edict which the cities held impracticable. It was resolved to consult the Emperor, now in Spain, upon the point, and until his opinion was received, a provisional arrangement was made: "Every State should so behave, rule, and believe as it should hope and trust to answer before God, the Emperor, and the Empire." [1]

This celebrated decision has often been described as the basis of territorial religion in Germany—of the principle, "*Cujus regio; ejus religio.*" It was impossible to get concerted action between an Emperor with other realms to think of and funds too small for his needs, a Pope led by political considerations, and Princes bent, if orthodox, upon secularising bishoprics, if Lutheran, upon the organisation of separatist bodies, and so this temporary arrangement did become a permanent basis. But it became so purely because of later facts and not because it was meant to legalise the ecclesiastical change that was widely carried out. It gave no legal footing to Protestantism within the Empire, but no legal sanction was needed in an anarchical realm for anything with vitality enough to exist. The Emperor could hardly approve the decision, but he acquiesced in its results. Some of his advisers recommended the abolition of penalties for heresy and the summoning of a Council to restore ecclesiastical unity. But war, politics and unity went badly together. In May 1527 an Imperial army sacked Rome itself, and the Pope was, in fact, a prisoner of the Emperor's. These strained Sack of Rome, May 1527. relations—only partly ended by the Pope gaining his freedom in November 1527 and only fully ended in June 1529 by the Treaty of Barcelona—allowed religious matters in Germany to settle themselves as might turn out.

Ferdinand had been at first strongly anti-Lutheran; he gained greatly in income from the Church in his duchies; he had

---

[1] Kidd, *Documents*, etc., pp. 181–185.

suffered much from the Peasants' Revolt, but events withdrew him from too active interference in Germany and gave him other interests. The Emperor Maximilian, following old dynastic aims and fortunate in their attainment, had married his grandson Ferdinand to Anna, sister of Lewis II, King of Hungary and Bohemia, while Lewis himself was married to Ferdinand's sister Mary. In battle against the Turks—the plague of Eastern Europe—Lewis fell at Mohacs (August 30, 1526). Bohemia elected Ferdinand as King (October 1526); he had to conform to the compact of Basle and promise if possible to secure an archbishop for the Utraquists, and hence at the Council of Trent he was found urging the permission of communion in both kinds. In Hungary, where Zapolya was a dangerous rival, Ferdinand's sister Mary secured her brother the throne, and in 1527 he was acknowledged as king there also. Thus the composite Habsburg territories were largely increased, and Ferdinand gained interests not purely German; above all, his new kingdom bound him to oppose the Turks with all his strength.

In Germany the organisation of the new religious bodies was now carried out in Electoral Saxony, Hesse, Ansbach, Anhalt (Köthen), Brunswick-Lüneburg, East Friesland, Silesia, and Schleswig-Holstein. East Prussia Albert of Brandenburg, Grandmaster of the Teutonic Knights, secularised under Poland (1525) into a hereditary duchy, which began a momentous history. The great cities of North Germany were also by this time mainly Lutheran. The new ecclesiastical organisation was in all cases made under the direction of the civil ruler and by his authority. The principle "*Cujus regio*; *ejus religio*" was so far accepted as to give large powers to the Prince, both in choosing the religion of his State and settling its details. Every prince, said the Strassbourg preacher Capito later, was head of the Church in his territory, appointed as such by Christ in his own place. The organisation of Saxony may be taken as a type.[1] Four commissions of laymen and clergy visited four divisions of the

The Reformed Body in Germany.

[1] Kidd, *Documents*, etc., pp. 185–232 for the organisation of the Lutheran Church, and the Saxon Visitation.

Electorate; stress was laid upon teaching, provided for by catechisms modelled upon earlier works, and upon preaching; superintendents of the clergy were appointed by the Elector, and these took the place of bishops. German was used, of course, in the services, and Luther's hymns added a further national element; the old portions of Scripture selected for epistles and gospels were kept; the continued use of the vestments (which were forbidden in Prussia), the crucifix and candles upon the altars, made the breach of continuity less noticeable.

The Zwinglian model (yet to be spoken of), which was to creep northwards in later years, made its entire breach with the past more apparent; the vestments and altar ornaments were removed; the polity set up was congregational and democratic; everything was cut down to the barest. But the rise of this separate movement and its historical importance have yet to be noticed.

After the meeting at Regensburg (1524) the suppression of heretical opinions had become much stricter in the lands of the Princes present there; nowhere, however, was it Its stricter than in the Netherlands, Charles's own Opponents. dominions. His dislike of Lutheranism grew; he and the Pope felt greater need of each other's help, and at length (1527) Clement promised a Council. The year 1529 marked the height of Charles's power: the Treaty of Barcelona (June 1529), signed by him and the Pope, recognised him as Emperor, while Florence was gained for the Medici and the Papal States secured. The Treaty of Cambrai which followed (August 5, 1528) gave up the French claims in Italy; all parties to these treaties bound themselves to extirpate heresy. The same year Charles was crowned, but at Bologna not at Rome (February 24, 1529)—the last Emperor crowned in Italy. The German Diets had of late years been either put off or been too poorly attended to do much business. Now, with the Pope and Emperor in league with him, and the ecclesiastical Princes upon his side, Charles resolved to attempt a settlement of the religious difficulties. The Lutherans, on the other hand, were not only alarmed at the turn of politics, but disturbed by rumours of plots against them. Otto von Pack, formerly a minister of

Duke George of Saxony, showed the Landgrave of Hesse a forged document indicating such a plot, and the Elector prepared for war. The discovery of the falsity of his information embittered both him and his opponents, so that the Diet of

Diet of Speier[1] (February 21, 1529) found parties even
Speier. more at discord than before. The Emperor was determined that the Decree of 1526 must be amended. Ferdinand was anxious to suppress all heresy. Inside the reformed camp a division, not merely one of the many shades of differences that later on led to diversity, but a real and fundamental division had arisen. The divergence of Zwinglian from Lutheran, and their hatred of each other, gave the Catholic party in the Diet a great advantage. Zwinglianism, moreover, struck at Habsburg power where it had old claims, not urged of late, but never given up in theory. Switzerland was a link between the Netherlands and Italy, and Milan could not well be held without control of Switzerland. Zürich, moreover, the seat of Zwingli's movement, was akin to the cities of Southern Germany; once an Imperial City like them, it had many ties of interest and relation with them; it now gave signs of extending its power northwards, and so politically was a special danger to the Empire. Thus the very division that weakened the Protestants (to anticipate the name they gained at this Diet) made Charles more desirous to suppress them.

At Speier the consent of the Pope to a new Council was declared, and it was proposed by the Emperor's representatives to revoke the Decree of 1526, replacing it by a declaration against any innovation. This change of policy was favoured by the majority of the Princes, who also wished to forbid any toleration of sects denying the Sacrament of the Altar. But the Landgrave of Hesse and some Imperial cities wished to leave things as they were—the liberty practically gained in 1526 had sent them much further on the paths of change. Attempts at mediation, in which one side was ready to sacrifice something —the territorial power of the Bishops, and the other side to throw over what they termed the "godless" followers of Zwingli led to no result.

[1] See Kidd, *Documents*, etc., pp. 239–45.

From their formal protest against the final decision, embodying an appeal to a free Council or a really national assembly, the party of change gained the name of Protestant. The protestors were the Elector John of Saxony (Frederick the Wise had died, May 5, 1525), the Margrave of Brandenburg, the Landgrave of Hesse, two of the Dukes of Lüneburg, Wolfgang of Anhalt-Köthen, and the cities of Strassburg, Ulm, Nüremberg, Weissenberg, St. Gallen, Constance, Lindau, Memmingen, Kempten, Nordlingen, Heilbronn, Reutlingen, Isny, and Windsheim. Their refusal to abide by the decision of the majority emphasised (although it did not begin) the break-up of the Empire: their declared intention to stand by the Decree of 1526 put an interpretation upon that which it had not been intended to bear. Their real appeal was to revolution, and to the individual's right to choose his religion for himself; this principle was not however extended, to begin with, below princes and cities that were almost republics. But it was in essence a repudiation of authority, and a declaration of freedom, such as Luther had made for himself at Worms. It involved first and foremost a repudiation of the Papacy and Papal power in any shape. Historically such a repudiation is the meaning of Protestant, although of late years the fashion has been to apply the word more loosely to bodies arising from the Reformation and in sympathy with its aims. In either case it asserts the freedom of the individual, and it has led to repeated divisions. The historic Church might claim one sanction of Divine authority: the individual conscience another like sanction. It was an evil thing that a difference between the two sanctions should be widely felt, and it was, so far as this difference arose from unreformed abuses, a reproach to the Church. But if the latter sanction, unchecked by the former, were to be the guiding element in religion divisions were bound to be multiplied. No appeals to the force of great leaders—such as Luther had now become—could well gloss over the dissension that arose from appeals made solely to the varying conscience of the individual. This was to be felt in later years.

The decision of this Diet of Speier, against which the pro-

The Origin of Protestantism.

77

test was made, stood as follows: The Edict of Worms should be enforced in the Catholic territories as before: in the territories which had become Lutheran no fresh innovations were to be brought in, and the Mass was not to be prohibited. No ecclesiastical body should be deprived of authority, property, or income. The sects which denied the Sacrament of the Body and Blood of Christ were to receive no toleration any more than the Anabaptists. The agreement of Emperor and Pope, the consolidation of the Catholic Princes, their dread of the growing movement, and, lastly, differences which had arisen in the movement itself, had brought about this result. It was a decided check to the Lutherans, for it set up again the jurisdiction of the Bishops, never legally abolished so far as the Empire was concerned. It is easy to point out the narrow limits of toleration set up, the recognition of religious differences, which it was yet wished to prevent from growing. But the problem now was a new one: the existence of religious bodies outside the Church, and in marked opposition to it. No State had hitherto been called upon to deal with so momentous a question: the Church, its limits and authority, had always been accepted as part of the normal conditions affecting civil life. It was a hard problem for any State to solve, especially when it received no help from the Church beyond a verbal condemnation of the novelty. It was a specially hard problem for the Empire, with its many local differences and its lack of central power. Political conditions had intensified the crisis; they seemed likely to make it permanent, for the Reformation emphasised the special weaknesses of German political life. Because of the shape into which these political conditions had forced the movement, and because of the personality of Luther, the Reformation, so far as it gave rise to separations from the Church, will always seem to many purely German in its origin and growth. But we should be on our guard against making it, whether in origin or in effect, too purely German.

Results of the Diet of Speier.

IV

THE REFORMATION IN SWITZERLAND AND ITS CONNECTION WITH GERMANY

THE cantons of Switzerland had gained their freedom after a long struggle with the house of Habsburg: the cities Lucerne, Berne and Zürich had histories like that of the Im- Swiss perial cities of the Empire, and indeed the last was History. itself an old Imperial town. Inside the Confederation there were rivalries between the city and country cantons, while the Federal tie was of the very loosest, lying in the Diets to which the cantons sent ambassadors with no powers for settlement except after reference to their cantons. The conquests of the Confederates, the Free Bailiwicks, and the Thurgau, were governed by the cantons in rotation, and this system was a later cause of religious strife. The peculiarity of the causes tending to freedom in the case of Switzerland has often been exaggerated: the fact that the overlords of much of it were the Habsburgs, absorbed as they were in Imperial politics, and that the land was well fitted for defence, gave the Swiss leagues a permanence not shared by the similar German leagues. This almost accidental growth of Switzerland led to its ecclesiatical unity being weak: of the dioceses Constance and Chur were under Mayence; Basle and Lausanne under Besançon; Sitten (Sion), until exempted by Leo X, under Tarantaise. The moral state of the clergy was low by comparison with other lands; both they and the monastic orders were less free from State control than was the case elsewhere.

The monks and friars were much mixed up in local affairs, and the Franciscans and Dominicans, who were especially so, were jealous rivals of each other. An incident in 1509 revealed a sordid life among them and became widely talked of. Four Dominicans were executed, after a long trial, locally and at Rome. They were charged with witchcraft and imposture by using one Jetzer, a journeyman tailor as a dupe: he had visions of the Blessed Virgin, and so the affair was fitted into the long controversy between the two orders about the Immaculate Conception. It was much and widely talked of, and we find even Sir Thomas More believing in their guilt. The story became part of the polemics of the day, and has a more modern literature of its own.[1] If it were worth while, modern jurisprudence and psychology might be used for an interesting treatment. But, apart from that, it revealed a sordid and unworthy life among the brethren.

Towards the close of the Middle Ages successes against Burgundy and in Italy gave the Swiss a great reputation, so that they were eagerly sought as mercenaries. Hence there resulted entanglements in outside politics, and a corruption of the old simple and mainly agricultural life of old. These complications, added to the division between Romance or French Switzerland and Teutonic or German Switzerland, gave the country a peculiar importance. For the Teutonic part looked towards Southern Germany with its Imperial cities, while the Romance part was entangled with France and Savoy. This twofold connection gave the Reformation in Switzerland a curious character: international in external relations, dividing Germany by the severance between Zwinglians and Lutherans, affecting French thought through Calvin, it was yet on its internal side involved in the Federal history. The career of Zwingli, however, not only checked the needed development of the Federal constitution, but divided the nation into hostile camps; the rivalry between Luther and Zwingli, growing into the fatal division of Lutheran and Reformed, added to the disunion of Germany and altered the currents of theological thought.

[1] See, e.g., *Die Berner Jetzertragödie im Licht der Neueren Forschung und Critik*: Georg Schuhmann: Freiburg-in-Breisgau, 1912, part of a discussion arising out of Janssen's History: it gives a Bibliography of the modern writings. When Ruchat wrote his *Histoire de la Réformation de la Suisse* in 1927 he passed over the matter but was so much reproached for what was held a great omission that he added a long account taken from the *Berner Chronik* of Valerius Anshelm, written twenty years after the trial (*edn.* Bern, 1825–33, and by E. Bloesch 1894–1904).

Huldreich Zwingli, was born (January 1, 1484) at Wildhaus in the Toggenburg Valley. His father was village bailiff, and his uncle Vicar, both elected: two uncles on the mother's side were Abbots, so the social state of his family was good. The Vicar left Wildhaus to become Rural Dean of Wasen (1487), and took his small nephew with him. The boy was sent for education to Basle (1494) and then to Bern (1498). At both places he got good classical teaching, and at Bern he was taught by Wölflin, the leading Swiss Humanist. After an interval at Vienna he came back to Basle (1502), graduated there (1504) and then taught at St. Martin's School. He was ordained (1506), and became Vicar of Glarus with its three hamlets; but on his appointment he had to pay a pension of one hundred gulden to a Swiss Guard at Rome who had bought the reversion from the Papal Court, and did a lucrative trade in benefices.

Huldreich (Ulric) Zwingli, 1484–1531.

Twice he visited Italy as chaplain to the army in the field, and formed a strong opinion against mercenary warfare; but his private life was morally lax and his standard low. By a different road and from another starting-point he, like Luther, reached a definite doctrinal position, but his career was only possible in a city commonwealth. Zürich was his field of work, and here, working on the basis of civic politics, he won over the Chapter and the citizens to begin with, and then developed his ecclesiastical system. It took its shape from the mould that contained it: the two Councils—the Small or Senate and the Great Council of two hundred—were the chief authorities in Church as in State; it was they who regulated worship, reformed or remodelled the great Chapter, and abolished the monasteries, gave the revenues so gained to a theological College and a School, called the Public Disputations which marked each stage of the Reformation at Zürich, and although mainly led by Zwingli, also conducted the religious policy of the city. Zürich was in the diocese of Constance, and the Reformation here took therefore the form of a city's revolt against outside episcopal control, and a seizure for itself of the direction of religious life.[1]

[1] See *Camb. Mod. Hist.*, Vol. II., Chap. X (by myself), and W. Köhler, *Das Buch der Reformation Huldrych Zwinglis* (Munich, 1926).

Mercenary warfare was a political matter at the time. The Swiss were reckoned the best mercenary soldiers in Europe, Mercenary and had proved their worth in the Italian wars: Warfare and they were old allies of the Papacy, and regularly Zwingli. as mercenaries fought for it. But the French were now competing for their help, and Switzerland was everywhere divided between French and Papal parties. Cardinal Schinner, Bishop of Sitten (Sion) was an energetic recruiting officer for the Papacy, and succeeded in keeping many Swiss faithful to their old service. But the French had more to offer, and pensions sometimes overcame patriotism. Zwingli, who loathed the corruption of old Swiss simplicity by political "pensionaries" and foreign wars, was not sparing in his criticisms, and held that the Papal alliance was the only one his country should permit itself. The defeat of the Papal forces at Marignano (September 1515) made most of the Cantons eager for the more profitable French alliance, but Zwingli at Glarus was against this change; as a result his life there became more disturbed. So he sought the Vicarage at Einsledeln, and obtained it (April 14, 1516), placing a curate at Glarus. He lamented the change, but ascribed it to "the wiles of the French."

At Einsledeln there were surroundings that suited him. Both the Abbot and the Administrator of the Abbey (who had appointed him) were on the Humanist side; the monastic library was well furnished and most useful to him. Although off the high road, his new home was celebrated as a widely-known place of pilgrimage, because of the miraculous statue of the Madonna and Child: many visitors, scholars, theologians and others thronged to it, and Zwingli, whose reputation as a preacher had already spread, was now able to reach a wider circle. At Glarus he had given his mind to Scriptural and Patristic studies; for the former Erasmus was his favoured guide, and the Fathers he studied widely with his improved knowledge of Greek. St. Augustine was his favourite Father, but he thought the Christology of the Greeks better than that of the Latins. His studies were directed mainly towards his preaching, and it was as a teacher he most excelled in the pulpit.

It may be noticed that he spent little time or energy in attacking abuses, preferring rather to give positive teaching, practical as well as doctrinal. In 1518 he was called to Zürich, as Vicar (or People's Priest of the Great Minster). This was to be his sphere of work, and his whole system of thought and leadership bears the stamp of a city commonwealth, and indeed was only possible in such surroundings.

He said he had learnt from Thomas Wyttenbach at Basle the supreme authority of Scripture and the glaring evils of Indulgences, and although he read Luther's writings and liked them greatly, he could, as he said, have easily learnt these two things at Basle or elsewhere. In later years he claimed to have been quite independent of Luther in the growth of his ideas. In this claim he was probably justified, although Luther's conclusions and his personal courage had gained Zwingli's admiration. In his broad conclusions he did not at first differ from Luther, but he started from the basis of a free and intellectual study of the Scriptures interpreted by the individual powers and for the individual needs. This was Humanism pure and simple, unfettered or unchecked, as with Erasmus, by regard for religious authority and the unity of the Church. In spite of his earlier unchaste life he had, even at Glarus, a sincerely religious spirit, which he kept, but his humanism and his firm belief in unchecked individualism, the inspiration of the individual by the Spirit of God, made him the revolutionary theologian of the Reformation. It was not accident that he, unlike Erasmus, was prepared to befriend the revolutionary and scandal-causing Hutten: it was not accident that the movement at Zürich had closer affinities with Anabaptism and with Socinianism than were possible for Lutheranism.

Zwingli's Opinions.

The Church was to Zwingli simply an aggregate of individuals, a local society based on a voluntary and reasonable agreement, moulded and coloured by the political condition under which it existed. Sacraments were merely signs, the efficacy of which depended solely upon the individual power of perception; all external aids to religion—images, pictures, pilgrimages, festivals, organs, things upon which the simpler

Christian had leaned—were hindrances to the individual life
the true support of which was to be found only in an en
lightened study of the Scriptures and a faithful attendance a
Sermons. The intellect thus played a part in his system fa
beyond that played by the emotions; the pulpit took the plac
of the altar. But given this basis of doctrine, and this view o
religion, an association of Christian men, borrowing less from
the ancient Church than did the Lutheran bodies of Germany
was, although of secondary importance, helpful for purposes o
study, prayer, and exposition. Thus the congregation found
place, and Humanism with its intellectual vigour and its in
dependent criticism was joined to a congregational systen
developed in a city state.

His theological writings had less effect on the city and out
side than his personal and political activity. But his standpoint
which was that of a critical Humanist, and his views, were mad
clear in them. His *Archeteles* (August 1522), although writter
Zwingli's   in haste, was in itself enough for this. Œcolam
Doctrines.   padius wished him to be more considerate: Eras
mus did the same, and begged him to act with others
About the same time he led ten priests in a petition to
the Bishop of Constance, in whose diocese Zürich was, fo
clerical marriage, a demand enforced by a very dark picture o
clerical morals. Already he had spoken emphatically on th
question of fasting, the choice and freedom of food (Marc)
1522). In this, as in other ways, all responsibility was laid or
the individual. The Church was a democratic body of Chris
tians, individually in spiritual contact with God, dependent fo
the truth upon the Scripture and the Holy Spirit's guidance
The organisation of the Church was a matter for the civi
executive authority. No place was allowed to the Pope, o
even to the ecclesiatical hierarchy. Any sacrifice in the Mas
was denied: the Eucharist was purely commemorative, and in
his writings he dealt with this doctrine at length. Confirmatio
and Extreme Unction he wished to retain as Rites, but not a
Sacraments. Auricular Confession he would discard. Th
churches and services were to be plain, without images, which
he held idolatrous, pictures or music. For the First Publi

Disputation (January 29, 1523) he had drawn up sixty-seven theses, stating these views, and in a German work *Auslegung und Begründung der Schlussreden* he expounded them for the unlearned public. The Bishop of Constance not unnaturally did not attend the Disputation, but his Vicar-General John Faber, a friend of Zwingli, was present and advised that no action should be taken until a General Council should meet. Before the Second Public Disputation (October 26, 1523) riots had broken out: he himself taught that to make changes in the public religion was in the power of the civil authority alone, but some of his followers would not wait: pictures and images were torn down both in town and country; some of the rioters were pardoned, but a leader Hollinger was banished for two years. And at the Disputation the Anabaptists appeared as an extreme party adopting his views, but more active in change. This made both him and the magistracy more cautious. But change in public religion and worship was carried out by the civic authorities with Zwingli behind them. He was the civic religious leader, if not ruler.

By the end of 1524 the religious changes at Zürich were completed; images were removed from the churches; pictures covered or washed over; the use of lights, bells, and organs was put an end to; the Baptismal service was simplified to bareness, while a con- gregational Communion in wooden cups and trenchers and round tables replaced the stately Mass. **The System Complete, 1524.**

Apart then from its religious importance, the career of Zwingli had a political side; he had a high conception of the pastor's office. In a democratic country, and even more in a city commonwealth, every citizen had his part in politics, and every minister—as a prophet to inspire and exhort, to sow ideas, and rouse men to act—had his leading part to fulfil: the sermons preached, not only to the citizens, but to the country people who flocked into the city on market days; the printed manifestos that were circulated in their thousands, for Zwingli was a political pamphleteer of skill, and the booksellers gave him a ready organisation to hand; the Public Disputations of January and October **Zwingli's Political Ideas.**

1523, to which representatives from other Swiss towns were invited—all these, although not peculiar to Zürich, gave Zwingli a useful machinery for forming and organising opinion. But the political circumstances of Zürich, a city which had aspired to be the leading state of Eastern Switzerland and followed an independent policy of its own, made these features of Zwingli's movement more significant. The Emperor and the French, and now the Pope through his recruiting agent, Cardinal Schinner, Bishop of Sion (Sitten), were competing for the support of Swiss mercenaries. Zwingli's Italian experience had made him dislike foreign service, with its easily earned wealth and corrupting influence; even at Glarus he had opposed the French faction, and this, joined to his renown as a preacher, had made the anti-French party at Zürich eager to secure him. The Pope had, as it seemed to Zwingli, who was appointed (1518) a Papal chaplain and offered further promotion and rewards, peculiar claims upon the help of Zürich. It was only (1519) when he differed from the Papal politics in the election of Emperor that he first became definitely anti-Papal, and doctrine had very little to do with this change. It is true that he, somewhat as Luther with Tetzel, had opposed Samson, a preacher of Indulgences, who came to Zürich in 1519; but the ecclesiastical authorities supported Zwingli and Zürich in the matter, and he was subsequently offered promotion at Rome. As regarded ecclesiastical organisation the Zürich movement was satisfied by the rejection of episcopal control; the Papal power presented itself more as a question of politics than of control or government, and it was as such that Zwingli, and Zürich with him, finally rejected it. But the Papacy, owing to its old relations with Zürich, and its desire to keep the city as an ally, treated Zwingli very differently from Luther.

Zürich had pretensions to the leadership of Switzerland in the East, and it had also close relations with the South German cities bound to it by commerce and democratic sympathies. Before long (1524) the religious ideal of Zwingli became bound up with politics; if his city gained greater power in the Confederation it could extend the Reformation; equally the Re-

Zurich and Politics in Switzerland and outside.

formation gave it a chance of increasing its power. In trying to urge Protestantism upon the subject lands it touched the Confederation where its system was weakest—in the government of these dependencies by the cantons in turn, each with a distinct religious policy of its own. Zürich's championship of the Reformation against the Forest Cantons (Lucerne, Uri, Schwyz, and Unterwalden), along with Zug, really broke up the Confederation into hostile camps. The problem of religious differences in a Federal State should have been less difficult to solve than in an Empire or Kingdom, but Zwingli presented it so as to bring Zürich forward. It was doubtful whether religion was a matter for Federal or Cantonal authority; it should have been possible to reach a solution which kept both Federal unity and local freedom, but Zwingli was too violent in his demands for religious supremacy. A further complication, therefore, came in when Zürich pushed or protected the Reformation in the subject lands. This put a strain upon the Federal constitution which it was not equal to bear, and (1529) war broke out. Bern, where a reformation roughly similar to that of Zürich had been carried out (1528), was on the side of Zürich for defence if not for attack. The First Peace of Kappel (June 24, 1529) only put off the struggle. Religious innovators in the subject lands were not to be punished (as the Catholic Cantons had desired); the majority in each community were to decide for the Catholic Mass or the Zwinglian substitute, as they preferred. Other causes of complaint, arising from previous violence on each side, were settled favourably for Zürich. It should be noted that in Switzerland, as elsewhere, the secularisation of the monasteries had before this been a leading object: at Zürich the funds so gained had been put to educational uses; at Bern to political; the popular desire for a share in the proceeds had in some places led to riots and been a link between the Reformation and the Peasants' Revolt.

By this Peace of 1529 the Catholic Cantons were forced to give up their alliance with Austria, which had indeed not led to the results expected. But the question of external alliances had been one which, apart from religion, went near to wrecking the Confederation. Zwingli had, even in 1524, looked to foreign alliances, notably to France and Savoy, as means for strengthening Zürich in the Confederation; when he came into touch with Philip of Hesse his political activity was quickened. The Christian Civic League (*das Christliche Bürgerrecht*)—a league of cities united for defence and war upon the basis of religious unity, began (Christmas, 1527) by Zürich and Constance, joined afterwards by St. Gallen, Biel, Mühlhausen, Basle, Schaffhausen, and, lastly, Strassbourg (1530)—partly realised the aims of Zwingli. But Hesse, in spite of Zwingli's endeavour, was not included; nor was the cause of Ulrich of Württemberg taken up as he wished. The Christian Union—a league of the Catholic Cantons under Austrian protection, meant to extend still further—was a reply to this earlier league. In Switzerland, as in Germany, the Reformation had thus divided the nation into two distinct camps. The Peace of Kappel recognised this division, and the clauses by which toleration was to obtain between the cantons led to disagreement. The Zwinglians thought that they might in future preach freely, not only in the subject lands, but in the Catholic Cantons as well; these latter thought they were left perfectly free from interference in religious matters. Of such disagreements the Second War of Kappel (1531) was the inevitable result. Dread of the Emperor and a little war on the Italian border hastened the end, but the demand of Zürich that preaching should be freely allowed everywhere showed the real aims of Zwingli. Bern, although tardily and with half its heart, was now on his side, but at Zürich itself lack of unity and spirit made itself felt. The battle (October 11, 1531) left Zwingli among the slain with many of his keenest supporters.

Through the mediation of France and the cantons not actually at war, peace was made (November 23). The victors did not press their advantage, but the Christian Civic League was put an end to: the Reformed communities in the subject lands were left alone, and everywhere Catholic minorities were protected. But the failure of Zwingli's scheme to force Protestantism upon the other cantons was significant: in Glarus, Soluthurn, and the Aargau Catholicism gained the

Second Peace of Kappel, 1531.

upper hand. Bern, influenced by Strassbourg—from its position and inclination a mediator between Switzerland and Germany—became more Lutheran. The dread of Zwinglianism which had led the Imperialist advisers to consider Zürich (1531) "the head of Lutheranism" was over. The city was still a refuge for Protestant theologians from Germany or England: the reputation of Zwingli made it almost a place of pilgrimage, and the diplomatic intercourse begun by him still continued, but its importance was immensely lower: Bern, and soon Geneva, under the dominating spirit of Calvin, outstripped it. The division of the Confederation was intensified by the progress of the Catholic reaction. Hugo von Landenberg, Bishop of Constance, and Christopher von Uttenheim, Bishop of Basle, had both been well abreast of the movement for better discipline, and Lucerne shared their impulses. Faber, Vicar-General of Constance, and the chief opponent of Zwingli in the Public Disputations, afterwards Cardinal and Bishop of Vienna, led the reaction with skill for some years. Cardinal Carlo Borromeo, Archbishop of Milan, drew closer an older link with Switzerland: his Swiss college at Milan, his introduction into the country of the Jesuits (1574–81), of the Capuchins (1581–8), and his establishment of a permanent nunciature at Lucerne, supplied the lack of organisation from which the local Catholics had suffered. The Lucerne statesman, Ludwig Pfyffer (1586), formed the Borromean League, a revival as it were of the Christian Union, including the Forest Cantons, with Zug, Soluthurn, and Freiburg. We are apt to be severe in judging the anomalous contrivances, "Interims," and Religious Peaces by which Germany partly patched up religious strife, but Switzerland did not even attain to these: religious divisions, unsoftened by such expedients, even when working on a less favourable field than incoherent Germany, had their own disastrous result.

The Anabaptist movement appeared in Switzerland also, and was there even more closely connected with The Anabaptists at Zurich. the Reformation than elsewhere. Andreas Carlstadt sought a new field of work when Luther returned to Wittenberg from the Wartburg (March 1522):

first at Orlamünde, near Wittenberg, and then in South Germany. Before leaving Wittenberg he had joined hands with Thomas Münzer, who had preached a socialistic iconoclastic religion at Zwickau, in Thuringia, and on being driven thence had gone to Wittenberg. These two men gathered around them the doctrinally and socially discontented. Bohemian influence gave the movement a strong anti-ecclesiastical direction: the hierarchy and Church orders were condemned, the impulses of the individual exalted to revelations, and the mystical or fanatical theories which had flourished in the Middle Ages gained new force when inspired by restless discontent and confronted by abuses often firmly fixed. This general movement, springing up in many centres where local causes made its growth easier and grouping itself mainly around a few special leaders, is broadly named Anabaptist. But although the varied elements combined or grew together they had no common origin; on a lower, less educated, and more fanatic plane, it is analogous in origin and history to the Reformation movement which grouped itself around Luther. But it can hardly be held, as some would have it, the logical issue of the Reformation. A short account of Anabaptism at Zürich brings out the main points in its history there and elsewhere.

Among those of Zwingli's followers who, by eating meat in Lent began the revolt against authority (1522), were the future leaders of local Anabaptism; a little later (1523) they outran the magistrates' action in the destruction of crucifixes and images. They soon appear as a distinct party, radical in their views but not bound together by any express doctrinal belief; their repudiation of infant baptism sprang rather from dislike to the methods of Christian organisation than to any doctrinal tenets. An agitation against the payment of tithes—a point on which the Peasants' Revolt was in sympathy with them—arose in many local centres near Zürich. Zwingli himself was embarrassed by the movement; its leaders had been among his earlier and most enthusiastic followers; in their denial of the efficacy of baptism, in their dislike to tithes, they would quote something of his teaching in their favour although he did not reach their practical conclu-

Anabaptism.

sions. When they began to found a distinct society, consisting solely of "converted" adults, he urged them not to weaken his hands; they, on the other hand, regarded him as "a lost leader": while they were bitter in their language, he had the magistracy on his side, and was thus enabled to be severe in his measures of repression. But the presence of Münzer at Waldshut (an Austrian town N.W. of Zürich where religious cabals were of importance in the relations of Habsburgs and Zürich), and of Carlstadt at Zürich, strengthened the Swiss Anabaptists locally and merged them in the wider movement. The well-deserved catastrophe of that movement at Münster (1533–34) discredited, and, on the whole, suppressed it, but here and there isolated strains of Anabaptist views survived and at times appeared on the surface.

The relations of Zwingli to Luther, and of their respective followers to each other, were significant in the history of thought, and became of great importance to Germany. Zwingli regarded no authority, and was bound by no traditions in his exegesis of Scripture: hence his anger against those who, as the Anabaptists, took an indvidual view other than his own. From the sacramental teaching of the Church there could be deduced the necessity of Holy Orders: the Sacraments and the Ministry were bound together. The necessity for the latter fitted in badly with Zwingli's view of organisation: the stress he laid upon the educated intellect made him averse from any ideas of grace conveyed otherwise than by spiritual or mental inspiration. But the exegesis by which the "is" in "This is my body" was explained as "signifies" was put before him by a Dutch theologian, Cornelius von Hoen, who considered its novelty made the suggestion worthy of being brought before theologians by a special messenger. Zwingli, who had not dealt with the doctrine of the Presence in his writings before 1522, adopted this exegesis, and made it peculiarly his own. But he felt it was needful that his views should be put forward, since Carlstadt, who, in some respects, shared them, was being taken as their chief exponent. For Zwingli, unlike Carlstadt, laid great stress upon the Church as a society (although of purely civic and

Zwingli and the Mass.

natural growth), and hence regarded the Communion as a corporate act: at one with Carlstadt in his denial of a supernatural presence, akin to him in the rites and form of administration he preferred, he differed widely from him in the stress laid upon the corporate nature of the Feast. It was, indeed, Zwingli's regard for the corporate life freely made up of individuals that made him, in opposition to the Anabaptists, lay stress upon the rightfulness of infant baptism. From the year 1524 Zwingli's view of the Eucharist, and especially his negative teaching, was vigorously put forth. Fitting in well as it did with his theory of organisation and his general system, it found a ready hearing. For it was both revolutionary and logical: it was easy to understand, and it gave a firm resting-place to those who approached the subject in a spirit of hostility to what the Church had taught. Even its very novelty—for the denial of any peculiar Presence in the Communion was novel—recommended it to many. Because he was the first great teacher who took this revolutionary view, and the one who taught it most effectively, the purely rational and symbolic view of the Sacrament of the Altar is always known as Zwinglianism.

Zwingli's doctrinal position was thus very different from that of Luther; he and his followers were both more thorough Doctrinal and more open to suspicion; while the Lutherans position. always claimed to hold the Catholic faith, and were sensitive to the charge that they did not, the Zwinglians held such a charge a trifle: ordination of ministers, Church organisation and doctrine, were all powerless before the individual's enlightened conclusions and the decision of the civic magistracy. Thus, in the second Peace of Kappel, the Zwinglians consented to give the Catholic Cantons the title of adherents of "Christian religion"; thus, too, Melanchthon and other theologians suspected Zwingli and his followers of a tendency to Socinianism. But sympathy with the Swiss and dislike of the German princes led the South German allies to adopt Zwingli's views: Ulm, Mainz, Strassburg, among cities; Wurtemberg, Hesse, and Friesland among territories were all Zwinglian.

The Lutheran Princes had not yet given up all thought of a

Reformed Papal Church with which they might be in accord. The suspicions brought upon Protestantism by the Zwinglians came as an obstacle to such a result. Hence the Landgrave Philip, with whom it was a great object to form a strong Protestant League, urged union, and arranged a preparatory discussion to prepare for it. At Michaelmas (1529) both Lutherans and Zwinglians met at Marburg, where the central point of discussion was the method of the Presence. Zwingli, while firm in his own views, was ready to make a league which would leave room for difference. Luther stood equally firm in his literal interpretation of the words of institution. It seemed as if the vital point lay here, but the real difference lay deeper; Luther was more ready to admit the supernatural than was Zwingli, who was a rationalist in his conceptions. They left the Conference with the doctrinal split more clearly realised than ever, and with the political split, imposed upon it, almost as clearly realised. This division was henceforth a leading feature in German life; the theological bitterness caused by it reacted on theology generally, and the many attempts at reunion, in which Bucer [1] was largely concerned (from the Wittenberg Concord, May, 1536, onwards), encouraged a loose use of language to conceal differences of view. But the importance which the Catholic Church attached to tradition and authority was given outside of it to names of great leaders. These leaders really differed essentially; the demand for their agreement was due to political needs although they might indeed have agreed in negations of Catholic doctrines. But such agreement was no real basis for a living and growing body. This was soon found out, and after the death of Luther (1546) Melanchthon was accused of whittling down his doctrine and tending towards reunion with Rome. The divisions that multiplied themselves made a full reunion of parties impossible, and wrought endless harm everywhere, but most of all in Germany.

Attempts at reconciliation.

---

[1] On Bucer see: *Martin Bucer*, by Hastings Eeles (Yale University Press, 1931), which gives a good doctrinal history. Cf. Schirrmacher, *Briefe und Acta zur der Geschichte des Religiongesprachs und des Reichstages in Augsburg* 1530 (Gotha, 1876).

As the Emperor's power grew divisions in Germany were becoming more marked; to the Catholic League formed at Regensburg corresponded the Protestant League of Torgau. The Emperor, now at peace with France and the Papacy, was yet bound along with them to suppress heresy, which, as a matter of faith and apart from political considerations, he loathed. There was now a further cause of fear, lest through the influence of Zwingli the cities of the Oberland, joining with the Swiss Reformed Cantons, should together throw off the supremacy of the Empire. This was the state of affairs when, in February 1529, the Diet (see p. 76) met at Speier. Here the consent of the Pope to a Council was declared, and it was proposed by the Emperor's representatives to revoke the decree of 1526, substituting for it a declaration against any innovation. The majority of the princes were in favour of this, and wished to forbid any toleration to sects who denied the Sacrament of the Altar. On the other hand, the Landgrave of Hesse and some of the Imperial cities wished to leave things as they were; they protested against having to surrender the liberty gained in 1526.

Church Politics in Germany.

In June 1530, at Augsburg, the Emperor in person opened the Diet from which so much was expected; he was anxious, he told them, to end the religious dissensions, if possible, without force; but irritation that had arisen through the Evangelical court preachers exercising their vocation in the very city itself promised badly for peace. And the issue corresponded to the omen. The Lutheran theologians had drawn up a Confession of their Faith on the basis of the seventeen articles agreed upon previously at Schwabach; the document, which contained twenty-one articles upon doctrine and seven upon abuses to be reformed, had been formulated by Melanchthon, and was read before the Diet. As an Apology (its title intended at the outset) it had a peculiar character; it was intended to conciliate the Catholics, and it tried, therefore, to defend the doctrines expressed from possible charges—those on the Eucharist from the charge of the Zwinglian conceptions,

Diet and Confession of Augsburg, 1530.

94

and others from the charge of Anabaptist tendencies—hence, as an expression of so-called reforming tendencies it was too cautious to be complete. Among the most important articles were—the sixth, which asserted that true faith had good works as a fruit, and that every man was bound to perform them, but could not depend upon them for salvation; the seventh, which asserted the existence of a holy Catholic Church, made up of all the faithful, and marked, not by a uniformity in ritual or rules, but by the effective preaching of the Word and pure administration of the Sacraments. By other articles the Real Presence was asserted, auricular confession retained along with absolution, but the need of a particular enumeration of sins was denied. The abuses noted were: the denial of the cup, clerical celibacy, the Mass as an offering for quick or dead, the conception of Confession and Absolution as a sacrament, the excessive number of ceremonies, the institution of monastic vows, abuses of ecclesiastical, especially of episcopal, power, which ought to be distinguished from the civil power it so often encroached upon.[1] It is noteworthy that there is no repudiation of Episcopacy.

The four Imperial cities of Strassbourg, Constance, Lindau, and Memmingen presented a separate Confession (Confessio Tetrapolitana), drawn up by Bucer and Capito, which differed from the Lutheran Apology mainly upon the Eucharist, in denying, although guardedly, anything of a bodily Presence or bodily manducation. A Confutation of the Confession prepared by Eck, Wimpina, Faber, and others was read and circulated; it was remarkable as showing signs of agreement with it upon the doctrine of justification by faith. Compromise upon this point was, in truth, less difficult than is often thought. Unless faith was taken to be the all in all, apart from means of grace or works, it was not difficult to reconcile justification by faith with the Catholic doctrine (often obscured by its advocates), according to which faith is a divinely implanted germ and leads

Confessio Tetrapolitana.

---

[1] Kidd, *Documents*, p. 259 *seq*. Ph. Schaff, *Creeds of Christendom*, I., 225. Th. Kolde, *Die Augsburger Konfession* (Latin and German, with the Marburg, Swabach and Torgau Articles and the Confutatio)(Gotha, 1911).

to a righteous life exhibited as its justification before God and men. Luther's view, which led to great practical abuse, lay in isolating the element of faith from life and from membership in the Church; on the other hand, some of his opponents departed equally from the Catholic doctrine in losing sight of the element of faith, or in obscuring it behind obedience to the commands of the Church. But the demands for reform as set forth in the Apology's Articles upon Abuses, and afterwards formulated at Rome, were a very different matter. It was upon these more than upon doctrine that agreement was impossible, and even had they been satisfactorily disposed of there remained the fact that new religious bodies, distinct from the Church, had already been organised. Doctrines may be defined and qualified, ceremonies accommodated and refined, but schism, easy to bring into being, is a hard fact to get rid of, a step difficult to retrace.

The Diet at its close gave six months to the Protestants for reflection; during that time Confession and the Mass were to be allowed in their territories and no innovations were to be made. But a Council was to be held, and even yet great hopes were entertained as to its work. Meanwhile the Emperor was determined to enforce the Edict of Worms. His brother Ferdinand, who, although personally unpopular with the clergy, was deeply pledged to the Catholic cause, was now elected King of the Romans, and as such became a more influential person.

The immediate result of the Emperor's action was the formation by the Protestant princes of the defensive league of Smalkald (1530). But the pressure of the Turks, whose defeat before Vienna (1529) had brought merely temporary and unexpected relief to the Emperor, was great enough to prevent internal war, and the Peace of Nuremberg (1532) postponed the settlement of the religious difficulty. By this peace all the German princes were to help against the Turks, and in return religious prosecutions were to cease. It was privately agreed that suits before the Imperial Court on account of the confiscation of ecclesiastical property should also cease. The effect of political considerations was thus very apparent in Germany itself, and in

Peace of Nuremberg, 1532.

these years of indecision the Protestants were led to turn, not only (as discontented princes had turned before) to France, but even to England, and still more strangely to the Papacy itself. For from a natural desire to avoid strengthening the Empire, the Papacy had to depend upon France: neither the Papacy nor France cared to see a council, which would be mainly Imperial in its authority and German in its constitution. Again and again, therefore, Clement, although pledged to a council, could plead the unwillingness of France: in Germany itself some of the Catholic princes—especially the Bavarian house—opposed the Emperor: had the Emperor been wholly free he would have dealt sternly with Lutheranism, while at the same time he would have tried to raise Catholicism everywhere to the spiritual level of earnestness and righteousness already reached in Spain. But it was to the interests neither of Pope nor Protestants that the Emperor should be free: both were thus led to depend upon his rival, France. Everything was political, and politics determined everything. There had been again and again men with opinions of a Lutheran type, with the same earnestness, with the same hatred of abuses, with the same disregard of unity, and the same readiness to shape a world anew. But never before—except in the prophetic case of Bohemia, where a religious leader had dexterously joined his religious movement with a national uprising—had political conditions tended to stereotype such a religious movement. Princes, Kings, Emperors, Pope, all now played with it as a counter in the game of politics: this was true of both the external and internal relations of Germany, and it was even truer when Protestantism spread to other lands. Clement VII did not rise to the religious earnestness of Adrian VI, and his conception of his power was that of diplomacy and politics. He had been an Imperialist; he became a supporter of France; he had borne the lot of a prisoner, and the experience lessened such strength for action as he possessed. Reform, a deeper earnestness, rose a little higher in the College of Cardinals, a little nearer the Papacy itself, but it did not yet reach the greatest height of all. It was no wonder then that Clement's Papacy saw the Western Church still further rent asunder.

Inside Germany, as we have seen, new religious bodies had been organised—Electoral Saxony, Hesse, Ansbach and Baireuth, Luneburg, Anhalt-Köthen, East Fries-land, Schleswig-Holstein, Silesia, Prussia, and among the cities Nuremberg, Magdeburg, Bruns-wick, Bremen, and Lübeck had all before 1531 adopted the Lutheran model with variations. A bold move of the Landgrave Philip of Hesse resulted in adding Wurtemberg to this number. The Emperor Maximilian had consolidated the territories of the Counts with a duchy (1495) under Eberhard V, and (1503) declared his successor Ulrich of age when only sixteen. But Ulrich would not join the Swabian League, which had long tried to secure local peace, nor was he really loyal to the Empire. A disgraceful amour with the wife of Hans von Hutten led him to murder that knight and to send his own wife, a Bavarian princess and Hutten's lover, back to her home. Quarrels of this kind and his general lawlessness led to Ulrich's banishment in 1519, and his territory was administered by the Imperial troops; the Duke's rule had been violent and reckless, but when (1534) the Landgrave attempted his restoration the old local loyalty proved itself strengthened by foreign rule. The campaign lasted little more than two months, and was ended June 29, 1534, by the Treaty of Kadan; the Duke was restored, although under the nominal suzerainty of the Habs-burg house, and was left free to introduce the new religion which he had adopted in his exile; this he accordingly did. The treaty thus practically put an end to the scarcely observed con-vention that the princes who had secured toleration for their own territories should not attempt to extend their religion beyond. Even more important was the concession that the Imperial Court (Kammergericht) should no longer hear cases concerning the confiscation of Church property. Secularisation had long been a common thing in Germany: it had often been carried out by the Catholic princes; the Protestant princes thought it a hardship that they must give up the privilege merely because it entailed in their case, a diversion of the endowment, not only from the original owners, but also from the religion it had been meant to serve. The process of secularisation would now be easier. The geographical result of the treaty was to place a strong Protestant state in South Germany among the leading Catholic powers, and near the great Sees of Würzburg, Salzburg, and Bamberg. About the same time the new religion was organised in Anhalt-Dessau, Pomerania and the cities of Westphalia. In Münster it developed from 1531 onwards into the socialist and immoral Kingdom of John of Leyden and his Anabaptists: excesses as distasteful to one religious party as to the other were suppressed by both in union. But the inevitable result was to discredit change of any kind.

V

THE REFORMATION IN SCANDINAVIA

BEYOND Germany the Reformation then spread into the Scandinavian kingdoms. Here, again, politics made the course of change easier, and religion and politics became closely bound together. But while in Germany the course of the Reformation weakened the Imperial power and further divided the nation, in Scandinavia it resulted in a strengthening of the Crown. Christian I, of the house of Oldenburg, King of Denmark, Norway, and Sweden, had found it hard to rule three disunited countries; and Sweden (1501) became really independent, in spite of the royal claims. When his son Christian II ascended the throne (1513) he found his power acceptable to the Danes, because his family was the nation's choice ; in Norway—where he had ruled before his father's death—he faced a nobility proud and discontented; he had filled all offices with Danes: even the Archbishopric of Nidaros or Trondhjem (1510) had been by Papal help and against the Chapter's wish given to a Dane, Eric Valkendorf, while the Bishop of Hamar had been imprisoned for years. The Norwegian Church were thus left without a leader, but their national spirit was still warm. Christian II, nephew of the Elector Frederic of Saxony, and married (1515) to Isabella, sister of Charles V, was rash, ambitious and cruel. In Sweden he availed himself of a dispute between Gustav Trolle, Archbishop of Upsala, who had joined the Danish party, and the Stures, the national leaders; he established his power, but the massacre at Stockholm (November 1520) of some hundred leading ecclesiastics and nobles aroused against him a national fury which led to the final freedom of Sweden. The excuse given that these deaths were the carrying out of a Papal excommunication was very transparent. This was the beginning of troubles, which, joined to Christian's ambition and the effect of the Reformation, split up the partly sundered three Northern kingdoms still further.

The Scandinavian Kingdoms.

Christian II of Denmark, 1513.

The Church in both Norway and Sweden, wealthy and aristocratic, in league with the nobles, had suffered from an isolation which, while against its vigour, had made it more national. The great wealth of the bishops (half of Denmark was said to belong to them), their foreign education (the University of Copenhagen, founded in 1478, was not yet important), and their ineffectual rule, invited attack. One outpost of Christianity—Greenland—had been all but lost; no bishop or priest had resided there for eighty years, and the sole relic of Christianity was a corporal, exhibited once a year, upon which a hundred years before the last priest had consecrated the Body of Christ. In Norway Archbishop Eric of Nidaros, however, was a wise ruler, and had circumstances allowed, the Church there, at any rate, might have kept its ground.

In Sweden, Gustavus Ericson, of the house of Vasa, headed a national revolt; he escaped from Denmark, where he was a hostage (1518), and in just revenge for the Stockholm massacre roused the Dalecarlians to revolt; a two years' siege gave him possession of Stockholm, and finally (June 7, 1523) he was elected King. But the nobles were jealous of him; the peasants, his chief supporters, were lawless; the commerce of the country was in the hands of the Hanseatic towns; he himself was heavily in debt. The Church, on the other hand—a preserve of the nobles—was rich, but the King's demands for money caused discontent at home and anger at Rome. The new Pope, Adrian VI, had sent an old pupil of his at Louvain, John Magnusson, a Swede by birth, and a Swedish canon, as Legate (1522). When he was elected Archbishop of Upsala his readiness to join Gustavus in the needed ecclesiastical reforms gave ground for hope. But Gustav Trolle, the old Archbishop, had merely fled, and was himself at Rome; a demand for his restoration led to threats on the King's part of a reformation carried out by his own power, and when (1526) Magnusson was finally confirmed by the Pope it was only after a quarrel between him and the King and when he was an exile. Both national and economic reasons now disposed Gustavus to a reform.

Course of Politics and Reform in Sweden.

Meanwhile, Lutheranism had entered the country. Two Swedish students from Wittenberg, Olaf and Lars Peterssen,

Spread of Lutheran- ism.

had returned home (1519), and their teaching, with its implied political possibilities, impressed the King, harassed by plots and difficulties as he was. Although endangered for a time by an Anabaptist movement, the new doctrines made way; public disputations, the marriage of Olaf Peterssen, although a priest (1525), a projected trans- lation of the Bible (1526), only completed for the New Testa-

Diet of Westerås, 1527.

ment and fully accomplished in 1540, emphasised their victory. In June 1527 the Diet of Westerås met, and here the King expressed his need for a larger income to be gained from the monastic and episcopal lands. As Gustavus threatened abdication unless his demands were fulfilled, there was nothing to do but yield; it was hopeless to seek support, as the bishops did, in the Papal authority.

The Recess, drawn up by the Council, but published in the name of the Diet, placed all monastic, chapter, and episcopal

Westerås Recess and Ordinances, 1527.

lands at the King's disposal for confiscation or religious use: land not subject to taxation and given to the Church since 1454 returned to its former owners; all taxed lands, whenever given, did the same. This settlement stood long, but the interests of nobles and peasants were opposed, and remained a cause of recurrent trouble. In trade, partly because of the gradual decline of the Hanseatic League, the country prospered and grew wealthier. The Word of God was to be the model for preachers; and a dis- putation, somewhat on the Zwinglian model, was to regulate all further points of importance. Subsequent ordinances gave the King the appointment of Church dignitaries and a general control over the Church. Henceforth, then, the bishops were under his control. The main object of the change had been the secularisation of Church property for State purposes; the con- sent of the nobles had been gained by the return (as mentioned above) to them of their old family gifts made to the Church. The royal control grew greater, and the Lutheranism of the now favoured religion was soon intensified when (1531) the Swedish Mass Book, Lutheran in doctrine, was published:

compulsory confession, and prayers for the dead were abolished, episcopacy continued although under royal visitation and with restricted powers. Gustavus' son and successor, Eric XIV (1560–8), was a Calvinist by choice, and under him the Church and clergy became laxer and more careless. His brother and successor, John III, began a reaction, and with him the Counter-Reformation made some headway. On the whole, the people followed the religious policy of Gustavus, which was for a national Church and wide royal control.

In Denmark, Christian aroused opposition: at length the rich and Lutheran city of Lübeck took up arms against him and supported his uncle and rival, Frederick, Duke of Schleswig-Holstein. Christian had, for political ^Denmark.^ reasons, taken up the anticlerical side of the Reformation, but doctrinal questions he was content to leave to the trading classes mostly influenced by German and Lutheran intercourse; these burghers and the peasants were thus his chief political supporters against the nobles. The clergy were heavily taxed, the nobles depressed in power; Codes, secular and religious, were issued (1521–2) by royal power. A Wittenberg theologian, Martin Reinhard, was asked over (1519): Luther was invited, but only Carlstadt came. The King's regulations were of a mixed type: monasteries were visited; priests were forbidden to be non-resident; ability to instruct was insisted upon as a qualification for minor orders; priests might marry, but must be chaste; cases of property were removed from spiritual courts, and a new royal court of appeal was set up at Roskilde, from which no appeal lay to the Pope. Christian's relations with the Papacy were thus strained, but the final success of Frederick (1523) lessened his importance. He fled, and an attempt to regain his power as a Roman Catholic (1529) and through wars and negotiations (1531–2) only ended in his treacherous capture and imprisonment (until 1559).

In Frederick's own Duchies Lutheranism was already strong; the Danish clergy had therefore insisted upon his taking an oath neither to introduce it nor to injure the Church. But his temporary and cautious neutrality was in itself a gain to the Lutherans. Not only did he foresee the gain to the

Crown from religious change, but he was himself a Lutheran
at heart. Diets at Odensee (1526 and 1527) discussed the
Lutheran- situation, but the King did much by his own power.
ism in Clerical marriage was common and was recog-
Denmark,
Frederick I, nised, but questions of doctrine were to remain
1523-33. until the meeting of a Council. Bishops were
to get confirmation from the Archbishop of Lund, not
from Rome: episcopal payments to the Pope were transferred to the Crown, as were also the fines inflicted by
Church Courts; all these changes arose out of the vacancy
of the See of Lund and a quarrel about it between King,
Pope, and Chapter. But consecration being disregarded, the
succession was gradually lost. The monasteries were deserted;
in Norway and in Denmark the higher clergy were against the
King; Christian's reconciliation with the Pope was a serious
danger, and his landing (1531) secured him all except the
fortresses. Foreign help from Lübeck and the Schmalkaldic
League, however, maintained Frederick's power, and his recognition of Sweden's independence removed one cause of
danger.

In Denmark, as elsewhere, there were some who like Paul
Eliaesen, Reinhard's interpreter, advocated a moderate reform—improved discipline, vernacular services, communion
Course of in both kinds, clerical marriage—with no doctrinal
Change. change. But Hans Tausen, the " Danish Luther,"
educated at Wittenberg and returned home (1524), a
married monk and popular preacher, headed a more extreme
party, which made a large and unconsidered use of the
New Testament (translated 1524). But the fact that the
Reformation was so largely carried on by royal power, and not
by popular tumult, resulted in the preservation to a larger extent than in Germany of ornaments such as the old altars and of
vestments. The death of Frederick I (April 1533) and subsequent disputes between his sons Christian and John, while
Lübeck fought for Christian II, changed the religious history.
Had not Lübeck suffered a revolution in which Wullenwever,
its great democratic leader, fell, and by which the Hanseatic
towns lost much of their importance, the city might have gained

on the Baltic the kind of power Zwingli had sought for Zürich in the South. In the end Christian III, the elder of Frederick's sons and a Lutheran, gained power in both Denmark and Norway, although many of the country districts in the latter remained Catholic. The Copenhagen Decree (1536) gave all ecclesiastical lands to the Crown; the secular members of the Council were henceforth to be Lutherans; the bishops, against whose order Christian had already as Duke of Schleswig-Holstein shown animosity, were removed and the episcopate abolished. Bugenhagen, the Lutheran organiser of Pomerania, was called in (1537) to draft a new constitution.

Seven superintendents (one of whom knew no Danish), with the place and even the name of bishops, were set apart by the laying upon them of Bugenhagen's hands: *The Danish Organisation.* this was the first inroad upon the Historic Episcopate. Under the new bishops were rural deans; nominally elected, both they and the bishops were largely chosen by the royal will. Side by side with the bishops stood financial officers representing the King, administering in his name the confiscated lands, and keeping the clergy under control. A liturgy was drawn up, and the gradual disuse of old ceremonies and institutions such as chapters and monasteries was hastened by the increasing local power of the nobles. The royal power, by its vigorous exercise, gave uniformity to the system: learning and theology were largely influenced from Germany, and the Augsburg Confession was made the basis of doctrine. But there was little national vigour in the movement, and the policy of drifting along which was thus begun has prevented religion having the force in Denmark which in Sweden and even in disunited Germany it mostly possessed. The death of Christian III (1559) saw Denmark Lutheran; Iceland had opposed the change bitterly, but was overcome: Norway had only tardily accepted it.

Into Norway Lutheranism was imported under Danish influence: monastic buildings were seized, and the bishops showed themselves feeble defenders of the Church. *Norway.* Christian III (1536) placed the Kingdom under Denmark, and thus its civil and ecclesiastical independence disappeared altogether. The Archbishop of Nidaros and the Bishop of Hamar fled (1537); the Bishop of Stavanger was imprisoned; the Bishop of Oslo reappeared as a Lutheran superintendent for Hamar and Oslo; the Bishop of Bergen became Superintendent of Stavanger and his own diocese. The old parish priests remained for the most part undisturbed, but were in the end succeeded by Lutherans, often foreigners, and of indifferent character and learning: for over fifty years the Kingdom suffered from religious revolution and ignorant pastors, but with the loss of political freedom she suffered sullenly, and it was long before the new teaching made itself at home.

The Scandinavian Reformation had thus some peculiar features of its own: clerical abuses had not been so prevalent, the Papacy did not count for as much as elsewhere: the doctrinal movement was imported and never very popular. The nobility was depressed, and the royal power raised as a result of the movement. Incidentally, trade, owing to its wider outlook and the lessened rivalry with the Baltic towns, flourished. Thus, when the religious connections with Germany gave Scandinavia a greater interest in German affairs, the royal powers were stronger, richer, and able to interfere with greater effect in the Thirty Years' War.

But the east of Europe seemed to lie apart from general history. The fear of the Turks, the growth of Russia, and the fluctuating state of the south-east marked it off from the rest of Europe. Furthermore, in religious matters, the existence of the Eastern Church kept Eastern Europe apart and gave it interest of its own. The proposals for union and the discussions upon it at the Councils of Ferrara and Florence had turned men's minds to the " Holy Oriental Orthodox Catholic Apostolic Church ": by its conservatism, its trials, and its historic interest it drew further notice to itself. It suggested the past to which theological controversialists made appeal; the Papacy had made tentative advances to it, and Lutherans sought its alliance. Political conditions in the east of Europe were changing rapidly: fishers in troubled waters of controversy and diplomacy thought something could be gained; men of devotion and zeal thought something could be done. Hence the sixteenth and seventeenth centuries have an importance for the east of Europe and the Eastern Church that lies even more in the fluctuations of relations than in permanent results. Sweden, Poland, Russia, and the Greek Church illustrate some aspects of the age which it is not so easy to see so plainly in other lands. Here we deal with Scandinavia.

In Sweden, with the imprisonment of Eric XIV (1568), who had raised the nobles to greater power, Calvinism lost a great chance of success in Sweden. The Lutheran settle-   Sweden. ment already made was open to the objection on   John III., one side that it had been too conservative in cere-   1568-92. monies and details, on the other side that it had given up essential doctrines. And it had not worked well: the priests were too often unlearned and unworthy; the Holy Communion was celebrated with slovenliness; the churches were in bad condition. Calvinists had hoped for much under Eric. It seemed that the placid Lutheranism of the realm would be invigorated by an infusion of their views and practice. But the poisoning of King Eric, for which the Diet gave orders, repeated in 1575 and in 1577, placed John III safely upon the throne. He was married to a Jagellon princess who had shared with him a long imprisonment, and he had hopes of becoming King of Poland—a Catholic country. He was something of a theologian as well as a linguist; and he had specially studied the writing of George Cassander (†1566), a theologian whom Ferdinand I had consulted, and whose significance exceeded his influence. Cassander had tried to lay down a basis upon which Catholics and Lutherans could agree: the Apostles' Creed, the consent of the Fathers, a thorough reformation of abuses, the permission for clerical marriage, and Communion in both kinds. A work of his, the *Consultatio* (upon points of difference) was reprinted at Stockholm (1577), and it was in his spirit of reconciliation that King John forwarded the Counter-Reformation. The new Archbishop, Gothius, worked with him; Cardinal Hosius directed the movement by correspondence, and two Jesuits were sent from Louvain (1576) with strict orders to present their views in a conciliatory and evangelical manner; they were to give the clergy instruction; the teaching of Prayers for the Dead and Invocation of Saints was reintroduced by order. It was fairly easy to raise the ritual, for the Lutheran Reformation in Sweden had been conservative in this respect, although the adoption of the " Augsburg Interim " (a compromise akin to that hoped for by John) had been refused (1549). The Red Book—the Liturgy in Swedish and Latin, based on the Roman Missal—was issued and enjoined. But it met with opposition; and on the other side the Pope (Gregory XIII) urged the King to become an open Catholic: he would not hear of any compromise and sent the Jesuit Possevin to influence the King. The Catholic attempt on Sweden was part of a crusade inspired by Spain, and Philip II took a warm interest in it. There was a difference of opinion between the Jesuits, who had hitherto guided the movement, and the Pope as to the amount of accommodation possible. After much pressure from the Pope and Possevin John himself was received (1578), but the policy of gradual change was not given up, Swedish youths were sent for training to foreign seminaries, the Catechism of Canisius replaced that of Luther, and the tone of thought was gradually affected. But the King's political schemes did not meet with the support that he expected from Rome. His Polish wife died and his second wife had Protestant sympathies. A change came. The Jesuits were expelled, but the use of the Red Book was still enforced with much severity. John died (1592), and his brother Charles, an able and decided man, who had kept his land of South Ermanland Lutheran, became Regent.

John's son, Sigismund, who had been elected King of Poland (1587), was a devoted Catholic, and wished to give up his claim to Protestant Sweden. Clement VIII, however, urged him to take the crown and with it the chance of a Catholic restoration. But under Charles's leadership the " Moot " at Upsala, an assembly of laymen and ecclesiastics, had made a new and stringent settlement (1593). The Augsburg Confession was adopted, the Red Book and the current compromise were forbidden; " no heresy, Papist or Calvinist," was to be allowed. A new Archbishop (Angermannus), a strong Lutheran, was elected, and a sudden revolution carried

through. Sigismund was compelled to accept these changes and
guarantee support to the Augsburg Confession. He came to
his coronation (1593), supported by a papal nuncio, Malas-
pina, and by a papal subsidy. The new King meant to favour
Catholicism, and in secret protested against the promise he had
made. The nuncio had opposed his making the promise, and
it was only with the written leave of the Jesuits he had done so.
Once more there was a disagreement between the Jesuits and
other Catholic advisers as to the accommodation it was lawful to
practise. The result was an open difference between the King's
promise and his performance: he favoured Catholics and allowed their worship in some places. Finally the nation threw off
their submission to him and Charles was elected King (1604).
The new ruler would for himself have preferred Cal-   Charles IX,
vinism, but the nation was so strongly Lutheran   1604.
that he fell in with its wishes, and the path thus taken was kept to.

The Reformation in Sweden had begun from the Crown,
and nowhere had the changes of the rulers a deeper effect upon
religion. In the end, Lutheranism was so strongly fixed that
Christina, daughter of Gustavus Adolphus, abdicated (1654) in
order to become a Catholic. But that was after Lutheranism
had been firmly re-established under Charles IX. The influence of mediating theologians upon John III is worthy of
note, and the failure of his attempt at a compromise is equally
so. The policy of the Jesuits, even their differences with the
Papacy in the midst of their success, is a significant feature of
the history. The final failure of the Counter-Reformation—
for the conversion of Christina was a poor set-off to the loss of
the land—was a heavy blow to a widespread movement. It
affected more lands than Sweden, for the north-eastern states
formed a system of their own, and the attempt to regain Sweden
was, as we have said, part of a wider movement. Sweden also
shows the practical failure of a movement that was great in
intellectual promise, but overlooked religious considerations.
It came very near to the adoption of what was really an
" Interim " of its own, and nearly carried out a " Counter-
Reformation." Royal inclinations counted for much, but not
for everything, and so the attempt failed.

VI

FRANCE AND THE REFORMATION

FRANCE, with a peculiar ecclesiastical past, had also in this period a distinct reforming movement of its own.[1] The Reformation in France is, however, always associated with the history of Calvin, so influential outside France, and with the so-called " Wars of Religion." The influence of Calvin cannot be estimated too highly: the Wars of Religion had little or no permanent effect upon the world except complicating its politics, secular and ecclesiastical. The kingdom of France had been formed through the gradual absorption of the great feudal possessions by the central power of the Monarchy. But the provinces kept their peculiarities: there was no really united France except as a thing of loyalty and government. Louis IX had brought the judicature, legislature and the executive into touch with the Crown. So the rights of the Monarchy were fundamental, and the nobility always stood close around the king. In the fourteenth century the system of Estates had grown up, because the king mainly depended upon them for his income. The English wars had left the country over-run by mercenary bands, lawless towards the people but disciplined under their captains. Charles VII gave them an organisation by districts, and, from their dependence upon the Crown thus brought about, there came into being a permanent army, which France alone possessed. Everywhere royal officials now replaced the old locally elected officials. Louis XI,

The Reformation and France. The French Church before the Reformation.

[1] For France see Mr. A. Tilley's Chapter IX in the *Cambridge Modern History*, II ; also W. H. Jervis, *History of the Church in France* (2 vols. London, 1872), clear and with much knowledge. Ranke's *Französische Geschichte*, 6 vols. (3rd ed., 1877); there is an old English translation by M. A. Garvey: *Civil Wars and Monarchy in France in the Sixteenth and Seventeenth Centuries* (London, 1852). In the *Helps for Students of History Series* (S.P.C.K.) Mr. Tilley has written two first-rate guides: *The French Renaissance* (No. 13), and the *French Wars of Religion* (No. 8). See also, his *Literature of the French Renaissance*, 2 vols. (Cambridge, 1904).

who seized Burgundy, after the death of Charles the Bold, set up Estates throughout his lands: he readily listened to their complaints, and furthermore favoured the towns with their growing trade and commerce. The curious combination of hereditary Monarchy having absolute power, and of Estates having much freedom and individuality accounts for the peculiar history of France. But the Monarchy was bridled by Parliaments, legal bodies of experts formed in the leading cities and districts everywhere, although the Parliament of Paris, with its right of making royal edicts effective by registering them, was a peculiarly strong check on the Crown. Hence the lawyers, " the gentlemen of the long robe," held great power in their hands, more than in any other country. It was so even to the Revolution and during it, when the lawyers, for the most part Jansenists, did much to influence debates and decisions. But for the whole of our period and indeed long after, the provinces, with separate organisations and different dialects, remained a bundle of territories only united by the Monarchy.

The Pragmatic Sanction of Bourges (1438) had, as we have seen, defined the position of the Church in France: it may be taken as the joint result of the Conciliar Theory (for France had eagerly championed the independence of the Councils against the Popes) and of the strong monarchical power. The Concordat of Bologna (1516) gave the appointment to ecclesiastical offices to the King: annates, previously all but abolished, were tacitly restored to the Pope. The Gallican Church had hitherto vindicated its liberty, but this meant that it was now under the control of the King, in whose favour the Pope had waived his rights. Henceforth the King was enabled to reward his favourites, and the evils of pluralities and non-residence were intensified. As regards discipline and religious life, France was as much in need of reform as other countries, and there, as elsewhere, earnest and educated men perceived the need. But the Reform movement in France began, more than elsewhere, with the Renaissance: although the Sorbonne had been at one time the leading theological body of the West, it was such no longer, and the Thomist revival of theology as seen in Spain had not affected Paris: the Sorbonne was strictly conservative, orthodox but not progressive in doctrine. It was the Sorbonne that opposed Erasmus, and the condemnation of his Colloquies by it ensured the sale of 24,000 copies.

The legal authorities, too, were guided by the Sorbonne, and,

Rise of Lutheranism.

when, on the rise of Lutheranism, it named a Delegation on matters of Faith, the Parliament of Paris followed its lead: heresy was, as in the Middle Ages, held a civil crime. But when Francis I, in the pursuit of Italian power, concluded the Concordat of Bologna to receive Papal support, the Parliament opposed this change. The versatile and unprincipled King, himself no heretic, although stained by many other crimes, was yet not prepared to follow the Parliament in its action against heresy, and thus at times appears as a favourer of what really threatened both his throne and the unity of his kingdom.

But it was not from Lutheranism that French Protestantism or Huguenotism arose. The clergy and schools were in close

Special origin of French Protestantism.

touch with the Church: the clergy were cultivated and leaders of the nation although sometimes satirised by writers; it was among these and among the higher classes that the French movement began, and Reform was for some years more a sentiment than a cause of action. Jacques Lefèvre d'Etaples (Faber Stapulensis), an opponent of Erasmus in a controversy on the Pauline Epistles, was a professor of mathematics who turned to theology, and, like Erasmus himself, commented upon St. Paul's Epistles (1512), on the Gospels (1522), and translated, after an older version, the Bible into French (1523–8). He had been a teacher of Briçonnet, Abbot of St. Germain-des-Prés, and when his friend and pupil went as Bishop to Meaux, he followed him thither by invitation (1516), as also did Guillaume Farel. At Meaux, Lefèvre and his pupils replaced the Cordeliers, and their preaching of Faith as distinct from obedience to authority, their denunciation of celibacy and prayers in Latin, drew upon them the anger of the Sorbonne. But the protection of the King's sister, Margaret of Angoulême, Queen of Navarre, and of the King himself, saved them. Finally,

however, stress of poverty and a grant from the clerical notables, on condition of his suppressing Lutheranism, led
Francis to sanction persecution (1526). But Farel, among the
Reformers, had gone too far for Briçonnet in his doctrine,
especially in denouncing prayers for the dead, and thus the
partisans of Reform went different ways. Provincial synods,
especially at Sens, now (1527–8) took up, as did Briçonnet
himself, the twofold policy of suppressing Lutheranism and
furthering moderate reforms.

But the movement now began to change slightly its character. There were still the Court preachers, most of them men of
good family, protected by Margaret. But Germany **Change**
now began to influence France, and the German **of the**
Protestants, to whom Francis was politically **Movement.**
favourable, negotiated as was their wont. The brothers
Du Bellay, one of whom was Bishop of Paris, held a
mediate position, and Guillaume du Bellay conducted negotiations with Melanchthon. Thus favour and fire alternated
fitfully as Francis changed his mood (1534). In 1535 the
Huguenot schism began when at Paris they founded a separate
place of worship, and thus the stamp of opposition to Church
and Crown alike was placed upon the movement. It was no
longer an attempt to reform the Church (indeed, the vigour of
the persecution at times made the hope of such a thing seem
vain): it was a movement of separation which at Paris and elsewhere in the cities (for the country places remained Catholic)
demanded toleration and safety. Thus the course of the religious movement in France was very different from elsewhere:
it originated in the Renaissance and biblical study; its Lutheran
associations were secondary and purely sympathetic; its treatment depended upon kingly and party politics; it was very
largely an affair of literature, sermons, and psalm-singing until
the popular enthusiasm and iconoclasticism of some of its followers alienated men like the hitherto sympathetic Rabelais.[1]
A curious feature in the literary war was the publication
(1544) by the Sorbonne of an *Index Expurgatorius*, which was
continued annually. But when violence on the part of its

[1] See A. Tilley: *Francois Rabelais* (London, 1907), Chaps. II–III.

promoters and persecution on the part of the authorities were becoming more marked, the masterful genius of Calvin appeared, and henceforth, whatever might be the play of politics and parties, French Protestantism and Calvinism meant the same thing.

John Calvin was born (July 10, 1509) at Noyon in Picardy, which had bred many reformers, notably Lefèvre and Berquin.

John Calvin, 1509–May 27, 1564. His father, Gerard, who died in 1531, was a lawyer, serving the Chapter and patronised by the local noble family of Montmor, two of whom, uncle and nephew, held the See for seventy-six years, the younger being suspect of heresy and on bad terms with his Chapter. For some cause or other Gerard Calvin also had trouble with the Church, and died under excommunication. But before his death he had gained for John, his second son, the endowment of two sinecure benefices, although the youth was later intended for the Law. In 1523 he went to the University of Paris, and there, after a legal course, studied more strictly for Law at the college of Montaigu. At Paris he fell under the influence of the Renaissance, and showed special taste for Greek. Among his closer friends it is significant to notice that some were scholars of that reforming type, mainly Scriptural, which marked the day in France. But Calvin himself was for some years more bent on scholarship than on theology, as he afterwards shewed (1532) by publishing a commentary on Seneca's *De Clementia*. From Paris he went to Orleans for a year (1528), and then to Bourges (1529), still nominally reading law, although with no special enthusiasm. Soon he gave it up, and took to reading the works of Luther and the *Novum Instrumentum* of Erasmus. The thought of the day was beginning to affect him and religion was now with many a matter of interested talk, even if not as yet of spiritual moment to him. Even his legal studies he had approached from the side of philological scholarship, and he was led by Valla to admire the Latinity of the *Pandects*. From Law he moved, still in the sphere of the Renaissance, to Ethics, and it was from this standpoint that he published his work on Seneca's *De Clementia*. Soon after the death of his father he returned (1531) to Paris, this time to the newly-

founded (March, 1530) Royal College there, which, somewhat after the model of Louvain with its Three Professorships of Latin, Greek and Hebrew, stood for the newer studies and the modern spirit. For a year or two the young scholar moved about, in Orleans, in his birthplace Noyon, and at Paris. He was influenced in thought and style by teachers like Mathurin Cordier, but he was now also reading for himself, in the New Testament of Erasmus, and in some Lutheran theology, and, more still, he was thinking for himself and looking on the life of the people around him with the judgment and the eye of a moralist, framing from his classics, his law and his theology a whole system of thought for himself. Among his friends of the time were the four brothers of the Cop family, all brought up under Erasmian influence, one of whom, Nicholas, became Rector of the University in 1533; this officer being the head of the Faculty of Arts, composed of the Masters. On All Saints' Day, 1533 he delivered his Rectorial address, which had been written for him by his friend Calvin and in its treatment of Justification seemed tinged with Lutheran heresy. The religious policy of Francis I had been very changeable: at times, when he wished for the friendship of the Pope, or received liberal subsidies from the clergy as he did in the Assembly of Notables in December 1527, he was ready to try and suppress " Lutheranism." But when (1534) he wished for the help of the Protestant princes of Germany, he favoured the Reformers. Sometimes at the Louvre there were Reformed preachings patronised by the Princess Margaret: sometimes there were burnings for heresy, as in 1526 and in 1529, when the Picardian, Louis de Berquin, perished: sometimes there were proposals for union between the Lutherans (for whom Melanchthon spoke) and the French Church, represented by William du Bellay, Bishop of Paris (1534). But Cop's address was likely to bring him into trouble: he fled and so did Calvin, whose journeyings soon became of moment. In Paris, the Sorbonne, the Theological faculty of the University, was invariably orthodox, and had thrown its weight Meaux.
against even the Erasmian reformers at Meaux, the future home of Bossuet: so its side was already taken.

In 1535 Calvin was at Basle, the home favoured by Erasmus until religious strife grew too bitter, and the scene where the gentle radical Oecolampadius (1531) and more violent reformers had triumphed. In the interval until his arrival at Geneva he drafted the *Institutio Christianae Religionis*, a work which went through many editions and translations, becoming the text-book of the Presbyterian bodies. It embodied the relentless growth of his very logical mind and rigid system: it had a legal order and logical completeness, and although his more peculiar tenets might be stated more completely in the later editions, from the very first it expressed thought both clear and revolutionary. In its French form (1541) it also holds a leading place in the national literature as " the first French book written on a regular plan ": it had a simplicity and restraint of style which fitted its clarity of thought: its characteristically French logic made its system of thought as clear to the reader as it was to the writer himself.[1]

The *Institutio*, in its completed form (1561), covered a wide field: it attacked with vigour many existing abuses of the Church, and so incidentally gave the impression that there was little in it save abuses. The outline of the work followed the divisions of the Creed: the first Book dealt with the knowledge of God the Father, externally in the world and internally in ourselves. The second Book treated of the Son, our Redeemer because

The Institutio Christianae Religionis.

---

[1] For Calvin see A. Tilley: *The Literature of the French Renaissance* (Vol. I., Chap. XI), (Cambridge, 1904); A. M. Fairbairn: *Calvin and the Reformation* (*Cambridge Modern History*, Vol. II., Chap. XI); Quirinus Breen, *John Calvin; a Study in French Humanism* (Grand Rapids, Michigan, U.S.A., 1931); and of course, many general works, especially A. M. Lindsay's: *History of the Reformation* (Vol. II, Chap. III).

The first Latin edition of the *Institutio* (1536) was enlarged in the second (1539) from six chapters to seventeen, and the matter trebled. In the edition of 1559 it grew fourfold, and was divided into four Books and eighty chapters.

In 1560 a new French edition—the seventh—came out, in which other scholars helped. The first English translation, by Thomas Norton, came out in 1561. The Edinburgh edition, by Henry Beveridge (for the Calvin Translation Society, 1845), gives in the preface much information about the various editions and translations into most European languages.

redemption was needed through original sin; from its power Christ is the only means of escape: He had to become Man in order to give us salvation. His Death, Resurrection and Ascension were considered. Free will was utterly condemned. The great benefit which Christ gives us by the Spirit is justification. Prayer is described as " our hand to grasp the word of promise." Here comes in the doctrine of election, of some to life eternal, of others to destruction. The Father reconciles us to Himself in Christ, so we come to the Church with its means of grace, Holy Baptism and the Lord's Supper: these are, as it were, Christ's sceptre by which He reigns in the Church and reaches to us. The third Book treats of the Holy Spirit which works in and upon us, being our bond of union with Christ. We are regenerated by Faith, and so (Chapter XI) we must consider Justification by Faith. Any righteousness of works is denied. By justification God receives us as if we were righteous, this righteousness being imputed to us in Christ. He holds that Osiander (the Lutheran minister of Nuremberg) erred in assuming a kind of transfusion of the divine essence into us to make us righteous, whereas our righteousness is a matter of imputation. Osiander held, too, that in the Lord's Supper Christ is eaten substantially by a carnal eating, and this is wrong. As little does Calvin accept the view, expounded at Trent, of a righteousness compounded of faith and works. He charges the Schoolmen with degenerating into Pelagianism, and he seems to reject a working of faith in us and forming, as it were, a germ of righteousness. In Chapter XXI of the third Book he puts forth nakedly and sharply God's election of some to salvation and of others to destruction.

Book IV treats of the Church, and is unsparing in its exposure of abuses, which are made to appear inseparable from its whole system. Existing ministries he condemned. In the primitive Church, there was always, as should be in lawfully existing institutions since, election of ministers by the members of the Church, but this has wholly vanished. The rightful mode of government is by a consistory of presbyters, some for teaching and some for censorship of manners. Thus there would be no grades in the ministry, for in all the existing grades he finds evils, whereas the consistory he depicts agrees, as he holds, with the primitive model found in Scripture in early days. " It was therefore a gross iniquity when one man, grasping the common power to himself, paved the way for tyrannical licence, robbed the Church of what was its own, suppressed and discarded the consistory ordained by the Spirit of Christ" (Chapter XI). This was the government by Consistories, which was afterwards to be so greatly developed in France, Scotland and England. The Primacy of the Popes was, of course, denied: St. Peter was never Bishop of Rome, and, if he had held a Primacy, Antioch and not Rome should be its place. So the Clementine tradition about Antioch as Peter's seat which had filtered through the Middle Ages and appeared in Marsilio now gained new strength. Moreover, the Pope was Anti-Christ. The authority of General Councils was put aside. To the jurisdiction and coercion by bishops with their numerous officials he objected. The administration of discipline means exclusion from the Lord's Table. Intrusion of civil governments into Church government is wrong. Stress is laid on the propriety of consistories ordering days of fasting and prayer (in which the Long Parliament copied them). Infant Baptism is right and scriptural. It is not enough to regard the Lord's Supper (Chapter XVII) as merely spiritual, or as a mere symbol with the Zwinglians. Transubstantiation and Consubstantiation are both mistaken doctrines. (But here we may note for ourselves that Luther did not himself use the meaningless label of Consubstantiation.) But in the Sacrament we do receive a reality: this too was to be held later on by his followers. He goes on to expound the true nature of Christ's Presence, which was not affixed to the elements of bread and wine, but still was truly there. It was " too high a mystery to comprehend." He speaks of the corporeal presence which the nature of the sacrament requires and which we can say is here displayed in such power and efficacy that it not only gives our minds undoubted assurance of eternal life, but also secures the immortality of our flesh, which is now quickened by his immortal flesh and in a manner shares in his immortality. Every part of the sacrament has reference to faith, and by participation of the body we nourish our faith (Chapter XVII). The Mass as a sacrifice he condemns: in it the priest offers up Christ; in the Lord's Supper Christ gives himself to us.

The *Institutio* is thus a powerful and clear treatise, complete on the side of doctrinal exposition, and severe in its denunciation of abuses which most men acknowledged to exist. If it grew longer and fuller as editions multiplied, the outline remained the same. It laid the foundation of a future Church polity, more decidedly perhaps in its exclusions than in its provisions; but the power of civil government in Church matters was limited to " entertainment " and support. In its attack on the Papacy and the hierarchy, and indeed on the Roman system as a whole, it was outspoken and easy to understand, only a little less so than his more occasional but more vigorous tracts. It was inferior to Hooker's great work in majesty and learning, but, like him, Calvin infused Latin influence into his native tongue. If Calvinism grew stronger as the century went on, while Lutherism grew gradually weaker, the coherence and scope of this literary masterpiece, compared with the more occasional and less coherent literature of Lutheranism, explain much of what happened. It became a text-book wherever Calvinism spread: it was so used for instance at Oxford.

There was a Prefatory Address (of considerable length) to Francis I, which proves Calvin's loyalty and patriotism; if it pleads for consideration of their cause (that of the " godly ") declares that they do not depart from the Fathers of the Church, and has much criticism of the Papacy and hierarchy; it is also a defence of the French Protestants. Throughout it is thoroughly loyal, and indeed Calvin never ceased, for many years, to urge upon his followers in France an abstinence from rebellion, although political schemers in the end overcame his influence. And the preface also shows us Calvin sympathetic with his fellow believers throughout France, and this sympathy naturally and quickly passed into control. The Huguenots everywhere in France looked to him, and so in his native land his word was law.

From Geneva, French in its sympathy but independent in its position, Calvin was able to dominate France, and to influence Europe both through France and independently. Geneva became a second Rome.

As time went on, he gained much the same influence in a larger field: not only to theologians did he write, and write with an authority almost apostolic, but to monarchs, to princes and to statesmen. Writing to Sir William Cecil in 1559, for instance, he rebukes him for being " more severe than was consistent with your courtesy " when he had promised himself much " from your regard towards me." And he also praised him for " his excellent disposition " and his other virtues. Theologians consulted him anxiously for his approval of what was being done; from England Grindal urged him, with the example of St. Gregory Nazianzen, who suffered in old age for his earlier austerity, to take more rest, remembering that he and Bullinger were the only chief pillars remaining to the Church.

Geneva, where the energetic Farel had laboured since 1532, stood between Savoy and Bern. Against the rule of its bishop leaning upon the Duke of Savoy, his Advocate, its democracy looked for help to Bern—reformed in a Zwinglian sense (1528), but at a later date more Lutheran— and (1526–30) had at last set up a republic. Internal strife and external troubles lasted, however, until (1536) Catholicism was abolished. The Bishop was driven out; sermons replaced the daily Mass; ordinary bread was used in the Eucharist, and a strict moral discipline—something on the Zwinglian lines— was introduced. This was the field to which Calvin was called, and where, after a short absence due to civic strife (1538–40), he lived until his death (1564). Here, too, he introduced the ecclesiastical organisation, largely original although much indebted to Zwingli, which was, perhaps, next to the Catholic model, most calculated to maintain itself and to impress righteousness upon a wayward people. The transformation of Geneva from a city noted for immorality to one noted for its austere piety is proof that his system possessed this quality.

Geneva.

Luther might start from a vivid personal experience; Zwingli from a humanism modified by local politics; Calvin—as became a lawyer and a logician—followed another Doctrinal method. Like them, he disregarded all previous basis of his theology (the sixteenth century was not, indeed, a system. theological age), but unlike them he went on to build up a theory of religion and life upon the sovereignty of God, for his theology was the basis of his polity to a greater degree than was the case with any Reformer, Catholic or Protestant. It was emphatically a legal conception, and man as the subject of God's law fell into his destined place. As did the Catholic Reformers, so he too went back to St. Augustine; but they, as became Thomists, seized on those conceptions of St. Augustine which fitted in with the Catholic faith and existing worship: he went back to the purely doctrinal and predestinarian side of St. Augustine's views, and upon this conception of law—the law of God, guiding and inspiring man as God's instrument for a destined work—Calvin based his teaching and his polity. It is a magnificent testimony to the breadth and force of St. Augustine's teaching that both the Catholic Reformers of Spain, who later on were the leading theologians of Trent, and Calvin himself, were indebted to him for the most vital parts of these divergent schemes.

In regard to the Eucharist, Calvin agreed with Zwingli in denying any bodily presence or any change of substance; unlike Zwingli, he held there was a real spiritual The grace given, a real union with Christ made; but Eucharist. these benefits were purely spiritual and connected with the Sacrament itself, rather than with the consecrated elements. It was on this view that the Second Helvetic Confession (1566), following upon Calvin and Bullinger's work, the generally accepted " Consensus Tigurinus " (1549) was based, and so finally and expressly united Switzerland.[1]

While Zwingli gave the power of excommunication to the State, Calvin kept it for the religious body itself in the

[1] Kidd, *Documents*, p. 652. Niemeyer, *Collectio Confessionum in Ecclesiis Reformatis Publicatorum* (Leipzig, 1840).

Consistory. The pastors had an almost unrestricted power ("new presbyter was but old priest writ large"), it was

Organisation and Discipline. for them to preach, teach, and administer the Holy Eucharist (with a ritual which was Zwinglian in its plainness). The pastors along with elected laymen formed the Consistory which exercised the moral discipline. It was in this association of the pastors, and in the strict supervision thus carried out, that the organic strength of the new system lay. It was a theocracy under God in which the ministers, His messengers, had the upper hand, and controlled even the State itself. It fitted in well with a democracy in politics, and hence it spread so as ultimately to absorb Zwinglianism in Switzerland and elsewhere; in France, the Netherlands, Scotland, and very largely in England, in districts of Germany, such as the Palatinate, it was " the Reformed " not the " Lutheran " type of Protestantism that finally had power.

In his later years the influence of Calvin reached far and wide; as a sort of Protestant Pope he received questions for

Calvin's influence in later years. decision, and wrote to sovereigns upon equal terms; his views governed a large territory of Protestant thought; and, until early in the seventeenth century an Arminian revival began, Protestant orthodoxy was judged by agreement with him. Such a large body of opinion affected thought beyond Protestant circles, and the tendency of speculation as Calvinism rose, and as it declined, was naturally towards the larger questions of God's government of the universe and the free-will or the limited power of man.

The religious history of France when, after 1550, French Protestants were Calvinists, can be best treated here. For

Religion in France. many reasons the Huguenots were opposed to the Crown; whether as led by great nobles of royal blood, or as demanding toleration and almost sovereignty in special districts and cities, or as a schism against a church dominated by the King, or as theoretical republicans, they took to opposition easily. But how far the Crown by its persecution or its energetic measures made their opposition active depended upon its mood, its policy, and its advisers.

There was always Spain, the national enemy, to be reckoned with, and after the revolt of the Netherlands (1572) opposition to Spain was inevitable: there were Popes of Spanish and French leanings to deal with; there were German Protestants to conciliate or delude; after a time there were armed camps, the League led by the Guise family, and the Huguenots, the triumph of either meaning ruin to the nation; that of the former meaning Spanish influence, that of the latter the reversal of all the nation's past. But the main interest of these wars is political, not in any sense religious. At the outset of the wars the moderate part of the nation was against the Huguenots; after the massacre of St. Bartholomew, 1572, it was rather against the Catholics; about 1585 a Catholic reaction began.

VII

GERMANY 1529–1555

CLEMENT VII, who had done little to encourage reform and during whose Pontificate Lutheranism had spread much more widely, died on September 25th, 1534, and was succeeded, after a Conclave of one day only, by Alexander Farnese —Paul III.[1] The new Pope, although only sixty-seven years old, had been a cardinal for forty years, and had narrowly escaped the Papal throne before. His sister Giulia had been the mistress of Cardinal Roderigo Borgia, and her daughter had married a nephew of Julius II, so that he moved in Papal circles. He had a humanist education at Florence and Pisa; under Innocent VIII he was out of favour but after 1491 rose rapidly: he was created a Cardinal Deacon in 1493, and held the Legations of the Patrimony (1494) and of Ancona (1502). His earlier life had its scandals: Julius II had legitimatised his sons Pier Luigi and Paolo, and he had also another son and a daughter. He had much knowledge of men and politics, and his judgment of them was mostly accurate and wise. In his last years, his nepotism was great. He was a patron of art and literature, easy and liberal in his views, and generous in his treatment of men: pledged to no party in politics, and by both person and tastes alike fitted for a dignified position. But he could not be reckoned an ecclesiastic or a theologian above everything else, and problems, ecclesiastic and theologic, were urgent. Yet he came to the throne when the greatness of the "German tragedy" was thoroughly felt: he was soon surrounded through his own choice by cardinals of a more deeply religious tone, and for some years it seemed as if the Papal administration was to be conducted in a very different way. But, like some earlier Popes, Paul cared overmuch for his family: his nepotism led him to invest his son Pier Luigi, who had been given Novara before, with the Duchies of Parma and Piacenza (August 1545), and this without Imperial sanction:

Paul III, 1534–49.

---

[1] Pastor's *History of the Popes:* XI. pp. 6–40.

which naturally led to friction with Charles V, and when Pier Luigi was murdered with the supposed connivance of Charles's deputy at Milan (1547), Paul claimed the duchy for Pier's son Ottavio. Another son of Paul III, Alexander, was a Cardinal.

In Italy there had at length been a reaction from the Paganism secret or avowed, of the Renaissance; "the Oratory of Divine Love" had been formed at Rome (1523) with the objects of prayer, biblical study and edification. Giberti, Caraffa (afterwards Paul IV) and some fifty others, many of them equally eminent, were its members. The movement aimed at the reform, not as earlier movements had done of monastic life, but of clerical. Its significance was, however, greater than its effect, for the sack of Rome (1527) scattered its members. It was characteristic that it embraced men of opposite extremes; but, broadly speaking, they were all united in a strong assertion of justification by faith—a doctrine which, however technically expressed and often erroneously emphasised to the exclusion of other truths, embodies the great principle that man is judged by God as what he essentially is. *Thought in Italy.*

Venice, to which in the political storm all people—Italians or refugees, such as Reginald Pole—flocked, became a centre of this newer school of thought. Here the whole Bible was translated into Italian; here, too, Gasparo Contarini, eminent in intellect as well as in piety, was laying in a small field that foundation of thought and observation which is the best preparation for lofty office. *Contarini and Morone.*

Sprung from a noble Venetian family, he studied at Padua: he was sent as Venetian ambassador to Charles V (1521) and afterwards to Clement VII. He was named a Cardinal (1535) while still a layman. He was looked upon as a leader of the "mediating" theologians and had many friends on many sides.[1] At Regensburg (Ratisbon) he was Legate, and so had charge of the difficult but important discussions on doctrine which formed a part, important but in- *Gasparo Contarini.*

[1] *Die Theologische Entwicklung Gasparo Contarinis:* Hans Ruckert (Bonn, 1926), *Kardinal Contarini: 1485–1542. Eine Monographie:* F. Dittrich (Braunsberg, 1885), *Studies in Venetian History:* Horatio F. Brown (London, 1907), *Contarini and his Friends*, II. 110.

effective, of the Imperial attempts at religious reunion and peace in the Empire (1541).

Giovanni Morone was born at Milan (1509): his father was a publicist and in the service of the Sforzas: after living as a youth *Giovanni Morone.* at Modena and Padua, he was made Bishop of Modena by Clement VII (1529) out of gratitude for his father's help in reconciling the Emperor to the Pope; but as the Duke of Ferrara, who ruled Modena, wished to gain the see for his nephew Hippolyte d'Este, the young Morone only entered on his episcopate in 1532, and had to pay his rival a pension of 400 ducats. His father had been favoured by the Farnesi, and hence Paul III took a great interest in the young man. He was much employed as a diplomatist, being sent after France (1529) to Germany (1536 to 1538); he was present at Bologna when Pope and Emperor met, so that his employment for German diplomatic relations, so delicate and important, was natural; in that country he travelled much, not only by himself but in company with Ferdinand I, at whose court he succeeded Aleander (1529). In this way his knowledge of men, and above all of men in high position, grew greatly. His piety, learning and high character gained him much influence in Germany, so that in the difficult conversations about unity in the Church and Empire he was perhaps the best representative of the Papacy at its best. He was created a Cardinal in 1542. In Modena there were some Lutherans and many sympathisers with the doctrinal turn the Reformation took in Italy: among them, as among others, as bishop he had to work, and belonging as he did to that company of theologians known as "mediating," he tried to see the good in every man. Stricter and narrower theologians might disapprove of his conduct in this way, but it is difficult to convert or change a man you boycott: as a diplomatist Morone had to meet all sorts of men in politics, and he brought something of this habit into his episcopal rule. His work in Germany in preparation for the Colloquy in 1541 of Ratisbon (Regensburg) needs larger treatment, and in recognition of what he did he was created a Cardinal by Paul III (June 1542). His varied activities in his own see and else-where brought him under suspicion with Paul IV (Carafa), who as he grew older had changed his earlier love of reform into strictness of the severest type, and was, moreover, fanatically anti-Imperial. He arrested Morone and handed him over to the Inquisition (May 1547); he was imprisoned in the Castle of San Angelo, where he remained until the Pope's death.

He had as tolerant an outlook on doctrine as on men, and in particular he liked that little Italian book *Trattato utilissimo del Beneficio de Jesu Cristo Crucifisso* which was widely circulated (1540) first in manuscript and then in print.

It was the work of a Benedictine, Benedetto, a Mantuan, and he asked Marcantonio Flaminio to revise it. He was a disciple of Juan Valdes and shared his mysticism, which inspired men to sink self and surrender their life wholly to God: hence came a union with Christ and a new life partaking of His grace and light. The tract seemed lost until Prof. Babbington found a copy in the Library of St. John's College, Cambridge, and printed an edition (1855). Its doctrine is not precisely Lutheran, as its standpoint was different, but it was classed as such.

But there was no justification for the charge of heresy brought against Morone, and it seemed almost ironical. On the death of Paul IV he was released by Pius IV (1560) and was afterwards Cardinal President of the Council of Trent, which he, more than anyone else, brought to a successful close.

He and Contarini were fellow-workers in the same fields of ecclesiastical reform, diplomacy or reunion and theology. But Contarini made his impression by his character and disposition rather than by his skill, great as that was: he won men by shewing them his simple self. Morone had more of the artistic skill of a trained diplomatist, consciously working on the men he dealt with. They were indeed noble brothers in their achievement if not in their character.

In Modena Morone taught the same doctrines, and brought into strong light the doctrine and the person of Christ. At the same time they and others held, along with Erasmus, to the unity of the Church and obedience to the Papacy. The latter presented itself as the most stable among the unstable political powers of Italy, and had, moreover, gathered around itself the ecclesiastical sentiments of the West. No corruption could, to

127

many minds, be great enough to justify a defection from the Church. It was better for each to try and reform what existed than to experiment in creating something new. It was best to bend all thoughts to improving the old and divine institution and curing its defects. Both Morone and Contarini, under Paul III, played great parts in Germany.

It was noteworthy that, on his accession, Paul III called to the College of Cardinals, Carafa, Sadoleto, Pole, Giberti and Contarini, all men of the type described, and all eager for reform.

The Pope himself, who saw reforms must be made, was sincere in his wish to call a Council, which was clearly needed and which he had promised at his election. There was a great work of reform to be done and he found many helpers, especially among the new Cardinals of his creation; Contarini, Sadoleto, Carafa chief among them. Reform, both of morals, and of the various offices of the Curia, were considered along with discussions about the General Council and as a programme for it. Then (July 1536) a Commission of nine was appointed to consider these matters. Their report, the celebrated *Consilium delectorum Cardinalium de emendanda Ecclesia*[1] (February 1537), was detailed and outspoken. Contarini was their president: Carafa (afterwards Paul IV), Alexander, Giberti and Sadoleto among the members; they condemned the abuse of Papal courts and jurisdiction by interested canonists. Money payments for dispensations were the causes of widespread evil. Good bishops and priests must be found: unfit men were no longer to be appointed: corruptions of all kinds were to be swept away. Simony must be uprooted: payments for, and pensions out of, benefices must not be allowed. Residence should be enforced on all bishops and parish priests. Evil life and scandals, even among the Cardinals, were denounced. In religious houses many abuses were to be found, and these must be put an end to. The report, founded upon wide knowledge and much consideration, covered the whole field of the Church's work. It was a private document, but copies got about: it was printed in Italy and

The Consilium de Emendanda Ecclesia.

[1] See Kidd, *Documents*, No. 126: pp. 307–18. *Cam. Mod. Hist.*, II. p. 643.

Germany, sometimes with notes, in ridicule or hostility. When Carafa came to be Pope he placed it on the Index. But unhappily the meeting of the Council was delayed, and so (April 20, 1537) the Pope appointed a new and smaller Commission of four Cardinals, afterwards enlarged (Contarini, Carafa, Simonetta and Ghinucci), to carry out reforms. Contarini was now full of hope, and he saw almost all the Cardinals on the side of reform. The Dataria, which controlled dispensations, graces, appointments in Papal patronage, and provided about half of the Papal income, was the first and also the most difficult branch of administration to be reformed.

While, in Rome, the Pope and his Cardinals were thus seeking to reform the Church, in Germany the Protestants were gaining ground. Würtemberg, where Ulrich was firmly seated after his restoration by the Smalkadic League Würtemberg. (1534), was extensively visited and organised.[1] The Duchy was a stronghold of Protestantism among Catholic states, and by the choice of its first pastors, especially of Brenz, became a centre for attempts at union among theologians. Loyalty to the old Ducal house was intensified by the romantic perils of Christopher, Ulrich's son and successor. On his father's expulsion he was placed under the care of Ferdinand of Austria (who had been invested with his father's Duchy): when he feared being taken to Spain in the train of Charles V, he escaped and his adventures made him a hero. So the old Ducal house acquired a romantic halo much as had done the medieval Billungs in Saxony.

With the territorial spread of Lutheranism, theologians of a secondary rank in comparison with Luther and Melanchthon became local leaders with much influence, and some reputation beyond their immediate sphere. Among them Martin Bucer and John Brenz may be taken as types of an increasing class, but there were many others, for the most part with humanist training, some of them with Zwinglian or Calvinistic sym-

[1] *Wurttembergische Visitationsackten:* Julius Rauscher (Stuttgart, 1932), Vol. I, 1536–1540. Kidd, *Documents*, pp. 305 f. For attempts at union: *Martin Bucer*, Hastings Eeles (Yale Univ. Press, 1931, pp. 162 f. For Christopher's adventures, Ranke, *Reformation in Germany* (Routledge, 1905), pp. 700 f.

pathies; interested in municipal politics, often dependent upon the Civil power.

Martin Bucer was born at Sélestat (Schlettstadt) in Alsace (Nov. 11, 1491). From his early days he took to classics
Martin Bucer, 1491-1551. When his parents went to Strasbourg he was left to the care of his grandfather, a shoemaker, who wished him to follow his own trade. But the boy, at that time ten years old, was eager to study, and this seemed possible only in a clerical life. His grandfather thought more highly of regulars than of seculars, and so, possibly a little against his wish, the young man became a Dominican. The house he entered was interested in the Thomist theology more than in classics, but when he was twenty-five he passed to the Dominican convent at Heidelberg, where he could follow his bent, not, however, with his fellow Dominicans, but at the University under John Brenz. Under him Bucer became a devoted Humanist. Study of Erasmus naturally led him to the New Testament, and along with it he read the Psalter in Hebrew. In these day he met Luther (1518) and talked with him much. Now he became a Reformer of the usual type. He visited Luther with an invitation from Sickingen (April 1521). After his ordination (Mayence 1519) he visited Basle, where he got to know Froben and Wolfgang Capito. His circle of friends was enlarging itself, and the many doctrinal differences among them possibly made him wish to draw them together. But the works and influence of Luther were the chief things in his religious growth. The army of Reformers, however, included not only Luther but Sickingen and Hutten: his intercourse with them and his Humanistic outlook brought him under the suspicion of the Inquisitor Hochstraten: his life was made uneasy and he left his Friary. He contrived, however, to get released from his vow (April 1521). For a year he was at the court of Frederic (brother of the Elector Palatine Lewis), as Chaplain; then Sickingen at Hutten's request gave him the parish of Landstuhl, where he married: he left it in the troubles of the Knights War, and was persuaded to settle at Wissembourg (Weissenburg). Here controversies brought excommunication, and he left (May 1523) for Strassbourg, and soon joined the local re

forming movement there, already begun. This was his future
home, and with that central and important city his name is
bound up.[1]

Education, in both lower and higher stages, needed improvement. A beginning was made (December 1523) when Bucer and
Capito became salaried lecturers. Thus began the University.
With the help of Jacob Sturm and in spite of some civic apathy,
six schools for boys and six for girls were founded: the expense
being met from the funds of the Chapter and the monasteries
(1525). A year later enlarged provision was made for higher
studies, mainly for ministerial training. In all these movements
Bucer took the lead, and the part he played in the Disputation at
Bern (1528) spread his renown outside his city. By an arrangement with the Chapter (January 1529) the magistrates gained
the right to appoint pastors, paid from the Chapter funds. In
this way the magistrates secured control of the ecclesiastical
organisation.

At Strasbourg Jacob Sturm was not only a leading city politician but something of a leader in German affairs generally.
He also had literary and historical instincts and it _Jacob
was at his instigation and with much of his help that Sturm._
Sleidan [2] wrote his history. The Sturms were respected and
notable in culture and civic politics alike: Wimpheling was a
family friend, Jacob went to Heidelberg and took his Bachelor's
degree there when he was fourteen. On Wimpheling's advice he
then went to Freiburg im Breisgau, where he studied law, and
visited Liège and Paris. From its position his city, with many
villages under it, standing where it did, had many outside
interests, and when he became its leading statesman he was of
necessity a diplomatist in the national field. He was an authority
in the League of Smalkald, and shared like others in the religious
politics of the Empire. His career [3] illustrates the importance of
the great cities and their statesmen.

---

[1] _Martin Bucer_, by Gustav Anrich (Strasbourg, 1914). _Martin Bucer:_
Hastings Eeles (Yale Univ. Press, 1931). The latter is fuller on the
doctrinal conferences for reunion.
[2] Sleidan: _Commentarius de statu religionis reipublicae Carolo V Caesare._
[3] _Die deutsh-protestanische Politik Jakob Sturms von Strassburg: In-_

John Brenz,[1] born June 24, 1499, at Weil (in Würtemberg), studied at Heidelberg, where he learnt Greek from Œcolam-padius, and also studied Hebrew, deviating, too, into Aristotle. Like others he was greatly influenced by Luther's visit to Heidelberg in 1518. In 1522, on the invitation of the Municipality, he went as a preacher to the Imperial city of Schwäbisch-Halle in Würtemberg, where he worked until the Augsburg Interim (1548). Here he gave up the Mass, and preached against the Invocation of Saints: it may be noted that he based his teaching on the doctrine of the Invisible Church. During his ministry there the Mendicants were expelled (1519). Some were sent in carts to Würzburg, some took to marriage and some got stipends. He threw himself into the Eucharistic controversy, where the views of Zwingli were opposed to those of Luther, who thought this controversy was revived by the revolutionary and violent Carlstadt, as he held, from evil motives. After Luther's unexpected return from the Wartburg to Wittenberg, in order to check the violent disturbances there (December 1521), Carlstadt had gone to Orlamunde. In 1524 Luther met him at Jena, to discuss with him about his Iconoclastic violence and Anabaptism: he, in his turn, charged Luther with heresy on the Eucharist. Pledged to a further discussion with Luther, he went to Basle and thence attacked his foe in his *Antichristian abuse of the Lord's Bread and Cup*: but his exegesis making out that Christ pointed to Himself as He said "This is my Body" was too forced to gain support. Luther replied in his work *Against the heavenly prophets of the Images and Sacraments*, in which he was violent himself because he saw disunion creeping into the ranks of the Reformers, chiefly through the disturber Carlstadt, whom no power could curb. The main lines of doctrinal division are easy to mark, but they should not be made too definite. Zwingli asserted that the eating and drinking of the Body and Blood of Christ was only done after a symbolic and spiritual fashion, interpreting

John Brenz, 1499-1579. {margin note}

---

augural Dissertation (Heidelberg, 42 pp.): K. G. von Langsdorf (Leipzig, 1904).

[1] *Johann Brenz: nach gedruckten und ungedrukten Quellen:* Julius Hartmann and Karl Jäger (Hamburg, 1840–42).

the word "is" in Christ's own words of Institution as equivalent to "signifies." Œcolampadius on the whole agreed with him. Each reformer seemed to think that he alone gave each element in the Sacrament its proper place and that all others erred more or less in one way or other. At Basle the Town Council asked Erasmus to give them his opinion, or, it might be said, his decision. In giving it he said that Œcolampadius had written well and in a pious way, but that for himself he must go by the universal doctrine of the Church. As the controversy went on, some dozen of the Swabian reformers along with Brenz wrote their *Syngramma*, pointing out that Carlstadt, Zwingli and Œcolampadius were not agreed among themselves: writers might indeed easily differ in defining what was to be taken literally and what figuratively when once the floodgates of discussion were opened. Besides the broad differences between Zwinglians, Lutherans and Calvinists there were many minor differences between individuals. But the Eucharistic controversy dominates the period.[1] Hence came attempts to unite opposed sections.

Even the Protestants had drawn together among themselves; under Melanchthon, the closer adherents of the Augsburg Confession, and under Bucer, the party of the Oberland theologians. Bucer, eager for compromise, hurried from one theologian to another, hoping to minimise their differences: even the Zwinglians approaching, although not reaching agreement. But the final result, the Wittenberg Concord (May 29, 1536), reached after much journeying to and fro, was not in the least a statement of agreed doctrine held by Lutheran and Zwinglian: in conferences theological diplomatists, like their political models, are too often content to produce a formula, satisfactory on the surface, but open to varying interpretations by different parties: in this way a real

The Wittenberg Concord, May 1536.

---

[1] Hagenbach, *History of the Reformation*, I. c. 15, discusses these differences. Beza's views and those of the Cardinal of Lorraine, given at the Colloquy of Poissy, are interesting: see H. O. Evennett, *The Cardinal of Lorraine* (Cambridge, 1930), pp. 296 *seq.* Beza's words at Poissy seemed more novel and extreme than those of Calvin.

solution is only postponed and made more difficult to reach in the end. In this case it only led to other formulæ (especially to the "First Helvetic Confession"),[1] which the curious may compare. After all there was a deep doctrinal cleavage between the Eucharistic beliefs of Zwinglians and Lutherans, and, as in some much later controversies, the final test of agreement came to be an answer to the question: What does the unworthy or the wicked partaker really receive? But it was something to the good that by meeting face to face, Zwinglians and Lutherans, too apt to hate each other, should become more tolerant or friendly. Even Luther himself waived what he sometimes insisted upon, a confession of error by his opponents. But it simplified the situation, ecclesiastical and political, when Lutherans and some Zwinglians met together. The Concord, however, was more of a lull, or even a truce in controversy, than a joint doctrinal profession. The verdict of an older and accurate historian and theologian (echoed by some later writers) is that "a union was very far from being effected, but an understanding, a mutual toleration, was arrived at."[2] Only a few extreme Zwinglians stood aloof. Illness, intermittent but severe, affected Luther greatly at this time and so he left much to Melanchthon: the real differences between them led to some inconsistencies in policy and statements. Princes and theologians, moreover, did not always see things in the same light. The Princes and their theologians met at Smalkald (February 1537) to discuss the coming Council. Luther had been asked to draw up for their consideration a Confession of Faith to be submitted to the Council. This he did, and its difference in tone from the Confession of Augsburg reveals the differing spirit of the writers. For Melanchthon had written for Augsburg, and he did so as one always seeking for concord and testifying to agreement. This was the spirit of the

[1] Schaff, *Creeds of Christendom*, p. 388.

[2] Hagenbach: *History of the Reformation in Germany and Switzerland chiefly* (trans., Edinburgh, 1879), II. pp. 230 f. Kidd, *Documents*, Nos. 127 and 128. *Martin Bucer:* Eeles, Chaps. XXI–XXII. Niemeyer, *Collectio Confessionum in Ecclesiis Reformatis Publicatarum* (Leipzig, 1840), I. p. 105. For the Articles of Smalkald: *A History of the Creeds of Christendom:* H. A. Smith and P. Schaff (London, 1877), I. p. 253.

Praecepta Germaniae, who died (April 19, 1560) with the prayer "Let them all be one, O Father" on his lips as it was always in his heart.

But Luther in these Articles of Smalkald was violent: he called the Pope Antichrist and the Apostle of the Devil. Unlike the Princes, however, he was ready to attend the Council: he had no fear, but his words (which even his apologists admit to be "spicy") were no passport to calm debate. The Wittenberg Concord had produced an article on the Lord's Supper which asserted that the true Body and Blood of Christ were present in it. The Smalkaldic Articles asserted that the true Body and Blood were present, given and received by impious as well as by pious Christians. So while these Articles, on the one hand, made reconciliations with Papalists impossible, on the other hand they threw over the not very far-reaching concord just made with the Zwinglians on the Eucharist. So the Articles of Smalkald have rightly been described as a landmark, if not a new departure, in the history of Lutheranism. Theological interest was henceforth mainly centred in Eurcharistic doctrine: Melanchthon,[1] for instance, said that never a day passed without his meditating on it.

Paul III, a politician of experience, anxious for a Council and pledged to it, found many difficulties in its way. Without the support of the Emperor and of Francis I it was impossible to hold it and it would be useless when summoned: negotiations for a lasting peace between them were long delayed by Francis. But the bad state of the German church itself, apart from the number of Lutherans, called for reform. Legate after legate reported the negligence and the evils they had seen. Even in the Austrian territories Morone found many parishes without priests; empty convents; religion neglected (1536); the whole state of the Church was deplorable and there was, above all, need of good bishops. Aleander found things the same later (1538), even in the same Austrian lands:

---

[1] *Die Versuche Melanchthon zur katholischen Kirche zurückzüfuhren:* Gustav Kawerai (Halle, 1902). Schriften von Vereins fur Reformationsgeschichte. *Die Kirchlichen Reunionsbestrebungen während der Regierung Karls V:* Ludwig Pastor (Freiburg im Breisgau, 1879).

135

at Innsbruck there were less than a dozen priests; worship and the Sacraments were neglected. Those Princes who were nominally Catholic hated the clergy and disliked the Curia: above all they also coveted the Church's property. The bishops lived in luxury and were merely officials; the monasteries were scantily inhabited; the secular clergy immoral and generally despised. It was a sad but true description.

An armistice with France (Nov. 16, 1537) gave Charles a little respite, and the Truce of Nice (June 17, 1538), to last ten years, left him free to carry out his plans for religious unity in Germany. But the Turks were still a menace, and the formation of a league against them by the Pope, the Empire and Venice (Feb. 10, 1538) had placed France in a bad light, as

Respite of Frankfort : April 19, 1539.

it was an ally of the Sultan. In this atmosphere of somewhat strained peace, Charles was able to deal with Germany, and the result was the Respite of Frankfort: by this the adherents to the Augsburg Confession were not to be subject to either persecution or prosecution at law for fifteen months: no action was to be heard in the Imperial Court: such actions had often arisen from the secularisation of Church property, and so the Lutheran Princes gained what they had long desired, comparative freedom to plunder the Church. On the other side the Protestants were not to molest Catholics. The effect of this Respite outlived the period fixed.

Much was looked for from the meeting fixed for 1540 at Speier: it was the prelude of a "lovely Christian union."

Diets and Colloquies.

But the Imperial Chancellor Seld had, before this met, formed (June 10, 1538) the Holy Alliance between Charles, his brother Ferdinand, the Archbishops of Mayence and Salzburg, the two Dukes of Bavaria and the two of Brunswick: the members of this League were to defend each other against attacks by Protestants. But even inside this League there were differences, for the Bavarian Dukes wished for war against the Protestants, while Charles wished for unity. There had been some changes among the Princes which affected the balance of creeds. Duke George of Saxony, a devout Catholic, died (April 15, 1539), and his duchy fell to his brother Henry, a devoted Protestant, but his rule was short and his death (1541) put his son Maurice, a Prince of great ability, in his place. Joachim II, the Elector of Brandenburg, who had refrained from any religious change so long as his father-in-law, Duke George of Saxony, was alive, now set up Lutheranism (October, 1539) in his territory. The Diet was moved from Speier to Hagenau (May 15, 1540), and afterwards to Worms (November, 1540), where representative theologians, Melanchthon, Bucer, Brenz and Calvin, represented the Protestants, Eck and Cochlæus the Catholics. Morone and Pozzio were now nuncios in Germany, urging on the Emperor the need for a General Council, but so greatly was the gravity of affairs in Germany felt that other nuncios were sent: Tommaso Campeggio (October, 1540) with special instructions not to imperil the Church by overmuch concession: also Cardinal Cervini (afterwards a Legate at Trent and Pope Marcellus II) and Cardinal Contarini (January, 1541). The choice of such able representatives was a sign of a change in policy: if earlier Popes had taken Lutheranism too lightly, Paul III and his advisers made no such mistake. Contarini and Morone were the very men for the task. But on some principles, such as the divine institution of the Primacy, the Sacraments and the practices of the Church, no surrender was to be made. As the Lutherans had already shown what they held, on their side, to be fundamental, to reach agreement seemed almost hopeless. The Emperor was represented by Granvelle, whose strength lay more in diplomacy than in theology and who was very ready to carry out Charles's policy of religious concessions which probably neither the Nuncios nor the Curia were likely to grant. At Hagenau Justification by Faith had been discussed: at Worms three days were given to Original Sin. But the Emperor postponed the discussions (Jan. 18, 1541) until the Diet of Ratisbon (April 5, 1541), where the presence of the Princes might be expected to weigh political interests more carefully and to dilute the draughts of theology. By the beginning of May four articles on original sin, free-will and justification had been agreed upon.

Diet of Ratisbon : April 1541.

137

Contarini had been sent as a Cardinal Legate to the Diet, and the higher authority thus given him was equalled by the great effect of his presence and character: his simple sincerity, humility and religion won all hearts even if votes were harder to change. So far doctrine, apart from ecclesiastical constitutions, had been discussed.

Morone rightly thought that agreement, if possible at all, would be more easily reached on doctrine than on the constitutional questions: shades of doctrine admit of blending much more than the hard facts of Church constitution: as a diplomatist of experience and insight he foresaw that certainly on the Primacy and probably on Episcopacy a breakdown must come. With doctrine, where refinements might seem to reclothe principles, there was some chance of agreement, and so this, along with friendly intercourse, might favour the following constitutional discussions. But on his instructions from Rome and in his own view, Morone was firm as to the impossibility of giving up anything on Church authority or the Primacy. On fundamental doctrines, especially on the Real Presence and on Transubstantiation, Contarini, so gentle and considerate, was equally firm. These were precisely the matters which the Lutherans held vital and where they had expressed themselves even more than strongly.

Diet and Colloquy of Ratisbon : April 1541.

At the Diet a Book was submitted by Granvelle, as the Imperial representative, which dealt under twenty-three heads with all these matters. It had almost certainly been prepared by John Gropper, a learned theologian of Cologne; as Eck had been kept by illness from the debate he would have loved and embittered, he had more to do and say than others. Contarini declared his personal approval as it emerged from the debate, slightly altered. But he could not vouch for its acceptance at Rome. The article on Justification had been accepted by both sides.

The Book of Ratisbon.

In the Book, Faith was said to be an inward motion in man, worked by the Spirit of God, and, along with love, poured into the soul of man from above. On this subject clever draughtsmanship had been shown in combining Catholic doctrine with Protestant expressions. This was, in reality, a duplication of Justification, for along with the inherent righteousness which men were made partakers of by the grace of Christ, a still higher righteousness, that of Christ Himself, was needed for perfect renewal. Neither Rome nor Luther was satisfied. Luther thought it a patched-up affair, and its rejection at Rome was as a heavy blow to Contarini and seemed to him a personal condemnation.

Contarini, who had thrown his whole admirable self into the discussion, and won golden opinions on every hand, was deeply disappointed. Yet of him no one said a word of blame. He returned to Italy, and it was some lightening of his trouble when Paul III made him Legate at Bologna (January 1542), and there he soon died (Aug. 24, 1542). He had striven for peace and by his character enriched the world of his day. The Colloquy of Ratisbon has always attracted men who seek peace and ensue it. But no other end was possible except what came. The Papal side had naturally defined the limits of concession as narrow, and the presence, still more the vote, of laymen in any Council to settle Church affairs was objected to. On the other side, the Princes were resolved to have their own way, and were intent upon secularising the Church's lands. In January 1540 the leading theologians, Saxon and Hessian separately, declared that the Confession of Augsburg must be upheld: that in any agreement the Pope and his followers must renounce their errors and give the true gospel full course. And the backs of the theologians were stiffened by the Princes.

The possibilities of conferences and discussions are limited. By means of them men who differ can come to see their differences in a clearer light: and they can keep the charity which controversy kills. But historic causes and results can only be but slightly altered by talk or speech: agreements lightly entered into can also be lightly broken or interpreted amiss. Convinced and honest men must keep the truths they have learnt, as they think, by the guidance of God. The process of history is long and it alone, like a man in his own life and work, can undo by time and its teaching what has been wrought, as it were, into the very fibre of its being.

But a great deal depended upon the concord between Pope and Emperor.

The Diet of Speier (Feb. 21, 1529) and the years following it had been critical for the Emperor. He had already faced difficulties in all parts of his vast and scattered dominions, but as Emperor and as King of Germany he had special responsibilities: both in his territories and outside. The religious affairs of Germany weighed heavily upon him, and the Edict of Worms had been his own special work. He was a sincere Catholic and, as such, heresy seemed to him a calamity in itself, even if Lutheranism had not yet threatened to divide the realm. But as Emperor he had a further special task of defending Christianity. No sovereign of his time had a deeper sense of duty: in his private life, and in his home, compared to other kings, he was moral and honest: to his wife, Isabella of Portugal (May 1, 1539), he was a faithful husband and cherished her memory until his death, and on his deathbed clasped her crucifix. Each of his scattered possessions he looked upon as a trust to be faithfully handled with due regard to its needs and its traditions: hence his policy for them differed from land to land.

As Emperor the defence of the Christian world was his special task: his rival Francis I might imperil Christianity by a league with the Sultan and by inviting him to invade Christian lands; he might be proud of his title of the Christian king, but his Christianity was purely titular and never affected his acts. With Charles it was different; Germany, Italy and Spain all lay open to invaders, and Charles took special measures of defence for each. His enemy Solyman, who had become Sultan in 1520, had already begun a victorious career: he had taken Belgrade (1521), and made the very important conquest of Rhodes, where the Knights Hospitallers had so long been a bulwark for Europe (1522); he had overrun Croatia and part of Hungary. To make Spain secure he made an expedition against Tunis (1535) and for the sake of Italy he attacked Algiers. In Tunis he restored the King whom the dreaded corsair Barbarossa had expelled. Next he turned to Germany, where the bulwark of Hungary always needed defence against the Turks. After Lewis II, King of Hungary and Bohemia, had fallen before Solyman at Mohacs (Aug. 30, 1526), Bohemia elected Charles's brother Ferdinand as King. In Hungary, his sister Mary, widow of Lewis, gained the throne there also for him, but he had a rival in Zapolski, Voivode of Transylvania, whom the Sultan Solyman supported: after ten years of strife Ferdinand allowed him to keep his eastern lands (1536); but he died in 1541 and so Ferdinand ruled the two kingdoms. The Emperor could thus leave Germany to the care of his brother, and although Ferdinand's interests were not always his, the brothers worked together in friendship. But his difficulties were complicated by the ambitions of Pier Luigi Farnesa, the legitimatised son of Paul III, who wished to hold Parma and Piacenza: this was not agreeable to Charles, and when Pier Luigi was murdered (September 1547), with the supposed connivance of Charles's governor of Milan, the Pope and the Emperor were definitely on bad terms. This was not only bad for the unity of Western Christendom, but retarded the assembly of the Council for which so many men looked.

The Emperor, who felt his responsibility, wished to defend his Empire, and indeed all Europe, against the Turkish invaders: this he could only do with help, in men and money, from the Princes. But it was hard to persuade the Lutherans; and yet their approval was needed not only for the anti-Turkish war, but for the coming Council which Charles thought might bring peace to his realm. The Pope had already fixed on Mantua as its seat. The Lutheran Princes met at Smalkald (February 1537), on the south-west border of Electoral Saxony, the birthplace of their defensive League. The Imperial Chancellor, Matthias Seld, and the Papal Legate, Van der Vorst, came thither to meet them and gain their promise to attend the coming Council. The theologians might have consented (Luther said he had no fear and was ready to go), but the Elector of Saxony was determined not to attend: other Princes followed his advice; so disappointment awaited Charles, and it was unfortunate for the Emperor's policy of Reunion that Luther, although more conciliatory towards the Zwinglians, whom at Marburg he had been so stern against, was more violently anti-Roman. The Pope was now to him more definitely Antichrist than ever: when saying farewell to some Lutheran theologians at Smalkald, which he was leaving for Wittenberg, he prayed that God might intensify their hatred of the Pope.

The Emperor would have liked to make the accepted Articles a kind of creed for the Empire—a step similar in substance to that taken further on by the Interim—but Contarini protested, and Luther, never lacking in the common-sense that so often accompanies self-will, rejected the proposal. But even had a satisfactory agreement been reached upon the points discussed there would still have remained the question of the Papal Power, and here any agreement must have been impossible. The Colloquy, although dictated largely by political needs, had, however, been a Christian effort, and even if little came of it, each party had seen something of the mind of the others. The discussion moreover and the clearer expression of Catholic doctrine greatly influenced theology of all types.

Before the Diet broke up a Recess[1] was agreed upon by which a truce was established through an Imperial Declaration.

Recess of Ratisbon, 1541.
The Catholic bishops were to press forward the reformation of discipline: the Peace of Nuremberg was renewed and also the Augsburg Recess: pending the assembly of a Council and of another Diet in eighteen months, Lutherans received protection for all ecclesiastical property they held: assessors from among them were admitted to the Kammergericht (the Imperial Court): their "reformation" of monasteries and their secularisation of monastic and capitular funds were legalised for the time. Charles' scheme of national union was thus seen to be hopeless;

---

[1] In the Recess after this Diet the term "Catholic" was given to the Papal side as against the "Protestants." In the second Peace of Kappel (1532) the Zwinglians had accepted the phrase "old undoubted Christian faith" as describing their opponents.

he was driven to work by political agencies to secure the
two objects nearest to his heart—the consolidation of a
reformed Church and the unity of the Empire. Charles
But he slowly came to the conclusion that against and a
the Lutherans force was his only remedy. With Council.
many people before and since he regarded belief and opinion
as secondary to practice and conduct: he was equally ready
to leave shades of difference to be fought over by theologians
subject to his royal decision: he could see that reform was not
only inevitable but desirable: he saw, moreover, that the only
way to gain it and make it acceptable was by a Council: if a
General Council could not meet, a German Council, at any
rate, could, and for his purpose the latter at least was essential.
But the Pope looked at the matter from a different point of
view: he was not so much bent upon reform as was Charles,
and he probably had a truer estimate of the obstacles formed
by theological differences. Nor was the condition of Germany
—for any improvement in which religious accord was needed—
of vital moment to him. Hence for some years after 1541 the
summoning of a General Council is the pivot upon which
ecclesiastical affairs chiefly turned.

In 1542 war broke out between France and the Empire,
ended only by the Peace of Crépy (September 1544). In
Germany leagues had been forming; the Imperial Politics in
Chancellor, von Seld, had formed a league of Germany,
Catholic princes (the Nuremberg Bond, June 10, 1542–55.
1538): the Emperor had granted the Lutherans toleration at
any rate for the time. Meanwhile, Protestantism made such
strides forward that in all Lower Germany only Duke Henry
of Brunswick-Wolfenbüttel remained Catholic. But events
worked together to give the Emperor increasing power. The
bigamous marriage of Philip of Hesse (March 1540), for
which Luther and Melanchthon with other reformers were
responsible, both shocked public opinion and put this
capable politician in danger of the Imperial ban. Not only
was Protestantism discredited, but Philip had to give up his
diplomatic schemes against Charles and to make his peace at
any price.

This affair, which began in September 1539, had serious political results and gravely affected Luther himself. Philip of Hesse had long been an active leader among the Princes. He had married (1523) a daughter of Duke George of Saxony, but he was a man of evil life and uncontrolled passions, and was consistently unfaithful to her. Diseased in body and remorseful in mind, for he dared not approach the Holy Table, he cast about for some excuse for himself and some expedient which, at the same time, would leave his conduct free. He pleaded that his wife was distasteful to him, but nevertheless he lived for years after with her: a second marriage, bigamy, in fact, seemed likely to give him the freedom he sought, while a divorce might lead to political trouble. It was a day when Princes were lascivious; and some theologians like Bucer (whose views Milton afterwards adapted for an English public) and some high officials at the Curia, dealt lightly with marriage.

When Philip met the young Margaret von der Saale, of a noble Saxon family, this course seemed to him absolutely right, and he talked the matter over with the girl's mother, Anna. She was willing, but insisted that the marriage should be recognised and public, and also that competent theologians should give a certificate that it was not against the law of God. Bucer had approved, and Luther, along with Melanchthon, gave a private certificate of approval to Philip. This was handed to the mother. The supposed wedding took place at Rothenburg on the Fulda (March 4, 1540) and Melanchthon was present. Neither the Landgrave nor his new mother-in-law treated the certificate as private, which its writers meant it to be. So the whole affair, which was a dirty and discreditable business, became public. Luther wished to deny boldly that such a marriage had taken place, but the lie would have been useless. The excuse sometimes made for his conduct, that he followed the line of the Roman Confessional, seems inapplicable to a Reformer. But Philip was in a dangerous position, as by the Law of the Empire bigamy was punishable with death. So he had to make his peace with Charles V, and dared take no part against him. Granvelle, the Bishop of

Bigamy of Philip of Hesse.

Arras, was an intermediary and Philip had to promise help against the Turks: he had also to join in Charles's plans for religious unity. Agreement was only reached in January 1541, and so Philip had to take his place in the Colloquy of Ratisbon in April of that year. But he was now the Emperor's man, and so the shameful matter had as much effect on politics as on the reputation of the Reformers concerned in it.

Furthermore, a disputed succession in the Duchy of Cleve divided the princes, and thus became of importance. Charles, Duke of Gelders—Charles' most determined enemy —had never gained recognition from him, and (1534) had formally yielded his territory to France. His subjects wished John of Cleve to be his successor, and (1538) the latter's son, William, was recognised as heir. On the death of the Duke of Gelders William easily gained possession of the lands, and on his father's death (1539) held Cleve and Gelders together. The Emperor claimed Gelders as a reverted fief, but as William's sister, Sibylla, was married to the Elector, John Frederick of Saxony, some members of the Smalkaldic League were likely to rally to his support, and a new cause of discord was thus found. Further to the west, Duke Henry of Brunswick-Wolfenbüttel, the Catholic leader of the North, had gained an Imperial Decree against the ancient town of Goslar for having destroyed some monasteries. When he refused to put off the execution of the Decree the Smalkaldic League began war against him, drove him from his territories, and introduced Lutheranism there (1542). The Palatinate (1545) and the city of Ratisbon also now became Protestant; Archbishop Hermann (von Wied), of Cologne, not only showed leanings towards Protestantism, but tried, with the help of Bucer and Melanchthon, to introduce it into his dominions (1536–42). His defection would have given the Protestants a majority in the College of Electors and would have stiffened the ecclesiastical opposition along the Rhine and northwards. Here the successful claimant, William of Cleve and Gelders, had introduced in his territories an eclectic reformation: Catholic in doctrine and organisation, but allowing communion in

Succession to Cleve and Gelders. Spread of Protestantism generally.

both kinds—a concession which the Venetian envoy, Guistiniani (1540–41), considered necessary if Germany was to be preserved Catholic. William, however, soon became decisively Lutheran (1542), just before the Emperor made an attack upon him that changed the fate of Northern Germany (1543). Philip of Hesse, to keep Charles' favour, had opposed the admission of William into the Smalkaldic League, which other members favoured. The League being thus divided, Charles was able to defeat William, wrest Gelders from him— thus joining to the Burgundian Netherlands what would otherwise have remained a purely German Duchy—and reintroduce Catholicism in William's lands. As a consequence, Protestantism in Cologne fell also. But in the North, where Saxony and Brandenburg had power, most of the Sees were by this time in secular hands; it was as yet only towards the Rhine that Protestantism was weakened. "We are daily becoming fewer," said the Catholic Cochlaeus.

But with a stronger position and now at peace with France (September 1544) Charles turned again to attempt a religious and political peace in Germany. Some Protestant theologians were ready to help him, but Luther, in a coarse but effectual way, gave his view of the obstacles to it in his treatise *Against the Papacy, as founded at Rome by the Devil* issued the very month (March 1545) when the Council was to meet. A second religious Colloquy at Ratisbon (1546) had no result; the Protestant princes refused to accept the decisions of the Council. But Protestantism was now divided by the very policies that had smoothed its earlier path. Duke Maurice of Albertine or Ducal Saxony (1541–53), son-in-law of Philip of Hesse, had been since 1542—both on his father-in-law's account and because of his jealousy of Electoral Saxony—an ally of the Emperor's: Joachim II, in Brandenburg, had carried out changes (1538–43) which gradually became more extreme, but he, too, in opposition to Saxony, stood apart from the Smalkaldic League and followed the Emperor's policy.

Growing power of Charles V.

Divisions in the Smalkaldic League.

Maurice of Saxony demands special study. He was born March 21, 1521, son of Duke Henry of the Albertine Saxon line and Catharine of Mecklenburg, a princess as energetic and able as her husband was indolent and pleasure-seeking: Henry's elder brother, George, ruled in Meissen and was a devoted Catholic, but Henry was guided towards Lutheranism by his wife. George was childless and Maurice seemed his natural heir. The youthful Maurice spent much time at Duke George's court, and also at that of the Elector John Frederick. So he came into close touch with both Catholics and Lutherans: belonging to a family of tangled politics and varied faiths, he was driven to judge for himself. Philip of Hesse, always a disturbing influence, was a friend of his parents, although they did not like their son's marriage to Philip's daughter Agnes. When Duke George died, Henry succeeded him, introduced Lutheranism, and had Lutheran councillors; but Maurice kept on good terms with his uncle's displaced advisers who were Catholics.

Maurice of Saxony.

Everything thus tended to give him a varied knowledge of men, and of their interests, religious and political: he saw how Lutheranism was changing the outlook of Princes and of people. He observed everything and so, at an early age, was much of a statesman, ready to act when the time demanded it, but from his character, not likely to act hurriedly; more inclined to let events and policies shape themselves, always quick to see, moreover, whither his interests led him. With the Elector, John Frederick, he grew gradually less friendly: his Hessian marriage and his refusal to join the Smalkaldic League (although he was ready to defend Protestants if attacked) increased the cleavage between them. Melanchthon had noted the beginning of this discord, which sometimes even threatened war. His father died in 1541. The Imperial politicians soon came to look on the young ruler as likely to be useful to them, and one Saxon minister, Carlowitz, who represented him at the Emperor's court, was in close touch with Granvelle. He had from these two warm assurances of the Emperor's regard for him.

Maurice had, however, objects of his own: on the episcopal

Sees, Magdeburg, Halberstadt, Meissen and Meiseburg he had cast his eyes: of the first two he was made conservator and guardian: moreover, he criticised the bishops for not introducing reforms. He was emphatically a man of his day, with none of the inherited loyalties and maxims of the older Princes. If he wished to act in any way, he was cautious and would run no risks: his plans, however, would always be well thought out and his mind clear, while not, in any way, clouded by scruples. In the end he came to differ from the Emperor: he would have no settlement of the religious question in Germany made by a Papal Council, nor would he leave it, as Charles wished, to a Diet largely manned by ecclesiastical Princes: he wished for a settlement by the lay Princes alone. Ferdinand, now advised by his able son Maximilian, would accept this. But Charles insisted on a Diet. Maurice made a treaty with France.

Thus when (December 1545) the long expected General Council met the spread of Protestantism had gone beyond its political power; the Emperor had never been stronger; he judged this the time to use again the weapon of arms that had answered so well against Cleve.

Charles hesitated long, but war was inevitable. John Frederick of Saxony and Philip of Hesse sent him a broken staff as a token of withdrawal of their fealty: it was addressed to Charles, "self styled the Fifth and Roman Emperor." The reply was the ban of the Empire against them for acts of violence and rebellion, attacks on Würtemberg and Brunswick. This was the inevitable climax and Charles, with Maurice as an ally, had sufficient military force for the fight.[1]

War in Germany.

The Pope regarded the coming war as partly religious—an aspect Charles was not wishful to give it publicly: he sent Charles money and troops and allowed him to seize for its expenses Church revenues in Spain. The Smalkaldic League was taken at a disadvantage, and the South German

[1] *The Emperor Charles V:* Edward Armstrong (London, 1902), II c. VI. W. Maurenbrecher: *Karl V und die deutschen Protestanten,* 1545–1555 (Düsseldorf, 1865), cc. 7, 8, 9.

cities were isolated. The Elector, John Frederick of Saxony, was defeated at Mühlberg (April 24, 1547): the Landgrave of Hesse surrendered at Halle (June 1547), and thus the two leading Protestant princes were prisoners. Maurice received much of his uncle's lands and became Elector of Saxony in his place: the Archbishop of Cologne, Hermann, had resigned his See (Feb. 25, 1547); Catholic bishops were restored elsewhere. The power of the Emperor—resting mainly upon the support of Maurice—was supreme. All the great Protestant cities surrendered, some on promise of toleration, and the Duke of Würtemberg followed suit. And further, Duke Henry was restored in Brunswick. Except in the further north, Charles was supreme: his triumph meant the success of Catholicism.

In the Diet at Augsburg (September 1547) the Emperor attempted a religious settlement: he was now out of friendship with the Pope, whose son Pier Luigi as already said had been murdered with the supposed connivance of Charles' governor at Milan. The Council had been moved, against his wish, from Trent to Bologna, and Charles was therefore more inclined to act by himself. His plan of settlement, the Augsburg Interim (May 1548), was drawn up by Pflug and Helding on the Catholic side, and John Agricola on the Protestant side: it was to serve provisionally until a Council could carry out reforms: in doctrine it was mainly Catholic, but it conceded clerical marriage, and communion in both kinds where it had been customary; on the other hand, Episcopacy, the power of Councils, the Primacy of Rome limited so as not to trench upon the rights of bishops, the Invocation of Saints, the seven Sacraments, the Mass as a true sacrifice—all these were asserted against innovators: justification was defined as the process by which a man is made just, and on such points as the encouraging of communicants at daily Mass there was an endeavour to meet a changing opinion. A Formula of Reform for the Catholic States prepared by Pflug (now Bishop of Naumburg) was also published and adopted by many diocesan synods. The Protestant States

The Augsburg Interim, May 1548.

received the document in varying ways: some approved; others, like Maurice of Saxony, hesitated; Maurice himself consulted the theologians, and a modified form—the Leipzig Interim (Dec. 24, 1548)—was the result. By this document

The Leipzig Interim: the Adia- phora. the lesser importance of ritual and ceremonies was asserted; but the controversy which arose as to the definition of these *adiaphora* (things indifferent) had a long history in Protestant theology. In its doctrine the Leipzig form was conciliatory: man's justifi- cation was declared to be solely due to the merits of Christ, but his conduct was not to be supposed mechanically controlled by God: the Mass was continued, but, as was favoured by reformers, canticles in the vernacular were to be sung during its celebration (in England the Puritans in the same way sang Psalms); the assertion of episcopal control was not in accordance with Lutheran practice.

Luther's life, with all its activities and influence, was now drawing to an end. He worked as strenuously as ever, and

Luther's last days. his characteristics, outwardly in ecclesiastical poli- tics and in his inner life, became more strongly marked. His opposition to the Papacy grew into a bitter hatred, on the lines of deep national feeling, the distilled essence, as it were, of the old *Centum Gravamina*:[1] in this, perhaps, even more than in aught else, he typified the German nation: his language was unbridled: the Pope was Antichrist, and his God was the devil: as he said in the tract, *Against the Papacy, as founded at Rome by the Devil*. This was in the outward field, but in his inner life his piety and his vision of God's Almighty presence were stronger and more expressed as his health decayed. But he was weary of life and his work seemed to him still unwrought; and indeed it had been more tumultuous than systematic. He said in a sermon (1545): "I am tired of the world, and the world is tired of me; so it will be easy for us to part company, as a guest leaves the inn where he has sojourned." Much that he saw in the life of Wittenberg distressed him: he wrote to hi

---

[1] Kidd, *Documents*, No. 61, p. 113, for these.

wife (1545): "Let us away from that Sodom. I would rather beg my bread than disquiet and torture my poor last days by beholding the disorderly doings at Wittenberg, with the proof they give that my toilsome but beloved labours have been in vain." He even left the city for Naumberg-Zeitz, where (Jan. 20, 1542) he had consecrated Nicholas Amsdorf as bishop, so making a new departure.[1] Only the prayers of the Elector brought him back.

Luther's discontent with the licence at Wittenberg.

The illnesses which had attacked his naturally strong body became more severe: some of his complaints, such as rheumatism and cataract, were constant: others intermittent.[2] He writes to a friend, James Probst of Bremen (January 1546): "I am old, decrepid, sluggish, weary, cold, and now also a one-eyed man, I who had hoped that by this time rest would be vouchsafed me, which, I think, would be reasonable. I am overwhelmed with writing, talking, doing and acting, to as great an extent as if I had never acted, written, talked or done anything before. But Christ is all in all to me: He can and does do all things. Praise be to Him eternally."

The end came through his friendship and repute. He was asked by his supporters, the Counts of Mansfield, to compose a family dispute about the mines which he had known in his youth, and went to Eisleben (January 1546) to do so. The journey thither was made hard and even

Luther's end.

---

[1] To begin with, one whom the superintendents and visitors found fit for the work and was called by the magistrates to a parish was installed before the congregation with laying on of hands and prayer, which Luther called ordination. In the Pomeranian Church Constitution (December 1534), Bugenhagen systematised this, saying it was an ordination, not only an installation to the church. We find Luther thus "ordaining" pastors in 1535 and 1537. Bugenhagen held that the examination was the duty of the superintendents, but at Wittenberg it had been that of the theologians. In this development Bugenhagen in Pomerania played a great part, but when he went for two years to Denmark (July 1537), Luther took it on. For a summary see Reu, *Thirty-five Years of Luther Research* (Chicago, 1917), a good and amplified Bibliography, pp. 97–100.

[2] Reu (as before), p. 97, for a list of his ten complaints, which critics have enjoyed discussing.

dangerous by floods; near Halle the Saale (as he writes to his wife) became "a huge Anabaptist, with billows of water and great cakes of ice, threatening to rebaptise them"; but he did not thirst for these waters and drank rather some good Torgau beer and good Rhenish wine. She need not trouble, he tells her, for God could create ten Dr. Martins, if the old one were drowned in the Saale. He bids her read again his Shorter Catechism, and so get a truce to her care. "I have One who takes better care of me than you and all the angels could. He lies in the manger on His mother's breast . . . and yet sits on the right hand of God, the Almighty Father. Therefore be at peace." In this spirit, of simple homely love, deep spiritual faith and readiness for any task laid on him, he met his end at Eisleben where he had been baptised. His agonising pains were intense, but through them all with simple words of heartfelt faith he commended his soul to God. Justus Jonas, a friend beloved, was at his bedside. The great leader and simple Christian died (Feb. 16, 1546) in his sixty-third year. So much for the man. We pass to the land he loved and the people whom he had moulded and led. Eisleben would have kept him, but Wittenberg called him. Everywhere vast crowds met the funeral procession which was headed by the Counts of Mansfield. Dirges, tears and civic solemnities marked the way. These were the doings of the day and of the people as they sorrowed for the life that had passed; so they bore witness to the work it had wrought. But it was more than this: it was a prophecy of what Luther was to be in the days to come for his Germany and the Lutheran Church he had moulded.

Germany at Luther's death was very different from the land at his birth, and we can hardly separate the changes in him and **Germany** in his fatherland. To him and his fellow-country-**after Luther.** men his first entry upon ecclesiastical politics had been chiefly an attack upon Papal administration and its abuses. Deeply religious though he was, doctrine, apart from his own individual concern for himself and for his flock faced by Tetzel, had not been the motive power behind the movement. But at his death, doctrine, and above all Justification by Faith alone, was the chief plank in the Lutheran platform. Thus when theological conferences and debates were in the air (1540–41), the Elector of Brandenburg in sending his theologians to such a discussion charged them to bring back to him the word *sola* or not come back at all. The Princes might agree upon showing a firm front to Papal claims, and they might have a steadfast eye on the Church's property and wealth. But Lutheranism was passing into what has been called the age of Protestant Scholasticism.[1]

This was a great outward change affecting Lutheran Germany as a whole. And in Luther's private life and spiritual struggles there had been something of a like Luther and change. He described, with some inconsistencies "Justitia." and variations at different times, the terrible despair into which he fell as he thought of the "Justitia Dei" (Romans i. 17). He thought, he said, that it was "the active righteousness" of God, that by which He condemned sinners, and for him there seemed no escape. But then suddenly, as he said, a great discovery came to him, and he was filled with joy and hope. It was not "the active righteousness" of God but "His passive righteousness" which He imparts in us and imputes to us. With the realisation of this he passed into a state of great peace and his soul was at rest. He believed and he was saved. This was his doctrine of Justification by Faith alone.

But the great scholar Heinrich Denifle, with his unrivalled knowledge of European libraries and their manuscripts, proved that this was no new discovery of Luther's, Denifle on but that all Western theologians from St. Augustine Luther. to Luther's own days had explained this "Justitia Dei" as the passive, not as the active, righteousness which condemns; the long *catena* of passages by which he showed this is a monument of learning, and he further showed that Luther

---

[1] This expression was a favourite one with Lord Acton. Before him it was quoted as used by Dean Farrar in his *Bampton Lectures: History of Interpretation*, p. 360, 1886, as my friend and old pupil Prof. G. R. Potter of Sheffield University tells me, but it might well be earlier. And an increased use of Aristotle by theologians of the time has been noticed.

in his lectures on the Epistle to the Romans (given A.D. 1515–16) had known and followed this earlier interpretation. Thus we find some contradiction and inconsistency in Luther's own story of his spiritual growth. We have no right to put these down to wilful dishonesty or deceit: it is always difficult to trace and describe clearly such changes and growth in one's self, and for Luther, with his tumultuous disposition, moving in new and quickly changing scenes, writing rapidly in critical days, it would be peculiarly difficult.[1]

But this doctrine was not historically the motive-power of the Lutheran movement: that must be found in the attack upon the Papacy with the Church constitution as it then was, and the abuses in its exercise. His "Primary Works" are decisive on this point. It was pointed out at the time, and Luther's dislike of the licence of life in Wittenberg proved it, that Justification by Faith alone might seem to lessen the obligation to a righteous life and to good works. Further, if justification were made to depend upon the sinner's own belief in it, this went to lessen the idea of God's grace. So the problem of the doctrine had many pitfalls for a Church formulating its belief upon it or for a Council striving to balance conflicting views.

Justification made the foundation doctrine only later.

Much has been written as to the way in which Luther reached his doctrine in its final form. It does not seem to me so difficult as it is sometimes made to appear. Luther always felt that he stood face to face with God in His presence. He had a horror of sin, and his conscience made him feel acutely his own sinfulness. He strove after holiness, and he hoped

---

[1] P. Henrich Denifle, O.P.: *Luther und Luthertum in der ersten Entwicklung* (I: Mainz, 1904), Vol. I. Part II gives the *catena* of passages on the interpretation of Romans, i. 17. After Denifle's lamented death on his journey to receive an honorary degree at Cambridge, P. Albert Moria Weiss, O.P., published the second volume 1906. There is an interesting review of Denifle's work by the late Dr. Figgis in *E.H.R.*, Vol. XXIII. p. 144: as he says, the magnificent scholarship shown in the *catena* goes far to atone for the regrettable violence of the biographical treatment of Luther, as an evil man of vicious life. But his verdict was that Denifle had destroyed the hagiographical view of Luther.

that as by God's grace he grew holier, he must become happier.
But the more he strove the more and more his conscience
troubled him. This was in his secret inner life. And so not
leaving, as it were, the settlement on the platform of his inner
life, he raised it to the higher platform of Heaven. If he really
believed in the reality of God's grace he could leave it all to
God. But the later "Protestant Scholasticism" tried to build
up the whole of Christian theology, the whole edifice of the
Christian Church, on a doctrine which was really different
from what had been with Luther a conviction in his inner
spiritual life.[1] Hence endless divisions and discussions sinking
to hatreds and perpetuating parties.

The Protestants affected to believe that the Interim was to
bind the Catholics also: Charles, who was on this occasion
less straightforward than usually, meant it as a limit to change.
While the States varied in their views, the cities emphatically
repudiated the Interim. In South Germany it was forced
upon them, and their pastors became exiles: in the North,
Magdeburg was a centre for fugitive theologians, by many
of whom Melanchthon was fiercely attacked: Philippists,
Gnesio-Lutherans, and Lutherans fought a many-sided duel.
The Pope condemned the Interim; and it was indeed an
exercise of regal power commoner in Catholic Spain, Protestant
Scandinavia, or in England than in Germany. But in spite of
the general unrest, diplomacy helped the Interim to survive.
Even Pope Paul III, in view of a possible reunion, hinted at
concessions as to clerical marriage and communion in both
kinds. His successor, Julius III, worked more harmoniously
with Charles, and when (May 1551) the Council of Trent met
again, several Protestants humoured the Emperor by attendance: Brandenburg, with an eye upon secularised sees, Würtemberg, and Saxony sent representatives, while the Protestant

---

[1] This is much the view of J. B. Mozley in his *Essays Historical and
Theological* (London, 1884), Vol. I ("Essay on Luther"), p. 325. Prof.
Mackinnon in his *Luther and the Reformation* (London, 1925) refers to
Mozley, misprinted as Mozeley, as having "a rather superficial knowledge
of Luther's Thought" (I. p. 208). But superficial was the last thing
Mozley could be on any subject he wrote about.

theologians prepared statements of faith. But the demands that these theologians should be admitted to vote, that the Council should begin *de novo*, and that the bishops should be for the time free from Papal control, were very sweeping. It did seem, however, as if concord were possible: it was a possibility which a subsequent crystallisation of doctrine and the fixed bareness for the most part of later Protestant worship leads us to underestimate. As we pass, however, in a city like Nuremberg from Catholic to Lutheran churches, the possibility mounts higher in our view, for the present buildings show us that the conditions of worship must at that time have been more fluid. But whatever the possibility was, the conduct of Maurice made it vanish.

The Elector Maurice was certainly the ablest and probably the most self-centred of princes when ability was rare **Maurice of** and selfishness common. Maurice was blamed, **Saxony.** not without some reason, for having betrayed his relative John Frederick. But his treaty with France and his deceit towards the Emperor Charles needs more excuse: it brought a great loss to Germany, for his calculated slowness of movement lost to France the three Bishoprics of Metz, Toul and Verdun. But his plans were not as a rule against the national interests: he had no old-fashioned loyalty to Charles and hated the presence of Spanish troops in Germany. With Ferdinand he had more in common, and their ideas of possible concessions in religious matters were much akin, although reached from differing starting-places. Charles's mingling of coercion in Germany and toleration at Trent might lay him open to suspicion; but the treachery of Maurice needs a better **Treaty of** excuse than this. A sudden treaty with France, a **Passau,** hasty march southwards, laid his benefactor Charles **Aug. 2, 1552.** at his mercy, and made him a fugitive (1552). The Council at Trent broke up, and the Treaty of Passau marked the failure of the Interim.

By this Treaty Philip of Hesse was set at liberty: until the next Diet an amnesty in religious matters was to obtain: this Diet was to settle how, whether by Council, by Recess, or a Colloquy, reform was to be secured. Maurice was bent

upon gaining for Lutheranism a legal recognition irrespective
of Trent or any other Council: Charles had to own his own
weakness, but would neither give up the unity of the Empire
nor the hope of ultimate unity. Had he acted otherwise,
the Catholic cause in Germany would have been nearly lost.
His war against France, however, went badly, and in 1553
he left Germany for good: the same year Maurice lost his
life in a fight against his former ally, the lawless Margrave
Albert of Brandenburg (July 9, 1553). He was only thirty-
two but already the foremost Prince of his land. Ferdinand
was left to make a lasting peace, for Charles could not bring
himself, faithful Catholic as he was, to legalise the work of
Luther.

In February 1555 the Diet which was to settle the religious
future of Germany met at Augsburg: the bulk of the Protestant
princes had previously agreed to maintain the Augsburg
Confession, irrespective of discussion or compromise: Ferdin-
and would have preferred a compromise that would retain
the appearance, at least, of religious unity: the Lutherans
demanded for the future full liberty to secularise Church
property, and a protection for their adherents in Catholic
States which was not to be given to Catholics under
Protestant princes. It was obvious how closely   Religious
the cause of Protestantism was bound up with   Peace of
the cause of princes against control from Emperor   Augsburg,
or Church. In the end all Lutheran princes received   1555.
Sept. 25,
security: the principle *cujus regio*; *ejus religio* was thus set up
inside the Empire: dissenting subjects were free to emigrate:
in Lutheran lands episcopal authority was surrendered: the
reservatum ecclesiasticum provided that in future bishops
becoming Lutherans should forfeit their territory. This
provision, although in the Recess, was really disregarded
by the Lutherans, and its feeble enforcement was one
cause of the Thirty Years' War. A royal declaration apart
from the Recess promised liberty of faith to Lutherans in
the states ruled by bishops: in the free Imperial cities
(where Protestants mainly prevailed) minorities were to be
respected.

This was a peace due to weariness of strife, and not to any recognition of principles. If the adherents of the Augsburg
Defects of Confession (it was not specified which of the many
the Peace. recensions was the model) gained recognition, it was due to the personal influence of Luther and the policy of princes: but their creed gained no sanction more than that of the Reformed which gained no recognition at all. Thus the Peace recognised the differences of Protestants as well as their power. On the other hand, it conceded to the princes the rightfulness of secularisation in the past while denying it in the future. It did not thus set up as a principle the inviolability of Church lands. It gave up the chance of regaining the secularised sees, which Pope Paul IV, for instance, would have gladly regained: on the other hand, it preserved the sees that still remained. It was a peace which neither side welcomed but both accepted until their weariness was past and their wish to infringe it freshly roused. It recognised the breakdown of unity, Imperial and Ecclesiastical, and so far it recognised facts sad but undeniable. If it was a Peace that contained the seeds of war (as every peace really does), it had at least been made by Germany alone. Neither Pope (the Papal legate Morone had refused to be a party to it) nor Council nor intrusive State such as France had aught to say in it. Moreover, it was the work of princes and politicians who saw the need for peace: the theologians were left outside, and continued to wrangle with increasing violence.

The first stages of the religious revolution past, the organisation of the Lutherans followed; the Saxon Visitation and
Organisation its results have been noticed already.[1] For some
of the years there was much disorder: in the great cities
Lutherans. the civic authorities called to the churches pastors as they chose: this did not seem strange, as in medieval days the connection between them and the churches had been close. The pastors thus chosen simply entered upon their work, and the disregard of episcopal authority often left city and pastors free: the existing state of religion had, as Papal legates repeatedly reported, been bad enough before

[1] For documents of the organisation, Kidd, pp. 121 *seq.*, pp. 185 *seq.*

and things did not improve quickly. It is true that the Confession of Augsburg had not rejected episcopacy; but both for doctrines and ceremonies there was laid down the condition that episcopal authority was not to contradict the Gospel. So the homage to episcopacy was only verbal: insistence on Lutheran doctrine and worship was implied, and much more scope was left to the individual conscience than to existing authority. The initiative and the lead fell to the secular power. When Luther had seen the state of religion in Saxony he urged upon the Elector that it was his princely responsibility and duty to settle matters: so his power lay behind all that was done and the appointment of superintendents to replace the bishops rested with him: he was the *summus* *episcopus* in his lands. To the Bohemian Utraquists Luther gave the advice to cast aside episcopal ordination and choose pastors for themselves.

Luther and Episcopal authority.

But there were local variations among German Lutherans which hindered their unity as a body. When their Grand Master, the Margrave Albert, had secularised the territory of the Teutonic Knights, Luther appealed

Prussia.

to the members of the Order to give up their monastic life and organisation, and so the way was clear for Albert to organise afresh, and he was the *summus episcopus* in his new Duchy. But here, in contrast to the case elsewhere in Germany, the bishops led the Reformation: in East Prussia the Bishop of Samland (who gave up his temporal power to the Duke) was strongly tinged with Lutheranism and commanded his diocese in that way (1524): in West Prussia also the Bishop of Pomerania was a Lutheran: he denounced the daily Mass as an abomination to God: he left monks and nuns free to marry: Festivals, except Christmas, Easter and Whitsuntide, were given up: bishops, he said, should be preaching bishops to expound the pure Word of God, not ordaining or anointing bishops: there were to be not seven, but only two Sacraments: Reservation and Processions of the Host were prohibited, and Confession was discouraged (1525). His brother of Samland, much in the same way, exhorted his clergy to read Luther's writings.

Speaking generally the Lutheran States varied in their systems. Würtemberg was not exactly like Saxony, which became the model and typical Lutheran State. But in Prussia the power of the Electors of Brandenburg, soon to be kings, was raised, and it was, from the first, connected with the Church system: hence it is not surprising to find Frederick I, the first King of Prussia, appointing two bishops, one for the Lutherans and one for the Reformed, much as the superintendents were appointed: they were to dignify his coronation (1701). The Consistory, too, which regulated Church matters, represented the King in his capacity of Supreme Bishop.[1]

The "Summus Episcopus." Later there followed negotiations about gaining for the Prussian bishops episcopal consecration from England in which John Sharpe, Archbishop of York (1691–1714), represented the English Church. Frederick William I (1713–40) had a large conception of his power and duty: Leibnitz was largely concerned, but it all ended in the Union Church under Frederick William III and Frederick William IV, which, as Lord Acton said, "added a new Church to the two original forms of Protestantism."[2]

Hesse, at first, seemed likely to have a more congregational system of its own. A synod met at Homburg (20 Oct. 1526)[3]: Hesse. not only pastors and jurists, but nobles and representatives of the towns attended: the scheme of Church government was the work of a French Franciscan, Francis Lambert. Scripture was to give the rule, and to each Christian community, therefore (it decreed), fell the right of choosing and removing pastors, and also the power of excommunication to be exercised by a weekly meeting of

[1] Ranke: *Memoirs of the House of Brandenburg and History of Prussia* (English trans. by Sir A. and Lady Duff Gordon: London, 1849), I. pp. 117–18 and pp. 463 *seq.*

[2] Lord Acton: *History of Freedom*, p. 345. He adds: "But strict Calvinism is nearly extinct in Germany and the old Lutheran Church has almost disappeared. It subsists not in any definite reality, but only in the aspirations of certain divines and jurists." See also my *Episcopate and the Reformation* (London, 1919), pp. 82–85.

[3] *Reformatio ecclesiarum Hessiae:* Kidd, *Documents*, pp. 222–30. Ranke, *Reformation* (English), pp. 468–9.

the pastor and his flock: for this purpose elders were chosen: there were also to be deacons elected by the members, to care for the poor: these were admitted to office by the laying on of hands: the pastor's. Over the confiscated revenues of the monasteries, however, Philip had more control. Large schemes for theological education were mooted, and, in particular, the University of Marburg, with a theological school as its backbone, was founded. But Luther (January 1527) persuaded Philip to change the nature of this democratic system, and the Saxon model was followed.

Brandenburg had its religious changes with a numerous princely house. Frederick the Elder († 1536) had ten sons: two of them, Casimir, whose wife was a Bavarian Branden- princess, and George the Pious, ruled jointly. burg. Casimir was Catholic and George was disposed to Lutheranism. Casimir held a Diet at Ansbach (1526), when it was decided to keep for the most part to the Mass in Latin, but it was ordered that the pure Word of God should be preached: Masses for the dead and fasts continued as before. There was thus much confusion, which was intensified by the former bishops carrying on their old jurisdiction and presenting to parishes as before. But Casimir died (1527) in battle against the Hungarians, and George, now sole ruler, introduced the whole Lutheran system, and changes in ceremonies were made: a Visitation, on the Saxon model, was held.

In this change the great city of Nuremberg had much influence. There the provosts had appointed Lutheran preachers: the Baptismal Service was translated into German, although the old ceremonial was Nuremberg. kept. The Chalice was administered to the laity. The Services of the old Hours and Masses for the dead were stopped. Against their diocesan, the Bishop of Bamberg, the city, rich in able and wealthy citizens, maintained its Luther-anism. Its beautiful old churches still keep much of their medieval state, and illustrate the more fluid condition of its past, and its civic independence controlling its religious life.

The year of the Peace (1555) marks the height of the success of Protestantism. Other causes were now working against it, and its own divisions were telling in the same direction. Electoral and Ducal Saxony, Holstein, Mecklenburg, Pome-

Progress of rania, Brandenburg (both electoral and Ansbach),
Lutheranism. Würtemberg, the Palatinate, nearly all Brunswick, Hesse, Anhalt, and nearly all the cities were either Lutheran or Reformed. Elsewhere in Catholic states, as Austria or Bavaria, many of the nobles and lower classes were also Protestant. But a reaction, not altogether due to force or persecution, was soon to begin, and to win back for Catholicism some whole states and many individual Protestants elsewhere. The main cause of this reaction was that the Church had risen to a truer sense of its mission and of the imperfections that had hindered its accomplishment.

In 1552, Maurice of Saxony (turned towards theology by devising his Interim, December 1548) wrote to the Cardinal of Lorraine, begging him to study the Confession of Augsburg. Help from outside against the Emperor would be useful, and religious sympathy might make it more likely. Nothing came of this, however, although the Cardinal had an eye on Germany, and was ready to utilise the differing Sacramental views of Lutherans and Huguenots.

Then afterwards the Cardinal cherished his vision of a French National Council and possibly of a Gallican revival to follow it. Anthony of Navarre had

Entangle-
ment of invited some German theologians to visit Paris.
religion with Representatives came from the Palatine and from
politics. Würtemberg, but the visit was disappointing and of slight importance, but when the Colloquy of Poissy was over, and the Cardinal had to look towards Trent, he thought again of German religion. Christopher of Würtemberg was known to the Duke of Guise, and he was asked to meet him and his brothers. They met at Saverne in Alsace, and, as asked to do, the Duke brought four Würtemberg theologians (two of whom, Bidermach and Andreas, had visited Paris) with him (15 Feb., 1562).[1] The Germans heard the Cardinal preach twice, he was eloquent, but also unexpectedly eirenic in tone and almost Protestant

[1] For an excellent account of the interview see Evennett's *Cardinal of*

in doctrine. On many points agreement was reached or supposed to be. On doctrine the Cardinal was vague, but in declaring his innocence of any persecution and his tolerant inclination he was diplomatically definite. His brother, the Duke, was just as definite as to his innocence, and he was not hampered by theology, which he left to the Cardinal. The two parties almost reached agreement on the Mass, which was hardly surprising, as the Cardinal seemed to give up any idea of a sacrifice in it. Brenz was delighted and he was a man experienced in such discussions. The short Conference broke up, but it was more significant than important.

It is well to note the different ways in which Contarini at Ratisbon and the Cardinal at Saverne approached theological discussion with a view to reunion. Compromise seemed easy to the Cardinal and he almost played with doctrines, while to Contarini a full statement of truth, embodying that which each believed, was the end to be reached. It was easier for the Cardinal to get what he wanted than for Contarini to reach what he sought. Political conditions might help the Cardinal, and he could take advantage of them. But Contarini moved in another sphere, and that which he sought seemed far away and hard to find, although it was what a Christian would wish, and the Church should strive for. International politics were severing nations and men, and with them religious issues were entangled. Beliefs had to be clung to by each theologian and each body of Christians: they were not to be lightly altered or used as counters in a diplomatic game. Men and churches must love the truth and peace. God alone can teach the truth and it is for those who do His will to hold the truth they have learnt in the fresh open air of charity and love.

Lorraine (pp. 429 seq.). It is based on a German account written by Christopher himself. There is a condensed French translation of the Duke's narrative in the *Bulletin de la Société du Protestantisme Français* for Aug.–Oct., 1855), pp. 184 seq., by A. Muntz. Christopher gives little of the theological discussion, but the story is a most interesting revelation of character.

VIII

THE COUNCIL OF TRENT 1545–1552

BIBLIOGRAPHICAL NOTE.—Many original sources for this Council have been published and much has been written about it.

1. Leclercq's French translation of Hefele's *Conciliengeschichte* (continued by Hergenrother) has now reached Trent; Vols. IX. 1 and IX. 2 (Paris, 1930 and 1931 respectively), *ed.* P. Richard, have been published, in which (pp. 1–18) the works on this Council are described.

2. The *Acta Concilii* of Theiner, who gave us the *Diarium* of Massarelli, Secretary of the Council, and the *Journal* of Paleotto.

3. The Görresgesellschaft has given us, not only studies, but also, in its *Concilium Tridentinum*, much material akin to that edited by Theiner.

4. Friedensburg edited the *Nutiaturberichte aus Deutschland*, important for the history outside the Council chamber.

5. Eder's works (e.g. *Die Reformvorschläge Kaiser Ferdinands I auf dem Konzil von Trient*) repay study.

6. Susta's *Das Romische Curie und das Concil von Trient* (Vols. I–IV, Vienna, 1904–14) gives us the important letters of Cardinal Carlo Borromeo. Incidentally I should like to add that the preface (19 pages) by Theodor Sickel gives the best account I know of the opening up of the Vatican Library by Pope Leo XIII.

7. *Jacobi Lainez Disputationes Tridentinae* (2 Vols., Innsbrück, 1886) are of great value.

8. Pastor's *History of the Popes* is a constant companion to the Council.

9. H. O. Evennett, *The Cardinal of Lorraine and the Council of Trent* (Cambridge, 1930), besides being a good and well-documented sketch of an enigmatic and leading character, has a very useful Bibliography covering the Council.

10. There are many editions of the Canons and Decrees in Latin: an English translation of them by I. Wordsworth (London, 1848) can be depended upon.

11. The place of the Council in the general "Counter-Reformation" is well given in Ch. XVIII, Vol. II, of the *Cambridge Modern History* (short but sufficient bibliography), by my old pupil, R. V. Laurence, an inspiring scholar, now unhappily lost to us by his recent death.

12. v. Ranke, that master of historical criticism, criticised the two histories of the Council by Paolo Sarpi, the Venetian scholar and publicist, and by Pallavicini in his *History of the Popes* (English translation by Sarah Austin, Vol. III, Appendix; Vol. III, section II, pp. 304 *seq.*). So much turns on these works that the criticism should be studied.

13. Sarpi's *History of the Council* may be used in the French translation by Courayer (2 vols., London, 1736, and 3 vols., 1751. The Italian translation was also published in London, 1619).

14. Sir Nicholas Brent's English translation of Sarpi has a magnificent English style (London, 1620, 1629). Some editions have Jewel's *Letter to Scipio* bound with them, which is, to my mind, his best controversial work. (Scipio was a Venetian who thought the English Church should have been represented at Trent.)

There had long been a demand for a General Council; the Lateran Council (1512–17) had just done enough to show that another Council might do more; not only the ever scantier supporters of the conciliar theories, but the more earnest theologians looked for it. Luther's appeal to a General Council and the hope that it might possibly conciliate some Protestants were to some people further reasons for calling it. As early as November 1526, the summoning of such an assembly had been discussed, and Charles—both as Emperor and as a private Catholic—was warmly in favour of the step. When urged to call it without the Pope he refused (1532), and he hesitated long before he would approve the proposed alternative of a German Council.

Demand for a Council.

Finally, however, the disordered state of Germany and the delay of the Pope to call a Council converted the Emperor to this plan, and at Worms (1545) Charles definitely promised a German Council if a General Council should not take up the work of reform. But there were nice calculations whether the state of politics would help or hinder the task of the Council, whether it might not alter the Church too violently: whether the Lutherans could attend or be listened to, or whether their presence might not affect the Council too greatly. Many men held that the practical evils which existed called for reforms only to be gained from a Council. Others wished for a clear and general statement of doctrine. Neither of these demands, however, was due solely to the Reformation. The earlier existence of the former we have shown already: the Thomist theologians, especially those of Spain, expressed the latter. The Middle Ages, in which popular theology had taken strange forms, in which speculation had been unrestrained and general, had left issues enough to be settled, even if the Reformation had not presented others more fundamental and important. The truth of theology and the existence of a Church imply that a close connection exists between theological truth and uprightness of life: only those who denied this connection could urge omission of either from the programme of the Council. Whether doctrine or discipline should take precedence was, however, a different question: truth affects the life: the surroundings of a man affect his soul; men equally honest could take different views of the relative urgency of the two tasks. Reform practical evils, and your very earnestness will make others listen to your beliefs and doctrines, said some: state your doctrines, and then the delicate lines between pious opinions and heresies can be drawn more firmly, said others. There will always be two classes of men— one thinking that a modification of opinions or a mild expression of truth will attract support, another thinking that the slightest possible sacrifice of truth in expression is a loss outweighing the gain of many adherents. It is often difficult to reconcile the claims of conscience and charity. It was certain, too, that some doctrines of great importance would need restatement or large modification to attract their critics or opponents. The widening of the creeds or their reinterpretation, the surrender of ancient and accustomed rites were very different things from a strengthening of discipline or the dealing with altered conditions of life. It was easy to expect too much from a Council: it was easy to fear it would do too much. It was hard to see how a Council could do all that all men hoped for from it: it was hard to see how anything could be done without it. Larger and more varied issues had never been placed before the Church: the minority of dissentients from the outset had never been so large. The civil powers were likely to control the Church more than ever, and had stronger reasons for doing so: the politics of the Curia would certainly influence the Council, as they had long retarded its' summoning. Controversy, schism, religious change, had all existed too long and been too violent to leave the minds and the reason of men sufficiently calm and spiritual for the issues that lay before the Council.

The Conclave that elected (1534) Paul III (Farnese) had made him promise to call a Council. His liberal education inclined this Pope to reform, although a Pope had Paul III and some reason to fear a Council, and it might give too the Council. much power to the Emperor, too many concessions to the Germans. But the *Consilium delectorum cardinalium et aliorum praelatorum de emendanda ecclesia* (1537)[1] seemed to pledge to reforms. Contarini and Morone—both legates with experience of Germany, and members of the Commission— Sadoleti, and many Germans pressed for a Council. Then the Colloquy of Ratisbon (1541) had shown both how far the Catholics and Protestants would go towards meeting each other, and how little could come of such a meeting. The Recess of the Diet of Ratisbon looked forward to a General Council or a National Assembly, and the Emperor was pledged to one of them.

If the need of a General Council was admitted on many sides: if it was even demanded formally by many who would not give it a heartfelt welcome, the atmosphere was

[1] See p. 128 *supra*.

favourable. But coming down from the air to the ground, there were many obstacles. The lack of "a European Concert" was one: the choice of the place for its Difficulties in the way of a Council. meeting was another. The Germans, especially the Lutherans, disliked a city in Italy: the Pope disliked one in Germany: the French liked neither. Mantua was first suggested, as early as February 1537, but the demands of its Duke for a large military guard proved excessive and too expensive. Then Venice was asked to grant one of its cities, and Vicenza was chosen (September 1537). Legates went there to pave the way (May 1538), but politics caused a prorogation to Easter, 1539. The prolonged discussions about a suitable seat, even one as awkward as Cambrai being suggested, illustrate the effects of discontented and discordant nations upon the Church's unity: to restore it must prove a most difficult task, but finally Morone renewed his former activities in Germany: the Pope had settled on Trent, but difficulties arose from the Lutherans and Francis I: Charles was moved by the unlikelihood of Lutheran attendance and his interest in the Council slackened while the Pope's grew keener.

The Pope decided to call the Council for 1542, and at Trent—an imperial city with an Italian population, and, as subject to its bishop, neither Papal nor German: a most suitable place. The Papal legates, Morone and Pole, the Emperor's ambassadors, Granvelle and Mendoza, all appeared, but few bishops could come, as the French war was on foot, and the assembly was adjourned (June 1543). The Peace of Crépy (September 1544) made its assembling possible; Charles had again promised at Speier a free Council (1544). Cardinal Farnese had been sent as legate to draw the Emperor closer to the Pope, and when this had been done the Pope felt he could safely and hopefully call the Council.

In May 1545, the members began to arrive at Trent: on December 13 the Legates held the formal opening. These were Cardinal Del Monte (to be, later on, Julius III), a Curialist by policy; Cardinal Cervini (Santa Croce, the later Marcellus II), a reformer and a theologian anxious to combat heresy, a natural diplomatist who often smoothed storms raised by Del Monte's hasty anger; Cardinal Pole, a cultivated scholar of supposed liberal sympathies, forced by his almost royal birth and martyr-like exile into a position beyond his powers. The bishops present were mainly Italian, five Spanish and two French:

The Council. Session I, 13 Dec., 1545.

under thirty in all; Charles and his brother Ferdinand alone sent ambassadors. Proxies from absent bishops, though suggested by Spain and Germany, were refused: only the Generals of Orders were given individual votes: three Benedictine abbots had a joint vote, theologians none at all: ambassadors could speak, but had no vote: the voting was to be in one body, and not as at Constance by nations—a point upon which the Legates consulted the Pope: the Italian majority, which the Pope could always increase by despatching Italian bishops from Rome, was thus decisive: there were three Congregations or committees who held preliminary discussions upon questions prepared for them by the theologians and canonists: the general Congregation or whole body then discussed the matter on report, and their decision embodied in a decree was afterwards announced at a public Congregation. Some discussion took place on the proposal to add the words, "representing the universal Church," to the Council's title, "the Holy Synod of Trent duly gathered together in the Holy Spirit under the presidency of the three apostolic Legates." These words, which would have recalled the claims of the fifteenth-century Councils to supremacy, were, however, rejected. It was thus clear from the outset that the Papal direction would be no mere form, and equally clear that it would have to reckon with the episcopal Order. The bishops were able, however, to prevail in some small matters against the monks. "We are here," said one bishop, "to destroy or to change rather than augment their privileges": and the Legates yielded gracefully. An attempt from Germany and Spain to get a few bishops present recognised as proxies for some absent was vetoed by the Council and rejected by the Pope.

The task of the Council had been defined as the propagation of the faith, the elevation of the Christian religion, the removal of heresies, the restoration of peace, the reformation of the clergy and Christian people, the overthrow of the enemies of the Christian name. The Legates had been instructed by the Pope that doctrine should be first discussed; this would be convenient as defining the Council's position, but not convenient if the Protestants were to be conciliated. The difficulty arose from the politicians, who in their wish for unity handed over to theologians the task of compassing it by definition and compromise. The Emperor, on the other hand, had instructed his party, led by Cardinal Madruzzo, Bishop of Trent, to insist upon reform being considered first. By a convenient compromise it was resolved to satisfy both Pope and Emperor and discuss doctrine and reform at the same time in different Congregations. But the preparation and manipulation of business, with their possession of the initiative, gave the Legates a great advantage: they were always in close communication with the Curia, and able to postpone difficulties until the Papal wish was known. The Spanish bishops, urged to attend by Charles, and led by Cardinal Pacheco, Bishop of Jaën, were keen equally for reform and for doctrinal orthodoxy. "It was necessary," said Fonseca, Archbishop of Toledo, "to strike at the same time against the erroneous doctrines of our adversaries and the bad morals of our friends." These preliminaries and their settlement filled three sessions.

Session II, 7 Jan. ; III., 4 Feb., 1546.

In the next four sessions (8 April, 1546–3 March, 1547), the Rule of Faith, with its sources—Scripture, its canon, interpretation and relation to tradition, original sin, justification, sacraments in general, confirmation, and holy baptism—were discussed. The Nicene Creed, as used in the Holy Roman Church, was stated to have its sources in Scripture, and in tradition (*a*) of Christ, and (*b*) of His apostles: the interpretations of Scripture held by Mother Church were to be maintained against private interpretations: it was significant of the variety of opinions that a few bishops urged Scripture alone as the rule of faith: it was a triumph for the opponents of the "poets" of an earlier decade when the Vulgate was affirmed as the authoritative

Session IV, 8 April; V., 17 June, 1547.

version.[1] Vernacular versions were, indeed, as the Spanish members urged, liable to abuse, not only in the notes sometimes appended, but in translation of terms: "Church" and "Congregation," "priest" and "elder" are, indeed, not synonyms, and the sixteenth century felt the difficulty which our own age knows too well. But the Church should itself have undertaken this work instead of putting it off and leaving it to chance: even the recommendation that the Vulgate should be printed with correctness remained ineffective until 1590, and was even then not efficiently carried out.[2]

A thornier subject was reached with "Original Sin," closely related as it was to the doctrine of "Justification." Men of different types of mind will always differ in the stress they lay upon spiritual processes and outward forms respectively, and in the relation of cause and effect they assume between them.

Original Sin, Session V, 17 June, 1546.

Luther had been by no means the first to discover either the importance of faith or its connection with justification. Both were to be found in Catholic and medieval teaching, but were there united with the facts of life and with the consistent practice of the Church's rule. Mystics and men of contemplative life laid comparative stress upon faith and the spiritual process, and it was this stream of doctrine that had revived the Augustinian Friars under Staupitz: the medieval view had not the defects which Luther charged it with.[3] But he underrated in comparison with faith the virtue of obedience and the obligation of a righteous life: his favourite phrase was "justification by faith alone": from this cause came the admitted laxity of German morals in his later years; and for this reason he was attacked not only by Catholics, but by some Protestants.

Luther and his Doctrine of Justification.

---

[1] *Der Kanon der Biblischen Bücher und das Konzil von Trient:* Dr. Albert Maechle: Freiburg im B., 1929.

[2] See Chap. X. p. 272.

[3] See A. Ritschl: *Critical History of the Christian Doctrine of Justification and Reconciliation:* English translation by J. S. Black, Edinburgh, 1872, of *Die Christliche Lehre von der Rechtfertigung und Versohnung* (3 vols., edns. 1–4, 1870–1895). The English translation is from the third edn., which is the same as the fourth: the history of the doctrine

That a man's justification depended upon his own conviction of its truth was a dangerous and unscriptural doctrine and deserved condemnation. On the other hand, the Nominalists towards the close of the Middle Ages had laid increasing stress upon the merit of obedience to the Church, merits in themselves, and of righteous conduct; thus they and their followers had somewhat lost sight of the spiritual side of religion. The multiplied cults of saints, the prevalence of special devotions and of indulgences made this view of religion commoner. It was hard to keep the balance between these differing schools, for their difference arose from differing types of mind, and resulted in opposite errors. Aquinas pointed out the risk of disproportion where so many elements were bound up together, and his followers attempted with success a balanced view; it does not follow, therefore, that everyone who laid comparative stress upon the spiritual side should be called a Lutheran or even a semi-Lutheran. The so-called "mediating" theologians should not, therefore, be held to have reached their view through a compromise with Lutheranism, but to have based it upon some of the many elements in the medieval views, to which the Lutherans themselves were also indebted. Luther departed from the view of justification as the beginning of a process (sanctification) actually wrought out in man's heart and life by the grace of God, and resulting in a righteous life; it became with him more of a forensic act by which Christ's righteousness is imputed to man, and man by his faith (which later tended more and more to be regarded as an intellectual assent and not as a complete surrender of the whole life and being), and by it alone was saved. There was thus involved in Lutheran doctrine the consideration of man's free will and of God's sovereign power. The Protestant bodies could not afford as could the

is in the first vol. Hanns Rückert: *Die Rechtfertigungslehre auf dem Tridentinischen Konzil* (Bonn, 1925, in *Arbeiten zur Kirchengeschichte*). Also Jos. Hefner: *Die Entstehungsgeschichte des Trientes Rechtfertigungslehre* (Paderborn, 1909): a Bibliography for the doctrine of Justification itself in A. E. Garvie: *The Ritschlian Theology* (second edn., Edinburgh, 1902: for German works p. 400, for English, p. 398).

Catholics to leave these doctrines to the decision of practical life, and it was thus that the Calvinistic controversies were of supreme importance to the Protestant bodies while such issues were more calmly weighed by the Catholic Church. But it was inevitable that the Council as soon as it entered upon the doctrine of Original Sin should place itself in sharp opposition to the teaching of Luther. For this reason the Emperor strongly urged that its consideration should be put off. In the end, however, this difficult point was discussed simultaneously with the equally difficult point of episcopal residence. The decree on Justification itself—which, as Harnack rightly says, is an admirably balanced statement of the doctrine, and if issued much earlier might have altered the course of religious history —belongs to Session VI.

Session VI, 13 Jan., 1547.

Pelagianism, when it began, forced fresh issues upon the Church. St. Augustine, never disregarding righteous life, held faith a gift of grace, which, infused into man, enabled him to produce works acceptable to God. St. Thomas Aquinas, developing this theory, regarded justification as an infusion of grace by which a man is made worthy of eternal life, and able to do works which have a merit in themselves. Justification is God's gracious view of sinful men, but a view taken by God must work itself out in deed and life. Luther, in whose favour was the technical use of the word to justify (to reckon, not to make just), laid too much stress upon the imputation of righteousness: and the faith which, in his view, saved (for he confused justification and salvation) was the scholastic *fides informis*, not the *fides formata per caritatem*. His attacks upon the artificial theories of varying merits were just, but his misconception of the meaning of Justification and his disregard of its bearing upon life confused the issues. Calvin was, as usual, more consistent and logical: he laid down firmly that without faith no one can possibly do works sufficient for or worthy of salvation. The Tridentine decree pointed out the defects of Luther's teaching, and asserted in a moderate but somewhat modified form that of St. Thomas Aquinas.

The Doctrine of Justification.

The decree upon Original Sin asserted that Adam's fall had degraded him, and through him all his descendants, in body and soul: that through the Saviour and His grace given in Holy Baptism the effects of this fall are taken away:
The Tridentine View. that the concupiscence left in man is not of itself sinful: these conclusions as to sin were not to be applied to the case of the Holy Virgin.

Justification was defined as the translation from the state in which man is born as a son of the first Adam to the state of grace and adoption as the son of God through the second Adam, Jesus Christ our Saviour: as not only the remission of sins, but sanctification and renewal of the inner man by the voluntary reception of grace and the gifts of God. Faith was said to be the beginning of man's salvation, the basis and root of all justification, without which it is impossible to please God. Luther, on the other hand, regarded faith as the essence of all justification and as salvation in itself. The theory of imputed righteousness, as begun by Luther and completed by Calvin, was condemned, as were also the classification of all works done before justification as sinful, and the assertion of the utter loss of man's free will.

In these definitions it was not only the exclusively Protestant view that had to be reckoned with: there were also the views of the German Augustinians, who really reasserted under new conditions of thought the views of St. Augustine. Seripando,
The Augustinians. their general, accepted the distinction between "imputed" and "inherent" righteousness, the former of which could alone justify, and was needed to make the latter satisfactory in the eyes of God. This mediating view was rejected: although it had been accepted at Ratisbon (1541), and might have some of the advantages of a compromise, it had too much of the weakness of scholasticism. The Fathers felt themselves hampered by a wish not to seem hostile to the views of Contarini in the Ratisbon Book. Pole, who favoured it, withdrew from the Council on the plea of ill-health, but the importance of his presence or absence was less than it would have been for his colleagues.

Opposed to the Augustinians stood the Jesuit theologians,

Lainez and Salmeron. Their learning, diligence, and facility of speech made them prominent and influential, and it was their view of justification which in the end prevailed. They were not pure Thomists as were the Spaniards. The Jesuit The doctrines of St. Augustine as elaborated by Theologians. St. Thomas left, as they thought, too little room for human freedom and Church life. When the Tridentine Decree placed the beginning of justification in the prevenient grace freely given by God, it was on the Thomist side: when it went on to speak of the recipient of that grace disposing himself for justification by co-operating with grace, it was on the anti-Thomist and Jesuit side. It must not be forgotten that the Dominican theologians followed Aquinas, and that the Decree, while excluding the definitely Protestant view, sought to combine the Jesuit and Dominican views. It was impossible to throw over St. Augustine and St. Thomas Aquinas, but the freedom of man and his power to possess merit apart from grace could not be asserted without some depart- Later Con-ure from these views. But the compromise resulted troversies. in a later controversy between the Jesuits and the Dominicans, which called for Papal interference.

In Louvain the tendency of theology became more and more Augustinian—that is to say, it laid more stress upon God's foreknowledge and man's lack of freedom, less stress upon the means of grace and the Church's economy. Michael Michael Bajus, Professor of Greek there, published Bajus, 1563 both before and after the last session of the Council and after. of Trent works which assailed Scholasticism, and were strongly Augustinian. His application of Original Sin to the case of the Blessed Virgin brought upon him an attack by her special advocates, the Franciscans. In spite of the endeavours of Cardinal Granvelle to suppress the controversy, it went on. Hessels and Cornelius Jansen (a theologian of repute, after-wards Bishop of Ypres and well known through the name of the Jansenists) had accompanied Bajus to Trent as representa-tives of the University, and were drawn into the controversy. Pius V (1567), and afterwards Gregory XIII (1579), con-demned certain of the tenets of Bajus—all of them grouped around Augustinianism, the chief one being the incapability of human nature by itself for well-doing: debate smouldered on until 1585. The Jesuits of Louvain, in their eagerness to oppose Bajus, rushed into Pelagianism; as a result they were reproved by the University of Louvain (1587) and enjoined by Sixtus V (1588) to keep silence. But the Spanish Jesuit, Molina, published (1588) a work on the points under discussion, condemning St. Augustine's doctrine, which, it was said, led logically to Protestantism. Molina, on the contrary, asserted that man may of himself co-operate in his own conversion and in the merit of good works. The Dominicans, especially Alvarez, attacked this position, maintaining that grace actuates the human will, and is irresistible. The controversy grew so warm that Clement VIII appointed (1599) the Congregation "De Auxiliis" to decide it. This Congregation lingered on under the next Pope, Paul V, until its suspension (1607), awaiting a decision, never arrived at, by the Pope himself. But although a quieter tone was enjoined upon the disputants, the dispute went on, its ground being slightly altered by the well-known Jesuit, Suarez († 1617), on one side, and Jansen († 1638) in his *Augustinus*, published two years after his death, on the other. The former distinguished between "congruous grace," which is always efficacious, and "incongruous grace," which is not efficacious, because man does not answer to its guidance. Jansen, on the other side, combined the Augustinian doctrines (as approved by the Sorbonne) of irresistible grace and predestination with a Catholic conception of the Church and its work. His works were forbidden by Urban VIII in the Bull "*In eminenti*" (1642) and condemned by Innocent X (1653). But the controversy which Spanish influence could control in the Netherlands became in France of political as well as doctrinal moment, and lies beyond the limits of our period. The side issue between the Dominicans and Franciscans, however, upon the Immaculate Conception of the Blessed Virgin remained open even until the days of Benedict XIV (1740–58), who declared the Franciscan doctrine favoured by the Church, although not yet affirmed as an article

Molina, 1588.

Jansen, † 1638.

of faith. The Immaculate Conception of the Blessed Virgin was decreed by Pius IX to be an article of Faith in his Bull "*Ineffabilis Deus*" (8 Dec., 1854). The Dominican supporters of Aquinas had, even upon this as yet minor point, less weight than the Jesuit theologians whose influence increased immensely at Trent.

These controversies, which are not to be regarded as arising out of Protestantism, and which ran a mainly independent course, sprang directly out of the earlier and chiefly Spanish theological revival. They have been mentioned here as illustrating the formation of parties in the Council itself, and as being to a large extent a continuation of the theological issues that began before or arose in it. Their continuance was made possible by the guarded and comprehensive nature of the Tridentine Decrees, which were meant to accommodate as far as possible opinions widely opposed, so long as these opinions were not Protestant. The smaller and endless discussions upon human merit were similarly the results of medieval teaching, and could be carried on within the limits of the Tridentine Decrees. *(side note: Relation of these controversies to medieval teaching and the Tridentine Decrees.)*

Discussions upon doctrine were less likely to go against Papal wishes than those upon reform. No scheme of reform affecting the Roman Court was to be discussed without Papal leave: in all matters of discipline Papal authority was reserved. The Legates, thus instructed, had soon come under the Pope's disapproval for allowing such discussions to go too far, and he had thoughts of removing discipline from the Council's consideration. But the Legates persuaded him to let the discussions proceed. *(side note: Reform and discipline : episcopal residence.)*

In these earlier sessions many questions of clerical manners and discipline had naturally been raised. In Session V, Don Francesco de Toledo, the imperial ambassador, had urged the priority of reform over doctrine, and at a later date (27 June, 1562) the Bavarian ambassador said the correction of doctrine was useless without a previous correction of clerical life, of which he drew a shameful picture. *(side note: Discipline and reform.)*

But quite apart from morals, the Church had not made ful
use of its powers for raising mankind. The provision made
for instance, by the Middle Ages for teaching both parochially
and in a graduated series from school to university was ample
and far beyond what is often thought; but, partly by the
apathy of parish priests and bishops, partly by the interference
of monasteries and priories with the ordinary ecclesiastical
machinery, this provision was badly made, and this too at a
time when the need for both spiritual and secular teaching was
deeply felt. In the fifth Session it was decreed that provision,
either by funds freshly raised (and an appeal was made here
to the generosity of princes) or by prebends devoted to the
purpose, should be made in all considerable churches for
catechisings or lectures upon theology and scriptures. In
some cases this meant a new effort, in others merely an enforcement of a duty already enjoined since the Lateran Council
of 1215. Cathedrals, churches, and monasteries were all
covered by this decree, and the Ordinaries were to enforce it.
Here, indeed, as in later decrees, the freedom of chapters and
monasteries exempt from episcopal control was lessened.
Some powers of this kind, it is true, were given to bishops
rather as "delegates of the Apostolic See" than in their own
rights, so that the same process which increased episcopal power
increased the Papal power still more. But even an exempt
monastery could not object to a visitation by a Papal delegate
where it certainly would have objected to one by a bishop.

The obligation laid upon bishops to preach was asserted
so strongly as to recall the old condemnation of Bishop
Pecock. All higher clerks and parish priests and
all monks engaged in parish work (this recalled
much medieval discussion) were also to attend carefully and
under episcopal supervision to this needed work. But regulars
were only to preach when licensed by their superiors and
their bishops. The "questers," the begging deputations of
the day, sometimes armed with Indulgences, were strictly
forbidden to preach, but it was left doubtful whether this
regulation applied to the begging friars or not. Heretical
preachers the bishop was to proceed against, but this, it was

Preaching.

significantly added, he was to do "by apostolic authority and as representing the Apostolic See." The discussion upon some of these points was more delicate than the bare decrees imply. Some bishops pointed in the style of Grosseteste at monastic exemptions as the cause of many evils. The monks and friars retorted that for many generations they had discharged the duty of preaching when it was neglected by the seculars. The Legates feared that a speedy decision against the regulars might lead to a schism, and so referred the matter to the Pope. But the Congregation was not inclined to exalt unduly the power of bishops, and in the end the interests of Pope and regulars combined, as in 1512, to keep up the exemptions with little change. It added incidentally to the discord between bishops and regulars that the former were mainly canonists and the latter mainly theologians. The preparation of the decrees on dogma lay mostly with the theologians, who formed the majority of the Congregation on Faith; the preparation of decrees on reformation similarly lay mostly with the bishops.

In the long interval (June–January) between Sessions V and VI the Smalkaldic war broke out in Germany. The Pope, who was bound by promise to give the Emperor help, openly praised the war as a religious crusade. *Imperial politics.* The Emperor, however, gave as reasons for it motives of State. But obviously it was now more than ever needful for Charles that a sincere reformation in manners and discipline (an object always near his heart) should be at least begun. It was as obviously undesirable for him that a consideration of those very points—justification by faith, and so forth—upon which Protestants differed from Catholics, should be undertaken. Some of the German Protestants were disposed to be neutral in the war: others it was possible Charles might win over. But either avoidance of reform or a strong insistence upon dogmatic differences made both of these results difficult to reach. Hence the turn of affairs greatly displeased the Emperor, his relations with the Pope became strained and their political interests in Italy differed. The interval of six months showed the difficulty of gaining what Charles needed

as a step towards unity in Germany, and also the wide cleavage
of opinion between Protestants and Catholicism in Germany
and elsewhere. It was not surprising, then, that Charles urged
the consideration of reformation before doctrine: it was
natural that the Papalists should feel or affect to feel fear
lest a war which caused marchings to the south of them and
battles to the north should make a sojourn at Trent unsafe.
Charles's promise to protect the Council needed not only an
intention, but also the power to make it effective or reassuring.

While the Emperor was dreading a dissolution of the
Council and the Pope wishing for delay, which, indeed, he
Difficulties recommended to the Legates (now two in number,
of debate. for Pole, on excuse of sickness ("catarrh of the
arm") had been relieved from attendance in October 1546),
the thorny subject of episcopal and clerical residence came
up. From the Spanish bishops especially came complaints
of the avarice and ambition of the Church. Some others,
however, saw and felt that if bishops were held forced *jure
divino* to reside in their sees, many at the Curia would find
themselves in hardships; the centralisation of power at Rome
would be checked, partly by the difficulty of rewarding supporters, partly by the lessened number of bishops there. In
their reports to Rome the Legates observed that the Fathers
were now treating *de summa rerum*, and that there were some
present who wished to humiliate the Apostolic See (October
1546). Meanwhile the Italian bishops were quickly leaving
Trent, and the Legates urged that attendance of bishops who
combined learning with respect for the Apostolic See should
be commanded. The task of the presiding Legates was in
truth a hard one. It was equally hard to keep their turbulent
flock together and to keep order when they were assembled:
a scene of actual violence between the bishops of La Cava
and Chiron (17 July, 1546); angry altercations, in which Del
Monte (who had a quick temper), Cardinal Madruzzo (Bishop
of Trent), and Pacheco (Cardinal-Bishop of Jaën) were the
leaders—these things intensified the hardness of the task.
Martelli (Bishop of Fiesole) and Nacchiante (Bishop of
Chioggia) were specially outspoken, and therefore came

specially under the anger of the Legates. But there were difficulties which lay in the subjects themselves. On some of the questions discussed, as was pointed out, the Fathers, tradition, and even later doctors gave no guidance. The Cardinal of Jaën proposed to ask the opinions of the Universities of Louvain and Paris upon justification; and this suggestion caused fresh division. It was found difficult to combine in one compact statement the search for truth with the enumeration of errors. The Bishop of Sinigaglia therefore proposed to separate the doctrines approved and those anathematised into two lists; and this plan was adopted. After Session VI, therefore, the former appeared as decrees and the latter as canons; and this rough separation between **Decrees** opinions plainly orthodox and those plainly **and Canons.** heterodox made discussion a little easier. The Cardinal of Jaën, supported by some twenty Spanish bishops, handed in their views in writing, owing, it was said, to the skilful manipulation of opinions (or even, it was alleged, of votes) by the Legates. Just before Session V the Bishop of Astorga, supported by the same cardinal, had tried to regain for the members of the Council the power of bringing forward subjects for discussion—a privilege which, after much heart-burning, was given them jointly with the presidents in 1563. It is no wonder that the Legates used piteous language to describe their plight. The ordinary machinery of debate and order—not very much elaborated by the Middle Ages—was greatly strained. Undercurrents of hostility, normally suppressed (such as that between the Spanish Dominicans—strictly orthodox and keen against heresy—and the Cordeliers, a section of Franciscans whom they accused of leanings towards Lutheranism), rose to the surface when the minds of men were much excited. But even as it was, the skill of Santa Croce (Cervini) was able to do wonders. Both by his control of the Council and his diplomacy in private dealings with its members he saved the situation for the Papacy, and his calmness of temper and knowledge of men stood him in good stead. But their correspondence with Rome was a great and constant anxiety to the Legates. Even in the third session the simultaneous discussion of doctrine and reformation had aroused the Pope's anger. His demands for a reopening of the whole discussion were evaded with difficulty, and henceforth subjects affecting the Roman Curia were allowed to be discussed only by Papal leave. The Legates—not for the last time—promised a protracted discussion of doctrine. The diplomacy of the old Conciliar days was thus repeating itself under other circumstances. But there were not wanting bishops who of their own will exalted the Papal power much as Cajetan had done at the Lateran Council. Now, as later, it was asserted that while the episcopal order was of divine institution, the obligation to reside, the jurisdiction, and therefore the real power of episcopacy, lay *jure divino* in the control of the Pope alone.

The decree on reformation issued at the sixth session left many details of residence to be dealt with later on. It was in five chapters. The first renewed all former canons against non-residence, and laid a penalty of one quarter's income upon any metropolitan or bishop absent without leave for more than six months at one time. The second imposed residence upon all clerks below the rank of a bishop; dispensations and indulgences as to residence were only to be given for fit cause (a Bull of Pius IV afterwards dealt with these matters more largely, and required the consent of the ordinary in all cases of non-residence). The third chapter ordered the punishment by the ordinaries of all excesses both of seculars and of regulars out of closure. The fourth entrusted the visitation of cathedral chapters and all churches to the bishops. The Council thus, and in other ways already noted, did away with many long-existing immunities and privileges of the chapters.[1] The historic interest lost was more than counterbalanced by the greater efficiency gained and the control exercised over a field where had been found the veriest homes of all abuses. The fifth chapter prohibited any pontifical rites or ordinations

Session VI, 13 Jan., 1547. Residence.

[1] On Chapters in Germany see Philipp Schneider: *Die Bischöflichen Domkapital, ihre Entwicklung und rechtliche Stellung im Organismus der Kirche:* Mayence, 1892.

being performed by one bishop in the diocese of another—
a regulation which checked the activity of titular bishops, and
so far restrained the Curia in the too free use of them. On the
whole, although the decrees thus issued were a promise of
better things, the defenders of abuse might well hold their
worst fears to have been unfounded. The subject of episcopal
residence was, of course, left still unsettled; but as some
compensation for the delay, the Pope, by a Bull, ordered all
cardinals holding more than one see to choose the one they
preferred, and to keep that alone. This was only partly
effective, and by means of pensions charged upon the sees
given up the loss was tempered to the offending and offended
Curialists.

The subject of divine grace led naturally to that of the
sacraments, another subject upon which it was not easy to
conciliate the Protestants of any school. But a Session VII,
wide divergency of views soon appeared in the 3 March,
Council. It was not likely that the extreme 1547. Sacraments and
Zwinglian views would find any support; but residence
without that and within the limits of orthodox of bishops.
definition there was still room for difference. The old (and
still ever new) discussion of the *opus operatum* and the *opus
operantis* came up, embodying the objective and subjective
views of sacraments, looking to the human and the divine
sides respectively. The intention of the minister was also
brought up for decision, and on some of these points debate
was warm. In the end, the Council, following wise advice,
proceeded by way of exclusion rather than definition, anathematising error rather than affirming truth. The thirteen canons
condemned variations from the ordinary belief; asserted the
number of sacraments to be seven, all instituted by Christ
Himself, varying in dignity, necessary to salvation and not
superfluous, not ordained merely to nourish faith, but capable
of giving grace to all, *ex opere operato*, and not through faith
alone. Baptism, Holy Orders, and Confirmation were said
to confer an indelible character. They were not all to be
administered by all Christians. In ministers celebrating sacraments an intention of doing what the Church demanded was

required. Mortal sin in the minister did not invalidate the sacraments. The rites of the Church could not be omitted or changed. The fourteen canons on baptism affirmed the necessity for the use of real water and of our Saviour's words. Heretical baptism, if in the name of the Three Persons, was held valid. Baptism was necessary to salvation. Some of the opinions condemned were those of the extreme Lutherans or of the Anabaptists, and the third canon is notable as affirming the Roman Church to be the mother and mistress of all churches. Canon XIV anathematised anyone asserting that adults refusing to ratify their sponsors' promise for them in childhood, should not be compelled into a Christian life by any other punishment than exclusion from the sacraments. This canon touched upon the medieval dispute between the Church and the State, which was expected to carry out the Church's sentence of excommunication, and therefore demanded in some cases a veto upon it. Some religious bodies have, in these later days, drifted into purely voluntary associations, with the very slightest powers of coercion, while the ecclesiastical courts, where existing, have been greatly restricted in power. But in the Middle Ages the Church exercised without hesitation its right of restraint and control. This canon ought not, therefore, to be held, as it has been by some, an *apologia* for persecution, even in an age when toleration was unknown. But it may be taken as a statement under changing conditions of the view held by the medieval Church. The limits of coercion were, however, really varying with varying conditions of life as widely as varies the theocratic tyranny of Geneva from a modern "Free Church" congregation. The three canons on confirmation affirmed that it was not an otiose ceremony—a species of catechism imposed at adolescence; that the attribution of virtue to the chrism was not derogatory to the Holy Ghost; that confirmation could be administered by a bishop only. The outcome of these debates, which had been wisely restricted, was thus not so complete as might have been, and the most difficult subject, the Holy Eucharist, was left over.

The decree on reformation, with its fifteen chapters, had

in its preamble the words, "always saving in all things the authority of the Apostolic See"—a condition essential for the Pope, who resented both the matter and the manner of the debates, and had already determined upon a removal of the Council to Bologna. Nevertheless, the restriction was irritating to some of the members, who openly expressed their view. It had been decided to begin the reform by removing impediments to residence, but in many ways existing canons were either re-enacted or slightly strengthened. It was thus evident that the evils arose, less from defects inherent in the Church itself, than from the slackness of those who should have enforced existing rules. The discussion recalls John XXII and his long constitution *Execrabilis* (1317);[1] it also reminds us of Colet's famous sermon before Convocation (1512) with its plea for the better keeping of existing laws instead of the enacting of new.

Bishops were to be of legitimate birth, grave in manners, and skilled in letters. No one was to hold more than one see, and those who then did so were to resign all but one within six months or a year. Inferior benefices were to be held without pluralities by worthy and fit persons, not only resident, but actually doing their proper work. Neglect of residence by a newly made curate (*curé*) was to entail deprivation upon himself and loss of patronage to the patron. Where pluralities were allowed by dispensation, vicars were to be appointed. The Ordinaries were to scrutinise rigorously unions of benefices and to visit those united. Those appointed to greater churches were not to postpone ordination beyond six months (the strict enforcement of this would have removed one of the greatest evils in the Church). Sundry safeguards as to choice of fit persons and against abuses in appointments were laid down. Civil cases involving seculars or religious living out of closure, even those of exempt monasteries, were put under

---

[1] See F. W. Maitland's *Canon Law in the Church of England* (London, 1898): Essay V, Execrabilis. Also I. Haller, *Papsttum und Kirchenreform* (Berlin, 1903), I. pp. 98 *seq.*, and Philip Ewald Müller: *Das Konzil von Vienne*, 1311–1312 (Münster in Westfalen, 1934).

the cognisance of bishops. The ordinaries were to see that hospitals were faithfully administered.

Notes upon the Eucharist had already been circulated among the members, and heretical opinions concerning it were already under consideration when the translation to Bologna was actually made. The Bull giving the Legates faculties for the transference was dated February 27, but the real decision had been reached much earlier. The Bishop of Capaccio died (March 6) of a fever, and there was much general indisposition about. This illness was seized upon as an excuse— a mere excuse said the imperialists. But panics were easy to create. The removal fitted in almost too well with the Papal policy, but the lessening number of those present was as marked as the difficulty of managing those present, and the removal was so far not unreasonable. Forty-two members voted for removal and fourteen against; but Bologna was to be only a temporary choice until another healthier place could be found.

Translation of the Council. Session VIII, 11 March, 1547.

To the Emperor, however, now on the eve of his victory at Mühlberg (April 1547), and profiting by the divisions of the Protestants, this translation to Bologna, lessening his influence and making the conciliation of even moderate Protestants hopeless, was a severe blow. He urged the Pope, even with threats of a national schism, to reassemble the Council at Trent, where the Spanish bishops, carefully inactive from fear of any doubtful action, still remained. At Bologna only Italian bishops were present, and these, by the Pope's desire, postponed all business until September. For a time the death of Francis I of France (31 March, 1547) made that kingdom less inclined to help the Pope against the Emperor, but the new king, Henry II, soon became more Papal, and a few French bishops appeared at Bologna. The Protestants of Germany consented at Augsburg (September 1547) to appear at a Council if it were free and not presided over by Legates, if they themselves were admitted under safe-conduct and with a right to speak, and if the decrees already made were open for reconsideration. Charles was ready to guarantee their safety and freedom of speech, but the Pope proved difficult, and the murder of his son Pier Luigi, made him more hostile to Charles. In January 1548, the Emperor's representatives, Vargas, Fiscal-General of Castile (whose letters throw much light upon the Council), and Martin Velasquez, with the support of the Diet at Augsburg behind them, protested against the Council at Bologna as void. Now that the Council had disappointed his hopes, Charles thought himself free to settle religious differences without the Pope, and the Interim (see p. 157) was his substitute for a Conciliar settlement when the Pope was loath to sanction the seeming minimum of concession, communion in both kinds and the marriage of priests. But the lack of adequate French support and the growing power of the Emperor combined *Suspension of the Council,* to force the Pope's hand; he consented to recognise through his Legates in Germany the provisions of the Interim, and after trying various expedients *17 Sept., 1549.* to bridge over the divisions of the Council, he formally suspended the sessions at Bologna. Once more the Pope had sacrificed the interests of the Church to his political needs. There was talk of a Commission of Reform at Rome, of decrees to be published there; but nothing came of it all. The death of Paul III, worn out by trouble and distress (10 November, 1549), was followed by the election of Cardinal del Monte, who took the name of Julius III. The *Julius III,* late Pope by his nepotism and inactivity had *7 Feb., 1550.* disappointed the wish for a true reformation. But there were difficulties from outside before the election and even after it. The Emperor wished for a speedy election while Henry II, for mere selfish reasons, wanted delay: the two great powers interfered in the Conclave excessively and unblushingly. Charles was bent upon the return of the Council to Trent. In Italy he was at war with the Farnesi family about their possession of Parma, which the Pope had promised to secure to them, and he also claimed Piacenza as an Imperial, instead of a Papal, fief, which Julius held it to be: Charles asked that the two cities should be given him by Papal investiture. Hence there were stumbling-blocks before the concord of

Pope and Emperor. That Charles should have a firm footing in Italy was not to the Pope's liking. Against the Germans the Farnesi looked to France and Henry II was only too ready to put a finger into Italian politics so as to counter Charles's plans. To help the Farnesi, Henry II even threatened a French National Council and a withdrawal of obedience. Italian politics moved towards war before the Pope's death. The cardinals who had a wish for that would have liked to see as pontiff the liberally disposed Cardinal Pole. He was also acceptable to the Emperor, and even with the influence of France against him only fell short of election by two votes. The Curialists would have chosen Cardinal Cervini, but to him the Emperor objected for having brought about the removal to Bologna. To Del Monte he had less objection, and thus the election was assured. The Conclave had agreed before the election that the new Pope was to reassemble the Council.

Pope Julius was more selfish and far less able than Cervini; his reputation for a love of pomp and pleasure added to a strain of weakness made him little likely to endanger his power and comfort by opposition to Charles. He knew, however, from his experience at Trent that reform was not only desirable,

The Council recalled, 14 Nov., 1550. but inevitable. Accordingly a Bull soon summoned the Council to meet once more at Trent. The Emperor promised that the Papal power should not be interfered with. The Pope, in return, consented to let the Lutherans attend, and was even willing not to insist upon the previous decrees, which Charles, with an eye on the Lutherans, disliked. There was some ground for the criticism that Julius was sacrificing everything to the preservation of his own power.

Sessions IX (21 April, 1547) and X (2 June, 1547) had been merely for prorogations; the first session now was **Sessions IX, X, and XI.** therefore XI (1 May, 1551). The presiding legate was Cardinal Crescenzi: many would have liked Cervini but his health was too bad. Pighino, Archbishop of Siponto, who knew Germany well, having lately been ambassador there, and was of the Imperialist party, who had been one of the Papal theologians at the first assembling of the Council, and Lippomani, Bishop of Verona, acted under him as Nuncios. Pighino also had been an ambassador to Germany: Lippomani was a Venetian, learned, pious and a patron of the Jesuits. Crescenzi's higher position was marked by his title of Presiding Legate *de Latere*. This expedient was meant to avoid disputes among the Legates themselves, while the choice of prelates who were not cardinals was likely to lessen friction between the presidents and the episcopal order. Cardinal Crescenzi had previously, in a Congregation of cardinals, advocated the reassembling of the Council, with the provision of such subjects and discussions as would leave no time for any attack on the Papal power or the Curia. It would be easy to secure the attendance of Italians, and to play off the Great Powers against each other. This was the policy of the presiding cardinal, and it was, on the whole, carried out. The Bull of Resumption (this was the term used to avoid its being held a new Council) claimed for the Pope the right of summoning and directing Councils, and after those present (only thirteen in number, excluding the presidents) had approved the resumption, the next session (XII) was fixed for 1 September, 1551.

Although the growing friendship between Pope and Emperor had alone made possible this second meeting of the Council, it was but a shifty foundation. Charles still wished for some changes in worship which might attract the Lutherans at least, and there seemed some chance of such a result. Melanchthon in particular showed a wish for a reunion and a readiness to explain points of difference which brought him much disrepute among his fellow Lutherans. But the Curia still wished the Council to mark definitely the errors of Protestantism. The outlooks of Germany and Rome were thus very different; and the latter was, by now, the more reasonable, for divisions of doctrine emphasised by differing political interests had really gone too far for reunion. The Emperor had prepared along with the Interim a scheme of reform in discipline which was of great interest, and served beyond Germany as a model in the Netherlands. Among other things, its provision for synods being held frequently would have quickened local life. But this scheme was wrecked by Papal opposition based not only upon difference of opinions, but upon the general principle that the State should not take the leadership in Church questions. The Pope, on the other hand, although he appointed (1550) two commissions, one to consider appointments to benefices, and another the reform of the conclaves for electing Popes, was bent more upon doctrinal than practical matters. It was inevitable that, as the course of the Council showed the impossibility of conciliating the Protestants and the real cleavage of beliefs between them and the Catholics, Charles and the Pope should draw apart. But, as usual, political interests forced the decision. France, under Henry II, had refused to recognise the Council, and was even threatening to withdraw the annates from the Pope. In Session XII the French ambassador Amyot, Abbot of Bello-

Session XII, zane, read a protest from Henry, addressing the
1 Sept., 1551. Council as "an assembly" (*conventus*), asserting it
French to be no true Council, but one called for merely
protest. private reasons, withholding for the present his
obedience from it in the interests of Gallican liberties, and hinting at strong measures of defence. And at the outset the choice of Legates—all either supposed Imperialists or known to the Emperor—showed a desire to conciliate the Empire rather than France. But in the war, Charles was not so successful against the French as against the Protestants, and his power in Italy, while more threatening to the Pope than that of Henry, proved not so efficient for protection. The little war (ostensibly for the control of Parma), in which Pope and Emperor were allies (1551), went against them. The Farnesi, striving to become a dynasty there, maintained themselves against them by the help of France. The Pope was therefore led to incline away from the Emperor to the most Christian king, and at length (April 1552) made a truce with Henry. After this his need of Charles's help was less. When, in 1562, the Council met for the third time after ten years' suspension, French influence was stronger in it than it had been before.

In preparation for the decree upon the Eucharist, some heretical propositions which it was easy to condemn, and which had been examined at Bologna, were con- Session XIII, sidered. The theologians were charged to go by the 11 Oct., 1551. testimony of Scripture, tradition, the canons, and The patristic authority. But some Italians, less affected Eucharist. by the humanist movement than the Germans (for in Italy humanism and religion had drifted apart), objected to this. Theology—which to them meant Scholasticism—was, they said, a matter of thought and discussion more than one of weighing authority, and they saw in the limitations proposed restraints upon ingenuity and development of system. It seems strange that objections against authority in the professed interest of the intellect should come from advocates of a system often held destructive of originality. But we are apt to forget how much dialectic preserved valuable thoughts and helped reason as opposed to caprice.

There was one pressing matter, however, which threatened to become a cause of division—the administration of the chalice to the laity. The withholding of this was a medieval custom, arising from the fear of irreverence, and supported by the doctrine that Christ was fully present in either species (as declared by the Fourth Lateran Council in 1215). But the Emperor, who was asking a safe-conduct for the Protestants and trying to secure their attendance, wished this special question to be deferred until they were present. The difficulties in the general subject of the Eucharist caused differences between the Dominican and Franciscan doctors; the Jesuits, along with the Spanish bishops, strongly opposed anything like concession to heretics; and this special question itself was a difficult one. It was possible to assert that the Church should not depart from the assumed actual methods of our Saviour's institution (although this was not urged at the Council). It was equally possible to assert that this was a matter within the direction of the Church. The weight of primitive example was on one side: the possible results of a change in present practice on the other; for it seemed to many a dangerous thing to allow that the Church should admit change on any such important matter, even if the Council of Basel had allowed it for a reasonable cause. It was no longer a question of a dispensation for one solitary prince or one body like the Hussites. The demand for change was widely spread, and to yield to it seemed to weaken ecclesiastical authority. The proposal of the Emperor to adjourn the question was therefore readily adopted.

The errors condemned in the eleven canons were: the Zwinglian view, that Christ is only present in the Eucharist as in a sign or figure; the denial of the true, real, and substantial presence of the Body and Blood, the soul and divinity of Christ; the remaining of the substance of bread and wine after consecration, or the denial of Transubstantiation; the denial of the presence of the whole Christ under each species; the limitation of the Presence to the actual use of the Eucharist, exclusive of its continuance afterwards as in Reservation; the limitation of the result of the Eucharist to the remission of sins; the denial of worship (*latria*) to the sacrament, or of processions with the Host, or of its exhibition for adoration; the negation of reservation; the assertion of a merely spiritual eating; the neglect of yearly communion, at least at Easter; asserting that the priest celebrating should not communicate himself; that faith is a sufficient preparation for reception; that sacramental confession where possible is not necessary in case of mortal sin.

Canons upon the Holy Eucharist.

The doctrine positively laid down (although more as an afterthought to the condemnation of errors, since the central doctrines were for the present left aside) in the eight decrees was: the true, real, and substantial presence of the Saviour in the Holy Eucharist, His sacramental presence not being inconsistent with His heavenly session; the institution of the Eucharist for a veneration of His memory and to show forth His death; for the spiritual food of souls; for an antidote to free us from daily faults and preserve us from mortal sins; that, like other sacraments, the Eucharist was a symbol of a sacred thing and a visible form of an invisible grace, but unlike them had a

Decrees upon Eucharistic doctrine.

sanctity independent of use as resulting from Christ's Presence; that the Body was present under the species of bread and the Blood under the species of wine, by the force of Christ's words, but that by concomitancy of the parts of Christ the Blood was also under the species of bread and the Body under the species of wine, and the Soul under both, and the Divinity was also there by its hypostatical union with the Body and Soul: hence the whole Christ is present under either species and in any part of it. Along with Transubstantiation, it was affirmed that the worship or *latria* due to God may be rendered to the Sacrament, and that the bearing of the Sacrament in procession is a pious and religious custom; that it may be reserved in the sacrarium, as by ancient usage, and also carried to the sick; that no one conscious of mortal sin should receive without previous sacramental confession; that there are three ways of reception—sacramentally only in the case of sinners, spiritually only in the case of those who eat by faith, both sacramentally and spiritually in the case of those who approach with proper preparation. The preamble to these eight chapters of the Decree assigned the plucking up of the tares of heresy concerning the Eucharist as one chief reason for holding the Council. By a strange coincidence, the ambassador from Protestant Brandenburg arrived about the time this Decree was issued. At the end of the Decree it was stated that not only the consideration of communion in one or in both kinds and the communion of infants, but also that of the sacrifice of the Mass, was postponed in order to hear the Protestant view. There was some difference of opinion on minor points. Some thought that to deny the need of Easter communion, an ecclesiastical but not a divine obligation, was schismatical rather than heretical; but it was agreed that as the Church had authority to impose the obligation, its denial was heresy. Some did not think the denial of confession as necessary before communion was absolutely heretical, although very erroneous. And there was some discussion as to what exactly constituted consecration—whether our Saviour had used some form of consecration other than the words of institution—a point which touched upon minor differences between East and West.

But detailed as the discussions were, the central conceptions of the Mass still remained for statement.

It had been decided to begin by removing causes that hindered the residence of bishops and weakened their power; frequent evocations of causes to superior courts, and specially to Rome, unduly limited the power of bishops, while the large number of exemptions narrowed their field of activity. It was laid down as a general principle that on the part of superiors charity was often forgotten in the wish to be dominant, while on the part of inferiors voluntary obedience was overlaid by murmuring. But to apply these excellent statements was hard. Appeals either against interlocutory sentences or in earlier stages of trial, whether criminal or visitorial, were no longer to impede episcopal courts. Appeals in criminal cases were to be made from the bishops to the Metropolitan, or in his absence to the nearest bishop or their vicars, never to inferior judges named by the Pope. The course of appeals was regulated; the process of degradation was simplified so that a bishop need not have other bishops present as required by the canons, the substitution of mitred abbots or suitable persons skilled in law being allowed. Bishops were allowed, as delegates of the Apostolic See, to take cognisance of the obtaining by false pretences graces to delay legal proceedings. Bishops were not allowed to be cited in person unless for a cause involving their deposition: a bishop punishable by deposition was to be tried in person before the Pope.

Reform. Episcopal jurisdiction.

Although these reforms were mainly made to safeguard the due power of bishops, and so indirectly to limit that of the Pope, their effect was likely to be considerable. For the pleadings of exemptions and delays interposed in ecclesiastical suits were great evils, and the Papal interference with lower and local courts had been so excessive as to paralyse ecclesiastical justice. For this the Pope himself was not, of course, to be blamed; it was rather his officials, largely dependent upon fees, who kept up the system. And the difficulty of enforcing degradation was so great as to encourage the worst class of offenders, an abuse against which the German bishops pleaded specially. Each of these chapters, therefore, was aimed at the removal of real evils. Gropper, a leading canonist and theologian, who had been employed at the Colloquy of Ratisbon (1541) and been a leader against Protestantism at Cologne, put in an earnest plea not only for the removal of abuses, but also for the revival of synodal jurisdiction as opposed to jurisdiction exercised by officials. Such a revival would have not only decentralised Church administration, but made it democratic. He was replied to by Castel from Bologna, who contended that the Church as it grew from infancy onwards had outgrown its system of government, and that therefore too much stress was not to be laid upon an appeal to primitive times when synodal government and other things now in comparative disuse had been common. But the bishops would not hear of any revival of synods in this enlarged sense. As it was, however, the new decrees were all serviceable if efficiently enforced. The difficulty with them lay, as with previous regulations, precisely in their enforcement, hindered as that often was by officials, sharp men of business, whose sphere was ecclesiastical, but who entirely lacked spirituality.

Without any delay the heretical opinions upon Penance and Extreme Unction were delivered to the Fathers, in twelve heads upon the former and four upon the latter. Session XIV, Many minor differences were found here, as upon 25 Nov., the Eucharist, but they resulted more from varieties 1551. of expression than mental distinctions. The order of speaking by classes and in groups, emphasised these differences by placing together those who usually thought alike. But in drafting the positive doctrines care had to be taken to avoid expressions likely to irritate or even condemn any of these various schools. Thus in discussing Penance it was necessary to avoid condemning the opinion of Duns Scotus, that the essence of the sacrament lay in the absolution alone, contrition and confession being merely conditions needed for its efficacy. But the lengthy debates upon doctrine due to these differences made any full scheme of reform impossible, especially since Cardinal Crescenzi had named July 1552 as the date by which the Council must end, and a full scheme of doctrine be prepared.

While these matters were under discussion, the ambassadors from Würtemberg had arrived; their conduct was cautious, Safe-conduct and, against the advice of the Imperial ambassador, for the they refrained from the usual call of courtesy Protestants. Politics and upon the presidents. A safe-conduct had already Protestants. been decreed for them at the thirteenth session in terms which seemed ample. But they asked for terms identical with those granted at Basel, as those in their view gave them a share in deliberations, and limited discussion by placing the Scriptures as decisive authorities. At the close of Session XV an enlargement of the former safe-conduct was therefore decreed, which gave more satisfaction. By that time Saxony and some imperial cities were represented; in particular, Strasbourg was represented by the historian Sleidan, who from the outset had no hopes of any good result from the negotiations. The day (24 January, 1552) before Session XV these ambassadors were received at a general Congregation; but although they were listened to with courtesy, their position was untenable and their demands extreme. They came to treat with the Council on almost equal terms, while in reality they differed among themselves (Würtemberg and Saxony presented slightly different professions of faith, both of which Strasbourg, a mediator as usual, signed), and had no historic position to warrant their claims. When, for instance, they demanded that the Pope should exercise no authority over the Council, and that the bishops for their better freedom should be released from their oath to him—they asked what was obviously impossible to grant. The same held good of their proposed reconsideration of former decrees. Moreover, the Emperor, although he had come to Innsbruck (November 1551), could exert little influence upon the Pope. Hence his request that all doctrinal discussions should be postponed until the arrival of the Protestant theologians, although favoured by the Council, was rejected by the Pope. But there was more delay; Crescenzi (Nov.) tried to hurry, and yet hinder, discussions by suggesting that the bishops should simply accept or reject what the theologians had formulated. But the Fathers rejected this suggestion, which would have given the Papal theologians, the Jesuits Lainez and Salmeron, the real control of the assembly. All these causes of difference, quickened by the pressure of politics, made the autumn and winter (1551–2) more barren of results than they otherwise would have been. In November, too, the Pope named six cardinals, none of whom were favoured by the Emperor. This disappointed the ecclesiastical electors, who, because of the outbreak of the war with France (March 1552), left the Council, fearing an attack on their territories. The Protestant princes had now leagued themselves with France, and the loss of the three bishoprics (Metz, Toul, and Verdun) by Germany was due to this treacherous act. When Maurice of Saxony marched against the Emperor and caused his flight from Innsbruck, the continuance of the Council was plainly impossible, and it adjourned for two years. Politics and the play of interests had once more stopped reform.

Meanwhile important doctrines had been discussed. The sacrament of Penance, it was decreed, was instituted to apply, by the ministry of the Apostles and their successors, the benefits of Christ's death to those who have fallen after baptism. It differs from baptism in that the minister is a judge and in involving labour on our part to attain a newness of life. For those who have sinned after baptism it is necessary to salvation. Its *form* consists in the words *"I absolve thee,"* to which the Church adds certain prayers. The acts of the penitent, contrition, confession, and satisfaction, are its *matter*. The thing signified and the effect is reconciliation with God. Contrition involves a sorrow for and a hatred of the sin, with amendment; and although sometimes it is so perfected by charity as to obtain reconciliation, this reconciliation is due not to contrition, but to the desire for the sacrament included in it. Attrition (imperfect contrition) is a gift of God which disposes the sinner to seek reconciliation through penance. Hence penance does not confer grace without any good motion on the penitent's part. Detailed confession of mortal sins is necessary by divine law, so that the priests may discriminate and observe equity in punishment; but confession of venial sins may be

Session XIV. Penance and Extreme Unction. 25 Nov., 1551.

omitted. While secret or auricular confession has always been in use, public confession is not divinely commanded. Confession should be made at least once a year, according to salutary custom at Lent. The absolution can only be given by priests, and even mortal sin does not deprive them of this power. But this absolution is of no weight if pronounced over one upon whom the priest has no jurisdiction, natural or delegated. Bishops and the Sovereign Pontiff can reserve certain cases for themselves. The guilt is never forgiven without the whole satisfaction being performed, and priests should enjoin suitable penance. We can make satisfaction to God not only by penance voluntary or enjoined, but also by patiently bearing affliction.

Extreme Unction belongs to the close of life; instituted by Christ (insinuated in St. Mark, but promulgated by St. James). In it the Holy Ghost forgives sins, and the sick sometimes obtains bodily health if it be desirable for his soul. It is to be ministered by priests. These nine chapters on Penance and three on Extreme Unction were guarded respectively by fifteen and four canons with anathemas, defining deviations from the positive doctrines. On Extreme Unction the identification of the sacrament with the expired gift of miracles of healing was condemned, and the identity of the Roman rite with that of St. James asserted. Otherwise there was nothing adding much to the decrees.

The fourteen chapters on reformation guarded holy orders against abuse by the ordination of any one interdicted by his **Reforma-** own bishop from such ordination, or against hasty **tion.** ordinations by titular bishops. By delegation from the Apostolic See episcopal authority over secular clerks was greatly strengthened, even against exemptions. The abuse of obtaining from Rome special judges, called conservators, who were often used to impede justice, was restrained. Clerks in holy orders or beneficed, not wearing becoming dress, were made liable to suspension, or on repeated offences, deprivation. Wilful murderers were never to be ordained, and accidental murderers only after episcopal investigation. No Ordinary was to exercise jurisdiction over clerks subject to another, and benefices in two dioceses were henceforth not to be united. For the future no right of patronage could be gained save by foundation or endowment. Presentation was to be made to, and institution by, the bishop of the place. Most of these regulations were in explanation or reinforcement of preceding decrees. They dealt with evils arising either from the excessive centralisation of jurisdiction or disorders: appeals on one hand and exemptions on the other had put the ordinary ecclesiastical legal system out of gear. In the sphere of Church law and judicature the same causes worked as in secular spheres—hasty applications of general principles, sometimes new and sometimes old; the difficulty of combining into a coherent body a number of decrees and decisions. Moreover, the Church was not now feeling its own unity so deeply as were the nations separately, and hence ecclesiastical affairs were in greater confusion than were secular. Mercenary men and bad men used various artifices for their own evil ends, and so intensified the evils.

For the next, the fifteenth, Session the Sacrifice of the Mass and Holy Orders were to be deliberated upon along with Reformation. But from what has been said already it will be seen that the end was drawing near, and discussion difficult. The Pope and the Legate differed absolutely from the Spanish bishops on the subjects of Papal and episcopal power. Germans and Italians were leaving the Council. The imperial ambassadors criticised the slowness and pettiness of the reformation undertaken. The presence of Protestant envoys and theologians could do little towards the almost impossible task of reunion. Session XV only met for a prorogation until St. Joseph's Day (March 19) and for enlargement of the safe-conduct for Protestants. The reason assigned for prorogation was the tardy coming of the Protestants, but there were real reasons in favour of the closing of a Council for which now no one but Charles really cared, which no nation would altogether obey, and from which even Charles could no longer hope for satisfaction of his desires—restored unity in Germany and a thoroughgoing reform.

Session XV, 25 Jan., 1552.

The Saxons withdrew (March 13), then the ambassadors from Würtemberg and Strasbourg, after many complaints (April): and the southward march of Maurice of Saxony hardly made up for their departure. Pope Julius bade the Legates to suspend the Council and send some bishops to Rome to help him there in the work of reform. But the presidents, Crescenzi being now fatally sick, preferred to leave the Fathers free, and the Council accordingly resolved "to be silent until better times," since "all places, and Germany above all, were ablaze with arms," and to suspend sessions for two years, after which, if the causes for suspension were removed, the Council should meet again without fresh Convocation. This seemed to them better than "wasting their time in idleness." And, indeed, with the Elector Maurice at Innsbruck and the Emperor in flight, a continuance in Trent was unsafe; even the citizens themselves were fleeing. The Council had been of late mainly German in composition. It was really for the needs of Germany even more than for general reformation that it had met. With the downfall of the Emperor's power and the success of the German Protestants, it became impossible to reach its ends. The political aims of the Pope had changed, and thus once again politics, and above all the politics of the Curia and of Germany, had spoilt the promise of a year before. Something the Council had done; but, like its predecessor of the Lateran, it had done only enough to show how much remained undone. It was not to meet again until nearly ten years had passed. And by then many things had changed.

Session XVI, 28 April, 1552. Suspension for two years.

IX

THE THIRD ASSEMBLY AT TRENT

WHEN the assigned interval of two years was over, everything was against a reassembling of the Council. In 1552, the war into which Spain and France had drifted in the backwaters of Europe reached the main stream, and it was not until April 1559 that the Treaty of Cateau Cambrésis brought back peace. The position of Charles V had been gradually changing; as he saw more and more the difficulty of reuniting Germany, and realised more and more the strength of the Spanish monarchy, his policy became increasingly Spanish, and he put the interests of his non-Spanish territories second to those of Spain. Meanwhile in the Empire Ferdinand, both by his own merits and the withdrawal of Charles, became a more important figure. He had been elected King of the Romans (January 1531), but at a later date Charles wished his son Philip chosen King of the Romans or even to become Emperor jointly with Ferdinand. In the end it was agreed (1551) by the family that Philip should succeed Ferdinand and the latter's son Maximilian, whose ability made him influential, should come next; but the electors would not agree to this, for they had more to fear from the Spanish prince than from his uncle. Ferdinand's policy in the Empire was very different from his strongly Catholic policy in his own dominions; in the Empire he was tolerant, and accepted the inevitable with a better grace than Charles had ever been able to assume; he was, moreover, strongly influenced by his son Maximilian, whose sympathies were distinctly Lutheran. Charles resigned the Netherlands to Philip (October 1555); he also gave him Spain (February 1556), and (27 August, 1556) he formally renounced the Empire to Ferdinand. The new Emperor's claims were at once admitted by the electors, and in spite of his non-recognition by the Pope he became at length fully Emperor (24 February, 1558).

Treaty of Cateau Cambrésis, April 1559.

Abdication of Charles, 1555–6.

Pope Julius III died 24 March, 1555, after a six-year pontificate of disappointed politics (for Ottavio Farnese kept Parma)
Marcellus II (Cervini), 9 April, 1555. and of family enrichment (his nephew Ascanio della Cornia founded a rich papal family in Umbria). His favouritism for Innocenzo del Monte, the seventeen-year-old son by adoption of the Pope's brother, was a glaring scandal. He made him Cardinal, in spite of disapproval from leading Cardinals. Pole spoke against it, and Carafa made a formal and strong protest. As the youthful Cardinal grew older, the scandals of his dissolute life were worse than before his creation. Julius' successor was Cardinal Cervini (Marcellus II), the former President at Trent, whose ability and moderation, together with his genuine goodness, led to great expectations, disappointed by his early death (April 30). His Papacy, beginning with bright hopes of an able, experienced and pious Pope, was a tragedy, compressed and confounding, like the longer reign of Adrian VI. But unlike that Pope, he knew Italy, Rome and the Curia. Had he been spared even for a few years, it might have altered the Church permanently and powerfully, for his goodness was bound up with strength and conviction. But it was not to be. A month later (23 May, 1555) Cardinal Carafa,
Paul IV (Carafa), 23 May, 1555. at the age of seventy-nine, and with a past of stormy energy, was elected as his successor. Of his piety and strictness (towards himself and others) there could be no doubt, but years had hardened his character, deepened his impulses, and strengthened his self-will. His early wishes for reformation had now become a hatred of anything suspicious in doctrine or novel in practice; his activity had thrown itself into the organisation of the Holy Office (or Inquisition) for Italy. In Italy the bishops resided at their sees less than was the case elsewhere, and the ordinary episcopal jurisdiction for correction of heresy or depravity was weak and fitful in itself, apart from the number of exemptions confronting it; the Dominicans also had lost much of their former zeal in this direction. Carafa had acquired during his nunciature in Spain a double portion of the Spanish spirit; he had seen the

Inquisition at work there and then himself acted as Inquisitor in Venice. When Paul III recalled him to Rome (1536), he urged the formation of an Inquisition under Papal control for all Italy, and (1542) his wish was gratified: six cardinals under his own presidency were appointed for the task. Episcopal jurisdiction in Italy was soon overshadowed, and they acted as a Court of Appeal not only for Italy, but for other countries also. They succeeded in suppressing the movement of thought, partly evangelical and partly revolutionary, which had appeared in Italy—the left wing as it were of that liberal movement in which Cardinal Pole and others had shared—standing in marked contrast to the paganism of the Italian Renaissance but having affinities with Socinianism. Carafa had as little tenderness for followers of this school of thought as for unworthy priests, and his stern measures of repression were successful in crushing out not only this form of thought, but other tendencies from which the Church might have gained. It was plain from the past that the Papacy of Paul IV would be marked by earnestness of purpose and an utter lack of desire to conciliate those opposed to him. "We promise and swear to try and bring about a reform of the Universal Church and the Papacy," were the words of his first bull. A congregation of three divisions was appointed for reform, and their programme submitted to the Universities. A Council for Reform would certainly have his sympathy, but never one intended to conciliate Protestants or negotiate with error.

The Pope's political tendencies pushed him in the same direction. He was a Neapolitan, of a family hostile to the Habsburgs. He had suffered official injuries from Charles V, and chafed at his indulgence of Protes- *Politics of Paul IV.* tants. He refused later to recognise Ferdinand as Emperor; and now when the Papal power was his, he felt bound to use it against its enemies, who in injuring it would, he felt, injure the Church itself. Hence it came about that a Pope intensely earnest in religion plunged himself into schemes which, except in his own judgment, had nothing to do with religion at all, and were founded on personal caprice. Under him Protestantism gained ground even in countries still in touch with the

Papacy. In Germany Ferdinand drew closer to the Protestants, and divison of religion became an accepted political fact. In the Netherlands the plans of Philip II for strengthening the Inquisition and increasing the number of bishoprics (1557), according to a policy begun by Charles, were approved by the Pope but led to revolt. In Poland the Pope's unsympathetic treatment of the Crown's request for some religious concessions and a needed revivification of the National Church missed a great opportunity. In England, under Mary, he insisted upon the full restoration of all ecclesiastical lands (a condition the landed gentry refused to grant), and tried to re-establish Peter's Pence, while his hostility to Spain or his dislike of Pole coloured all his relations with the Queen. When Elizabeth came to the throne, a gentler touch might, possibly, though not probably, have kept hold of the somewhat slender cords of connection. Precisely when the nations were realising their individuality and intensifying their differences, one of the most religious Popes since Adrian VI pressed his power beyond everything else, and in his intentness upon his own spiritual and personal ends would neither see nor hear the wishes of others. The worst and indeed most astounding use of his arbitrary power was his imprisonment, as already mentioned, of the upright and most respected Cardinal Morone on an unfounded charge of heresy: the practical refusal of an open trial was disgraceful. The Pope and he had formerly been fellow-workers, alike in views and aims. The imprisonment lasted until the Pope died, and then, to the general joy, Morone was released, and grew still more respected.

It was not likely that his plan of a Council to meet at Rome would win the approval of princes he disregarded or opposed. The Council. Only when Rome was threatened by a Spanish army under Alva, and his wars had turned out disastrously, would he make peace with Spain (September 1557). Then, too, when he no longer needed the help of his most unworthy nephews in war or diplomacy, he foreswore the nepotism that had blemished his reputation, and threw himself into the work of reformation with the impatient zeal of one soon to die. The year before his death left its mark on Rome in the removal of abuses and a change of tone; it was as important for the paths of reform he indicated as for the things he actually wrought. Towards the end of his Papacy (he died 18 August, 1559) Spain, France, Venice and German Catholics expressed their conviction that a Council was needed, not now to reconcile the Protestants (for that seemed hopeless), but to save the Church itself. The religious politics of France even alone made one desirable. The growth of Calvinism had been rapid, and the Crown alternated between a wish to overthrow and attempts to conciliate the Huguenots. There was talk of a National Council which might grant concessions, favoured by the French bishops, but disliked by the Papacy. This was the scheme of the Cardinal of Lorraine. Such a step would have fixed for ever the semi-independence of the Gallican Church, and the Papacy therefore had a special reason for watching with anxiety the internal affairs of France. In the conclave that followed the death of Paul IV each cardinal promised, if elected, to call a Council and to undertake reforms. Even these reforms which the Council had decreed in its earlier sessions had proved almost a dead letter, and the theologians of Louvain had pointed out in an address to Philip II the neglect shown for the Conciliar Decrees. A new assembly was needed to preserve the results of the old, not to speak of evils that must be overcome.

The Conclave, which lasted four months, was remarkable as the first in which Spain claimed the right of excluding or vetoing a candidate—a privilege already secured practically if not formally by the Empire and France. Philip II gave the cardinals to understand that no Carafa or partisan of the late Pope would be acceptable to him. His ally, Duke Cosimo of Florence, contrived to secure the election of the Milanese Gianangelo de Medici, unconnected with the noble house of that name, and brother of a cruel mercenary leader once in the Imperial service. The new Pope himself was a jurist of popular manners, skilful and experienced in administration—a cardinal created by Paul III, but disliked by Paul IV. Yet marked contrast as he was to his predecessor in manners and tone, terrible as was the righteous punishment

Pius IV, 26 Dec., 1559

he meted out to the Carafa family (two of whom, the Cardinal and another, were put to death for crimes, including murders), there was no change of atmosphere, and Rome itself remained "more like a well-ordered monastery," as it was said, than before Pope Paul's reforms. Nepotism as a system of Papal government, able to plead for itself the risk of depending upon strangers or possible rivals, had been ended by the swift revolution when Paul IV had learnt the treachery of his nephews and dismissed them the Court. If Pius IV afterwards leaned much upon Carlo Borromeo, the saintliness of the nephew, inclined to refuse all honours but those of toil, and the prudence of the uncle, averse from scandal, and too careful to cause it, stayed all complaints. Bishops were admonished to return from Rome to their sees; a higher ideal lessened the scandals of ecclesiastical life. The prudence and worldly wisdom which even more than any spiritual conviction led to this result also caused the Curia to adopt a more conciliatory policy towards the sovereigns of Europe. The Pope was personally inclined to call the Council demanded by the general voice. "We might," he said frankly, "amuse the world for years with difficulties;" but he had already spoken of concessions that must be made to secure unity. There was, moreover, no longer any fear of Imperial power overshadowing the Papacy in Italy. Inclination and politics therefore worked together. It was decided (March 1560) to call a Council. Those were invited who (as the Eastern Christians) had an independent history of their own, those who (as the English) had separated from the Papacy, and those who (as the Lutherans) had separated from the Church. Elizabeth advised the envoy who bore the invitation not to cross the Channel. From Switzerland only the Catholic Cantons cared to come. The invitation was for the most part either evaded or refused.

Invitation to the Council. Nov. 1560.

Difficulties in getting the Powers to agree upon practical points somewhat lessened the Pope's zeal for a Council. France and the Emperor not only objected to Trent as the seat of it, because of its nearness to Italy, but also demanded a freedom of discussion larger than the Curia cared to allow. It was now the

States that lagged behind the Church, and had not the near prospect of a French National Council given the Papacy a new reason for hastening the summons, delay might once more have put off the meeting. An even more important question was raised, but left unsettled: should the Council start (which France and the Empire wished) as a new assembly, or should it be held (as Philip II demanded) a continuation of the former Sessions? Papal diplomacy had its utmost to do in getting the Great Powers to agree to a Council with Trent as its seat, and could not deal at once with all these difficulties. The meeting was fixed for 6 April, 1561. The legates appointed (14 February, 1561) were Cardinal Gonzaga, Bishop of Mantua, and Cardinal du Puy, Archbishop of Bari; but the latter, in ill-health when chosen, died before reaching Trent. At a later date (March 10) there were added Hosius, well known for his learning and activity; Seripando, once General of the Augustinians, a well-known and moderate theologian; and Simonetta, a canonist of repute. The choice was suitable, and likely to be successful. Gonzaga was an Imperialist, able and upright in character; Hosius in particular, from his wide experience in Germany and Poland, deserved his post; and the whole combination, although differences arose later among the colleagues, was peculiarly strong. It was not materially strengthened by the later addition of the Pope's nephew, the young Cardinal d'Altemps, whose alleged qualifications were his German birth and his possession of the See of Constance.

On the appointed day (April 6) few, either bishops or ambassadors, were present. A proposal to consider an index of prohibited books was discussed, and when it proved hard to get any subject agreeable to all, it was suggested the Fathers should choose their own topic. Nothing came, however, of either discussion, and the Council was postponed until 18 January, 1562. At that date one hundred and six bishops, four abbots, and four generals were present; this new period of the Council, it may be noted, was marked throughout by both a larger attendance and a higher level of discussion. The Jesuit theologians, among whom Laynez, now General of the Society, stood first,

Session XVII, 18 Jan., 1562.

exercised great influence over the assembly, and he once took up the whole of the sitting by his speech. Salmeron, another distinguished Jesuit, was among the Papal theologians, but four of his colleagues were Dominicans. The state of flux through which theological thought had passed was now over. The prevalent uncertainty had been illustrated by the changing careers in varying directions of many humanists and doctors, such as Beatus Rhenanus, Pole, and Staphylus (who, forsaking Protestantism, became an adviser of the Emperor Ferdinand and his helper in the "Libel of Reformation"). A large body of popular opinions (such as those about Indulgence) had for many years floated around the kernel of authorised doctrine; from the ferment of reforming tendencies and new forms of critical studies, opinions of various kinds, some merely well-intentioned, some revolutionary, had emerged. But these opinions were of all shades of intensity, and were variously held in differing combinations, so that it was often hard to classify their holders as distinctly Catholic or distinctly Protestant in tendency. Gradually, however, views and opinions crystallised, and it became easier to classify a man as distinctly on one side or the other. But at the same time religious earnestness, a hatred of moral corruption and real liberality of thought were found as widely on one side as on the other (if indeed in the case of liberality it should not rather be said as rarely). Of this crystallisation of views and doctrinal sympathies the Jesuits were the best examples.

The Jesuits at the Council.

The Nominalism which was prevalent at the close of the Middle Ages had been essentially sceptical, and in its love of the intellectual had often lost sight of the spiritual; it had questioned dogmas and drawn distinctions; controversy, indulged in merely for the love of disputation and the exercise it afforded, brought with it a worse revenge than did even controversy just redeemed from sin by the touch of earnestness. These speculations had ended by taking probability and existing facts as guides. As their philosophy became more refined, the Nominalists came to accept the existing conditions of ecclesiastical life as better, owing to the mere fact of their existence, than anything likely to replace them, and drew

Medieval thought.

distinctions between truth in reason and in theology. The Thomistic (Aquinist) philosophy, on the other hand, had started from the unique pre-eminence of divine grace and the spiritual importance of a living faith. But since all truth was one, Revelation and Reason must, it was held, ultimately agree. In its insistence upon the importance of Church life it realised much of the abiding power of Christ, and found a stronger motive for energy than was afforded by mere negations. Here lay the strength of the Spanish Catholic Reformers, and it was by this valuable element rather than by the royal support or by the machinery of the Inquisition that they had brought about their reformation. But even the Thomistic philosophy had a weakness of its own; it had been unable to complete its task of systematising the many discordant elements of medieval thought: still less was it able to assimilate the newer thoughts and vigorous tendencies of the Renaissance. It combined with its essential Christian thought an extreme conservatism, and a too rigorous adherence to its original methods; hence it sometimes grew (especially in Spain) into a hatred of new and therefore possibly risky forms of thought. If it was pious, it also became narrow: if it was devout, it also lost touch of the life around it; it turned (as did the Spanish Church and Carafa) to repression instead of persuasion; it would take men by force and make them Christians.

But if this school of thought was narrow and had to answer for much that was harsh and cruel in ecclesiastical methods, it was effective within its limited sphere, while its moral earnestness raised it far above the accommodating Nominalism or the easy Humanism of the day. One of its characteristics has been noted already—its followers, with few exceptions, such as Cajetan, were not Curialists of the type so common in Italy. To the Italian Curialists, the whole of the organisation and machinery, centred in the Papacy, was to be supported because it existed. They had not the deeply religious view of Papal responsibility and Papal power that had sanctified the Hildebrandine movement: the divine origin of the Papacy might be spoken of to the multitude, but for themselves it remained merely a convenient system.

Nominalists and Curialists.

Hence it could be supported by means and methods that were at any rate worldly, if not worse. The contradictions of the Middle Ages—that immense variety of thought which we, from our distance, so often fail to see—had thus resulted in two leading types: the enthusiastic Aquinist, devout, and often learned, but sometimes narrow and bigoted; the Curialist, an ecclesiastic more than a theologian—diplomatic, a man of the world, skilful, but not always scrupulous. Nor should we forget how greatly the system of Canon Law and its study had tended to produce men of this stamp; so that the opposition in the Council between theologians and canonists was something more than a mere professional variance. And, on the other hand, in regard to the Papacy, the Spanish theologians fell back on the theory of Episcopacy, so that at this time the divine right of the Episcopal Order rather than the divine right of Councils was the theory that mostly opposed the Papal sovereignty.

But the progress of the Jesuits had resulted in a third type —freer in its treatment of doctrine, not keeping too closely to traditional methods, but conservative in its results. No shadow of unorthodoxy rested upon them, while their learning and ability was equal to that of the strongest among their rivals. But they were as little ready to conciliate Protestants as were the Spaniards themselves. Dislike of the new teachers, who brought disunion and heresy behind them, drove the Jesuits back into still deeper devotion to Catholic doctrine and Papal headship. This devotion was both religious and intelligent, while it seemed to give an apparent remedy for two distressing characteristics of the time, variety of doctrinal deviations and disregard of Church organisation. The Society had placed itself at the disposal of the Papacy, because this was their spirit to begin with, and the policy thus chosen was one that in the existing political circumstances could not fail to be successful. Their success intensified their devotion, and thus the interests of the Papacy became as dear to them as to the Italian Curialists. But to them the Papacy was the only possible centre of unity, and not a mere convenience of practical politics. Their support of its claims

Position of the Jesuits.

was due to a passionate conviction of their truth, and not to a calculation of existing facts. Gradually, moreover, the Society came to see that learning, intelligent and free, was their best ally for their purpose. This had hardly been part of their original programme, but soon it became one of their characteristics.

A Council was needed, in the view of many (especially of the princes), to conciliate or overawe the Protestants. Hence had arisen the dislike expressed to the early treatment of Justification, and hence the repeated demands from France and Germany for Communion in both kinds. But a Council was needed, in the eyes of Catholic theologians, for another end, to define and, as it were, codify Catholic doctrine. This had to be done partly because of the mass of scholastic material and of questions already discussed, partly because of the existence of Protestantism, with its outspoken criticism and negations; for Protestantism, whether of the Lutheran or Calvinistic model, was, in its negation of Catholic doctrines, and its assertion of individualism against the corporate authority of the Church, a clear and consistent system. The same could not be said of medieval Christianity until it had digested, selected, or rejected scholastic materials and speculations. Hence new definitions of doctrine were needed, but not, as it seemed, definitions which would compromise with Protestantism. It was natural, however, that the order followed in the discussions should be that of the Augsburg Confession, for it was on the points where discussion had most arisen that definition was most needed. In the previous discussions upon justification different views had existed in the Council, and the result had been a compromise between the views of Jesuit and Dominican theologians. In this third meeting of the Council the influence of the former was greater than it had been before, although the persistence of the Spaniards, led by Guarrero, Archbishop of Granada, and the course of events, prevented their triumph from being complete.

The theological necessity of the Council.

The conduct of business was now, on the whole, better than before; and, in particular, all matters of precedence and procedure were carefully arranged. The order of debate was that of the Seven Sacraments. The decrees on faith and doctrine were prepared by the deputation of theologians, and Order of business. then polished by a few of the Fathers. Those on Manners and Morals were discussed primarily by the Legates, and this, of course, meant their constant communication with the Pope. The assembly gradually grew into a knowledge of its own machinery, and things went more easily. But a wish for reform was in the air. It was necessary, said the Cardinal of Mantua, to improve doctrine by the eradication of heresy, and to correct the depraved manners of the faithful. In the discussion preceding Session XVII the Archbishop of Granada, supported by Vargas, the Spanish ambassador at Rome, strongly objected to the words "on the proposal of the Legates and Presidents" (*proponentibus legatis ac Presidentibus*), which seemed to deprive the Council of any initiative. He also urged that the Council should be declared a continuation of the former one—a matter which the Papal Bull seemed to leave in doubt. For the present, the latter difficulty was got over by the Legates explaining this to be the real meaning of the bull, although an explicit statement of the case was impossible if the presence of Protestants was to be hoped for.

Session XVIII was fixed for 26 February, 1562. The three subjects of the Index of prohibited books, the invitation to the Session XVIII, 26 Feb., 1562. Council of those who had written suspected books, and a safeguard for the Protestants had been prepared for the session. The third might have been settled without much trouble; but when the Archbishop of Granada pointed out that the original form of the safe-conduct would interfere with the jurisdiction of the Inquisition in Spain, the enactment was deferred, and entrusted to a General Congregation with powers equal to those of a Session. In the end the form used under Julius III was used again, but its provisions were enlarged so as to cover the case of countries which were not in communion with the Roman Church. The Emperor significantly urged that the Augsburg Confession should not at first be placed on the Index or condemned, lest it should hinder the Protestants from attending. The Archbishop of Granada also requested that the words

212

"representing the Universal Church" should be added as in previous Councils to the title of the Council, but the request, supported by the Spanish bishops, was disregarded.

On the question of the Index different opinions were expressed. The Archbishop of Granada thought the task difficult, and likely to lead to the neglect of more important subjects; the Archbishop of Braga would have The Index. preferred to leave it to the Universities to settle. But the general opinion went with the Patriarch of Jerusalem, who held the work to be needful and likely to be best performed by a deputation of those present. The way had indeed been shown by other bodies. At Paris the Parliament (1542) drew up regulations for the press. In February 1544, some books, among which Calvin's *Christianæ Religionis Institutio* was chief, were publicly burnt, and the Sorbonne issued an Index which was afterwards registered as a decree by the Parliament of Paris. This was not the only list of local force. Cardinal Carafa (Paul IV) when Grand Inquisitor of Italy had put forth (1543) a severe edict against printers and publishers of heretical books. Lists of forbidden books had been issued at various times since 1524 by other inquisitors or governments. The University of Louvain prepared (1546–50) for Charles V a list of its own which was truly "expurgatorial," since it essayed the difficult task of correcting isolated passages instead of merely indicating unsound books. So long before as 1479, Sixtus IV had empowered the University of Cologne (which in 1549 published an Index of its own) to punish all printers, publishers, and readers of heretical works; Alexander VI (1501) enlarged this jurisdiction for them; Leo X (1515) gave the same power for the Papal States to the Master of the Palace. The bull *In Cœna Domini* (1527) included in its excommunications all readers of heretical books, and (1559) Paul IV, using his past experience as Inquisitor, issued for the whole of the Church a comprehensive Index of Prohibited books. It named authors all of whose works were prohibited, and also single books condemned as heretical, impious, immoral, or merely unwholesome; publications from seventy-two presses were forbidden, and presses which had published any heretical book were interdicted. Among other writers Erasmus, censured often before, had a fortune which varied curiously in succeeding lists, the treatment of him and his works illustrating the spirit in which the task of selection was approached. Paul IV with special emphasis included all his works; the Council of Trent saw that a list so sweeping needed revision; under Pius IV (1564) only a few of his works were mentioned; Sixtus V (1590) once more condemned all his writings, but Clement VIII (1596) returned to the milder judgment of Pius IV.

It should be noticed that there was at the time little objection expressed to the principle of such a list; its formation might even be held a duty of spiritual authorities, who were to guide those under their care; or, on the other hand, of Universities which had the needed learning and habit of discrimination, or (better still) of both powers together. This was the principle on which the work proceeded. Some restraint of the press was recognised as needful; the exercise of this restraint was at that time naturally considered an episcopal function, a fact which the history of the censorship in England illustrates. The Universities, moreover, were naturally regarded as literary and theological advisers. When the Inquisition gained power it approached the work, however, more from the side of repressing heresy than of guiding thought; less leniency was shown, and in cases of doubt the tendency was to condemn a suspected book. But it should be noticed that objections brought against the Index apply in reality more to the spirit in which it was built up than to the principle of control itself.

It is convenient to deal here with the later history of the Index. In Session XXV the matter was brought up on the *Later history of the Index.* report of the Congregation. The Council was then hurried, and a discussion likely to go into details would have been wearisome; the list prepared by the committee was therefore ordered to be submitted to the Pope for publication after he had passed his judgment upon it. Ten rules, afterwards enlarged (1593) by Sixtus V to twenty-two, were laid down for its use; these were moderate, although they left a heavy task in the intended expurgation of works only partly allowed. Versions of the Bible in vulgar tongues, "since more harm than good arose from their indiscriminate use as experience showed," were only allowed to those whom the Ordinary held likely to benefit from their reading. This Index was accepted in Portugal, the Spanish Netherlands, Bavaria, and much of Italy. Pius V organised a special Congregation for the Index, which up to that time had been controlled by the Inquisition, and it was this body that prepared the Index of Sixtus V (1590). Clement VIII in publishing a new Index (1596) returned to the original ten Tridentine rules, and his Index— which was largely based upon the Spanish Index, and was in itself a triumph of the more zealous cardinals over the Pope— was double the size of the Tridentine list. It was not always those who did most for the extension of the Church who approved of such drastic and yet ineffectual methods. Canisius, the learned and energetic Jesuit, pointed out that the true remedy against error lay in widely diffused learning, while force alone was useless. Where the Index was most effective intellectual life sank lowest; authority gained a victory at the expense of energy. Instead of guiding its world to higher planes, the authority of the Church forced it down to a level where it was well regulated, it is true, but lower and less rich than might have been. If the Catholic were to remain a schoolboy instead of a man, he could never do the work of a man, although he might seem to escape some of a man's responsibilities and dangers.

The interval allowed between the sessions seemed to many Fathers too long, but Seripando was anxious for reform, and the Imperial ambassadors were pressing for it. The delay was therefore utilised to draw up a scheme of reform. While Seripando had the chief part in doing this, the actual drafting was left to Simonetta, who was more skilled in canon law and procedure. Among his chief helpers was Paleotto, afterwards a Cardinal and a useful recorder for this part of the Council. Seripando wished to begin by attacking abuses at Rome, but the majority wished to deal first with questions of apparently wider scope. Accordingly Simonetta drew up twelve heads for discussion. The first raised the old question of episcopal residence. Others

Session XIX, 14 May, 1562.

dealt with fees for Holy Orders, divisions and unions of benefices, their visitation, and the questers. Under all these heads
grave abuses existed, and there was a general desire to reform
them. Those connected with benefices were evidences of a long
lack of supervision and of a Church failing to meet the needs
of a changing time. They may be compared with those found
in England after the long inaction of the eighteenth century,
and the technical nature of the reforms should not blind us to
their real importance. The fundamental question of episcopal
residence, however, was an essential one for the Curia, and it
had aroused many storms before. Simonetta wished, therefore,
to postpone it; but the Imperial ambassadors represented that
to do so would be trifling with their master. The discussion
therefore went on. A division, which might have been fore-
seen, appeared among the Legates: Seripando and Gonzaga
would have left the decision to the Council; Simonetta, whose
letters to Rome were hardly loyal to his colleagues, and whose
advice was largely followed by the Curia, wished to leave it to
the Pope. A mere declaration of the obligation of residence
would have been of little use unless the exercise of Papal
privileges, which so much interfered with it, were also restrained. In the congregation on April 7, which was carried on
until the 18th, the discussion began; and it seemed as if (in the
words of Paleotto) an evil demon had infected the Council:
calumnies and accusations of all sorts flew about. At length,
when the debates had filled many days, the legates resolved to
take the votes as to what should be done. To simplify the issue,
a simple *placet* or *non-placet* was to answer the question,
Should the debate go on? Sixty-seven voted *placet*, thirty-
eight *non-placet*; thirty-four wished the Pope to be consulted
before going further (April 20).

The main lines of the discussion, notable more for its length
and importance (alike in itself and in the side-issues involved)
than for other features, were fairly obvious. The Council had
grown rapidly in its knowledge of its own procedure and in the
habits of legislative bodies. Procedure was better known; a
tradition of business had been formed, and was followed. But
at the same time parties were becoming more defined, and not

only the leaders of these parties, but also the rank and file, felt bound to deliver their opinions. Hence, in spite of the fact that the Council, as a rule, both knew its own mind and its own methods better than in earlier sittings, the debates became longer and more involved. It was certainly so in the present case. The heads of discussion were: the evils arising from non-residence, the need of residence, the obstacles to residence and the means for their removal, penalties for the breach and reward for the observance of it, the machinery for enforcing the decree to be passed. Some urged that, in view of the evils arising from its breach, the law of residence should be declared of divine obligation, so as to bind the consciences of bishops more firmly. Such a declaration would still leave the Papacy free to impose moderate restraints or allow moderate exceptions to the general law—in other words, to regulate its application. But it was objected to this that, as a matter of fact, the laws of God were broken as widely and as often as the laws of the Church, and that to declare episcopal residence of divine obligation merely in order to ensure its enforcement might lead to the inference that laws purely ecclesiastical as opposed to divine could be broken with impunity. Such an inference was nearly inevitable, and yet savoured of Protestantism. It was better in the eyes of some to throw the whole weight of the Church upon the removal of obstacles to residence and its encouragement by rewards. In Italy, where non-residence was common, evils were, it was said, less abundant than elsewhere; but it was evils of heresy rather than of immoral life that this argument pointed to. It was also truly said that often the demands of princes and the ambition of bishops caused non-residence, by employing them in secular business at courts. The existence of the abuses was generally admitted, but opinions—swayed, some by doctrine, some by self-interest—differed as to the way to deal with them.

Meanwhile, the arrival of ambassadors from Spain, Bavaria, the kingdom of Hungary, from Venice and Switzerland, and the expected arrival of de Lansac from France, enlivened and interrupted these discussions. France, under Charles IX (or really Catharine de Medici), was, though for the moment only, complaisant and willing to let the Council rank as a continuation of the former sessions. Owing to its religious wars, France was now replacing Germany as the centre of ecclesiastical politics, and it was also becoming more important for the King either to make terms with his rebellious subjects or else to get all possible help against them. He was anxious (as Charles V had been in earlier days) that the general trend of Papal policy should not place outside difficulties in the way of his power at home. De Lansac was unable to arrive before the date fixed for Session XIX (May 14), and therefore asked for its adjournment. Instead of this, however, the only Decree passed at the session was one indicating June 4 for the next session.

The relations between the Legates and the Curia had by now become important. The Pope had already begun his reforms in Conciliar the Curia—an indication not only of his own diplomacy. wishes, but of the conviction that reform was needed there. The first department attacked was the Penitentiary, then the Apostolic Chamber, and the Chancery; the reforms, however, were only slight compared with the evils that existed (4 May, 1562). But the Curia was greatly disturbed at the turn affairs were taking at Trent. The Pope, facile, easily led and now influenced by the permanent officials, was displeased, and at first wished the debate cut short. He spoke of sending three new Legates, one of whom, the Cardinal of San Clemente, was senior in rank, and would therefore outweigh his colleagues. The Bishop of Ventimiglia was also sent as Nuncio to Trent, in order to keep the Pope more fully posted in the course of affairs. On the question of continuation the Pope wished the Legates to secure a declaration in its favour. But at more leisure and in calmer moments, wisely advised, moreover, by Venice, he soon reconsidered these decisions. He consulted the cardinals (May 9), and finally left liberty to the Council at the discretion of the Legates; he put off sending a new commission to supersede them, and declared he was willing to approve a decree on residence, provided it were not termed expressly of divine obligation. At the same time, difficulties caused by the ambassadors also pressed on the

Legates. The French ambassadors, de Lansac, du Ferrier (the President of the Parliament of Paris), and de Pibrac arrived (May 18); the orations they delivered (May 26) were very free in their tone, and also urged that the present Council should be considered a new one. France had never recognised the second meeting of the Council, and did not wish to have its decision forced; in this the Imperial ambassadors supported them, but the Spanish, with equal firmness, opposed such an admission. The Pope was, as a matter of fact, pledged to Philip on the point, as were the Legates both verbally and in writing to Pescara, the Governor of Milan; but it was clear that to settle it one way or another would at that moment mean the dissolution of the Council. It was supposed, too, that the cardinals at Rome, who pressed the Pope to act as Philip wished, did so with a real wish to force a dissolution. The Legates were, however, equal to the crisis; they persuaded the Emperor to withdraw for the present a scheme of reform (the Libel of Reformation) which he had presented, and they contrived to put off an express decision on the question of continuation. It was easy to convince the Spaniards that facts were on their side, and that the proceedings of the Council both should and did assume identity with the older meetings; the French and Imperial ambassadors (the former of whom were strongly suspected of heresy) had to rest content with not having their view expressly negatived. It was a real triumph of diplomacy, and the credit of it belongs partly to Delfino, the Nuncio in Germany. From this time onwards unusual importance attaches to the influence it was possible to exert upon the Emperor by representatives at his Court.

In the next session little was done beyond returning a reply, friendly and not contentious, to the French orations, and proroguing to June 16. The Legates had decided, in keeping with their pledge to Spain that doctrine should be taken up at the point where it had been left, to begin with the Holy Eucharist. The attention of the Fathers was thus concentrated upon a fresh point, and bitter divisions arose. The Spanish were against

Session XX, 4 June, 1562.

any concessions in administration or doctrine; the French and Germans pressed for them. The Legates proposed for consideration the following questions: Was administration in both kinds necessary?[1] Should any exception be made as to administration in one kind only? Should the administration of the chalice be conceded to any kingdom, and if so upon what terms? Is less grace received through one kind only than through two? Should those under age be allowed to receive? The Archbishop of Granada held that the Council of Constance had settled the whole matter, and that no compromise was possible. The prevalent opinion among the theologians in their preliminary debates was that Communion in two kinds was not a divine institution, and that the Church had full power to order or authorise as it held best. The Legates, seeing the difficulty of a settlement, would have put off this special division of Eucharistic doctrine as a matter of economy rather than of faith, and therefore to be treated along with reform. The Hussites and members of the Greek Church had been allowed to receive in both kinds; Paul III had authorised the concession in isolated cases in Germany much as Clement VII had been ready to yield it in 1532; Pius IV himself was not disinclined to grant it, and his nephew Cardinal Borromeo had advised his yielding. From Spain, where the grant was not demanded, and where orthodoxy was firm, came the strongest opposition. Canons were drafted in answer to the questions proposed, but on this one point it proved impossible to agree. Primitive custom was admittedly in favour of administration in both kinds, but the Church had, it was held, a right to change the methods of administration as it had done in the case of baptism; we may remind ourselves that the preference of affusion to immersion was a practice irrespective of climate, and essentially a mark of original Roman obedience. It was also argued that priests as successors of the Apostles were alone included in the original administration of both kinds. Now it was important that when such questions arose there should be confidence between the Pope and his

Reception in two kinds.

---

[1] G. Constant : *Concession à l'Allemagne de la communion sous les deux espèces :* (2 vols., Paris, 1923).

Legate. Gonzaga had thoughts of resigning, and withdrew himself from the debates under plea of sickness, but the Archbishop of Lanciano, sent from the Council to Rome, and the Bishop of Ventimiglia at Trent, sent from Rome to the Council, smoothed matters over. When the Legates were given a free hand, when the Curia was itself divided, the Pope almost alone being for concession, it was possible to evade a settlement. Papal diplomacy at Vienna contented the Emperor (who had just consented not to present his Libel of Reformation to the Council, but to forward it privately to the Pope and to confine his demands at Trent to general terms) with a written promise of a future settlement. Ferdinand was hardly decided enough in action to suit his policy; earlier training and theological preferences struggled in his mind against political necessities. The French were equally undecided, but for a different reason; their Court had hardly determined as yet what policy to adopt finally with the Huguenots, and so delay was not distasteful to them. Religious War had now broken out (March 1562), and until its close (February 1563) war, and not diplomacy, was to be attended to first.

The Decree *De Communione* laid down four chapters of doctrine: (1) Laymen and clerks not celebrating were not bound under divine law to receive in both kinds. Although Christ had instituted this sacrament in bread and wine, He had not by so doing made reception in both kinds compulsory; nor is reception in both kinds to be inferred from His discourse in St. John vi (the existence of varying patristic interpretations of this chapter was noted to please the Archbishop of Granada); in other passages, too, He spoke more particularly of eating. (2) The Church has power to alter what does not affect the substance of the sacrament and to dispense with it for the purpose of utility, and of this nature is the already decreed reception in one kind only. 1 Corinthians iv. 1 was quoted to prove this authority of the Church, but a criticism by Salmeron, the learned Jesuit, and Turrianus, who afterwards became a Jesuit, led to a limitation of it as "not obscurely" seeming to mean this. Considerable difference indeed appeared in the

Session XXI, 16 June, 1562.

interpretation of Scripture, and this is only one instance out of many where the Jesuits departed from the traditional interpretation. The same theologians wished to state that the command, "Do this in remembrance of Me," applied only to the celebrants as successors of the Apostles, and not to Christians generally, but this, although approved by Hosius and Gonzaga, was struck out on the day of session. (3) The whole Christ and the true sacrament is received under one kind, and those so receiving are not defrauded of any grace (a large number of Fathers, however, thought that more grace was received under both kinds than under one). (4) Children are not bound to receive, although antiquity is not to be blamed for sometimes observing this custom. There followed four Canons against holders of contrary views. A note was added to the Canons that the Council deferred the examination and definition of two articles—whether the Church's reasons for communicating in one kind were so weighty as to permit of no exception, and further, if for reasons of honesty and Christian charity the use of both kinds were permitted to any person or nation or realm, upon what conditions it should be allowed. This Decree and the Canons were the result of careful consideration and redrafting. The Decree on doctrine had been entrusted to Seripando, Hosius, Patavinus, General of the Augustinians, and three bishops; as the cases of Cyprus and Candia, where reception in both kinds was usual, and as the example of the French kings, who received so at their coronation, were brought up, great care had to be taken in the wording. These cases could not be condemned and yet the closing words of the second chapter really seemed to assert the sole rightfulness of the prevalent use against an apparent innovation which could plead in its favour primitive usage. The Canons on heresies and the Decree on Reformation were entrusted to Simonetta, Patavinus, and two others. It might be noted that the Bishop of Brescia proposed to forbid altogether the communion of children.

The nine chapters on Reformation dealt with various abuses: (1) Bishops were to confer Holy Orders and the tonsure, and give letters testimonial and dimissory without fee (a stronger assertion, that to receive voluntary gifts for ordination was simony, had been struck out), and official fees, which were to be paid to unsalaried officials only, were regulated (a homely abuse was here struck at which has in some places passed unscathed through storms of re-formation). (2) No one, however suitable, should be ordained as a secular in Major Orders unless with a sufficient benefice or with private means sufficient to satisfy the bishop (this decision, although widely disapproved, was held needful to prevent the scandal of a penniless priesthood dependent upon alms). (3) In those churches where there was a body of clergy sharing the dividends, a third part of the income was set apart for daily distribution among them; thus penalising priests neglecting the daily services. (4)–(8) Bishops were to make new parishes or unite old, as needed; incompetent rectors were to have vicars, and scandalous rectors be deprived; bishops were to visit strictly, and see to the restoration of churches requiring it. (9) The name and the use of "questers" were abolished because of their "wicked abuses" and since the repeated decrees against them had proved useless; the bishops were to publish indulgences, and two of the Chapter were to receive the alms arising from them without reward; all were to understand that these proceeds of an indulgence were to be applied to pious uses. In spite of admitted abuses, some of the Fathers did not wish to abolish "questers," but gave way when they heard that in any case the Pope would use his power to do so.

Gradually matters settled and the heat cooled down. Public opinion at Rome grew easier, and political causes tended to make the ambassadors less pressing. Simonetta and Gonzaga were reconciled, and the inherent diffi-culties of the position made many think that the settlement of peculiarly vexed questions (such as residence) were better left to the Pope. But the demand for administration in both kinds—even from such a strongly Catholic State as Bavaria—was continued; and as this point, along with the Sacrifice of the Mass, was to come up in the next session, a long interval until September 17 was allotted. The deputation that prepared the doctrinal decrees was also to

Reforma-tion.

Session XXII, 17 Sept., 1562.

report upon abuses that had crept into the celebration of the Mass. Once more the French ambassador wrote home urging the need for the French theologians to appear. On hearing that forty were to arrive in September, he begged the Legates (but without result) to postpone the session.

As so much variance had arisen and the faithful needed clear guidance, it was held better to define the doctrine of the Mass at length. It was elaborated in eight chapters, to which were added nine Canons and a Decree concerning the things to be observed and to be avoided in the celebration of Mass. (1) Christ at the Last Supper gave power and command to the Apostles (whom He then made priests) and to their successors in the priesthood to offer His Body and Blood under the species of bread and wine, thus leaving to the Church a visible sacrifice, by means of which the power (*virtus*) of the sacrifice completed upon the Cross (which is here represented) is applied to the remission of those sins which are committed daily. (2) Since in the Sacrifice of the Mass the selfsame Christ is contained, and bloodlessly offered, as on the altar of the Cross, the sacrifice is truly propitiatory, and is therefore fitly offered, according to the tradition of the Apostles, for the sins, punishments, satisfactions, and *other needs of the living* (these words were objected to by twenty-six bishops as likely to encourage superstition), and also of the dead in Christ not yet fully purged. (3) Although the Church is wont to celebrate Masses for the memory of saints, the sacrifice is made not to them, but to God alone. Their protection, however, and intercession may be sought. (4) The Canon of the Mass, instituted many years ago by the Church, is in agreement with the words of the Lord, the traditions of the Apostles, and the pious ordinances of the Holy Pontiffs. (5) The alternations of tone, the benedictions, lights, incense, vestments, and other adjuncts of the Mass commend the majesty of the Mass itself, and in adaptation to the nature of man (which is only raised to thoughts of heavenly things by external means) lift up the minds of the faithful to celestial things. (6) Although it is to be wished that the faithful should be present at every Mass and communicate by participation sacramental even those Masses

The Mass.

in which the priest alone communicates are not to be condemned as private, but approved as truly public, not only because in them the congregation communicate spiritually, but because they are celebrated by a public minister of the Church, not only for himself, but for all the faithful. It may be noted that great disapproval was expressed of "*Missæ Siccæ*," in which there was no consecration, but on account of ancient use they were left untouched. (7) Water is to be mixed with wine in the chalice because our Lord presumably did so: water and blood flowed from His side: and (Rev. xvii. 15) "the waters are peoples," the mingling thus signifying the union of Christ with His Church. (8) Mass was not to be said in the vulgar tongue, but priests were to expound, frequently, and specially on Sundays and Saints' days, what was read. The nine canons were ushered in by a prolegomenon (9) noting the abundance of errors and the unanimous voice of the Fathers in condemning them. These ran as follows: those were anathematised who denied the doctrines asserted in the decrees above; also those who said that the Roman rite, in which part of the Canon and the words of consecration are said in a lowered voice, is to be condemned, or that only the vulgar tongue should be used, or that the mixed chalice should not be used. An additional Decree dealt with evils arising from avarice, irreverence, or superstition. Fees for celebrating Masses were prohibited and current abuses were sharply spoken of. Wandering or criminal priests were not to be engaged to say Masses. Music of unsuitable nature was forbidden (there were some who would have abolished music altogether). Priests were not to celebrate at irregular hours or with forbidden ceremonies. A fixed number of certain Masses and of candles was to be done away with as tending to superstition (this somewhat vague clause seems to condemn the popular abuse of "the sacrifices of Masses"). Exhortation and teaching were to give the Mass its proper position.

These Decrees had been formed after much deliberation from July 20 onwards. In August the Pope asked the Legates to yield to the Emperor's demand for the concession of the chalice. All the Imperial ecclesiastics urged it. There were proposals of using the concession so as to strengthen the Catholic faith numerically, for the Archbishop of Prague, Anton Bruns, saw in it a chance of regaining the Utraquists. Gonzaga and Hosius favoured it, and gradually the idea gained ground that it might be made generally by a Decree, and each particular case left to the Pope for decision. This was the goal towards which the Legates worked, and in the end it was reached.

On July 1 the Fathers had begun giving opinions upon the doctrine of the Mass before a large audience, estimated at 2,000 people. The old difference between Jesuits and Dominicans appeared in Salmeron's assertion and Soto's denial that our Saviour gave Himself for us at the Last Supper. This point, and the expediency of preparing a full statement of Catholic doctrine, were the only causes of long discussion. Salmeron's great supporter was Laynez, about whose theology there was a modern ring, although much of it could have been found in medieval writers. His erudition was used with effect. He based his contention on the ground that we were saved, not by Christ's death alone, but by His life and death together—a series of acts to which His death formed the climax. This view, he held, did not derogate from the Sacrifice of the Cross. The Spaniards objected that the derogation was real—that the Last Supper was only a sacrifice of praise and thanksgiving, not propitiatory. As in the Decree upon Justification, the final decision was a compromise, embodied in the Decrees and Canons summarised above, which said that in the Last Supper Christ offered Himself to God under the species of bread and wine, but did not affirm anything further as to the nature of the offering or its relation to the Sacrifice of the Cross. But the compromise inclined to the Jesuit view, and allowed variations in theology. The Archbishop of Granada, followed by some thirty other bishops, strongly and repeatedly opposed the Jesuit view that the priesthood was instituted by our Lord's command, "Do this," advocating the view that it was rather instituted at Pentecost. Upon no other points did much discussion arise, so that although the suggestion to give the Decrees the force of Canons was not acted upon, the

unanimity of the Fathers gave them a very real force of
their own.

The first of the eleven Decrees for Reformation was general.
It ordered all clerks to bear themselves soberly and discreetly
in manner and dress, avoiding all worldly business,
keeping themselves far from dice and games.
The second ordered bishops to be of legitimate
birth, of character approved by superiors, and
certified by testimonials or university standing as fit to teach.
The third (much like Chapter III of Session XXI) dealt with
the daily distribution in Chapters, and ordered the share of
members not fulfilling their daily duty to go to the fabric of
the church or to some other pious use. Other Chapters
provided that only those should have a voice in chapters,
cathedrals, or collegiate churches who were at least sub-
deacons. Anyone nominated to a post must within a year
qualify himself by ordination as needed. In future only those
of suitable age and honest life should be appointed. Dispensations for use outside the Curia must be shown to the Ordinaries
in order to be effective. Legates, nuncios, and metropolitans,
in cases of appeal, were to follow the procedure as laid down by
Innocent IV and other Popes. Bishops, as delegates of the
Apostolic See, were to take charge as executors of all pious
gifts or legacies to colleges, schools, hospitals, etc., and should
be visitors, except in foundations under royal protection.
Administrators, ecclesiastical or lay, of all churches, hospitals,
guilds, etc. were to render yearly accounts to the Ordinaries.
Any offender who from cupidity wronged pious foundations
should be excommunicated until he had made restitution
and been absolved by the Pope. These reforms have been
condemned as slight, but they deal with evils most apparent
in the Church at large, and the number of discussions upon
them raised by commentators is possibly the best measure of
their importance. They laid upon the bishops heavy but
rightful burdens which their predecessors had often shirked,
and it really mattered little in practice if their authority was
noted as a delegation from the Papacy. Some of the provisions
as to wills and visitations of foundations seemed likely to

*Reforma-
tion.
Eleven
Decrees.
The clergy.*

lead to conflict with secular powers, but this would arise not so much on the general principles, for such powers would be recognised as belonging to the Church, but in the details of administration and in special cases.

The important question of the concession of the chalice had now to be faced. A paper giving reasons in its favour had The been drawn up by the Bishop of Fünfkirchen in chalice. Hungary, and presented to the Legates for the benefit of the Council. To satisfy the Emperor and the French, the Legates thought first of introducing two decrees, one declaring that for sufficient causes the chalice might, in the opinion of the Council and the Pope, be conceded, and the other that the authority to concede it should rest with the local bishops under certain conditions. The Pope, but not the Fathers as a body, approved this course. It would have been easy as proposed, to limit the concession to the Emperor's dominions (his Italian fiefs were, however, expressly excluded by his ambassadors); those receiving it were to accept Catholic doctrine and worship, and to promise obedience to the Decrees of the Council; the clergy were to teach with the utmost care that communion in one kind was right; confession as usual was to precede communion; it was also suggested that the administration in two kinds might only take place on certain days; special care was to be taken against possible irreverence in the use of the chalice, and reservation of the wine was to be forbidden. The matter came before a general congregation (August 28), and it was easily seen that the Fathers would never make the concession. Laynez, in particular, distinguished himself by a speech in which he urged the Fathers to disregard the Emperor, and to cast away the fear of princes. When the voting came on (September 6), opinions were divided; fourteen voted to defer the matter (as the Archbishop of Granada had recommended), thirty-eight for refusing the concession, twenty-nine for granting it, twenty-four for referring it to the Pope, nineteen would limit it to Bohemia and Hungary alone (thus excluding Germany), thirty-one would concede it if the Pope alone were to execute the Decree and determine its application, ten voted against it while leaving the decision to the Pope. The Bishop of Fünfkirchen now became anxious that the Legates should get the matter left to the Pope. The Legates drafted a request to the Pope to concede the chalice, "such a concession, upon condition of its pleasing him, being wished for by the Council"; but (September 15) this was opposed as seeming to limit the Pope's power of action without the Council, and was lost by seventy-nine to sixty-nine; therefore a milder form was adopted. After referring to the two questions proposed and deferred in Session XXI, "the whole matter was referred to our most Holy Lord, who, by his peculiar prudence, should do that which he should judge useful to the Christian Commonwealth and salutary to those seeking the chalice." This Decree was carried by ninety-eight to thirty-eight (September 16), but only with difficulty, and by the intervention of Simonetta. This Decree was added after those on Reformation.

To the Emperor this proposed settlement was distasteful, for a Papal concession would have less weight in Germany than one from a General Council. His ambassadors, along with those of France (still pleading for delay), urged the immediate consideration of reforms in discipline. The Imperialists presented the "Libel of Reformation"; the French, a somewhat similar scheme of reform; both of them documents meriting some description.

When Ferdinand, for the sake both of his hereditary lands and the Empire, began a policy of conciliation and tolerance, he instituted a commission of bishops and others *The Libel of* to prepare for him (September 1561) a scheme of *Reformation.* Reformation. This commission proposed to lessen the power of the cardinals and their number, to divide them equally among the nations, and take away from them the election of the Pope. The authority of the Council—the reassembling of which was just then looked for—was to be supreme, and to limit that of the Papacy. The ecclesiastical centre of gravity was to be moved from Italy, and the Princes were to undertake the task of reform, redistributing funds which seemed to the lay eye superfluous. The significance of the scheme lay not so much in the reforms proposed as in the assertion of national independence and a national share in the government of the Church; even more significant still was the right of the Prince to direct a reform—a principle which filtered downwards from Wyclif into many streams of thought, and had caused antagonism between Charles V and the Papacy.

This report, drawn up by the commission, was obviously too extreme for submission to the Council, and so the Emperor asked a few advisers (including Staphylus) to prepare another document for the Council. This followed the lines of the other, but went into detail. Beginning with the reform of the Curia, it would have had only twenty-six cardinals. Residence was to be enforced upon bishops; simony, exemptions, and dispensations were to be abolished; excommunications were to be limited; the Mass was to be put into the vulgar tongue; the chalice to be administered to the laity; the Service-books were to be revised; the use of flesh during Lent and of clerical marriage were to be allowed. It was this document that the Emperor sent (22 May, 1562) to his ambassadors at Trent. At first it was quietly dealt with, forwarded to the Pope, and a few points in it selected for consideration. It now reappeared as a definite programme (Sept.). The French "Libel of Reformation," presented at a later date (8 January, 1563), when the Huguenots had been for the time defeated, was in thirty-four articles. It asked that the characters and attainments of those to be ordained priests and bishops should be tested carefully; that the teaching work of the Church should be enlarged by a reform of monasteries and convents, the institution of frequent sermons, and the publication of a good catechism; that pluralities, pensions on benefices, and sinecures should be abolished; that dispensations for matrimony should be suppressed; the vulgar tongue introduced into the services of the Church; the chalice administered to the laity; excommunications limited; abuses of images, indulgences, pilgrimages, and relics restrained; diocesan councils should be held yearly, provincial every two, and general every ten years. This scheme dates back substantially to instructions given to the Cardinal of Lorraine (November 1562), which are the same in outline. It will be noticed that the French and German schemes differ: the Germans dealt more with constitutional and national grievances; the French aimed at a higher standard of knowledge and thought. For practical purposes, however, they agreed; and as the German scheme acquired a renown little inferior to that of the oft-reappearing *Centum Gravamina* of earlier years, and the French scheme was printed and widely circulated, their effect was great. Other States were known to sympathise with many of the demands, and a scheme of reform under some ninety heads had been presented previously for papal consideration by Italian bishops.

Immediately after Session XXII, when the question was brought urgently before them by the Imperialists and the French (the latter still awaiting their Cardinal of Lorraine and theologians, who would, it was rumoured, make a strong stand for the independence of the Council), the Legates handed over the Libel to Simonetta and four others to extract definite proposals from it. But the Libel in all its nakedness they declared hostile to Christian piety and impossible to submit to the Council. A careful selection of points was made by leave of the Pope and Cardinal Carlo Borromeo.

Meanwhile the theologians were divided into six classes, three being set to prepare Decrees on Holy Orders and three on Matrimony. The heretical propositions it was proposed to condemn were that (1) Holy Orders are not a sacrament, but (2) a human figment; (3) not one sacrament with lower orders as steps to the priesthood; (4) there is no hierarchy, but all Christians are priests, and a call from the people is necessary; a priest can again become a layman; (5) there is no priesthood in the New Testament, and the only ministerial office is that of preaching; (6) unction and the other ceremonies in Ordination are vain, and the Holy Ghost is not given in Ordination; (7) bishops are not superior to priests, and can confirm and ordain no more than priests; those who have not had canonical ordination can be true ministers of the Word and Sacraments. In discussing these various heretical propositions the speeches of the theologians

Orders. Seven Canons.

were limited (not for the first time) to half an hour, as prolixity had been growing of late.

Many vital questions arose out of these propositions. Holy Orders could not be discussed without Episcopacy, and thus by a side wind the old point of residence came up again, as well as the relation of bishops to the Pope. The Spanish bishops wished to assert the divine origin of Episcopacy, and asked the Legates to introduce a Decree drafted by Cardinal Crescenzi at an earlier date asserting the Episcopate to have been instituted by Christ, and to be, by divine law, superior to the priesthood. The Legates were able to reply that they were merely discussing points raised by heretics, and not other speculations. The Confession of Augsburg, they argued, recognised the divine origin of Episcopacy, but erred on the accessories. Passages brought from heretical works were, as Seripando (now acting as chief legate) thought, not aimed at Episcopacy in itself, but against the rightfulness of existing bishops. In reply it was pointed out that Calvinism certainly denied the divine origin of Episcopacy, and that the Council had to deal with all heretical views, not merely those of the Lutherans. In discussing Episcopacy, Salmeron denied that election had ever belonged to the people, wherein his old opponent Soto contradicted him, while yet admitting, however, that this merely administrative point could be altered by the Pontiff; as to the part the voice of the people played opinions differed in debate. But many agreed that the Episcopate was a distinct order and should be recognised as such. Some admitted this distinction in order, but found no independent jurisdiction, as all jurisdiction was derived from the Papacy. Others contended that bishops derived both office and jurisdiction from God, but that the Pope regulated the scope and use of both. Much discussion followed. Laynez spoke for one whole day, placing all jurisdiction in the Pope, from whose grant bishops derived their jurisdiction. One hundred and eighty-one other Fathers spoke also on this fundamental doctrine. Here was raised the question of Papal and episcopal power, upon which had hinged so much of the history and the development of the Middle Ages. The original draft of the Canons underwent much change, and it was seen how many points had been left undecided by the scholastic teaching.

The Legates were now begged to fulfil their promise of allowing the subject of residence to come up with that of Holy Orders. Philip of Spain was also influencing the Kings of France and Portugal to join with him in demanding the removal of the words "on the proposal of the Legates" (*proponentibus legatis*) from the Acts. It was found that the initiative in the hands of the Legates was too strict a limit upon discussion. The Legates pressed the Pope to end the question of residence once for all, and Pius decided that heavy punishment should be assigned to non-resident bishops and curates, but that nothing should be said as to the divine obligation. A Decree to that effect was submitted in Congregation (November 6). The former Decree against non-residence was extended; good causes for non-residence were named; loss of revenue and incapacity for office were to follow persistent non-residence.

An attempt was also made to draft a new Canon on Episcopacy in which all would agree; but the Spaniards, to whom it was shown privately, refused it. Bishops were declared to have been instituted by Christ, and this they approved, but the omission of any further statement was distasteful to them. They were willing to declare bishops subject to the Papacy by the law of God, and bound to obedience; but they insisted that the divine origin of Episcopacy, derived from Christ Himself, should be fully stated. The Canon was therefore modified twice. One form said episcopal jurisdiction was conferred by Christ in His Vicar, the Roman Pontiff, which jurisdiction is derived by bishops from him when they are assumed into a part of his oversight. But again the Spaniards objected, and Seripando himself thought the wording ambiguous—a fault which the Pope specially wished to avoid. Further alterations again failed to commend the draft. As a matter of fact, it was difficult to find a form of words to gloss over a fundamental difference of view—a truth which Lutherans and Zwinglians had before this discovered for themselves.

But the arrival of Charles of Guise, Archbishop of Rheims and Cardinal of Lorraine (as he was called), altered the conditions of the Council. The Congregation (November 9) put off the session fixed for November 12 until his arrival. He reached Trent on November 13, along with fifteen French bishops and some theologians and eight abbots (a few others arrived later). He was a perfect type of the ecclesiastical statesman of the day; interested in everything, with a Frenchman's charm of manner and adaptability, something of real diplomatic ability, and something also of an ambition to make a great figure. He was soundly educated, an efficient prelate, and had the advantage of competent advisers. A combination of the knowledge of the Sorbonne and the legal traditions of the Parliament was just what was needed in the Council. The Cardinal had been expected with fear and with hope, both tinged with uncertainty. He had no past conciliar associations of party or cabals to hamper him, and he was free from too embarrassing scruples when he had once decided on his policy. He was an accomplished player, and, backed by skill and ambition, he had now come to encounter the best players of his day in what was to him a game, not always to be had, with high stakes and much excitement. On his first appearance he described the state of France, torn by wars and bleeding from religious discord. A reformation such as the Council might make could alone restore to her unity and peace. He had some personal right to speak for the national Church, for his oration at Poissy had perhaps saved the situation. Since then his advocacy of the concession of the chalice and his broad sympathy had given him a unique position, well suited to an advocate of Gallican independence. But his eye looked not merely over his own country, but over Germany also, as his interview at Saverne with Duke Christopher of Würtemberg had lately shown: he was ready to make use of differences between Calvinists and Lutherans to suit his large designs, the nature and limits of which are hard even to guess, still less to know. With all his advantages, his position and his personality he soon became the central figure of the Council.

Arrival of the Cardinal of Lorraine.

234

A stormy debate, in which the Bishop of Guadix (near Granada) argued the Papal institution of bishops not to be essential, giving as an example the suffragans of Salzburg (confirmed by their Metropolitan and not by the Pope, a survival from earlier medieval centuries, when Metropolitans, as a canonical rule, confirmed their suffragans until the Pope claimed and came to exercise the right) was chiefly remarkable for the Cardinal's speech in defence of Episcopacy. His general attitude, cautious and diplomatic, was that the matter of order was in itself difficult: he wished, therefore, to introduce some mention of the imposition of hands which, strangely enough, had been purposely left out. He was not anxious expressly to define Episcopacy as of divine origin, for to do so might now seem an attack on the Papacy just when it needed support. The new arrival of French representatives seemed to increase the difficulties of the Legates; it was impossible to carry out the command of the Pope, that his power must be assumed in any definition as fundamental and supreme. They talked of closing the Council, and he wished it done, but these questions had to be settled. It seemed no gain when the Legates turned the Council away from the subject of Episcopal Order to the equally difficult one of Residence. The debates were so long that the session fixed for November 26 was further put off until December 17, and again and again; once more in the course of the delay Congregations met twice a day instead of twice a week as at first.

The Legates sought advice at Rome; Cardinal Borromeo sent three forms of Canon VII (see p. 231) placed in the order preferred by the Pope. They might pass a Decree on Residence, which the Cardinals of Trent and Lorraine had been set to consider, but it must on no account be defined as of divine obligation. In the course of the debates an eighth Canon on the Primacy of Rome was also proposed, which enlarged the discussion. In this proposed new Canon the Pope was described as ruler of the Universal Church (*rector universalis ecclesiae*), and to the French bishops this seemed to imply an inferiority of the Council to the Pope; moreover, they denied their dependence for Order upon the Pope, and were doubtful if they depended upon him for jurisdiction. The Cardinal of Lorraine in all these matters showed a dexterity as a draftsman which partly explains his power over assemblies; a version of Canon VII proposed by him, for instance, met with the approval of the theologians except Laynez, although the Canonists and Simonetta disliked it. Further postponements of the session were necessary (4 Feb. to 22 April, 1563). The final form of Canon VIII stated the legitimacy of " bishops assumed by" Papal authority.

In March the Cardinals Gonzaga and Seripando died (the latter of fever), both of them respected and lamented.

Deaths of the Cardinals of Mantua and Seripando, 2 and 17 March, 1563.

There were intrigues set afoot for the appointment of the Cardinal of Lorraine as president, but Seripando's last request had been for a man of ripe years and experience. Simonetta was distrusted by the Spanish, and had played too decided a part for him to exercise any great control; Hosius could do little for the opposite reason that he had been too colourless; the Cardinal d'Altemps had previously left the Council for Rome: Cardinals Morone and Navagero were therefore appointed (7 March, 1563). But the change was of less importance, as the Legates and Lorraine had by this time spoken frankly to each other, and the influence of the latter was now thrown not against, but along with their authority. Canons VI, VII, and VIII on the Hierarchy in the form afterwards passed were the results of these negotiations and debates.

Of the new Legates, Morone took precedence; he had mixed in German politics as nuncio more than once, especially

The new Legates. Morone, Navagero.

about the time of the Colloquy of Regensburg, and none had more nearly approached a reconciliation. He had been a friend of Contarini's, and sympathised with his views of Justification; under Paul IV (as already mentioned)[1] he was not only accused, quite wrongfully, of heresy, but thrown into prison, which he only left on that Pope's death (1559). Like some other members of this Italian school of thought, he had become a zealous Papalist, scarcely trusted by all his fellow-cardinals; but his

[1] See pp. 126–128 *supra*.

German experience was likely to help him at the Imperial Court. Cardinal Navagero was a Venetian of good birth, who, as a layman, had been ambassador at various Courts, and only as an elderly widower had sought ordination; he had (1561) been created cardinal, a dignity he deserved by ability, literary and general, and had earned by his devotion to Papal interests.

Morone had hardly done more than arrive (13 April, 1563) and deliver his address, when he left Trent for Innsbruck (April 20), where the Emperor had been for some time, and where the Cardinal of Trent, the Bishop of Fünfkirchen, and the Archbishop of Salzburg, as well as the Cardinal of Lorraine (12 February, 1563), visited him. Ferdinand had been much influenced by Canisius, and as he gradually discovered the incapacity and unwillingness of the Council to satisfy him, he turned to the Pope. Morone's journey was to ratify the compact, and thus once more Papal diplomacy shot ahead of the Council. But there were difficulties in the position. It was needful, as the Cardinal of Lorraine advised the Emperor, to strengthen the non-Italian element in the Council, and to ask that the ambassadors should make their proposals directly to the Council—the latter being a point which had been urged upon the Legates by the ambassadors at Trent. Philip II had (March) sent to Rome Don Luis de Zuñiga to reinforce Vargas, and the main point of his instructions (December 1562) was to insist upon the sessions continuing until all matters of faith and heresy were defined: novel opinions should be sternly condemned, and no concessions—such as that of the chalice— should be made. The Spanish ambassadors at Rome also took up the complaint of the Spanish bishops at Trent, pressing for the abolition of the clause which gave the Legates the initiative, so that the Council might really become free. But the issue of the Council depended upon the unity of Europe, and that was now once more broken up. Spain rather preferred to see France divided into parties and at war in itself. The peace between the French king and the Huguenots (March) made the former desire peace; he was even willing for the Council to be transferred to some city in Germany. The position of Lorraine, after the death of his brother the Duke de

Guise (18 February, 1563), was altered, and he was now anxious to bring the council to a successful end. He returned to Trent (April 20) from Innsbruck and gradually drew nearer to the Legates and the Papal policy, until by the middle of June he acted cordially with the Legates. The change in his views made him more inclined to an agreement on the matter of episcopal residence and he was now anxious above all to bring the Council to a happy end with credit to himself. The Pope found a grievance in the peace with the Huguenots, and the French ambassadors at Rome were very busy (under a Bull of April 7 some French bishops were cited to Rome for sympathy with Lutherans). The Lorraine family were striving Differences to marry their niece, Mary of Scots, at one time and with an Imperial, at another with a Spanish prince; diplomacy. and so family interests, tinged by an infusion of religious politics, brought England (where a manly queen must either be married or excommunicated) and Scotland (where a self-seeking nobility and a Calvinistic democracy might be checked) within the diplomacy of Trent. For a time, however, Rome held its hand. But when Morone returned to Trent from Innsbruck (27 May, 1563), he had really won over the Emperor; the Pope was to be supported, and, in return, as soon as the Council had ended the chalice should be conceded; Morone had promised large reforms; the Pope had issued some more reforming Bulls dealing first with the Rota (27 September, 1562, and then 1 January, 1563) with other departments, notably reducing official fees. The Emperor was now seeking for the acknowledgment of his son Maximilian (a strong sympathiser with the Protestants, and most desirous of communion in both kinds) as King of the Romans. He had been elected 24 November, 1562; had been just previously recognised as King of Bohemia, and (September 1563) was soon to be crowned King of Hungary.

X

THE CLOSE OF THE COUNCIL

DURING Morone's absence, when diplomacy was busy and the theologians inclined for rest (they had finished the considerations of Matrimony in March, and by the end of April the Decrees on the abuses in Holy Orders were ready), things moved slowly. In the middle of May Congregations began again; the theologians presented their drafts. Titular bishops (whom one prelate roundly declared to be an introduction of the devil), the cessation of the Minor Orders, the election of cardinals were commented upon among other things. The Cardinal of Lorraine took the part of a moderator, and mostly set an example of brevity. The Archbishop of Granada spoke much and often as before. On Morone's arrival many minor quarrels were composed, but the postponed session was put off again and again, and finally reached the distinction of being postponed eight times. Two proposals were made to facilitate business: Morone suggested that what was agreed upon should be passed, and the rest left over: the French ambassador, Du Ferrier, proposed to close the Council and leave the task of reform to national synods, whose decisions should come before the Pope for approval. Lorraine and some of the Legates approved of this. The Pope was supposed to be inclined for it; but the course of affairs in France and the danger from Germany made him anxious to close the Council speedily. He therefore left the Legates a free hand even in matters touching the Cardinalate and bishops titular and coadjutors. The Decrees on Reform were recommitted, the election of bishops being left over and the condemnation of titular bishops left out. Before the Canons could be passed, a conference of leading Fathers had to be held, at which it was decided to go back to the late Cardinal Gonzaga's form of VII (taken with VI and VIII) on the place of bishops. On June 9 these long-debated Canons were accepted, although even then the Archbishop of Granada, supported by others, stood out to the end for an assertion of the institution of the hierarchy by Christ, instead of its divine ordination (which might mean, it was said, indirectly through the Pope). When the session was finally held the Canons and Decrees passed with little dissent and slight alteration.

Session XXIII, 15 July, 1563.

The enunciation of Faith, in four chapters, asserted: (1) The union of Sacrifice and priesthood. Christ, therefore, gave to His Apostles and to their successors in the priesthood the power of consecration, of offering and administering His Body and Blood, and also of remitting and retaining sins. (2) To show the veneration of so great a Sacrifice seven Orders have been in use from the first: among them subdeacon, acolyte, exorcist, lector, ostiarius. (3) Holy Orders is one of the Seven Sacraments, since grace is conferred in it and this is accomplished with words and signs. (4) Orders confer an indelible character. Not all Christians are priests. Bishops, the successors of the Apostles, specially pertain to the hierarchy. They are superior to priests, can confer Confirmation, and Ordain. For the promotion of bishops, priests, and other orders, no consent or calling by people or secular power is needed.

Decrees on Holy Orders. Minor Orders.

An incident in the preparation of the Decrees on Holy Orders illustrates the Council's difficulty of being sufficiently detailed for precision, and yet not being too minute. The Legates had prepared a long Chapter on the seven Orders, and when this left the hands of the theologians it included long definitions of the duties of each Order. This involved much detail, and the minuteness was reasonably objected to. The Cardinal of Lorraine suggested that the care of the details might well be left to the bishops, who should now be charged to exercise a stricter control. The lengthy provisions were therefore left out. But where, as in many matters touching benefices, new regulations were desired, a like course could not be taken. A large assembly, in which nearly every member understands even the details of the matters dealt with, finds great difficulty in coming to a conclusion.

In the explanation of the Conciliar Decree under Paul III it was explained that all, even cardinals, should reside (this extension to them was due to the Cardinal of Lorraine), unless for causes approved by the Pope, the Metropolitan, or his deputy. Absentees were to receive no income. All those appointed to cathedral churches, even cardinals, are to receive consecration within three months of their appointment, under pain of losing the income. Six months' delay shall entail deprivation. Major and Minor Orders were guarded by rules as to the need of testimonials, character, knowledge, and vocation. Fraudulent withdrawal from secular jurisdiction by receiving the tonsure is to be guarded against. None under fourteen years of age, even if in Minor Orders, is to receive a benefice, or to have benefit of clergy (*i.e.*, exemption from secular jurisdiction) unless holding a benefice and wearing the ecclesiastical dress and tonsure. A knowledge of Latin was demanded, except in special cases, for Minor Orders. The lives of those admitted shall be watched over, and none shall be admitted who are not likely to proceed to Major Orders. For promotions in Orders proper interstices of time are to be carefully observed. Ages for the Major Orders were fixed—twenty-two for subdeacon, twenty-three for deacon, twenty-five for priest. Strict regulations as to testimonials were made, and the lives of those ordained were to be marked by piety, continence, and frequent communions, special emphasis being laid on the sacredness of the priesthood. No one shall be ordained in future unless attached to a particular church, and no wandering priest without letters from his bishop shall be allowed to celebrate. To further the restoration of the Minor Orders, which in many places had fallen into disuse, no unordained person was to perform their special offices. Bishops were to try and restore the Minor Orders in parishes of sufficient population and revenue, assigning stipends to those ordained. Failing unmarried clerks, competent married men, if not twice married, and if wearing the tonsure and clerical dress, might be employed. All cathedral churches are to be bound to keep and educate a number of youths of the diocese proportional to their means and the size of the diocese, in a neighbouring college chosen by the bishop. These youths are to be twelve years old and likely for the ministry. A preference is to be given to the poor. Wealthy children desirous for the training are to pay for themselves. The boys are to wear the tonsure and clerical dress, attend Mass daily, act as servers, confess once a month, and receive the Communion at their confessor's direction. Their education is to be liberal as well as ecclesiastical. These seminaries are to be under the bishop's care. Besides funds set apart for education, a certain part of capitular, parochial, and all ecclesiastical revenues is to be taken for their maintenance. These rules were to be enforced. To lessen the cost of teaching, Ordinaries may compel scholastics to teach as they direct. In cases of poverty, one seminary may be provided from two churches. In case of a wealthy diocese, two seminaries may be founded.

The new diocesan seminaries.

Provisions for ecclesiastical order and for education had once been ample, but had been corrupted or laxly enforced. These difficulties were now intensified by the number of monks who were leaving the monasteries and by the controversies of the Reformation. These Decrees were a fair endeavour to reform abuses. The existence of unfit priests, scandalous ordination, clerical exemption from jurisdiction, negligence of bishops—all of which had wrought untold mischief—were now to be restrained. The pressing need of efficient education for clergy was now to be supplied by these episcopal seminaries. It was a return to primitive and early medieval models, although the boldness of the financial provisions savoured of an age of secularisation of benefices. The episcopal seminaries, thus ordered, are often spoken of as a new departure in clerical education. Such they were not, for cathedral schools and seminaries had a long medieval history. In England, for instance, Canterbury, York and Lincoln may be mentioned. Canterbury takes us back to Theodore of Tarsus and the Abbot Hadrian, not to speak of St. Augustine himself. York was great enough to produce Alcuin to illuminate the Continent under Charles the Great. At Lincoln, Remigius (1067) who came from Fécamp,

Effect of these Decrees.

attended to learning: under St. Hugh, William de Monte was drawn thither from Paris: of Grosseteste's day there is no need to speak. Many bishops had in the youths and young clerks of their household, what was really a bishop's school: we may recall the training of Thomas Becket. The Council of the Lateran in 1215 ordered all cathedrals and great churches to set apart one prebend for providing a teacher, and English Councils, for instance, repeated this command. It was these schools which gave training for the clergy, and the schools for boys at the cathedrals were the types of all medieval schools for boys. It may be noted that St. Dominic founded his Order primarily not for the Inquisition but to remedy the evils of a low clerical training.[1] Although there were some great monastic schools, it was the great churches that did most for education generally. Henceforth, if bishops did their duty, there could be no lack of fit ordinands. On the one hand, some have traced the greater coherence of dioceses, the heightened respect for the priesthood, the higher standard of clerical life, to this particular Decree for the founding of seminaries. On the other hand, some have seen in it a cause of the too common separation between clergy and laity—an aloofness, sometimes exaggerated, of one from the other. Probably there is truth in both contentions. But of the importance of holding up clerical vocation before the young there should be no question, even if individual cases prove failures. For a special work, needing not only gifts of disposition and learning, but also of spirit and self-sacrifice, a special training is needed. The fault, if fault there were, did not lie here. It was easy for small institutions to drift into a low state of education. The seminaries could not rise higher than the aims of the bishop himself, and were liable to abuses not so likely to arise in larger colleges. Seminaries have done an immense work in providing for the needs of the Church; but they have too often suffered from an unreality of tone and a too great

[1] See A. G. Little, *Studies in English Franciscan History* (Manchester Univ. and London, 1917); P. Mandonnet, O.P., *Revue d'histoire ecclésiastique*, Vol. XV, pp. 34–50. On English Schools generally, Leach, *Medieval Schools in England* (Antiquaries Books (n. d.)).

conservatism in methods. The conception of their foundation was happy: the method of their administration has sometimes fallen short of it. No provision did more for the efficiency and the adequate machinery of the Church, but there was need of a constant adaptation to the needs of the time and of a high ideal of education, spiritual and intellectual. Some German dioceses, and notably Würzburg, were soon to become illustrations of the good working of this Decree, and it fitted in well with the work of the Jesuits.

When so much had been done, the Legates began to think of closing the Council speedily, but De Luna (the Spanish Ambassador) opposed this, and also Morone's scheme (afterwards adopted) of preparing business by two small committees of theologians and Fathers respectively. Since the beginning of the year directions from Rome had enjoined upon the Legates conciliation of Lorraine, and their policy had accordingly changed towards him. His visit to Rome (September 18) set a seal to the attempt to come to terms with him. But there was now arising between the Spanish and the French a jealousy which was illustrated by an incident of St. Peter's Day. At Mass a special chair was placed for De Luna, in obedience to the Pope's command, to give him an equality with the French representative. Lorraine and the French threatened withdrawal, and even a renunciation of obedience to Pope Pius. After much consultation, the incident was closed, but it had caused much heartburning, and left some behind it. It was partly a sequel to this that the Spanish Court once more raised the question of the initiative about subjects, proposing to throw it open to the Council at large, and even (which would have been an innovation) to the ambassadors (September 1563). But all desired the end, and preparations for the next session went on, although the Count de Luna pressed for schedules of reform being prepared by the bishops of each nation and then discussed. In the end, a French, a Spanish and an Italian committee were appointed to digest the business, with a view to an early ending.

Before the end of the Council, Massarelli, the invaluable secretary of the early sessions, returned to his old office

[margin note: Jealousies arising.]

(November 1563): he had previously gone to Trent (April 1551) to arrange for the resumption of the sessions. For the early sessions we owe him a great debt because of his Diary: his information is invaluable. It is hard to say how much such an assembly owes to a competent secretary, and such he most certainly was.

The details of marriage, rather than the general principles, led to debate. Broadly speaking, the original and correct view of the Church was to regard the union of man and woman as a natural sacrament, sanctified by, and Marriage. corresponding to, the union of Christ and His Church. Therefore the Church blessed it, and grouped around it ceremonies which not only recognised its holiness but emphasised it before the world. From its original sacredness, and from Christ's words, there resulted its inviolability, except for some previous obstacle to marriage between the parties. And, in spite of an increasing tendency to base the sacredness of marriage upon the Church's blessing Re-marriage on it rather than upon its own sacramental force, after the sacredness of marriage had, as a rule, been well divorce. taught, and firmly maintained, by the medieval Church. The Lutherans and other Protestants had, however, lowered the conception of marriage, and proposals to allow remarriage after a divorce following adultery, and to allow desertion or crime to annul marriage, had found favour with them. But with one exception the Council had no wish even to discuss anything of this kind. That exception was when some of the Venetian bishops would have liked to allow remarriage to a man divorcing an adulterous wife. In the Eastern lands subject to Venice this was done by dispensation from the Eastern Church, and they therefore wished not to condemn the practice. To meet their views, merely those who condemned the Church for her stricter view were anathematised, not those who only differed from her; at the same time the permanency of marriage even in this case was reasserted as the Church's view when the assertion was of peculiar value. The Council did much for the world in this one respect alone and at a time when it was badly needed.

But while the general principles were clear, the machinery of the details of matrimony was complicated, and much in need of reform. The gradual extension of the doctrine of affinities, natural, spiritual (by the relation of sponsorship), and irregular through sinful connections, had complicated Church law; the jurisdiction of Church Courts, and the issue of dispensations, were both at their worst in matrimonial causes. There were further national differences in use, such as the English steady denial of the legitimatisation of children by their parents' subsequent marriage, only lately retracted, and the French denial of validity to clandestine marriages. The discussions were therefore of necessity long, while the matter was of the utmost importance, social and religious, and especially so in an age of growing licence and lessened restraint. So keen was the discussion, and so desirable was it to get a perfectly free opinion, that all non-voters were excluded from the final congregation (November 10).

The much-prolonged debate from July to September caused an adjournment of the session from September 16 to November 11, the first General Congregation on Marriage being held on September 7. The majority thought that marriage, even when not blessed by a priest, was a sacrament, and that possibly in annulling a marriage, clandestine or irregular from lack of consent, the essence of the sacrament might be interfered with. It thus became with some of the Fathers a matter of faith; and Hosius, who held strong opinions of this kind, would not attend the session itself.

Marriage was declared a sacrament, instituted by Christ Himself and not by men, and therefore conferring grace; polygamy, dissolution of marriage by heresy, incompatibility, or desertion were condemned. Not only the Levitical degrees of consanguinity and affinity, but others set up by the Church are valid, and from some of the Levitical prohibitions the Church can dispense. The Church can establish impediments to marriage; matrimony contracted, but not consummated, can be dissolved by one party making a profession of religion (*i.e.*, taking vows). The Church

Session XXIV, 11 Nov., 1563. Holy matrimony. Twelve Canons. Ten Chapters.

had not erred in declaring that the bond of matrimony cannot
be dissolved by adultery; the innocent party cannot remarry,
to do which is adultery. The Church can, for many causes,
decree separation *a mensa et thoro* (sometimes loosely called
divortium). Clerks who have vowed chastity cannot marry,
and the feeling of a lack of the gift of chastity (which God is
able to give) does not justify the breach of vows. The state of
virginity, or celibacy, is to be preferred before that of marriage;
prohibition of marriage at certain seasons, and the benediction
and other ceremonies used by the Church in marriage, are not
superstitions. Matrimonial causes belong to ecclesiastical judges.
These affirmations were made by Canons anathematising
those who maintained opposite opinions.

The Decree of Reformation of Marriage declared the
Church's dislike of clandestine marriages, and of those made
without the leave of parents, although such marriages are valid
until declared otherwise by the Church; validity does not depend upon parental consent; as a safeguard, triple publication
of banns and marriage by the parish priest before witnesses
and in the face of the Church are decreed. Marriage celebrated
otherwise was void, and the priest punishable: it must be
celebrated by the parish priest or his deputy; any other priest
celebrating a marriage is *ipso facto* suspended; a register of
marriages is to be kept; confession and reception of the Holy
Eucharist are to precede marriage. Pious provincial customs
other than these are to be kept also. This decree was to be
explained carefully, and published in every parish, and to
come into force thirty days after publication. Spiritual affinity
was restricted by the regulation that one, or at the most two,
of each sex should receive the infant from the baptism (*i.e.*, as
sponsor); spiritual affinity was to exist between them, the
priest baptising, the baptised, and the parents of the baptised;
the names of these godparents were to be registered; so, too,
in confirmation, substituting the sponsor there for the sponsor
in baptism. The impediment of public honesty was restrained.
Affinity arising from fornication was confined to the first and
second degree. Marriage within the prohibited degree, unless
through ignorance, was to lead to separation, without any

hope of dispensation. Dispensations for marriages were to be given rarely, for good cause only and gratuitously; they should be granted within the second degree in the case of great princes only, and for a public cause. Marriage was prohibited from Advent to Epiphany, and from Ash Wednesday to Low Sunday.

In addition to previous Decrees, the creation of bishops was further regulated. Vacancies were to be the subject of prayer.

Those who appointed were to remember their responsibilities and choose suitable men satisfying the Canons. Each province in its synod was to prescribe suitable forms of scrutiny, to be approved by the Pope. When the scrutiny was satisfied, the result in a document should be sent to the Pope, who should then confirm. All the documents should be examined by a cardinal, with three other cardinals as assessors. They should report to the Consistory, declaring their conscientious belief. In the next Consistory (unless the Pope should regulate otherwise) the sentence of appointment should issue. Like regulations were made for the College of Cardinals, who were to be chosen out of all the nations of Christendom. Finally, his solemn responsibility in these appointments was urged upon the Pope. It should be noted that these Decrees as to the confirmation of bishops were made more precise by Gregory XIII (1591) and Urban VIII (1627). Before 1563 the whole process had taken place in Rome. The Pope usually set in charge of it one of the cardinals—for choice the Protector in the Sacred College of the nation concerned. He or his secretary received the evidence—information from persons then in Rome for the purpose or by coincidence—and presented the result (often embodying details as to situation and condition of the Church) to the Consistory, which, as a rule, immediately passed the confirmation. But after 1563 an investigation was made on the spot by a Papal commissary, in most cases the nuncio to the nation. A protocol drawn up by him and forwarded to Rome was then considered by a committee of cardinals, who brought it and their recommendation before the Consistory. The new process was less of a formality,

Reformation. Twenty-one Chapters.

Election of bishops and their confirmation.

and while more satisfactory on the local side, greatly strengthened the control of the Papacy. The improvement in bishops
of this new type is illustrated well by the case of some German
dioceses.

Provincial synods were to meet every three years, diocesan
every year. Bishops not subject to a Metropolitan were to
attend some neighbouring synod. All bishops were   Duties of
to make yearly visitations (even exempt churches   bishops.
were to be visited). In the larger dioceses two years were
allowed for the circuit. All inferior visitors were to be regular,
and report to the bishop. Too great luxury and pomp in
visitations were forbidden, and their true purpose was emphasised. Fees for visitations were limited to food that was
needed, or its equivalent. No appeal or delay was to suspend
Decrees for correction made by visitors. No honorary titles or
offices, Papal or royal, were to withdraw their holders from
episcopal control. Bishops were to preach in their own churches
themselves or by deputies; in parish churches, the parish priests
or persons chosen. Sermons were to be given on all Sundays
and festivals, and in Advent and Lent daily, or every other day
at least. Children were to be instructed at least on all Lord's
Days and festivals. Grave causes against bishops were to go
before the Pope, others before provincial councils. Cases
reserved for absolution by a bishop were defined. Bishops and
priests were to explain the sacraments in the vernacular, if need
be, and in a form to be prescribed in a catechism. A public
penance was to be laid on public sinners, and a suitable Penitentiary, with a prebend annexed to his office, should be
appointed for confessions in all cathedrals. Suitable men were
to be chosen for canons and archdeacons. Anyone appointed
to a benefice was within two months to make a profession of
faith in the presence of the bishop or of his official, and swear
obedience to the Roman Church. Holders of cathedral offices
were also to do the same in chapter. Regulations were made to
shut out unordained, too young, or absentee holders of
cathedral offices, and the behaviour of chapters was regulated.
If convenient, half of the cathedral offices were to be held by
doctors, masters, or licentiates in theology or law. Provision

was made for the union of parishes where it was desirable. No pensions or reservations were to be fixed on churches with less than a certain limit of endowment, and no charges on stipends except for pious uses. The previous regulations against pluralities were repeated. The nomination and institution of parish priests were regulated, and those appointed had to satisfy selected examiners. Mandates *de providendo* (provisions) were forbidden even where cardinals were to benefit. Expectatives (grants in expectation) were forbidden, and also mental reservations (those which specified no name). All ecclesiastical cases, except those which by Canon or evocation went before the Pope, were to go first before the Ordinary, and to be decided within two years. Matrimonial and criminal cases were not left to archdeacons and lower judges, but reserved for bishops. Legates were not to interfere with episcopal justice or even proceed in cases without episcopal cognisance. Other regulations improved procedure. Certain words (viz., "on the proposition of the Legates and presidents") were not to be understood as changing the routine of business in General Councils. (This was the settlement of the much-debated phrase.)

Much discussion had arisen upon the reformation of princes. The Middle Ages had such a vivid conception of the Church as an entity—the division between spiritual and temporal was so much more a division between functions than between the men who exercised them —that the medieval theory of Church and State was very different from the modern. The State had to attend to religion; the King had to act for the Church; although neither the State nor the King could perform spiritual functions. The Church had allowed the State to do much in matters we should now call purely ecclesiastical. It had expected the State to give it a large and indefinite amount of help in cases of heresy (as in the anti-Lollard laws), or those where force was needed. The Middle Ages could quite well see a bishop acting spiritually in one of his capacities and acting temporally in another; he had, as it were, a double personality. The monarch in a State could similarly act in his civil and

The Reformation of princes.

Medieval thought.

in his religious capacities. There was here what some modern
critics would call a confusion, and it seems easier to us to
divide society into sharply defined classes of spiritual men and
temporal men. Church and State become at the same time
opposed corporations instead of different aspects of the same
thing. Exemptions of clerks from secular jurisdiction, interference of princes in religious and ecclesiastical matters, were
natural but opposed results of the medieval theory. To deal
properly with the whole matter of Church and State there
would have been needed a theory clearly thought out and an
adequate review of existing facts, for medieval institutions and
growths needed some enlargement and some adaptation. But,
on the one hand, the bishops at Trent were urgent for a reform
of secular princes—and this meant to them much interference
with the jurisdiction princes exercised and rights that they had
long enjoyed; on the other hand, political interests made it a
very difficult matter to curtail the privileges of princes. The
Conciliar theories of the fifteenth century had expressed in the
ecclesiastical sphere the sovereignty of the people. The growth
of the Papal monarchy had, on the other hand, negatived that
sovereignty in the same sphere. There had seemed nothing
strange a century and a half before in a Council all but solely
composed of ecclesiastics legislating for Christendom. But
now, as soon as the Council undertook the reform of princes,
they were told it was wrong for them to legislate for the laity.
The growth of national sovereignty was one characteristic of
the day, and it answered with something of defiance to the
other theories of the Papal monarchy and of Conciliar power.

In July the whole question of reform had been discussed
with the representatives of the three nations, and especially the
French and the Imperialists. All three were very *Course of*
strong upon the reform of the College of Cardinals. *the nego-*
Forty-two Chapters on Reformation were pro- *tiations.*
posed, but, by omitting six, were reduced to thirty-six. Those
omitted concerned tithes, lessening the number of Masses, excommunication, the prohibition to the clergy of mingling in
secular matters, the control of the revenue of vacant benefices,
and impediments to reform caused by secular persons. The last

of these was the celebrated Reformation of Princes. These thirty-six Decrees were considered (August 21), and reduced to twenty, to which a twenty-first, explaining the "proposal" clause (about the Legates' initiative), was added. The Emperor and Philip of Spain protested against the Decrees about the temporal power. The King of France (with many causes of complaint, and now not well served by the Cardinal and his bishops, as instanced by their not supporting in the debates the French demand to allow marriage of priests) ordered his ambassadors to protest, and if their protest were useless, to withdraw: so they withdrew (September). De Luna had added to the embarrassment by bringing up the question of the "proposal" clause. On the other hand, one hundred bishops signed an engagement to stand aloof from the Council if this reform of princes were left aside. But when the Cardinal of Lorraine came back from Rome (November 5), the Pope bade the Legates close the Council speedily, pass the Decree on clandestine marriage as best they could, and deal firmly with difficulties. As to the reformation of princes and jurisdiction over ecclesiastics, they were to renew the ancient Canons and add no anathema. If difficulties arose upon other articles, they were to refer to him, and for the rest they were to work with the Cardinal, who knew his mind. The previous Decrees were to be confirmed; the continuity of the Council throughout all its sessions declared; the Papal power was not to be touched: the Council was to ask for Papal confirmation of its Decrees; the Fathers were to sign the Decrees, and the ambassadors to do the same for their masters. When the twenty-one clauses had been disposed of in September, the remainder came up for discussion, so that questions arising out of the Decrees afterwards passed in Session XXV were now causing irritation before Session XXIV.

This Chapter proposed for the reform of princes asserted that clerks were not to be judged save by ecclesiastics; all cases touching the Church were to go before ecclesiastical judges; temporal judges were not to sit upon ecclesiastical cases, and clerks admitting their jurisdiction were subject to suspension; temporal authorities were not to command an ecclesiastical judge either to withdraw excommunication or to suspend judgment; emperors and princes were not to make decrees for ecclesiastical persons or cases, but were to lend their help to ecclesiastical courts; the jurisdiction of ecclesiastical judges was not to be disturbed; subjects of ecclesiastics were not to be called before secular judges in temporal cases. Princes were not to promise benefices by brief or importune bishops and chapters for their bestowal. They were not to seize the fruits of vacant benefices or appoint to them vicars or stewards. They were not to force payment of taxes upon Church property or the private property of ecclesiastics, except where ancient custom in the case of war against infidels justified their doing so. They were not to touch the goods of communities or of the Church. Proclamations and edicts of Church courts—especially those from Rome— were to be published at once, and without waiting for a *Placet* from the State. The right of claiming hospitality from monasteries was taken away from princes and magistrates. Any realm or province claiming exemption from these rules was to enter the claim within a year, so that it might receive Papal confirmation; otherwise the claim was bad. By an addition to the clauses, all previous Decrees upon clerical exemptions were renewed.

Chapter on Reformation of Princes.

This lengthy and exhaustive Chapter—represented in the result by Chapter XX in Session XXV, which merely recommended clerical communities and the rights of the Church to the care of princes and renewed all previous Canons—would have made permanent some of the worst medieval defects, and would have been as ruinous to the Church as to the State. It was small wonder it caused opposition, and it was happy for the Church that it all but disappeared.

But there were minor difficulties to be dealt with. The Spanish bishops, already in opposition to the Legates on many points, objected strongly to the manipulation of the Chapter on Reform by the deputation, composed mainly of Italians. They further wished to see less independence given to cathedral chapters (Chapter VI, Session XXV, was also under consideration now), and the provision by which

The Inquisition.

criminal charges against bishops were to be dealt with at Rome seemed to strike a blow at the Spanish Inquisition. The Portuguese bishops raised a like objection, and it was felt even more strongly by the monarchs of the countries. About this time the rumours of the intended introduction of the Inquisition into Milan caused great anger among the Italian bishops, who feared for their own jurisdiction. Hence the bitterness between Spanish and Italian, due to many causes, intensified the Italian opposition, fostered by letters from officials at Rome, on the question of reform. But the Legates showed a great desire to come to terms, and Visconti, Bishop of Ventimiglia, left Rome as Papal Ambassador to Spain (end of October). After many attempts at drafting, a satisfactory wording of the Chapter on the initiative of the Legates was happily reached. The Legates could not risk having Spain also against them, as now Du Ferrier, along with some bishops, had withdrawn to Venice soon after his protest (September 22). The Pope's action, indeed, was now very hostile to France. The condemnation of the Queen Jeanne of Navarres (October 22) for heresy and the deprivation by the Pope of the six French bishops previously (April 7) cited to Rome had increased the tension between the Curia and France. All the diplomacy of Lorraine was needed, and he found it well to come back by way of Venice so as to procure Du Ferrier's return to Trent. In this, however, he failed. (It may be noted that another ambassador, De Luna, was never able to leave Trent, for he died there (December 18) of an illness ascribed to the evil effects of fruit and bad water.) Some of these differences were seen on the day of session itself. The Bishops of Naples and Lombardy expressed their fears about the Inquisition, and the Cardinal of Lorraine, by a formal protest at variance with his secret professions, saved the ancient rights of the French Crown and Monarchy. But, as a matter of fact, the Gallican liberties had often been a euphemism for royal control. It was more significant that he also added that he received these reforms as part of a more general scheme. In many respects such an expectation was vain. It seemed, for instance, that, under Session XXIV, Chapter

XIV, annates would disappear, but they were still levied by right of the Papal privilege under Session XXV, Chapter XXI.

Other incidents at that time made it only natural that bishops should feel their position uneasy. Bartolomé de Carranza (born 1503) had been a zealous and prominent Dominican at Valladolid (where he was professor), in England under Mary, and in Flanders. He had been Imperial Theologian (1546–7 and 1551–2) at Trent, and, after twice refusing sees, became in 1557 Archbishop of Toledo, in which dignity Paul IV readily confirmed him. In this office he was zealous and able, and gave the last rites to Charles V. The publication of a catechism at Antwerp in 1558 brought him under notice (August 1559) by the Inquisition, the rival Dominican, Melchior Cano, and Ferdinand de Valdez, Archbishop of Seville and Grand Inquisitor, already having enmities against him. His trial lasted two years, and after the prisoner's condemnation a difference arose between the Conciliar committee for the Index and the Spanish Inquisition. His theology was certainly Erasmian, and was held Lutheran. Tried by the Spanish standard, it was heterodox in 141 propositions; to the Fathers at Trent it seemed vague but harmless. A Papal Bull had authorised his seizure; but the Archbishop appealed to the Pope. The Fathers at Trent decided against the Inquisition's judgment, and asked Pius IV to interpose. Philip II resisted this interference, and the case went on until Pius V, under threat of an interdict (December 1566), forced the King to send the Archbishop to Rome. Under Gregory XIII judgment was at last given: Carranza was to abjure sixteen articles, perform certain penances, and remain in an honourable captivity, while his catechism was forbidden (14 April, 1576). Three weeks later he died, recanting his errors and receiving Papal absolution. That he had not always conducted himself cautiously might be true, but he suffered mainly because he carried opinions on justification, at one time common, into a day when they became both uncommon and suspected.

The Patriarch of Venice had also brought himself under suspicion, but his trial by a commission of twenty-five bishops led to an acquittal (1563). He too was accused of Lutheran and

Calvinistic heresy, but he, too, like Carranza, had brought upon himself much ill-will by his strict enforcement of clerical discipline.

There were thus difficulties enough without debating the detailed Reformation of Princes. It had been feared already that some Decrees of Session XXII on last wills and appointments might lead to trouble with the princes, and these fresh topics did more. There was great activity in private congregations, and much diplomacy centring around the Cardinal of Lorraine. In the end, two-thirds of the Fathers approved of the Decrees for Session XXIV, but some wished to leave disputed matters to the Pope. But this was done, not merely in the interest of any theory or doctrine of his Primacy, but rather as a detail of organisation and as a means of escaping the give-and-take and the compromise of a popular assembly. There were also those who strove, not from any conscious prejudice, but from a belief in their position, to preserve their privileges. Some bishops, for instance, sought to restrain their Metropolitans, and they were, indeed, now freed from the onerous duty of visiting their superior Metropolitans once a year. There were also regulars who objected to the power over them given to bishops—which was something of an innovation, though one greatly needed. But everything was now hurrying to an end. The theologians had already been considering indulgences and vows, although an attempt to encourage brevity by demanding their views in writing had merely resulted in the production of lengthy documents. The next session was fixed for December 9, or earlier if possible.

The Pope was greatly pleased at what had been done, and urged equal speed again. The leading cardinals and prelates—twenty-five in number—met and digested the business that remained. The subjects of Purgatory, Invocation of saints, and the use of Images needed little fresh Conciliar explanation; but an utterance of the Sorbonne upon Images presented by the Cardinal of Lorraine was highly praised. On November 15 the General Congregation began, and the unanimity now seen contrasted greatly with the differences before the last session.

Preparations for the close of the Council.

On an urgent representation by Lorraine that coadjutor bishops were of great service in France, especially in monasteries (their existence made easy the abuse of appointing merely nominal abbots, sometimes even laymen), their office was not abolished; but their appointment was to be only for grave cause; such could, unhappily, often be alleged as an excuse. Among the additions made to the original draft were those on the manner of episcopal life, the possession of tithes by laymen, the use of excommunication, and the provision of a record office in each diocese. On reformation of regulars twenty-two Chapters were prepared, and their discussion only lasted four days. By December 2 everything excepting a Decree upon Indulgence was ready, and it was suggested that this difficult and contested subject had better be left out. The news of the Pope's illness that came from Rome made everyone wish to close, and De Luna's intrigues for postponement became useless. Some thought the Chapter on secular princes insufficient, but the insufficiency was intentional. Most of the business was agreed to at the session upon December 3, but an adjournment was made to the next day for everything to be included. The Legates, anxious to please, and conscious that the subject merited a decision, drafted in the interval a Decree upon Indulgence; and this again passed with slight change. It had contained a clause forbidding the payment of any money for the procuring of an indulgence; but the Spaniards pointed out that this would apply to the Spanish Cruzada—a form of indulgence for Spain the proceeds of which, gained by the compulsory purchase of copies of the Bull, went to the King. Although some twenty bishops wished to keep the words, they were therefore struck out. The zeal of princes for reform did not go very deep, and both France and Spain had been lately seeking from the Curia leave to alienate or tax ecclesiastical revenues at the moment of their sharpest differences with it.

Session XXV, December 3-4.

The Decree on Purgatory referred to the previous Decrees of Sessions VI and XXII affirming the existence of Purgatory, wherein souls are helped by prayer of the faithful, especially by the Mass. This doctrine was to be explained to congregations, but more subtle questions or uncertain points were to be left aside. Anything savouring of filthy lucre was to be prohibited. All works of piety for the faithful dead were to be duly and devoutly rendered. The Intercession and Invocation of Saints, the honour paid to relics, and the use of Images were also to be expounded. Saints were to be invoked and their aid asked in gaining benefits from God through Christ, the only Redeemer. The relics, a source of benefit to men, were to be honoured. Images are to be retained (specially in churches) and honoured, not as having any virtue or divinity in themselves, or to be invoked, but because honour paid to them is referred to their prototypes. Paintings and other representations instruct people, and miracles also attest their value. All abuses as to Images, by which false doctrine could be taught, the Council wished abolished. Unlettered people were to be taught that they could not represent the Divinity. All superstitions, all filthy lucre, in the Invocation of Saints, relics, and Images, were to be abolished. A too sensual beauty in works of art and revelling or drunkenness in celebrating Saints' days were to be avoided. To gain these ends bishops were to use diligence. No unusual image is to be placed, no miracle acknowledged or relic recognised without episcopal leave, and assessors might be called in by the bishop in deciding such matters. If questions arise or an abuse has to be ended, the bishop shall await a provincial council. Nothing new or unusual in the Church shall even then be done without consulting the Pope. It may be noted that in these two Decrees signs of hasty drafting are to be found, not only in their inconclusiveness (strangely at contrast with some earlier Decrees), but also in the mingling of condemnations of erroneous views with enunciation of those affirmed as true. This method was not so clear as that of separating the views condemned in Canons.

Opinions will always differ as to the state of monasteries before the Reformation. The diversities of countries, orders, and local influences should be allowed for, and when that is done generalisations are obviously dangerous. Monastic

Purgatory.

Invocation of Saints.

Orders, like everything else, need both reorganisation from time to time and a constant renewal of their early enthusiasm. In many cases the needs they had once satisfied had either disappeared or changed their shape, and so the Orders lacked their former stimulus. But it was admitted—and no one had put the case more strongly than had monastic reformers, and nowhere was it stated more vigorously than at Trent—that reform was needed: not the reform the German princes spoke of, which was merely secularisation or diversion of funds, but a reform based upon spiritual objects and discipline of life. It was now decreed that all regulars were to obey their Rule strictly. Superiors, in chapters and by visitations were to see to this. (This had been done by episcopal visitation before.) Individual monks were restrained in their possession of property. The number of inmates of a monastic house was to depend on its income, and no new houses were to be formed without the leave of the diocesan bishop. Closure was to be strictly enforced, and elections of superiors were to be by secret voting. All monasteries directly under the Pope must within a year form themselves into congregations with suitable statutes. If they did not carry out this Decree, the Metropolitan was to see to it. The control of bishops over exempt nunneries, monastic patronage parishes, and other details, was made stringent. Episcopal censures, interdicts, and feasts were to be published and observed in their churches by regulars. All those disputes about precedence which so often caused scandal were to be settled by the bishop. No man or woman was to make profession under the age of sixteen and before a year's probation, and renunciations of property were carefully guarded against abuse. Girls above twelve wishing to take the habit were to be questioned then by the ordinary and before making their profession, and left free from coercion. Since abuses sprang from maladministration in monasteries (most of the evils, we may note, could really be traced to this), the Council trusted that the Pope would make it his care to see that over those monasteries held *in commendam* there should be appointed regulars of the same order and suitable

Reforma-tion of Regulars. Twenty-two Chapters.

for their task. All these Decrees were to be carried into effect at once.

Considering the disorder into which monastic life had fallen through the numbers breaking their vows, the above scheme was a capable and conscientious effort at reform. It greatly enlarged the powers of bishops and lessened the evils of exemption. So far as legislation could, it restored discipline and the observance of rules. Some of the regulations, such as that which made the numbers of inmates in the poorer houses depend upon their revenue, struck at real evils, for it was in the smaller houses that evils mainly flourished. Others, such as those for visitation and administration, were meant to prevent the financial disorder and the embezzlement which had ruined so many houses. But these Decrees, however admirable and far-reaching, needed a high ideal on the part of those administering them and of those governed. It was of the utmost importance, therefore, that they were issued just when the ideals of episcopal care and spiritual life (as seen in the widespread monastic revivals) were being greatly raised. The Decrees for reformation strengthened the hands of those who were raising these ideals. They, in their turn, prevented these Decrees becoming what other Decrees, as well meant if not so thoroughgoing, had often become—a dead letter. These Decrees were not in themselves a monastic revival, but they reflected the spirit of a revival which had already begun.

There were many things in the life of the Secular clergy, too, that had not yet been reformed; and these were next dealt with.

Further reformation of seculars and chapters. Cardinals, bishops, and all holding benefices were to shun nepotism and live simply, remembering that their lives are a sermon. In the next provincial synods everywhere all the Conciliar Decrees were to be received, obedience to the Pontiff to be professed, and all heresies named in the Canons anathematised. In future all bishops were to do the same in their first provincial synod. All beneficed clerks and those with University charges were to take oaths to these Decrees. Universities were to be corrected and reformed by the visitors, and the Pope would take care this was done for Universities under him. Excommunica tions were to be sparingly used, and, when meant as enforcements of admonitions, by bishops only; in criminal cases only after two monitions and public notice; interdicts also were only to be a last resort. In the case of churches where the number of Masses to be said is excessive, the Bishop or General should regulate as he thought fit, provided all the departed founders be commemorated. All conditions or obligations attached to all benefices or prebends should be observed. The procedure of episcopal visitations in exempted chapters was regulated. No access or regress (rights of accession after a vacancy and resumption after a term of years) should apply to benefices. Coadjutor bishops or abbots should only be appointed by leave of the Pope. Hospitality was enjoined upon all holders of benefices, and the administration of hospitals was further regulated. Titles to patronage must be proved; privileges not proved were abrogated except when assigned to cathedrals, kings, and Universities. Unfit persons presented by the patron might be rejected by the bishop; endowments were guarded against patrons. Synods were to appoint persons from whom the Pope should select judges to try local cases. All judges were exhorted to decide cases speedily. All farmings out and leases of ecclesiastical offices were prohibited. Tithes should be properly paid under pain of excommunication. The procedure against clerks who kept concubines was regulated: a fine of a third part of their revenue, and, after two admonitions, deprivation was to be imposed by the bishop. Bishops offending in this way and not heeding the admonitions of the Provincial were *ipso facto* suspended, and left to be punished by the Pope. Illegitimate sons of clerks were excluded from benefices or churches connected with their fathers. Bishops were not to be servile before kings and nobles, but to maintain their office. Canons were to be strictly kept, and dispensation from them given only for fit cause. Duelling was prohibited; those involved in it should be excommunicated. The immunities and all rights of the Church were recommended to all secular princes, to be observed by them, their subjects, and officials. All ancient Canons in favour of ecclesiastics and the liberty of the Church and against its violators were renewed. And, lastly, all things decreed in the Council for reformation under Paul III, Julius III, and Pius IV were to be so understood as not to touch the authority of the Apostolic See. This last was a reservation which covered much ground and had a wide effect.

It should be noted that some of these Decrees formed part of the original forty-two, discussed in Sessions XXIV and XXV: some of them partly repeated, partly enlarged previous Decrees. A tightening of ecclesiastical authority in the Pope and in the bishop marks many of them. Some, like that against duelling and that for clerical immunities, could not well be enforced without the help of the temporal power; but here the Council, like earlier assemblies, claimed to be legislating for Christendom. Not only, however, were there lands where its authority was not regarded, but the temporal power everywhere was taking up a new position with regard to the Church's commands. It was otherwise, however, with the Decrees dealing with persons or matters solely within the ecclesiastical sphere. Here, even if the Decrees, such as those against concubinary priests and those enforcing the Canons, only repeated medieval Decrees, it was certain that they would be now more strictly kept; public opinion had some weight. The Council, in spite of difficulties, had tried to give coherence to the Church organisation. It had benefited by the spectacle of religious organisations, especially the Calvinistic, which had a logical order and a certain effect. Henceforth the spirit of the Spanish Church and its ideal of strictness were to be those of the whole Roman obedience. But many allowances had to be made for local variations and customs. The exception by which the Papal authority, capable of great uses, and equally of great abuses, was left untouched was so large that the working of the Tridentine scheme could not be expected to equal its ideal. But there was hardly a blemish of ecclesiastical life that was not dealt with. It remained a fair attempt at a large legislation.

Strangely enough, the subject of Indulgences, upon which much had been said and written inside and outside the Council, remained to be somewhat hastily dealt with. Morone would have left it out altogether as too difficult. Their use was defined as ancient, and granted by Christ; Decree on Indulgence. as most salutary for Christians, and approved by Councils; but moderation was to be observed in granting them. Desiring to correct the abuses which had led heretics to blaspheme, the Council abolished all evil gains for obtaining them—a prolific cause of abuse. As to all other abuses, proceeding from superstition, ignorance, irreverence, or other cause, all bishops were to collect them and report them in the first provincial synod. After review there they were to be reported to the Pope, so that he might ordain suitably. The gift of indulgence would thus be piously and incorruptly dispensed to all the faithful.

Chapter IX of Session XXI had dealt with the questers and regulated the publication of indulgences: the present Decree added somewhat. The doctrine was left as it had been before, and so was still indeterminate upon some issues. With the disappearance of the questers the worst abuses went, but the machinery of the last Decree was cumbrous, however excellent its intentions were. It laid a heavy burden upon the Pope, which it might have been better to leave upon the diocesan bishop, but to do this was in accord with the tendency of Papal centralisation. The working of the Decree had to be left for future history to test; and even then there were many causes at work other than the Decree likely to alter, not the doctrine, but the practice. The doctrine remained as before. It was to be taken along with the Decree on Purgatory in the same session, Canon VI, Session VI, and Chapter II, Session XXII (on the Sacrifice of the Mass as a propitiation). The existence of a purgatory, penal in its nature, during their sojourn in which souls are helped by means of prayer (*per modum suffragii*), and mostly by the Mass, was asserted: the Catechism stated it more definitely. But the continued issue of indulgences, even when freed from the worst abuses, left the demands of reformers still unsatisfied. The more primitive view, restricting the indulgence to the temporal penalty imposed by the Church, was supplemented by the later medieval view (due rather to specula-

tion supporting practice) extending it to the guilt carried into
the other world. Nothing but a distinction clearly made between the temporal penalty (*poena*) and the eternal guilt (*culpa*)
would have sufficed, and this distinction was not drawn. A
practice of general Western growth (for such indulgences were)
was therefore left existing, but under careful supervision, and
the doctrine upon which it was based was left broad enough
to protect the practice. Further niceties were put aside and discouraged. The Council avoided condemning some of its supporters who had been unwise, but the views of its critics did
not here meet with the anathemas they encountered in other
fields of theology. Those who thought the Decree on Purgatory insufficient had right on their side. Another point—the
choice of meats—upon which the Reformation at Zürich had
begun, and which had been raised in requests to the Council
itself, was also now dealt with. All Church observances were
recommended to the faithful, especially those tending to
mortification (as the choice of meats and fasts) and those tending
to piety (as festivals). As the Index was all but ready, and could
not now be judged, the work of the Commission was (as
already noted) to be laid before the Pope, and by him to be
looked over and published. The same was to be done with
the Catechism and the Missal and Breviary. No act of the
Council and no assignment of places in it was to create prejudice among ambassadors or ecclesiastics for the future. And
lastly, it was decreed that as through the malice of heretics all
parts of the faith had been defiled, the Council had therefore
made it its chief care to condemn the heresies of the day and
deliver the Catholic doctrine. So many bishops could not have
been absent from their flocks so long without hurt, and there
was no chance that the heretics so oft invited would come
later. Therefore the Council urged all princes to guard its
decrees against the heretics and procure their observance; but
as difficulties of reception or explanation might arise from its
decrees, the Council trusted the Pope would meet these needs
by calling to his help assessors, specially from provinces where
difficulties have arisen, or by a Council, or some other
way.

At the close of the Council all the Decrees from the first were read, and thus the question of its continued existence was settled. The Fathers were then asked if they wished to end the "Sacred Œcumenical Synod" and to ask confirmation from the Pope for all and singular the things decreed. The "Placet"—which the Archbishop of Granada alone refused—was possibly as significant as anything done by the Council, and closed for effective purposes a controversy of 200 years upon the relations of Council and Pope. Acclamations after the Oriental model followed, composed and led by the Cardinal of Lorraine—to the memory of the departed and the welfare of the living among the popes, emperors, kings, legates, and prelates concerned in the Council; to the Council, its Faith and its Decrees; to the anathematising of all heretics. All those present, including proctors of absent prelates, then subscribed the proceedings, as they had been enjoined to do under pain of excommunication—four legates, two cardinals, three patriarchs, twenty-five archbishops, 168 bishops, seven abbots, thirty-nine proctors of absent bishops, and seven generals. But the ambassadors did not sign as wished, for De Luna refused without the leave of his King, and Lorraine's acceptance for France had no force. Roughly speaking, among those present the Italians were in the later sessions six times as numerous as any other nation. Some bishops, especially German and French, had left, and when the end came there was a sense of relief and gladness. The Pope ordered a thanksgiving, which was celebrated on December 15. It is no strange thing in a large assembly for contentions to increase and appear insuperable. Then suddenly the mood changes, and in a short space, sometimes with a loss of what is important, all the business is settled amid general agreement and with a sense of relief. It had been so here.

There were some at the Curia who would have been glad to deny or defer the confirmation given. Pope Pius IV (whose illness had hastened the close, and whose recovery speedily followed it) expressed his genuine approval, and named Cardinals Morone and Simonetta, along with Cardinals

[Marginal note:] Session XXV, 3–4 December, 1563. Recitation of all the Decrees for Sessions I–XXV.

Carlo Borromeo, Cicala, and Vitelli, to discuss the means of carrying out the Decrees. Then (by the Bull *Benedictus Deus*, 26 January, 1654) he confirmed the proceedings in Consistory at the request of the legates and cardinals. The printing and circulating of the Decrees was ordered, and all difficulties or questions arising out of them were to be brought to his decision. Bishops were ordered to return to their hungering dioceses. A little later (2 August, 1564) a Congregation of the Council of Trent was appointed, composed of eight cardinals, and the work of this congregation was long and effective. It was reorganised and made permanent under Sixtus V (1588), but its work was, of course, confined to discipline.

In the sixteenth century it was not as it had been earlier: for a Council to decree was one thing; for the Decrees to be enforced was another. It was hardly to be expected that all the States would fall into line. Venice, though not always friendly to Rome, strangely enough led the way, and (although with a reservation in favour of its own customs) volunteered obedience. Portugal, with no restriction, and Spain with a detailed reservation of royal and ecclesiastical privilege, followed (2 July, 1564); then Sicily, Flanders, Naples (with reservations of the royal power); Poland (7 August, 1574) accepted them by the King, although the Diet refused them because the country had not been represented at the Council. The Swiss Catholic Cantons accepted them, and the Emperor did so for his hereditary lands, but not for the Empire. Germany was too much divided. The spiritual Electors did not, as the Emperor, favour the concession of the chalice. This concession, made by the Pope (16 April, 1564) at the discretion of German bishops, is dealt with later. But (1566) the Elector of Mayence declared, in spite of the Emperor and the Nuncio Commendone, that the Empire could not receive all the Decrees on discipline, although they accepted those on faith and worship. France too did not go so far as the Cardinal of Lorraine (whose influence was now smaller) had promised. The Decrees were never published there, and some of those on discipline were objected to. The Parliament of Paris gave its reasons in

Acceptance of the Decrees.

detail: some Decrees were against the rights of the Crown, others against the liberty of the Gallican Church. In 1565, when both Pope and Spain urged consent, it was again refused. The bishops, however, were allowed to carry out in their dioceses all Decrees not against the national laws or customs, and the Profession of Faith was generally made. Provincial synods at Rheims, Cambrai, Rouen, Tours, Bordeaux, Aix, Bourges, and Toulouse adopted the Decrees in substance. They were thus ecclesiastically binding upon the clergy. Clerical assemblies or their representatives sought to gain the enforcement of the Decrees by the State no less than seven times before 1596, but they were unsuccessful. This difference continued to be a grievance between the King, the Papacy, and the Gallican Church.

The reform of the Breviary, which the Pope had now to carry out, had long been needed. The older Roman office for seculars, dignified and well proportioned, had long been superseded by a more modern office, *The Breviary.* appearing in the twelfth and thirteenth centuries, marked by shorter lessons, often from inferior writers; by such a number of Saints' days as to obscure the seasons, and by a freer use of hymns. Under the Avignon Popes, and largely through Franciscan influence, this later Breviary was authorised. It needed simplification: it was overburdened with special offices for festivals, overshadowed by additional offices (the Little Office of Our Lady and the Office of the Dead); its rubrics were incomplete and unsystematic. It was this office that the cathedral chapters so widely neglected attending, and so often scamped when they did attend. The Council saw the need of reform, but others had seen it before. A higher standard of devotion among the secular clergy ought to be accompanied by a better book of devotion for them to use.

The Humanists had wished for reform of the Breviary, but mainly in the direction of more Ciceronian Latin and greater elegance. Leo X gave the task to Ferreri, *Ferreri.* Bishop of Guardia, who, as a beginning of it, *Quignon.* published (1525), with the approval of Clement VII, a hymnal, pretty in its conceits, classic in its language and mythology. After Ferreri's death Clement VII asked Cardinal Quignon (a Spanish Franciscan, General of his Order) to reform the Breviary after ancient models, purging it of prolixities, and making it better for use. The new Breviary appeared (1535), first in a tentative form, criticism of which was welcomed and freely given, and it passed through six editions within two years. The object aimed at now was edification and instruction rather than devotion—objects which are not, of course, inconsistent, but which are best reached by different means. The German Reformers were admittedly stronger than the Catholics in teaching and preaching. This was confessed by Contarini at Ratisbon in 1541, although thirty years later the balance shifted. Quignon's Breviary was, on the whole, more Protestant than Catholic in its tendencies of this kind. The strength of the Church lay more in its system than its men, and its system of prayer was what Quignon disregarded. With many devout composers since, he disregarded liturgic tradition. The versicles and responses were left out; and even antiphons (perhaps better spared) did not appear in the first edition. The Psalms were more uniformly distributed, on a plan which was edifying, but not ancient. The Lessons, three in number, were biblical, with the exception of one on Saints' days and days with a proper Mass. The changes on Saints' days were less marked. Edification was thus the object mainly sought rather than a formed and formal habit of devotion. It has been called "a Breviary for busy people," and, in spite of its defects, "a Shortened Service" ensured popularity at the cost of devotion. Paul III gave leave to many of the secular clergy to use it individually, and the Jesuits found it an easy form to recommend for daily prayer. Canisius, to induce negligent clerks to perform their private duty, gained leave for many to use it. It crept into public use even in some Spanish cathedrals; but the Sorbonne, traditional even where tradition was less excellent than it was here, condemned it. A dislike of it was expressed at Trent. John de Arze, a Spanish theologian, sent in a memoir (August 1551) in which its faults were shown and a plea made for liturgic tradition. Paul IV was like-minded, and (8 August, 1558) stopped further issue of the new Breviary. Thirty years before he had taught his Theatines to seek a reform of the Office (1529), and his ideal although different from that of Quignon, was earlier in its date. A revision dealing with the lessons and hymns was made, but not published, and afterwards the Spaniards (November 1562) asked Pius IV to take it as a basis of reform. Councils both in France and Germany had also sought for change. Pius therefore asked the Council to appoint a Congregation to consider it. When the Council closed and handed its unfinished tasks to him, he called Marini, Archbishop of Lanciano, Calinio, Archbishop of Zara, and Foscarari, Bishop of Modena—three of this Congregation—to Rome to complete with the help of others this great work. From the Bull (Pius V, *Quod a nobis*) which approved the final result, it seems that the Congregation studied MSS. of early Breviaries, struck out what was of foreign origin or of uncertain authority, but left the essence untouched. In the end the Ferial office was less eclipsed by that for special days, the additional offices were made more occasional, and the Pope went even beyond the rubric in making the use of some of them optional. The regular Psalms were less interfered with, and more of the Bible brought in. When this Breviary came out (July 1568), that of Quignon was prohibited. Local forms in use for over two hundred years were allowed; and thus Aquileia contrived and Paris struggled to keep their own local use. Gregory XIII, Sixtus V, who thought of an ampler revision (to cover the Missal), and Clement VIII added some festivals. The last, after seeking the advice of the leading Catholic theologians, asked Baronius to prepare a memoir on the subject. Learning of all kinds was now commoner, but a greater timidity of changes prevailed, and a Commission suggested by Baronius (1592) made but few and slight changes. Urban VIII appointed a congregation to purify the text, and a Commission of four Jesuits, with whom he worked himself, to amend the Hymnal (1629); but the result of the latter was not adopted everywhere. The form as left by this Pope has maintained itself since, although, notably in France, wishes have been expressed for further change. The importance of the work thus ended cannot be overstated. Some of the Reformation bodies which had thrown over tradition in forming new models of their own have since felt a need, even a longing, for more liturgic forms. It has been increasingly found that devotion is a matter of habit, and habit a thing that must be formed. The Roman Breviary, once in danger of excessive change, has handed down to less devout ages the discipline of more prayerful days, and its piety has appealed to pious souls beyond the limits of its own communion.

The revision of the Missal appeared later (1570). There
The   had been much variety in local use, as well as
Missal.   various texts; but there was less change made here
than in the Breviary. It too underwent revision under Clement VIII (1604) and Urban VIII (1634).

In nothing more than in Church music had the weakness of the fourteenth century and the frivolity of the Renaissance
Church   shown themselves. The most religious minds, and
Music.   not even only the most severe among them,
Palestrina.   thought that the music of the day could not be harmonised with religion, and the sternest Catholic reformers (here as elsewhere curiously akin to Puritans) talked of its total disuse. The Emperor Ferdinand, speaking for the Empire, had complained of the singing of the day. And at the same time Lutheranism, more open than Calvinism to the influence of outside helps to religion, was forming its simple congregational music. The Council spoke strongly upon the defects of Church music, and Pius IV appointed a Commission to consider the question. The musicians then, as often since, regarding the voice as secondary, declared that its distinctness and appropriate accompaniment could not be furnished artistically. But the Commission did not despair: Palestrina, at S. Maria Maggiore (formerly of the Julian Chapel at St. Peter's, but ejected by Paul IV as a married man), was asked to prepare a Mass at once religious and artistic. His well-known Missa Papae Marcelli prevented a divorce between the Church and music (1564). His *Improperia*—Passion music—has perhaps gained an even higher praise; and other composers, Italian

and Spanish and Belgian, carried on his traditions worthily, and rivalled the Flemish musicians of the fourteenth century. About 1600 Opera began to make Italy its home, and had not Church music been reinforced by the compositions of Palestrina's school, along with the Biblical oratorios founded by St. Philip Neri, even worse things might have been in store for it. Happily, the severer type of earlier days, into which life was breathed by the counter-reformation, lived on to show that ecclesiastical tradition and congregational singing could go together. National schools of music have since then given some rich gifts to religion and art alike, but they have been slow to learn the infinite possibilities of art inspired by devotion. It was his vision of these, as shown in his motto, *Domine, illumina oculos meos*, that made Palestrina able to preserve for us the tradition of sacred music.

The extent to which plain instruction had been given parochially in the Middle Ages is often understated. But the frequent inefficiency of the clergy and their neglect The of rules had made the provision ineffective. On the Catechism. other hand, the Catechisms—on a somewhat larger scale, although formed after medieval models—of the Protestant teachers had great effect, and were most efficient means of teaching a plain morality. The Catechism of Canisius is mentioned elsewhere, but the issue of the Roman Catechism, smaller in circulation, although more official, had been handed over by the Council to the Pope. Pius IV entrusted its preparation to the three prelates already at work upon the Breviary along with Fureiro, a Portuguese theologian. All these, except Calinio, were fellow-Dominicans of the Pope's, and the Catechism—whether a draft laid before the Council was used or not—favoured the Dominican views on Grace where they were opposed to the Jesuits, and thus met with prejudice. Carlo Borromeo and Poggianio revised the Latin original, which was published under Pius V in September 1566, and afterwards largely translated. It was intended for the purpose of instruction in accordance with the Decrees, was lucidly and well drawn up, and (1572) was divided into four parts, treating of the Creed, the Sacraments, the Decalogue, and the Lord's

Prayer. Its definition of the Papal power went perhaps a little beyond the documents of the Council in terming the Pope Universal Pastor and in some of its expressions. The scheme and scope of the work was hardly what the Decree (Session XXIV, Chapter VIII) seemed to imply, being more for the teacher than the taught; but the translation into vernacular had been expressly ordered. Cardinal Bellarmine also published (1603) another Catechism, used largely by missionaries. In Germany, the Catechism of Canisius was most widely used. The Roman Church was thus meeting its opponents on their own ground of popular instruction with excellent weapons and great results.

Another work the Council had enjoined (Session IV) was the purification of the Vulgate: the authority given to this
The Vulgate. version, due partly to the existing stage of scholarship and partly to the traditional love of its rhythm, was unfortunate, and played into the hands of the school that opposed Erasmus. After the invention of printing, many individuals had edited the Vulgate; between 1471 and 1599 no less than 179 Latin editions, including the Complutensian, appeared, some of them translations independent of the Vulgate. There were thus many texts and much uncertainty. Pius IV created a Congregation of Cardinals and Theologians *pro emendatione Bibliorum*, but its scope was limited to the recovery of the original text of the Vulgate, and its work went on intermittently until 1588. Various editions had appeared (1455–1541). Meanwhile the theologians of Louvain (where an edition had been published in 1547) had been working at a critical edition of wider scope which appeared (1573) at Antwerp, and was reprinted more than once. An edition of the Septuagint, under the patronage of Sixtus V, was printed at Rome (1587), and the Commission which produced it was afterwards set to the Vulgate (1588 onwards): the original Vulgate, the Louvain text, and also deviations from the correct Hebrew and Greek, were considered, and the result has been held better than the Louvain edition itself, which was the best up to that date. But Sixtus V was dissatisfied with it on the score of its deviation from that edition, the critical defects of

which he could not appreciate; he therefore made a new edition (published 1590) himself, with the help of Toletus, a Jesuit, and Rocca, an Augustinian. The introductory Bull (*Aeternus ille*) prescribed this edition as the true, legitimate, authentic, and undoubted exemplar, solely to be used in public and private, and not to be superseded. The work and the correcting of the proofs was a great enjoyment to him, but his scholarship was not equal to the task, and great controversy upon Papal power and infallibility has since then raged around it. The Congregation *de emendatione* complained (1591) to Gregory XIV of the disregard shown to their work and of the defects in the Sixtine edition, a prohibition of which was recommended by some of them. Bellarmine tells us that he, on the other hand, recommended a buying up of the copies and the issue of a new edition, under the name of Sixtus, with the correction of the numerous mistakes as if mere printer's errors, and not due to Sixtus himself; the course he commended, with his reasons for it, was more creditable to his regard for the Papacy than to his candour or accuracy. A new Commission (February 1591) was appointed, and the result of their work after a supervision appeared under Clement VIII (1592), but it too contains many misprints. The intention of the Council in this matter has been sometimes misrepresented: an authorised version was to be prepared, which was to be both accurate and official, but the discouragement afterwards shown to critical labour lay not with the decree itself, but with a feeling and policy independent of it, and gradually gathering strength. But this feeling, akin to that which had opposed Erasmus, was not shared by the Jesuits of the sixteenth century. It should be noted that while the list of Canonical Books (Session IV) is made a matter of faith and confirmed by anathema, the chapter on the use and interpretation of the books has no anathema attached, although a breach of the restraints upon printers might make offenders liable to anathema or fine.

Decrees had ordered (XXIV, 12, and XXV, 2) that all bishops and holders of benefice should make a public profession of faith according to the doctrine of the Council. Such a profession was now (1564) drawn up for the Pope, to whom its preparation had been left, by a commission of cardinals. It

consisted of twelve Articles, the Nicene Creed being the first, and the eleventh a reception of all things decreed by General Councils, including Trent. The intervening articles assert apostolic and ecclesiastic tradition and all the observances and constitutions of the Roman Church; that the Scriptures are to be taken in the Church's sense and interpreted by the unanimous consent of the Fathers; the seven Sacraments, with the ceremonies attached; the Decrees on Original Sin and Justification; the Mass as a sacrifice; transubstantiation; invocation of saints; images and indulgences; the Roman Church, as the mother and mistress of all churches, with an oath of obedience to the Pope. The twelfth article affirms the impossibility of salvation without this Catholic faith, and ends with a personal promise to retain it and to do the utmost that it shall be held and taught by all under the person making the profession. The Bulls *Injunctum nobis* (13 November, 1564) and *In sacrosancti beati Petri* (2 December, 1564) made this form binding upon all priests and teachers in seminaries and colleges. It also came to be widely used for converts, although other differing forms have been used for that purpose. This profession brought home to individuals that definiteness and closing up around Rome and the Papacy which had marked the Council. There was no longer any vagueness as to faith or any looseness of organisation. The doubtful questions of Scholasticism were thus closed, at any rate superficially, and the power of the Papacy, which was essentially a medieval growth, was asserted in a form both popular and clear. The attitude of the Council towards the Middle Ages was marked: it summed up and emphasised their results.

So much has been said already of the gain in organisation and discipline due to the Council that no more need be added. But it was significant that important details affecting both worship and life had been left to the Pope for settlement. This was the upshot of the continued but practically settled strife between Pope and Council. Nothing had been done to make easier the return of the Protestant dissentients to the Church. Nothing could well have been done. A generation bred in Lutheranism had by this time risen, and the Calvinists cared little to seek a unity which went against their theory of an invisible Church. But when the Council condemned much that was unreal and evil in the life of the Church and so made it gradually disappear, some of their ground for dissatisfaction had been cut away from the Protestants. High ideals of life and sound morality were henceforth characteristics, as they ought always to have been, of the clerical life in the Church. One concession, showy but not really important because temporary and sporadic, had been made—the concession of the chalice. But even this had been made by the Pope more than by the Council, and in regard to worship the Papacy had shown itself, notably in the case of the Breviary, more open to change than the majority of the higher clerics. It was more significant that the Curia and the College of Cardinals remained, in spite of a continued outcry, almost unreformed. The exhortations of the Council to the Pope in this matter had been vague. They were either disregarded or scarcely carried out at all. Even here, however, higher ideals of duty had their effect, and the improvement, carried out by various popes, was gradual but firm. The Curia and the College of Cardinals had gained a power not strictly based upon anything written, but yet a power without which or against which any Pope would find it hard to hold his own. The power of the Pope had been greatly strengthened; the view that Bishops were his delegates had been partly assumed, partly but often expressed; with the organisation now set up it was easy to develop this view still further. The Bishops thus lost much of their old independence. It was now easy to control the Roman Church, but it was harder to keep its hold upon the vigorous life of nations. Yet another power, equally undefined, but based upon real importance and great achievement, had now appeared—that of the Jesuits. And this Society had left the Council with a reputation enhanced and with new paths of

Summary of effects of the Council.

activity plainly marked. It had sometimes seemed as if Rome had lost its power and its hold upon the Western World. The Council made it clear how far or how little that was the case. Politically and religiously—even more so where the two spheres met—Rome was now far more powerful than before. The Council of the Lateran (1512) and that of Trent stood far apart in their importance and their results. The one compared with the other left the Papacy in a different state and with a very different forecast for the future.

MONASTIC REFORM AND THE JESUITS

THE beginning of the sixteenth century saw not only a widespread wish for reform, but an attempt to bring it about. This attempt, based upon the revival of both classical and patristic learning, and upon the study of doctrinal theology, was most successful in Spain, where it gained *Medieval* control of the whole Church. Here the strictest *Reform.* orthodoxy was found joined to a renewed study of Aquinas and a high ideal of clerical life. Like conditions existed elsewhere, and, although apparently less successful in controlling national life or clerical discipline, were as significant for the future of the Church.

In Italy the Monastic Orders and the Friars felt the new impulses; the Benedictines (as already mentioned) were reorganised (1504). Among the Camoldolites— *Monastic* the hermit Order to which Peter Damiani had *Revival.* belonged—a separate and stricter congregation arose (1523), under the leadership of Paul Giustiniani, a zealous Venetian. Among the Franciscans Matteo de Bassi tried to restore the life and spirit of their founder, thus repeating the attempts of the strict Observants which divided the Order and disturbed the Church politics of the Middle Ages. This old strife between Conventuals (who dwelt together) and Observants had been ended by Leo X (1517); his allowance to each party of its own General led to peace. Even among the Observants, however, there were varying degrees of strictness; a quarrel with them drove Bassi to attach his followers to the Conventuals, but as a separate congregation. By leave of Clement VII, he organised them with the special view of preach- *The Capu-* ing to, and working among, the poor, whom they *chins, 1528.* largely drew to themselves, and whose lives they influenced widely. These Capuchins, so called from their pointed hoods, were deservedly popular long before they were made (1619) an independent Order; the check they suffered when their Vicar-

General, Bernardino Ochino, fell into heresy (1542) was only temporary, and they have done much for religion in poor and common life. Akin to the poor in their sympathies, they were also often like them in their prejudices and superstitions. In Milan, the Barnabites were organised for mission and parochial work by Antony Maria Zaccaria (1530). Placed to begin with under the Archbishop of Milan, they were afterwards placed directly under the Pope. Among this Order St. Carlo Borromeo—Archbishop of Milan—not only chose his confessor, but made his retreats. Thus, in Italy, at its worst, the religious life was upheld, and the licence of the upper classes was balanced by the increased devotion of the lower. Of like movements in Germany enough has been said already.

But among the higher and more cultured classes also the same religious impulse was felt. Some fifty priests of high position at Rome, cherishing a high ideal of life, founded an informal society—the Oratory of Divine Love. The Oratory of Divine Love ; the Theatines. Sadoleti, Giberti, Carafa, with others, whose later paths diverged most widely, were members of it; many others, like Contarini, were in such close sympathy with them as to be reputed members; nor was Rome their only centre, for their influence reached to Vicenza, Verona, and Venice. But this purely personal and semi-academic movement took a more practical turn when (1524) Count Gaetano di Tiene, aided by his abler friend Carafa (afterwards Paul IV), Bishop of Chieti (Theate), founded the Order of Theatines. The special object of this strict society was to train parish priests, but a secondary aim was the suppression of heresy. Many of its members were noble, marked both by birth and talents for the high office they reached, and the Order thus gained an influence in Italy beyond what its mere numbers warranted.

Among female Orders, the Ursulines, founded (1535) at Brescia, by Angela di Merici, for the reclaiming of the fallen, soon turned to the education of girls, and after their formation (1544) into an Order, spread widely and did well in their special work. But Spain, as was natural, gave to the world the most noted woman monastic reformer. St. Teresa was both an example of mysticism, more medieval than modern, and a leader of reform. She was herself a Carmelite, and founded (1562) a new Order of barefooted Carmelites, which, owing to her mysticism, met with opposition. Medieval mysticism had, on the one hand, touched theological study and the devotional spirit; on the other hand, it verged not only on heresy and contempt for means of grace, but even licence of life. St. Teresa's visionary mysticism was of the most spiritual and devoted type; but, nevertheless, it brought her under the suspicion of the Inquisition, always on the watch for peculiar forms of energy overflowing established limits, and in this case incited to action by her own older Order. But both by her life and her teaching she showed how the union with God—the basis of her mysticism—could be realised, to be a light to the world.

The Ursulines. St. Teresa, 1562.

Of great importance in monastic reform was the life of St. Philip de Neri. This young Florentine on leaving college devoted himself to the service of the sick in Roman hospitals; in 1548 he founded the confraternity of the Most Holy Trinity, and soon built a large hospital for pilgrims. But the Oratory in which lectures in divinity were given to these pilgrims became so crowded that a church was given for their use (1558). In 1574 the congregation of the Oratory, as it was called—composed of both priests and laymen, bound by common aims but by no vows—was authorised. The later history of the society—some of its members, like Baronius, its second general, and author of the *Annales Ecclesiastici* († 1607), famed for learning, and some like the founder, for pre-eminent piety—was worthy of its conception. A French society, the Oratory of Jesus, founded by Cardinal Bérulle (1611), quickly spreading and including many learned members, gave rise in its turn to similar movements.

St. Philip de Neri, 1513–95. Cardinal Bérulle, 1611.

Nor did Cardinal Bérulle stand alone, for the French Benedictines, fallen from their old estate, now underwent a great revival. Didier de la Cour, placed when young (1596) as Prior over the Abbey of St. Vannes, at Verdun, prepared himself by a long course of study for his work, and then roused his brethren to sacred study, joined to a strict observance of their rule. The movement spread, and (1618) all the reformed monasteries joined to form the congregation of St. Maur,[1] which grew to the number of 180 houses. No revival ever bore better fruit in learned men, especially in patristics and ecclesiastical history. To it we owe Mabillon, Martène, Durand, D'Achery, and many others to be noticed later.

Benedictines of St. Maur, 1618.

In spiritual matters and in ecclesiastical politics, no one was a greater figure than Carlo Borromeo; this saintly prelate and cardinal, a nephew of Pius IV and a director of the Papal counsels, was led by the laxity of clerical life to strive for a higher ideal. Not even his rapid promotion—he became Cardinal and Archbishop of Milan when twenty-two—could spoil his character or bring him enemies. Nor did he lose the statesman in the saint, for his government of the States of the Church committed to his charge was model. His influence spread far beyond the limits of his diocese, where the revival of Church life was complete, although the Oblates, founded (1528) by him at Milan, did not extend as far as many other orders. Whether owing to his experience of politics, or to his natural disposition, he was noted then, and has been rightly condemned in later days, for his undue severity and intolerance against Protestants. Even so far north as Switzerland, he furthered the Counter-Reformation; his Swiss college at Milan, his introduction into Switzerland of the Jesuits (1574-81),[2] and of the Capuchins (1581-88),[3] and his foundation of a permanent nunciature at Lucerne, had consolidated the Catholics of the country, and the Borromean League (1586) of Lucerne, Uri, Schwyz, Unterwalden, Solothurn, Freiburg, and Zug, for the defence of the Catholic Church, kept his name alive. His saintly life and unwearied diligence gave an example, fruitful both at Rome and Milan.

St. Carlo Borromeo, 1538-84.

---

[1] For the Benedictines of St. Maur, see Jervis, *History of the Church in France*, I, pp. 333 *seq.*

[2] In Lucerne in 1574 and Fribourg in 1581.

[3] In Altdorf, Staas and Appeazell.

Many of these orders or congregations (for the looser form was often preferred) differed from medieval types in being practical rather than contemplative; the individual search after perfection, the brotherhood of the common life, did not inspire them so much as did a wish to check the evils of clerical life and raise the priesthood. But the motives of work- **Features** ing among the poor or suffering and among un- **of these** believers were not wanting; and thus the spirit of St. **Movements.** Francis was reproduced. Gradually, too, as the century went on, France, whose disturbed religious politics caused and upset so many nice calculations, took the place of Spain and Italy at the birthplace of these movements. The impulses which caused them were widely spread, and spiritual links between them were common. Thus St. Vincent de Paul had joined the Oratory of Cardinal Bérulle before he founded his own society; St. Francis de Sales was influenced by his Jesuit director, Possevin. In an atmosphere favourable to their growth these orders arose and gave rise to others. No age, indeed, is richer in special types of saintliness than the one we are dealing with. The variety of practical objects aimed at is also worthy of note. Education stood foremost with the Piarists or Brethren of the Pious Schools, founded (1600) by Joseph Calasanze, a Spanish priest in Italy. They were recognised as an order (1621), and become second only to the Jesuits in their influence upon schools. Other minor orders had the same end in view. The care of the sick was the aim of the Brothers of Charity (Brethren of St. John of God), founded at Seville (1540) by a Portuguese monk, John of God. It should also be noted how the spirit of association was spreading from the regular to the secular clergy, who wholly or partly formed many of these bodies.

Many of these activities were combined in the rich and saintly career of St. Vincent de Paul. A Gascon, born at Pouy, near Dax, by the Pyrenees, the son of poor **St. Vincent** parents and himself a shepherd, he studied under **de Paul,** the Franciscans near Rome, and then at the **1576–1660.** University of Toulouse. After his ordination as priest (1600), he spent some years in teaching and in study, until his acpture by Barbary pirates placed him as a slave at Tunis. His last master, a renegade Christian, was led by pity and remorse to give him freedom, and together they returned to Christendom. After a visit to Rome, St. Vincent went on a mission to France, where he joined the Oratory of Cardinal Bérulle. In obedience to commands laid upon him, he first took parish work, and then a tutorship in the family of the Count de Joigny. His experience of country places and their needs led him to the idea of Missions for their good (1617), which took shape in the College des Bons Enfants for that purpose. He also became Chaplain-General to the galley-slaves, over whom the Count de Joigny was General, and in this sad field his work was intense. But the needs of the clergy and of parochial life were still before him, and (1632) he founded the Priory of St. Lazare for the Society of the Mission. These Missioners, besides their natural work, largely took charge of the seminaries so widely set up after the Council of Trent. Before long, Missions in Italy, Switzerland, Poland, Ireland, and even Madagascar witnessed to the need St. Vincent had seen. When a bishop complained to him of the number of drunken or immoral priests in his diocese, St. Vincent resolved to deepen the sense of Vocation in candidates for the priesthood; Ordination Retreats (Lent, 1631) were the result. Then from the conferences held to carry on the work so begun sprang a confraternity with the same objects, of which Bossuet was an early member. While in parish work (1617), he had felt the urgency of cases needing help, and seen the great waste in relieving them: this led him to organise the Confraternity of Charity composed at first of wealthy ladies. But he like many later reformers soon saw that charity must be organised permanently, and not left to amateur administrators; thus he was led to found the Sisters of Charity. This led on naturally to the training of nurses; that, again, to help in hospitals and the care of homeless infants. The foundation of the hospital of the Name of Jesus (as an almshouse), and then of the Salpêtrière (for the same end, but on a larger scale) were merely incidents in a life crowded with good works. From his death-bed (1660) he could look back upon a number of varied works, any one of which would save an ordinary name from oblivion.

The special note of his life beyond his saintliness is the ready provision of means for coping with evils met in his daily life; so little by little he was led on from one great deed to another. His master's motto, *Coepit facere et docere* ("He began to do and to teach"), was true of himself; he was always beginning some new form of doing, some new form of teaching; and his life completed is the best of lessons.

Yet another type of saint was shown in St. Francis de Sales. The eldest son of a noble family of Annecy in Savoy, he felt his vocation from childhood; when only St. Francis eleven he took the tonsure, but his father meant de Sales, him for the career of law, and with that in view he 1567-1622. was educated at Paris. In 1593, much against his father's will, he was made Provost or Dean of Geneva, and ordained priest. His great wish was to carry always with him the atmosphere of the altar; thus his care for souls as Confessor, and his heartfelt sermons with practical lessons, had a force beyond themselves, and he showed that better side of mysticism which had been so strong in Spain not long before. He was sent (1594) to carry on a mission in Chablais, a district just gained by Catholic Savoy from Protestant Bern, and here his devotion succeeded beyond all hope; he soon became Coadjutor-Bishop of Geneva, to which see he finally succeeded. His claim to remembrance lies not only in his foundation of a female order —the Visitation of the Blessed Virgin—or in his spiritual writings—as the *Introduction to the Devout Life*—but also in his model episcopate, a pattern and a wonder far and wide; his private piety and his public work were blended into one almost perfect flower.

It is a tribute to the importance of the Jesuits that their rise should have obscured that of these other societies, energetic and useful as they were. The personality of the The Jesuits. founder, with his background of Spanish chivalry and crusading zeal; the skill of his organisation perfected by succeeding generals; their success in the work, undertaken partly through their definiteness of aim, partly through the opportune moment of their appearing—all these gave them importance. But the personality of Ignatius Loyola should not make us forget the history of Spain that made his career possible; the success of the Jesuits should not lead us to forget that other societies, with similar aims and success only inferior to theirs, had also arisen. It is an error to regard the appearance either of these other orders or of the Jesuits as due to a mere reaction against Protestantism; their appearance takes its proper place as one event in a long series beginning with the earliest movements for reform and for a more vigorous life, strengthened by the religious side of the Renaissance, and finally issuing in the reforms of Trent. It sounds paradoxical to say that Protestantism and Jesuitism should have arisen partly from the same causes, but, so far as each was due to a positive wish for revival and an impatience of evils, such was the case. The causes that made the one a support to the Church and the other an attack upon it are not far to seek; they lie partly in the leaders of the movements, partly in the way in which they were met, and partly in the political atmosphere that surrounded them.

Inigo Lopez de Recalde was born at the château of Loyola in Guipúzcoa (1491); as a younger son he was brought up to arms, and began his career as a royal page. When in
Ignatius command of Pampeluna (1521) he was forced to
Loyola, surrender to the French, and being wounded was
1491–1556. sent home to recover. During his long illness he turned from the tales of chivalry he knew to books of devotion, the Flowers of the Saints and others; Spain was the land of chivalry and mystic devotion alike, and he shared the national sympathies. When he left home, healed but lame for life, the energy of his knighthood was turned into new channels; he went (1522) to Montserrat, which the late Abbot Dom Garcia de Cisneros, a nephew of Cardinal Ximenes and the author of a devotional *Exercitatorium Spirituale*, had made a centre of influence; thence he passed to Manresa, a resting-place for pilgrims to Montserrat, and the traditional scene of the conception of his Society. The sojourn there, where visions and meditations gave a tinge of mysticism to his zeal, was a crisis in his life. After a vigil much like that of a knight, he meant to journey to Jerusalem to convert the heathen; he made the voyage, but on arrival found he could do but little:

his lack of knowledge and his powerlessness when alone was borne in upon him; he returned to equip himself for his venture and to seek for companionship. Years not only of study but of teaching and preaching also at Barcelona, Alcala, and Salamanca taught him his powers and his methods of work; in each place he gathered followers around him; both at Salamanca and at Alcala he fell under the suspicion of the Holy Office (Inquisition) as a mystic—a charge based on truth— and spent some weeks in prison. He was bidden to study theology for four years before he could preach or teach; so he betook himself (February, 1528) to Paris with the idea of a brotherhood already in his mind; he had a singular power, not only of arousing enthusiasm in others (which is easy), but of dominating their whole thought and life; soon he gathered his first real band of disciples, Pierre le Fèvre, a Savoyard, Francis Xavier and Iago Laynez, both Spaniards, and others. On 15 August, 1534, the little company, seven in number, together before an altar, took oaths of celibacy, poverty, and a spiritual crusade in Syria. If this last could not be carried out they were to place themselves at the disposal of the Pope for employment where and how he pleased. It was this condition that in the end marked out for the Jesuits their great task and their stupendous future.[1]

Looking at St. Ignatius himself, we can see clearly marked stages in his life and work. We begin with his conversion, and his individual mysticism, based on self-sacrifice. This stage is centred in himself and his spiritual growth on a soil of Spanish zeal. Pilgrimages, such as that to Jerusalem (1523), were natural in such a mood. Then there came to him, as there had come to the Celtic monks who sought solitude among foreigners, the wish to help others in gaining what he himself had come to hold. Therefore he began to gather disciples, at first among the ordinary people he met, and then afterwards among those more like himself and so most likely to share his work. To train such converts by his *Spiritual Exercises* was, as it seemed, the best that he could do. This stage was a natural enlargement of his great vision, for he could not do for the world all that he wished if he stood alone and worked alone.

[1] For literature, see Note at end of Chapter.

This was his second stage. But something nobler and larger loomed ahead. If he was to change the world, mere zeal, either his own or that of his earlier disciples, was not enough. The Spain of Ximenes and the religious work of the Universities which they knew suggested something further. Learning in sacred letters must be brought to help. So he went to schools and Universities: to a school in Barcelona (1524–26), to the newly-founded University of Alcala (1526–27) and then to the dominating University of Paris (1528–35), cherishing always the enlarging vision that was unfolding itself before him: striving, too, to train others through his *Spiritual Exercises* to share his hopes: to be, as it were, one with himself in work and aim but always, beyond their leader, one with God and with the Church. This was the third stage and so the Society of Jesus began. The little brotherhood was fortunate in its members, marked, as they were, by variety of gifts inside the compact unity of aim. For their work was to be many-sided, if their purpose one.

Venice was to be their starting-point for the East; here the The Order, comrades met (1537), and here Ignatius came into 1534–40. touch with Carafa and the Theatines, whose objects and methods may have impressed him; here too, after an interview held by some of them with Pope Paul III at Rome, those not already priests received ordination. At length giving up their Eastern voyage, they betook themselves singly to Rome, each on the way thinking over the organisation they should adopt. Ignatius himself gave them, besides the main idea, their name, " the Company of Jesus," "like a cohort or century gathered to fight spiritual enemies, as men devoted body and soul to our Lord Jesus Christ and his Vicar on Earth." On reaching Rome they set to work; as at Venice, so here they preached, and did it with success. Paul III employed them for teaching and preaching in his schools and colleges. Papal and popular favour drew jealousy upon them, and to place themselves in safety Ignatius gained recognition (1538) from the Pope. Gradually their organisation took shape; their General was to have unlimited power, and to hold office for life; he was to be venerated as if Christ were present in him. The whole life and strength of every member was to be given in warfare for Christ and the Pope, carrying out at once and without reserve all the Pope should order in any place or land, among heretics or heathen. This was the constitution approved by the Pope and was the very thing that was needed; Protestantism had attacked the Papacy which to the closing Middle Ages had come to stand for Western unity; hence the Jesuits had come to its support. Ignatius only slowly realised what his order could do, but gradually the problem of the reconquest of the Protestant West instead of the heathen East shaped itself before him; the difficulty of a new problem gave to his order, as it had formerly done to the Franciscans, an impulse to overcome it. "The finger of God is here," said Pope Paul. When the three Cardinals appointed to examine the new order and its constitution were going to report unfavourably, the Pope himself (like Contarini favourable to them) gained their approval for it. The new society was sanctioned (27 September, 1540) on condition its members should never exceed sixty in number, a condition afterwards removed (1543). As preachers, directors of consciences and teachers of the young, the company was to serve the Church; and to further their work many privileges were afterwards given them.

If obedience to the Papacy was, to begin with, the most striking feature of the society, the absolute power of the General was to be of the greater moment later on. In the original constitution as approved by Paul III, the advice of the Council was a slight check upon the General, but before many years this was done away with (1550); the General, sole disposer of the destinies of the members, stood alone. *Peculiarities of the Society.*

Loyola had great personal power over others, and, of course, specially over those he trained. But while he lived this sway over his disciples was a personal gift: it was only afterwards under his successors that it grew into a constitutional fact: this growth, too, was gradual, for Laynez and St. Francis Borgia, the second and third Generals, had great trials of insubordination to *Working of the Society.*

face. The founder himself had some trials of conflict,
Loyola and as his relations with Laynez show, but his succes-
Laynez. sors had more.

Loyola was quick to see the special gifts his followers had,
and so to give them special tasks which suited them. Laynez
was a great scholar and an equally great teacher and organiser.
Hence to him was given the control of the Jesuit schools in
Italy, where they began. But trouble arose as his best
helpers were quickly taken away from him for other work,
and he complained to the General. He got a sharp rebuke
and his answer by letter to St. Ignatius is a remarkable
document.

In the bowels of Christ he begged Loyola to punish his
sins and to conquer the disordered passions, which had caused
them, by withdrawing him from office, from preaching and
study, even so far as to leave him his Breviary as his only
book: he prayed that he should be ordered to travel to Rome
as a mendicant and to be employed until death in the lowliest
of household work, a task which formed part of the Jesuit
training: if he were thought unfit for this, he asked to be told
off for teaching the elements of grammar during the rest of
his days. In every way he asked that no regard should be
shown to him but that he should be treated as the offscouring
of the earth. Opinions may differ as to the sincerity of the
submission: it may have been the loyalty of a convinced
member of the Society filled with its spirit and mindful of his
profession: it may have been the proud withdrawal of one who
knew the importance of his work and the utter impossibility
of taking him from it. If Loyola was the official superior
we may remember that there was much of autocracy and
caprice in his later rule and that the inferior had a breadth
of scholarship and an experience in teaching which made him
more able to form schemes of education than his master.
But fortunately St. Ignatius did not act upon the abject submission made to him: he merely bade Laynez compose a
Summa Theologia, a task which after all was left scarcely
begun. As a concession two excellent assistants were given
him for the work of teaching. Thus both the discipline of

the Society was preserved and a valuable instrument kept for one of its most essential works. The "incomparable Laynez," as Ignatius called him, was kept for better things.

Ignatius himself was naturally the first General (5 April, 1541). Before his death (31 July, 1556) his society was firmly rooted if not full-grown; he himself had at any rate in the main devised the lines of its constitution, although it was only under Laynez—the next General—that it was definitely settled in details: the differences from older foundations were probably not favourably regarded by the Curia, and only gradually gained approval. Julius III (1550–5) was very friendly to them; under him and by his liberal help the Roman College, a teaching body of great ability and much influence, afterwards moved to the Gèsu, and the German College (1552), for the special training of German youths, were begun. Marcellus II was even more friendly still, and had he lived longer the order would probably have gained that supreme power its critics seemed to fear. His early death brought to the papal throne (1555), Cardinal Carafa (Paul IV), who distrusted the order both as too Spanish and as sufficiently akin to his Theatines in object to make their separate existence unreasonable. There followed the first of the many struggles between Pope and Jesuits, complicated by internal strife between Laynez, the acting Vicar, and some of the members. The Pope wished to make the regular recitation of offices in choir compulsory for the society, which would have forced it into resemblance to other orders and made their peculiar work more difficult; he also wished to limit the General's term of office to three years, which would have seriously weakened his position. The next Pope, Pius IV (1559), removed these restrictions, which the society had never heartily adopted.

The constitution of the society had not been formed hastily; its ideas were the mingled result of the meditations and long experiences of St. Ignatius himself. The years of waiting and the changes of scene had borne their fruit, and as the exact nature of his task opened itself out before him he adapted most

Its Constitution. Its Growth. The Exercises.

skilfully the means to the end; in the last stage at Rome itself something must have been due to Laynez. Both under Loyola and Laynez there was opposition, from inside as well as from outside, to the hardening absolutism of the system. The latter while acting General (August 1556–July, 1558) had to face the charge of delaying in his own interests the publication of the constitution. St. Ignatius died 31 July, 1556, and for some years before his death he had been considering the Constitution which he was empowered to draw up. He worked at it with the help of Codure, after whose death he still went on and began to make notes of it (1547). He consulted his earlier followers, and was helped much by his secretary, Polanco. The enlarged form was approved by Julius III (21 July, 1550), and in that year what may be called the Founder's first draft was ready: he called to Rome those members who could come: the Constitution was then considered, with many alterations as a result: here again Polanco was helpful. But the work was not completed and the wording of it he altered from time to time. In 1558 the Congregation approved it, at the assembly which elected Laynez as General (2 July, 1558).

There was certainly a long time spent in making known the Constitution, which was stated to be the work of Ignatius himself, and critics have therefore thrown doubt upon the genuineness of the Ignatian authorship, and attributed much to Laynez. But apart from the fact that Polanco helped Laynez in draughtsmanship as he had helped Loyola, it is likely that the bulk of the Ignatian work was somewhat disordered and that much in it may have needed to be made coherent and consistent. For Loyola was not a modern politician who might undertake to draft a constitution for a city or an Empire at the shortest notice.

Then we must remember the antipathy of Paul IV for the Jesuits: a long Papacy could not be expected, for Paul IV was already seventy-nine at his election: he was fanatically anti-Spanish; the Society had difficulties of its own in Spain, and there were more than hints of divisions, fomented by some

Spanish members. Delay was diplomatic. Laynez might well wish "to gain the benefit of time," as a Cardinal once expressed it. There seems nothing extraordinary then in the long delay. Laynez was elected General (2 July, 1558) after he had been acting as such since August 1556.

The outside policy and outside success of the society must be ascribed to Laynez, while to St. Ignatius was due the internal preparation that made that success possible. The *Spiritual Exercises of Manresa*, next to the *Imitatio Christi*, the most powerful work of its class, unlike the *Imitatio*, not the outpouring of a soul but a spiritual guide for others, is the basis of the internal preparation. It is mystic and spiritual, but it never loses sight of the active work with the need of strength for its fulfilment; it is thoroughly practical and common-sense in its wise and full treatment of detail. The passages upon bodily discipline and postures in devotions, for instance, give apt illustration of these features. In the book, as in the society itself (to begin with, at any rate) it is hard to divide fairly our admiration between the exalted spirit raised above the world and the perfect knowledge of the world with the adaptation of everything to it. Self-sacrifice and wisdom, ardour and calculation are not easy to combine; but in this book as in the society they are blended with the utmost skill. The man who passes through the four weeks or divisions into which the exercises are divided has (1) got rid of his evil self and also of his personality so far as it is a hindrance to his great aim; (2) he has taken Christ's life as the model of his own; (3) he has realised Christ's sufferings for him as his own; and (4) he has entered into the triumph and the joy of Christ; while self-surrender, docility, and obedience of all the faculties in subordination to one great end have been learnt in the process. The spirit and method of the Exercises are the spirit and method of the society.

According to the Constitution, *novices* were to spend two years in study and the Exercises, under the constant watch of their superiors, who thus came to know their natures and

Laynez and the Constitution.

capabilities. At the end of the novitiate they took the vows of poverty, chastity, and obedience, along with a promise to remain in the society and do the work appointed by the General. The next stage was that of *scholastic*, spent in the study of arts for five years, followed by a term of some years' teaching. An *approved scholastic* might, after a four years' course of theology (in which he also studied the Exercises for himself) and a second novitiate of a year, receive priesthood and become a *Spiritual Coadjutor*. In its ample provision of education, training in obedience, and humble work, as well as in the higher business of life and knowledge of men, the scheme was very complete. In practice it was elastic enough to develop the talents of the individual, while neither the oversight of superiors nor the personal sense of vocation was ever relaxed. If not ordained the scholastic might become a *Temporal Coadjutor*, engaged in the secular business of the society much as lay-brethren in other orders. Beyond the Spiritual Coadjutors were the Professed with their three ordinary vows, and also a fourth of special obedience to the Pope to go wherever he might send. These Professed made up but a small part of the society; at the time of the death of St. Ignatius they numbered only thirty-five out of a total of a thousand. From among the Spiritual Coadjutors and the Professed were chosen, by the General, the officers of the colleges and the Provincials. All these held office for three years only, while the General, elected by the congregation, held his for life. All these officers sent to the General yearly reports, and thus the centralisation of knowledge as of power was complete. By the side of the General stood a Council of six assistants elected by the congregation from the assistancies of Germany, France, Portugal, Spain, Italy, and Poland. It might seem as if there was here an absolute tyranny, the guidance of a single mind. But even over the General there was a watchful guard, and he, as other members, had become part of the great tradition and the system it involved. There was no risk of a General working too much upon an individual line, while yet all the advantages of his individual energy and

The margin notes:
The Novices.
The Coadjutors.
The Professed.

wisdom were made use of. In the same way the advantages of other orders were combined with the utmost liberty in such points as dress, and the relaxation of rules when desirable for important ends. The regulation by which no Jesuit could without leave accept any bishopric or high office in the Church ensured to the society the constant help of its most gifted members and put a check upon merely personal ambitions.

Among the early Jesuits, Laynez was the one who, next to Loyola himself, left the greatest mark upon the age. Iago Laynez [1] was born at Almazon in Castile (1512): he was thus much younger than Loyola, and some six years younger than Lefèvre and Xavier: in birth he was inferior to them, for although his family had been Christian converts for three generations, it needed four to make *conversos* fully recognised: this stigma of birth brought on him some scorn and dislike, which, with his talents and scholarship, he was able to disregard. His knowledge was immense, and he was able to say, probably with truth, that he never quoted from any work which he had not read through. His ability and his command of oratory were equal to his learning; overcoming all his disadvantages he became a power in the Church and even in the secular world. In 1552 he was made Provincial for Upper Italy; and the growth and wise control of the Italian Colleges and schools must be ascribed to him.

Laynez, 1512-65.

In Italy, as was natural, the society spread rapidly; it appealed specially to the cultured classes, and its influence among the small princely families soon made itself felt. Venice, where they founded a college (1542), became a Jesuit centre, and even in its time of political decay, its importance as a literary and intellectual centre was great. Faenza and Bologna were also Jesuit strongholds. The school at Messina, which was the first to be founded (1539), and where the studies followed Parisian models, became the type of the excellent schools set up by the society. In other countries also the society gained power. Spain, where the Emperor

Spread of the Society in Italy.

Spain.

---

[1] His *Disputationes Tridentinae*: by Hartmann Grisar, S.J., I–II Innsbruck, 1886, with a short Life and Introduction, is an excellent work.

Charles V. had a reasonable distrust of papal policy, and where the Dominicans disliked Jesuit intrusion, was slow to receive them, until Francis Borgia, great-grandson of Alexander VI, Duke of Gandia and Viceroy of Catalonia, became their patron, and at length after joining them (1548), rose to be General (1565–72). Although the Archbishop of Toledo refused to allow his clergy to have any intercourse with them, and they were excommunicated at Saragossa, Borgia's influence turned the scale in their favour. To begin with they gained influence among the lower classes, while later on they pushed their way into the Universities, first at Gandia (under Borgia) and then at Alcala and Salamanca, at which last place they had a college of their own. In the Netherlands they gained a footing (1556 onwards) under Philip II and the Viceroy Margaret of Parma, and in 1584 the restrictions there which had so long vexed them were removed. Their college at Louvain intensified and carried on the Catholic traditions of the University. Portugal welcomed them more warmly than Spain had done. Thence St. Francis Xavier sailed for the Indies, but not before he had begun a work destined to give them complete control of Royal Family and kingdom. The Jesuit colleges or houses were all modelled to secure "perfectio religiosa": the establishments at Paris, Louvain and Cologne illustrate this. But just as monasteries in the Middle Ages had found difficulty in combining schools for the novices and for outside pupils, so did the Jesuits. A definite separation had to be made between the two: in this way the novices were thoroughly trained for the life of the Society, and for the external pupils a separate definite system grew up: Jesuits with an aptitude for teaching took up the work, and so the Society gained its great influence on the outside world.

In France the Chancellor du Prat, and the Cardinal of Lorraine, introduced them; but both the Sorbonne, the theological faculty of the University of Paris, and the Parliament of Paris, that legal body which had grown into a national power, opposed them. The latter, indeed, declared them enemies of Church and State, and the

In the Netherlands.

In Portugal.

In France.

former condemned them as disturbers of the Church's peace and overthrowers of monastic orders. Many bishops, led by Eustace du Bellay of Paris, shut them out of their dioceses, and the parish clergy followed their official leaders. Only when a War of Religion was ready to break out did the bishops consent to receive them (1561), and even then they stipulated for their subordination to themselves. It was Laynez who, while in France for the Conference at Poissy (September, 1561), procured their admission. The College of Clermont, then founded at Paris, soon gained distinction, but the society has nowhere undergone more vicissitudes than in France. Germany, owing to the spread of Lutheranism, In had been marked out by Loyola as a field for Germany. the society. Lefèvre, Le Jay, and Bobadilla were the first workers there; the first soon passed into Spain. Bobadilla, who incurred the Emperor's anger by his opposition to the Interim, took Bavaria for his sphere: Albert V, brother-in-law of Ferdinand, founded a college for them at Ingolstadt (1549), and another at Munich (1559). Le Jay, in Austria, gained the ear of Ferdinand, and after he had been joined (1551) by others, Vienna became one of their strongest settlements.

Peter Canisius, who succeeded Le Jay as Rector there, was a leading theologian of the day. As a young man he had shared in opposing the attempt of Hermann von Wied, the reforming Bishop of Cologne, to Protestantise Canisius, his see (1542–7); then for four years he was trained 1520–97. under Lefèvre. He was the first German to join the Society. As Rector at Ingolstadt (1549) he carried on the learned and reforming traditions of John Maier, of Eck. When only thirty-two years old he was called to Vienna, there to become Rector of the Jesuit foundation and to found a seminary for priests. Two professorships in the University were allotted to the society; and here, as at Prague, Freiburg-in-Breisgau, Trier, Mayence, Salzburg, Bamberg, and Constance, their system of education produced great results. It would be difficult to localise the activity of Canisius, who travelled widely from Switzerland to Poland, working both upon the Universities and the general public. His learning was equalled by his activity and industry: Aquinas he studied closely. He was a Ciceronian, well-read in the Fathers, as he proved by editions of Cyril of Alexandria and of Leo the Great. Equipped with this learning he had a great career as teacher at Cologne, Ingolstadt and Vienna, where, as said before, he became Rector. He had a hard struggle to escape the charge of the See, first as Archbishop and then as Administrator, for he felt that his true field was education. The monasteries were bad, and the secular clergy, as a rule, ignorant, and therefore ineffective. For their instruction he wrote his Summa. He was at the Colloquies of Regensburg and Worms, and at the Diet of Augsburg (1559): he helped the Legate Commendone to keep on good terms with the Emperor Maximilian II, whom he persuaded to avoid strong steps against the Calvinists, while remaining on good terms with Lutherans (1566). It was somewhat difficult to combine the relations, but the jealousies of the two Protestant parties played into the hands of the Counter Reformers. It was really due to the advice he gave to Emperor and Pope that the decrees of Trent were accepted in the Empire wherever Habsburg influence was strong. One part of his work, which he felt needed, was the controversy with the Centuriators: he thought the duty forced on him. His *Summa Doctrinæ Christianæ* (or larger Catechism), was the theological text-book of the Catholic revival, with two hundred and eleven questions leading to page-long answers. His small (1556), with one hundred and twenty-two questions, was written at the request of the Professors of Louvain in Latin to begin with and was translated into many languages. The Age, which is often called one of Confessions, may as truly be called one of Catechisms, which were numerous and had long useful lives. His smaller Catechism (1559) provided for Catholics means of teaching, in which for some thirty years they had been excelled by Protestants; five hundred editions and many translations are sufficient proofs of its success.[1] His activity was rewarded by his becoming Pro-

[1] The usefulness of the Catechism was shewn, when at the Vatican Council of 1870, the German bishops did not wish, like others, for any

vincial (1556) of the newly erected Province of Upper or Southern Germany, including the Habsburg territories, Bavaria, Suabia, and Switzerland. Under the inspiration of a letter from Loyola, he founded an Archducal College at Ingolstadt for the special work of educating young nobles and to the German College at Rome he sent twenty-two young Austrians: for Switzerland he founded a seminary at Fribourg. There was no bound to his activity: he worked in Poland, Hungary, the Netherlands and Switzerland; colleges at Dillingen, Freiburg-in-Breisgau, Saverne and Fribourg in Switzerland were among his foundations. As a preacher he swayed multitudes with lasting effects, and not merely for the moment. At Augsburg, above all, he worked wonders and was called "the Apostle of the city," and there by his statue in front of the cathedral he is remembered gratefully and graciously. The Province of Lower Germany remained however comparatively unworked.

The activity of the society in England during our period falls into two divisions, in the earlier of which, under Elizabeth and James I, its members devoted themselves rather to private administrations not different in kind from those of other priests, and in the latter of which they were more concerned with diplomacy and attempts at influencing people of importance. In the former period arose between the Jesuits and the secular priests, both of them in captivity at Wisbech, the struggle known as the Arch-priest Controversy.[1] This sprang from the attempt of the Jesuits to rule by an "Arch-priest" over both the regulars and seculars; the strife led to great bitterness, and tended to place the Catholics who kept to the Papal obedience still further outside the main currents of national life. But however unfortunate the political results of their activity, in England

In England, 1580.

---

new Catechism, because that of Canisius was found and proved just what was needed. They wanted no new one and could wish no better one.

[1] See T. G. Law: *A historical sketch of the conflicts between Jesuits and seculars in the reign of Elizabeth, with a reprint of Christopher Bagshaw's "True relation of the faction begun at Wisbech" and illustrative documents* (London, 1889).

as elsewhere the Jesuits gave proof of the greatest persistency and devotion, and in spite of their connection with politics some of their members truly earned the rank of martyr. In the second period of their activity, although their influence was, like their diplomacy, rated too highly at the time, their field of work was more the Court than the country at large, and even here they were overshadowed by members of other orders, esteemed more suited to the special task. In some other countries, such as Poland, the progress of the Counter Reformation was due, wholly or mainly, to the work of Jesuits.

NOTE ON BOOKS

The best modern life of Loyola is: *Ignatius Loyola* by H. D. Sedgwick (London, 1924), with accounts of the earliest Jesuits, good characterisations and references to authorities. See also Bibliographies in *Camb. Mod. Hist.* II, c. XVIII, and in Evennett: *Cardinal of Lorraine.* Larger works are B. Duhr: *Geschichte der Jesuiten in den Landern deutscher Zünge im XVI Jahrhundert* (Freiburg-im-B., Vol. I, 1907; Vol. II, 1913), and H. Fouqueray: *Histoire de la Compagnie de Jésus en France* (Paris, I, 1910; II, 1913). For England much material in H. Foley: *Records of the English Province of the Society of Jesus* (7 vols.; London, 1877–84). A. W. Ward: *The Counter-Reformation* (Epochs of Church History: London, 1889), a small and sympathetic summary. B. J. Kidd: *The Counter-Reformation; 1550–1660* (London, S.P.C.K.), 1933).

XII

THE FRENCH WARS OF RELIGION

THESE Wars [1] filled the history of France from 1559 to 1598.[2] The military details of the wars can be left aside here. There were few great and fewer decisive battles such as Wars of Dreux (Dec. 19, 1562), St. Denis near Paris (Nov. 10, Religion. 1567), Jarnac on the Charente (March 13, 1569), Moncontour (Oct. 3, 1569), Coutras (Oct. 20, 1587), Arques (Sept. 21, 1589), Ivry (March 14, 1590). And there were some long intervals of uncertain peace: slaughter in battles and assassinations removed some leading men, while the interplay of plans and politics was unceasing. Through all the desultory campaigns (which did not end with the Seven Wars), the old local divisions of dialects and habits persisted, now intensified by differences of faith and worship. Poitou, Guienne and Lower Languedoc were Huguenot; Brittany and Picardy (whence some Huguenot leaders came) were Catholic; Paris, which now as of old played a decisive part in French history, was also Catholic. Huguenots[3] (a word of uncertain but clearly

---

[1] See *Camb. Mod. Hist.*, Vol. II. c. ix. (A. Tilley). Also the same author's excellent booklet, *The French Wars of Religion* (*No.* 8 in *Helps for Students of History* (S.P.C.K.); *Camb. Mod. Hist.*, Vol. III. c. i., A. J. Butler; *The French Wars of Religion*, E. Armstrong (London, 1892) is an excellent short summary; *The Period of the Reformation* (1517–1648) by L. Haüsser (Eng. trans. by Mrs. G. Sturge (London, 1873), Vol. II. cc. xxv. to xxix.); Ranke *Französische Geschichte* (3rd ed., 1877—an Eng. trans. by M. A. Garvey, London, 1852); E. Lavisse, *Histoire de France Illustré*, Vols. V. 2 and VI. 1 and 2; *The French Monarchy*, A. J. Grant (2 vols.: Cambridge, 1931). For the French Church generally, W. H. Jervis, *History of the Church in France* (London, 1872), sound and well-informed.

[2] The Wars, usually given as seven in number, began (1) 1562, (2) 1567, (3) 1568, (4) 1572, (5) 1574, (6) 1577, (7) 1580. But peace did not come with the end of them.

[3] The name first appears around Tours about 1560; names from general or local leaders were used earlier, such as "those of Meaux": Beza called his history: *Historie des Églises Reformées:* so the name "Reformed" spread and was used for the Calvinists in Germany. As Calvin's influence spread they had naturally been called Calvinists. For the name "Huguenot" see Preserved Smith, *Age of the Reformation*, p. 208.

of French origin) were mainly found in the towns, among tradesmen and workmen and among the lower country gentry: in a few cases University students and even teachers were also affected, especially at Paris, Orleans and Nîmes. Estimates of the number of the Reformed varied. It was said that by 1558 there were 400,000 of them! thirty-four churches had been organised in Paris or elsewhere: as Calvin himself directed the whole, it was efficient. After the national organisation had been completed at the Paris Synod of 1559, the number rose rapidly and later on converts among the higher classes joined them. But events in Paris soon caused bitterness and strife. A statue of the Madonna was mutilated (1528) and Placards, coarsely denouncing the Mass, were posted up (1534): the passions of hostile mobs were stirred. There were mutterings of storms to come. Some twenty-three were executed: Louis de Berquin, a well-known scholar, from whom much was expected, had been in trouble over the possession of heretical books (1523): he was thrown into prison (1528), then released by the King but burnt later on (1529). A liberal grant of money from the Church, and the hope of help from Lutherans in Germany, were pushing the monarch in different directions. Flirtation with heretics abroad, joined to a real passion for the wealthy orthodox at home, made for instability in a sovereign's rule.

Much then hung on the characters and inclinations of the monarchs. Francis I himself was disposed to be tolerant, and The Waldense. was ready to negotiate with the Lutherans in Germany so as to weaken his rival Charles V.

But the persecutions of the Waldenses in Provence had happened under him. These simple folk, followers of Peter Waldo (c. 1170, who had given up his trade at Lyons to become an evangelist), survivals of the sects dispersed by the Inquisition, lived in thirty villages on the Durance: they were stirred by the beginnings of Lutheranism and Zwinglianism and sent messengers and a confession of Faith to the Reformers: they planned to have the Scriptures in French, and also take up new evangelistic work. The Inquisitor for Provence, Roma, took steps against them, and they appealed to

Francis: he gave them his protection, and Roma fled (1531). Then the Archbishop of Aix took it up and ordered seventeen villagers of Merindol to be burnt; the local Council was doubtful what to do, and the whole affair ended for the time being in the King promising them their lives if they abjured (1541). But later the Parliament of Aix, led by a new President, were against them, and, after Francis had protected them for three years, got the help of Cardinal Tournon, Archbishop of Lyons.

The King was told that they were rebels and threatening Marseilles. He withdrew his protection and ordered all Waldensian heretics to be exterminated. In two months some three thousand were killed, women and children as well as men: some of the latter were sent to the galleys and many survivors fled to Switzerland (1545).

So suffered these simple people, peaceful citizens guilty of no crime. They were preparing to spread their religious faith, but it is no justification for the severity used to put them down. The burning at Meaux, after trial at Paris, of fourteen who had organised a Church at Meaux, showed the same spirit of severity (Oct. 7, 1546). The King's tolerance was not a deep-seated mood. He had now changed his mind and, like the people of Paris, naturally angered by the mutilation of the Madonna's statue and the insult of the Placards, was now set against the Reformers.

When a truce ripened into peace with Germany, Francis was free to order his realm as he pleased; he had met Charles V at Aigues-Mortes (July 14, 1538), that impressive fortress in its desolate land, with its memories of St. Louis and its outlook towards Spain. The result was the Peace of Crépy (Sept. 18, 1544).

Edicts of persecution marked the change; there had been an edict of amnesty (July 1535), but now, after cruel persecutions, the Edict of Fontainebleau (June 1, 1540) organised trials for heresy, and its provisions remained substantially in force for some nine years. The Cardinal of Tournon, the Inquisitor-General (Ory) and the Parliament of Paris vigorously supported the King in his new policy. But after an illness of two months Francis died (March 31, 1547) and was succeeded by his only living son, Henry II, a more convinced Catholic. The new reign was to carry out with more consistency the policy of persecution already begun.

Henry II had a high view of himself as the Christian King (although he felt free to negotiate a Turkish alliance); he **Henry II,** expressed his conception in a severe repression of **1547–1559.** heresy; a special tribunal was set up, the so-called *Chambre Ardente*, an offshoot of the Parliament of Paris. The ecclesiastical courts were jealous of civil interference, but the Edict of Chateaubriand (June 27, 1551) gave jurisdiction to the civil courts in cases of heresy. Five French scholars of Lausanne were put to death at Lyons, which they had visited on their way home: after a year in prison they were burnt (May 1553). Many larger numbers had suffered elsewhere, but as these men had done nothing in act, the case caused much fear and distress. Meanwhile the Protestants were growing in influence, largely owing to their aristocratic leaders, and also in organisation of new churches in many important towns: Calvin had sent to France by 1566 over one hundred and twenty pastors of his choice and training, which was a guarantee of their efficiency.

Much depended not only upon the kings, but also upon the leading men. First among them came the Princes of the Blood: **The Princes** two of the house of Bourbon, Antony, King of **of the** Navarre, and his brother, Louis, Prince of Condé : **Blood ; the** the former was unstable, and easily tempted by offers **Bourbons.** (if not chances) of regaining the part of Navarre lost to Spain. Both brothers became Huguenots. Margaret, sister of Francis I, had married as a second husband Henry II of Navarre, and their daughter Jeanne d'Albret married Antony, Duke of Bourbon and Vendôme. The memory of Margaret's friendship with the early reformers of Meaux would predispose the house of Navarre towards the Huguenots, and about 1557 Antony joined them, as did Louis de Condé. Condé was the firmer of the two: he was easy-mannered and popular: his morals were not those of Geneva, but the general French public was not too critical. When his brother (*c.* 1661) became a Catholic it was natural that Condé should take his place as

Huguenot leader: he was not a great general although brave and venturesome. Antony died of wounds at the siege of Rouen in 1562, and, after Condé's death at Jarnac (1569), Antony's son, the future Henry IV, brought up by his steadfast Huguenot mother, was now regarded by her and her fellow-believers naturally as the leader of the party: he was only sixteen, but quickly matured both as general and statesman.

Catharine de Medici, wife and widow of Henry II (who died in 1559), had, like most of her family, a taste for politics and a wish for power: she inherited the traditions of Lorenzo the Magnificent and the maxims of Machiavelli. While her husband lived she was over- Catharine de Medici. shadowed by his mistress, Diana of Poitiers, but his death and the accession of her son Francis II gave her a chance to make up for lost time. For politics, in the Italian sense of balancing rivals against each other for her own gain, she had an instinctive and decided turn, but into the sphere of ethics she had not entered. Hence, although she was not a monster of cruelty and did not delight in it for its own sake, any movements and combinations, which she directed, might easily become proverbs of cynical bloodshed, as was the Massacre of St. Bartholomew on a large scale.

The family of Guise, owing to its Catholicism and its abilities, played a great part in this history. René of Lorraine, in the days of Charles the Bold, left his lands there to his elder son Antony, and his French territories, The Family of Guise. in Normandy and elsewhere, including the county of Guise (later on raised to a duchy), to his second son Claude. At Marignano (1515) Claude had fought bravely, and while Francis I was a prisoner he had steadied the kingdom, and especially Paris, in face of ferments and an invasion by Charles V. Like many Lorrainers he and his descendants were equally at home in diplomatic chambers and fields of battle. He left daughters, one of whom, Mary, was married to James V of Scotland, an alliance which made the family strongly anti-English, as was to be seen in later years. Of the sons, Francis, the eldest, was an able soldier and had conquered Calais from the English; but he was assassinated at Orleans by a Huguenot,

Poltrot de Méré (February 1563): the murderer under torture said that Beza and Coligny had instigated him, and although this was untrue it left with the family a deep hatred of Coligny.

The second son, Charles, was marked for the Church: he had helped Henry and was made by him Archbishop of Rheims (1538). As a prelate he was, certainly on the secular side, and in many ways on the ecclesiastical, all that could be wished: he drained marshes, gave his timber for buildings, founded a University (1548), a theological College, a seminary and a convent for lay brethren. The youngest of French cardinals he was also the best, moulded by the counter-Reformation. He gave up hunting and always kept a yearly retreat. But he relied overmuch on his real skill in diplomacy, and as men always have the defects of their qualities, he gave the impression of being too much for himself and never disinterested: a Venetian observer thought he was never trusted. But he became dominant in ecclesiastical France. For some time he was bent on a National Council which he hoped would bring about a united France: probably he did not appreciate the thorough-going earnestness of the Huguenots, and hence was too sanguine in his hopes for unity. But while a National Council might unite and strengthen France, it would have weakened Papal power there, and hence the Cardinal and the Pope were opposed in politics:[1] his brother Louis († 1578) was less important. In the next generation State and Church were again represented; Henry, Duke of Guise, the eldest, was an able general; Charles, the second son, was Duke of Mayenne; the youngest, Louis, was another Cardinal of Guise.

The Cardinal of Lorraine.

On the Huguenot side the chief figure was Gaspard de Coligny,[2] the Admiral, a thorough patriot, an able leader and statesman: high-principled by nature, his disposition was raised and strengthened (perhaps hardened) by

Coligny.

[1] This is well brought out in Mr. H. O. Evennett's excellent work, *The Cardinal of Lorraine and the Council of Trent* (Cambridge University Press, 1930); the conflicting policies and the contending personalities are well described with knowledge accurate and wide.

[2] A. W. Whitehead's *Gaspard de Coligny* (London, 1904) is not only an excellent biography, but one of the best books on the Wars.

the discipline of his religion: he is, perhaps, the only character of the Wars deserving of great and sincere respect: by his side, on a much lower platform, was his brother d'Andelot.

While Catharine de Medici might move towards toleration through her policy of balancing opposed parties, more detached observers were moved in the same direction by cool reasoning. Some members of the Parliament of Paris thought banishment a more fitting punishment for heresy than was death. Chief among these was de l'Hôpital, whom Catharine called to her help (May 1560); when she made him Chancellor in June, he was able to guide *De L'Hôpital: the Politiques.* affairs as he and she, for their differing reasons, wished. But Henry II had disliked this new school of thought, and might have reacted against it, had not the fatal tournament (July 10, 1659) ended his life and brought to the throne Francis II, husband of Mary of Scots, a sickly youth, who was *Francis II* crowned at Rheims (September 18, 1559): his *(1559-1560).* reign, however, was short as he died after a short illness (December 13, 1560). But even while it lasted the divisions of parties had become more clearly marked. Naturally the Guises had been all powerful: the Duke in the Army and the Cardinal of Lorraine in the Church. There were many who thought that the chief places in the Council should belong to the Princes of the Blood: the King, however, left everything to the Guises, and announced that he was doing so. This step quickened the latent dislike felt for a foreign family, and discontent began to simmer. But Calvin kept a restraining hold on the extremists who wished to come out into open resistance. He would do nothing not authorised by the Bourbons, and he gave more weight to the decisions of the Parliament of Paris than the Huguenots liked.

French parties were also becoming more entangled with those of other lands. In the Netherlands the Provinces were striving for their freedom against Philip II of Spain, and now when religious sympathies were joining together men of different races and realms, the Huguenots, who had their own fears and suspicions of Spain, kept their eyes on the struggles of the Netherlands. Thus on the North as on the South, where Lutherans and Calvinists could help, the Huguenots had possible allies. The situation in France itself needs review.

HenryII had always been in need of money and wished to order his realm as he chose. This need made him dependent on the Estates and specially upon the Church, which could and did give him liberal grants. This dependence of his on the Church kept persecution alive, although on a small scale and mostly against men of lower rank. But it seemed the moment to give up unrealised dreams of power in Italy, and this was done by the treaty of Cateau Cambrésis (April 12, 1559). By this treaty one chapter of history was closed, but the acquisition under it of the Three Bishoprics (Metz, Toul and Verdun), seized earlier in 1552, carried another chapter a stage further. The pretext for this border gain was a wish to protect the German Lutherans, who on their side had no scruples in joining with the national enemy. But the Huguenots feared that a treaty with Philip II behind it must mean an assault upon their religion. And now they had not only organised local churches with preachers, and Consistories of elders and deacons, at Strasbourg, Tours, Angers, Bordeaux, Nîmes, Poitiers, Orleans and elsewhere, but had also held a National Synod at Paris (1559).

State of France under Henry II.

For some time an idea of toleration had been growing stronger: the separations due to religious differences were slightly bridged over by social and commercial intercourse. Some members of the Parliament of Paris, for instance, came to think banishment a more proper punishment for heresy than was death. But the King resented their support of this view. By his Edict of Chateaubriand (June 1551) he ordered more extreme measures and greater zeal on the part of judges: no one was to be a magistrate or hold office unless of warranted faith. A later Edict, that of Compiègne (July 1556), expressly ordered the punishment of death for heresy. The Parliament of Paris was specially active against heresy and houses where conventicles had been held were razed: offenders were sent to the galleys, banished or put to death. The populace of the city, too, sometimes took matters

Religious Toleration.

into their own hands of violence. What happened in Paris also happened under the Parliaments of Toulouse and Aix in Provence. On the other side there were riots of Huguenot mobs in which churches were desecrated and despoiled: at Caen, for instance, *L'Abbaye aux hommes* suffered severely, and its tomb of William the Conqueror wrecked.

The Guises were by many disliked as foreigners or not Frenchmen of the old brand. They were hated by the Huguenots as their cruellest enemies, and a later Massacre incident turned hate to passion. When the Duke of Vassy. of Guise with his retainers lit on an unauthorised Huguenot service at Vassy (March 1, 1562), his soldiers burst into the building, slew over twenty of the worshippers, and wounded many others, this turned the ferment of strife into the explosion of war. Condé seized Orleans, to be for a time the Huguenot centre of war: massacres of them at Sens, Tours and Toulouse balanced their iconoclastic riots in various town, and the Parliament of Paris proclaimed them to be outside the pale of law. Recognised warfare was perhaps better than such a state of things, and even if ordinary life was shaken and fields left desolate by the marches of troops, the wars were punctuated by treaties of peace embodied in Edicts marking, with fluctuations, an approach to a settlement. The Wars, indeed, may be compared with the numbered and dated Crusades, which were less separate movements than crises when smoldering strife burst into war.

In June 1559 the Parliament of Paris discussed religious affairs. A speech by Anne de Bourg against persecution awoke the anger of Henry II: he was cast into prison and executed under Francis I. Owing to his position and his dying speech, his death won much sympathy for his cause. The Huguenots were now forced to feel that they were at the mercy of arbitrary and fitful power, wielded by relentless partisans. The Guises came in for most of the blame. If Vassy with its bloodshed was still to come, du Bourg's death had spread fear. There was much whispering and some open talk, in which Godefroy de Barry, Seigneur de la Renaudie, was mysteriously active: he had a grievance as his brother-in-law had been strangled by the

Guises without trial. Rumours filled the air in the winter of 1559. But Henry II, in his time, had begun a policy of severe repression: it seemed likely to go badly for the Huguenots, and the rise of a new party urging toleration would not have weakened the King's will. His death removed the controlling hand and opened the way for rivalries at Court; ambitious country politicians might see a chance of making use of these rivalries for some desired end. The outlook was now wider than merely national; there were Scots parties and plots with wily English diplomatists behind, while on the French borders were tangled movements in Germany and the Netherlands. This wider and darkened field gave a mysterious background to French intrigues, and a profitable path seemed open even for lesser political gamblers. The Duke of Guise, a good soldier, was supreme in war, and the Cardinal of Lorraine administered Church and State. The Queen Mother was at first not very influential, but was able to get help from Michel de l'Hôpital when he became Chancellor in 1560.

On the Huguenot side there were some soldiers of fortune; many rumours of active moves and plots, such as Calvin had condemned, spread everywhere; in March 1560 these came to a head. The Guises were growing more unpopular, and there was talk of seizing them. After a winter of rumours it was decided to carry this out at Amboise (March 1560). The Tumult of Amboise. The leading spirit was La Renaudie, who as already mentioned had just grievances against the Guises. There were many rumours of help from outside; Elizabeth of England and theologians in Germany were vaguely said to be interested and Condé was precisely hinted at as the real leader. But the Duke of Guise was told about it, and the affair ended in a mere demonstration of horsemen against Amboise. Some were slain and some prisoners executed. But many had armed for the plot, and the vengeance taken embittered feeling without doing more. Meanwhile Calvinism was spreading and the Government becoming more oppressive: it was also forced to demand large grants to meet arrears and so grew more and more unpopular. It then began to hesitate, and by the Edict of Romorantin (May 1560), prisoners, except preachers and the seditious, were set free. Bishops were to try cases of heresy (which made an organised Inquisition unlikely): assemblies for worship and conventicles were held to be matters of police, and left to the civil authorities. Thus liberty of religious opinion was allowed, but not liberty of worship; and this was what the Huguenots thought they might reasonably ask. Catharine's policy of conciliation was in the air. In April, as noted before, she had made Michel de l'Hôpital Chancellor. The Bishops of Orleans and Valence, and the Archbishop Marillac of Vienne, denounced clerical corruptions and abuses as the real causes of the heresy. A National Council was suggested as the remedy.

An Assembly of Notables was held at Fontainebleau (August 21, 1560). Both Catharine and l'Hôpital were for toleration, she from expediency and he from principle. **Discussions, Civil and Religious.** Moreover, the Cardinal of Lorraine was also on the side of clemency, since he was now bent on a National Council. At Fontainebleau this was decided upon and a reformation of clerical discipline, which seemed to many more a matter for a National than for a General Council, was urged. Coligny, for the Huguenots, presented a petition against persecution, asking liberty to build "temples" (the name still in use) for their worship: he claimed that he had many followers especially in Normandy. Further assemblies were fixed; for the laity in December, and for the clergy in January. But at this moment came rumours of a Huguenot plot for a general rising in the South. Even Calvin knew of it, but the supposed headship of the Bourbons reconciled him to it much as he disliked strife and loyal as he was.

The States-General met at Orleans (December 1560): L'Hôpital appealed for toleration: beyond this the **States-General of Orleans, 1560.** nobles and the third Estate attacked the Church for its wealth and power. Further discussions were arranged, and in August 1561 the States met, the **Assemblies: Civil and Ecclesiastical.** laity at Pontoise and the Clergy at Poissy. There a Conference between the two sides was to be held. At Pontoise constitutional changes of a feudal type were suggested, and a payment of State debts out of the Church's wealth; this meeting too had some constitutional significance. The election arrangements differed from those of 1481. The three Orders now elected their representatives separately instead of all together: they also sat separately. For the laity the unit of election was the *bailliage*. These changes were a sign of the lessening national unity and coherence between classes. But Poissy was a scene of greater interest and of doctrinal importance.[1] The Cardinal of Lorraine was as much interested as Catharine and the Chancellor. He depended greatly upon his learning and real debating power. Yet it may be doubted if he realised the hold which their beliefs had upon the Huguenots. But it was skillfuly diplomatic to turn (as he did) debate upon Eucharistic doctrine, where Lutherans and Calvinists differed so widely as to hate each other fervently. Germany, where, from Lutherans, military or political help was looked for, was important to the Huguenots, and the more they committed themselves to a denial of the Real Presence, the deeper a wedge between the two Protestant bodies was driven. We must remember, however, that there are many to whom the Presence in the Eucharist appeals strongly, and Henry IV said later that this was so with him. For the Huguenots, Theodore Beza, the most aristocratic and personally impressive of French reformers, took the lead. After nine years of ministry at Lausanne (1549–1558), for which he had forsaken his legal education at Paris, Orleans and Bourges, he had become Calvin's coadjutor (and was to be his successor) at Geneva. He had much classical learning, and if, like Æneas Sylvius (Pius II), he might reproach himself for his *Juvenilia*, no one was likely to bring it against him now as Gregory of Heimburg had done against the Pope. His sincerity and devotion was undoubted, and after Calvin's death he, alone among the Genevan ministers,

Colloquy of Poissy, Sept. 9, 1561.

---

[1] See H. O. Evennett, *The Cardinal of Lorraine and the Council of Trent* (Cambridge, 1930), especially Chap. VIII. Also in the *Cambridge Historical Journal* (1927) and in the *Revue Historique* (May–June 1930): *Claude d'Espence et son discours du colloque de Poissy*.

For Beza see *Theodore Beza* (Heroes of the Reformation): H. M. Baird (1899). *Histoire des Églises Reformées sur Royaume de France*, par Théodore Bèze (3 vols., Lille, 1841–1842).

did his faithful duty in an outbreak of plague. By his side stood
Peter Martyr (Vermigli), an Italian, a former Austin canon,
then married, a convert to Zwinglianism, and now a preacher
at Strassbourg and to have later a short career in England
under Edward VI. There was also present for the
Catholics, Laynez, General of the Jesuits, most learned as he
proved at Trent, and here effective in France. His Society had
been coldly looked upon there, but after French experience of
it at Poissy it gained a footing and their college of Clermont (in
Paris) greatly influenced the French Church. Thus learning
and theological oratory were well represented. The greatness
of the learning shown, the scope of the debate, was more than
the lasting effect. Incidentally Beza had made an impression
which, to his countrymen, put his cause in a better light.
But little was gained for reunion, if something was for
toleration.

The Guises feared for their power, and the more so as the
inherent loyalty of the nation favoured the Princes of the Blood.
The Bourbons had an army of their followers and there were
signs of civil war; they were moving on Orleans, which was
important from its central position. They had declined the invitation to Fontainebleau, but when he was now summoned
to the Court, Condé obeyed: he was arrested and condemned
to death. The King of Navarre was less heroic, and played
a somewhat ignoble part, almost fawning upon the Guises.
But Condé was saved, although narrowly, when (November 16)
Francis II was taken ill and died three weeks later (December
5, 1560). Civil war was now not to be avoided, Death of
and the excited feeling of the people was both ex- Francis II:
pressed and stimulated by pamphlets at this time, Dec. 5, 1560.
which specially attacked the Guises. The French have always
excelled in clear logical pamphlets of political thought, and also
in vigorous popular tracts. One of the latter was the "Epistle
to the Tiger of France," attacking the Cardinal. Popular
favour for the time centred on Catharine de Medici and at
first events went in the same direction. Antony of Navarre
had given up all claims to the Regency, and was paid much
honour, expressed later (March 27, 1561) by the title of

Lieutenant-General of the Kingdom, which gave him little real power but some prestige and much leisure for his scandalous love affairs. His religious career was fitful: he now became a Catholic, but when he died of wounds in the siege of Rouen (November 1562), he is said to have returned to Protestantism. Condé lived longer, but at Jarnac (March 13, 1569), he was wounded and on his surrender shot faithlessly. As a leader he had been a failure, although always popular.

Short as the reign of Francis II had been, it had fixed the rivalry of the Bourbon and Guise: it had tangled up the affairs Charles IX, of Scotland with France, it had opened a path for 1560–1574. the political ability of Catharine: it had made civil war inevitable, and had also brought forward the problem of religious toleration. Now with the new King Charles IX only a boy of ten, his mother was the real ruler : opposite to her stood the Admiral Coligny, an experienced soldier of skill, steadfast in his religion and patriotic in his outlook. The triumph of Protestantism was as dear to him as the independence of his country, so his Protestantism was more than national, and his devotion to it led to what was now un-Pamphlets avoidable, opposition to Catholic Spain, bringing of the War. with it a wish to help Protestants in the Netherlands and, what was more hurtful on the national side, an alliance with England, whose naval power soon became the great help of the Huguenots, especially at Havre and then at La Rochelle. Into such an atmosphere there came now a stream of pamphlets which deserve mention and repay study[1] where space allows: after the Massacre of St. Bartholomew (1572)

---

[1] On these pamphlets see: A. Tilley, *The Literature of the French Renaissance* (Cambridge University Press, 1904); Vol. II: cc. XXIV and XXV. Also his article, E.H.R. (XIV, 1899), 1, p. 451: *Some Pamphlets of the French Renaissance.* And an earlier article by E. Armstrong, *The Political Thought of the Huguenots*, E.H.R. Vol. IV (1889), 1, p. 13. E. Barker, *A Huguenot Theory of Politics:* Huguenot Society of London: XIV (No. 1): also in *Cambridge Historical Journal: The Authorship of the Vindiciæ Contra Tyrannos*, Vol. III, No. 2 (1930). For a life of Plessis Mornay, see Raoul Patry, *Philippe du Plessis Mornay* (Paris, 1933). Also see *Camb. Mod. Hist.*, Vol. III: *c.* ii (A. Tilley), pp. 62 *seq.* and *c.* xxii (J. N. Figgis), pp. 754 *seq.*

the Queen Mother and no longer the Guises were aimed at, for the latter had saved the lives of some Huguenots.

Among the writers Jean Bodin may be mentioned first. He was essentially a *Politique*, and fixed his eye on sovereignty and the body politic. His *Six Livres de la Répub-lique* (1576) showed great historical learning, Jean Bodin. discussing such topics as slavery and national character over a large field. He decided that a monarchy on the French model, not a tyranny, hereditary and limited to males, was the best form of government. He saw, as was clear, that the Huguenot movement tended against the monarchy. He himself was a Catholic and assumed that the State must have one religion; but he would have other religions tolerated. This was the ordinary view of the *Politiques*: thus he wrote as a Catholic of tolerant mind. It should be noted that this book had much influence outside France. Bodin's own Latin version (*De re-publica libri sex* 1586) was soon followed by translations into Italian (1588), Spanish (1590) and German (1592). The Eng-lish translation by Richard Knolles, *The Six Books of a Commonwealth*, appeared in 1606.

Another writer was François Hotman, whose *Franco-Gallia* (1573) was also founded on a long historical survey. He laid stress on the Teutonic element in French con- François stitutional history and for it he had great admiration. Hotman. Like some more modern English historians he delighted in the popular election of the monarch. From this election naturally came the idea of a contract between King and people. The democratic foundation of polity was thus enwrought into the constitution, and his view reminds us of some early writers of the Investiture contest, notably of Manegold of Lautenbach. Incidentally he dislikes the excessive regard paid to Justinian's legislation. The Salic law, the origin of which he places rightly, is discussed, and he decides that while it shuts out women, it did not so treat a female line (a judgment which Edward III would have welcomed). But an obvious application of this was to the displacing of the Valois line by the house of Guise, who had a descent of this kind from Charlemagne: there were now Huguenots who thought this change might be of service to them, since the Duke of Guise had saved some lives at St. Bartholomew. But there were others who held the house shut out by the Salic law, and the same exclusion was applied to the claim of a Spanish Infanta which Philip II suggested. As the pamphlet put forward all these views it was naturally decried by some as disloyal to the Valois and as republican in effect. But this was unintentional. It should be noticed that in this current pamphlet literature there was much dislike of Machiavelli, whose *Prince* was naturally connected with Catharine de Medici. Thus an early translation of the *Vindiciæ* printed the *Prince* as an appendix. But the royalist and Catholic side had its strong and able supporters, chief among whom was the lawyer Louis d'Orleans, who when the accession of Henry IV was imminent wrote an apologetic work in which an English Roman Catholic was made to depict the position of English Romanists under Elizabeth.

One of the most interesting pamphlets was the *Vindiciæ contra Tyrannos* (probably written and published in 1579), The Vindiciæ to be attributed, perhaps with help in its matter, to contra the Huguenot diplomatist, Du Plessis Mornay, the Tyrannos. well-travelled adviser of Henry IV. This book, as its title shows, went straight to the practical question of the rights of oppressed subjects against an oppressive ruler: it also treated of the interference of foreign States in emergencies that arose. So it dealt with urgent difficulties, and did so in the light of Scripture, reason, the law of nature, and existing usage: it reminds us in many ways of the medieval discussions of Dominion, and there was a feudal tone in the exaltation of a national nobility, and indeed there is obvious continuity in the growth of political thought. Opposition to rulers, even to their death, could even claim some scholastic support. Like some other of these treatises it, too, had some effect in England.

Such a literature turned in France naturally to satire: naturally too the language in the end became the current The Satire French instead of the learned Latin. The cele-Ménippée. brated *Satire Ménippée* was the work of a group of learned and able *Politiques* in Paris, and after a preliminary history was printed in 1594 and passed into many editions. In form it pretended to be the speeches of orators in the Estates of 1593: the speakers are made to speak in their individual characters, and to give with those their true aims, and this is done with a skill and popular appeal that reminds us of the *Epistolæ obscurorum virorum*, and it had much the same popular effect. Of the group of authors, Pierre Pithon, a Protestant who had become a Catholic, was perhaps the most important of the writers, for his book *Les Libertés de l'Église gallicane* became a text-book of a school linking together Conciliar tradition and the later learning of Thomassinus and Fleury: incidentally it had a momentous bearing on the reception of the Tridentine decrees. But in its vivid French, contrasted with the Latin of earlier books, and in its popular touch the satire had a place of its own.

After she had gained an edict declaring the young King of age the Queen Mother began a tour of his court (March 1564) which lasted till late in 1565: it was intended to strengthen the royal hold on the nation, and in its course she met at Bayonne her daughter Elizabeth, now Queen: the warrior and statesman Alva was there too, and popular rumour assumed a discussion of severe measures about religion. Alva gave this advice, but the later assumption that a massacre was then and there decided upon was mistaken. At the time such a proposal was likely, but that Catharine agreed to carry it out is not true. Alva, even if ready to help in France, had his more pressing task in the Netherlands.

Between the government and the nation there was only slight sympathy. There were some long intervals of peace, such as that following the Peace of Amboise (March 1563), which lasted until September 1567. By this Treaty, which, like the other Treaties to follow, had the force of an Edict, the highest nobles were allowed Huguenot worship for their households and dependants: lesser nobles, for their households only. Liberty of conscience was allowed to all, and towns which already had their services could continue them; but Paris and its neighbourhood were excepted. One town in each *bailliage* might hold Huguenot services: an amnesty was promised for past offences of religion.

This settlement, from its nature, was only provisional and

incomplete: it was only to hold good until Charles IX came of age, and the looked-for General Council had pacified the religious world. When the Peace of Longjumeau (March 1568)

Long- repeated the same terms they were to hold good
jumeau. until a unity of religion covered the realm. By that time the Council of Trent had ended, and all hope of a world-wide religious peace from it was at an end.

Through the whole term of the wars and Treaties the Huguenots looked back to "the January Edict" (1562), by which they were granted liberty of preaching, although they were forbidden to build "temples" in towns, but might worship in private houses. Again and again they spoke of this as what they wished, although it had its restrictions. The Edict was not due to any conviction of the rightfulness of toleration, but to the "balancing" policy of Catharine, who at the time was well disposed to Condé and Coligny. But there was nearly always a scattered local warfare: fields were neglected and the social atmosphere was thunderous. Condé marched on Orleans but then diverted his force to Normandy, where Huguenots were numerous and English help at hand. While Henry of Guise was besieging Orleans, he (as said before) was assassinated by the Huguenot fanatic Poltrot de Mére (February 1563): this was a heavy blow to his side and it was little to the credit of Coligny and his comrades that they rejoiced at the evil deed. But the removal of Guise enabled Catharine to arrange the peace she desired and it was so the Peace 'of Amboise came about. Though favourable to the Huguenots it was not more so than the Ordinance of Orleans (January 1561), which had stayed all persecutions for religion and released all prisoners.

A new complication on the ecclesiastical side arose on the close of the Council of Trent. The last Session (XXV) was

The Council held on December 2, 1563, and the Pope, Pius IV,
of Trent: confirmed all the Decrees on January 26, 1563; but
its decrees. the acceptance of them by the various nations was only partial. France for itself had two scruples, the rights of the Crown and the Gallican liberties; the Parliament of Paris led by legal tradition formulated its reasons for refusing

acceptance. But the hierarchy, and notably the Cardinal of Lorraine, wished for reception, although their influence was not strong enough to get their will (see p. 266), and bishops were allowed to carry out in their dioceses such of them as were not against national custom. Eight provincial Synods approved the Decrees, and repeated attempts to gain their reception were made up to 1596. The strengthening of Papal power due to the Council and its reformation of discipline was, however, not without its natural effect on France. This question of the Decrees long remained a triple-headed grievance, between Pope, King and national hierarchy. But the introduction of diocesan seminaries as ordered by the Council, mainly under skilful Jesuit control, gave a higher tone and a closer coherence to the French Church. This improvement was noticed, with praiseworthy candour, by Bishop Gilbert Burnet in his *Pastoral Care*,[1] as a pattern for Restoration England.

On the political side both Catholics and Huguenots were closing their ranks. And the shadow of the war in the Netherlands was over France; the Huguenots feared war at home, which some others hoped for. They armed simultaneously in many places and one band planned a seizure of the King, who was near Meaux, but Catharine surrounded by Swiss mercenaries fled to Paris, as did the Cardinal of Lorraine to Rheims. War broke out again: the Constable Montmorency was killed in the battle of St. Denis (1567); Henry, Duke of Anjou, was made Lieutenant-General, and war in which Condé had the support of German mercenaries would have gone on had not Catharine made the peace of Longjumeau (March 1568), renewing the Treaty of Amboise. But peace was in the air rather than on the ground.

Catharine drew nearer the Huguenots, and Coligny, now at Court, was much with the King, who was attracted by the warrior's fame and conversation. The Catholics were drawing closer together and forming leagues, one of which in Picardy was a model for the later national league, and, as that was afterwards to do, they looked

<small>Catharine de Medici: diplomacy.</small>

---

[1] *A Discourse of the Pastoral Care*, by Gilbert, Lord Bishop of Sarum (4th edn., London, 1713), p. 49; the last he revised.

towards Catholic Spain for help if needed. Fear of Alva oppressed the Huguenots, but it seemed possible by fighting Spain in the Netherlands to save France, and Lewis of Nassau had a scheme for dividing them between England, Germany and France, leaving to Spain nothing of the old Burgundian heritage.

It was an age of diplomatic schemes, and of marriages to found or cement alliances. Charles IX had just married Elizabeth, daughter of the Emperor Maximilian II (1570). The Huguenots would have liked to see Henry of Navarre married to Elizabeth of England, which might lead to a Gallican Church independent of Rome. But Catharine wanted her for her favourite son the Duke of Anjou, and this courtship, more diplomatic than ardent, lingered along its way. Catharine feared a breach with Spain, for its result would be uncertain. However, she now revived a marriage scheme of her husband's suggestion, that of Henry of Navarre to her daughter Margaret: religion was the only obstacle and the death of the Queen Jeanne of Navarre (June 9, 1572) removed a steady Huguenot influence on her son. He with the younger Condé had conformed to Catholicism after his father's death: then he had returned to his earlier faith, but these more outward changes had no deep roots.

This marriage proposal disturbed many. Pius V, ascetic, severe in discipline, the sainted Pope of the Counter-Reformation, disapproved of it, and later, during the Wars of the League, Sixtus V excommunicated Henry, although afterwards he resented the dictation of the Leaguers in the matter.

Henry, now for over two months King of Navarre, was married to Margaret of Valois on August 18, 1572. Many

Henry of Navarre: his marriage. Huguenots had flocked to Paris for the celebrations and a time of peace seemed coming. But Catharine was disquieted at the growing influence of Coligny on her son, who had been won over to approve an attack on Spain in the Netherlands. Coligny had sent thither an army under Genlis, but (July 19, 1572) it was utterly defeated. Catharine felt that more risks from Coligny must be avoided, and she therefore attempted the Admiral's assassination

(August 22, 1572): it was to her a mere incident of politics, expedience being her only consideration.

But the murderer's shot only broke the Admiral's left arm and mutilated his right hand. It was an inconvenience for Catharine, but to the Huguenots it was much more and they naturally cried out for vengeance. Catharine's dream of peace and a united France gained by Coligny's removal was at an end, and she had to form another and a larger plan. This again she did as another political expedient to which morals and human lives must give way. If the Huguenot leaders were put out of the way, it seemed possible to over-awe the rank and file, and the removal of Coligny would also hinder any danger of an open break with Spain. So she hurriedly held a small council (August 23), and it was decided to kill all the leaders except Navarre and the younger Condé. It took some time to persuade the King to agree, but in the end he did so, and on a given signal the massacre began (St. Bartholomew, August 24, 1572). The Duke of Guise himself saw to the murder of the wounded Admiral, whose body was treated with gross barbarity: the King, with the hysterical passion of a convert, shot Huguenots from his window, and a general massacre went on in the city all day. Then, by royal order, the same bloodshed followed in cities from Meaux to Toulouse. There was a greatness and yet a vagueness about the number slain which deepened the horror, felt and expressed in many lands except in Italy, Spain and Switzerland. Estimates of the number vary from 10,000 to 100,000 (which is far too high); the smaller number is nearer the mark: in Paris itself about 2,000 perished.[1]

Massacre of St. Bartholomew, 1572.

In judging the massacre and fixing the guilt for it, we must recall the maxim so dear to Lord Acton that, for the historian, moral laws and standards do not vary from age to age; we must not be misled into the miserable mistake of excusing it

[1] For the massacre: see Lord Acton: *History of Freedom and other Essays*; Essay IV: *The Massacre of St. Bartholomew*. A. W. Whitehead: *Gaspard de Coligny c.* XV: and *c.* XVI, p. 276. *Problems of St. Bartholomew* (noting that Lord Acton had not to his hand some important Spanish documents). C. Häusser: *Period of the Reformation*, Vol. II, pp. 33 *seq.* Ranke, Lavisse VI. I. pp. 121 *seq.* and *Camb. Mod. Hist.*, Vol. III, p. 19.

because such crimes, although on a smaller scale, were common in that day. For fear, passion or sudden impulse, excuses might, of course, be made, but the horror is even raised by the coldness of calculation and absence of passion with which it was conceived.

Many points and problems about the massacre have been much debated. But it was certainly due to a sudden resolution of Catharine's and had not been decided upon long beforehand. Most certainly Catharine was its author, and to her, horrible as it must seem, it was a mere matter of politics; but its effect was a disappointment: it neither gave her more power nor united the kingdom. Much that has been written about it has camouflaged the terrible truth. Charles IX said (August 24) that it was the Guises who devised it: then (August 25) he said that it was carried out suddenly to counter an alleged Huguenot plot: this had been a pure invention of Catharine's, used at the Council, to over-persuade the King, and there was no foundation for it: finally (August 26), Charles claimed it as his own work: the government gave the explanation that the King had forestalled an attack upon himself. Truth, however, could hardly be looked for where humanity was lacking.

Some minor questions can now, with the volume of evidence before us, be easily dismissed. The Papal Court had not known the measure beforehand, but welcomed it when it came. Gregory XIII (May 13, 1572–April 10, 1585) wished to illuminate the city at once and was only prevented from doing so by the French ambassador Ferratz, and he spoke of it as a Divine mercy. In France itself the clergy, with few exceptions, do not seem to have encouraged the massacre or shared in it.

The Huguenots now organised themselves afresh for defence: troops and commands were put on a local and democratic footing for which their religious associations had given them a model. War began and soon centred on the siege of La Rochelle, but Catharine wished for peace and offered terms which led to the Peace of La Rochelle (June 1573). Protestant worship was allowed at La Rochelle, La Rochelle. Nîmes and Montauban: the greater nobles were allowed baptisms and marriages with assemblies of ten persons attending: liberty of conscience and an amnesty were promised. Catharine had family cares to see to. Charles IX was slowly sinking, and remorses for responsibilities he, all untrained and unfitted for them, had to bear, saddened his nearing end, which came May 30, 1574.

Catharine's ablest and favourite son, Henry of Anjou had, by her diplomacy (May 1573), been elected King of Poland. On the death of the last of the great Jagellon dynasty, Sigismund (1572), the throne had been made elective: religious toleration, to which the cities, with Roman Catholics (of the State religion), Orthodox and Protestants, were used, was part of the constitution and had to be sworn to by the King on his election; but the nobles, who were the electors, had the real power. But France, and most of all Paris, Henry loved: the roughness of his new surroundings and the proud freedom of its nobles displeased him. Catharine had taken great trouble to gain him the throne against a German rival:[1] it would give him power and a political sphere, which to her were the greatest of prizes, but he only felt the drawbacks of his new position, and as a war with the Turks seemed to be coming, he feared that his subjects would insist on his leadership to justify the military reputation they had heard of: fearing to be kept by force, he took to an ignoble flight, only relieved by a gorgeous reception at Venice, and so reached Paris and the throne of France. *Henry, Duke of Anjou, becomes King.*

The outset of the reign saw a new trouble for Catharine: many moderate Catholics in Languedoc had joined forces with the Huguenots, and Damville, the Governor there, was really independent: he allowed the Huguenots their worship freely, and proclaimed a policy of religious toleration. In opposition to this the more fervent Catholics formed a closer league. Henry III wavered, but after seeing his mother, gave out that his realm must only harbour one religion. War almost at once began, and Alençon gained a useful success by

---

[1] There is a curious account of the embassy entrusted to Montluc, Bishop of Valence, in Isaac Disraeli's *Curiosities of Literature*, III, pp. 346–363: it is written by his secretary Choisnin: I remember it from reading it when I was a boy of eleven.

his capture of La Charité, the Huguenot stronghold on the Loire, thus closing the way to the expected German allies. The sixth war had lasted from January 1577 to September, when the Peace of Bergerac ended it with terms slightly less favourable for the Huguenots: although they were allowed their worship in one town in every *bailliage*.

But the King really counted for little: Philip of Spain supported the League, and the League followed his policy: they Influence of agreed (1585) that heresy should be suppressed, no Philip II. heretic should hold the throne, and the old Cardinal of Bourbon was declared its heir: Philip gave the League a subsidy, and they embodied his terms in a Manifesto. Thus while Navarre really ruled in south-western France, the League held Paris and the north. Henry III had to choose between them and he joined the League. He decreed that all heretics must conform or else leave the realm: the Parliament registered this decree and so it was fully law. The Pope excommunicated Henry and declared him incapable of succession. War—"the War of the three Henries"—was inevitable. Henry III was supreme least of all in his beloved Paris. A Council of Sixteen held all power there, dominated by the League and city preachers. In the country there was war: Navarre had Swiss and Germans marching to his help: the King sent one of his vicious and incapable *mignons*, the Duc de Joyeuse, against Navarre, but he was utterly defeated at Coutras (October 20, 1587) and himself slain: this was the first Huguenot victory in battle and was due to the skill of Navarre, even against odds.

From Henry III much might have been looked for: he was the most gifted, in both mind and appearance, of the brothers. Henry III, But dissipation, in the sickly atmosphere of an 1574–1589. immoral court, had eaten away his mental and moral fibre: he might have risen to greatness and command, but he sank to trickery and deceit. When King, he passed fitfully from devotional displays to degraded debauchery, and his court was the most vicious France had known. His brother, Alençon, who succeeded him in Anjou, might outdo him in trickery and plots but he himself was the most contemptible king of the line he was to end, although for the legislation of his reign much good might be said. The pair were parodies of the Medicean type with its love of politics and power. Anjou was disappointed in turn of the hand of Elizabeth, which held England so tightly in its grasp, of a promised province in the Netherlands (where his career ended in an attempt to seize Antwerp by force); so he turned to his native land, and there "the Peace of Monsieur" (published as an Edict from Beaulieu, May 1576), which ended the fifth war, was ascribed to his diplomacy and called by his official title; it is the one good thing recorded of him.

By this peace Reformed services were permitted everywhere except in and around Paris. *Chambres mi-parties*, as before, were set up. Eight places were to be garrisoned by Huguenots, and the States-General were to meet in six months. There was nothing new in the terms, but the state of the country had changed greatly since the wars began.

The Huguenots were no longer growing: the austerity of Calvin's system was now felt more than its lofty appeal. On the other side Catholicism was stronger and felt the new enthusiasm of the Counter-Reformation. The *Politiques* might see no chance of a realm with only one religion and so choose the remedy of toleration; but this the Catholics, remembering their past power, were not ready to grant; and the Huguenots still cherished hopes of supremacy for themselves, distant as it might be. Changes in the State of France.

The Catholics were now headed by Henry of Guise; his brother, the Cardinal of Lorraine, having died two years before: Henry was a devoted Catholic, and had all the popular gifts his monarch lacked: a personal fascination adorned in him the political and military ability common in his family: he was a good general, the best rider, fencer and swimmer in France. He was bent on making France an entirely Catholic land, and under his leadership the older model of a League was invigorated and enlarged. Huguenots had organised themselves, now their opponents Henry of Guise.

did the same. Between 1563 and 1568 Leagues had been formed at Angers, Dijon and Bourges: in 1576 a larger one was formed at Peronne with the special object of resisting Condé's claim on Picardy, and Guise was its natural head. In Europe at large Spain was now the champion of Catholicism, and, looking outside their own land, the League looked to Spain: and gradually it grew more dependent on this willing outside help. If Spain were dangerous to France, it had on its side, however, something to fear in Portugal.

The League.

The States-General meeting, demanded for reform, met at Blois (November 1576). Neither of the two parties was anxious to support the Royal power, and the assembly was dominated by the Guise party and demanded religious unity at all costs; the two higher estates took a lofty tone and were on their dignity. The Huguenots had taken no share in the elections and only one deputy belonged to them. It was proposed that the Royal assent should not be necessary for laws passed by the States, and that the majority of his Council should be nominated by them. Henry III was ready to abjure religious toleration, and his apologies for having granted it were both degrading and useless. He was ready for war and prepared for it, but an adequate money grant he could not gain. The diplomacy around the meeting was greatly tangled even for the France of the day, while religious and political discontents worked together. Damville had proposed a National Council including Huguenot deputies, "so that, through a real reformation of the clergy, the wrath of God might be appeased." It was to be, as it were, a second Colloquy of Poissy but with legislative power. But before long Damville was won over by Catharine's diplomacy and deserted his Huguenot friends. The clergy, who a little later at Melun (1579) asked for the reception of the Tridentine decrees and free election of bishops, were told by Henry to reform themselves, but his prerogatives and rights under the Concordat he would not surrender. The King could not suppress heresy by force as the leading Estates demanded; he could hardly raise money enough to pay for his needs and his pleasures, and financial abuses, such

States-General at Blois, 1576.

as the sale of offices, multiplied. There was desultory warfare, and on the whole the Leaguers had the upper hand. But the Treaty of Bergerac (September 17, 1577), came to stay a more destructive campaign. By this treaty Huguenot services were restricted to one town, with its sub-urbs, in each *bailliage*, and to those towns where they had been practised up to then. Paris with a neighbourhood now enlarged was excluded as before: they were allowed fewer *Chambres mi-parties*, and the proportion of their representatives in those left to them was now a third and not a half: they were allowed to keep six of the garrisoned towns assigned to them before. This Treaty was later renewed by that of Fleix (November 1580). But Henry III tried to strike a blow for his power by decreeing the abolition and illegality of all leagues henceforth and throughout the realm. He was so far pleased with it that he proudly called it *his* Peace in contrast to that of Monsieur. As a permanent foundation for a settled realm it was not enough: as a temporary reshifting of parties it was less favourable to the Huguenots. It was published as an Edict from Poitiers.

Treaty of Bergerac (or Edict of Poitiers), Sept. 1577.

Henry of Navarre had his grievances, and raised his reputation by conquest of beautiful Cahors with its famous bridge across the Lot: it was part of his wife's dowry but not been given to him. This short spell of war, ended by the Treaty of Fleix (November 1580), was known as the Lovers' War: Henry III had ridiculed the love episodes of the Court at Nérac and this was resented more than a deserved moral reproof might have been.

Philip II had reasons beyond religious interests for building the power of France. In 1580 he claimed the throne of Portugal: its King, Sebastian, had perished (August 4, 1578) in an attempted conquest of Morocco; the rich possessions of Portugal in the East Indies made it a desirable gain. Sebastian's successor was the aged Cardinal Henry, but Philip contrived to hinder his getting a dispensation for marriage from Rome, which might have given him, as he hoped, a chance, though slender, of founding a dynasty, and he died (January 1580). There was a claimant, Antonio, Abbot of Crato, certainly half-Jewish and uncertainly legitimate: he found some support in his country and was encouraged by Elizabeth in England and Catharine in France as a set-off against Philip of Spain: in league with Catharine he fitted out a mercenary fleet to capture the Azores (October 1581). Both this and a second attempt were disastrous failures, but Antonio lived for some years in an obscurity which might any time be lightened by schemes against Philip. Hence arose fears which quickened Philip's support of the Leaguers in France.

The Duke of Anjou died (June 1584) and dying has been called the most important thing he ever did. Its import-
Death of Anjou, June 1584. ance lay in the fact that Henry of Navarre was now by accepted law the heir to the throne, since Henry III was childless, but the Curia, Spain and the League were all loath to recognise his claim. But his beginning of war in 1580 and the growth of his reputation as a leader made Navarre a dangerous rival for the League. On the other side the popularity and power of the Duke of Guise brought him into the field as a likely rival of ancient lineage which was proved by current genealogies. From Lorraine came one special work, the *Stemmata* (1580), urging the claim of the Guise family as the rightful heirs of the Carolings. It was the work of Francis de Rosières, a high ecclesiastic of Toul, who had travelled much in company with the late Cardinal of Lorraine. So French politics showed once more the national tendency to justify the facts of life by the logic of theory.

Paris has more than any other capital settled the fate of its country, and now Paris set up its own branch of the League (1584): a lawyer, Hotteman, was its leader, and its officers became a central committee acting also as a controlling committee (for the guilds and local associations) called "The Sixteen." And Henry of Guise was the idol of the Parisians. So events and theories were leading him into rebellion.

Then came pressure from Spain, whose ambassadors came to him at Joinville (January 1585), and a secret agreement was made. Spain and the League were to root out heresy in

France: to admit no heretic or favourer of heretics as king: to recognise the Cardinal of Bourbon, who was the uncle of Navarre, as heir to the throne: he was an ecclesiastic of great age and childless; this put off the difficulty of decision, which Guise felt strongly from his dislike of rebellion. He sought Papal advice, and Gregory XIII answered that if the cause of rebellion was a religious one only, he could bless it. As the Duke was eager above all to make France solely Catholic he could now feel reassured.

Philip had promised a yearly subsidy, and the League (March 31, 1585) published a Manifesto, stating the points agreed upon and, still further, promising to maintain the constitutional rights of the nobles, the Parliament and the civic bodies; taxes were to be lowered and the States-General to meet every three years.

The monarch seemed shut out from this strictly constitutional programme, and in fact neither in Paris nor the realm at large had he any power. Henry of Navarre had a faithful Huguenot following in the south-west: northwards and in Paris the League was the supreme power. Queen Elizabeth gave Henry III, as one might expect, most manly advice, which he naturally rejected.

But Henry III, like Guise, had strong Catholic convictions. By the Treaty of Nemours (July 1585) he joined the League, and in a spasm of hopefulness promised to pay their army. He abjured all his former promises of toleration, and decreed that all who were of the new religion must within six months confess the Catholic faith, or else leave the kingdom. Two months later Sixtus V excommunicated Henry of Navarre; he was never to become King of France, even if he should become a Catholic.

Thus began "the War of the Three Henries"; it was rightly so called, for the three personalities more than any principles caused its outbreak. In the months which followed, **The War of** Henry III and Henry of Guise were really hostile **the Three** though allies. The degradation of the monachry, **Henries.** the anarchy throughout the land, the headstrong turbulence of Paris, with its "Sixteen" controlling everything there, with its ecclesiastical orators such as Jean Boucher, the one-eyed curé, remind us of France and Paris in 1793.

Navarre could depend upon help in money from England, whose Queen, with her excellent credit, could borrow from Italian or German bankers at a much lower rate than could any other monarch: from Germany and Switzerland he could hire mercenaries. And his own French troops were devoted and thoroughly trained.

A sluggish tide of success for the League was checked by Navarre's victory at Coutras (October 1587), when the King's army under his favourite, the incapable Duke de Joyeuse, was utterly defeated and its leader killed. But this victory, not properly followed up, was partly counterbalanced by a victory won by Guise over the foreign mercenaries of Navarre. On the other side, Henry III was suspected as half-hearted by the Parisians; he angered the Guises by giving to two of his favourites the governments of Normandy and Picardy which Guise desired for himself and his uncle, the Duke of Aumâle. The King gradually lost any influence he had, and his good faith was suspect. At the end of 1587 he came to Paris. Guise, whom he forbade to come there, disobeyed and came (May 1588): the King was overshadowed by him and the "Sixteen." When the King called his troops to his help the citizens rose in riot: his troops were overpowered and the streets were

The Barricades: flight of Henry III. barricaded. The King saw nothing before him but flight, and so by night he fled from Paris. But he still kept to the League: once more by an Edict he declared his intention to stamp out heresy: all

Edict of Union, July 1588. officials were to be sworn Catholics, and the power of the "Sixteen" in Paris was recognised. Also he made the Duke of Guise his commander-in-chief.

The States-General were called together at Blois, September 1588, and the Château there was to add tragic interest to its famous architecture. The King, who had the gift

The States-General of Blois, Sept. 1588. of occasional eloquence that often marks inferior statesmanship, made a powerful speech at the opening. The representatives were disappointed at the postponement of the reforms, and angry at the excessive expenditure, largely on unworthy favourites. The King was ready to admit restraints on his power, yet spoke loftily of his prerogative, a gift from Divine power. Yet he repeated his former Edict of Union. But the Assembly was inspired by theories of another kind: the Royal power was to them a creation of the people's will and the Church's choice. They demanded lower taxation, but at the same time larger military measures against the Huguenots. The King would yield about finance, but the attack on his power, enforced by the lofty tone of Guise, was another matter: it was a crisis much like that of 1793 even if based on memories of the Merovings. Too feeble, even with his passing spasm of brilliance, to act as a King, Henry thought that he might save himself by becoming an assassin. So he arranged to murder Guise when he was summoned to attend him. Despite his rank, the Cardinal of Guise was put into prison and murdered the next day: others of the family were imprisoned. Henry felt able to write and say "Now I am King"; for he had killed "the King of Paris." His mother was lying ill, and when he told her of his great deed, she sadly said: "God grant that you have not made yourself King of nothing." All she had schemed and wrought for was at an end: the thread of her life was broken and she died (January 5, 1589). *Murder of the Duke of Guise, Dec. 23, 1588.* *Death of Catharine de Medici, Jan. 5, 1589.*

Her fears were well founded: all Catholic France was roused to anger and hatred. Paris was furious: the Sorbonne, like a medieval Pope, declared that Henry had by his act released his subjects from their allegiance. The lawyers lagged behind the ecclesiastics, but the governor of the Bastille arrested sixty of its members and the rest then reasonably agreed with the Sorbonne. Sermons and processions roused the Parisians to fever-heat, and extinguished tapers symbolised their prayer for the extinction of the last of the Valois. The older generation took up the task of the younger dead: the Duke of Mayenne, uncle of Guise, was declared Lieutenant-General of the Royal State and Crown of France (March 13, 1589). A Council General of Leaguers and civic representatives took the direction of affairs at Paris. So religious differences had been forced by politics into the foremost place, and yet it was really civil war.

The King, who had massacred the Huguenots and murdered the Catholic leaders, had no choice left him except a change of sides. A truce with Henry of Navarre ripened into a league made appropriately enough at Plessis-lès-Tours with its memories of Louis XI. Protestants were not heretics, said the King: the Gospel was the bond of Christians: small differences should not make enmities. The King of Navarre showed real greatness of mind by greeting his brother-in-law as a king should be met. They joined their forces and they had Swiss mercenaries to help them. They marched upon the capital and gained a success at Senlis. If the King was not yet in Paris, he could at any rate sleep at St. Cloud. The passions of the Parisians calmed, but fanaticism had its children: Jacques Clément, a Dominican of feeble mind, was inspired by strong political theories and was ready to sacrifice himself if he could slay the tyrant. He contrived to get admitted to present letters to the King: he stabbed him but was himself killed at once. It was the very day (August 2, 1589) on which an assault held sure to be successful was to have been made. So ended the line of the Valois kings.

Assassina-
tion of
Henry III,
Aug. 2, 1589.

Henry of Navarre was the one outstanding leader left: he had the shape of greatness and much of its spirit. But his task was even greater now: a kingdom lay before him: he might have some support behind him but the realm had yet to be conquered: strangely enough the changes of faith which his professions had shown, the grave moral defects of his character and life, made it easier for him to reconcile different creeds, and revive by personal popularity the loyalty which had made the monarchy. But the standard of Navarre was not as yet the flag of France. If we judge from the religious standpoint, to barter a creed for a crown condemns a man and his nature, but an immoral life, such as Henry had led, dims the spiritual sense and eye. A man to whom that has happened cannot rise to the highest pitch of judgment. This lack of deep religious conviction

Henry IV and
his religion.

made him ready to respond when the growing rift between the Spanish and the national French groups of Leaguers widened, and some of the latter turned to negotiations with him. It became clearer that his Huguenotism was the one thing that went against him. His wise adviser, Sully, himself a Calvinist of the strictest life and thought, advised him to change. Political reasons, then, for Henry's becoming a Catholic were many and strong (January 1593).

With his experience, and his friendship with men in both religious camps, the change of creed probably seemed to him no extraordinary step. At Paris in the States-General his side was well represented by the Catholic royalists, especially by Renaud de Beaune, Archbishop of Bourges. There was a wish for a conference between the parties, and despite frantic efforts at the last moment from the side of Spain, and attempts by the Papal Legate Caetani to hinder any approach to heretics, it was carried through. Deputies were chosen and the conference began at Suresnes (April 29, 1593); they Conference left Paris amid loud cries of "blessed are the peace- of Suresnes, makers." A fortnight later it was announced that April 1593. Henry had decided to become a Catholic: he received instruction (July) at Mantes: among the divines who instructed him were the Archbishop of Bourges and the learned skilled controversialist Du Perron, whom Casaubon called "a thunderbolt of a man": the King is said to have shown unexpected knowledge and acuteness. About this time he said to one of his chaplains that he saw neither order nor devotion in the Reformed religion, which was a mere preachment, and that without the Real Presence in the Sacrament, religion was a mere ceremony. On some points he had his doubts: Invocation of Saints: Auricular confession and Papal Supremacy, but on the whole balance his mind was made up. And behind these theological discussions there was the shadow of his distracted land and its many sufferers. There was no hypocrisy on his part and there was something of self-sacrifice, for he moved slowly to decision, a man of action rather than of argument and reading, he did not promise one thing while he believed or intended another. He went honestly by his lights, but they shone rather from the earth beneath than from the heaven above.

He signed his Abjuration and, after a sad and solemn farewell to some Huguenot ministers, was received into the Church at the Abbey of St. Denis by the Archbishop of Bourges and seven other bishops (May 25, 1593). At Paris the States-General still sat and Mayenne still behaved as before, but neither had much effect. City after city, noble after noble, came over to Henry: late in the year the young Duke of Guise joined the crowd. Then (February 27, 1594) came the coronation at Chartres, where he had for a time held his court, not at Rheims, rightly the historic and traditional cathedral for coronations, as that city still held aloof from him. The tide was still with him, the skilled diplomacy of Sully and du Mornay was active: some leaders, like Villars, the able and obstinate defender of Rouen (to be killed later as a traitor by the other side in the coming Spanish War), and Brissac, the omnipotent commander of Paris, got, like Guise, large gifts of money. At length (February 22, 1594) Henry could enter Paris and feel that he was King indeed.

His absolution had been given by the Archbishop of Bourges, even to-day the most medieval of French towns. This See-city had been the cradle of the Monarchy; its Archbishop had, by a gradual growth, gained great power, Metropolitan and even wider in the realm at large; fostered, to begin with, by the Papacy, as a channel for its own jurisdiction, their power had gradually become more independent. So the present Archbishop inherited Gallican traditions and acted on them. He had given the reception into the Church conditionally (*ad cautelam*), but he held that to give it was fully within the rights of the national Church. The Curia thought otherwise. There had long been a tendency to reserve cases for Papal decisions: this process, by which spiritual powers were gathered more and more into the hands of the Pope, was a long one stretching from the Middle Ages and quickening in post-Reformation centuries with their Quinquennial Faculties, held by bishops as delegates of the Papacy and not as inherent

His Abjuration and Reception, May 25, 1593.

rights of their own. It was also part of the long history of Gallicanism, beginning with the Conciliar period and to reach down to Jansenist days.[1]

It was not until later (September 7, 1595) that the Pope, Clement VIII (1592–1605), accepted the Absolution and Reception, and even then only guardedly. He be- *The Papacy* longed to the exiled (and therefore anti-Medicean) *and Henry.* Florentine family of the Aldobrandini: as Cardinal and Nuncio he had been of service to the Habsburgs, and he owed his election not only to his legal learning and experienced wisdom, but to the support of Philip II. He felt it his duty to help the great champion of the Church, and this coloured his actions in French affairs. But Henry held his own, and although conciliatory and deferential, abated nothing of his royal rights and dignity. The Parliament of Paris, always the watch-dog of the Constitution, was firm for Henry's cause. A young man, Jean Châtel, tried to assassinate but only wounded him: when questioned he gave philo- *Nov. 27,* sophic doctrines as his justification and the Jesuit *1594.* College of Clermont as his place of education. The Parliament took the matter up, closed the College, and banished the Jesuits from Paris and the realm as enemies of the State. But the Southern Parliaments did not do the same, and the King, later on, recalled the Society (1603).

Some conditions had been made by the Pope on confirming the Absolution. He had wished to enforce "rehabilitation" or the restitution of royal rights, an inherited medieval claim to Papal control over temporal Princes. But the French representatives at Rome, Du Perron, afterwards Bishop of Evreux, and Cardinal d'Ossat, along with the Duke of Nevers, would not admit this power. It was feared at Rome that Henry, with examples before him and Gallican traditions behind him, might make the French Church really national

---

[1] The growth of Metropolitan jurisdiction of Bourges has been well sketched by L. de Lacger in the *Revue d'histoire ecclésiastique* (Vol. XXVI, 1930, January and April); *Le primitié et le pouvoir metropolitain de l'archéveque de Bourges au XIIIᵉ siècle.* For the Quinquennial Faculties see Leo Mergentheim, *Die Quinquennal Fakultäten pro foro externo* (Kirchenrecht-lichen Abhundlungen, ed. Stutz: I–II, Stuttgart, 1908).

under a kind of Patriarch of its own; so negotiations followed, in which the French envoys stood firm on main points while yielding on lesser. Of Du Perron more must be said later, but d'Ossat, less of a scholar and more of a diplomatist, was as great in his own line. Son of a blacksmith, educated by charity, and a student of law, he was made Secretary and then *Chargé d'affaires* at Rome: Bishop, first of Rennes and then of Bayeux, he lived at Rome: made a Cardinal in 1598 he did the greatest service to Henry, being as much at home in the Curia as in French politics.

The conditions, which were not made public, were: the re-establishment of Catholic worship in Béarn and wherever it had been suppressed since 1585: holders of benefices, if heretics or laymen, were to be displaced, a preference was to be given to Catholics for offices of State, and the King was to show his wish for the establishment of Catholicism as the religion of the State. And according to Sully the recall of the Jesuits was promised, which took place in 1603.

France could now be held won, but if its miserable plight was to be remedied its surroundings must be secure, and Spanish interference was more than an outside fact: Spanish troops were yet in the country; they had only just left Paris, peaceably it is true, but were still encouraging discontent. War with Spain could not be escaped from and was declared (January 1595). Perhaps the odds were against Henry, even if Philip II had borne many blows of late: 700,000 Frenchmen were said to have perished before 1580, and many more since then: fields were untilled and the peasantry, one great part of the nation's life, were in misery. One of the last incidents in the War made Amiens all-important, as it has been so often since: the Spaniards captured it by a clever stratagem, and Henry had to retake it by arms. At last came the Treaty of Vervins to end the strife: it followed the lines of Cateau-Cambrésis: each side giving up its conquests: two details were of importance: Spain got Cambrai, and France recovered Calais. France had to conclude peace without the allies to whom she was bound, Eng-

Margin note: War with Spain: the Treaty of Vervins, May 2, 1598.

land and the Netherlands. It was difficult to deal with the restless and scheming Duke of Savoy: he had conquered Saluzzo and even formed large designs on Provence (1590). This part of the treaty was left to Papal arbitration, but the localised war broke out again: the Duke had to sue for peace (1601) and was allowed to keep Saluzzo.

The Pope was now friendly to France: Henry had shown sincerity. Philip II had died (September 15, 1598) with all his schemes and hopes unfulfilled. More could be won from France by diplomacy, especially by Roman diplomacy, than by war. Henry was in- *The Papacy more friendly to Henry.* duced to recall the Jesuits, who indeed, despite their origin, were no longer Spanish in their sympathies. By a curious provision one of the Society was to remain at Court as a sort of honourable hostage for the Society, and Fr. Cotton became the King's Confessor: he and his brethren were often useful to him. The influences around the King were indeed mainly Catholic, and he was probably happy under them: he had never cared for Calvinist doctrine, and if France were to be drawn into unity, its King must have, as in better days, the Church's help. But the Church, like the country, was in a sad state. Three-quarters of the churches were said to be without a priest: nearly half of the *State of the French Church.* Archbishoprics and a third of the bishoprics were vacant: many of the monasteries were pillaged by lay patrons who cared little for their needs: by a system of "confidences," as the term ran, an Abbot or Prior was appointed who paid the patron an annuity. Hundreds of churches were in ruins; in Orleans, for instance, there was not one left standing. If the King was to deal with these evils, it was essential that he should be on the best of terms with Catholics, and not only seem to be but to be so in very deed sincere. There were many ecclesiastics who could help him in this needed work, and even in civil matters, but for him to throw himself (as he did) whole-heartedly into it naturally raised suspicion and distrust among his former Huguenot friends. They were disappointed, and difficulties for the King now arose from them, no longer from the Catholics. They hardly gave him due credit for having swept away restrictions on their worship which the Leaguers had formerly enforced. By the Edict of Folembrai, made with Mayenne four months after the Pope had accepted Henry, the League had come to an end, and the King got the Catholic nobles to swear fidelity to the new policy of toleration. It was true that the Declaration of St. Cloud (August 4, 1589) had only authorised Huguenot worship where already carried on, and that offices outside such places were only to go to Catholics. By the Edict of Folembrai, Mayenne, from the other party, had been very well treated: he got a large indemnity and six places of security: he and the Leaguers were handled very gently. Old advisers like du Mornay, and a lesser herd who may have hoped for profit, were naturally disappointed. That the King allowed their worship in all royal towns seemed only a slight concession, friendly though it was. Disappointment grew to anger.

At Mantes in the winter of 1593 the Huguenots held an assembly, and swore anew allegiance to their faith. Later (May 1594) they held another assembly at Ste Foy without the King's leave, alleging that many complaints had come to them. They went on to organise themselves by dividing the whole country into nine provinces each with a council: every year an assembly of deputies from these provinces was to meet for discussions on their business. This was an extension to the whole country of a practically republican system adopted before at Nîmes and La Rochelle. Next year at Saumur they went still further by demanding admission to all offices on a level with Catholics, the setting up of *chambres mi-parties* throughout the land (except at Grenoble) and the permanent possession of all the places of surety which they were to hold only for a limited time. Henry was slow in replying, for it was really rebellion; some of the leaders, moreover, had deserted the royal army. Their assembly met each year up to 1597, and the extreme leaders published a complaint of the injustices done them, and even thought of seizing Tours as a kind of capital.

Henry had insight and instinctive ability joined to a

Organisation of the Huguenots.

knowledge of men. He was ready to face facts, and so he negotiated with the party instead of treating them as rebels and using force, which he might have done. For some time Huguenotism had not been as flourishing as formerly: a Venetian envoy had noticed the great falling off in their numbers. Henry asked their assembly to send four deputies to him with full power to treat and settle. His action, though risky, was generous and kingly: the result was the Edict of Nantes.

By this Edict the Huguenots were allowed their worship except in Paris and its near neighbourhood: in all places where it had been carried on in 1596 and up to August 1597; in two towns of every *bailliage* and in the castles of a limited number of the smaller nobles: Huguenot officials of Court might have their worship in their lodgings but they were not to sing the Psalms too loudly. They were admitted to Universities, schools and hospitals and might leave or give money for such foundations of their own: for their schools the King gave grants. They were given equal rights with Catholics in marriages, in buying and selling: for all such matters they were promised protection. *Chambres de l'Edit* were set up in the Parliaments; in that of Paris there were always to be six Huguenot members out of sixteen; in those of Bordeaux, Toulouse and Grenoble they had half of the members: these Chambers were to settle all causes arising under the Edict. They were to have all civil rights with full protection. They might hold political assemblies on getting royal licence. They might also hold synods, general and provincial, for doctrine and discipline: afterwards, owing to clerical criticism and resistance, leave had to be sought for these synods too. For eight years they might keep a large number of towns (some hundred or so) already in their possession: some of these were fortified strongly, like Rochelle and Montpellier: the garrisons of these the State was to pay. It may be noticed that Mayenne had received on a much smaller scale security of the same kind. Such a provision had its dangers, but it remained up to Henry's death.

Edict of Nantes, April 13, 1598.

The dawn of tolerance had come: but before it came Henry had to appeal to his Huguenot past and his memories of St.

Bartholomew. He had said to the Pope that if he did give favours to his Huguenot subjects he had in his mind the gain to the Catholic Church. But the case was not over yet: he had also to meet resistance from the Catholics, clerical and lay. Some ecclesiastics urged that liberty of worship should not hold over the whole realm. Henry made them some concessions, but this demand he could not agree to: Catholic worship was re-established in the towns held as surety, and for some time a rule that synods were not to meet without licence was in force. The Parliament of Paris, moreover, resisted registration: its President, Villiers-Seguier, a lawyer rightly respected, was hostile, but was conveniently honoured by being sent as ambassador to Venice. The King met the Parliament (January 7, 1599): he recalled the horrors of the past intolerance: he spoke of the love which he, even more than they, had for the Church, the eldest son of which he was. The speech had its effect. The King made some concessions: only one Huguenot member was to sit in the Parisian Chambre de l'Édit: at last the Edict was safely registered (February 27, 1599); the Provincial Parliaments, with much the same moods and difficulties, slowly followed suit.

Religious intolerance might be curbed but it was not dead: charity may be encouraged but cannot be created by law. There were political dangers, too, in the recognition of an organisation which had its political side, its political interests and its branches over the whole realm. But the Edict was to work and endure. It was Henry's own achievement and by it his kingship must be judged.

The League, as a political body, had done much harm by its entanglement in policies dangerous to the real interests of France. And now the Huguenots, by their organisation, were doing the same. They were doing it, moreover, when their cause was on the decline. On the other hand, the greatest period of French Catholicism was, as will be seen later, just beginning. The scholarship of Du Perron did not stand alone, although Fleury and Bossuet were still to come. Du Perron had already made many converts: the revolt against Calvin's dominance in religion was working in France as it did in

England in the days of Hooker. Calvin had been a French patriot always, but Geneva was now international and less of a centre for France. Hence came much discussion and theological unrest, on a background of difficulties and complaints about the working of the Edict. Henry's old adviser Mornay, somewhat dissatisfied as he was, yet did much to help him when the Huguenots had to complain of the Parliament of Paris: among his Huguenot brethren he had such an influence that he was called "the Huguenot Pope." In 1598 he brought out his *Traité de l'Eucharistie*, defending the Calvinistic doctrine of the Eucharist from Scripture and the writings of theologians. Based on some five thousand quotations, it was widely circulated in France and outside: at the dinner-table of the Princess of Orange, Du Perron, to whom Sully had sent a copy, gave to a minister who was about to change his creed his opinion of its apparently massive learning: he said it was superficial, as many of the quotations were incorrect or falsified. Du Perron knew his way in controversy; at Mantes (December 1593) he had met a Huguenot minister in a debate on the sufficiency of Holy Scripture for salvation: his opponent had the manliness to confess that he had been overcome: among his converts was Palma Cayet, who has told us so much of the times. When Mornay heard of this conversation he was naturally eager to defend himself: under the patronage of the King and the presidency of distinguished Theological courtiers a public debate (May 4, 1600) was arranged debate. at Fontainebleau, much like those in England under the Stuarts. Sixty passages for discussion were reduced to nineteen, but only six were dealt with, as after the first day Mornay, whose health was bad, fell ill. But before that he had paid the penalty of one who takes unverified quotations on trust. In two cases, for instance, the passages from scholastics were statements of objections to be refuted, not affirmed. During the debate the King said to Sully, "What do you think of your Pope now?" and the reply was, "It seems to me, Sire, that he is more of a Pope than your Majesty thinks for, he is now giving the red hat to the Cardinal of Evreux:" (du Perron) indeed he only had to wait for it until 1604.

Persecution had naturally made the Huguenots discontented and bitter, in religion and politics alike. Equality, even with some inconveniences, and religious liberty naturally tended to charity, even if incomplete. Political equality had the same effects. But the tendency of Presbyterians to Republicanism had shown itself in France as it did in England and in Scotland. On the side of doctrine two points on which much was to be said in England, Scotland and Germany had already emerged: the sufficiency of Scripture by itself for salvation and the central conception of the Eucharist.

Henry IV might owe much to his great minister (Maximilian de Béthune, Baron de Rosny), the Duke of Sully: order brought into the national finances from an unacknowledged bankruptcy; agriculture fostered in every way and France led into rural paths of industry which it has trodden ever since. Taxation was not oppressive and it was just. Many injustices were removed, and contentment succeeded to complaints. In all this Sully's help and his uprightness, Huguenot in its stern simplicity, were invaluable. On the side of the Church, however, it was Henry's own work which made possible a recreated France: it could be rebuilt as so many of its cathedrals and churches were. Every inch a King: with him every instinct, every word was that of a people's leader. Fitted by his nature, even sometimes by his very faults, he restored, almost without seeming to do so, the Absolute Monarchy which the Religious Wars and the kings during them had discredited and debased. On the whole, with some drawbacks, he had the love of his subjects. The Monarchy once more was the centre and the symbol of the nations' life.

"Henry IV is, or was before the Revolution, a national hero: he was a thorough Frenchman, with the good and bad qualities of the race well developed; he was a Frenchman of the old régime . . . we must allow that there was a want of fixed principle in him: he was not the man to be the martyr of any cause, and like the statesman of the present day, he had not the slightest difficulty in training his conscience to believe that the course most expedient for him at the moment was the one which his higher nature recommended to him, which the development of his own views showed him to be the right, nay, which under a different form was the course which he had always intended to hold. A second most serious fault was his relations with women, his utter incapacity for restraining his passions in that direction. Henry IV was not the slave of passion, but he was a thorough-going seeker of pleasure. . . . Now for his good points. He had a true love of his people and a clear perception of all their best interests. To them he was a good king, the only good king since St. Louis."[1] His great minister, the Duke of Sully, was the administrator in the restoration of prosperity. Faced with an immense burden of debt he cleared it off, swept away abuses and corruption, brought in a time of efficiency, and ensured it by his careful over-sight.

The rivalry with Spain remained and Henry was preparing for war against it when his life was cut short. On the chessboard of European politics the two countries were henceforth the dominating rivals. But France now had her position assured, and his second marriage (after he had divorced Margaret of Valois) to Marie de Medici (October 5, 1600), gave him an heir.

Henry was on the point of setting out, with strange forebodings and some justified self-reproach, for the war. The Queen, who was to be Regent while he was away, had been crowned (May 13, 1610); when he went to Paris, and on his way to visit Sully he was stabbed to death by one Ravaillac, who did the ill deed because the King was about to make war on the Pope. Assassination, and the miserable pretext of religion,

---

[1] This passage comes from a master of historical portraiture. *Lectures on European History*, by William Stubbs, D.D. (ed. by A. Hassall: London, 1904), Section II: Chap. IX: *Henry IV's Place in the History of Europe*, p. 241. I read this work when it came out, and was greatly impressed by it. My great teacher, Sir A. W. Ward, told me that he and two other historians (whom I knew to be authorities) thought it a great work: he, in particular, thought it was the best treatment of the Habsburgs in English. It abounds in vivid sketches of character.

were relics, as it were, of the Wars of Religion which Henry himself had ended. There was an interval of years and then Richelieu[1] became the great King's real successor, if not in immediate time yet in policy and spirit, mingled of good and evil, but in every way great and of world-wide effect.

[1] Henry IV as the restorer of Absolute Monarchy and the forerunner of Richelieu is the theme of Lecture IX in Lord Acton's *Lectures on Modern History* (London, 1907).

XIII

GERMANY: 1555–1648

For nearly seventy years (1555–1618) the history of Germany was dominated by the religious question. The peace had merely been a truce, and it had serious weaknesses of its own. The Catholics and the Lutherans accepted it so far as it suited their own ends, and so far only: each party protested against the benefits enjoyed by the other, and the Calvinists, **Defects of the Religous Peace.** standing outside the peace, could only enter it by the door of the Augsburg Confession. Of the two essential parts the Ecclesiastical Reservation and the Declaration of Toleration, the one had not full effect, and the latter depended merely upon the Emperor's word. Meanwhile the Imperial power grew weaker, the Habsburg house became more purely Austrian in its aims, and the central power was ineffective: local princes over-shadowed it alike in their religious policies and their foreign alliances. The Reformation helped the growth of princely power and the influence of local Courts. The Empire, as a whole, had no policy of its own. Thus in the absence of political progress the interest of German history lies mainly in religious matters: the influence of Papal Nuncios, the progress of the Counter Reformation, the early revival of the Augustinian Friars and the later growth of Jesuit influence, the reform and organisation begun at Trent; these were the chief features on the Catholic side. On the Protestant side, there were the attacks upon the *Reservatum Ecclesiasticum*, the attempts at union and the growth of discord between Lutherans and Calvinists, and the constant secularising of Church estates. Meanwhile political danger from France coquetting with the Protestant princes, dynastic dangers from Spain, the existence of religious wars on the frontiers in France and the Netherlands, with the constant pressure of the Turks on the East, threw the Emperor upon the princes for help, and made him realise increasingly the disastrous

effects of religious discontent. Hence the Emperor Ferdinand
had a distinct policy of his own for internal affairs,
not quite consistent with either his strong
Catholicism or his religious policy in his hereditary
lands. His German instincts and his Catholic principles
combined, and the resultant expressed the political needs
of the nation. When (March 14, 1588) he was crowned
Emperor, the maintenance of the Religious Peace was included
in his Election Covenant; the defiant policy of Paul IV towards
him endangered his relations with the Church, but politically
the mediating (or to the Protestant view, the timid) policy of
Electoral Saxony under Augustus (1553–86), working with the
Catholic Electors of Mayence and Trier, secured his position.

Policy of Ferdinand I. (margin note)

Not only in politics, but in religion there might have grown
up a mediating or combined party, satisfying the Protestant
demand for reform (so far as that demand was genuine) by
small changes and concessions as well as by
liberality and piety of spirit, yet not departing
from Catholic lines. On the Catholic side, Julius
von Pflug (who had been elected Bishop of Naumburg
in 1541, but was opposed by Amsdorf, the candidate
supported by the Elector and consecrated by Luther) is a
fair example; he was ready, as was also Gropper, to adopt
large and inclusive definitions on the Mass and Justification,
and to concede clerical marriage and the chalice; there were
not wanting like-minded men, such as George Calixtus
(† 1556), on the Protestant side. Even the Lutheran services
in some places resembled those of the Catholics: a Breviary
used by them at Halberstadt up to 1801 might well have
belonged to the Catholics. But such cases were exceptional.
Such a party would not have satisfied the Papacy (for they
were scarcely Papalists), the orthodox Spaniards, or the
majority of Protestants, and before the third assembly at
Trent if not earlier, the reconciliation they hoped for had
become impossible. But before that the dividing lines between
Catholics and Protestants, either in thought or in practice,
were not drawn so rigidly or clearly as since and elsewhere:
had the policy of the Papacy and of the Princes been different,

The Mediating Party. (margin note)

had politics not given Protestantism a vitality it did not possess of itself, had not the Counter Reformation closed up the ranks of Catholicism and given it a more rigid test for discrimination, above all, had not controversy hardened into hatred, Germany might have been united instead of divided. As it was, ecclesiastical politics tended more and more to war. The wonder was not that the Thirty Years' War came when it did (1618–48), but that its coming was so long delayed.

The division between Calvinists or Reformed (as they came to be called after the *Formula of Concord*, 1577), and Lutherans grew. The Landgrave Philip of Hesse, more Zwinglian than Lutheran, but more a politician than either, would have gladly united the two parties; the Swiss Protestants were united nearly by the *Consensus Tigurinus* (1549), and fully by the *Second Helvetic Confession* (1566). In Germany division grew, the strength of Melanchthon (which some thought weakness) was thrown on the side of peace, but an extremist party headed by Flacius Illyricus was formed against him. Some of the Protestants wished to combine against the *Reservatum Ecclesiasticum*, but theological differences outweighed even the love of gain: a colloquy (one among many) at Worms (1557) failed to bring about peace. Duke John Frederick of (Ernestine) Saxony had taken a strong line, and made the University of Jena a stronghold against the Crypto-Calvinists (as Melanchthon and his followers were now often called). Flacius was called thither that same year, and ruled the religion of Ducal Saxony. The Electoral (Albertine) line under Augustus (always afraid of a restoration of the other line to its rights) took the opposite side. Melanchthon had already by his treatment of the Interim given rise to the *Adiaphoristic* controversy (on things of lesser importance and the limits of toleration in worship): much in ritual, much in organisation, even to a limited papal supremacy, he was ready to accept. To this controversy were added others. On the positive doctrine of the Holy Eucharist he was somewhat more Calvinist than Lutheran, but in the express negation of the Catholic view he was less decided than Luther; on the question of Predestination—now rapidly coming to the

Divisions of Protestants.

front—he was somewhat opposed to Calvin; he allowed more effect to the will of man and some efficacy to good works; with him as with the Jesuits reason made itself heard; here altogether were themes for ample difference. Melanchthon left the colloquy at Worms knowing himself an object of attack. At Ratisbon (1556-7) and afterwards the Protestant party found itself divided. "Better Catholic than Calvinist," said Lutherans. "Can Calvinists be saved?" asked a Lutheran consistory from a pastor. Calvinism was blasphemy; to defend Calvinists was to serve the devil; Calvinists are not our brethren, but the enemies of God, said one Lutheran Court preacher. A three weeks' colloquy at Naumburg (January 1561) broke down because the theologians of Jena would have nothing of the union sought by the Palatinate and Würtemberg. Under Frederick III (1559-76) the Palatinate became Calvinist, a change of great political importance. A board—on the Calvinist model—was set up to manage religious affairs, and the Heidelberg Catechism, to have a great future of its own, was composed (1563). Melanchthon had originally directed the Lutheran organisation in the Palatinate, his early home, and he had counselled Frederick III to quell the bitter disputes raised by the rigid Lutherans. But after Melanchthon's death (1560) the new tendencies gained ground, and Heidelberg became the centre of German Calvinism. At Augsburg (1566) the Elector made a manly defence of his creed, attacked as it was by both Catholics and Lutherans, and his stand did something to gain him respect. But its religious isolation, no less than its local position, turned the Palatinate towards foreign friends and foreign schemes; from the day (1567) when Frederick III sent his son John Casimir to help the Huguenots until the Thirty Years' War, its outlook was abroad, and its policy brought disaster upon the country.

It is well to review rapidly the outlines of religious changes under the accepted principle "*cujus regio ejus religio.*" The *Territorial changes in religion.* North German States were all but solidly Protestant; the exception being the Duchy of Jülich-Cleve, where, under the Emperor Ferdinand's son-in-law, Duke William, who became Catholic (1570),

Catholicism gained ground once lost. Among the cities, Aix-la-Chapelle and Cologne alone were Catholic. In Saxony the Grumbach feud (1558–67) brought the Ducal (Ernestine) territory under the care of the (Albertine) Elector Augustus, who then drove out the extreme Lutherans, thus making all Saxony of a uniform religious type.

This feud, a typical process, needs notice. Wilhelm von Grumbach had the native lawlessness of a Franconian knight deepened by the training of his dead leader, Albert The Grum-Alcibiades of Brandenburg, whose traditions he bach Feud. kept up. For a raid on the See of Würzburg his lands had been confiscated, and in a further raid for revenge the Bishop was slain (1558) and the Chapter forced to give back his lands to Grumbach. After this Grumbach gained the patronage of the Ernestine Duke, John Frederick, at Gotha, who clutched at any chance of regaining the Electorate; Grumbach, helped mentally by magic and materially by France, formed plans to replace the Elector Augustus by the Duke, and his brother-in-law Frederick II of Denmark by the Duke of Holstein. These wide and wild schemes simmered on; the Elector Palatine, Würtemberg and Bavaria strove for peace. Ferdinand II put the ban on Grumbach and bade John Frederick withhold his help. When Maximilian came to the throne he put the ban on the two allies; the visions of magic grew more splendid and the Imperial throne itself was whispered of for the Duke. The pacifists stayed inactive, and only Augustus, with so much at stake, would act: with an army of 16,000 he took Gotha (1568): Grumbach was executed and John Frederick imprisoned until his death (1595). Lack of control at the centre; selfishness at the separate Courts; disregard of law, and everywhere disorder, all flourished in an atmosphere of foreign interference, always threatening if not active.

The Elector Augustus himself, however, became later (1574) jealously Lutheran, saw Crypto-Calvinism everywhere, but specially in the Philippists (or followers of Melanchthon); after this Wittenberg became a centre of the Flacianists; with some later variations Saxony remained consistently and strongly Lutheran. Brandenburg, with which (1571) the

347

Ansbach territory and (1618) the Prussian Duchy were joined, was also Lutheran, and (1566) a Court preacher Funck was executed for Calvinism. But the Elector John Sigismund (1608–19) himself became Calvinist (1614) and his creed was, of course, tolerated: the people were mainly Lutheran, but the politicians sometimes Catholic. Although he claimed the control of religion as the highest royal prerogative, he did not exercise it. But these differing types of faith intensified political jealousy between Brandenburg, with its peculiar condition, and Saxony.

The obvious need of unity led to further attempts to gain it, and these resulted in the *Formula of Concord* [1] (1577, published 1580): it was a wordy document, discussing at great length the distinction between Human Nature and Original Sin: it reflected disputes and suggested differences instead of stating doctrines clearly as such a Confession ought to do. It had been drawn up by six theologians, and signed by fifty-one princes and lords (the Electors Palatine of Brandenburg and of Saxony being among them), thirty-five cities, and over eight thousand theologians and pastors. Among the assenting States were the two lines of Brunswick, Mecklenburg, Ducal Saxony, Ansbach, Baden, Würtemberg, and the Neuburg Palatinate. But those of Pomerania, Anhalt, the Zweibrücken Palatinate, Holstein, Hesse and Nassau, with most of the Imperial towns, refused to sign. Among the last were Nuremberg, Frankfort-on-the-Main, Speier, Worms, Magdeburg, and Strasbourg (which, however, became Lutheran in 1597). Under John Casimir, by a chance of much political importance, the Rhine Palatinate became exclusively Calvinist, and the Neuburg Palatinate mainly so. By 1605 all Hesse was also Calvinist. Thus German Protestantism was divided into two great camps, and among the Lutherans of the *Concord* themselves dogmatic quarrels arose. Outside Germany, Sweden and the Hungarian Lutherans adopted the *Formula*, while Denmark rejected it. All these associations affected the future, and gave rise to further complications. The broad result was that the German Lutherans were parted off from most Protestants outside Germany.

The Formula of Concord, 1577.

[1] Schaff: *Creeds*, III. pp. 93, *seq.*

The secularisation of bishoprics, an old evil, and the growth of Calvinism, leading to some defections from the *Formula*, summarise much of this German history. The princely families had set up a lien upon the sees near them; the Elector of Brandenburg had long nominated to Brandenburg, Havelberg, and Lebus; he also succeeded in gaining Magdeburg and Halberstadt, both of which were Protestantised (1561–3). The sees of Merseburg (1561) and Naumburg (1564) came to Alexander, the boyish son of Augustus of Saxony; the Elector soon administered not only these sees, but also Meissen. Bremen, Verden, Lübeck, Minden, Schwerin, Ratzeburg, and Cammin were also held by Protestants. Joachim Frederick of Brandenburg was elected Bishop of Havelberg when seven, and Archbishop of Magdeburg when twenty; in 1570 he set about the extinction of Catholicism in his dioceses, and when Pius V asked for his deposition, the Emperor Maximilian felt himself unable to enforce it. On his succeeding to the Electorate (1598) his son Christian William followed him at Magdeburg, just as he himself had followed his uncle Sigismund. Henry of Saxe-Lauenburg was Archbishop of Bremen at seventeen (1567), and afterwards gained Osnabrück (1574) and Paderborn (1577). These were great evils, but it should be borne in mind that they arose partly from the degeneracy of Chapters, that the spiritual responsibility of bishops had been too often lost sight of, and their offices looked upon as mere possessions; Catholic dynasties indeed did not differ greatly from Protestants in their treatment of sees. But it was a strange result of all this when (1557–73) Hildesheim, with its medieval monuments and memories, was the only Catholic see in Northern Germany. This abuse was made possible in the following way: when the Chapter had made the election, often forced or corrupt, the elected bishop sought an indult from the Emperor, which freed him from the immediate necessity of going to Rome for Confirmation; the delay was often prolonged, but as meanwhile the Emperor gave him the regalia and he could enjoy the revenue, he did not feel deeply his ecclesiastical incapacity.

Marginal notes: Politics of Protestantism. Abuses of bishoprics. Indults.

The great Sees of the West seemed likely to follow in change. Cologne had a varied history: three bishops (1556–67) were either Lutheran or laxly Catholic; the next, Salentin von Isenburg, resigned in order to marry (1577), and Gebhard Truchsess von Waldburg, a man of evil life, was elected by the mainly Protestant Chapter; he was forced by her brothers (1582) to marry his mistress, Agnes von Mansfeld, a canoness of Görresheim, but meant still to hold his See. The Chapter and the city were divided for and against him, so were the Electors. The Pope deprived him of his See, and Ernest of Bavaria, Bishop of Freising and Administrator of Hildesheim, who had been defeated in the election by two votes, succeeded him. But the dispute grew into a war. The question of the Ecclesiastical Reservation was here raised in an emphatic way, but much as they disliked that clause, the Lutherans disliked union with the Calvinists more, and John Casimir of the Palatinate was Gebhard's only effective supporter. The dispute was made more important by the constant influx, owing to the war in the Netherlands, of Dutch Protestant immigrants, who founded Protestant congregations. The failure of Gebhard's attempt, which had much chance of success, was due more to the divisions of Protestants than anything else. He retired to his deanery of Strasbourg, where he died, while his wife went to England, where she incurred Elizabeth's displeasure through her relations with Essex. But the failure came at a critical time, and the restoration of Catholicism in the bishopric, which naturally followed, encouraged other attempts to regain sees for their rightful use. Two other incidents helped to the same end. Joachim Frederick of Brandenburg, elected Archbishop of Magdeburg (1566), had never received an indult, but at the Diet of Augsburg (1582) he claimed, in spite of this, to vote as Administrator, although not as Archbishop. The claim was reasonably disallowed, and thus a blow was struck at a discreditable system.

The third incident was at Aix-la-Chapelle, which had pledged itself to remain Catholic. Flemish immigrants, however, won over a majority of the citizens to Protestantism, and these

Cologne, 1583.

Magdeburg, 1582.

now demanded (1581) the free exercise of their religion, which was refused by the Catholic Town Council. An appeal to an Imperial Commission was decided in favour of the Council, and riots, in which the bishop's authority was defied, followed. Technically the Religious Peace only protected minorities in towns where they had existed before 1555, and it had not provided for future changes of creed. The Emperor was threatening force, and the Duke of Parma had marched troops across the frontier: the citizens brought their case before the Diet (1582). A new Commission was appointed (1595), and decided against the Protestants, whose worship was prohibited (1598). Thus on all sides the Religious Peace was causing difficulty, and the Catholic Reaction was able to use its legal interpretation in its own favour.

Aix-la-Chapelle, 1581–98.

In Trèves the Archbishop was driven from the city (1559), and it was not until his successor's time (1567–81) that Catholicism was restored. The Archbishop of Mayence just contrived to hold his own, and in the end even drove the Protestants from his lands of the Eichsfeld (north of Mühlhausen). Both these prelates made great use of the Jesuits, and the ubiquitous Canisius left his mark there as elsewhere.

Ecclesiastical lands. Trèves. Mayence.

The territory of Fulda, the senior abbey of Germany, was largely Protestant, but the Abbot Balthasar Gravel (1571) brought in the Jesuits to found a school, and then expelled all the Protestant ministers. He met with opposition from the nobility who had wished to found a Protestant school, and the Chapter, whose evil lives he had tried to reform, forced his resignation. An appeal to the Emperor brought about his tardy restoration (1602). Bishop Julius of Würzburg too took up the Catholic restoration in his bishopric. He enforced Catholicism (1584) with the alternative of emigration. A hundred and twenty preachers were driven out, and the Jesuits who took their place are said to have reconciled over sixty thousand to the Church. The Franconian knights asked (1582) for the expulsion of the Jesuits, who had been introduced in 1564;

Fulda.

Würzburg.

for the bestowal of a church upon the Lutherans, and leave for the local priests to marry, but they did not stay the reaction, which was greatly furthered by the bishop's model life. In visitation, confirming, and all his duties, he set a model which surprised the Protestants; his zeal was not purely negative and repressive as it was with some. For education he also cared, and the University was reformed (1582), while preparatory colleges were erected. Everywhere popular schools were restored or begun; processions and pilgrimages revived; new parishes were formed; three hundred churches were built or restored; hospitals and almshouses sprang up freely; other bishoprics changed like Wurzburg: Paderborn (1585), Münster (1588), Salzburg (1588), Bamberg (1595). Not all these bishops, however, were holy men or deeply spiritual. Sixty years before men of a worldly or indifferent type would have drifted into Lutheranism, now they drifted by the force of their surroundings into Tridentine zeal. The ideal of the Episcopate was restored, and a new life was breathed into the Church. Popular tendencies were now towards Catholicism, and the views and the organisation it presupposed. It was the same in education. The best systems and the best teachers were no longer found chiefly among the Lutherans. Among them religious controversy had done its evil work and sapped their power. A new Scholastic had sprung up among them, and its technical science had more to do with speculation than with life. In some places their preachers condemned or did not encourage the study of the dead languages, and there was then as in all days of growing trade a set against studies of no immediate profit.

In the South the cities and lower nobility were mostly Protestant, although the latter did not like to see their superiors, the Princes, enriched by secularisation. But the bishoprics, as seen above, were mostly kept for Catholicism, and Augsburg, under Bishop Otto van Truchsess, Cardinal and (1556) Legate *a latere*, was a good example. He was an ally of Bavaria, and followed its policy. The High School of Dillingen was connected with the College of St. Jerome, which he founded (1549) and generously en-

South Germany. Augsburg.

dowed, partly for general education, partly to train priests for
his diocese. Dillingen was (1551) made a University by
Julius III, and handed over (1564) to the Jesuits. The college
(1565) passed also into their charge as a clerical seminary of
the Tridentine type; afterwards the Fuggers (who owed much
wealth to Rome and had profited by the shameful traffic in
benefices and indulgences) founded at Augsburg a large
college and a gymnasium. Gregory XIII (1585) placed a
seminary at Dillingen, and the diocese became an important
centre of activity which worked against the evil living amongst
the clergy as well as against the Protestant propaganda. In
fifty years (1559–1610) the number of Easter communicants in
the city (to take a familiar test) rose from eight hundred to
six thousand seven hundred.

In Salzburg George von Khuenberg (1580–7) had done his
duty well as a coadjutor and then Archbishop. His successor,
Dietrich von Raittenau (1587–1612), was less conscientious. He bade all non-Catholics to leave his   Salzburg.
land, but, when the Jesuits rebuked his concubinage, he
threatened them likewise; no kind of religion flourished. The
next ruler, Marx Sittich von Hohenembs, was earnest in work,
but coped with the increase of Protestants by the easy way of
expulsion. Many changed outwardly, but the Archbishop's
own life of ease and gaiety did not set a good example. In
Passau, which took in much of the Austrian lands,   Passau.
the preachers were driven out and heretical books
forbidden, but this unhappy stringency was accompanied by
the provision of Catholic schools and teaching. Everywhere
the Counter Reformation did most where its bishops were
truly pious and enlightened. On the other hand, it was where
episcopal rule or Church organisation was weakest (as in
Switzerland, North Germany, and the Netherlands) that the
anti-Catholic movements spread. Stringent measures (common
on all sides, and therefore needing no apology then, while
gaining ready support from the law *"cujus regio ejus religio"*)
often failed, where not backed up by positive teaching. The
German method of persecution was expulsion as opposed to the
Spanish *auto-da-fé*. Although cruel and sad it was the milder

of the two, and it was not as a rule until some years after the
Council of Trent that more cruel persecution of the Spanish
type arose. The Emperor, Ferdinand II, for instance, during
the Thirty Years' War, strictly forbade bloodshed, although
his measures were stringent.

In the Austrian lands there was no political cohesion and a
mixed state of religion prevailed. The Crown and the nobles
held the patronage of benefices, and had seized
most of the revenues. The Estates had allowed
(1555–6) the administration of the chalice and also
clerical marriage. In Hungary the Lutheran organisation had
been introduced (1550); in Transylvania (1545); the large
powers of the Estates here made any division dangerous, and
religion intensified the tumult due to Turkish attacks. In
Bohemia Lutheranism had grafted itself upon the Bohemian
Brotherhood; monastic houses had been widely secularised.
The University of Prague, following its old traditions, had
become Lutheran, but the influence of the Jesuits, who came
to the city in 1555, changed things greatly. The personality of
Ferdinand I (1564) only served to increase the disorder. He
himself was genuinely tolerant in administration, but a condition founded upon accident and not on principle could not
bring about toleration. His son and successor,
Maximilian II, had been greatly influenced by a
secretly Lutheran Court preacher Phauser, and was
suspected of Lutheranism. Up to 1570 he was
strongly anti-Spanish, but in that year he and Philip II became
friends. The latter took Maximilian's fourth daughter Anna as
wife, and the death of Don Carlos had left Philip sonless (1568),
so that visions of Spain came to Maximilian. But his reign, like
others, was darkened by the Turkish danger, while on the west
the war in the Netherlands brought risks and temptations.
Inside the empire he held the balance fairly between the two
parties, refusing alike the suggestion of Pius V to attack the
Protestants, and of the Protestants to expel the Jesuits. Tolerant in himself, he yet set toleration before himself less as
a principle than as the line of least resistance, and he just failed
to hold religion as something above all else; he let the nobles
take their own line on their own estates.

The Austrian lands.

The Emperor Maximilian II, 1564–76.

There was in him much of greatness, yet with a weakness which his circumstances might excuse. He enforced neither the Ecclesiastical Reservation nor the Declaration of Toleration. He grew, like his father, and not merely under Spanish influence, into stricter conformity to the Church. For the rest the Catholic reaction gained strength as did Protestant disunion. Against the designs of the Elector Palatine he gained (1575) the election to the Roman Kingship of his son Rudolf (already elected a month earlier King of Bohemia, and King of Hungary, 1572). All these elections meant concessions to the Protestants. The three lay Electors, now Protestant, insisted that Rudolf should confirm the Religious Peace with its Declaration of Toleration. The three Archbishops, on the other hand, denied the validity of the Toleration, which was however maintained against them. In the end the jealousies of Saxony and the Palatinate weakened the opposition, and Rudolf was crowned unconditionally.

At Ratisbon (1576) it was proposed to remove the Reservation, and make the ecclesiastical lands thus thrown open bear the cost of Turkish wars. This scheme was rejected through opposition from the counts, who did not wish to see the princes strengthened. In this and other ways the religious divisions brought the constitution to a standstill, and led to loss of power abroad, although at home the country grew in wealth. Towards the end of Maximilian's reign the care of Gregory XIII (1572–85) did much for Germany. So constant was his thought for it that he was said to have "a German heart," and he never said a Mass without intercession for its welfare. Six months after his accession he created a Congregation made up of Germans or Cardinals with local knowledge. A much-needed reform of German Chapters was one object set before it. Nunciatures at Munich for South Germany (1573), in Styria (1580), and at Cologne (1584) strengthened the connection between Germany and Rome. Special diplomatic attention was paid to the Princes, and here the Jesuits (now beginning careers as court diplomatists) were useful. Political relations tended to war, and religious controversy was hardening to hatred. The practical work and very definite aims of the Jesuits, above all, tended in the same direction. Where energy, unaccompanied by constant recurrence to breadth of thought and simplicity of first principles, is thrown largely into organisation, the narrowing of object and the immersion in a system are apt to produce hardness and severity. The lines of the coming struggle were clearly laid down. Maximilian could not avert it, but he did at any rate gain peace in his time (1564–76).

He had conceded a free exercise of the Augsburg Confession to the nobles of Lower Austria (1568), and with intent possibly to please the Protestants and still suit the Catholics, a book of worship was drawn up (mainly by Chytraeus of Rostock) as a compromise, and revised by the Emperor. Ferdinand I had already (†1566) consulted George Cassander, a Dutch theologian living in Germany, who had formulated a *viâ media*, and drawn up for the Emperor a *Consultatio* with that aim (1564). Styria was much as Lower Austria. In Upper Austria Maximilian reaped a harvest of difficulties due to the double dealing which had gained him the Empire, pledged as he was both to the Pope and the Lutherans, able however to put off the latter more easily. A papal brief (16 April, 1564) allowed all the German bishops to grant the administration of the chalice to laymen desiring it, provided they professed belief in the sufficiency of communion in one kind, and renounced all the doctrines that had separated Utraquists from the Roman See. In the Austrian lands this was gratefully received, for the upper classes were mainly Protestant, although the lower classes were Catholic. In some towns in these duchies Catholics were even excluded from the councils, and in others (as in Grätz) had but one or two representatives. So late as 1578 Protestantism was the prevalent religion in all these territories except the Tyrol, which remained thoroughly Catholic.

But in 1598 when the Catholic revival affected Passau, a diocese including much of Austria, the bishop was able to refuse the chalice to the laity and in Salzburg the archbishop had refused the concession. In Styria, with Carinthia and Carniola, Charles, son of Ferdinand I, was ruler, and the great advance of Protestantism had led him to invite the Jesuits (1573). To Grätz and three other cities he allowed (1578) freedom of worship, which

Catholic reaction. Austrian lands.

in the case of Grätz was abused by almost depriving the Catholics of citizenship. Under Charles the reaction was slow in spite of ready help from the Papacy and the Jesuits, but his son Ferdinand (1590), strictly educated and with a conscientious devotion to religion and duty, was a man of sterner stamp than his father, and became the leader of the Catholic movement. His sense of religion and duty was his own, but the mould into which these qualities were cast was that of the Jesuits. He shrank from no severity if bloodless; he expelled all Protestant teachers and preachers (1598), and rescinded the allowance of freedom of worship. Thus the measures of Protestant Princes were met by retaliation. The examples of these relatives of theirs affected the Emperors, and the course of affairs in Bavaria had the same effect.

The peculiar Church conditions of Bavaria have already been noted (pp. 64–5). William IV (1508–50) had ruled not only strongly, but well, caring for the welfare of the peasants and keeping up the standard of **Bavaria.** Ingolstadt as a centre of learning, second among Catholic Universities only to Louvain. Albert V (1550–79) laid the foundation of the celebrated library and the other collections still adorning Munich. The Jesuits by ducal invitation came to the city and founded a college there (1542–56). The Estates complained of the bad discipline of the clergy (1553), and asked (1556) for communion in both kinds and relief from the obligation of fasting; afterwards also permission for clerical marriage. Thus the Duke was in opposition to his nobles, and only when he had overthrown them was he able to carry out his policy. To conciliate the Estate she had to support their demands at Trent; for a moral reformation he was as anxious as they were. But early in 1564 the Duke by violence suppressed for a time Protestantism in the Ortenburg territory, and although his action was not supported by the Reichskammergericht, the fear of his doing the same elsewhere made the nobles submissive. In a few years the government, exercising powers properly belonging to the bishops, had, by strict visitation and care for education, changed the country greatly.

In the Empire as a whole, the central power was weak and the general condition bad. Foreign trade, with nations hostile if not actually at war, was fitful and lessening; home industry, harassed by evils in the currency, was growing weaker. Class-hatreds were becoming bitterer, and on this confused and depressing social background, the shadow of religious differences lay dark. Bohemia especially, with its old Utra-quist traditions, had a never-slumbering fear of losing its hard-won national freedom.

The Emperor Rudolf—deeply interested in art, literature, and science, but from the first moody and reserved—grew more solitary in his later years. He had been brought up in Spain, and his inclinations were for repressing Protestantism, but his first attempts—he expelled the preacher Opitz from Vienna (1578), and tried the same course elsewhere—met with opposition, and he drew back. It was the persistence and success of his cousin Ferdinand (1597) in Styria that led him to revive this earlier policy, and it was this revival that led to the Thirty Years' War. Melchior Klesl—Cardinal and Bishop of Vienna—was the director of a conciliatory policy. As a poor child he had been trained by the Jesuits, and his ability did credit to their teaching: his skill is not to be blamed for the disasters due largely to Rudolf's growing insanity. The Catholic organisa-tion was restored in Austria (1597), in Styria and Carinthia under Ferdinand (1600–2), and the prohibition of Protestant worship and teaching was strictly carried out. In Bohemia Rudolf (1602) re-enacted a former (1581) edict banishing the Bohemian brethren, and made it cover Calvinists as well. When a synod (1605) adopted the Decrees of Trent, the Bohemians began active opposition. In Hungary also an attempt to reverse the change of churches to Protestantism intensified the national dislike of the Emperor, and to save the realm both Lutheranism and Calvinism had to be allowed. The death of Duke John William of Jülich-Cleve (1609) once more brought up the disputed succession there, and it was only settled after long disputes by the Treaty of Xanten (1614) between the Neuburg and Brandenburg claimants. In the

The Emperor Rudolf, 1576–1612.

course of the negotiations and fightings the Empire showed its weakness, and religious division its bitterness.

The rightfulness of the secularisation of Church property after 1552 had been questioned in many cases, and notably in those of four convents: Frauenalb, Christgarten, one at Strasbourg, and Hirschhorn. The Kammergericht had ordered their restitution, but an appeal for revision was now to be decided. There could be no doubt as to the result, but the Calvinists (inspired by Christian of Anhalt, a wandering and restless soldier-politician, an official of the Palatinate, filled with hatred of the Habsburgs) decided to dispute its enforcement, and to admit in religious disputes no authority but the Diet, the most unlikely body to settle anything. The law was clear on the one side, and the facts were clear on the other. Maximilian of Bavaria, bold and energetic, was ready for his own policy to oppose the Habsburgs, but here his inclination agreed with the Emperor's power, for it meant going with the flowing tide of Catholic reaction to enforce the law. The opposed policy of the Calvinists really meant the breakdown of the Empire, and the matter led to their withdrawal from the Diet (1603). *The decision about the four convents, 1598–1603.*

By this time Rudolf's insanity had become plain, and the succession—in which both Spain and the Papacy took an interest—was merged in the question of his removal. His brother Matthias, who had arranged a peace in Hungary by granting religious freedom to Lutherans and Calvinists, was adopted by the family as their head (April 1606), and their candidate for the Empire. The discord between him and Rudolf put both of them at the mercy of the Estates.

In 1604 a disputed election to the See of Strasbourg, which had gone on since 1592 between a younger Cardinal of Lorraine and John George of Brandenburg, came to an end after lengthy wars and disputes, but only by the arbitration of Henry IV of France. No sooner was this settled than another dispute broke out. The people of the imperial city of Donauwörth had been, since 1555, *Donauwörth.*

mainly Protestant: processions held for many years by the Benedictines there were suddenly forbidden by the Council when, against regulations, they became more elaborate: the monks persisted and riots arose: the case came before the Supreme Courts, and a commission was issued to the Duke of Bavaria to inquire into it. Finally the city was put under the ban which the Duke Maximilian was to execute. He took the town and restored Catholicism. This set the Protestants on the alert: the Diet (1608) came to an open rupture. The Protestant States formed at Anhausen (16 May, 1608) a Union, renewed and afterwards enlarged, from which Saxony, however, kept apart. Meanwhile Matthias forced Rudolf to cede to him Hungary, Austria, and Moravia along with the succession in Bohemia. He granted freedom of religion to Austria, and finally Rudolf, in Bohemia (which could not forget its history), legalised by the Letter of Majesty the Augsburg Confession. The nobles, knights, and royal towns were allowed to build Protestant churches where needed: on royal domains the people themselves might do the same. Trouble afterwards arose because the Church lands, being managed by the royal treasury, were treated by the Protestants as if they came under the same provision, a mistake which was technical but far-reaching. Silesia received like privileges, and only Ferdinand in Styria stood out against it. In July 1609, the formation of a Catholic League was the reply to the Evangelical Union. Rudolf was forced to resign Bohemia (1611), and died (20 January, 1612) in the midst of wild schemes for regaining power, which had thrown all his subjects, and specially the Bohemians, upon the side of Matthias. The latter was elected Emperor (18 June, 1612), but the Electors made favourable terms for themselves in the transaction. He had made a mistake in bidding for the support of Protestants with whose principles he did not agree, and he favoured the Catholics more than once. The Protestants had built churches at Braunau on land belonging to the Abbey, and at Klostergrab on the lands of the See of Prague, and to this their superiors objected. It was replied that ecclesi-

The Evangelical Union, 1608.

The Catholic League, 1609.

Emperor Matthias, 1612–19.

astical lands, as controlled by the Crown, ranked as royal, and therefore admitted the building of churches. But Matthias took the other and more legal view. He contrived to get his determined relative Ferdinand (of the Styrian branch) elected King of Bohemia (June 1617) and of Hungary (1618); in yielding to this Bohemia had owned the hereditary right of the Habsburgs and ran a risk of losing its freedom, for it had hoped to elect a Protestant. The expected death of Matthias (which took place 20 March, 1619) could no longer bring relief to his lands. Ferdinand was stricter and more sincere; his subjects would not gain a milder rule by waiting. The church at Braunau was soon closed and that at Klostergrab pulled down; feeling grew more intense. Under the leadership of Count Henry of Thurn (23 May, 1618) a national revolt, hastened by outside diplomacy, broke out. The Religious War had at length begun. Christian of Anhalt had been intriguing and reckoning upon it. The war might, with France and Spain at rivalry and keenly interested, become European; at any rate, the German Catholics were only too likely to be thrown upon the side of Spain as the Protestants upon that of France. In Maximilian of Bavaria and Ferdinand the Catholics had leaders of higher type and stronger fibre than any found on the Protestant side. Unhappily these leaders had now resolved to meet innovation by force. It is not our purpose to follow out the war in detail; many features already noted reappear in its course. The dark shadows of France and Spain hide German interests; the Protestant divisions, the weakness of the imperial constitution, the pertinacity of the Counter Reformation are seen again and again. In its later years religion is quite lost sight of: it is a war of mere politics and often of barbarity, which worked untold harm and made misery a thing of daily life. It was not only great events such as the sack of a great city like Magdeburg (20 May, 1631), when it was burnt and ruined, although the cathedral was saved by Tilly's efforts. The marches and barbarity of armies, largely mercenary, brought the war to the peasant's cottage as to the lord's castle. The chief seats of the actual warfare

Emperor Ferdinand II, 1619–37.

The Thirty Years' War.

might change, but the suffering and want it caused were almost everywhere.[1]

The War falls into strongly marked periods, the first of which is the Bohemian War (1618–1624). It was natural that Bohemia, with its long history of religious strife behind it, and now struggling for its old freedom under unsympathetic Habsburg rule, should lead the way. But, unfortunately for them, their Diet had accepted Ferdinand of Styria, chosen by the Habsburgs as their candidate for the Empire, as the future successor to the Bohemian throne (June 1617): they were unready and unequal to the diplomatic skill of Cardinal Klesl. Ferdinand's rule in his own duchy left no doubt that his Imperial and kingly policy would be sharply Catholic. In Bohemia, however, freedom of conscience, though not of worship, had been allowed under Rudolf and Matthias: the regulation of church-building and worship had been left to the Estates—that is, to some 1400 feudal land-owners and about 40 towns; on the royal lands, however, church-building had been left free, a concession against which Rudolf and Matthias had striven vainly. On the Protestant side, the able and restless Christian of Anhalt had been intriguing for a Protestant king of Bohemia, preferably a Lutheran Saxon Prince or, failing that, the Calvinist Elector Palatine Frederick V. But this was now impossible in view of Ferdinand's certain succession. The Bohemians could not escape the handicap of their first and worst mistake.

Matthias, with legal correctness, interpreted the Letter of Majesty not to cover ecclesiastical lands, whereas the Utraquists held them to be grouped with the royal lands, as the crown had special interests in them: this was one of those popular confusions which often cause trouble. And trouble came with a darker prospect when Ferdinand was elected for Hungary

Periods of the Thirty Years' War.

---

[1] I owe much to the chapters in the *Cambridge Modern History* (Vol. IV), by Sir A. W. Ward, and also to his lectures before I came to Cambridge. I may refer here to the Bibliographies in Vol. IV, which are very full, and include the pamphlets of the time in the Acton Library, which Miss A. M. Cooke arranged. In the *Epochs of History* (Longmans, 1894) there is an excellent small book on the War by S. R. Gardiner.

(1618), a year after his Bohemian Election, and finally as Emperor (1619). Their prospects were darker because now behind the Habsburgs stood the power of Spain ready to help the Catholic cause at need. But Christian of Anhalt was also looking abroad: he had hopes of English help, for the Elector Palatine had married the brilliant and beautiful Princess Elizabeth, daughter of James I: the wed- *The Elector* ding, with its Protestant halo, had stirred the Eng- *Palatine,* lish poets into song, and through the future Hano- *Frederick V.* verian succession was to leave its mark on English history.[1] The certainty of Ferdinand's accession forced the Bohemians to choose between a tyranny and a revolution. A body called *Defensors* had legal power, at their discretion, to call a Diet: this they now did (March 1618). In it they drew up a statement of their grievances, including the rankling sores of Braunau and Klostergrat: this document was sent to Ferdinand, and his reply declared their meeting illegal, and justified the government action in the cases complained of. This reply the Diet wrongly attributed to two of the Regents, Slavata and Martinitz: the only hope seemed to be instant action, and under the leadership of Count Henry of Thurn, revolution, already prepared for, was decided upon. The defence of their traditional liberties was just, but the vengeance, planned and dealt out to the two obnoxious Regents, was on a lower level: what ought to have marked a great historic occasion was made violent and disgraceful. Thurn led his armed followers to the Hradschin (palace), and there they denounced the two Regents as authors of the reply and showed *The De-* their sincerity by dragging them to a window and *fenestration* hurling them to the ground some fifty feet below: *of Prague,* an innocent secretary Fabricius was also seized and *26 May,* thrown below. In spite of the fall and of being afterwards shot *1618.* at, not one of the three was killed, and, later, they escaped from the city.

Thirty Directors were chosen to carry on the government:

---

[1] See S. R. Gardiner, *History of England* (1603–42), Vol. II., chap. XV. Also Sir A. W. Ward, *The Electress Sophia* (London, 1909).

a few obnoxious ecclesiastics were expelled and so were the
Jesuits in a body. But defence had to be provided for, as
Ferdinand had forces behind him. A Diet met, voted
taxes and ordered a levy. But the levy fell through
and the tax was not collected. Foreign help seemed
the only hope. James I, the most interested and
most likely friend, had home difficulties to face, and in any case
preferred the shades of diplomacy to the open road of war.
Savoy did something by lending 2000 mercenaries under the
command of the Count of Mansfield, an experienced leader, but
with followers noted for plunder and a terror to the land.

*The Bohe-
mian Revo-
lution: War,
1618–22.*

The Bohemian Diet, along with representatives of Upper
and Lower Austria, now met again (31 July–19 August,
1619): it affirmed the Bohemian Kingship to be elective:
then it dethroned Ferdinand, replacing him by the
Elector Palatine, Frederick V (26 August, 1619).
To the sorrow of wiser heads at his Court, he
accepted the crown, and went to Prague, "taking
with him" (as said his mother, Louisa Julia, a daughter of
William the Silent) "the Palatinate to Prague."

*Frederick,
the "Winter-
King" in
Bohemia,
Aug. 1619.*

The Emperor Matthias had died (20 March, 1619) and
Ferdinand was his successor, chosen unanimously by the Electoral College, a result only due to the jealousy
between the Lutheran John George of Saxony and
the Calvinist Elector Palatine: had they only been
able to agree, tolerant terms might possibly have
been gained for the Protestants: Ferdinand knew his own
difficulties, and might have proved conciliatory in such a crisis.
But Frederick's election at Prague had been, at any rate, a
rebellion in Germany: war, certainly local and probably much
more, was inevitable. The state of Germany, and the interest
of powers outside in its politics, religious and dynastic, were
only too likely to make such a war disastrously great, not
merely national, but European in scope and effects. Behind the
Habsburgs stood Spain. Among the Protestants there was a
lack of unity, partly dynastic, but especially between Lutherans and Calvinists: Frederick's removal from the churches in
Prague of ornaments which he disliked but Lutherans ap

*Ferdinand II,
Emperor,
28 August,
1619–37.*

proved, went against him. Moreover in a meeting at Mühl-hausen (March 1620) the Catholic League had promised not to attempt the recovery of episcopal lands held by Protestant administrators or of secularised Sees in the north, provided the holders were loyal to the Emperor. The Lutheran Princes, with this bribe before their eyes, were not likely to act against Ferdinand: profit from such lands was one of their dearest interests. The offer left them sure of something, and disregard of it might lose them their States.

Frederick was not well supported: the Union, which had promised neutrality towards the League (3 June, 1620), left him to his fate: James I had too many troubles at home to send help abroad, and his theory of kingship went against encourag-ing rebellion. At first the war in Bohemia and Austria went well for the new king, but fortune soon changed. Maximilian of Bavaria, the ablest German Prince, whose family had always chafed at their exclusion from the Electoral College, was won over by the promise of Frederick's seat in it: he was also allowed to keep Upper and Lower Austria in pledge for his expenses in the war. The League's Army was led by Tilly, a Walloon by birth, upright in character and sincerely Catholic, trained in warfare under *Tilly.* able leaders and in varied fields, but his mercenary troops, like others, were noted for plunder. Early in November he drew near Prague, and (Sunday, 8 Nov., 1620) de-feated Frederick's army in the battle of Weissen-berg (the White Hill) near the city. "The Winter-King" fled through Silesia, and at length reached *The battle of Weissen-berg, 8 Nov., 1620.* the Hague: his short dream and shorter reign were at an end. The victors received the submission of the capital and of the leaders, to whom Tilly gave a chance of escape, not taking which they were executed: wholesale confiscations followed, and newcomers, German and Catholic, sprang up as a new nobility: among them was Wallenstein, of an older family, soon to become great and wealthy. Bohemia, as a whole, was easily conquered: Glatz, the last place to hold out, fell in November 1622. The conquest was used *Conquest of Bohemia, 1622.* for religious interests: the Bohemian Brethren were expelled, and the Jesuits came back to carry out the Counter-Reformation in a severer way, since now heads were heated and swords were swinging.

Thus, on both sides, the war was rapidly becoming a religious one, and all hopes of toleration disappeared. Along with the hopelessness of toleration went prospect of an effective national settlement. Frederick's election to the Bohemian throne might have been treated as a rebellion of a kind not unknown before, and punished as such. But the policy followed by the government and the persecution carried on, left bitterness behind: sectarian hatreds grew on all sides, and the sufferings of minorities gave excuse for foreign interference in a country already divided enough in itself. The Emperor, ruling over Habsburg territories, artificially joined together as they were, came to depend more and more on his kinsmen in Spain. Local memories of days of sadness always linger long. Bohemia especially, rightly blamed as it might be, had its national memory seared by a reeking sword. Before Peace came, its population fell, according to native estimates, believed generally even if not accurately proved, from 4,000,000 to 80,000. Easter, 1626, was fixed as the date by which all non-Catholics were to leave the country, and 30,000 families are said to have gone. And Bohemia was not alone in its suffering, nor was the suffering on one side only. The passage of ruthless mercenaries left havoc and desolation behind.

After Bohemia was conquered, the Imperialist army went on to attack Frederick's ancestral lands, first the Upper, and then the Rhenish or Lower Palatinate. The Upper and part of the Lower were given (1623) to Maximilian, the former of these Bavaria was, in the end, to keep permanently. Here, as elsewhere (in the Emperor's lands for instance), Catholic worship was restored with sternness, the only allowed alternative to conversion being emigration. In these campaigns the Emperor not only gained ground, but made his central power more effective.

In the spring (1622) the hostile armies were marching to the Lower (Rhenish) Palatinate, where Sir Horace Vere, in command of English volunteers, was acting for Frederick, who had been put under the Ban of the Empire (22 Jan., 1621). Mansfield and the Margrave of Baden were able, for a time, to hold Tilly, until Gonzales de Cordova with Spanish troops came to his help. But Mansfield and the Margrave could not agree, and the latter was heavily defeated at Winpfen (6 May, 1622) and Mansfield, with a hungry army, marched to Alsace. It was clear that the Protestants were as much disunited in the field as in the council chamber. Meanwhile *Protestant Disunion.* diplomatists were negotiating at Brussels, and Frederick kept wavering in mind and plans. His older and ancestral Palatinate had been finally conquered and his Electorship was handed over to Maximilian. John George of Saxony could thus see that his fellow Protestants of the West were as hopeless as in the East. France seemed the only Power that could check Spain and the Emperor together. But Richelieu had always to consider Huguenot hostilities, and was at times too busy at home to act abroad. Heidelberg was taken (July 1622): Tilly could enforce proper treatment of the defeated garrison but the city suffered much. One result was an injury to learning, for the famous Library, with all its treasures, was now carted to Rome, there to be housed (as the Palatina) in the Vatican. It was a *Destruction of Heidelberg, July 1622.* mean revenge, wrought, too, upon memorials of medieval learning. So the War in Germany went on, with hopeless disunion among the Protestants, and with foreign Powers eagerly watching and likely to intervene.

Christian IV of Denmark was the first to act: he was the hereditary Duke of Holstein, and had himself seized the Sees of Bremen and Verden. He was a political Protestant with natural interests in Germany: he had been chosen as Director of the Lower Saxon Circle, where lay most of the secularised Sees. But the *Danish Intervention, Christian IV, 1624–29.* Danish intervention did not work much. At Dessau (25 April, 1626), Mansfield, who was helping Christian, was defeated. Christian himself was defeated by Tilly at Lutter (27 August, 1626). The theatre of war was large, and things went badly for Christian: his own lands were in danger: he complained, with reason, of the little help he got from England,

and before long (22 May, 1628) he made peace with the Emperor at Lübeck. Thus another period of the War was ended.

One most important matter was the appearance on the scene of Albert of Wallenstein, or Waldstein. He belonged to an old **Wallen-** Bohemian family, of great descent but scanty **stein.** means. His parents, who were Lutheran, died when he was twelve, and he was left to the care of an uncle, a strict member of the Bohemian Brethren, and him he left for the Jesuits at Olmütz. Religion made no special appeal to him, but the training he got under them sharpened his great ability. He made a wealthy marriage and turned to a military career. He aimed at raising an army of his own, living on the lands where it encamped: looking on a disordered land he saw its only hope in a strong central power. He was enough of a patriotic German to find that power in the historic Empire. And the army of his vision, the tool for his own career, was to be placed at the Emperor's service and restore his power. It was a far-sweeping vision, and his great practical abilities might well make it possible. But for the religious matters and differences which filled the minds of many, he cared nothing at all. Catholics and Protestants of all kinds were to find freedom in the closely knit German Empire of his vision. He was made Duke of Friedland (January 1627) and seemed likely to found a strong northern power. After Christian IV had made peace with the Emperor (1629), the Emperor, the army led by Wallenstein, the League represented by Maximilian, and the clergy inspired now above all by the Papal Nuncios (such as Carafa), were now the leading forces on the Catholic side, and the interests of their parties were rapidly growing apart. By this time Ferdinand had put down Protestantism in his own territories—Austria, Moravia, Silesia, and Bohemia. He was determined to re-establish not only Catholicism, but the power of the House of Habsburg over all its territories and to make the Imperial authority a reality. His high-handed proceedings alarmed even his Catholic followers, but they dared not oppose him then. That he went too far is shown by the fact that in Hungary at a later date (1645) Ferdinand III was forced to restore some churches to Protestants. Behind the soldiers who saw to the expulsion of ministers and teachers came the Jesuits and the Monastic Orders; emigration of dissenters and instruction of those who remained completed the process. The first stage of the Emperor's policy was now finished; his own lands were secured for his own religion. It seemed as if he might even go further, win more of Germany for the Counter Reformation, and along with that restore the imperial power to its former greatness. This policy was expressed in the Edict of Restitution.

The abuse of episcopal Sees for the enrichment of princely youths was disgraceful, and so the Edict had some moral justification. The career of Duke Christian of Brunswick-Wolfenbüttel is an instance of the abuse, although Christian's character had streaks of attractiveness, such as his devoted admiration for the exiled Queen of Bohemia. He was titular Bishop of Halberstadt (1616–29). He had been a captain of dragoons before his election, and he was indeed more at home as a leader of cavalry than on the outer circle of ecclesiastical affairs. An English letter hit on the happy description of him as a "temporal bishop," but even as a leader of mercenaries he fell below the best. He might remind us of the medieval apologist for the use of fire in warfare who said that "fire was to warfare what the Magnificat was to Evensong." Christian would perhaps have agreed with this sentiment as far as warfare went, but the correct liturgic language might have been beyond him.

This Edict enjoined that all bishoprics, monasteries, and other Church lands not held directly from the Emperor which had been secularised since 1552 were to be restored to the Catholics; all those held directly which had passed to Protestants since 1555 (and therefore contrary to the Reservation) were also to return to Catholics. All Catholic princes could compel their subjects to adopt Catholicism, or to leave the country on receiving money to do so. The Religious Peace was only to apply to Lutherans; Calvinists and Zwinglians were not to be tolerated. This Edict applied to some fourteen Sees and one hundred and twenty

Edict of Restitution, 6 March, 1629.

other foundations at least. If it had been carried out it would have done for North Germany what had already been done for the South; but it was carried out only in Alsace, Franconia, and the Lower Saxon Circle. Incidentally the Emperor could thus provide for younger members of his family, such as his son, the Archduke Leopold, who was now elected Bishop of Halberstadt. But the Elector John George of Saxony, hitherto loyal, and the League, strongly Catholic but also anti-Habsburg, were turned against the Emperor by the Edict. Maximilian of Bavaria suggested its postponement for forty years, and the Elector asked its repeal. All parties united against Wallenstein, who was likely to make the Emperor too great and destroy the freedom of Germany. While the Edict only interpreted the existing law correctly, it did not allow for existing facts and for processes hard to undo; it put hardship upon some who were not to blame for the original fault. It was well that greedy princes should be reminded of their limitations, but there were some of humbler rank who suffered more. And the manner in which the Edict was enforced—along with the proscription of Protestantism elsewhere—really retarded the cause it was meant to serve. Here and there, as in Prague and the Upper Palatinate, the new clerics were surprised at the ease with which the masses returned to Catholicism, but the true cause of this was that their previous Protestantism had been founded upon persuasion rather than conviction, and was often the result of princely or baronial influence rather than of spiritual change. But in many cases a real and lasting harm was done to religion by the use of force to coerce the conscience, instead of merely removing a hindrance to its freedom of play. It was strange that Urban VIII—a Pope led mainly by political considerations, unlike Gregory XV, who had subsidised the Emperor and urged him to persevere—did not welcome Ferdinand's increase of power. For a time he refused subsidies, and would not allow the war to be called religious; he would not even allow Ferdinand to name the first holders of the benefices regained, and he did not approve the handing over to the Jesuits of recovered foundations, since this removed them from episcopal control. It was more politically important that the imperial success roused France to new efforts and interference, first by diplomacy and then by war.

With the intervention of Gustavus Adolphus, King of Sweden, comes the central part of the War. In Sweden the power of the Crown and the stability of the Constitution had been founded on the secularisation of Church property, parochial and monastic. By this alone the Crown was enabled to meet its expenses. The story of the royal family founded by Gustavus Vasa was tragic: he was a Lutheran, but his son Eric XIV was a Calvinist, and under him ecclesiastical rule grew slack and politics disturbed: when he was poisoned his brother John III took the throne. John had keen interest in theology and corresponded with George Cassander, a divine who was bent on the reconciliation of Catholics, Lutherans and Calvinists, and whose *Consultatio*, formulating his views, was reprinted at Stockholm. King John, helped by his archbishop and Cardinal Hosius, worked for the Counter-Reformation: he issued the Red Book, a Liturgy based on the Missal, but his plans were not effective or popular. His son Sigismund, a strong Catholic, was elected King of Poland, a Catholic country. On John's death (1592), Sigismund had a disturbed kingship and his uncle Charles IX was elected king: himself a Calvinist, he fell in with the wishes of the Lutheran nation: he was succeeded (1611) by his son Gustavus Adolphus.

The War and Gustavus Adolphus of Sweden, June 1630–Nov. 1632.

This Prince had been thoroughly trained: as a boy of twelve he attended the Diet and learnt its ways, in the European languages he was at ease, and he had a military education, which was needed, since after his accession he had to pass through three wars to give his country peace. Danes had overrun it, Poland and Russia were enemies on its coast and borders. But when his three wars, against Denmark, Russia and Poland, were over, his land was free from spoilers and the Baltic was a Swedish lake. The army was supplied by the nobles and their service: this had been given grudgingly up to his day, but by his tact and political instinct he made them proud to serve under his banner.[1] His mother

Gustavus Adolphus, 1611–32.

---

[1] For Sweden see Chapters V and XVI, pp. 100–9 and 461–81.

and his wife were Germans, and both in politics and religion Sweden had many links with Germany.

But although such reasons might have led a politician to interfere in a German civil war, Gustavus Adolphus was more than a mere politician, and other reasons swayed him. He had a deep but restless nature, much imagination as well as practical ability. With such a man and with such responsibilities, religion was a profound reality and the very foundation of life. If Protestantism, in the form he held, was to be saved against the power of the Habsburg Emperors, backed by the influence of Spain, foreign help was needed, and so in the spirit of a Protestant Crusader, Gustavus Adolphus entered the War. And he came when the Edict of Restitution had shown what Protestantism might expect, and what the Emperor meant to carry through: he landed (4 July, 1630) and the War at once passed into its greatest stage, dominated by his personality.

Gustavus Adolphus has been called a Protestant Crusader, but the description must not mislead us: he also stood for His religious liberty of conscience, which, had he realised his plan policy. of a *Corpus Evangelicorum*, an association of Princes under his own control, would probably have been the rule within its bounds. Although Gustavus, looking towards Poland and his cousin Sigismund, had to be cautious in guarding his lines of communication, he had foreign support, for he concluded a treaty with France (at Bärwalde, Jan. 1631) Treaty of by which Richelieu promised help for various Bärwalde things, including the security of the Baltic. But between the German Protestants did not rally to him as he France and Sweden: expected, and even his brother-in-law, the Elector 23 Jan., of Brandenburg, George William, was, as he 1631. announced, neutral: he remained so until the Emperor pressed him too far. Wallenstein, of whom the Catholic Princes were jealous, was dismissed from his command (Sept. 1630), and so it was with Tilly that Gustavus had Sack of first to cross swords, and he succeeded in driving Magdeburg: him back. But he was not quick enough to save 20 May, 1631. the great city of Magdeburg, from its fall and sack, a memory of horror which not only the never-taken "maiden city" itself, but the whole of Germany never forgot. Tilly was not to blame for the worst outrage, the burning of the great cathedral. Tilly had to retreat towards Saxony: he threatened to deal with Leipzig as he had done with Magdeburg: the threat made the Elector join Gustavus at once, and the Swedes marched towards Tilly. The armies met at Breitenfeld, near Leipzig. The Swedes, though outnumbered, were too mobile, and used their artillery too well for the Leaguers, who had to retreat, which they did in an orderly way. It was a crushing defeat for Tilly, due to the tactics and skill of Gustavus; his reputation and his confidence were never the same. The war was moving westwards: when Tilly was trying to stop the Swedes from crossing the Lech he was mortally wounded, 14 April, 1632, and died at Ingolstadt. Wallenstein, who with the licence of a German Prince, had been negotiating with Gustavus, was restored to his command, first temporarily and then permanently (April 1632). From the neighbourhood of Nuremberg, where Gustavus failed to carry Wallenstein's lines, Wallenstein went to Saxony. Gustavus followed him, and the armies met at Lützen: the Swedes broke the German line, but it was restored in the centre. Gustavus had a wound not fully healed, and so could not wear his armour: he rushed to the dangerous centre, and there was wounded twice, and then shot fatally. The battle went on, Bernhard of Weimar taking the King's place. Pappenheim, Wallenstein's dashing leader of cavalry, was slain. Victory at last settled down on the side of the Swedes. But no victory could make up for the loss of the great general, his eye for tactics and his grasp of politics. After him the War seems to move on a lower plane.

Battle of Breitenfeld: 17 Sept., 1631.

Battle of Lützen: 16 Nov., 1632.

The months before Lützen have difficulties of their own. It is often difficult to see clearly what Gustavus or Wallenstein is aiming at. Probably Gustavus was looking more on political than on military matters. South Germany, with its great cities, showed him a side of the nation's life very different from what he had seen before. Wallenstein for his part, was striving to preserve his army, meant to be the weapon for securing his future greatness. All his plans, which might incidentally be for the good of the nation, centred on himself and his interests. Intrigues, diplomacy, and warfare were mingled, and when later on he was charged with treason, it was impossible to say that he had not crossed the line.

Both Gustavus and Wallenstein had formed great plans for the future of Germany. Those of the latter verged on treason in spite of his real veneration for the historic Empire. The *Corpus Evangelicorum* of Gustavus would have made a permanent division of the Empire on the foundation of religious differences, although toleration might soften them. Historic traditions would have been violated, Napoleon's map of Germany anticipated, the breakdown of the Empire hastened. Foreign infusions would have weakened the stream of national life.

Under the not too cordial diplomatic guidance of the Swedish minister Oxenstiern and the military command of

The war after Gustavus. Bernhard of Saxe-Weimar (by whose side stood Horn, the trusted general of Gustavus) the war went on. The League of Heilbronn (23 April, 1633) united under Sweden the circles of Swabia, the Upper and Lower Rhine and Franconia (where Bernhard hoped to form a duchy out of Bamberg and Wurzburg). Wallenstein's great success and too great power had led to his second dismissal. The Princes were jealous of him, Spain disliked him, and the Emperor, convinced of his treason, had him assassinated at Eger (1634). This living cause of jealousy removed, Bavaria and the Habsburgs became more friendly. Saxony, no longer threatened by his army, made a preliminary peace with Ferdinand at Prague (1635). Spain was more active than before on the Catholic side, when France, stronger at home under

French intervention, 1635-48. Richelieu, and long the secret supporter of the Protestants, now plunged openly into the war. Thus a disastrous and blighting struggle, which might have ended in 1634, was prolonged for fourteen years. But the Peace of Prague foreshadowed its end, and this peace came after the disastrous Protestant defeat at Nördlingen (6 September, 1634).

By this peace the Elector of Saxony made peace for the Lutherans, and for them alone. So far as they were concerned the Emperor gave up the Edict of Restitution. They—that is, those of the Augsburg Confession— were allowed liberty of worship in the Empire except in Bohemia and the Austrian hereditary lands. Peace of Prague, 30 May, 1635. All mediate Church lands (*i.e.*, those not held of the Emperor) were to remain as in 1552. If secularised then they remained so. All secularised immediate Church lands, reconquered since 11 November, 1627, were left to their secular holders (thus most of the northern Sees were left to the Protestants). Thus the Emperor really compromised with the Lutherans and surrendered much, so that they were practically bought. He also gained support for his son as successor in the Empire, and secured the See of Halberstadt for his younger son Leopold. The Pope (Urban VIII) disapproved of the peace; the Capuchins, now coming to the front and marked by a national feeling lost among the Jesuits, approved. Among some Jesuits the opinion was that the peace was really a snare for Saxony, that the concessions made were more apparent than real, and would only divide the Protestants.

The religious element in the war was now overlaid by the political. The Treaty of Paris (November, 1634) had secured for the Protestants the help of France (now and since August, 1624, guided by Richelieu), but to gain this help Alsace was to be given up. Thus religious divisions played into the hands of France. On Ferdinand's death (15 February, 1637) he was succeeded by his son Ferdinand III, King of Hungary and (since December 22, 1636) King of the Romans. Ferdinand and III., 1637. The new Emperor was strict and regular in habits, careful and discreet, and although pious lacked the enthusiasm of his father. The war under him was utterly merged in the duel between Spain and France, while Germany was weary of war. Bernhard of Saxe-Weimar died 8 July, 1639. Negotiations for peace had begun in 1645, and in 1648 the Treaty of Westphalia, made up of the Treaty of Münster between the Empire and France, and that of Osnabrück between the Empire and Sweden, was completed. With the political terms, forming a basis for European politics during one hundred and fifty years, we have little to do; the cession of land to France and Sweden, and the influence given to these powers in the Empire, were disastrous to the national life of Germany.

The secularisation of Sees was confirmed. Sweden gained Bremen and Verden; Brandenburg took Halberstadt (the Archduke Leopold exchanged it for Strassburg), Minden, Cammin, and in the end Magdeburg also; Mecklenburg received Schwerin and Ratzeburg; Brunswick-Lüneburg the alternate nomination to Osnabrück. Many secularised abbeys were similarly used as " compensations." The recognition of the independence of the Swiss and of the United Provinces acknowledged facts less open to criticism than these secularisations. The old *reservatum ecclesiasticum*, the cause of so much trouble, was done away with, and for most of the Empire the term (January 1624) was taken as the norm. All benefices were to remain in the hands of the religion then in possession. For the Palatinate, Baden, and Württemberg the date 1618 was taken, but had this earlier year been taken throughout the Empire, the changes in the Habsburg hereditary lands would have been disallowed as later in date. If in future a holder of an ecclesiastical State changed his religion he was to lose his office. A State was to remain as it was at the normal date. The right of reformation was given to the princes, only to be exercised with the approval of the people, and where direct sovereignty was possessed, so that this right was denied to the imperial cities; in them the dominant religion was to remain as such. This right of reformation gave to the princes great powers of interference in religious matters, and by implication adopted a system of State relations often assumed in practice if decried in theory, but it was rarely brought into play. Thus all the tendencies of religious strife and political greed so long at work were crystallised and made a permanent part of the constitution. Religious toleration was

Treaty of Westphalia, 1648.

gained, and Calvinists were now at last treated the same as Lutherans of the Augsburg Confession and Catholics. Many regulations guarded the rights of Protestants in Imperial relations and judicial suits. Then the Empire settled down to the tremendous task of repairing the desolation and healing its misery, but religion remained for long a thing of territory and politics rather than of the inmost life. The Empire had been sacrificed by Austria to its religious and dynastic aims, by others to their less lofty greed. Inside the Austrian lands Catholicism held undisputed sway; in the Empire religion was free. In comparison with the policy of others, that of the Habsburgs is just redeemed from vulgarity and selfishness by its vision of the ancient Empire and their own religious earnestness. For the rest the princes seemed now to have become everywhere the keepers of religion, and real spirituality was likely to perish under their care as had the national life.

In the negotiations for peace papal legates—four, one after the other—were present, but the conditions upon which they insisted were disregarded. Church property should *The treaty* not be dealt with; Sweden and the Elector-Palatine *and the* should not be allowed to gain; but their protests to *Papacy.* these ends were of no use. Europe had now passed out of political tutelage to the Pope; the legate Chigi protested against the Peace, and Innocent X (*Zelo Domus Dei*, 20 November, 1648) annulled it so far as it was against the See of Rome, the Catholic Church, or clerical discipline. But the treaty itself had provided that the opposition of any power, temporal or spiritual, should be disregarded, and the condemnation had thus no result except as the beginning of a policy which has sometimes since then placed the Papacy in opposition to national wishes and interests in Germany and elsewhere. The Papacy had chosen to make political results its great end. The Council of Trent had, on the other hand, strengthened its spiritual powers, and these remained unaffected by the treaty or its rejection; its political claims were, however, openly disregarded. Spain, too, which earlier in the year (January 1648) had made peace with the Netherlands and acknowledged their independence, protested against the treaty. This was no wonder, for in Spain more than anywhere else the hope of un-doing the work of the Reformation had been cherished, and henceforward that hope in its largest shape was impossible, in spite of the very great progress of the Counter Reformation. But just as a century earlier Catholicism had gained by the hatred between Lutheran and Calvinist, so now Protestantism had gained by the rivalry between France and Spain. Political, and not religious problems were to be henceforth the primary difficulties and duties of States; this was an axiom princes had been forced to learn, but which the Papacy had chosen to dis-regard. The Treaty of Westphalia laid a purely political basis for the future, and it was not without significance that the Holy Roman Empire—the distinctive dream of the Middle Ages as an embodiment of spiritual unity expressed in politics—had now by this treaty changed its character and lost its power.[1] Thus Germany, by this Treaty, did its part in creating a new Europe, as Scandinavia, the Netherlands and other States were also doing. And along with the territorial changes the influence of the new Science of International Law, so mightily taught to Europe by Grotius, did its share in forming a Europe, if old and a little weary in some ways yet eager and hopeful in others and with great powers of new growth.

[1] The effect of the war upon population varied locally: Magdeburg, for instance, suffered greatly. So estimates vary too. Sir A. W. Ward, in a *Lecture at the Royal Institution* (5 March, 1912), mentions that in Franconia monastic vows before the age of 60 and clerical celibacy were prohibited by law: laymen were allowed two wives apiece.

XIV

THE NETHERLANDS, FRANCE AFTER THE WARS, THE JESUITS

The Netherlands played a great part in the history of the Reformation,[1] but, in its beginning, this was due not to religious differences but to the struggle for freedom against a foreign oppressor. That foreign oppressor was Spain, the champion of Papal Catholicism, the ally and patron of the Inquisition, and so the political conflict inevitably became religious also. It is true that there were reforming bodies, Lutheran and Calvinist, but they were small and unorganised, and did not cause the wars, which mark so tragically the Age of the Reformation in the Netherlands.

The religious, like the political, history of the Netherlands was peculiar. Their political unity was dynastic, not national or local, and their ecclesiastical organisation was both weak and complicated. The bulk of the territory lay in the three dioceses of Tournai, Arras and Utrecht, but part also in those of Terouenne, Cambrai (both French Sees) and Liége. As the controlling Archbishops of Cologne and Rheims also belonged to foreign countries, no organisation could be more confused, and it was impossible for religious coherence to exist. Charles V had again and again urged upon the Papacy the formation

[1] Popular ideas of the Revolt of the Netherlands are mainly derived from Motley's *Rise of the Dutch Republic*, 1535–84 (3 vols., London 1856) (also in Dent's Everyman Edition) and his *History of the United Netherlands* (4 vols., London 1860–7). Some fundamental criticism of these has been made by Prof. Pieter Geyl, in *The Revolt of the Netherlands* (1555–1609) (London 1932) and *The Netherlands Divided* (1609–48) (London 1936); both based on his *Geschiedenis van de Nederlandsche Stam* (Wereldbibliotheek, Amsterdam 1930–4). His work is that of a trained historian and valuable for its wide knowledge. In the *Cambridge Modern History*, Vol. III, CVI, *The Revolt of the Netherlands*, and CVII, *William the Silent*, by the Rev. George Edmundson, are clear and accurate and have a full bibliography.

of new Sees, as the existing organisation worked against the unity he desired, but the death of Adrian VI and the hostility of later Popes hindered him. When Philip II (1557) proposed to found and to endow out of monastic funds, fourteen new Sees, with three Archbishoprics, the scheme aroused great opposition because it was supposed to be in the interests of Spain. The Netherlands had also had a peculiar history in regard to tendencies of thought. The revival of learning had greater hold in the region of the Brethren of the Common Lot,[1] but their sound religious influence had been counter-balanced by that of more fantastic and mystic theologians or heretics, among whom the medieval Kathari (*c.* 1162), the Beguines and Beghards and the Lollards (*c.* 1300) were numbered. Some of these bodies combined excellent practical impulses with teaching opposed to that of the Church. In districts where the dioceses were too large for oversight and lines of trade brought wandering teachers, these vague popular movements soon degenerated, a process which was greatly hastened by the influence of the spiritual Franciscans. It was not surprising then that in the Netherlands Anabaptist teaching found a ready soil; Luther's writings soon became popular in the cities, and there as elsewhere strengthened underground currents of revolutionary thought; the Augustinians, who were locally strong, naturally favoured his views. But before long Zwinglian and Calvinistic tendencies gained the upper hand. It was from a Dutch theologian, van Hoen, that Zwingli first got his sacramental views, and the nearness of France made Calvinist influence stronger than Lutheran; incidentally, too, this school of thought was more suited to rich and democratic towns. When the Anabaptist movement was ended two classes of religious communities were found in existence; firstly, a number of "quieter" Anabaptist bodies somewhat akin to the English Friends and organised (especially in Friesland) by Menno Simonis (*c.* 1542) as a select people, separated from the world, secondly, a number of Calvinist bodies spreading from the Walloon provinces (the lands of Hainault, Artois and Namur) northwards: with

Religious thought.

[1] See p. 26 *supra,* where they are called "Brethren of the Common Life."

these Calvinist bodies lay the future of the Netherlands. Thus the religious state was confused.

Charles V was not hampered in the Netherlands by the political conditions which thwarted his will in Germany and he was determined to put down Protestantism with a heavy hand. In April 1522 he organised an Inquisition of his own, and, with Papal leave, a layman, Francis van der Hulst, was placed at its head. When this was superseded, in 1524, by the Papal Inquisition, the Emperor continued to issue Placard (or Edict) after Placard and to order their enforcement by the secular authorities, especially in those provinces where local privilege prevented the introduction of the Inquisition. These Placards culminated in the most severe one of 1550 by which death was made the penalty not only for preaching heresy but also for attending conventicles and reading heretical books. The process of repression—an exercise of sovereignty rather than a consequence of personal bigotry on the part of Charles—continued for many years, but, though it produced its tale of martyrs and of refugees, it was never wholly effective, as is shown by the large rewards offered to informers in the Placard of 1550. In fact, the persecutions here, as elsewhere, influenced men profoundly in the direction of reform; but the movement was as yet unorganised. It was not until Charles V's reign was over that the forces of opposition broke into revolt.

On 25 October, 1555, there was an assembly of unique importance in the great hall of the palace at Brussels. Charles V, worn out prematurely by his incessant toils, there abdicated the thrones of his many dominions. To him the essence of the ceremony lay not in its pomp and glory but in the surrender of the responsibility which had been the burden of each single possession. He had sought to discharge that responsibility fittingly before God and man; and now, about to lay it aside and to pass into semi-monastic retirement, the Emperor, a Netherlander by birth, chose to seal his surrender in the land he loved the best. There were assembled the representatives of the seventeen provinces, with Mary of Hungary, Governess of the States

Charles V and his rule.

Abdication of Charles V, 1555.

(whose husband, Lewis II, had fallen in 1526 at Mohacs) and Philip, now to succeed his father. The wearied Emperor, having heard Mass and signed the Deed of Abdication, entered, walking feebly and leaning on the shoulder of a favourite page, William of Orange-Nassau. It was strange and indeed prophetic that the two, William and Philip, whose conflict was to make so much history, should both be present at this dramatic scene. Charles asked from the Netherlanders for Philip the loyalty he himself had received from them and urged them to obey the Church. When, concluding his farewell with a request, half-faltering, for forgiveness of any error or fault in his rule, he invested Philip with the government of the Netherlands, it was at once made clear that their new ruler was a foreigner. Philip had no tongue but Spanish, and Peronnet de Granvelle, Bishop of Arras, spoke for him. The personal touch which had softened Charles's large demands was lacking, and so Philip's continuation of his father's policy was resented as a tightening of Spanish bonds.

The States-General met at Brussels (March 1556) and Philip's request for a nine-years' subsidy was resisted; the States **States-** asserted their right to control the levy of money **General—** themselves, and stipulated that, as peace had now **March 1556.** been made with France, the justly detested Spanish troops should be withdrawn from the Netherlands. Philip was forced to yield, but for this rebuff he blamed William of Orange and with reason. His patriotism was revolted by the presence of the Spanish troops and he did not shrink from boldness in his speech. Philip left for Spain in July 1559, and, though he often promised to return to deal with their problems, delays lengthened and the Netherlands never saw him again.

His sister, Margaret, Duchess of Parma, was left as Regent or Governess; she had the advantage of being the daughter of a **Margaret of** Flemish mother and of being brought up in the **Parma and** Netherlands, but she had little real power. Author- **Granvelle.** ity was in the hands of Granvelle, whom Philip had made President of the Council of State, and who became, in 1559, Archbishop of Malines, Primate of the Netherlands and Cardinal. He, with Viglius, a determined Catholic and believer in persecution, who had been responsible for some of the severer Placards, and Barlaymont, an impecunious Walloon nobleman, formed an inner council, acting directly under Philip's orders. Not only did this lead to delay (for Madrid was far off) but it alienated the great nobles of the Netherlands, who, though members of the Council of State, were only nominally consulted; jealousy of Granvelle was not unnatural with them. He was a masterful man, much like Wolsey, knowing all the details of administration and of unwearied diligence. He took control of public business from the Regent. The agitation against him, though it arose from the introduction of the new bishoprics, was political rather than religious and when, in 1564, Philip ordered him to withdraw from the Netherlands, it was a triumph for the national resistance to Spain.

That the movement was still political and not religious is shown by the fact that its leaders were all Catholics. William of Orange, it is true, was of Lutheran parentage; but, when he inherited the lands of his cousin René of Orange (which made him one of the chief nobles in the Netherlands and, in virtue of his tiny principality in the Rhone Valley, a sovereign prince), the Emperor stipulated that he should be brought up as a Catholic. Lamoral, Count of Egmont, was a great popular figure, rich in lands and in military glory as victor of St. Quentin (1557) and Gravelines (1558) and a Catholic of fervent conviction. Philippe de Montmorency, Count of Horn, was as firm a Catholic as he. Yet the fact that the King of Spain whom they resisted was the champion of the Counter-Reformation, led inevitably to religious conflict also.

The removal of Granvelle, a most capable minister, but only a minister, hardly lessened the discontent with Spanish rule and Philip's Edict (8 August, 1564) ordering the publication of the Decrees of Trent, intensified it. William of Orange said in the Council of State, "However strongly I am attached to the Catholic religion, I cannot approve of princes attempting to rule the consciences of their subjects and wanting to rob them of the liberty of faith."[1] He and the other great nobles withdrew,

Leaders of the Opposition to Philip.

Growth of Discontent —the "Compromise," 1565.

[1] Geyl, *Revolt of the Netherlands*, p. 78.

for the time, from public affairs, but a league called the "Compromise"[1] was formed by some of the lesser and rasher nobles to demand the withdrawal of the Inquisition. Its leaders were Louis of Nassau, brother of William of Orange, free, as a German prince, to be Lutheran, Marnix de Ste Aldegonde, a Calvinist, well-read and a writer of great ability and the Count of Brederode, a turbulent noble. The league was joined by large numbers, both Catholic and Protestant.

In April of 1566 the league gathered in Brussels to present the "Request," drawn up with help from William of Orange, **Les Gueux, 1566.** to the Regent. Two hundred and fifty noblemen wearing, in reference to a sneer of Barlaymont's, the badge or even the dress of "Beggars," professed loyalty to Philip, but demanded the abolition of the Inquisition, the withdrawal of the Placards and a settlement of the religious question by the King in concert with the States-General. Yielding to their pressure, Margaret consented to suspend the enforcement of persecution and to refer the "Request" to Philip. His reply to the Regent—that he did not mean, as was feared, to introduce an extreme form of the Spanish Inquisition; for himself, he disliked bloodshed and would seek some other way of punishing heresy—encouraged the Protestants to believe that he was yielding. The seeming success of the opposition encouraged many refugees to return hoping for happier times.

Protestantism was openly preached and the Reforming movement spread rapidly. In the Northern Netherlands **New Religious Influences.** the Protestant movement centred in Emden in independent Friesland, where John a Lasco had been active since 1540.[2] Son of a Polish noble family and nephew of the Archbishop of Gnesen, Primate of Poland, John was educated by his uncle, and, after passing through the Schools

---

[1] Formed, so Cardinal Granvelle wrote, on the plan "de la Ligue que les Huguenots ont fait en France et dans les mêmes fins." Poullet, *Correspondence du Cardinal de Granvelle*, t. I, p. 303; quoted in *Revue d Histoire Ecclesiastique*, Jan. 1933, Tom. XXIX, N. 1.

[2] There is a full (or even diffuse) *Life of John a Lasco*, by Dr. Hermann Dalton (Gotha 1881); English translation by the Rev. Maurice I. Evans (London, 1886). The spelling of the name varies: I prefer Laski or a Lasco.

of Cracow, he had travelled widely. He visited not only Rome, Venice and Paris but also Zurich and Basle, where he came into contact with Zwingli and Erasmus. He settled in Emden in 1540 and there organised a reformed Church. For their use he drew up a Catechism, Calvinist in tone, which had to be expounded by ministers in the churches, and to be taught to children, while a knowledge of its doctrine was required of communicants. Each church had elders, deacons and a consistory. Later, when Charles V's victory over the Schmalkaldic League drove John a Lasco from Emden, he fled to London, where he drew up in Latin (later translated into Dutch) a Confession of Faith[1] for the Church in Austin Friars established for refugees from the Northern Netherlands. On Mary's accession (1553) he returned to Emden (for Charles V had been defeated in Germany) and made the city a centre of Protestant influence. Preachers were sent out through all the Dutch-speaking Netherlands. Calvinism in the Walloon provinces came later. The Peace of Cateau Combrésis (1559) opened the way not only to trade but also to missionaries from the Calvinist Church by then secretly organised in France. Their preaching had great effect and the doctrine was accepted in many parts of the Southern Netherlands, a Confession of Faith was drawn up for them in 1561,[2] and by 1566 there was in existence a complete Calvinist organisation with its headquarters in Antwerp.

Thus openly or secretly Protestantism advanced and, encouraged by Philip's dilatoriness, the popular movement became violent. Government was almost at a standstill and the Iconoclastic riots of August 1566 were barely checked. Protestant violence, however, caused many Catholics, especially amongst the nobles, to withdraw from the national movement or to support it half-heartedly, because they feared for their faith. And the violence made it more William of difficult for William the Silent to carry into effect Orange. his views and his policy. Behind all the disorder and tumult, we

[1] For the Confession, see Niemeyer: *Collectio Confessionum in Ecclesiis Reformatis publicatarum* (Leipzig 1840), p. 360; also Schaff, *Creeds*, etc., III, p. 383.   [2] See p. 393 below.

can trace his growth in statesmanship and political influence. He saw, as most others did not, the real aims and the real character of Philip, he saw also what, in the end, would have to be done against him, but until the time came, he could take no action. Many of the nobles maintained, as he no longer did, the old loyalty to the Habsburg house; moreover they were ready, as he was not, to accept Philip's word when he promised to withdraw the Inquisition and to grant religious toleration "so far as might be with the Catholic religion."[1] For himself, William was a convinced believer in religious toleration; it had been the chief factor in his own religious development and it was necessary for him if he were to be at peace with himself.[2] The Protestants offered as many difficulties as the Catholics on this subject. When, on a sudden summons from the Regent, William had to leave Antwerp, where he was Burgrave, mobs broke into the churches and wrought havoc. William and Egmont between them restored order, and it is significant that at this time William referred to himself as a Christian, taking the name neither of Catholic nor of Protestant. Warned by his agents in Madrid of Philip's intended vengeance and knowing that he could not yet impose his policy of union and toleration on the Netherlands, he withdrew in April 1567 to his native Dillingen. It was, after all, a good recruiting ground, and, while he watched the influence on Germany of the interplay of religion and politics, he could plan to gain what he now saw to be essential, the help of foreign powers, France, England and the German States.

The recklessness of the Protestant rioters and the narrow patriotism of the nobles, each inclined to stand for his own province rather than for the Netherlands as a whole, were serious obstacles to national unity. But when William had retired to Alva, Dillingen, Alva arrived in the Netherlands armed 1567–73. with full powers as Captain-General and determined to take the strongest measures against rebellion and heresy,

[1] Philip's private message to the Pope disavowing this as a "mere form of words" is referred to, *Camb. Mod. History*, Vol. III, p. 208.

[2] He was deeply influenced by Coornhert, on whom cf. B. Becker, *Bronnen tot de kennis van het leven en de werken van D. Coornhert* (Hague 1928).

and his reign of terror welded the Netherlands together in hatred of Spain. The arrest of Egmont and Horn, the Council of Troubles—"of Blood" as the victims called it—and the ruthless pursuit of heresy defeated their own ends. William was proclaimed an outlaw (24 January, 1568) unless he submitted to the Council, and his eldest son, Philip William Count of Buren, kidnapped from the University of Louvain and taken to Spain when William defied Philip.

William's *Justification* which denied the jurisdiction of the Council, was one among many political pamphlets[1] which influenced the Netherlands during this time. Huguenot tracts had been circulated widely in Flanders and they dealt with a position much like that in the Netherlands. Du Plessis Mornay and other Huguenots[2] had taught that the wrongdoing of a ruler freed his subjects from their allegiance. This appeal to the theory of the Original Contract, historically unsound though it be, is useful as a rough guide to political action. The Netherlanders remembered how Philip had sworn to respect their liberties and how they had sworn allegiance to him. If he failed to keep his word, were they not freed from their duty? On the other side, the Catholics taught that the first and greatest duty of a ruler was to protect true religion. This view commended itself to many, especially in the South. A curious view urged by one writer was that Philip should be opposed because he was aiming at a Catholic world-domination: there was some truth in this, but it was a remote assumption with which to support political action. There were not only French tracts, some leaders themselves wrote as well as acted, notably the very able Marnix de Ste Aldegonde, whose anti-Papal pamphlet *The Beehive* is of importance, and who was probably also the author of the war-song, *Wilhelmus van Nassouwen*, a noble expression of steadfast

Political Pamphlets.

[1] There is an interesting article in the *English Historical Review*, Vol. XLIV (1929) on *Some Pamphlets of the Revolt of the Netherlands*, by R. N. Carew Hunt, which deals with French influence. There is also an article on *Les théories politiques des calvinistes dans le Pays Bas à la fin du XVIe et au debut du XVIIe siecle*, by Ch. Mercier in the *Revue d'Histoire Ecclésiastique*, Vol. XXIX (1933). [2] See p. 314 *supra*.

patriotism. This, and the *Appeal to the People of the Netherlands*,[1] published under William's name, though without his knowledge, show how the Prince of Orange had come to be recognised as the leader and the embodiment of the national resistance to Spain. The majority of the Netherlanders were Catholic, but they found the leaders and the organisation of their resistance to Spain in the Calvinist minority. Orange, tolerant by conviction, was moving now, in his exile, in the direction of the Calvinism he embraced later in 1573.

It was during these years that he was negotiating with Coligny, now in the ascendant in France. Elizabeth had **Brille and St. Bartholomew, 1572.** proved unwilling to do more than allow the Sea Beggars to use her ports, the German princes would furnish mercenaries, but Coligny pledged himself (1568) to help the Netherlands, when liberty of conscience was gained in France. The "Sea Beggars" carried letters of marque from Orange, and on April 1 gained a signal success by the capture of Brille. This gave William a foothold in the State of Holland, which he had recognised as the best centre of resistance to Spain, defended as it was by rivers, and open to the sea, where Spain had little power. This success and the capture of Mons by Louis of Nassau gave hope of early liberation with French help, but in August came the crushing news of the Massacre of St. Bartholomew. From 1572 to 1576 the States of Holland and Zeeland defied the power of Spain unsupported, and William, now restored as their Stadtholder, had difficulty in curbing the Protestant zeal of his allies, the "Beggars," and securing any kind of toleration for the Catholic majority. The rest of the Netherlands was cowed by Alva's brutality, and, even after his withdrawal in December 1573, the Spanish success continued until Leyden was saved in 1574 by the cutting of the dykes and the grim determination of its defenders. The new Governor, Requescens, sought to make peace by abolishing Alva's tax (the Tenth Penny) and offering a general pardon; but this was not

---

[1] It was written by Jacob van Wesembeke, ex-Pensionary of Antwerp, a lawyer, who devoted himself entirely to the national cause and became William's adviser in 1570.

enough. The Netherlanders now demanded religious freedom and on that point Philip was immovable.

The death of Requescens (5 March, 1576) led to the mutiny of the unpaid Spanish troops and the collapse of Spanish power. This was Orange's opportunity to secure that unity of the "entire fatherland" which had been his aim from the beginning. The Council of State, power- *The Paci-fication of Ghent, 1576.* less to control affairs, had sanctioned the summons by Brabant of a States-General to which all States but those actually at war— Holland and Zeeland—were called. This meeting of the States-General, representing Brabant, Flanders, and Hainault, was a real act of rebellion against Philip, and was made by Catholic States, under no pressure such as the "Sea Beggars" had exercised in Holland and Zeeland. The States-General declared the Spanish mutineers to be public enemies, and then, needing troops to resist them, turned naturally to Orange with his tried forces. Negotiations began at Ghent in October 1576 and proceeded slowly, for, agreed as the delegates were on the expulsion of the Spaniards, the religious question was a stumbling-block. They were, however, forced into rapid agreement by news of the sack of Antwerp by the mutineers— the "Spanish Fury"—and in November the Pacification of Ghent was signed. The Catholic states recognised William as Stadtholder of Holland and Zeeland, promised to suspend all persecution until the foreigners were driven out, and agreed then to submit all questions, including that of religion, to the States-General. Holland and Zeeland undertook not to attack the Catholic faith outside their own boundaries. In effect, then, national unity was based, for a time at least, on a promise of religious toleration. The attempt to defy the States-General by the new Governor, Don John of Austria, failed, and he had to accept the Pacification and withdraw the Spanish troops. William warned the Netherlands that Don John's promises were not to be trusted and when he took Namur and tried to seize Antwerp (July 1577), the States-General called William to Brussels and hailed him as the national leader. Some Catholic nobles, jealous of William's influence and democratic ideas, invited the Archduke Matthias, Philip II's nephew, to become Governor of the Netherlands, but this served only to strengthen William's position. The States-General named him Matthias' lieutenant, and he clearly had the real power.

National unity was broken not by political action but by religious intolerance. The Walloon Provinces, already doubt-

The Mal-
contents.

ful of the sanction given to heresy by the Pacifica-
tion, were alienated by the stark intolerance of the Calvinists, not only in Holland and Zeeland, but in Flanders. This state they had recently acquired, and there, in despite of the States-General's proposal for religious peace, by which a second religion was to be practised wherever one hundred families desired it, they forbade Catholic worship. Some mutinous Walloon troops, calling themselves the "Malcon-tents," were carrying on a minor civil war with Ghent, now a fanatically Calvinist state. Their name was adopted by the Catholic nobles of the Southern States, who already, notably in Hainault, were considering a Union for the defence of the Catholic faith. The arrival of Spanish reinforcements under Alexander Farnese, Prince of Parma, enabled Don John to win a signal victory over the army of the States-General at Gemblours (31 January, 1578) and drove William to leave Brussels. He went to the Northern States, where Gelderland had now accepted his brother, Count John, as Stadtholder, and where his Hollanders had taken Amsterdam; but the re-moval of his influence from the South, and the activities of John Casimir, Elector Palatine, who used the forces raised to help the Netherlands against Spain, to help the Calvinists against their Catholic fellow-countrymen, led to the formation on 9 January, 1579 of the Union of Arras, by which the

Arras and
Utrecht,
1579.

Walloon Provinces of Artois and Hainault bound themselves to maintain Catholicism. In reply the Northern Provinces, Gelderland, Holland, Zeeland, Utrecht and Friesland formed on 23 January the Union of Utrecht by which they bound themselves "to be forever one" and to respect the Pacification. The member States were free to settle their own religion, but no one, it was stipulated, was to be persecuted for his belief. At first, William would not join this "Closer Union," seeing it as a disruptive force, but the success of Alexander of Parma in winning over the Southern Netherlands made it necessary for him to accept it. The lines of separation for the future were laid down.

Encouraged by Parma's successes, for in May he came to terms with the Union of Arras, Philip put William of Orange to the ban as traitor and miscreant. William's **End of the** reply—the *Apologia* (1580)—asserted the right of **Revolt, 1609.** the people to overthrow a tyrannous government, and this was followed in 1581 by the repudiation by the Estates of their allegiance to Philip. William's ill-starred attempt to gain help from the Duke of Anjou, Matthias having withdrawn, ended in failure, and the independence of the Netherlands owed little to direct foreign help. William's assassination in 1584 only stiffened the national resistance; his young son, Maurice of Nassau, proved himself a better general than his father, and Oldenbarneveldt, Pensionary of Rotterdam, was William's worthy successor as statesman. The victory won by England over the Spanish Armada in 1588 and the diversion of Philip's energies from the Netherlands to France after the accession of Henri IV in 1589,[1] altered the whole nature of the struggle. After Parma's death in France in 1592, Spain had no outstanding general and diplomat, and, though the Netherlands were not included in the Peace of Vervins (2 May, 1598), Philip's death in September of the same year, and Maurice's successes in the Netherlands made it inevitable that Spain should acknowledge the independence of the United Provinces. This was virtually recognised by the truce of 1609 and formally confirmed by the Treaty of Westphalia (1648). The territory thus acquired by the Netherlanders was compact and strategically strong. The chief towns of the Netherlands and its ports were in their possession, and to them flowed the trade which had formerly centred in the S. Netherlands.

Apart from its political importance, the revolt of the Netherlands had vast influence on European **Thought in** thought. The country stood as an example to **the Nether-** resistance to tyranny in religion, and it had to face **lands.** difficult problems of its own. The Swiss Federation—the

[1] P. 330 *supra*.

loosest of organisations—had almost broken up on the question of governing dependencies. Was religion a federal matter or one for the cantons to settle for themselves? Was the Federation to regulate the religion of the dependent or subject lands, or was each canton to follow its own policy when according to the Constitution its turn came to administer the dependencies? These had proved hard problems to settle, and similar difficulties arose in the Netherlands. In the Federation between Holland and Zeeland (1576) William the Silent undertook, as ruler, to defend the Protestant Reformed Faith and to put down all beliefs which were contrary to the gospel; but he meant to tolerate Catholicism. The Union of Utrecht (1579), which united the Northern Provinces, bound them together against foreign oppression, but left each province free to settle its own religion, although nobody was to be persecuted for his belief. Catholic worship, however, was not really free until much later, although Catholics were certainly not in a minority, and Lutherans and Anabaptists, while allowed liberty of conscience, had not freedom to proselytise. Iconoclasm as at Ghent was as far from toleration as was the Inquisition. Under these fluctuating conditions an acute controversy arose over the power of the State to control religion.

The earlier tendencies to learning had been even quickened by the impulses of national vigour. Leyden, in return for its **Learning.** brilliant defence against the Spaniards (1575), had been allowed to choose a favour for itself, and had thus gained the right to found a university, which soon became the leading one among Protestants. When Lipsius (the celebrated professor of Roman history there) joined the Roman Catholics the more famous scholar Scaliger was asked to take his place (1593). Feeling, as he said, that civil strife had banished letters from France, he accepted the offer and found himself the centre of a learned company, among whom he discerned the brilliant promise of Hugo Grotius. It was only natural that in a country where Calvinism was supreme and intellectual life vigorous grave questions should arise by way of reaction.

In the Netherlands Calvinist organisation presented itself in a special form. The rich towns with their close corporations were the very soil for a Presbyterian growth, and here it took on a strictness not reached in France. France had developed the synods, but the Netherlands, where the Church organised itself in the face of persecution and primarily as a religious body apart from the State, followed a more purely theocratic model. When the end of the war came it found a Presbyterian system completely organised, claiming to be independent of the State, whereas the cities and those who were building up a State sought to exercise some control over religious matters. Zwingli, in Zürich, had been willing to leave the power of excommunication to the city-state. Calvin moved slowly to the latest model, but his organisation of elders and the greater rigidity given to Church discipline marked a step in advance. The French Protestants emphasised the idea of synods already brought forward by Zwingli for Switzerland. The Netherlanders had now a unique chance of organising a system which was to have no relations with the State and to share no powers with it.

The foundation of these claims to ecclesiastical independence was laid in the Calvinism of the Belgic Confession, prepared (1561) by the Dutch refugee and martyr de Brès, The Belgic along with Saravia and others, and presented to Confession, Philip II.[1] In this Confession the discipline of 1561. the Church for the punishing of sin, with its power of excommunication and the duty of magistrates to protect it, was firmly laid down (Articles XXVII–XXXVI). But the controversy which arose between Arminius (professor at Leyden, 1603–9) and his fellow-professor Gomar upon predestination soon became joined to the other question of the right of the State to control the Church. And here they went back to the controversies at Heidelberg connected with the name of Erastus. Erastianism is commonly defined as the ascription to the State of the right to control religion, a theory rarely affirmed in its extremest forms, though often approached in practice.

[1] Geyl, *Revolt*, p. 82, has *de Bray*. The Confession was "presented" to Philip II by being thrown over the ramparts of Tournai castle.

Erastus [1] himself merely went so far as to deny to the Church the power of excommunication, and to give coercive powers only to the State; this, moreover, in a country where only one type of religion existed. He thus made a protest against the new clerical interference which at some times and in some places recalled and rivalled the Inquisition. But his writings and those of others were applied to the controversy which now arose under very different circumstances. Upon no subject were theories more confused than upon the relations of Church and State. Upon the Catholic side "Interims" and the Spanish method, upon the Protestant side the Lutheran rule of princes, might be contrasted with the high papal view of spiritual supremacy and the Dutch or Scots view of a Church wielding a rigid discipline; but no side seemed to have thought out its system completely. Catholics and Protestants alike agreed, as the Westminster Confession worded it, that erroneous opinions and practices, "whether concerning faith, worship, or conversation," or "destructive to the external peace and order which Christ hath established in the Church," might be proceeded against by the censures of the Church and by the power of the civil magistrate. But as to the methods by which the civil power should be kept in the right path opinions and practice differed widely. The true path of toleration was as yet undiscovered; most men, like Baxter, were disposed to "abhor unlimited liberty and toleration of all," even if not able, as he claimed to be, "to prove the wickedness of it."

Arminianism in Holland in its reaction against the prevalent views of Calvinism became not only more tolerant even

Arminian- towards Rome, but also readier to admit the inter-
ism.   ference of the State in matters of religion. The Cal-
vinists wished to have a united Church left free to control religion throughout the land. But Uyttenbogaert, chaplain to Prince Maurice of Nassau and successor to Arminius in the leadership of the party, after having presented five Arminian Articles (1610) on doctrine (known as the Remonstrance), asked that a national synod (not purely ecclesiastical) under

---

[1] See *Erastus and Erastianism*, by J. N. Figgis in the *Journal of Theological Studies*, Vol. II, pp. 66 *seq*.

civil authority should meet and settle these points. They declared the existence of the Church as an equal body beside the State to have been a failure and inferred the need of State regulation. But the Counter-Remonstrants asserted for their part the strongest Calvinist tenets and the independence of the Church. They advocated the existing rights of the provinces, while their opponents wished to develop the rights of the central federal power. The struggle became political. The great statesman Oldenbarneveldt supported the Remonstrants: Prince Maurice, led by motives of policy rather than conviction, supported their opponents. Oldenbarneveldt was executed (1619), his party was scattered, its most prominent member Grotius escaping; and the Synod of Dort, at which some English, Scotch, Swiss, and Germans were present (although not all as delegates), met (November 1618–May 1619). The theological canons formulated were rigid in their Calvinism, but the very triumph of their assertion marked the beginning of a stronger reaction not only on the Continent, but in England. It was not pure co- **The Synod of Dort, 1618–19.** incidence that Laud, tolerant in his views and accused of leanings towards Rome, should have relied upon the arm of the State, for the same was the case with those Dutch scholars, defeated at Dort, but having the future upon their side, with whom in theology and temper, although not in views of discipline, he had so much in common. A few years later the expelled Arminians were readmitted and tolerated even in Holland; their learning exercised great influence, but their theology was afterwards suspected, not without justice, of Socinianism. Meanwhile the victors were content to develop at their leisure a Calvinist Scholasticism of more than local power, which became more formal as it slowly lost touch with life. The Netherlands had become for a time the centre of this controversy, which was a vital one for Europe. When political circumstances vary but little men may be content to act without clearly thought-out principles or policies; but when change and even revolution comes, then it is essential that these problems should be discerned and solved. To drift and do nothing more is a sign of weakness, not of strength or intelligence.

We are beginning to see that the age of the Reformation was one in which these problems arose from the course of events, but not one in which statesmen or thinkers or theologians for their own part did much to solve them. We have inherited something of their conditions of life, something also of their confusions of thought and vagueness of theory.

Spain, at the beginning of our period, stood before other countries in the revival of theology and the ideal of clerical life. Charles V, and after him Philip II, had stood forth with their nation's support as champions of Catholicism, although, as the Spanish bishops at Trent had plainly shown, of a Catholicism differing from that of Italy. From Spain had come out not only Ignatius Loyola, but also St. Teresa (1562), and Melchior Cano (1560), types of pious mysticism and learning respectively, and also great missionaries like Las Casas (1474–1566). Their lives show the power and variety of Spanish Catholicism. The policy of the kings was always, although in varying proportions, dictated by religion; even if at times, and especially under Philip III (1598–1621), by selfishness also. We should then expect the religious influence of Spain to have been much greater than it was. Its religious promise at the outset of our period is undoubted; its political supremacy half-way through is equally undoubted; at the close of the period the lingering decay which to many minds sums up the history of Spain has undoubtedly begun. The influence of the Inquisition, so often assigned as a cause of this strange outcome, is by itself insufficient to account for it. The Inquisition, indeed, was but one instance in the special field of religious administration of the general Spanish method of government, absolute and bureaucratic, unsympathetic and rigid, founded on force, not leadership. Protestantism in Spain was a feeble and exotic growth which it did not take a great institution to suppress.

There were other causes at work, affecting both the political and the religious history of Spain. The country was all but ruined by heavy taxation, begun by Charles V and continued after him. It had been drained of both money and men for lengthy and useless wars. The privileged classes, noble and ecclesiastical, escaping the burdens that fell on others, were often idle. The wealth that flowed in from the colonies seemed to make great enterprises possible, but it was badly used and dearly bought, and the government, through its incapacity to see great issues, failed to use its opportunities in the New World. No country can live upon mere traditions and conformity applied by force. Widespread idleness and national extravagance form but a bad atmosphere for religion to breathe. The Church in Spain, moreover, relied upon force and observances instead of persuasiveness and ideals, and therefore failed more there than elsewhere to control and to utilise the new forces of life around it. But the intellectual influence of Spain upon Europe was great upon the side of literature, especially in the two separated departments of devotion, where the work of St. Ignatius Loyola and of St. Theresa shaped European experience, and of fiction, where Cervantes ushered in a new epoch with *Don Quixote*. What was achieved here should, under other conditions, have been achieved in other fields of thought also.

The ecclesiastical history of France ran on lines very different from those of its great rival. The religious wars had caused great desolation. The harm wrought by them to learning is illustrated by many details in the life of Scaliger, and by nothing more than by the common scarcity of books. The clergy reported to the King (1595) that from six to seven out of fourteen archbishoprics, thirty to forty out of one hundred bishoprics, were vacant; that 120 abbeys had no heads, but were managed by laymen; that three-fourths of the parochial churches had not proper priests. The interference of the Royal Council in preferments and grants of dispensations for marriage and pluralities was greatly complained of. When Henry IV restored peace, 150 great and hundreds of smaller churches had to be rebuilt, and yet the consolidation of the Huguenots as a corporation apart from others and their concentration in certain towns had left the Catholics elsewhere room to work freely. So sharp was this separation that some of the Protestants cherished the idea of a separate republic, possibly under

France after the religious wars.

English protection, but the idea was discouraged by the best of their leaders. When Lewis XIII supported the counter-Reformation by force, war broke out again, and the Edict of Grace of Nîmes (1625), while confirming the ecclesiastical and civil rights, withdrew the political rights given by the Edict of Nantes. Protestantism in France, like Catholicism, seemed to decay when in opposition to the Crown and to lose its independence when attracted to its side.

It was a striking tribute to the vigour of French thought that, even when hampered by the civil wars, it was both so rich and widely influential. Of the leaders in clerical education we have already spoken.[1] But there were other great thinkers and men of activity who kept alive the old traditions of Paris and reached something of the later intellectual supremacy of Pascal. Among these, Jacques Davy Du Perron,[2] Cardinal and Archbishop of Sens, was a striking figure. Sprung from a family of Normandy Calvinists who had emigrated to Switzerland, he naturally turned to the controversy which divided France, and as a result of his study became a Catholic. He was ordained in 1557, and in 1591 joined the Court of Henry IV. Consecrated as Bishop of Evreux, and sent as envoy to Rome, he soon became distinguished as a disputant, and his great argument with Du Plessis-Mornay, who got hopelessly lost amid Calvinist quotations and misquotations from the Fathers and Scholastics, achieved a great renown.[3] In this dispute Casaubon was one of the moderators, and Du Perron's influence was probably a factor in preserving him from Huguenotism. To the end Casaubon's attitude in religion was cool and deliberate. "I do not condemn you; do you not condemn me," he said to his son, who became a Capuchin. And in the like spirit Scaliger could say, "All controversies in religion arise from ignorance of criticism." This was the tone of French thought—predominantly intellectual—which the wars overpowered. Many leaders were scattered. Robert Étienne (1526–59)—whose son Henry was author of the *Thesaurus*—head of the great printing-house at Paris, who made the division of

Thought in France. Du Perron.

[1] Pp. 281, *seq.*, *supra.*   [2] Pp. 333 *supra.*   [3] Pp. 339 *supra.*

the Bible into verses, found it needful to remove to Geneva, although his sons kept on his Parisian Press. Religious controversy, added to war, made the quiet pursuit of letters impossible. In France this was a special loss. Nowhere were learning and intellect more abundant, and she was about to become the leader of European politics.

Many of these controversies concerned the Jesuits. We have already noted[1] the opposition to their entry into France, as into Spain. The contest upon Augustinianism,[2] begun by the Jesuit Molina and carried on by Suarez against the orthodox Dominicans, intensified this feeling. Molina (1588) contended that assuming pure Augustinianism the doctrines of the Protestant reformers followed logically, and hence he was led to assert that man may in some measure help both in his own conversion and good works. Suarez (1617) modified this view, asserting that grace congruous to man's nature is efficacious; incongruous grace, on the other hand, remaining ineffective although sufficient. Aquaviva, General of the Jesuits (1581–1615), who had previously (1586) issued a revised Rule of Studies (*Ratio Studiorum*) for the Society, now (1613) ordered this view of grace to be taught in their colleges. To this discussion, which the popes tried in vain to still, a whole series of other conflicts was added.

The Jesuits in France and Spain.

Most of the earlier Jesuits, like St. Ignatius, Laynez, and Borgia, the first three generals, were Spaniards. Upon Borgia's death (1573) Gregory XIII suggested to the Society that a General from another nation should be taken, but his nominee, Mercurianus, proved incapable and the Society somewhat fell to pieces. Aquaviva, the fifth General, an energetic and youthful Neapolitan of French sympathies, found himself opposed by a disappointed Spanish faction, although, through the constitution of the Society and his power of appointments, he was able to hold his own. But this opposition first made clever use of the feeling caused by the *Ratio Studiorum*, which was circulated (1586) after some years' preparation and placed before the provinces for discussion, and then turned to the Inquisition for help.

Jesuit difficulties. Aquaviva, 1581–1615.

[1] Pp. 294.   [2] Pp. 176.

The provincial along with others was arrested for venturing to deal himself with a crime reserved to the Inquisition, and the statutes of the Society were brought under review. None knew exactly what was at stake or what would result, and a royal visitation exercised through the Bishop of Carthagena was begun. But the influence of Aquaviva was strong enough at Rome to gain both the evocation thither of the cause and the prohibition of the visitation. Yet a little later (1592) Clement VIII ordered the summoning of a General Congregation; Aquaviva at once made a satisfactory defence before the Society, but some suggestions of Philip II, by which they had to give up the rights of absolving from heresy and of reading prohibited books (here they conflicted with the Inquisition), and by which novices were in future to surrender their property or benefices, had to be complied with. The Pope also insisted upon the King's further demands that the superior officers should be changed ever three years and general congregations should meet once every six years. Some of the faction opposed to Aquaviva, and specially Mariana, had also warmly opposed the general deviation from the teaching of Aquinas. The stress laid in the *Ratio Studiorum* upon adherence to the Thomistic doctrines in most points was qualified by exceptions; in practice the exceptions were emphasised, and this was certainly a new departure. The Dominicans, always jealous of the Jesuits, keenly opposed the novel views on grace and free will, and a public discussion at Valladolid (1594) attracted much attention to the dispute. Thus an air of uncertainty prevailed, and in Spain the Society was supposed to be under a cloud.

Many ecclesiastical and political difficulties of later times arose from the fact that medieval thinkers had rather made

Political contro- versies.

assumptions than laid down theories upon the relations of Church and State. Gradually and insensibly these assumptions became unworkable through the growth of great nations and the divisions of religion. Hence had arisen the disputes at Trent upon the "Reformation of Princes"; hence also arose the difference between Philip II and the Papacy. Philip II continued to act as the kings of the Middle Ages had always acted. The

Papacy, met by denials of the powers it claimed, acted upon its former assumptions. But unfortunately for both parties, altered circumstances had made impossible the tacit compact by which Pope and King had worked together in the Middle Ages. At the same time there were not wanting theologians who, as we have seen, formulated in the plainest way the theory of papal power in itself. The Jesuits went a step further, and when theories of the State and Monarchy were put out as replies to the papal theory, discussed the origin and limits of the State itself. No controversy was more far-reaching in effect than this, for the theory of the State underlay all discussions of ecclesiastical matters and any progress towards religious liberty.

The Spanish Jesuit Mariana in his *De Rege et Regis Institutione*[1] had maintained (1599) the lawfulness of tyrannicide and praised Jacques Clement for his conscientiousness in assassinating Henry III of France. Laynez at Trent had asserted that while the spiritual power was derived immediately from God, the temporal power was only derived mediately from Him through the people. From the superiority of its origin the Church thus gained the power of not only advising, but controlling the State. This was the view which Mariana developed. The Sorbonne issued (1610), against this justification of tyrannicide, a decree which the Jesuit Father Cotton,[2] confessor of Henry IV, stated his Society accepted frankly. But the discussion on the relations of civil and ecclesiastical power was a many-sided one. English Roman Catholics were required (1606) to take an oath that the alleged right to depose excommunicated princes was a damnable opinion. The English seculars, under Blackwell, were ready to take the oath. The Jesuits opposed it. Paul V forbade the taking of the oath; a letter by Bellarmine, explaining his views, led to an expansive controversy between him and James I, seconded by abler but lesser writers. Bellarmine by his denial in his earlier controversies of the extreme position that the Pope was direct lord of the whole world had angered Sixtus V, and led him to include the volume containing it

[1] See *Political Theory from Gerson to Grotius* by J. N. Foggis (London).
[2] P. 335.

(until it should be corrected) in the Index (1590). But his later services to the papal cause outweighed the reputation of this earlier hesitation. These theories as to tyrannicide and control of the State were of more practical importance in France than in Spain; hence when (1594) Jean Chastel, a Jesuit pupil, tried to assassinate Henry IV, fresh strength was given to the movement that already existed against the Jesuits. The Parliament of Paris, followed by those of Rouen and Dijon, resolved to banish them from their districts. But at the King's wish (1603) they were afterwards readmitted, although even then the Parliament of Paris hesitated to register the Decree. Restraints were, however, placed upon their action both as to localities and methods; one such restriction, the compulsion to have one of their members at Court, was skilfully turned to their advantage and Father Cotton became a power. Henry IV was anxious for France to be Catholic, but its Catholicism was to be superintended by himself, and the Jesuits were able instruments of his policy.

The University of Paris had been (1600) reformed by the State. Richer, once a prominent Leaguer, but now a Gallican and afterwards (1608) Syndic of the Sorbonne, was one of the

The University of Paris. reforming Commissioners. At a Chapter of the Dominicans (1611), the year after the murder of Henry IV, there were laid down for discussion three theses, asserting that: (1) the Pope is infallible in faith and moral doctrine; (2) a Council is not above the Pope; (3) the Pope confirms or disallows the decisions of Councils. Richer, who was an opponent of the Jesuits and also of papal claims, attended and forbade the discussion on the ground that these theses were opposed to the Decrees of Constanz, which the University from its old traditions supported. But as an outcome of the discussion Richer now published his *De Ecclesiastica et Politica Potestate*, which ascribed all ecclesiastical jurisdiction to the Church as a body and to the Pope and bishops only as its instruments. Infallibility was said to belong to the Church only as a whole. And the papal power was limited by the Canons and not able to contravene them. The temporal jurisdiction belonged to the State, and in no wise to the Church. A lively controversy now arose in which Du Perron took a part. At first the Jesuits seemed likely to suffer, but in the end and after many complications Richer resigned. The lengthy proceedings were a curious mixture of literature and litigation, but they illustrate the importance attached to the question, which showed great vitality. At the first States-General under Lewis XIII (1614) the Ecclesiastical Estate sought the reception of the Decrees of Trent, to which the Nobles, but not the Third Estate, agreed. On the other hand, the Third Estate drafted a *cahier* which included a repudiation of the right of any power to depose sovereigns or to absolve their subjects from allegiance. To this it was suggested that all professors, teachers, and preachers should subscribe; while the opposite opinion was to be declared contrary to the Constitution of France and all persons supporting it were to be pronounced enemies of the State. But the attitude of the Third Estate and their firmness, even when confronted with learning and ability such as Du Perron's, showed the national feeling. A diplomatic arrangement evaded further conflict, but it was sufficiently evident that the plainer statement of papal claims had called forth a clearer expression of national sovereignty. For two centuries at least Frenchmen had been foremost in political thought, and hence the assertion of principles if not the adoption of policies was peculiarly forcible among them. When Richelieu desired friendship with the Papacy he had to curb the expression of these views, and a few years later (1626) he had to meet a request to forbid Jesuits to enter the pulpits of France. But that great statesman was no rigid partisan, and if at times he protected the Jesuits, at others he earned their disapproval. The ecclesiastical atmosphere of France remained after him, as before, a peculiar one, and tended to become even more so. At times Gallican liberties remained in the background, but their reassertion was often a convenient weapon in politics.

Towards the end of our period controversies upon Probabilism and on Casuistry became keen. The former did not concern the Jesuits alone, for it was a Dominican (de Medina, 1577) who first propounded the view that if an opinion was probable it was allowable

Change in Jesuit teaching.

403

to act upon it, while the probability was made to lie in its being supported by some teacher of repute. The Spanish Jesuits for the most part supported this view; some leading Jesuits like Bellarmine opposed it, but before our period closed it was generally held by members of the Society. In itself it was the systemised outcome of the later medieval Nominalism, and was allied with that confessional casuistry which Pascal afterwards attacked. Interest in casuistry had been revived and was shown elsewhere, as for instance in England by Bishop Sanderson (1587–1663) as Professor at Oxford in his *Lectures upon Conscience and Human Law*, and Bishop Hall; in Germany, F. Baldwin and Buddæus treated of it also. That the Jesuits were driven to this special method of casuistry resulted from the combination of their philosophy and their position as confessors, often of influential people. It was an accommodation to the spirit of the world quite foreign to the mind of St. Ignatius himself. Much, probably too much, has been written of it, and the process has found able apologists, although it must be regarded as a sign of decay. But a complete discussion of it belongs to a later period, although the beginnings of it have to be noted here.

The *Ratio Studiorum* systematised the Jesuit methods of education, but did not make any sudden change. Intelligence, adaptability, and directness of aim had marked their methods and continued to do so; but the system aimed too much at results and tended soon to become traditional and deadened. As the Society grew and its work became more complex, centralisation became more difficult for it. Aquaviva had refused to travel as his predecessors had done, and instead merely received reports at headquarters. Under this method the provincials naturally became more independent. At the same time the Society changed in other ways. Members without the keen sense of vocation which had been possessed by the original members lowered the spiritual tone of the whole body. Its practical work and the number of tasks to be accomplished intensified this effect. The professed members too now began to hold offices before held by coadjutors—as rectors and provincials.

Changes among the Jesuits.

They had before this stood apart and exerted a peculiar influence upon the Society; now they became absorbed in affairs just as the other members and lost their distinction. Vitelleschi (1615–45), successor to Aquaviva, was gentle, but weak. Under him the older members formed an inner body with ambitions, but with an easier life of their own, while the younger members did the work. Thus it is to be noted that towards the close of the period, when the Society sank somewhat in reputation, the tie of submission to the General and the internal coherence of the Society were weaker than had been the case earlier. The activity of the Society, the controversies in which it was engaged, and the antagonism it aroused, sum up much history after the Council was over.

NOTE ON THE BOLLANDISTS

One enterprise of the Jesuits in the realm of scholarship merits a separate description—the publication of the *Acta Sanctorum* by the Society of Bollandists. In 1607 a Belgian Jesuit, Heribert Rosweyde (1569–1629), issued a prospectus of a proposed critical edition of the manuscript lives of the saints in the libraries of Flanders. On his death the unfinished material was handed over to Jean Bolland (1596–1665) for completion. Bolland was subsequently joined by Godefroid Heaschen (1601–81) and by Daniel Papebroch (1628–1715), under whose inspiration the scope of the work was enlarged and the standard of criticism raised. Publication began in 1643 with the issue of the *Acta Sanctorum Januarii* in two folio volumes, and was continued by successive generations of scholars in the Jesuit house at Antwerp. The work was interrupted by the suppression of the Jesuits in 1773, and the French Revolution caused the dispersal of the valuable library and the loss of all the notes accumulated for future volumes. It was only in 1837 that a fresh group of Jesuits was able to resume work in the Collège St. Michel at Brussels, where it is still carried on. What was originally conceived as a few years' work by one man, has grown into a co-operative enterprise that is still unfinished after

300 years. The *Acta Sanctorum* now consists of 66 volumes (the latest, issued in 1925, is *Tomus III Novembris*) arranged according to the calendar. Under each day is included a list of the saints commemorated, practically all the available lives and detailed critical studies. The Bollandists are universally recognised as the creators and masters of the study of scientific hagiology. [See H. Delehaye, S.J., *A travers trois siècles, L'œuvre des Bollandistes* 1615–1915 (Brussels, 1920)].

R. E. BALFOUR.

[When I was preparing this chapter for the Press, I could only find a brief outline by Dr. Whitney and a note that he wished for a note on the Bollandists, so I applied to Mr. Balfour, who kindly supplied this note. M.T.S.]

XV

ENGLAND

WHEN Henry VIII [1] came to the throne (1509) he typified in wealth, popularity, and power the new monarchy that had arisen. If the country was thus strong at its summit, it was even stronger at its base. No State could compare with it in the coherence and liberty of its local life. There Henry VIII, 1509–47. were many problems left for solution, many difficulties to be dealt with. But the Middle Ages had been greater in building up institutions than in defining ideas, and this was no disadvantage; more problems are solved by the man of action than by the man of thought, although they may press more acutely upon the latter. The Middle Ages, however, had been slow to perceive contradictions in its system unless practical difficulties presented themselves. There had been of old conflicts between the Papal and the kingly power, just as there had been inevitably between the political and religious hierarchies. Statutes, such as that of Provisors, limiting the Pope's right to fill up English benefices with chosen occupants, and that of Præmunire forbidding the bringing into England of Papal Bulls, had expressed but hardly composed these conflicts. Impatience had been often felt at the Papal jurisdiction, and the way in which it was exercised; tested by its utility in action or on behalf of morals it could not be rated highly. At Rome, says

[1] For Political History, see Vol. V (*Political History of England*, ed. Hunt, W., and Poole, R. L.) *Henry VII and Henry VIII*, Fisher, H. A. L. [London, 1906]; *Henry VIII*, Pollard, A. F. (London, 1934); *The Tudors*, Conyears Read (London, 1936) ; *Letters and State Papers of the Reign of Henry VIII*, Brewer, J. S., and the *Reign of Henry VIII* (Introductions to the Letters and State Papers), by Brewer, J. S., revised by Gairdner, Jas. (London, 1884) are indispensable for the period.

Macmillan's *History of the Church*, Vol. IV, Gairdner, Jas., *The English Church in the Sixteenth Century from the Accession of Henry VIII to the death of Mary* (London, 1902) is an accurate record of the facts, but does not do justice to the positive spiritual impulses of the day.

[Cf. also Dr. Whitney's *Bibliography of Church History*—published for the Historical Association (S.P.C.K., London, 1923). M.T.S.]

the English chronicler, not himself a worthy man, Adam of Usk (1402), "everything was bought and sold, so that the benefices were given not for worth, but to the highest bidder . . . and therefore as when under the Old Testament the priesthood was corrupted with venality, the three miracles ceased, namely, the unquenchable fire of the priesthood, the sweet smell of sacrifice which offended not, the smoke which ever riseth up; so I fear it will come to pass under the New Testament, and methinks the danger standeth daily knocking at the very doors of the Church." It was the Roman jurisdiction, brought home to everyone by the sway of Wolsey, thus exercised which had aroused so much feeling in England; the non-resident holders of benefices to which they had been "provided" kept alive the irritation of an old grievance; the ever-growing number of ecclesiastical lawyers, then as always the bane and degradation of the Church, found in the Roman Canon Law [1] a complete system, which, however, presupposed authoritative Papal legislation. Technically the Canon Law (which may have allowed for local customs) had no force in England unless accepted by the national synods and allowed by royal permission; but practically, and in legal theory, as might have been expected, the lawyers trained in its principles always sought to apply it. Along with the unity of the Western Church went the acceptance of its Canon Law. The ecclesiastical courts, with their inquisitions into private lives and petty details, were increasingly unpopular. Alike to the ecclesiastical lawyer who approved and to the ignorant laity who disapproved of them, the ecclesiastical courts formed a pyramid, converging in the Curia. But the feeling of England towards the Papacy at the beginning of the sixteenth century was rather one of indifference than of active dislike.

Beyond the anti-papal legislation there had been other signs of coming difficulties and contests between papal and royal

Royal and Papal Relations.

power; the question of the King's supreme power had been raised as early as 1515 in the argument between Convocation and the popular Minorite,

[1] Cf. Maitland, F. W., *Collected Papers*, ed. Fisher, H. A. L., Vol. III, pp. 65–77 and 137–156 on Canon Law in England.

Dr. Standish (later on an opponent of Erasmus). "We are," said Henry VIII, "by the sufferance of God, king of England, and the king of England in times past never had any superior but God." Yet, when the king wrote his *Assertion of the Seven Sacraments* against Luther in 1521, Sir Thomas More, to whom he showed it, found the arguments in support of Papal authority so strong that "I said unto his Grace, 'I must put your Highness in remembrance of one thing, and that is this. The Pope, as your Grace knoweth, is a prince as you are, and in league with all other Christian princes. It may hereafter so fall out that your Grace and he may vary upon some points of the league, whereupon may grow breach of amity and war between you both. I think it best therefore that that place be amended, and his authority be more slenderly touched.' 'Nay,' quoth his Grace, 'that shall it not. We are so bounden unto the See of Rome that we cannot do too much honour unto it.' " [1] To Henry's mind at that time his relations with the Papacy could not be too close, although with varying politics he might vary in the warmth of his affections. Sir Thomas More had seen indeed that Papal Supremacy was to be the crucial question of the day, and had therefore studied it carefully; [2] in the end he came to the conclusion, different from that of many others, that the Papal Supremacy was grounded in Scripture and essential to the Church. But it was significant that so acute an observer had singled out the point as important. For the present Henry was firm in his attachment to the Papacy, but how long he would keep so was yet to be seen. "I am," he said to Giustinian, the Venetian ambassador, "the Pope's good son, and shall ever be with his Holiness and with the Church, from which I mean never to depart; and I think I have sufficient power with his Holiness to warrant hopes of my making him adhere to whichever side I choose." This was of Leo X in 1515, and again in 1517 he could say, "*Pontifex est meus.*" Clement VII also had a personal affection for Henry, due not only to favours received, but to hopes for the future. And yet

[1] *Thomas More*, by R. W. Chambers (London, 1935), p. 194.
[2] More said, in a letter to Cromwell, "for *ten* years," Chambers, p. 195.

in 1525 Wolsey could hold out a threat that the whole realm of England would become Lutheran. So far had ecclesiastical relations, the growth of ages, taken for the most part on trust, become matters of political convenience; so fast had a crisis in these relations developed.

As to the general condition and efficiency of the Church in England strongly opposed statements are often made. It Condition of should not be forgotten that too great reliance upon the Church. the Monastic Orders and the friars tended to put the ordinary machinery of the Church out of gear; soreness often arose between the diocesans and the secular or parochial clergy; while the laity were inclined to take part in the struggles. The popularity of the friars, as shown by legacies left to them, was far greater than that of either secular priests or monks; the friars, coming with their popular sermons (or sermon, if their stock-in-trade was limited) and their easy manners, were a welcome change from the parish priests. The bishop and the archdeacons, always remote and often involved in quarrels over local jurisdiction, were never very popular and often very unpopular. Thus there resulted a dislocation of the ecclesiastical machinery which needed more regular visitations and a more favourable atmosphere to work efficiently in the absence of a great enthusiasm. The comparative rarity of synods and the tendency for visitations to become matters of form (if not worse matters of fees) were indeed signs of a lack of enthusiasm and of something closely bound up with it, the preoccupation of the higher clergy in affairs of State or secular business. This evil was undoubteded, and nothing did more to lower the respect felt for the clergy. The higher clergy, as individuals, were not popular or even influential. But the Church as a body was still respected and obeyed; the form of its working machinery, synods, and visitations, continued sufficiently for a revival in the hands of reformers. In ecclesiastical as in constitutional history it is of the utmost importance that forms capable of being revived should remain, even if for a time ineffective.

The Monastic Orders may have lost their former zeal, but they had not sunk to the low level of life that satirists and unfounded traditions ascribed to them. Although Warham's Visitation (1511) showed in many cases financial mismanagement, defects, and sometimes small dishonesties in housekeeping or care of property, there **The Monastic Orders.** were few moral evils and certainly no widespread corruption. Some monasteries needed reproof and received it (as St. Albans had in 1499). Numbers were diminishing, and for many years new foundations and additional endowments of the old had nigh ceased: pious founders preferred to endow hospitals or chantries. Thus from Henry IV to Henry VIII only eight monasteries were founded, but about sixty colleges or hospitals. The variation in the endowments of chantries (where a single priest said masses for the founder) is instructive: for Yorkshire, A.D. 1350–1400, the number was forty-eight; 1400–50 it was twenty-eight; 1450–1500 it was sixty-one; from 1500–50 it was forty-seven; the drop in the fifteenth century, if due to Lollard influence, had been only temporary, and eventually the old doctrines had lost no favour. If the feeling of piety then remained the same, the lessening zeal for monasteries is still more significant; clearly they no longer met a need of the age, and indeed the visitations and all our evidence show no very high standard of usefulness or devoutness of life. Broadly speaking, society felt the need of a life of retirement less than it had done in bygone ages; many men and women took up the life of rule without a distinct vocation for it; there were many houses that were places of pleasant retirement for the rich, and others that were places of easy life for the poor. While there were, as Erasmus said, types of the highest life to be found in monasteries, they no longer preserved, as of old, a higher general standard of life than the outside world. Recent research has shown that the monasteries did little service to education. The nurture of such sons of gentlemen as were sent to be bred up in the abbot's household, the training of a few poor boys in choir schools, and the teaching of novices—this was the sum of their work; and the actual teaching was often done by laymen appointed for the purpose, where, especially in the case of young monks, it was not neglected althogether. The nuns, on the other hand, ran successful boarding-schools for wealthy girls, though the standard of education was not high. The monks were still, though with less economic and agricultural success, landlords of fairly generous views; but their religious functions were not so well performed. The need of reform had been widely felt; Archbishop Morton (1487) under Henry VII had planned, and Archbishop Warham (1511) had partly carried out an important visitation: the results of which agree with the above statements.[1]

If we turn to the secular clergy, we find the leading churchmen belonging to them, and not as earlier to the Monastic Orders; their general level of life was, as always, dependent upon that of the outside world and a little above it. But their great immersion in politics and business, where they were sometimes successful rivals of laymen, went against them and lessened their efficiency as a class. There is no reason to accuse them of any widespread immorality, but there was a wide difference between the Church's standard of clerical celibacy and the frequent concubinage punished lightly, if at all. The teaching power of the Church was, of course, not limited either to sermons or to catechisings. The frequency of preaching is often underestimated, and the collections of medieval sermons show a readiness to preach; the popular mission sermon was a creation of the friars, and not of the Reformers. But the teaching assigned to the parish priest, apart from the more secular instruction often given by the chantry priests, was often most important. Every parish priest was bound[2] to expound to his parishioners the chief points of Christian doctrine and practice; for a public mostly uneducated, these expositions were of necessity simple, and they were so far the ordinary rule as to escape frequent mention.

The Secular Clergy.

[1] Cf. Gairdner, Jas., *Lollardy and the Reformation*, Vol. II (London, 1913) [*The Fall of the Monasteries and the Reign of the English Bible*]; Dixon, R. W., *History of the Church of England*, Vols. I and II (London, 1884); Gasquet, Cardinal, *Henry VIII and the English Monasteries* (London, 1906); but the best treatment of the whole subject is a book of which Dr. Whitney thought very highly—Baskerville, G., *English Monks and the Suppression of the Monasteries* (London, 1937). See pp. 36–44, on Monastic education (M.T.S.).

[2] Cf. *Instructions for Parish Priests*, by John Myrc, Early English Text Society (London, 1868), ed. Peacock, E., pp. 8–17.

But the number of manuals for use in such instruction shows the importance given to it, as do the large proportion of religious works issued by the early presses. The religious controversies of the Reformation could not have arisen or have been popular among people untaught or ignorant of Christain creed or duty. The point then disputed was not whether a priest should preach or teach, but what, and in what manner, he was to preach and teach. The simple piety of the English people, their regular attendance at church, where on week-days they said their offices as monks did elsewhere, and their frequency at mass, struck a Venetian ambassador (1500) as remarkable. Not improbably this widespread love of the Hour Offices led in later days to the popularity of the Morning and the Evening Prayers modelled upon them. The Sarum Offices had a beauty of their own, even if they were more complicated than the Roman Use.

The New Learning had perhaps penetrated as deeply, if not more deeply, into the life of England than of any other country, Italy excepted. But whereas in Italy it was the pagan side of the movement that went the deepest, in England it was the theological and religious. This was partly because England had only two Universities, in both of which the revival of learning gained firm footing at an early date. Colet,[1] at Oxford, came rather in the second generation of teachers of this class, and his lectures upon the Greek New Testament were in the spirit of what Erasmus called "sound learning," reverent, practical, learned, and not widely speculative. English Universities and English scholars seemed to have changed their character since the time when brilliance and paradox had been held the characteristic of English thought, as solidity and accuracy were of French. Sir Thomas More,[2] whose *Utopia* has carried his name where neither his learning nor martyrdom could have done, was the central figure of the English movement: the host of Erasmus, the friend of Colet,

The New Learning.

[1] Seebohm, F., *The Oxford Reformers* (Dent, Everyman's Library).
[2] For More see the recent and admirable life, *Sir Thomas More*, Chambers, R. W. (London, 1935), with useful bibliography, *The Life of Blessed Thomas More*, Bridgett, T. E. (1891), and *Thomas More*, by Holles, (Christopher 1934). More's *Utopia* in Everyman's Library (Dent).

the pupil of "sound learning" in high judicial and political place. But two features of his life are to be noted. First, his theology was essentially medieval; he had no sympathy whatever with the doctrines of Lutheranism; he had a fierce hatred of all heresy, as he showed in his "Dialogue concerning heresies" (1528), which called forth an answer from Tyndale.[1] And, secondly, he must be judged by the simplicity and Christian peace of his Chelsea home. It is a perfect picture of a Christian household, and it shows us on the very eve of the religious revolution what medieval Christianity invigorated by the New Learning could not only idealise but actually produce. More's theology was the theology of the movement in England. This theology cannot be gathered from the *Utopia* alone; his household was the type of practical life the movement aimed at producing. And for many years under Henry VIII and Warham it seemed as if this movement, which Wolsey's administration and scholastic foundations helped to some extent, would control or shape the Church in England. That it did not so in the end was due to two causes—the matter of the King's divorce and the adverse influence of the Lutheran movement abroad which outside the doctrinal sphere was food for politics.

Recent studies of the "Divorce"[2] or, as it should be called, a suit for the nullity of marriage, have shown that the real cause "The King's is to be found not in any doubts or scruples felt by Matter, himself or others, but in Henry's desire for a 1527–29." legitimate heir, and in his passion for Anne Boleyn. As early as 1514 a Venetian had noted the rumour that "the King of England means to annul his own marriage and will obtain what he wants from the Pope as France did,"[3]; but in 1516 Mary was born, and Henry hoped he might yet have a son, so the idea of annulment was dropped for a time. By 1520, however, it was clear that Katherine could have no more

[1] Tyndale, W., *Answer to Sir T. More*, Parker Society, No. 30 (Cambridge).

[2] On the "Divorce," see Pollard, A. F., *Henry VIII*, pp. 172–307, *Cranmer*, pp. 24–60, *Wolsey*, p. 151 onward. Byrne, M. St. C., *Letters of Henry VIII* (London, 1936), pp. 42–139.

[3] Louis XII's dispensation from Jeanne of France to enable him to marry Anne of Britanny (1499) and to retain that great fief for the Crown.

children, and Henry regarded a male heir as essential to the peace of the kingdom. He considered securing the succession for his illegitimate son, whom he made Earl of Richmond in 1525; but by 1527 he desired ardently to marry Anne Boleyn, and the first step, of submitting the validity of his marriage to the Pope, was taken then. Wolsey, who hoped to strengthen his own position by a marriage between Henry and a French princess, was active in the matter. The negotiations with Clement VII give a low idea of Henry's character and of his opinion of the Papacy. The Sack of Rome, May 1527, when Clement became the prisoner of the Emperor Charles V, Katherine's nephew, rather than any question of right and justice, controlled the issue. The Pope dared not offend Charles by an insult to his aunt, nor could he afford to alienate Henry by a direct refusal "to show itself (the Apostolic See) compliant in forwarding our just and sacred cause." He therefore proposed that Henry should obey his own conscience and wed again, if he considered it lawful. He could do so on the Legatine authority of Wolsey. But Henry did not propose to allow his new marriage to be open to any question of its validity, and so, after endless shifts, and against his judgment, Clement signed a decretal commission giving Wolsey and Campeggio power to try the marriage case in England (8 June, 1528). Campeggio did not reach England until October of 1529, and then every pressure was put on Katherine to yield. It was proposed that she should enter a nunnery, or take a vow of chastity, and when she refused the first and would only accept the second if Henry did likewise, Wolsey made the amazing and dishonorable suggestion that the Pope should allow Henry to take such a vow "only thereby to conduce the Queen thereunto" and that Henry should then be absolved and "proceed *ad secunda vota cum legitimatione prolis* as aforesaid." But if that were not possible, would the Pope not "dispense with his Grace, upon the great considerations that rest herein, to have *duas uxores* [1] " ? He went on to threaten unequivocally

---

[1] Cf. a note by Arundell Esdaile in the *Athenaeum* for 11 May, 1907, on notes in Henry VIII's handwriting on the margin of Augustinus de Ancona's *de Summa Potestate Ecclesiastica* on this point.

that Henry, if not satisfied, would with "many other princes, his friends and confederates withdraw their devotion and obedience from your Holiness and the See Apostolic." Katherine refused to yield to any pressure, and the Court was formally opened on 31 May, 1529. The Queen appealed to Rome, and when that appeal was over-ruled, withdrew from the Court. The case dragged on until July, by which time her appeal had reached Rome and been admitted, for Clement was now in alliance with Charles V, and, when Campeggio adjourned the Court until 1 October, it was a declaration that the Pope would not satisfy Henry. "Catherine could hope for no justice in England, Henry could expect no justice in Rome. . . . It was intolerable that English suits should be decided by the chances and changes of French or Habsburg influence in Italy, by the hopes and fears of an Italian prince for the safety of his temporal power. The natural and inevitable result was the separation of England from Rome."[1] Henry had been balked, and his anger was roused. Wolsey, the greatest of English ministers, fell a sacrifice to the King, who was now learning his strength. Events hurried rapidly on. It was necessary to put a decent gloss upon the King's cause, and hence the appeals to the universities of Europe, not on the legality of the original dispensation but on the power of the Pope to pronounce upon such a case at all. And finally an obedient Parliament, little unwilling to take such action, supported by a Convocation much the same in temper, put an end to all ecclesiastical relations with Rome. There had been many matrimonial causes as dishonourable to the kings concerned, some of them honourable to Popes who had stood for righteousness; there had been few so dishonourable to all concerned save to the suffering Queen and her advocate, Fisher. There had been none, small as the incident in itself was, destined in a world of inflammable politics to bring about such a vast and permanent result. For henceforth, if Catholicity depended upon the admission of papal jurisdiction and connection with Rome, the Church in England was to lose her Catholicity. That is, in one sense, a theological question upon which at the

[1] Pollard, A. F., *Henry VIII*, pp. 226, 227.

very outset Eastern and Western Christians might hold differing views; it is, in another sense, a historical question, the answer to which is to be sought from the early rather than from the medieval Church itself. But to most Englishmen of that day it presented itself as a change in external relations and in those alone, not affecting their worship or belief.

Wolsey was indicted for breach of Præmunire (9 October, 1529) and replaced as Chancellor by Sir Thomas More: of all his offices he was only allowed to keep his Arch-bishopric of York, to which See now in his disgrace **Wolsey's Fall.** he journeyed for the first time. While awaiting his installation he received a summons to London on a charge of high treason, and it was on his journey to the Tower that he died (St. Andrew's Eve, 1530), at Leicester Abbey. His had been a striking figure: the able statesman of low birth ranking among princes, but prouder and grander than they, entering into their politics with a skill which has been questioned and a wisdom which has been construed as selfishness. He played in England the part that some Popes of the day—respectable, but not spiritual, patrons of learning but not models of religious life—played in Rome itself. But his career shows how politics were supreme, how even to men not paltry in their minds or ignoble in their aims everything turned upon the relations of dynasties and kings. The tide of religious earnestness was rising even now if the air was still full of strife and bitterness. The Lutheran movement had thrown much of that earnestness upon the side of disruption; earnestness on the Catholic side had yet to find its centre. In England the death of Wolsey removed the one ecclesiastical statesman who, had he kept his hold on Henry, might have directed the currents of the time instead of being swept away by their force.

Henry VIII now entered upon a career of absolute power, and was guided by himself alone. He still kept his love of learning, but learning, like commerce, flourishes **Henry** best in quiet atmosphere, disturbed by little change. **VIII.** He never altered his doctrinal faith, although Lutherans from the Continent looked to him for help, and were sometimes encouraged for political reasons. If, on the one side, he left untouched the internal organisation of the Church, developed its growing national tendencies, and carried out the policy of independence indicated by kings before him, on the other side his hand was heavy and his greed was great. The power he claimed and exercised in ecclesiastical matters was in truth little more than could be seen at work in Spain or Bavaria or in France with its Gallican liberties; but his assertion of the royal power against that of the Papacy, was a bolder and stronger one than other kings had cared to make. Other kings, Catholic and Protestant, had freely applied confiscation to ecclesiastical property, and it had been the main motive of the Swedish Reformation.[1] Other kings had played with ecclesiastical problems as pawns in the game of politics. But the peculiarity of Henry's policy was to combine all these characteristics into one effective whole. He did it too with a reckless force that did not stop to consider consequences; at times he risked everything, and his bold front was often the strongest support of his throne; he was often unpopular, and rebellion often came near to success. So that his personality counts for even more in the changes of his reign than is sometimes supposed; his persistent courage no less than his capricious selfishness needs to be emphasised. The past history of the English Church may account for much that happened, but only when other countries are taken into account can the changes of his reign be understood. He could do what he did, not only because he was king in the England of Henry II, of Edward I, and of Wolsey, but because he was living in the Europe of Charles V, of Christian II, and Gustavus Vasa—the Europe where Julius II and Leo X had just been buried, and where Clement VII was a political influence.

In November 1529 a Parliament was called mainly for ecclesiastical legislation; "there was holden," says Hardyng, "a Parliament wherein was reformed divers enormities of the clergy." It is, however, noticeable that in a list of bills for this Parliament, it was "proposed to renew the bill put up to the king in his Parliament A.D. 1410 concerning the temporal possessions being in the

The Reformation Parliament, 1529.

---

[1] See p. 102 *supra*, Ch. V.

hands of the Church"[1]—the famous proposal of Henry IV's "Unlearned Parliament" to secularise all Church property—and in Darcy's memoranda for Parliament there is a note "that it be tried whether the pulling down of all the abbies be lawful and good or no."[2] When the Parliament met its spirit was seen to be hostile to the clergy, or at any rate, to the ecclesiastical courts. Fees for probate cases, mortuaries (fees paid at burials), pluralities of benefices (even if held by papal licence), and non-residence were specially attacked. Some of these abuses both Warham and Wolsey had tried to reform, and the Convocation, which met at the same time, made some provisions for reform in life and clerical discipline. But a heavy and unexpected calamity now fell upon the Church. In 1531 the whole Church and clergy were accused of Præmunire for having recognised Wolsey's Legatine Court. It was worth noting that Wolsey's appointment as legate[3] (1518) had been made at the King's special request, and that a judge like Bishop Fox of Winchester had looked for great reforms through the power thus conferred. For this offence the clergy paid a fine equal to two million of modern money, levied as a subsidy. Still more, they admitted that the King was Supreme Head of the English Church and clergy so far as the law of Christ allowed. The title (yielded after a struggle) might mean either some new or only the old powers claimed by former kings and by Henry himself in a proclamation (September 1530) on the rigid enforcement of the Statute of Provisors. An explanation furnished by the King favoured the latter sense. Protests were not wanting, as, for instance, that made by Tunstall, the learned Bishop of Durham, and the course of the discussion was tedious. The final result was that whatever the king's new title might mean, the Church was powerless in his grasp. In 1532 the Commons, secretly moved by royal influence, complained of the clergy's legislation, and also of the ecclesiastical courts.

The Petition of the Commons, modelled upon four drafts, still

[1] Brewer, J. S., *Letters and Papers*, Vol. IV, Part 3, p. 2692.
[2] Dixon, R. W., *History of the Church of England*, Vol. I, p. 2. With references to *Brewer Letters Foreign and Domestic*, *IV*. Part 3, p. 2554.
[3] See Pollard, *Wolsey*, Ch. V, pp. 165–74 for Wolsey as Papal Legate.

THE REFORMATION

extant with corrections by Thomas Cromwell, and *The Answer*
of *the Ordinaries*[1] are blast and counterblast, but
both blew softly on the kingly power. The laymen
begged Henry to "do the most princely feat" and
grant their prayer, while the Bishops prayed "his accustomed
and incomparable goodness" to remain their chief protector.
The Commons complained of canons being passed by the
clergy alone, of excessive fees and many hardships in administration, but it was the inquest into heresy which troubled them
most, both in its scope and its execution. The Bishops denied
that any canons had infringed upon the prerogative, minimised
many of the hardships alleged, but spoke of the prevalence of
heresy as needing restraint. Much of their defence was sound
but it was delicate sailing between a formal answer to the Commons and a real reply to the Court. Individual wrong doings
they admitted, but thought the Church at large should not be
blamed; the feeblest part of their defence was a plea for the
presentation of those "of young age or infants" to benefices if
the income were given to the maintenance of the Church or
God's service or in alms or for training the candidate. In any
case, what was a default in any one was "in spiritual men most
detestable," but it was the default of particular men, not of the
whole clergy.

A controversy between king and Convocation followed,
which ended in the Submission of the Clergy[2] (15 May, 1532).
By this it was agreed that no new canons should be
made without the king's consent and that the Canon
Law should be revised by a half-clerical, half-lay body of 32.
In 1534 and again in 1535 the king was empowered to appoint
this Commission; in 1544 this was done once more, but with
little effect, except that Cranmer began his studies for a Code,
to which he afterwards returned under Edward VI. In 1549 a
committee of eight, half clerical and half lay, did the preliminary
work, and in 1551 the full body of thirty-two was named and a
draft prepared. Under Elizabeth, Parker, with his unfailing

Petition of the Com-mons, 1532.

Canon Law.

[1] Gee and Hardy, *Documents Illustrative of English Church History*
(London, 1896), pp. 145 and 154.
[2] Gee and Hardy, p. 176.

wisdom, returned to the work. The Commons agreed to the appointment of a new Commission on the lines of the old, but the Lords did not. It was left for the Archbishop to act: Elizabeth preferred the Church to act for itself, and disliked the discussion of such matters by the Commons, some of whom had a high idea of their competency and many of whom wanted more sweeping changes. Medieval bishops had relied overmuch upon Papal authority, and there was always the royal power, sometimes to utilise, sometimes to fear; now there were varied streams of thought, some conservative, but more revolutionary, to be reckoned with. Authority was never more needed, but it had a difficult world to deal with. It was happy that Parker had an ideal, to which his long study of the Early Church and the Fathers gave body, while his knowledge and love of the English Church in the past gave colour. Some large scheme such as Cranmer had begun and Parker elaborated was needed. The days of Henry had expressly left in force such parts of the Canon Law as did not assume the Papal power or contradict the national laws. The material to be studied was vast and the disentanglement of the many threads was difficult, and consequently, in spite of Cranmer's intentions and Parker's attempt, no complete code was elaborated. The canons actually passed (1571) covered but part of the field: much of the old Canon Law which had passed into a working system was retained, as for instance in patronage and benefices, the regulation of which is substantially due to Alexander III (1159–81): many difficulties were afterwards dealt with as they arose from time to time. This gradual process, at once conservative and accommodating, marked the Reformation in England.

The labours of Cranmer and Parker remain for us in the *Reformatio Legum Ecclesiasticorum*, printed by the martyrologist Foxe in 1571 after a difficult manuscript history, which leaves the share of the two Archbishops somewhat uncertain. The system here elaborated was strongly conservative on the hierarchical and disciplinary side, which made it unacceptable to the Elizabethan Puritans, while on some matters, such as Divorce, it was laxer than the actual Canons of 1571, thus conceding something to the looser and Lutheran ideas of the day. It testifies to Cranmer's firm belief in the necessity of a complete synodal organisation, but its disappearance as a legal whole is not to be regretted. In face of discordant and revolutionary criticism, as well as of pressure from the State, it was a bad day for building a great ecclesiastical edifice.

To return, however, to the events of 1532; it should be noted that Convocation, the assembly of clergy, not kings or princes **Convocation,** or parliaments, had already marked out the path of **1532.** wise reform, as Colet had done in 1512. Bishops were to be stricter in their visitations, both of parish priests and monasteries; greater stress was to be laid upon clerical residence and a higher standard for Holy Orders was to be kept up; episcopal officials were to be restrained in their exactions of fees; teaching and preaching were to be better provided for; clerical offenders strictly punished; heresies put down and heretical books suppressed; the parochial poor better relieved. These were prevalent evils; but this clerical Reformation, anticipating the best results reached later at Trent, was thwarted by the Submission of the Clergy and the attacks of the King and Commons upon their liberties. The presentation of the Submission to Henry on 15 May, 1532, was one of Warham's last public acts; the next day Sir Thomas More resigned his chancellorship. The Church of Englnd was passing into drifts and currents which he had no wish to enter.

Meanwhile Henry's suit was not yet pronounced upon at Rome, and the relations of King and Papacy were fluctuating **Anti-Papal** and undeveloped. The Statute of Provisors had **Legislation.** been diligently enforced, and a proclamation for that purpose had been issued (19 September, 1530). In 1532 the payment of Annates (the first year's income of a spiritual living, levied first in the twelfth century by some bishops, then more commonly in the thirteenth century, and from 1306 onward by the Pope himself) was conditionally restrained, and the king was given power to enforce or retract the Act at his pleasure. It was only after Henry VIII had used this clause to exact from Clement VII the bulls recognising Cranmer as Archbishop of

Canterbury in 1533, that he did make the restraint absolute.[1] It was confirmed in 1534 by Statute.[2] After this the anti-Papal legislation, a gradual but sweeping process, was wrought out with much discussion and ponderous repetition. The Statute for Restraint of Appeals (1533)[3] laid down all the legal principles of the English Reformation. England was, it declared, an empire, to whose supreme head and king, a body politic, "compact of all sorts and degrees of people, divided in terms, and by names of spirituality and temporalty," owed obedience. Under this royal authority, "that part of the said body politic called the spiritualty, now being usually called the English Church," had power to declare, interpret and shew all causes of divine law or spiritual learning. So too the temporalty did the like in its appropriate sphere, while thus "both authorities and jurisdictions do conjoin together in the due administration of justice, the one to help the other." Thus we get a fine expression of the medieval conception, one great Christian society, organised in its fundamental unity as St. Augustine, had expressed it long ago, but with its twin yet separate magistracies, ecclesiastical and civil, working together, "the one to help the other"—a conception, fated slowly in the course of generations to yield before the modern idea of two societies, separated and often opposed. That great change was to be wrought out slowly, as the independence of the Church, affirmed for instance by Elizabeth in England, faded before the heavy hand of monarchs or the heavier hand of the modern State.

This Act for Restraint of Appeals, after glancing at the laws of Edward I and III, Richard II, Henry IV and other kings against "the annoyance of the See of Rome," spoke of the dangers and inconvenience of appeals to the Pope, confined all appeals to the king and within the realm: and "eschewing the said great enormities and inquietations," ecclesiastical cases were now to follow the sequence of archdeacon, bishop diocesan and Archbishops of Canterbury and York: the

[1] Cf. Pollard, *Cranmer*, pp. 54–6.
[2] Gee and Hardy, pp. 178–86 and 201.
[3] Gee and Hardy, p. 187.

prerogatives of the Archbishop of Canterbury were saved, and ecclesiastical causes touching the king were to come before the Upper House of Convocation.

Then there followed (1534) the Act forbidding Papal[1] dispensations, which purported to be due to the prayer of the faithful Commons, declaring the realm free from all laws of man not passed within it, and substituting the Archbishop for the Pope in dispensations. Minute regulations as to taxes for dispensations were made, prelates were left their existing and customary rights of dispensations, the control of the King over all ecclesiastical causes was asserted, but it was stated that the Act was not meant to indicate any variation from the Catholic faith of Christendom. The visitation of monasteries was reserved to the King; and all exempt monasteries —those directly under the Pope—were to come into the King's jurisdiction and not under the Archbishop. The Act was to come into force on the next Nativity of St. John Baptist, and in the interval the King was given power to annul or abrogate any part of the Act by letters patent. The power thus conceded is significant and the peculiar attention given to monasteries foreshadowed their coming doom.

The final Act for the Restraint of Annates (The Ecclesiastical Appointments Act, 1534)[2] put the appointment of bishops on its present footing, the royal nomination, election under the *congé d'élire* and confirmation in office "without suing, procuring or obtaining any bulls, briefs or other things at the said See of Rome or by the authority thereof in any behalf." At the same time Peter's Pence and all other payments to Rome were abolished.

In the same year the first Succession Act,[3] which events had made necessary, was passed: the King's first marriage was condemned, and that with Anne Boleyn, which had already taken place (some time in January, 1533) was sanctioned. To this Act, to its justice as well as to its legality, all persons might be called upon to swear, and it was for refusing this oath, from

[1] Gee and Hardy, pp. 209–32.
[2] Gee and Hardy, pp. 201–9.
[3] Gee and Hardy, pp. 232–43.

natural scruples of conscience, that More and Fisher were committed to prison. Their subsequent deaths, for which no valid excuse could be offered, is perhaps the darkest blot upon a reign clouded by many stains.

In November 1534 came the Act of Supremacy,[1] which "for increase of virtue within this realm of England and to express and extirp all errors, heresies and other enormities heretofore used in the same" declared the King "the only supreme head in earth of the Church of England, called *Ecclesia Anglicana*," although he was this by right and justice and so acknowledged by the clergy in Convocation. Therefore to the imperial crown was given, in sonorous phraseology, power to exercise this right. As the claim had been already made and allowed, the Act might seem to add but little, but very significantly the saving clause which Convocation had adopted, "so far as the Law of Christ allows," was left out in the phrase of Headship. The political change from the Roman to the royal obedience was completed.

Henry VIII had now realised the extent of his power, and he proceeded to use the weapons with which Parliament had armed him in these Acts. He proposed to show that no man, however illustrious, might defy him with impunity; and Sir Thomas More and Fisher, Bishop of Rochester, were committed to the Tower, charged with misprision of treason, because they refused the oath tendered by the Commissioners under the Act of Succession. While they were in prison, Parliament passed a new Act of Treasons[2] which made it treason to deprive the King of any of his titles, including now, of course, that of Supreme Head. Although they continued to assert their loyalty to Henry, neither could, in conscience, approve his claim to Supremacy, and they were marked for death therefore. Had Paul III not enraged Henry by bestowing the Cardinal's hat on the imprisoned Bishop Fisher, it is possible that their fate might not have come so swiftly, but, as it was, Fisher was executed on 22 June, and More on 6 July, 1535. The eminence

Bishop Fisher and Sir Thomas More.

---

[1] Gee and Hardy, pp. 243 and 244.
[2] Gee and Hardy, p. 247.

of the victims struck fear into the hearts of Englishmen and caused more horror abroad than Henry's defiance of the Pope. More, a humanist and scholar of European reputation, and Fisher, saintly and learned, had been sacrificed—*Ira regis mors est*. Fisher's friendship with Lady Margaret, his great services to the University of Cambridge, of which he was successively Vice-Chancellor and Chancellor, his eminent learning—all these weighed nothing against the fact of his championship of Katherine, whose confessor he was, and whom he had supported through the weary course of the Divorce. The plea that Fisher had been a centre of conspiracy against the King, an accusation of which he declared himself innocent, can be rejected with safety; but Henry's apologies for the execution, widely circulated and elaborately made to Rome and in Germany, betrayed his uneasiness while they showed his inventive skill and his eagerness to prove himself legally in the right.

Warham had died on 23 August, 1532 and Cranmer, then on an embassy to the Emperor, was recalled to England to be his successor. He arrived in Jan. 1533, was immediately instated as Archbishop-elect, and, the necessary bulls having been extracted from the Pope, was consecrated on 30 March. Almost at once he concluded the "King's Matter" by declaring Henry's marriage to Katherine void from the beginning and pronouncing (28 May) the marriage of Henry VIII and Anne Boleyn lawful. He was godfather to their daughter, Elizabeth, born 7 September. He had been in contact with Protestants on the Continent; but his appointment did not imply any change in doctrine. In his eyes, as in those of most English reformers, the need was rather for a revived knowledge of the Scriptures and a higher standard of personal religion.[1]

Cranmer, Archbishop of Canterbury, 1553.

There was little reason why bishops or clergy should, at that time, defend the Papacy. Gardiner—himself a former emissary to Rome in the King's matter—was no less strongly a supporter of what had been done than was Cranmer himself. For the present there was, no sympathy with the Lutherans, although efforts at an alliance with Lutheran princes were made.

[1] Pollard, A. F., *Cranmer*, p. 96 (1927 edn.).

The inducements to such an alliance were political, the obstacles were doctrinal. Henry's attitude towards the Papacy was, however, not without weight in deciding the Lutherans against the Council at Mantua, to which Paul III had invited them. But, as regards England, the separation of the realm from the Papacy was, as yet, something that it seemed possible for later events to reverse. It depended mainly upon the King's disposition, and was parallel to separations, less permanent because of local conditions, that had taken place between the Papacy and other powers, such as France.

Although Henry for his own purposes might encourage heresy and was often glad to let agitation weaken the Church's influence, the changes of his reign were mainly in ecclesiastical relations and very little in doctrine. Under the Act of Supremacy Thomas Cromwell, an able adventurer, a former soldier of fortune in Italy and money-lender in London, a useful servant to Wolsey, and a statesman of sordid ambitions, was made Vicar-General (1535), and as such wielded a large, tyrannous, and unscrupulous power over the Church. It was through him, if not due to him, that the Dissolution of Monasteries was carried out. Wolsey had systematically suppressed monasteries, on the strength of a bull issued to him as Legate *a latere* in 1518, empowering him to reform them; and this precedent Cromwell followed, his position as Vicar-General giving him the same power as Wolsey had exercised, while he had the King, more immediately effective than the Pope, behind him. In 1535 he undertook a Royal visitation of the Monasteries, the main object being to discover the exact resources of the Church, and the result was not only the *Valor ecclesiasticus* but a vast store of information on the internal state of the monasteries. Bad though the conduct of the visitors was, especially in the matter of taking bribes, they were no worse than the visitors under Wolsey—in fact they were frequently the same men. The smaller houses were dissolved (1536) by a process of visitation and surrender which anticipated the Act. Their alleged evil condition was made an excuse for transferring their inmates to larger houses where religion "is

Thomas Cromwell.

Dissolution of Monasteries, 1536 and 1539.

right well kept and observed,[1] but (1539) these larger houses
soon followed their brethren. Altogether some 350 smaller and
200 larger houses were dissolved, some 5,000 and 3,000 persons
respectively affected. There should have come to the King an
income of some £200,000 a year, or a capital of some £4,800,00
in the currency of the day, and in modern value of ten times
that amount at least. But so much was wasted to enrich
courtiers and officials, the new nobility subservient to the
Crown, that the results were far below this sum. Six new
bishoprics were created at Westminster, Bristol, Chester,
Gloucester, Peterborough, and Oxford, the first of which had
only a short existence. It is to be noted, however, that the pensions arranged for the dispossessed monks and nuns were
regularly paid by the local receiver of the Court of Augmenta-
tion and that benefices were usually found for any monks that
were in priests orders.[2] The endowments of a few Professorships and much rearrangement of foundations earned the King
a reputation greater than he deserved. He has indeed been
called "the founder of all that he left standing." A great revolution was wrought, and by the Suppression a richly illuminated
page of medieval history was turned over almost for ever. The
completeness of the process, which the reaction under Mary
could not reverse, left England with its monastic buildings
destroyed and desecrated, while its parish churches stood often
damaged but preserved. The suffering and discontent thus
brought about were one cause of the Pilgrimage of Grace, the
most dangerous to Henry of all the risings of his reign (1536)
which was cruelly put down. The injury done by the suppression to the higher interests of national life is hard to
estimate. The monasteries had been the supporters of much
labour and skill that could not maintain themselves alone, and
nowhere was the change more felt than at the Universities
where the number of students was sadly lessened. Society and

---

[1] Gee and Hardy, p. 258, *Act for the Dissolution of the Lesser Monasteries*, and Pickthorn, K., *Early Tudor Government—Henry VIII* (Cambridge, 1934). Chapters XIV and XVIII.

[2] Cf. Baskerville, G., *loc. cit.*, pp. 254 *seq.*, and (on monastic employment
of lay artists, architects and masons), pp. 42–4.

agriculture were dislocated, and the resultant economic change (a third of the land in England may have changed ownership) led to uncertainty and to a race often unscrupulous, for wealth and power. The Abbey landlords were often kind if not always wise. The keen business methods of the new landlords, and the need of poor-law legislation under Elizabeth, emphasised the change.

Henry's legislation in some respects remained unchanged in later times. The election of bishops by *congé d'élire* was no great change from medieval practice, and recognised a royal privilege of ancient standing which was exercised elsewhere, for example, in France. The removal of Papal Confirmation destroyed what had been sometimes a safety to the Church and sometimes an excuse for tyranny. The King's legislation and his correspondence show that he had not at first meant his breach with the Pope to be final, and indeed the legal renunciation was only completed in 1536. His chief object was the enforcement of his own will, and both the papal power and the independence of the English Church stood in the way of this. Gradually his breach with Rome became permanent; the weakness of the Papacy and the politics of the day made it easy for him to hold a position which was theoretically anomalous. The new power, different in degree rather than in kind from that exercised in other lands, was as dangerous to civil as to religious liberty, and met with much dislike and some opposition, for the most part ruthlessly put down. It also changed the position of the Archbishop of Canterbury. Church and State had hitherto worked so closely together that it had become difficult to discriminate between the secular and ecclesiastical position of the Archbishop, between his functions as leader of the Church and as chief adviser of the King.[1] Moreover, there had arisen the same difficulty in separating his powers as *legatus natus* and as Archbishop. The suppression of the former office partly gave him a clearer field of insular authority, partly left him weaker as against the King.

Relations to the Papacy.

Royal Supremacy.

Powers of the Archbishop.

---

[1] Cf. Dixon, R. W., *loc. cit.*, Vol. I, p 251. Gardiner alleged that if Cranmer were no longer Legate, he was no longer Primate of all England.

Both these features are easily seen in Cranmer's archiepiscopate (1533–36).

It is difficult to judge the character of Cranmer fairly; for there was in him so much of weakness and caution, so much of of a mind open to temporary influences, with at the same time, **Thomas** so much of constructive power, of historic **Cranmer;** appreciation of the past with its organisation and **Character.** liturgic riches, and of literary sympathies with the newer national and popular spirit of the day, that the results of the combination are often contradictory. Always he had the great virtue of an open mind. His subserviency to the King in the matters of his divorce and later marriages may be set against the spiritual influence of his literary workmanship in the English Prayer-book and his caution in directing the Reformation. His views especially upon the Holy Eucharist may have changed from time to time under outside influences, yet were more consistent than is often said, but to him is due the conservatism of the English Reformation in its constitutional changes: and it should be remembered that his ideal of a reformed Church included both frequent synods and a working code of canon law (see *Reformatio Legum* and especially *De Concionatoribus*, cap 5). Had his idea been carried out in these respects, the English Church might have regained more quickly its old self-government, and so recovered from its temporary paralysis through Henry's Supremacy much as the Parliament did from his civil tyranny. Elizabeth's changed style of Governor for Head, even if with a chance of retreat in an added *etc.*,[1] her repudiation of any spiritual functions, and her care for the independence of the Church as against Parliament, were significant and influential, but even they did not make up for these grave defects, which Cranmer had wished to supply. It is impossible here to separate the varied influences that moulded Cranmer. The earlier revival of learning was, as his own library shows, one of the strongest. "Little Germany" and the White Horse at Cambridge (1523–27) counted for something. At a later date Ger-

[1] Maitland, F. W., *Collected Papers*, Vol. II; *Elizabethan Gleanings*, p. 159.

man influences were strong. A mind so receptive as his joined to a disposition so pliant, was naturally swayed by the tendencies both of current theology, in Germany as elsewhere, and of national thought.

In the later years of Henry's reign it is needful to bear in mind the course of affairs abroad, where the leading features were clamour for a Council, the growing import- Henry VIII, ance of political and religious Lutheranism and Cal- 1536–47. vinism, a demand for reform even by cardinals themselves, and papal avoidance of a Council.

Much controversy arose upon the King's position. Gardiner's celebrated *de Vera Obedientia* (September 1535)[1] asserted strongly the complete authority of the King over "his English Church and Congregation" (to use the terms of the Articles). He there rated the *authority* of Rome highly, but he used the word "in the sense of Cicero," implying popular estimation rather than legal right. He even admits a Roman Primacy, but he goes to the Scriptures to define its nature, which is one of service and use, not of dominion or disrespect to others.[2] A treatise on the same subject, more official although inferior in force, was Sampson's *de Vera Obedientia præstanda*, which drew forth Pole's well-known *de Unitate Ecclesiæ*. Pole's almost royal birth, his liberal and discursive education, his destination for high office (he is said to have refused the Archbishopric of York after Wolsey and before Lee), and his correspondence with the Spanish Court, made his views important. But his affirmative answer to the question whether "the superiority which the Pope claimed for himself in many ages was of divine origin " checked his English career. He charged Henry with breaking the unity of the Church and with usurping spiritual functions. His support of these charges—for which he was condemned by Bishop Tunstall and others— made a breach between him and Henry. His creation as a cardinal (22 December, 1536) launched him on a new, and now a definitely clerical career.

[1] *Dixon, loc. cit.*, Vol. I, pp. 427–9.
[2] Muller, F. A., *Stephen Gardiner and the Tudor Reaction* (London, 1926), pp. 61–5.

Three doctrinal documents of Henry's reign have great importance. The Ten Articles were the first definition of the
Ten Articles Faith issued under the Royal Supremacy and the
of 1536. first of many attempts to maintain, on a wide basis, the unity of the Church of England. Their composition was preceded by a command from the King to compose the disturbance of the realm and by much discussion between Cranmer and Stokesley, Bishop of London, mainly on the definition of Sacraments. The first five of the Articles included things necessary to salvation. The Creeds and Bible expounded according to the Doctors of the Church were the basis of faith. Opinions condemned by the Four Œcumenical Councils were to be rejected. The Sacraments of Baptism, Penance, and the Eucharist were left undefined. Baptism was declared to be necessary for everlasting life, and to be the remission of Original Sin. In adults, penitence and faith were conditions of baptism. Penance, with its three parts, contrition, confession (auricular confession being retained), and amendment, was declared necessary for the salvation of the baptised after deadly sin. The real and corporal presence of Christ under the form of the elements was asserted, although Transubstantiation was not. Justification was defined as remission of sins and our reconciliation with God, that is, our perfect renewal in Christ, to be reached by contrition and faith working through charity. The other five Articles concerned laudable ceremonies of the Church. Images were to be retained, as were veneration of saints and prayers for their intercession, but superstitious abuses of these were to be avoided. Many popular ceremonies associated with special days were explained in a simple way. Prayers for the dead were required, but the abuses connected with Purgatory (Masses, pardons, and so forth) were to be put away. The Ten Articles were a real advance towards the purification of the life of the Church in England, with their emphasis on amendment of conduct rather than on ceremonies. The same year Cromwell issued for the King injunctions to the clergy, which differed slightly in their tone towards some of these ceremonies. Demands made in them upon the clergy for instruction and pecuniary help for scholars were meant to

repair the ravages of the Dissolution. There is a ring about this document that suggests Spain or Bavaria rather than the England of the past—royal control is so much taken for granted and the path of clerical duty so emphatically shown. By these injunctions a copy of the Bible in Latin and English **The Bible** was to be placed in the choir of the churches. The **in English** order may have been ineffective, but it marks (as did **Churches.** the Ten Articles) a transitional stage. As yet there was a desire not to discard Latin, the language of medieval unity, but there was also an impulse towards a national Bible. The English Bible was as closely bound up with the English Reformation as the German Bible with the German Reformation.

In 1537 Henry licensed the use of Coverdale's Bible, and, in 1538, at Cranmer's instance,[1] the "Great Bible" based on Tyndale's version, was ordered to be set up in all the Churches; though another Act in 1543 regulated its use and limited its readers.[2]

The two other doctrinal documents also deserve mention. The first, the Institution of a Christian Man (1537) called the "Bishop's Book"— a paraphrase and explanation at length of the Creed, the Lord's Prayer and Ten Commandments, the Sacraments and the Hail Mary. With great literary power and with logical accuracy the Institution defines the **The Insti-** position of the English Church much as it might be **tution of a** done to-day. It embodies the doctrinal parts of the **Christian** Ten Articles, but the four lesser Sacraments are now **Man, 1537.** defined, though as being of less dignity and necessity than the others. Much of the exposition of them was indeed **The** used in the later Book of Common Prayer and **Necessary** the Articles. The second work—the Necessary **Doctrine and** Doctrine and Erudition of a Christian Man (1543)[3]— **Erudition,** was largely a revision of its predecessor, and it has become **1543.**

---

[1] "I pray you, my lord, that you will exhibit the book unto the King's Highness, and to obtain of his Grace, if you can, a licence that the same may be sold and read of every person." Cranmer to Cromwell, 4 August, 1537. *Letters*, p. 344.

[2] Gairdner, *Jas., Lollardy and the Reformation* (London, 1908), Vol. II, p. 302.

[3] Gairdner, Jas., *loc. cit.*, Vol. II, pp. 354–6.

known as the King's Book, since it has a preface in the King's name and had been fully considered by Henry. An article on faith was added. In the part on the Sacraments Transubstantiation was affirmed. On the whole subject of Orders, with its divisions and ceremonies, the later book kept closer to tradition. Generally there was here sign of doctrinal reaction.

The changes in England had been hailed with enthusiasm in Germany, and Cranmer, already sympathetic with Lutheran ideas, welcomed the arrival in 1538 of Lutheran deputies, who aimed, in a conference with English bishops, at attaining a religious union, parallel with the political alliance which Cromwell desired. The three points, however, which the Lutherans made as a preliminary to any discussion—the concession of the Cup to the laity, the abolition of private Masses and the marriage of the clergy—were all refused by Henry, who remained Catholic in his doctrine. The attack on the Church had been limited to its government and its property. "He had abolished the Pope but not Popery"[1] and he would here go no further than his subjects, who desired no change.

Conference with the Lutherans, 1538.

The same reaction as was shown in the "King's Book" had been seen in the so-called Six Articles (1539): a reassertion, by parliamentary authority under royal impulse and after discussion in Convocation, of the older theology. Here again the advantages of unity were insisted upon. Transubstantiation, the non-necessity of Communion in both kinds, the celibacy of the priests, the obligation of monastic vows, the use of private Masses in the King's English Church and Congregation, auricular confession, were all asserted. Rigorous machinery for inquiry into heresies was made by the Statute, but harsh as its provisions were, the use made of them was slight. The Statute really came from the King, and was passed under Royal pressure. It marked his repudiation of heresies and agitations which he had sometimes encouraged but now found inconvenient. Controversies had arisen as to England's isolation, and her orthodoxy needed assertion. About the same time the old Service Books were

Statute of Six Articles, 1539.

[1] Hooper, *Original Letters*, Parker Society, Vol. I, p. 36.

being considered with a view to greater unity of use. A vernacular Book of Prayers, following after the many   Book of
English Primers or Manuals of Devotion (a notable   Prayers.
instance of which was put forth in 1545, the last of a long
medieval series), was both popular and desirable. A reissue of
the Sarum Breviary (1541), which was ordered for sole use in
the Southern Provinces, was a step towards unity. The public
reading of a chapter in English upon Sundays and Holy-days,
and the issue (1544) of the Litany in English[1] (much as now)
marked the extent of change. Various drafts of services were
being considered when the King's death brought Edward VI
to the throne (28 January, 1547).

The reign of Henry had altered the foreign relations of the
country, especially in Church matters, although probably the
vigorous Bull of excommunication (1535) composed   Results of
by Paul III was never published.[2] Even more was   Henry's
the country changed in domestic affairs. The heavy   reign.
hand of the King exercised a tyranny as complete in the Church
as in the State, but in both cases the constitutional machinery
remained. Some theologians, and especially Cranmer, had come
under German influence, as yet of the Lutheran, not Zwinglian
type. The King had sometimes talked of a political league with
the German Protestants, but in its formularies and organisation
alike the Church remained unaffected, save in a few lesser
points upon which differences of opinion and practice were not
peculiar to England. An extreme case among these was the
destruction of shrines, beginning with that of St. Thomas of
Canterbury (1538). The relics and the jewels were conveyed
to the King's treasury, and images "used superstitiously" (a
term admitting differences of definition) were removed. This,
like the use of the familiar Latin, now beginning to be less
understood and also rivalled by the vulgar tongue, was something that affected the multitude. While the more learned part
of the country sympathised, some with moderate reforms such
as were later wrought at Trent, others with the differing

[1] See Brightman, *English Historical Review*, Vol. 24, Jan. 1909, on the
Litany.
[2] Cf. Dixon, Vol. II, 93–6.

reforms of Germany, the bulk of the nation remained little affected by the doctrinal discussions of the outside world. Changes in devotion, however, uprooting venerable habits and local traditions, aroused an opposition not provoked by anti-papal legislation, and the new reign had to reckon not only with a growing national spirit, somewhat dissociated through Henry's tyranny from loyalty to the Crown, but with tendencies even stronger and more dangerous. Doctrinal strife had gained intensity and was now reaching England. Martyrdoms on both sides had disgraced Henry's rule. Ecclesiastical changes had become bound up with private selfishness, and gentle families in England, as princely families in Germany, could make their market of religious differences. Statesmen wishing to copy Thomas Cromwell had a new career opened to them under an infant King, and the lower classes were to learn from experience that their religious habits and spiritual interests were to be the sport of politicians. A time of social change and commercial growth is not the best for religious changes that are dangerous even if necessary.

The politics and alliances of Henry's reign had made it clear that England and Scotland were to form henceforth, as once before in the earlier Middle Ages, one almost independent system. Scotland had, it was true, passed ecclesiastically by the formation of an independent province of St. Andrews (1472), under more direct papal control. The Tudor policy aimed at bringing Scotland into closer touch with England, an aim which, at a later date, first French and then Spanish rivalry made even more to be desired. On the other hand, a feeling of Scots independence was aroused in opposition to England, and thus there was a battle of diplomacy. But the course of the Reformation movements in Scotland and in England became inevitably intertwined, and the smaller country, once under Elizabeth and again under Charles I, decisively influenced the larger.

In no country was the Church in a worse condition than in Scotland.[1] The greater Church offices were the booty of royal

[1] See Macewen, A. R., *History of the Church in Scotland*, Vol. I (London, 1913), Chs. XIX and XX.

and noble families. The gentry, jealous of the greater nobles, were ready for foreign (*i.e.*, English) alliance and revolt from the Church. Clerical efficiency and even morality were at the lowest ebb. The feudal treatment of the Church and its offices had lingered longer in Scotland than elsewhere, and the political constitution was more rudimentary than that of England. The parishes were pillaged for the abbeys and the abbeys were pillaged for the nobles. Lollardy may have slightly affected the country from its English starting-place, but the Scots Church suffered not so much from energy misplaced as from a lack of any energy at all. When Lutheranism arose its books reached Scotland, and Patrick Hamilton (1528) was a martyr to his Lutheran creed. David Beaton, Cardinal and Archbishop of St. Andrews (1539), was a leader of the anti-English party, and the great upholder of the Church; but, like Wolsey, he belonged to politicians and statesmen rather than to theologians or religious leaders. His execution (1546) of George Wishart,[1] a Zwinglian layman, who had been both in Switzerland and in Cambridge, gathered congregations in Haddington and Forfar, and may have been mixed in English intrigues, is an epoch in the Scots movement. Three months later Beaton himself was surprised and slain in his castle of St. Andrews. John Knox, then middle-aged, was a disciple of Wishart's, and acted as preacher to Cardinal Beaton's murderers at St. Andrews, and with them, surrendered to the French. After his imprisonment he escaped to England and, on Mary's accession, fled to Geneva and then to Frankfort. Religious changes in Scotland and friendship with or hostility to England were henceforth closely intertwined.[2]

It was unfortunate that the tender age of the new King (he was only nine), marked him out as a plaything for politicians, and that he came to the throne when religious   Edward VI. factions, within and without the land, were keenest.   1547–53. The personal piety of a boy was of small avail. His precocity

---

[1] Cf. for Wishart, Hume Brown, P., *History of Scotland*, Vol. II (Cambridge, 1905), p. 204, and Macewen, A. R., *loc. cit.*

[2] Cf. Maitland, F. W., *The Anglican Settlement and the Scottish Reformation*, Ch. XVI (Cambridge Modern History, Vol. II).

and openness to outside influence made him easily led. His early training amid theological discussion and vagaries of tyranny increased the danger from his pliability. The Augsburg Interim (May, 1548), which drove many German ministers, Lutherans, and Calvinists from their homes, brought some of them to England.[1] The reign of Edward, therefore, with its background of a Court and King ruled by ambitious and self-seeking statesmen, was that in which foreign influence reached its height. Change was rapid and not controlled by regard for religious interests or national welfare. The reaction against ecclesiastical statesmen had lessened the possible power of the leading bishops. The robbery of the Church continued. The destruction of the chantries (with their provision for prayers for the dead, and often, incidentally, for village education) and the confiscation of the property of all guilds and religious societies brought the evils of rapacity and misrule more closely home to individuals. Education suffered, over two hundred grammar schools being swept away and but a few refounded. The pillage of the enclosures and the debasement of the coinage; the selfishness of rulers who depended upon mercenaries for their support—all these made a bad atmosphere for a constructive religious policy. As yet there was no outcry for the restoration of papal power, but a rule such as that of the Council, was likely to create a demand for any possible alternative that seemed to promise stability. Force, that could not plead legality, and overshot the general conscience of the nation, was certain to cause a reaction.

In the Council marked differences appeared. There was a conservative party, the theological leader of which was Gar-
Parties in the Council. diner, Bishop of Winchester (1531 to 12 November, 1555). But he and Wriothesley, Earl of Southampton and Lord Chancellor, were soon excluded from power and superseded. Gardiner, a learned man, who had risen by his diplomatic and political ability, had been a thorough-going supporter of Henry. He now deprecated changes in worship and dealings with doctrine until the King should come of age.

[1] For example, John a Lasco (see Ch. XIV, *supra*), Martin Bucer and Peter Martyr.

In regard to the Holy Eucharist he upheld Transubstantiation, and he had opposed changes in view insinuated in the Bibles published (by private enterprise, although with later royal approval) under Henry. He now took his stand upon "the Pacification" intended by Henry. He opposed changes, symbolised by the removal of "unabused" images in favour of the royal arms, or accompanied by mutilation of images here and there, by violent sermons and changes that ran ahead of law. Cranmer's sermon at the Convocation, which greatly magnified the office of the King; far-reaching words of Henry's executors now in charge of the realm; the publication of the First Book of Homilies, prepared by Cranmer as early as 1542,[1] but only now issued by the Council; the Injunctions (July, 1547), which, when enlarged by decree (Sept.), did away with all images and shrines and with processions and ordered the saying of the Litany in English by the priests and choir kneeling—all these things heralded greater change, opposition to which landed Bishops Bonner and Gardiner in the Fleet. Parliament, which met in November, passed an Act against ridicule of and disputation in the Sacrament, to which was added an order for Communion in both kinds. Other Acts did away with the *congé d'élire* in the election of bishops, made the bishops' courts directly depend upon the Crown, and gave to the King all chantries not yet dissolved.[2]

A most important Act of 1547, reflecting perhaps Somerset's tolerant nature, repealed Henry VIII's Act of the Six Articles, reduced the definition of treason to reasonable limits and allowed full liberty for religious discussion.

The history of Convocation is a troubled one. The Bill of Communion in both kinds had been added to a Bill against ridicule of the Sacrament, and after passing the Commons, gained the unanimous consent (verbal, not as usual, written) of Convocation. The Southern Lower House petitioned that Convocation should have its proper share in the legislation about religion and the Church, and also began to move for a revision of services and the fulfilment of the Commission of 1532 for a code of canon law. And lastly, they

Convocation.

---

[1] Dixon, *loc. cit.*, Vol. II, p. 422.   [2] Gee and Hardy, p. 328.

decided for clerical marriage, a Bill for which was passed in 1549.[1] Thus Convocation, while chafing at its loss of power, which was only regarded as temporary, showed itself inclined to changes of the kind favoured not only by Lutherans, but also by Catholics in Germany and France.

But the ritual change which was to end in making the Anglican Use the type of a new family went on. The adoption of Communion in both kinds necessitated a change in the Holy Eucharist. The old form was left in Latin, but a Communion for the people in English was added for Eastertide, 1548, and further changes were under consideration. Some ceremonies— such as the blessing of palms, creeping to the cross, carrying of candles at Candlemas, and ashes on Ash Wednesday—were forbidden (January 1645). Cranmer's own draft of a service book—was again brought up for discussion; so too was the Rationale—the explanation of Anglican ceremonies prepared by the Commission of 1540, and since then laid aside. The publication of a Communion was necessary, and the choice of English was a concession to the growing love of the vernacular. The enlarged use of epistles and gospels and daily chapters in English had been a move in the same direction, and was intended for the positive instruction on which the Reformation, like the Middle Ages, laid much **Book of** stress. But the issue of the first Prayer Book (1549) **Common** went further. In its conception it was reverent and **Prayer, 1549.** conservative. It bore traces of the Consultation of Harmann of Wied (Bishop of Cologne), and of the Breviary of Quignon, but, in the main, was a revision of the old English Service Books. The use of the Breviary of Quignon has been described as almost " irenical" in its intention, for that Breviary was favoured by the Pope and largely used among Continental Catholics. The existence of parallel revisions abroad, papal and Lutheran alike, is significant of the need of such a work. The attempt to secure unity in the realm was meant for "pacification," and the measure of its success affects our estimate of the wisdom of the attempt. Whether Convocation was consulted

[1] Gee and Hardy, p. 366. Act of Parliament confirming this vote of Convocation.

upon the Prayer Book or not has been greatly discussed; the loss of its records and the balance of opposite inferences from existing evidence perplex the verdict.[1] It is certain the bishops had been consulted upon the doctrinal questions. Something that might be taken for approval had been gained from them, although Thirlby, Bishop of Westminster, denied before the House of Lords that they had done more than consider it in disputation. But even had Convocation been free to use all its theoretical powers of self-government, the *jus liturgicum* lay not with it, but with the bishops. The questions presented to them for decision show that as large a basis of unity as possible was desired in making a new departure.

The first Act of Uniformity (21 January, 1549),[2] which enforced the use of the Prayer Book, was an emphatic enlargement of Henry's policy of uniformity. However Act of Uniformity, desirable in the interests of peace such uniformity formity, might be, the change of usages and language— 1549. especially when accompanied by the removal of images and the active interference of the Council—was unpopular. Rebellion—partly due to these religious changes and partly due to social and economic causes—increased the difficulties of the unscrupulous leaders. Their manipulation of doctrinal disputes, like their indulgence in greed and plunder, recalled the worst days of Henry VIII. The fall of Somerset (October 1549) only increased the uncertainty and intensified the evils of the nation, for his successors were worse copies of the same bad type.[3]

The bishops found their authority interfered with by the State and despised by the multitude. Foreign theologians and those Englishmen who, like Coverdale, had lived long abroad, gained more influence, and the wish to reform the English Church after "the model of the best reformed Churches abroad" began to appear. Bishop Ridley's visitation of London,

---

[1] *Cranmer's Liturgical Projects*, by Legg, J. Wickham (Henry Bradshaw Society. 1915).

[2] Gee and Hardy, p. 358.

[3] But see Pollard, *Cranmer*, p. 246, for a different estimate of Somerset, and the same writer's *England under Protector Somerset*.

where he had irregularly replaced Bonner (May 1550), marked a new tendency. He ordered the removal of altars and the erection of tables, and otherwise outstepped the limit of legal change. The objection of Hooper—chosen as Bishop of Gloucester (April 1550)—to the episcopal vestments, retained in the ordinal when various ceremonies were left out, was an indication of future troubles as to vestments. The Prayer Book had to reckon with those who preserved within its limits as much of the old practice as they could, and with those who moved as far towards Calvinistic worship as possible. It was impossible then, as now, for a book to be a complete directory of worship, and much was left, even within the limits of uniformity, to personal taste. In these circumstances, foreign and unsympathetic criticisms prepared the way for the second Prayer Book. This book, authorised by Parliament (14 April, 1552), was to be used on All Saints day, 1552; and went far beyond what the nation was prepared to accept. It is unnecessary to dwell upon the differences of the two books, but the part played by John Knox—now a licensed preacher in England—in gaining the addition of the so-called Black Rubric deserves notice. Knox objected to kneeling for the reception of the elements, and gained the Council to his view. Cranmer, whose pliancy has been often overstated, protested, but the Council added the Rubric on kneeling, which was afterwards omitted under Elizabeth (1559), and restored with a verbal but vital alteration in 1662. The death of Edward (6 July, 1553) found this Prayer Book hardly in use, while uniformity had been nowise reached. The fact that the new book had declared the old "agreeable to the Word of God and the primitive Church" gave a safe footing to those who preferred the old, and the reaction under Mary restored the conservative party who had, up to now, been overborne where not imprisoned.

The political schemes of Edward's Council came to naught, and Mary's success at once removed the Council's claimant, Lady Jane Grey, from the throne. Wyatt's rebellion (1554) led to severity against some of the leaders and the flight of others. Political discredit discounted

Mary,
1553-58.

their religious views. The Queen's religious preferences were well known, and the reaction against Northumberland made her popular. The laws passed in Edward's reign concerning religion were repealed in the first Parliament (1553), and thus at once a large step backwards was taken.[1] But it is evident that the new Queen at first meant to be tolerant, and in justice to her it should be remembered that the attacks upon her by the Protestants in exile passed all bounds.[2] Wyatt's rebellion was a political turning-point in her treatment of the opposition, for it led her to regard treason and heresy as the same thing.

The Emperor, whom Mary consulted from the first, advised caution and mildness to begin with, but after this rebellion he thought her timid in punishment, and he even suspected Gardiner, now in power as Chancellor, of treacherous advice. Julius III had made a natural choice in appointing Cardinal Pole legate for the reconciliation of England (August 1553), but neither Pope nor legate quite understood the temper of the realm. There was, as Mary confessed, much opposition to "the re-entry of papistry." Parliament clearly distinguished between the religious changes it approved and the papal authority it disliked; and the restoration of the monastic lands proved an impossible step to take. Pole's reception was long delayed, and when at last he came (20 November, 1554), it was as ambassador, not as legate. All statutes against papal authority passed since 1528 were repealed, and the country was formally reconciled. But the process had been irregular, and the The Catholic counter-revolution, like the revolution, had dis- Reaction. regarded proper forms. The Council and Parliament had anticipated the papal authority and acted of themselves.[3]

Before this had been done Mary's marriage with Philip of

[1] For the Marian Acts see Gee and Hardy, pp. 277–85.

[2] *E.g.*, Knox's " First Blast of the Trumpet against the Monstrous Regiment of Women." Knox, *Works*, Vol. IV, pp. 373 *seq.*

[3] See Frere, W. H., *The Marian Reaction in Relation to the English Clergy* (Church Historical Society, London, 1896). "Mary, with every wish to exhibit at once an entire reversal of her father's policy of religious independence, had, in fact, to begin her reign with a series of actions which had no public papal sanction but were done by royal authority " (p. 138).

Spain had marked a new English policy, and brought much odium upon the English Court. It was, however, so necessary for Spain to gain the political help of England that nothing of the Spanish rigour against heresy was recommended in England by Philip or his attendants. But events moved towards the persecution that has stamped the reign. Cranmer and other bishops had been thrown into prison (September to October 1553), and the bishops formerly displaced by them were restored. Gardiner was not only released from the Tower, but sworn of the Privy Council and on 23 August made Lord Chancellor. Apart from these cases the rate of episcopal change from natural causes was heavy throughout the reign. The married clergy were also deprived or allowed to part from their wives. Shortly before the repeal of the anti-papal laws, the statutes against Lollardy were revived, although not without some opposition. But the mild treatment of the prisoners for religion did not continue. Gardiner, in a sermon at St. Paul's declared that the heresies which had arisen through the Royal Supremacy had made him alter his stand and support the Papal authority. He was not a persecutor by disposition and only five heretics were condemned by him, the first to suffer under the revived heresy laws.[1] He had already got rid of a number of heretics, foreign and English, by giving them opportunity to escape abroad. After his death (12 November, 1555) the persecution became fiercer.

> **Marian Persecution.**

The martyrs were mainly either bishops or men of lowly rank. Some of them faced death for the private interpretation of Scripture; others for the Common Prayer Book or the principles it embodied. The tragedy of Cranmer, however, raised a different principle—the papal authority. It is true that a belief in Transubstantiation might possibly have saved his life. So far he was revolutionary, but his doctrinal attitude, on the other hand, was, perhaps, most strongly given by his practice and almost dying words recommending confession as good. In the course of his trial, his weakness, no less than his inner fibre

[1] Muller, J. A., *Stephen Gardiner and the Tudor Reaction*, p. 267, and pp. 278–85. See also *The Letters of Stephen Gardiner*, by the same author (Cambridge, 1933).

of consistency, was shown with dramatic force, and in the end he died heroically rather for a system he had helped to form than for any single point (21 March, 1556). Cardinal Pole succeeded him as archbishop. Upon him and the poor Queen, embittered by her life as an oppressed maiden and a neglected wife, the chief guilt of persecution must rest. The Marian persecution was neither unique nor without palliation. Seditious language and heresy—regarded by all sides as a crime—could not be redeemed by morality or sincerity, but the persecution wrought a change in English opinion which nothing else could have done. The policy by which Paul IV opposed Philip and had revoked Pole's commission was a curious comment upon the reconciliation of the realm. The first meetings at Trent had fallen in the reign of Edward, and England had then naturally stood aloof. Paul IV, however, made a close union between England, even under Mary, and Rome unlikely. But Pole had, even so, already had a great opportunity of shaping a Church in accordance with his best ideas. A Synod met (December 1555), and a large programme was laid before it: a newly translated New Testament, new Homilies, a completed code of canon law, a wide reform of abuses. The twelve constitutions presented to it were meant to rival those of Ottoboni, and dealt with many abuses afterwards reformed at Trent—the duties of bishops as to preaching; non-residence; reform of chapters; avoidance of luxury; due care in ordinations; diocesan seminaries, and so forth. The reforming movement begun by Convocation in 1532 was thus to be revived. Unhappily, however, Pole's labours were mainly literary. He extended a glorified copy of the proposed constitutions for the eye of the Pope in his *Reformatio Angliæ*, but the Synod itself was put off again and again until in the end nothing came of it. Hence once more Pole thus showed an excellence of intention joined to weakness of execution.

The death of the Queen and of Pole on the same day (17 November, 1558) opened the way to the changes now desired by the majority of Englishmen.

Elizabeth, on her accession, found an England actively opposed to the Papal supremacy. Of the new Queen's

popularity there was no doubt, and it was generally expected
Elizabeth, that her ecclesiastical policy would be like that of her
1558–1603. father. The dread of Spain was upon the land, and
the dislike felt for that dominant power was both religious and
national. Elizabeth and her statesmen (especially Cecil) felt
that the one thing needed was to carry a united nation along
with her in what was to be done. It was to be clear that she
stood for England, through peace if possible, but if necessary
by war against the Papacy and Spain. It was to be clear that she
wished to conciliate all Church parties, but that she would not
risk peace to conciliate the most extreme. Caution and diplomacy, carried even to dissimulation and cunning, were to mark
her policy, and its aim was to be comprehensive. Too much is
sometimes made of the phrase "the Elizabethan settlement."
In details much was changed at a later date, and the true permanent settlement belongs to 1662; but the spirit which has on
the whole since then marked the English Church inspired the
policy of the Elizabethan leaders, slowly as their policy shaped
itself. And as regards outside powers, the significance of the
date of her accession must be noted. The Tridentine settlement was not yet completed; it was therefore possible to
cherish hopes of a full reunion.[1] Meanwhile France and Spain
might be played off against each other, and England was of so
much importance that nothing rash was likely to be done
against her; indeed, so late as June 1563, the Fathers at Trent
hesitated from policy to condemn Elizabeth, although urged to
do so by the theologians of Louvain.

Thus circumstances favoured a somewhat tentative policy,
the broad lines of which were laid down, although the details
Elizabeth's were open to variation. It was not the papal policy
policy. that drove Elizabeth and her advisers into opposition to Rome. That they intended from the first. As external
success met that policy, it grew bolder; but it became more evident from the action of the Pope upon his English followers,
on the one hand, and from the deeds of the reformers upon the
other, that complete success in the full union of a compacted

[1] Cf. Pollen, J. H., *English Catholics in the Reign of Elizabeth* (London,
1920), pp. 75–7.

realm could not be reached. It is clear, from the tight hand kept upon the preachers and innovations, and from the records of discussions upon important points, that the Crown meant to lay down the religious policy of the country as a whole. Alterations adverse to "the Pope's religion" were to be made, but on the other hand, small regard was paid to the extreme reformers. Moderation, uniformity, and a dexterous use of politics were first to found and then to defend a religious edifice. The composition of a "book" was to be the chief of the means chosen. The plunder of the Church for the State was, although with less intensity than under Henry or Edward, to continue, and did so until James I, to his credit, stopped it. The Queen's supreme power was to be rigorously used, but within these limits the right of the Church to its self-government in its own assemblies was carefully guarded. It was significant that the title of Supreme Governor took the place of Supreme Head. It was unfortunate that episcopal authority—upon which large calls were to be made—was not popular, and that its efficiency had been interfered with, both by the Crown under Henry and Edward, and by the Papacy and legatine influence under Mary. Nothing is more notable than the way in which this authority recovered itself, although its assertion of its rights was to cause strife, and even warfare.[1] Strangely enough, no less than ten Sees were vacant by death in Elizabeth's first year. Her choice of Matthew Parker as Archbishop of Canter-   Parker, bury was wise. He had the needed learning, he   1559–75. was likely to command the sympathy of reformers, and his moderation was undoubted. In his case, however, moderation did not spring from timidity or uncertain views, but from personal conviction. Great care was taken to secure the episcopal succession. In the appointment of bishops the usage of Henry's reign was restored; viz. election under *congé d'élire*, confirmation by the archbishop and consecration. But revolutions had left

[1] Whitney, J. P., *The Episcopate and the Reformation* (London, 1917), Ch. IV, pp. 127–49; *Elizabeth's Defence of Her Proceedings in Church and State*, by Collins, W. E. (Church Historical Society, 1899); Frere, W. H., *The English Church in the Reigns of Elizabeth and James I* (London, 1904); Kennedy, W. P. M., *Elizabethan Episcopal Administration*, Alcuin Clubs (London, 1924).

legal uncertainties, and so in Parker's case the Queen, by a special clause in the Letters Patent for his confirmation, "supplied all defects"; so the needs of the civil law were satisfied, and every care was taken to comply with ecclesiastical law upon the other hand.

When the exiles returned from Germany and Switzerland, they brought with them views other than those they had held on The exiles' leaving England. The importance of "the troubles return. at Frankfort" (1554–7),[1] a double dispute, firstly on the question of using during exile the English Prayer Book, and secondly on the question of discipline, cannot be overlooked. For these incidents marked a division between those who wished to reform the Church of England on a Calvinist model and those who (like Parker) preferred a Catholic and yet national line of their own. It was the former group that caused the earliest difficulties of Elizabeth and Parker. They only accepted—if their partial use were an acceptance—the settlement in the hope of further change in their direction. The views of the rulers were different. The Prayer Book The Elizabethan of 1559 was based upon the Second Book of Ed- Prayer Book, ward. In combining the words of administration at 1559. the Communion from the two books of Edward, it attempted an inclusive form which definitely excluded for their sacramental views only those to whom the Sacrament was a mere symbol. By its Ornaments Rubric ordering the vestments which were in use in the second year of Edward it indicated the type of service chosen. The preservation of episcopacy (upon which only the exigencies of controversy have thrown an utterly unfounded doubt) and the provision of Canons (1571) kept continuity with the older days. Thus the dangers to which the Church had been exposed under Edward seemed now passed. But it proved hard to secure uniformity from the returned exiles. So difficult was it to enforce the vestments that the Advertisements of 1566 allowed the use of the surplice as a minimum. The Queen did not care for the Advertisements;[2]

[1] Macewen, R. A., *History of the Church in Scotland*, Vol. II, p. 67.
[2] Gee and Hardy, p. 467.

the bishops regarded them as temporary, and a step towards general obedience to the Rubric. The opinion of the foreign divines was quoted against the Prayer Book, and the deliberate policy of the bishops was for the time to keep a standard of ritual in theory and to enforce a lower one in practice. But Parker's attempts at enforcing obedience and discipline—in which he was but badly supported by some of his colleagues, and often thwarted by the puritanically disposed statesmen and by lack of royal support[1]— were suddenly checked by a more important controversy, one that questioned the whole ecclesiastical constitution. But before this arose, the Thirty-Nine Articles, reduced, with some changes, from the Forty-Two of Edward, had been adopted by Convocation and published by the Queen's Council. Save for a slight revision in 1571, they were much as they now stand. No like document has remained so long practically unaltered. Their genuinely comprehensive character, with their boldness of assertion against the decrees of Trent and the doctrines of the Puritans on opposite sides, deserved this fate.

The Vestiarian controversy replaced by that of Episcopacy.

The apparent success of the Advertisements only led to a keener strife. The extreme faction fell back upon the position that everything done in the Church must have Biblical support. This principle, easily disproved later on by Hooker, was used to express their real dislike of ceremonies, and to justify their non-conformity. That no "rags of Popery" were to be kept was a feeling equally intense and fruitful in results. A definite doctrinal position was thus reached,[2] and while on the one hand separated religious bodies appeared (1567), on the other hand academic Presbyterianism, especially at Cambridge, where Cartwright, a leader of some learning and far-reaching influence, taught, took a peculiarly English form. It was not so complete an organisation as Scotland showed, for there Genevan principles, hitherto worked out in a large city, took a

[1] *Correspondence of Matthew Parker* (Parker Society, Cambridge), No. 33, p. 246 and pp. 280–1.
[2] Read, Conyears, *Walsingham* (Oxford, 1925), Vol. II, Ch. X, "Catholics and Puritans," pp. 258 *seqq.*

larger form, suited to a land which lay at their disposal. Scots Presbyterianism is thus the most developed type of its class.

Varieties of Presbyterianism. The same principles on French soil had developed and emphasised the synod, but Scotland added to the French model a complete system of tribunals. In England, however, possibly owing to the strain of episcopal authority, Presbyterianism turned itself into an attack upon Episcopacy as an evil and anti-Biblical system, while the need of a popular call to the ministry was insisted upon. Its doctrinal side was thus strongly developed.[1] But the sacerdotal spirit of the Presbyters was as strongly marked in England as it was in Scotland. Side by side with the existing Anglican organisation a Presbyterian system was thus formed; the prophesyings or preachings were something that came to the surface, but the organisation of "classes" was more important, although deeper down. It was this attempt to Presbyterianise England which Archbishop Whitgift (1583–1604) suppressed with full success; for the Presbyterianism appearing under Charles I was a new introduction, a Scottish and not an English growth. But it is important to notice tendencies of thought as well as schemes of organisation, and there remained in England a widespread tendency to refer to the Bible, and to it alone, for authority. This tendency existed inside the Church among many of its members, while outside it Congregational bodies and Baptist bodies were formed with the same conviction. A uniformity which concealed underlying diversity was thus to a large extent reached inside the Church, but with the result of leaving separated bodies outside it. The problem of religious liberty was thus forced into a new stage; not looseness of thought or organisation within the Church, but toleration for differing sects was to be the outcome. But it was long before the sects, who would have preferred their own supremacy, saw the necessity of this solution.

Religious change in Scotland had also quickened its pace. Protestant opinions had been spreading, and on the other hand some attempts at improved discipline and instruction had been made; but the conditions were unwholesome and the reforms

[1] Frere and Douglas, *Puritan Manifestoes* (London, 1907).

were slight. John Knox returned (1555) to find a Scotland in which Catholicism was bound up with subserviency to France. Two years later the First Covenant was signed, and the leading nobles began to look to England for help. The Parliament (1562) adopted a Calvinist Confession, prohibited the Mass, made a call from the congregation an essential for the ministry, and did away with both papal and episcopal jurisdiction. Under a book of discipline a system was afterwards organised for the whole country, and when this was completed (1592), Scotland was devoted to the doctrine of the divine right of Presby- Presbytery, to a government by ministers and terianism elders. But before this came about, Mary of Scots[1] in Scotland. had ended her stormy and sad career. The result, a closer union between the two countries, was now certain. It simplified their politics and embarrassed their religion. The English speculations of Cartwright and his followers produced in Scotland an organisation, while in its own home it remained a mere tendency of thought. During the Civil War this Scots Presbyterianism was imported into England, but the original English Presbyterianism died out, and indeed it was, perhaps, of too academic a nature to flourish everywhere. But when the English Parliament during the Civil War needed help from Scotland, they pledged themselves to the introduction of Presbyterianism, with the result that the nation, impatient of the old ecclesiastical courts, was soon equally impatient of the new clerical jurisdiction. But much turned upon the Scots' dislike of Episcopacy. James I had tried to maintain titular bishops, who had slight authority and were little more than representatives of the Church in Parliament. He had an archbishop and two bishops consecrated (1610), for Scotland in England. But James's real struggle in Scotland had Episcopacy been to resist the claim of National Assembly and in Scotland, Presbyters to control the State, and in this resist- 1616–38. ance he had, at first, the majority of the nobles and gentry upon his side. When he went further, however, and tried to interfere with the existing worship, trouble began. It was possible, by

[1] On Mary cf. Pollen, J. H., *The Counter Reformation in Scotland* (London, 1921).

violence or by skill, to manage the General Assembly, and its approval was gained for the preparation of a new Liturgy (1616), which proved abortive. But the Five Articles (1616) were another thing. By these James proposed to introduce the great festivals, Confirmation, kneeling at the Holy Communion, Communion for the sick, and private Baptism. These were accepted by a majority of the Assembly, and confirmed by Parliament (1621) but the opposition was stubborn and continued. The attempt intensified the existing dislike of royal interference. The national sympathy, which had been veering round to Episcopacy as against Presbyterianism, was alienated by the royal policy. The plan of a new Prayer Book

Scotland 1629-33. was revived under Charles I (1629), but the suggested introduction of the English book was unpopular, and (1633) the matter was postponed. Meanwhile, bishops of a higher ecclesiastical tone were chosen, and (1635) a new Prayer Book, modelled upon the English book of 1549, and Canons were drafted. The former was, without reason, objected to as popish. The latter were disliked as exalting bishops and instituting diocesan synods, and directing ritual changes already enforced in England (1637). But the main point was that through the old unwise policy the Book and the Canons were forced upon the Scots by royal authority. In the tumult that arose power passed from the King to the nation, and Scots Presbyterianism was bound up with the cause of national liberty. The political organisation of Scotland was weak, and the ecclesiastical organisation made up for this lack by the strength it possessed. Whatever might be the merits or defects of Scots Presbyterianism, it was national throughout, a position forced upon it by the Crown. The Episcopacy, which was defended by the Stewarts, represented the earlier reforming tendencies. It was, however, discredited by its association with absolute monarchy, and it also ran counter to the growing Calvinism of the Scots. The Catholics who kept to the papal obedience formed a large minority, and tradition, which, to some slight degree, was in their favour, made up to them for the loss of national sympathy, which turned more and more to Presbyterianism. The course of politics—which lie outside our

452

period—added strength to this clerical and yet democratic Calvinism.

Meanwhile the guidance of the English Catholics from Rome, and the growing boldness of the English Government, raised difficulties on the side remote from Puritanism. The Elizabeth's first attempt at ecclesiastical rule had Papacy and been an "Interim," and like all such attempts, was Elizabeth. to depend upon the conciliatory dispositions of parties and the power of the Crown. Bound as they were under fine to attend their parish churches, the English Catholics who clung to the Papacy would have liked to keep their peace with the authorities at home, and yet maintain their separation. But the dread of Spanish influence, the certain existence of internal plots connected with religion, and the effect of the Tridentine reformation made their position harder. Acts of growing stringency were passed against them, and the agitation which centred around Mary of Scots intensified the bitterness of religious feeling. The question was asked at Rome of the authorities whether consent could not be gained to the attendance of English people at Matins and Evensong, although not at Communion. Obviously those who asked hoped to gain permission, but (October 1562) the answer was not what they expected. The process against Elizabeth at Rome, and her excommunication and deposition by the Bull *Regnans in excelsis* (25 February, 1570),[1] seemed to put before English Roman Catholics a choice of loyalty to Queen or obedience to Pope. The severe persecutions carried on by the Government—even the imprisonment of the Marian bishops was said by some to have been harsh—took advantage of their dilemma. The foundation of the English College at Douai (1568), and the similar College at Rome (1576), increased the differences of view between the English Catholics of the Roman obedience and their spiritual leaders abroad. In 1574 the first batch of priests left Douai for England, and from that time onwards the unhappy stories of worship forbidden but carried on with devotion, of priests bearing their lives in their hands because accused, and often

[1] Pollen, J. H., *English Catholics in the reign of Queen Elizabeth* (London, 1920), pp. 147–51.

with reason, of conspiracies, became more common. The troubles at Wisbech (already mentioned, Ch. XIV) showed divisions of opinions among the priests of the Recusants, between the Seculars and Jesuits. The more English party did not like the energy and the political restlessness of the new school. But now and again, as at the time of the Armada, and when Charles I raised his standard, the Roman Catholic gentry showed that loyalty which English law made difficult, and the papal bull made irreligious for them.

The primacy of Grindal (1576–83), with the rise of the "prophesyings" disliked by the Queen, but approved by him,
Grindal, 1576–83. furthered the spread of Genevan doctrines, and encouraged the underground Presbyterian organisations. The Council drew his attention (1579) to the distinction drawn between "preaching" and "ministering" clergymen, and to the designation of some as "no-sacrament" ministers, neglecting the sacraments.[1] In consequence of all this, his successor found a hard task awaiting him. After Whitgift's stern
Whitgift, 1583–1604. repression of these organisations and his enforcement of discipline this doctrinal influence grew even stronger. Calvin's Institutes was the text-book at Oxford, and Cambridge was even more Calvinistic in tone. So decided was this tendency, that the Lambeth Articles (1595), meant by Whitgift as a compromise between the views of the Articles and the prevalent opinions, seem in these days to be extreme. A dispute as to final perseverance had arisen at Cambridge, and these Articles, happily never sanctioned, are Whitgift's modification in the interests of peace of a suggested strongly Calvinistic statement. But a school was arising which was both to depart from Calvinism and to claim for the episcopate its
Reaction against Calvinism. proper historic place. It was the work of Hooker to lay in majestic English a new foundation of Anglican theology, giving to reason its full authority, and yet attaching due weight to scripture, tradition, and patristic teaching. "The English Church had many learned theologians and great writers in the reign of Elizabeth, but in nearly every

[1] For his sequestration and disgrace see Frere, *English Church in Reigns of Elizabeth and James I*, pp. 194–5.

way Richard Hooker excelled them all. An accomplished
writer, claims that he first revealed what English   Richard
prose might be. Sir James FitzJames Stephen   Hooker,
says of the *Laws of Ecclesiastical Polity* that "in rela-   1553–1600.
tion to the age and the state of thought prevalent at the time of
its appearance, it will perhaps be considered one of the most
remarkable books in English Literature."[1] His learning was
massive and his style majestic. When Clement VIII had the
First Book read to him (in Latin) he is reported[2] to have said:
"There is no learning that this man hath not searcht into:
nothing is too hard for his understanding . . . his books will
get reverence by age, for there is in them such seeds of eternity,
that if the rest be like this, they shall last till the last fire shall
consume all learning." His life of only forty-seven years was
all too short, but he impressed himself upon the English
Church in a critical age, and since then not only theologians,
but secular historians, have done the same. S. R. Gardiner,
from the standpoint, as it were, of the next generation, calls
him "the representative man of the Church of England."[3]
This was one element in the Anglican system. Bancroft, first
at London, and afterwards Archbishop of Canterbury (1604–
11), partly by a return to older doctrine, partly as a reaction
against the depreciation of Episcopacy, insisted upon the
importance of the historic episcopate, and this made another
element. This view agreed well with that held by James I,
whose Petition showed his personal convictions. An Arminian
reaction set in, especially at Oxford, where Laud, before he
began his career as a restorer of ancient discipline,   Laud, Arch-
and the realiser in practice of the Prayer Book ideal,   bishop,
had attacked the prevalent Calvinism. Both de-   1633–45.
partments of his activity—his enforcement of discipline and
order, his repudiation of Calvinism—brought him up against
strongly fixed opinions. Those who had neglected order, and
those who taught Calvinism, hated his conception of the

---

[1] *Horae Sabbaticae*, Vol. I, p. 145 (First Series, *Article V*).

[2] Walton's *Life of Hooker*, Works of Hooker in the Oxford edition
(1888), Vol. I, p. 71.

[3] *History of England:* 1603–42 (London, 1883), Vol. I, p. 40.

Church, shadowed in the Prayer Book as it was, partly because it contradicted their views, partly because its realisation made for ever impossible that Calvinist system to which they had long hoped to bring the English Church. When four English Churchmen were sent by James I to the Dutch Synod of Dort (Dordrecht) in 1619, they found their outlook very different from that of their hosts. The small result from their visit marked the decay of Calvinism in England, and the disappearance of any ground for hopes of joining the English Church "with the best reformed bodies" abroad. But Laud, innovator though he seemed to many in his own age, was really recurring to a type of Churchman common in the day before Edward VI. He represented, in his controversies with Papists and Puritans alike, the course the English Reformation might have run steadily and throughout, but for foreign and temporary influences. He has often been blamed for his want of sympathy and for some narrowness in his aims, but this lack and this limitation sprang from his central idea of discipline. Training himself by a system, he also enforced, often with a rigour that was fatal to his ends, this discipline upon others. But he did not only represent these earlier tendencies of thought. He further represented, among the Anglican Catholics of England, the movement of reform which the Roman Church had wrought out for itself at Trent. It was, however, the misfortune of the English Church that the course of English politics, the pressure of the Royal Supremacy, and the force of Puritanism prevented its realising for itself, and in a connected whole, a reform of its system comparable to that of Trent. It was wonderful, under the circumstances, how abuses such as the holding of ecclesiastical offices by laymen, or by those not yet in Holy Orders, simony, and so forth, gradually disappeared. But the Church suffered much and long from the fact that this process was piecemeal and desultory, instead of considered and complete. The Canons passed by Convocation in 1640 were Laud's beginning of an attempt at such a legislative reform; they showed his ideal and put the keystone upon his system. But they overshot the national inclination, and their formation was one of the charges that led to his martyrdom.

Ireland was a complicated problem, with its small English pale, its fringe of denationalised English, and its larger Celtic population. Government had been weak, civilisa- Ireland. tion backward, and religion, as was natural, at a low ebb, even before the shock of the Reformation made things worse. The Tudor policy was to make the country follow England, but it was easy for disloyalty or racial enthusiasm (as the same thing might be variously called) to seize upon the Pope's cause as an excuse for what it did. Hitherto Crown and Pope had worked together against the Irish; now they were opposed. In defence, Henry VIII hit upon the plan of bribing by grants of land Irish chieftains to support his policy, religious and secular. In succeeding reigns changes of policy intensified discontent. Under Elizabeth the Irish Parliament passed Acts changing things as had been done in England. Most of the Marian bishops lived on in their offices as before: only two out of twenty-six were deprived for refusing the Oath of Supremacy. But the Act ordering the use of the English Prayer Book (1560) began the severance of the Church from the people, and the appointment of bishops directly by the Crown (as in some Continental countries), though of course those appointed received valid consecration, increased royal influence overmuch. Successive settlements of Scots and English brought in fresh elements, and when the Restoration came, it found a country in which the Roman Catholic cause had grown, by its own wisdom and the mistakes of others, into a close union with Irish feeling. The rise of Puritanism had added bitterness to theological strife, and both the Civil War and the Irish rebellion (1641) left incurable wounds upon the land. Neither the country itself, nor the Church system which England proposed to support, had been given a fair chance of vigorous life. With a rule from England, fitful and intolerant, and mainly exercised in the interests of a minority, it was easy for the Counter Reformation, working with the elements at its hand, to build up, in spite of the great names of some Anglican bishops in Ireland, a hierarchy under Roman obedience that not only led but raised the people. The work of the body so built up has often added to the political evils of distressed Ireland, but it has also given to her a real religious enthusiasm and strong, effective, moral guidance.

The causes and the progress of the Civil War do not call for discussion here, but what has been said upon Laud's ideal, The Civil cherished by Charles I, as well as by himself, ex-War. plains some antagonism between the King and the nation. It had been an evil result of her position, for which, perhaps, the recent history of the Church was more responsible than Laud himself, that Laud, intent upon realising his ideal, should have leaned so greatly upon the royal power. In the end he who had taken the sword of the State perished by it. Dark days came upon the Church. The triumph of the Independents, i.e., the Army, showed that religious toleration had been farther from their thoughts than religious supremacy. The Parliament, which had always longed to settle not only Church organisation, but doctrine, also gained its wish, and completely revolutionised the religious and ecclesiastical life of England. For a time the needs of the war made it buy the help of Scotland at the cost of setting up a Presbyterianism Pym and his friends alone admired, 1643.[1] But the enforcement of it was never thorough, and was in no way permanent. At length an Independent Congregationalism, slightly modified through a uniting pressure by the State, was set up (1653–54), and not only the learning, but the devotion of England, seemed lost in the days when its Church was dismantled and its worship made penal. A religious tyranny, that considered itself tolerant because it was merely indefinite in its thought, shut out Anglican and papist from the protection of the law. But in the end the disturbed state of religion was one of the causes that led to the Royal Restoration, and with the King the Church returned.

The time of its suppression had left a mark behind it upon the Church, although its orders and its succession remained. A generation that had not known baptism had grown up, and a form of adult baptism had to be added to the Prayer Book. The discontinuity of religious life had left gaps even more important than the loss of traditions which had long supplied the

[1] Gee and Hardy, p. 569.

place of Rubrics. But there was now no real question as to what model of a church should be restored. It was brought back as Laud's vision had seen it, one with the past not only in its unbroken descent, but in the devotion that was inspired by its altars and breathed in its prayers. Before its persecution it had attracted not a few foreigners like Adrian Saravia, and Isaac Casaubon, who felt the force of its appeal to antiquity as against both Geneva and Rome. Sacred learning was a necessity of its life *Isaac Casaubon in England, 1610–14.* which it could not forget, and in the men of its restoration, Andrewes, Ken, Jeremy Taylor, and their not unworthy fellows, it realised a type of Churchman not possible for it at the Reformation. Their manuals of devotion were the richest fruits of the age; some, like Laud's own prayers, were not meant to see the light. The existence of the souls and the minds which produced them was not .possible among those who looked on the past with horror and dislike. It still bore the scars of its struggle. There were still some who leant over-much upon the State, and the State had somewhat forgotten the limits of its power. There was still a strong current of Puritanism flowing beneath the surface, but suffering and exile had deepened the reformation which Laud's stringent discipline had begun. There was still much of intolerance left, but it showed itself more in the State than in the Church, and in the end England, which had been taught much by its constitutional life, solved the problem of religious toleration earlier and better than did other lands. That this was possible was due partly to the peculiar course of the religious wars in England, and partly to the close connection of the Church with the national life. If the Church suffered often and heavily from the limitations placed upon it, it learnt something at least from them too. In later days it was to find out the value of having kept—what might have been so easily lost—a wide sympathy with varied currents *Unique position of the English Church.* of thought, and above all, a national coherence and independence for its episcopate: the union of these advantages with the carefully guarded validity of its orders, which so many other countries sacrified,.gave it a unique position and a many-sided future. The breach which it had to face was, as its formularies proved, as its ablest advocates argued, and its later history was to show, a breach with the papal Catholicism of Trent, but not a breach with the Catholicism of earlier medieval days, still less with the Church of the Fathers.

Books to be Consulted (in addition to those referred to in the chapter).

1. *Bibliography of British History. Tudor Period.* Read, Conyears (Oxford, 1933), especially England—Ecclesiastical History, pp. 121–63; Scotland—Ecclesiastical History, pp. 345–9. Ireland—Ecclesiastical History, p. 371.

2. *Bibliography of British History: Stuart Period.* Davies, Godfrey (Oxford, 1928). Vol. IV, Religious History, pp. 135–81.

3. *The Oxford History of England: The Reign of Elizabeth.* Black, J. B. (1936), especially Chs. I and V.
   The Early Stuarts. Davies, G. (1937), especially Chs. III and VIII.

4. *Records of the English Bible.* Pollard, A. W. (Oxford, 1911).

5. *The Church of England and Episcopacy.* Mason, A. J. (Cambridge, 1914).

6. *Studies in Tudor History.* Kennedy, W. P. M. (London, 1918).

7. *La Réforme en Angleterre.* Constant, G. (Paris, 1930).

8. *Records of the English Province of the Society of Jesus* (7 vols.). Foley, H. (London 1877–84).

9. *Early Tudor Government.* Pickthorn, K. W. M. (Cambridge, 1934).

10. *Constitutional History of the Church of England.* Makower (Eng. Trans., London 1895).

11. *Queen Elizabeth.* Neale, J. E. (London, 1935).

XVI

POLAND, RUSSIA AND MISSIONS

POLAND, with its large and tumultuous Diets, where each noble had the right of veto, with powerful neighbours eager to interfere in its politics, had a peculiar history in the Reformation period. It was the leading kingdom of north-eastern Europe and was closely connected with Sweden. Its growing territory and its military force were a bulwark against the Turks. Its attitude in religious matters was thus also important, and its religious history significant. *Poland.* A large part of the country towards the east belonged to the Greek Church, Lithuania and Galicia being mainly of that profession. On the other hand, it had ecclesiastical connections with Germany, while Russian Christianity again was thoroughly Eastern in origin and type. A separation was made (1415) between the two provinces of Lithuania and Eastern Russia, with Moscow as its head, by the creation at the old seat of Kiev of a new Metropolitan, depending upon Constantinople. Kiev had indeed been the original seat of the archbishopric until, upon the inroad of the Tartars, the See was transferred, first to Vladimir and then to Moscow. It was now restored to its old place, and thus the Greek Church in Poland gained more independence. About half the inhabitants of the kingdom thus looked towards the East, while the other half looked towards Rome. Hussite influence in Poland had once been active, but, lacking national support, soon died away, although it left traces behind. The establishment of the University of Cracow (1400) gave Polish learning a home of its own, independent of Italy and Prague, and the culture of the nobles soon justified its boasts. The Renaissance in truth had a strong hold upon the country, which drew to it the sympathy of Melanchthon, and these new currents of life, in strange contrast to the sluggish paganism and political backwardness of the country, made the course of its history peculiar. The standard of civilisation attained by some Poles was high. In 1573, for example, the Polish ambassadors surprised the French Court by their ability to converse in Latin, French, German, and Italian. There was, at times, a general toleration of religious differences; thus, one city had its three bishops—Greek, Armenian, and Roman—and all the Reforming bodies printed their books freely. Moslems were at liberty to build their mosques and Jewish merchants abounded. Eighty-three towns had printing presses, which flourished in an atmosphere of freedom. Lutheranism entered Poland from Germany, and by way of the cities. Danzig (1524) distinguished itself by its adoption of the new teaching and its violence in enforcing it, but Sigismund I (1506–48) suppressed the movement (1526). Another influence to be noticed was that of the Bohemian Brethren, who were exiled from their own country (1548) and partly settled in Poland. Here they formed about eighty congregations, and many of the nobles sympathised with them. The liberty of the nobles, which verged upon licence, was afterwards a cause of political anarchy, but it was already a cause of religious disunion. Each noble thought he had a right to choose his own faith and force it upon his inferiors. Owing to the various religious tendencies in the surrounding lands—notably the Lutheranism set up by Albert of Brandenburg in ducal Prussia—Sigismund took up a firm attitude against religious change. He was not a bigot; he was lord, he said, of the goats as well as of the sheep, but repeated edicts in his reign repressed heresy until his successor's days. The moral state of the Church was bad. The bishoprics and higher offices were (by a decree not rigidly kept) reserved to men of noble birth, and thus made less useful. Under the influence of the Queen, Bona Sforza, the Renaissance took an Italian colour, in both its morality and scepticism. Her confessor a Franciscan, Lismanini, became first a Calvinist and then a Unitarian. Some of the bishops who had bought their offices from her were noted for their evil lives.

Calvinism, more closely connected with the Renaissance than was Lutheranism, and also less German in origin, was better received in Poland. Among Polish Calvinists John Laski (a Lasco), nephew of the Archbishop of Gnesen, after his work at Emden,[1] became a leader of change in Poland (1556). He had a varied life and suffered much from sectarian hatreds. He joined in himself many and diverse influences and he strove energetically to unite the Protestants of his own land. Besides Laski many of the great nobles had adopted Calvinism, and under shelter of Calvinism Socinians found a refuge; their school of thought naturally found a ready welcome where Jews had been greatly favoured and were very powerful. In spite of the firm rule of Sigismund I the Church fell into disrepute, and the nobles showed a great and growing jealousy of her privileges and powers; ecclesiastical courts were complained of; annates were abolished (1543); Church lands were taxed (1544), and the clergy subjected (1565) to the ordinary courts: the reception of dignities from the Pope had been prohibited (1538), and it was proposed to remove bishops from the Diet on account of their oath to the Pope (1559); on the other hand, ecclesiastics began to feel their responsibilities and seek for new means of efficiency: as means of Church defence a Synod (1527) recommended the Inquisition and an increase of teaching. The accession of Sigismund II brought on a crisis. He wished to marry Barbara Radziwill, a Calvinist. The bishops consented to his doing so (1550); the King in return issued an edict supporting the privileges of the clergy and the unity of the Church and promised suppression of heresy. But the renewed vigour of the Church courts led to their suspension for a year (afterwards extended to ten) in the interests of the gentry (Diet of Piotrikow, 1552). In this revival of the Church Hosius, a remarkable figure, was the leader. He was descended from one of the many German families who had settled and formed trading colonies in the Polish towns. He studied at Padua and Bologna, he became Bishop

John Laski, 1499–1560.

Sigismund II, 1548–72.

Cardinal Hosius, 1504–79.

[1] See p. 384 *supra*.

of Culm and then of Ermland, was ambassador to Germany and a distinguished writer and controversialist. He was made cardinal and a president at Trent (1561), and after a life of great devotion and unwearied labour he died at Rome (1579). It was on his invitation that the Jesuits came to Poland. Canisius visited the country (1558), and Laynez sent a permanent mission thither (1564). These allies of his helped Hosius to raise the standard of ecclesiastical efficiency, but, unlike him, they also made use of the changing and disturbed politics of the country. He was the leading figure in the Synod of 1551, which not only decided upon a strict enforcement of the heresy laws, but adopted his well-known *Professio Fidei Catholicæ* for subscription by the clergy and tried to force it upon the laity also.

Upon the opposite side, and especially as an advocate of clerical marriage, an equally striking figure was that of Stanislaus Orzechowski, formerly a student at Wittenberg, but now a canon and married. To gain his support at this crisis the bishops suspended his excommunication for marriage and promised to submit his case at Rome. Upon the death of his wife, however, he changed his views, and from an ardent supporter of the national independence against the Papacy became an equally violent advocate of extreme papal control. His violence and his fickleness are characteristic of Polish thought and ecclesiastical politics. He played a great part at the Synod of 1552, many members of which had received a mandate against ecclesiastical courts. The suspension of these courts meant religious liberty, for while the determination of heresy was left to the clergy, no civil results were to follow unless secular courts (mainly Protestant) took the matter up. It was afterwards decided (1655) that excommunication itself should not cause any loss of civil rights. Wrongfully believing the King, who was in reality a moderate but firm Catholic, to be on their side, the Protestants took great advantage of the suspension of the courts. The Diet had further allowed every noble the right of worship at his pleasure, within scriptural limits, so that religious anarchy prevailed. The Calvinists and Bohemian Brethren had united themselves (1555), and by the *Consensus*

Orze-
chowski.

of Sandomir (1570) the Lutherans joined with them in a Federal Union. On the doctrines of the Trinity, the Person of Christ, and Justification, they reached an agreement. As a summary of their some- *Consensus of Sandomir.* what different views on the Holy Eucharist they adopted the Saxon Confession of 1551, which had been drawn up by Melanchthon for the Council of Trent. In the Communion and in organisation they recognised their independence and kept their own rites. A Federal Council was arranged, pulpits were to be interchanged, but the existing organisations were preserved. It was an interesting experiment, for which Laski had prepared the way, and it was fitting that it should adopt a Profession drawn up by the gentle and peace-loving Melanchthon. At later Synods, especially at Thorn (1595), this *Consensus* was confirmed, but the Lutherans gradually identified themselves with the Formula of Concord, began to quarrel with their brethren, and finally dissented. An experiment, which in later ages has been sometimes suggested as a novelty, was thus tried and failed. A further dissension was due to the rise of the Anti-Trinitarians. Lælius Socinus had spread these views in Poland (1551). Stancari, an *Socinians.* Italian and professor of Greek at Cracow (1554), and Peter Goniondzki (Gonesius) (1556) had followed him. In 1562–63 the holders of these views were expelled from the Polish Church, and (1565) they organised themselves into the Minor Reformed Church of Poland. Faustus Socinus, the nephew of Lælius, visited Poland (1579) and remained there, doing a great work of organisation until his death (1607). His predecessors had varied in their positive views, although agreeing in their negations, but he systematised their doctrines. Italian scepticism, working upon a Calvinistic basis amid the freedom or, rather, anarchy of Poland, thus became powerful; the Racovian Catechism, published at Racov in Southern Poland, became the recognised text-book of the sect, which in Poland suffered much persecution from Lutherans and Jesuits alike. The Senate decreed (1638) the destruction of their leading school and the exile of their ministers; later (1658) they were expelled as a body.

There had been in Poland a strong national movement, demanding (1547 onwards) a national council; Sigismund II, with the general approval of his nation, had sought from the Papacy the Mass in the vernacular, communion in two kinds, and the convocation of a national council for the remedy of abuses and the union of the many sects (1556). This national feeling now died away, partly through the dissensions and anarchy of the Protestants and partly through the success of the Counter-Reformation led by the papal nuncios and Jesuits. The Jesuits did the work, but even here we must not overlook the native leadership of Hosius. The nuncios Lippomani (1555), Berard, Bishop of Camerino (1560), Commendone, Bishop of Zante (1563–65, and again in 1571), in their respective ways did much in inspiring the King to greater firmness, in gathering around them a Catholic party, and in reforming the abuses in the Church. Before Sigismund's sudden death (1572) he had refused in the Diet to put Protestants on a legal equality with Catholics, but when Henry of Anjou was elected [1] after an expensive contest of diplomacy and intrigue, the Compact of Warsaw granted religious liberty to all *Dissidents* or Dissenters (23 January, 1573). Unhappily the nobles had the right to punish any disobedience among their dependants, and thus the principle of territorial religion was extended in Poland to every landed estate. This compact Henry had to accept before his coronation (May, 1573). His flight to France was followed by great confusion which was ended by the election of Stephen Bathory, Prince of Transylvania (1576), although the nuncio Laureo did his utmost to secure the election of Emperor Maximilian II. The new King proved to be a liberal sovereign, a strong Catholic, and a great warrior. His foreign policy turning mainly on the acquisition of Russia was supported by the Jesuits, especially by Possevin. Inside the kingdom, the King used the Jesuits widely for his great schemes of education in schools and for his new university of Wilna.

Marginal notes: National-ism in Poland. / Henry of Anjou, 1573. / Stephen Bathory, 1573.

[1] See p. 321 *supra*.

Stephen was followed by Sigismund III, son of John III of Sweden [1] and Catharina Jagellon. He was, as already said, a devoted Catholic, and he gradually changed the Sigismund tone of the Senate by his appointments. Under III, the influence of the nuncios, a kind of Edict of 1587–1632. Restitution was enforced by the courts, restoring to Catholic worship churches that had been perverted by Protestant landowners. This, with the education of the young nobles in the Jesuit schools, soon changed the thought of the country. Furthermore, Catholics and Protestants were eagerly striving to absorb the Greek Church. Sigismund, partly Synods of by threats of excluding from the Diet those bishops Bresc, who did not submit to Rome, persuaded a Synod 1594–96. of the Greek Catholics in Poland to discuss union. The terms proposed by some of the bishops, whose reputations did not commend their opinions, and afterwards approved of by Clement VIII, were the preservation of Eastern ritual and discipline, the use of the Sclavonic tongue, and the recognition of the Council of Florence. But these terms left much discontent behind, and the Polish hierarchy was consequently divided into Orthodox and Uniat factions. The union was forced with so much severity that it soon alienated the Cossacks of the Ukraine and drove them towards Russia. In the same way Protestant parts of the land were driven towards Sweden. Thus divisions in religion complicated Polish politics. The Polish King was the champion of Rome in eastern Europe. So great had been the change wrought in the country that a legate could say (1598) that "heresy was being driven to the grave." The joint action of the Papacy, the Jesuits, and the Crown had been successful. Nowhere does religious history give more instructive lessons than in Poland. The internal anarchy of the country, and the interest taken by its neighbours in its affairs, ultimately (1772) proved its political ruin. The same causes worked in religious history and tended to their natural result.

The rise of Russia disturbed the balance of power in the North-East. Poland, hampered by internal anarchy, gave

[1] See p. 107 *supra*.

place to this new rival. In the struggle that ensued, Sweden championed Protestantism, Poland Roman Catholicism, and Russia Eastern Orthodoxy, but their aims were not only religious. The struggle was for power, and for territory, such as the secularised state of the Knights of the Sword in Livonia. Here the Grand Master, Gotthard Kettler, turned Lutheran (1561), giving up most of his territory to Poland,

Russia and Eastern Europe.

but keeping Courland as a secularised duchy for himself, after the precedent of secularised Prussia.[1] The natural antagonisms of these states were intensified by events in Europe: the rise of Protestantism, the revival of the Papacy, the energy of the Jesuits, the schemes of Spain. Politically, there was the unsuccessful attempt to secure Sweden for the Counter-Reformation and the successful attempt to secure Poland. Religiously, the success in uniting Lithuania with the Latins—a movement which was supported by persecution and caused much bitterness—was balanced by unsuccessful attempts at the union of the whole Eastern Church. Besides all these disturbing factors, the influence of the Turks must not be forgotten; but in the latter part of our period the Sultans became mere figure-heads. The Christians under them enjoyed fair liberty, given for political reasons. The Patriarchs of Constantinople were recognised by the Sultan and paid him large sums on election, but they were liable to deposition for alleged disloyalty, and one Patriarch, the well-known Cyril Lucar,[2] was deposed and restored five times. These changes and this subserviency naturally weakened the power of the patriarchs and degraded Christianity.

The rise of Russia begins with Ivan the Terrible, whose energy, cruelty, and deeds of massacre, followed by fits of

Russia. Ivan IV (the Terrible), 1553–84.

penitence and devotion, recall the Frankish kings of old. He was great in war. He was victorious over the Tartars, but failed to gain a hold upon the Baltic. Ivan III had already declared himself the Protector of all Greek Christians, and his grandson, Ivan IV (the first to take the title of Czar), tried to realise this

[1] P. 159 *supra*.   [2] P. 472 later.

claim. The Jesuit diplomatist, Possevin—sent to gain him for Rome—was not very successful, and Ivan made political use of his country's growing wish for religious independence. The Metropolitans of Moscow had been originally either consecrated or approved by the Patriarchs of Constantinople. The Metropolitan of Moscow, Isadore, had supported at Florence the union with Rome, and returned (1439) as a cardinal and a legate, but he fell into disgrace through this action, and finally died at Rome. After the fall of Constantinople the Metropolitan of Moscow was consecrated at home. Russia thus became more independent, and the later union of Lithuania with the Latins met with no support in Russia. Ivan's treatment of the Church, however, was fitful and barbaric. Hearing of the piety shown by St. Philip, Igumen (or Abbot) of the Monastery of Solovetsky, he forced the Metropolitanship upon him; then, when the prelate remonstrated against his cruelty, he had false charges brought against him, cast him into prison and strangled him. Ivan burnt some churches and plundered monasteries, but he built others and endowed them. After a life of bloodshed and lust, redeemed by days of penitence and alms, he took the tonsure just before death and so died a monk. Russia, in its kings and its type of Christianity, its missionary successes, enthusiasm, and barbarism, carries us back to the Europe of the eighth century. Yet Ivan's reign had done something to strengthen Christianity. A Synod at Moscow (1551) passed the Stoglav, or Hundred Chapters. Monastic life was reformed, clerical property regulated, and the revision of the Liturgic books ordered. Some needed good was done, but the State held too much control over the Church.

Ivan was succeeded by his son Feodor (1584–98), but the real power lay with his brother-in-law, Boris Godonof, who poisoned Feodor's brother, Prince Demetrius, and was afterwards elected king (1598). Under Feodor, Moscow became the seat of a Patriarchate. The old number of five Patriarchates was held essential— The Patriarchate of Moscow, 1589.
Antioch, Alexandria, Jerusalem, and Constantinople; Rome, it was contended, had forsaken the faith, and Moscow should

take its place. The Patriarch of Constantinople—Jeremiah—plundered of all Church property by the Sultan, was on travel to collect funds, and happened to visit Moscow. His poverty and the prospect of help doubtless influenced him in consenting to the suggested new arrangement, which answered not only to the growing power of Russia, but to the needs of the Church. For Russia was, and proved herself to be, a capable protector of the followers of her faith. The political advantages to herself of this protection were obvious, but she was not the only one to gain. The Metropolitan Job was consecrated as the first Patriarch (23rd January, 1589). At the same time four bishops were made Metropolitans, and new Sees were founded. Next year the Patriarchs of Constantinople, Antioch, and Jerusalem, with about eighty other bishops, confirmed this change. An important step was thus taken, and as a result the Eastern Church was better able to keep its independence against Papacy and Protestantism. The Lutherans had shown a wish to approach the Eastern Church, as it seemed to them that their common opposition to the Papacy was a bond of union. Melanchthon sent to Joseph II, the Patriarch of Constantinople (1555–65), a Greek translation of the Augsburg Confession. But nothing came of it under this Patriarch, whose troubled lot illustrates the difficulties of the day. He excommunicated the Metropolitan of Cæsarea for visiting Rome to bring about union, but he himself was deposed by a Council for simony—a charge that flourished in the evil air of the Turk. Some years later, Jacob Andreæ and Crusius, professors at Tübingen, sent printed copies of the same confession in Greek, with letters and sermons upon it. Jeremiah II (1572–94), then Patriarch, replied with the criticism they invited; one of his letters, his *Censura Orientalis Ecclesiæ*; being very lengthy. In the Lutheran document he found statements to commend only upon regard for the Œcumenical Councils and the marriage of priests. All distinctive Lutheran views he condemned, and the Synod of Jerusalem (1672) long afterwards officially sanctioned this letter. A Lutheran reply could not draw the Patriarch into

The Lutherans and the East.

further controversy. The Eastern Church rejected Lutheranism and Calvinism as decisively as it did papal supremacy.

Although more than one Pope had failed to bring over Russia, and Boris Godonof claimed for Moscow both the Patriarchate and the name of "the true and orthodox Rome," events seemed to favour the cause of ·The false Rome. A pretender appeared in Poland, claiming Demetrius. to be Demetrius, son of Ivan. He joined the Roman Church and received the help of Sigismund III and the papal nuncio for political and religious reasons respectively. He promised to do his utmost for the Papacy if he gained the Russian throne. Boris was defeated, and died soon after. Demetrius became King (1605); but the arrival of his wife, a Polish princess, and a large company of monks, destroyed his popularity. The Swedish faction dethroned him, and after a struggle in which another Demetrius appeared, Ladislas, son of Sigismund III, became Czar. The struggle between Poland and Sweden for power over Russia evoked there a combined political and religious resistance. Bishops and clergy headed the people and bore the holy icons before them. They marched upon Moscow and drove out the Poles (August, 1612). Once more we seem to be in the Middle Ages. The House of Romanof was raised to the throne. Its The head, Philaret, Metropolitan of Rostov, was too old Dynasty, to rule, and so his son Michael, aged 16, became 1613. Czar, while he was brought from prison and made Patriarch of Moscow. The union of Church and State, peculiarly close in the Byzantine world, was thus specially close with the new dynasty. The organisation of the Church was strengthened and its tone raised. The power of the Patriarch was increased, and the clergy, who were allowed many privileges, were placed more strictly under his control. The Orthodox Church in Russia had not only saved the nation, but in doing so had identified itself with a power which was to grow beyond all expectation.

During the earlier years of the Turkish Conquest the ancient Church of Constantinople enjoyed a modified tolera-

tion from the conquerors.[1] The most prominent figure of the
seventeenth century in the East was Cyril Lucar.
This remarkable man, somewhat like Cranmer in
his receptive mind and in his national zeal, like him
too in a varied life and an unhappy end, was a
native of Candia and educated in Italy. In the course of his
travels he came to Geneva and developed a sympathy with
Calvinism. He became successively Patriarch of Alexandria
(1602) and of Constantinople (1621). His foreign experiences
made him anxious to raise the level of education at home, and
he helped this by translating the New Testament into modern
Greek; but he was also desirous of modifying the Eastern doctrines in a Calvinist sense. He had sent young men to European
universities, and he carried on a wide correspondence with
theologians (it was he who presented the celebrated Codex
Alexandrinus to Charles I); and he imported (1629) a printing-
press from England, a country which helped him with friendship and money. The politics around him were involved, and
his own course was not only far from straight, but also
troubled, for he was five times deposed and restored. His Confession, written in Latin (1629), and then in Greek, restated the
doctrines of his Church, with Protestant additions. On Justification by Faith he compromised; Transubstantiation he rejected. He affirmed the inerrancy (or infallibility) of the
Scriptures, the existence of only two Sacraments. He rejected
Purgatory, and upon the Holy Eucharist he was Calvinist.
The authenticity of the Confession has been doubted, but
without much reason, and it fairly represents Cyril's position.
He had many enemies, and much diplomacy, Jesuit and English, centred in his removal or support; and (1638) he was
charged with disloyalty to the Sultan and strangled on board a
ship. A Synod at Constantinople, under his successor and
enemy, Cyril of Berœa, afterwards condemned him, as did
other Synods at Jassy and Jerusalem. Metrophanes Crito-
poulos, whom he had sent to study in England, where he had
been supported by Archbishop Abbot at Balliol College, and

*Cyril
Lucar,
c. 1572–
1638.*

[1] See Vol. V of the *History of the Church Universal*, ed. Hutton, *The Age of Schism* (London).

in Germany where he had published at Helmstadt a strongly Calvinist creed of his own, joined in his condemnation, changed his own views, and afterwards became Patriarch of Alexandria. Cyril of Berœa, who was strongly inclined to the Roman Church, if indeed he did not belong to it, perished a year later, just as Cyril Lucar had done. His successor, Parthenius, was strongly anti-Latin. Thus the changes and struggles of the Reformation influenced the East.

The same wish to put forth confessions and catechisms prevailed in the East and West. With labours of this kind is connected the name of Mogilas, a soldier of noble birth, educated at Paris, who became a monk and is called the father of Russian theology. He was Mogilas, 1647. chosen (1632) Metropolitan of Kiev. To strengthen his Church against all attacks he composed (1640), in the form of a catechism, the *Orthodox Confession of the Catholic Apostolic Church*. It was revised by a Russian Synod at Kiev and a more general Synod at Jassy (1643), at the latter of which Meletius Striga, Metropolitan of Nicæa, corrected and reshaped it; it was afterwards signed by the Eastern Patriarchs. From Russia there thus came forth the general creed of the Eastern Church. Mogilas also wrote (1645) a *Short Catechism* and corrected the office books, adding explanatory notes upon them. His interest in general learning and his labours rank him with the great Western leaders of the day. The East was unhappy and disturbed, backward and conservative, but these epithets are far from summing up its history. It had to face keener foes than had the West, and yet the West has often dealt hardly with it, forgetting its troubles, which gave it scanty time for such constructive work.

This document is in three parts with an Introduction, arranged in question and answer. Starting from what an Orthodox and Catholic man should hold and observe in order to gain eternal life, in the The Orthodox Confession. First Part it explains Doctrine at some length, in Part II it expounds the Lord's Prayer and the Beatitudes under the head of Hope, and in Part III under that of Love the Ten Commandments. It was thus both practical and theoretical, and also lengthy enough to give a connected view of theology. It is said to have been meant as a counterblast to the Protestants and the Latins, but it had a positive aim of its own.

Through the ignorance of copyists and the introduction of printing, the text of both Bibles and Liturgies had become **The Liturgic Books.** corrupt and discordant. As early as 1520 a learned corrector had been brought from Mount Athos and set to work in Moscow at correcting the Sclavonic Bibles. The Synod of 1551 had affirmed the correction of service books to be needed, and thus the East felt the same needs as the West. But in the West greater movements cause us to forget that many a process which we ascribe to them, such as the revision of books of prayer, was natural and inevitable. The fulfilment of the task was left, however, for Nikon, a great **Nikon, 1605–81.** ecclesiastic and patriarch under the Czar Alexius (1645–76). Nikon was upright, devout, and scrupulous in life and worship, with much of the strength and grandeur of the great medieval Popes. It was not unfitting that after he had fallen into disgrace one of his monkish admirers should dream of an enlarged and strengthened Russian hierarchy with Nikon as its Pope. This celebrated man, sprung from a peasant stock, had entered a monastery at the age of twelve; but he returned home to close the eyes of his grandmother, married, and became a parish priest. Some years later his children died, his wife took the veil, and he himself began a new and more rigorous monastic life (1625). His strength of character and his rigour made his career a troubled one, but at length he became Igumen of a monastery at the mouth of the Onega. In 1646 he met the Czar Alexius, who was youthful and needed an adviser; devout and careful in worship, and therefore able to appreciate a conservative reformer like Nikon. The Czar made him his friend and promoted him rapidly. He became archimandrite of the monastery where the Czars were buried, Receiver of Petitions (an office which gave him political importance) and (1649) Archbishop of Novgorod. After three years' active friendship and service in Church and State he became Patriarch (1652). He had so far worked along with a Czar like-minded with himself.

He now began a new career, doing for Russia what Laud did for England, attempting reforms akin to those of Trent, and at last falling in a struggle against the State. But his story falls outside our period.

The Reformation period was thus for the Church in Russia, as in the West, a time of stress and change; a growing national and social life made new demands upon her; she started from a level lower than did the Church in the West; she had to struggle against ignorance and inertness rather than against perverted energy and speculation, but she more than kept her place and her hold upon the nation's life. She was affected by the troubles of the West, but she was able yet to mould the destinies of the East.

The new life that stirred in the Church soon carried its zeal into wider fields. The discovery of the New World both opened up new lands and revived the spirit of Christian enterprise. The Society of the Jesuits Missions. was peculiarly active and self-sacrificing, but the older orders ran them close. No period saw more beginnings of great missions, but Europe, as in the old Crusading days, most unfortunately carried its quarrels into its new battlefields. It was not only that religious controversies often thwarted missionary efforts, that the religious divisions of the Old World were reproduced in the New, but also that political feuds also reappeared there. Nothing is sadder than the quarrels of Spanish and French in South America; nothing is sadder than to see the intolerance of the Inquisition leading to cruelties like those of Menendez in Florida. France, like England, had conceived the idea of giving religious discontent an outlet in America, and the result was that Huguenot colony in Florida which the Spaniard Menendez destroyed. Philip II endorsed his official's report of the slaughter, "as to those he has killed, he has done well." In the English colonies the religious divisions of home were reproduced, and those who had claimed tolerance for themselves failed to show it to others; too much, moreover, was left to chance and private enterprise, and the neglect of the episcopate, due to the State, but not remedied by the Church, was a grievous error. These are the evils which it is easy to see; on the other hand are the heroisms and martyrdoms, as well as the quiet persistence of unrecorded effort so easy to overlook.

The Papacy made many attempts to bring about union with the lesser religious bodies. For the Maronites a college was founded at Rome to educate their clergy. In 1522 a division took place among the Nestorians of Persia—an off-shoot from the Partiarchate of Antioch—now commonly called Syrians or Assyrians. Rival bishops, Simeon Barmama and John Sulakas, were elected, and the latter to gain support paid allegiance to Rome, which his successors, who moved to Ormia and under the title of Mar Shimun kept their jurisdiction, preserved until the eighteenth century. This body is well known in England, as the Assyrian Christians. The other body, which also offered allegiance to Rome (1607) and whose "Catholicos" or Patriarch lives at Mosul, is now the Uniat Church of Chaldæa.

Among Eastern bodies. Nestorians.

The Copts of Abyssinia had fallen on evil days of Mohammedan persecution, and Queen Helena as Regent sent to Portugal for help. The next king, David, procured the consecration of a Portuguese, John Bermudez, as Metropolitan, whom Paul III afterwards not only confirmed, but also made by his own authority Patriarch of Alexandria. The Emperor Claudius, however, in more settled days, quarrelled with Bermudez and sought a Metropolitan from Alexandria. The Roman obedience was all but lost when (1557) a Jesuit Mission was sent, one member of which, Oviedo, became Patriarch. Civil wars followed, in which finally the party of the Emperor and Jesuits were victorious. The Emperor Seltan-Segued (1626) joined the Roman communion, after Gregory XV sent a Portuguese Jesuit, Mendez, to be Patriarch, and communion with Alexandria was broken off. But the extreme rigour of the Mission, and the proscription of Monophysitism under pain of death, led to rebellions. The Emperor proclaimed liberty of conscience, and his son Basilides expelled the Latin Patriarch and the Jesuits. So as the Abyssinians sang, "the sheep of Ethiopia were

The Abyssinians, 1525-1632.

476

delivered from the hyænas of the West," and the Copts of Abyssinia and Alexandria were reunited. Negotiations through the Jesuits under Paul V with the Coptic Patriarch of Alexandria led to nothing.

The congregation *De Propaganda Fide* founded by Gregory XV (1622), brought unity into the control of missions and placed them under the Curia's direct care. This was a natural result of the new position given to the Papacy at Trent, and the system proved successful in practice, both in control and the administration ganda, of funds. Isolated and badly directed efforts are apt to die away and leave no results. But here there was something very different; the organisation was made continuous, and its growth carefully guarded. Much of the success of the Roman missions is due to this admirable organisation. Under Urban VIII (1627) the *Collegium Urbanum* was founded for the education of missionaries of all nations, and thus the plan of seminaries already used in European dioceses was utilised for the mission field. Once more the monastic orders proved their vast usefulness. Its first foundation was due to the generosity of a Spaniard, Vires, a papal official, but other donors enriched it with special gifts for different lands. Urban VIII (1641) placed the institution under the control of the Propaganda. It is worth noting that the Greek College, founded at Rome by Gregory XIII, had opened the way to those efforts in the East which have been noted, and the definiteness of aim thus illustrated was not long in making its mark.

The New World had been divided by the Pope between the Catholics of Spain and Portugal. Religious impulses were mingled with commercial. Dominicans and Franciscans followed the traders; in some cases, as in North America, they went before them. In the East Indies the Portuguese founded the first bishopric at Goa (1534), made an archbishopric (1557). For some time the work was mainly among the immigrants and the Nestorian Christians, until S. Francis St. Francis Xavier, a splendid example of missionary zeal (1542), led other Jesuits thither, he afterwards visited Travancore, thence he passed to Japan (1549), and started towards China, on the threshold of which he died (December, 1552). His labours had been apostolic and unwearied, and his last words were from the Te Deum, "In Thee, O Lord, have I trusted, let me never be confounded." His converts were numbered by thousands, but their edification had to be left to others. Not so much his permanent success as his disregard of self and his burning zeal made him a pattern missionary. In Japan 600,000 natives became Christians, but a change of policy by the Government (1612) led to fierce persecutions and many martyrdoms. Even thus early the problem of how to treat native customs and religions presented itself, and some Jesuits erred on the side of accommodation to such habits, as did Nobili in Malabar and Ricci in China. A keen dispute between Dominicans and Jesuits on the rightfulness of accommodation to native customs arose, which was submitted for settlement to Gregory XV (1623). The learning of the missionaries, especially in mathematics and astronomy, it may be noted, was greatly in their favour and impressed the peoples.

In America the evils of the slave trade (1506) greatly retarded the growth of Christianity, and the worst features of the Spaniards showed themselves in their treatment America. of the natives. These were assigned to different owners as servants (*repartimientos*) under condition of Christian instruction, but this condition was soon disregarded: the natives were said to be of different natures and useless to be taught. Paul III had to state (1537) that he held them fit both for the Catholic faith and for the Sacraments. The Spanish rulers, it is true, had set before themselves the Christianising of their new subjects. The laws for their protection, civil and religious, were admirable, but the King was far away, and there was every temptation and opportunity for unjust officials. Peculiar powers in ecclesiastical matters had been granted to the Spanish Crown by Pope Alexander VI (1501). The King became legate in America, the Church in Mexico was self-governing under the Crown, and there was no appeal to Rome. The Christian missions in these countries had thus local coherency and independence, but their connection with the

Crown and the administration wrought harm as the monarchy decayed. Six Jesuits under Nobrega set out to the Portuguese colony of Brazil (1549); a bishopric was founded at San Salvador (1551), and many of the natives who had been cannibals became Christians. The most unusual of the missions, however, was that in the Spanish colony Paraguay. Here the earliest missionaries, Franciscans (1580-2), were not very successful, but the Jesuits (1586) quickly identified themselves with the country. Philip III (1602) allowed them to form a native state which they administered for him; he allowed them to exclude all other Spaniards from their "reductions." The Jesuit rule was patriarchal, but worked for happiness and prosperity, although not fully developing the native character. Disputes, however, arose between them and neighbouring bishops; the Jesuits were charged with being too intent upon amassing wealth, just as later they were charged with too great intentness upon trade: the sequel of this curious ecclesiastical state lies, however, beyond our period. In Mexico and in the West Indies the work of Las Casas was untiring, Bartolome and remarkable not only because of his interest Las Casas, in the natives (for that he shared with others), but 1474-1566. because of the principles upon which it was based. He had gone out (1592) to Hispaniola (San Domingo), and like other settlers he owned slaves. Touched by the preaching of some Dominicans he received holy orders. One day a Dominican refused him absolution so long as he held slaves; he thought the matter out and threw his whole restless energy into the fight against slavery. He found opponents in some of the government officials (although Cardinal Ximenes and Loaysa, confessor to Charles V and afterwards Archbishop of Seville, were exceptions), in some local bishops, and generally in the colonists. Charles V himself inclined to Las Casas' view; in 1517 and again in 1542 he legislated in its direction and gave Las Casas an official right to protect the Indians. The position which Las Casas took up was that personal liberty was inalienable and that slavery was against the gospel. It was a noble protest to be raised in an age when cruelty was common, and it had a great effect. Missionaries however then had to face the same problems as now; relations with colonists of their own race and with natives of others were difficult and delicate. Missions supported by a State are greatly handicapped and it was often difficult for others to exist.

In New France the mission work was very different, but its full history lies outside our period. Priests accompanied the early settlers, and even when the Huguenot de Monts went to Port Royal (Annapolis, N.S.), he had with him, besides his own ministers, Catholic priests for the savages (1604–5). Little, however, was done in Acadia until the Jesuits came (1611), and even their success was limited by the ill-fortune of the colony. Champlain brought into the St. Lawrence district four Récollets, as the French Franciscans of the strict observance were called. They ministered in lives often lonely along that great river and far west to the Ottawa. Jesuits came to their help (1625), and after the temporary loss of Quebec to the English (1629) the Society went on working after its restoration (1632). From their station at Sillery (1637) they founded missions on the Kennebec southwards towards New England (1646), and the mission at Tadoussac, the centre for the fur trade, stretched its influence up the Saguenay and east to Labrador. Other stations were Three Rivers (1633) and Montreal (1641). Récollet brethren (1620–3) undertook missions to the Hurons, and afterwards (1634) the Jesuits joined them in what was to be the greatest mission of New France. But, like the colonists, the missionaries suffered from the all-devouring Iroquois, and cruel, lingering deaths often ended lives of privation. Finally the missionaries were driven back, first to the Isle of Orleans, and then to Lorette, near Quebec. Out of twenty-nine missionaries seven had been martyred. The Iroquois destruction seemed to have ended their work and to have blocked the way for missions to the colonies. But a new day dawned when these very Iroquois (1653–5) opened negotiations and invited the missionaries to their territories. No missions have a story of more self-sacrifice; none have a more romantic background, in the land itself and in the Indian races who dwelt there, than have those of New France. The

Canada. The Jesuits ; the Récollets.

French Canadian Church of to-day by its high standard and its influence upon daily life has shown itself worthy of such a past.

By their extent then and by their spirit the missions of the period had wrought much and promised more. The evils of European life, its intolerance and its divisions, appeared in them, it is true, but so did a devotion and Results. a love of Christ, which, although often hidden, ever beat strongly in Europe too. The Catholic Church must be judged, sometimes to its loss, but here to its gain, by its missions as well as by its life at home, by its extensions as well as its intensity.

CHAPTER XVII

THE PAPACY AFTER TRENT

AFTER the Council a marked change came over the Papacy itself. There were Popes of varying character, some spiritually minded, others of a political stamp. But even these last did their
The duty conscientiously, for they, like the bishops in
Papacy. Germany, were affected by the spirit of reform. Nepotism of the old style was impossible. No Pope was able to form a principality for his family. Paul V and Urban VIII enriched their families, the Borghesi and Barberini respectively, and papal nephews were used for the management of affairs, but that was all. The Popes attended to their office with a sense of responsibility, and were careful in choosing bishops and in guarding ecclesiastical interests in different lands. The great objects of papal policy were no longer purely territorial, although even in this way the reigns of Clement VIII and Urban VIII were fortunate in the gain of Ferrara (1598) and Urbino (1631). The Popes had high ecclesiastical, although not necessarily spiritual aims, such as the recovery of lands lost to their religious leadership. Subsidies intended to benefit Catholicism were lavishly given; to provide these heavy taxation was put upon the Papal States. Nearly all the offices of State were sold and fresh offices were created mainly for their sale. Loans secured upon certain taxes were raised. Sixtus V, who systematised the finances in this way, had by these means saved a large sum, but Gregory XIV quickly spent much of it. In the Middle Ages the financial system of the Papacy had been the mainstay of commercial Europe, filling the same place in it that the great financial houses hold to-day. Hence many interests had centred in the Papacy, and those who were discontented with the organisation of society had drifted into opposition to it. For this reason, among others, opposition to the Papacy was so often found in cities, where commercial conditions were changing

rapidly. In France, for instance, even more than elsewhere, anti-Papal movements and the Huguenot party were products of the cities, and were bound up with the rise to wealth of new classes. The Popes almost alone among medieval rulers had always command of ready money, and this had secured their power. Thus too at the beginning of modern Europe the wealth of the Popes, and the subsidies they could afford, made them important and able to reach their aims. Pius V in his organisation of the league against the Turks, which resulted in the victory of Lepanto (1571), recalled the days of his namesake Pius II, and Gregory XIII continued the policy. We should not forget that Mohammedanism was a living dread, as is testified by one of the most touching of devotional books, *The Sufferings of our Lord Jesus Christ,* by Father Thomas of Jesus, an Augustinian friar. He had been taken prisoner by the Moors in Africa (1578), at first suffered long imprisonment himself and then ministered to other prisoners, whom his devotions were meant to help. Stories of imprisonment like his and that of St. Vincent de Paul were common, and the Papacy therefore did well to try to rouse Europe to this war of defence. For this political leadership the Papal States, now consolidated, gave the Papacy the means. Accordingly the Papacy became in the period after the Council of Trent distinctly a political force. The Popes, with the exception of Innocent X (who was disgraced by his subservience to a greedy sister-in-law), were diligent and conscientious rulers; Pius V actually reached the official standard of saintship, being canonised by Clement XI, and Gregory XIV deserved it.[1]

The organisation of the Curia was of great importance, but its history, upon which much light is now being thrown, is difficult to trace. A memoir of the year 1574 by Giovanni Carga, one of the officials, illustrates the organisation and also its confusion. In the earlier Middle Ages the business habits of ecclesiastics were better than those of laymen. After a time secular business became better organised and secular men showed more business capacity. Hence there often resulted disorder in ecclesiastical

Organisation of the Curia.

[1] v. Ranke, *Popes*, Vol. II, pp. 229 *seq.*

matters as compared with those of civil life; hence too came the tendency to employ ecclesiastics less in business of State. The history of religious as compared with civil jurisdiction, and the government of ecclesiastical (and notably of the Papal) States, are proof of this. There was accordingly much that was haphazard in the organisation, and there was much confusion, especially, perhaps, in the preservation of documents. The arrangements of the Curia in the earlier Middle Ages excelled those of temporal courts; in our period they fell behind. Martin V first assigned to the secretaries a fixed stipend. Calixtus III and Paul II reserved the title of Secretaries for six officials. Innocent VIII added to the existing six no less than twenty-four colleagues, these offices being saleable and forming a college. We also find a domestic secretary whose office grew in importance and was very confidential. Leo X founded a Secretaryship of Briefs, and at a later date we find three secretaries of Briefs, along with six for Italian letters. These officials formed a kind of college, apart from the domestic secretary. Then above all and in a unique position we have the Cardinal Superintendent, who is not merely a confidential minister, but has a real effect upon the papal policy. There had thus been a process of differentiation between what we may call affairs of State—with which the Secretary and the Cardinal Superintendent supported by many lesser officials had to do—and the affairs of business and routine belonging to the colleges, such as that of the secretaries of Briefs. Business had vastly increased, and the Curia, although its intelligence is often praised, had not met the increase with the wisdom shown by some temporal courts. There was much confusion, and the use of offices as means of raising money by their sale led to their useless multiplication and made reform or simplification difficult, if not impossible. On the one hand there were interruptions of policies, changes due to the varying personal habits and wishes of Popes, and these worked along with the conservatism and tradition natural to departmental work on the other hand, to prevent reform and cause confusion.

When Pius IV had closed the Council of Trent his labours

seemed to be ended. In his later years he somewhat disappointed the more earnest spirits who wished to carry out the reforms at once. The chance of his death (9 December, 1565) was used to elect in Pius V a Pope of a different stamp, sternly and severely religious, Micheli Ghislieri, a Dominican *Pius V, 7 Jan. 1566– 1 May, 1572.* and a former Inquisitor in Italy, whose life after his appointment as Cardinal, as it was when Pope, had been simple and ascetic. He brought to the Papacy something of the spirit of the Inquisition itself. Muretus could praise him as " thinking life unworthy unless spent in purging heretics of their errors or the world of their presence." At the same time he carried out reforms both in the Curia and in the granting of dispensations. It was his task to translate the ideas of Trent into facts of life. The Breviary and the Missal belong to his rule, and the sentiment of the day was thus consolidated before passing away. In his dealings with sovereigns, however, he was contrasted with Pius IV, who had skilfully drawn rulers to his side. He ordered the bull *In Cœna Domini* to be read every Maundy Thursday (whence and not from its opening words *Pastoralis Romani Pontificis vigilantia* it gains its name) in all Christian lands. But as this bull, besides excommunicating all heretics and Protestants, claimed for the Church all its medieval privileges, many states refused to obey the command, and thus international relations were disturbed. His spirit which infused rigour into the politics of France, the Netherlands and England, was thus far from wholly admirable; but his piety was undoubted, and he gave unity and coherence to the papal policy (1 May, 1572).

His successor, Cardinal Buoncompagni, was by nature an easy-going ecclesiastic, who yet, under the influence of the new spirit, was fairly rigorous about discipline. By a sound instinct he systematised the government of the Papal States, checking the banditti and forcing the nobles to justify their titles to their lands; thus a surer basis was gained for the support of external undertakings. The old system of government by the advice of the whole College of Cardinals assembled in *Gregory XIII, 13 May, 1572– 10 April, 1585.*

consistory was proving ineffective; either its members were divided in views or else one or two able men gained undue influence; furthermore, in a world of changing states and policies, pressing matters came up oftener than of old. Hence the method of Congregations was systematised, and under Sixtus V was further developed. There now existed seven of these: for questions arising out of the Council; for the Turkish War; for affairs of Germany (this Gregory himself added); the Inquisition; the Index; the Segnatura or final tribunal, regulating all lower courts and granting graces; the Consulta, which was administrative. As special objects became important or lost their importance, new Congregations were formed or old ones ceased; and Sixtus V added to the number, making fifteen in all, among them being those for the University of Rome (the Sapienza), for liturgies and new bishoprics. Gregory's new permanent Nunciatures for Styria, at Munich and at Cologne have been already mentioned and were a natural development of the old organisation, used not only for ecclesiastical business, but for diplomacy. All these institutions made for watchfulness, and built up a more effective centralisation, essential if the conciliar reforms were to be carried out. His intense interest in colleges in Germany to which he was an unwearied benefactor, has already been noted. But his reform of the Calendar (1582), which by the older system had become so disarranged that Saints' Days were falling out of their old seasons of the year, is for ever bound up with his name. Religious dislike hindered its adoption. It was taken up by the Protestants in Germany in 1699; and then in Switzerland, 1701; England, 1752; Sweden, 1753; France, Holland, Catholic Germany and Switzerland (1583–4), Spain and Portugal adopted it from the first (1582). By this needed change Gregory meant to claim the Pope's ancient leadership of Europe, but division had gone too far for agreement to exist even in science.

The Gregorian Calendar, 1582.

The exhaustive means adopted by Gregory XIII to raise funds had brought discontent and trouble upon the Papal States, and the Pope himself became feeble and unhappy. His successor Felice Peretti, Sixtus V, was above all things strong and full of belief in himself. Sprung from a peasant family, he had joined the Franciscans as a boy, and had risen rapidly by his talents. He had formed friendships with men of the deepest saintliness, Cardinal Caraffa, SS. Philip Neri and Ignatius Loyola, and also with men of learning. As Cardinal he had begun at Milan an edition of St. Ambrose, which was afterwards printed at Rome. As a preacher, a theologian, an adviser of the Curia in theology, and, under Pius V, as Vicar-General of the Franciscans, a stern reformer, he became famous. At Venice, where he was Councillor to the Inquisition, and in Spain, whither he accompanied Cardinal Buoncompagni for the investigation of Carranza's case (p. 255), he gained experience of affairs and made some enemies. Pius V (1570) made him a Cardinal (di Montalto). He utilised a period of disgrace under Gregory XIII, who disliked him, for building and for study. He was interested in Canon Law as well as Patristics and the Bible, as he testified by a work upon Gratian and encouragement of Cherubini's *Bullarium Romanum*. He owed his election as Pope to his own strictness and the self-control shown in his retirement. The story of his age (he was sixty-four) and infirmities being his recommendation, and then being suddenly cast aside, is mythical. His rise had been rapid and great, and he had scarcely learnt the limitations of events. He was something of a fatalist and more of a believer in himself. There seemed to be no limit to what he, or rather the Papacy could do. Hence he formed vast plans, and miscarried in his political schemes alone. His vast schemes of buildings, the additions to the Vatican, the library, were all part of a great scheme. Pagan Rome was to be overshadowed by Christian Rome, once more the capital of the world, rising out of the past and making use of all possible knowledge and learning. A printing-press was added to the library, and here the Septuagint and Vulgate were to be printed. Sixtus was not very friendly to the Jesuits, whose rules and very name he had changed, although his successores revised his Decrees, but he understood, as they did, the need of enthusiasm and the work that had to be done. He was not inclined to stand upon prerogative;

Sixtus V, 24 April, 1585– 27 Aug., 1590.

he closed up some differences of a smaller kind, and abolished the Congregation upon ecclesiastical jurisdiction, from which many disputes had arisen. He reaped the reward of peace with his neighbours and could devote himself to greater aims.

His European policy was not successful. It was marked by largeness and firmness, but he hardly knew what he could **His foreign policy.** effect and what was beyond him. He was driven into the arms of Spain, the power of which had the same religious aims as himself, and yet a power which, from its tendency to dictation and its influence in Italy, was most distasteful to him. France was distracted, and he was averse from treating with the future Henry IV; he therefore supported the League and Spain. Against England he joined with Spain, and the defeat of the Armada was a bitter although not an unexpected grief to him. But there was a difference of view between the Pope and Spain: the Pope did not wish to destroy France as an independent state; Spain wished to make France subordinate to itself; and hence in regard to France the two allies were not always closely at one. When Venice ventured to congratulate Henry IV of France upon his accession, seeing in him a possible help against Spain, Sixtus was furious against the Republic, and would at first hardly listen to the explanation given by the special ambassador from Venice, Leonardo Donato; but as he gradually cooled down he veered round towards Henry IV, who might after all become a Catholic. High as was Sixtus' idea of the papal power, he had a lack of perseverance in his firmness. His very face is that of a dreamer rather than that of a man of action. He was always consistent in his ends, but not always so in his way of reaching them. Thus he now received the French envoy with friendliness. But when Olivarez, the Spanish envoy, protested against this action (March 1590), urging the excommunication of all the followers of Henry IV and his utter exclusion from the throne of France (which the Pope had previously declared in 1585), further backing this request by a threat of renunciation of allegiance to the Pope, Sixtus yielded and for a time inclined to Spain. His ultimate policy was yet uncertain, and he was vacillating from one side to the other when he died (27 August,

1590). So much had Spain become identified with orthodoxy that the suspicion of unorthodoxy which had floated around Sixtus in earlier years had grown stronger in his later years, when he worked less well with Spain. He had been a great, if not a wise, Pope, guided in policy by ecclesiastical interests, but his feelings and views were perhaps in the first place ecclesiastical rather than religious. Europe was passing into a period when it was easy to treat religion as a principle which dictated leagues and excited wars rather than moulded life and hallowed souls.

The relations between France and Spain made the conclave of election momentous. And yet unlike the old days in which France and Spain had formed parties in the College of Cardinals, the divisions now found there were made on a new principle. The family and the "creatures" of the late Pope—that is those cardinals whom he had "created"—formed one party; his opponents, those who had suffered from him or been passed over by him, formed another. The cardinals had now more freedom and their divisions were used politically. As a rule the party opposed to the late Pope carried the election; thus changes of policy, temporal and ecclesiastical, became almost a rule. In the present case the creatures of Gregory XIII carried the election of the Genoese Cardinal Castagna (Urban VII), a strong supporter of Spain. The new Pope lived only twelve days, and on his death Philip II named seven cardinals whom he would accept; no others would be agreeable to him. Some of these names were rejected by Cardinal di Montalto, grand-nephew of Sixtus. In the end both parties agreed upon Cardinal Sfondrati, Gregory XIV (5 December). Cremonese by descent and attached to Spain; a mystic of deep devotion, he threw himself heartily into the cause of the League and Spain, commanding all Catholics to stand aloof from Henry IV and sending subsidies to his enemies. The fate of France seemed settled, for a determined Pope able to use the treasure saved by Sixtus V could have done much; but after a rule of only ten months Gregory XIV died (15 October, 1591).

Urban VII, 15 Sept., 1590.

Gregory XIV, 5 Dec.

The new Pope (Fachinetto), Innocent IX, again one of seven nominated by Spain, was Spanish in sympathies, but old and sickly. After two months he too died (29 October–29 December, 1591). These repeated conclaves had resulted in an understanding between Cardinal di Montalto and the Spanish faction, but it was clear that a strong and energetic Pope was now a necessity. It was supposed that Cardinal San Severina (Santorio) would be elected. He was suitable in years and strength, an extremist of the Spanish faction, but a man feared for his severity. On the very point of the election some of his supporters hesitated, and the conclave fell back upon Cardinal Aldobrandini, a "creature" of Sixtus V, but one to whom the Spaniards had no objection. He belonged to a learned Florentine family, had been a Roman official and a nuncio in Poland. He was diligent and regular in his devotion and his business. Under him for thirteen years the Papacy at length enjoyed a steady rule of unbroken tradition.

Innocent IX, 1591.

He let himself be formed by his office instead of moulding it to himself. His treatment of the French question was cautious and wise. The reception and recognition of Henry IV came about gradually, and thus the danger of separation on the part of France was avoided. This alone would have marked his Papacy, but it had other claims to importance. The publication of the Vulgate has been mentioned, alterations in the Breviary (in which Baronius wished great changes), and the controversies on grace, for which the Pope appointed the Congregation *de Auxiliis*, also marked this reign. Clement was unwearied in all his duties, so much so that the congregations sank in importance and the advice of the cardinals was often collected privately instead of in a body. He was also a priest of deeply spiritual life and regularly heard confessions. His rule was thus open to few objections, personal or political, and these years of peace did a work of the utmost importance. He left the Papacy secured from Spanish control, not only through the influence of France, but by its own stability and power.

Clement VIII., 20 Jan. 1592– 5 March, 1605.

The growth of a French party in the Curia, a natural result

of the conversion of Henry IV, was shown by the election of
Cardinal de Medici, Leo XI, a connection of the
French royal family, but he only lived twenty-five   Leo XI,
days. Upon his death Baronius, who had been   1–26 April,
made a cardinal by Clement VIII, was nearly   1605.
chosen, but Cardinal Borghese (Paul V) was   Paul V,
elected (16 May). The new Pope was of a legal   1605–21.
mind, as so many Popes from Gregory XIII onwards had
been. He had few enemies and had seen little of active life,
although versed in the quieter business of the Inquisition and
papal offices. He enforced rules upon others, even upon the
cardinals—as he did upon himself. Any rights or powers
which he conceived to belong to the Church he, unlike Sixtus
V, was determined to enforce. His Papacy was therefore
marked by struggles with states, and the famous contest with
Venice—the old rival of Rome in ecclesiastical and political
matters—was of more than local or temporal importance. For
Venice, like France, had contributed much to the history of
thought, and had filled a great place of old.

The endeavour to carry out the Decrees of Trent, no less
than the new spirit of ecclesiastical zeal, drew the Papacy into
dangerous currents. Very often diplomacy had   Venice
smoothed over the difficulties that met it, but   and the
Paul V was firm rather than diplomatic. Naples,   Papacy.
Savoy, and Genoa, with all of which he was embroiled in disputes as to ecclesiastical rights or jurisdiction, yielded to his
insistence. But Venice was a different state. Here some churchmen had been tried for disgraceful crimes before the ordinary
courts. By a new law a veto was claimed upon the erection of
new churches in its territory; the acquisition of property by
the Church was also restrained. To all these irritations were
added boundary disputes with Ferrara (now a papal de-
pendency), and complaints against exemptions granted by the
Pope from payment of tithes. There had always been an anti-
papal party in Venice, and these discussions made it more
active. Its leader, Leonardo Donato (who had been ambassador to Rome under Sixtus V), was elected Doge in 1606.
To Pope Paul's demand for the cession of the ecclesiastical

offenders mentioned above and the repeal of the new law, the Venetians replied by demands that all bulls published in their territory should be first approved by the State, that only Venetians should be appointed to their benefices, and that no taxes should be levied in their state for the Curia. Venice had lost something of its old importance as a state, and quarrels with it might therefore seem of little significance; but the ability of her statesmen and the literary power of her writers still remained, and these added to her old traditions made this incident seem large. Fra Paolo Sarpi (1552–1623), Provincial of the Servites, proved an advocate of peculiar skill. His *History of the Council of Trent*, in spite of some defects, partialities, and errors, is perhaps the most considerable work of our period. This contest with the Papacy was only an incident in his life; an occasion for stating his views rather than an influence that formed them. The religious types of mind favoured by Spain and the Jesuits were distasteful to him; the political power of Spain, the theoretical claims of the Papacy, were so also. He had much sympathy with thought in France, and was also somewhat English in his ideas. This explains the curious fact that his *History of the Council of Trent*, brought to England in manuscript by de Dominis, Bishop of Spalatro, should have been published there. He had composed other works and had borne a part in other controversies; but this, his chief work, written, of course, with a bias, is the key to his position. His thought was a criticism of all that the Council had resulted in. He was in ecclesiastical politics much what Machiavelli had been in civil, a critic and an assertor of far reaching theories by his negations rather than by his assertions.

At the age of fifteen Sarpi had joined the Servites and had soon become known for knowledge of all kinds, theological, historical, and scientific. At sixteen he disputed at Mantua on the authority of Councils and the Papacy; at twenty-four he lived in Milan under Cardinal Borromeo; when twenty-seven he became Provincial of his Order and was ordained priest. As Procurator-General of his Order he lived for three years at Rome and had redrafted in a strict sense the rules of his Order. Thus he had been

Sarpi's life, 1552–1623.

brought into touch with the best and most influential Church movements of the day. At Venice, moreover, political thought and experience were almost a tradition. The little society of "the Ridotto Morosini," where he knew the leading Venetians of his day, combined the best traditions of the Renaissance and of Venetian statecraft. In knowledge, insight, and character Sarpi was a typical Venetian product. It is especially worth note how he turned to study fully the great peculiarities of the Gallican Church with respect to beneficiary matters and particulars of royal jurisdiction; its history and its theories had a great fascination for him, as the alliance of France had for his State in politics. English thought was also of great interest to him. Sir Henry Wotton (envoy to Venice) and Dr. William Bedell (afterwards Bishop of Kilmore) were close friends of his; from the latter indeed Sarpi (himself according to Wotton "one of the humblest things that could be seen within the bounds of humanity") said he had learnt more of theology and practical religion than from anyone else. These things define the positive views taken by Sarpi; negatively his strong dislike to the Jesuits and his abhorrence of the Pope's temporal sovereignty and claims to control over states were equally strong. When the Papacy demanded that Venice should withdraw the law she had passed and asserted that the election of a Doge by excommunicated citizens was invalid, the pride of Venice and her leading adviser (for Sarpi was now theologian adviser to the State) was touched upon the tenderest point. The Pope (17 April, 1606) solemnly excommunicated all the authorities of Venice if they did not speedily recant; and the territory of the Republic was to be put under a strict interdict. The Doge replied by a proclamation that the Republic owned no superior in temporal powers but God, and that the clergy, regarding the sentence as void, would carry on their cure of souls and worship of God. The papal commands were disregarded except by the Jesuits, Theatines, and Capuchins, and these, unable to obey the State, left the territory for Rome. It was even proposed at Rome to carry on war against Venice. Had France and Spain been ready, as some of their subjects wished, to take sides in it,

Papal Attack on Venice.

the war might have happened, and the last interdict of a medieval pattern might have led to a papal war of a similar type. The two great powers, however, mediated. Venice delivered up the ecclesiastics it had tried, and adopted a form of words which the Curia could take as a withdrawal of offensive laws, but she firmly refused to readmit the Jesuits; Spain would not defend the Society, and therefore the Pope yielded the point. A further dispute arose as to the need for absolution, which Venice, not recognising any offence as having been committed, regarded as superfluous. In the end it was privately pronounced. Thus the Papacy was on the whole victorious. But the method of the quarrel, conducted by the Papacy in medieval forms, showed how far and how greatly the world had changed; the dispute, while showing the strength of the Papacy in practice, had called forth a clear assertion of anti-papal views. The diplomatic triumph was a defeat in the history of continuous thought.

The well-known attempt on Sarpi's life—significant, like the assassinations of the time, of a bad state of morals—involved persons near the Pope, although there are no grounds for accusing him. But Sarpi (himself an advocate of assassination) might feel justified in considering the wound inflicted *stilo Romanæ Curiæ*. The other charge, however, against the Pope—which Sarpi himself pressed home and which was generally credited—of unduly enriching his own family, the Borghesi, must be held true.

Paul V died 28 January, 1621, and Gregory XV (Ludovisi), elected (9 February) as his successor, was too old and infirm for his work and had to leave most of it to his cardinal nephew Ludovico. But he was able to do something for peace in Italy, and uniting France and Spain (8 July, 1623). His successor, Cardinal Barberini (Urban VIII), was ardently French in sympathies, partly because he had been a nuncio in France. He was strong and indefatigable, and the objects of his interests were the Church and his family. He more than provided for his own in regard to wealth, and his foundation of the Congregation of Immunities showed his

Gregory XV, 1621–3. Urban VIII, 6 Aug., 1623– 29 July, 1644.

wish to guard the privileges or rights of the Church. But on the whole he owed more to chance than to wisdom. He was swimming in a current of French influence under Richelieu that was stronger than his stroke. War between the Habsburgs and France was inevitable, and Richelieu meant it to be so. The unity within one political league of the Catholics in her communion was no longer possible for Rome, since Richelieu carried to extreme the old French policy of leagues with Protestants against their Catholic rivals. And finally all political rivalries were swallowed up in the Thirty Years' War. The political inclinations of the Pope were now of more importance than the religious. His sympathy with the Emperor, who was doing so much for the restoration of Catholicism, was slight in comparison with what he felt for France in its purely political schemes. Urban would not regard the German War as one for religion, and was unwilling to spend money upon it. Spain protested against the Pope's indifference and great indignation was professed. The interests of Catholicism were not now sacrificed, it is true, to consideration of the mere Papal States, but to those of wider politics. And the final result of such a policy was that the Papacy was shut out from the Peace of 1648, and its protest against it was useless. No theoretical claims were yielded or withdrawn, but the lessening of its political importance affected the general influence of the Papacy. It was driven back upon purely spiritual weapons, and the restricted area of the Catholic restoration was largely due to the papal policy. The Popes of the earlier Counter-Reformation might have had visions of a world restored to their leadership. To the Popes of the seventeenth century this was impossible, largely because of the mixture of temporal with spiritual aims in the papal policy. Urban VIII, busied not with theological science or ecclesiastical law, but with plans of fortifications and temporal cares; no ascetic, but frankly a man of the world; a temporal ruler above all, himself typified the change. The spiritual influence of the Counter-Reformation had reached the Papacy, and then seemed to lose its power.

The next Pontificate, that of Innocent X (Pamfili), illustrates the temporary lessening of papal power. He was elected after a

Innocent X,
16 Sept.,
1644–55. stormy conclave, in which the Barberini family made a hard fight for power, and finally, by an agreement with Spain, agreed upon a choice adverse to France. Feminine quarrels in his family, and the corrupt influence of his sister-in-law, degraded his court. An inquiry into the administration of the Barberini resulting in heavy fines; small Roman politics upon a background of Italian difficulties and alliances; filled his reign. The Pope was becoming more and more a small Italian sovereign to whose office spiritual duties were annexed.

The attitude of the Church towards learning had in many ways changed. She no longer dreaded the study of classics,

The
Church
and
Learning. and the Jesuits fostered them in schools. The Bible, Patristics, and theology were also closely studied. Early (1507–22) in our period, de Vio (Cardinal Cajetan) had revived instruction on the somewhat neglected Aquinas, and combined with it Biblical study, carried out in his commentaries with great freedom of criticism. Afterwards in the middle of the century theological study lapsed. In Ingolstadt after Eck's death (1543) there was only one theological professor, and in Cologne theological lectures were discontinued. But the influence of the Jesuits, who as a rule preferred Aquinas to Peter Lombard, revived the study; Petavius, Maldonatus, and Estius were distinguished names amongst them. The great Dominican Melchor Cano (†1560) had systematised the study, and the equally great Jesuit Bellarmine (1542–1621) developed it in a specially controversial sense. Another Jesuit, Cornelius à Lapide, collected Patristic interpretations in his commentaries and so popularised them. In a like way ecclesiastical history was studied. Love of the past, as well as the needs of attack and defence, had forced the writers of the *Magdeburg Centuries* to collect material, and their rival Baronius followed suit. The critical insight of all these writers often fell below their good intentions, and Bellarmine, for instance, had to criticise Baronius sharply in his treatment of records and events. But these writers laid an admirable foundation, and criticism eventually followed collection. The same love of the past was seen in England, notably in the case of Archbishop Parker: a mere enumeration of names, large as it might be made, is of little use, but it is easy to underrate these writers and the work they did.

The study of science lagged far behind that of theology and history. Copernicus (1473–1543) dedicated his work *De Revolutionibus Orbium Cælestium* to Paul III, but his view that the sun was the centre of the universe Science. seemed strange and even absurd. Luther thought him a fool. The Congregation of the Index suspended his book until corrected and pronounced his view a contradiction of the Scriptures. Kepler (1571–1630), whose belief in astrology stands in strange contrast to the insight of his celebrated laws, took a step in advance and began a new era. He assumed the theory of Copernicus, but his relations with many theologians, and especially with the Jesuits, were friendly; both when professor at Gratz and when elsewhere he had a great reputation. The Copernican theory itself, however, was still assailed. Galileo Galilei, professor at Padua, attracted much Galileo notice by actual observations, and in his published 1564–1642 works (1612) he too argued upon the Copernican system, professedly as a hypothesis, but with a real belief in it. The Inquisition condemned the teaching of the system and forbade him to support it. He submitted for a time, but when Urban VIII, a friendly ecclesiastic, became Pope he once more advocated this hypothesis (1623). A little later he gained the Pope's approval for a scientific dialogue, but the Jesuits now took up the case against him, as the Dominicans had done before. During the process, every detail of which has been discussed in an extensive literature, he abjured the system, but was punished by a not too rigorous imprisonment for some years. The dealings of the Church with science have often been unsatisfactory, and in the case of Galileo there were special and general elements that combined to cause difficulty. The general element was the dislike which the Church in its imperfect wisdom has so often shown to novel scientific theories or truths. This spirit has shown itself often and in other cases, and has not been peculiar to the Inquisition. Then to this element were added special elements peculiar to the time and the surroundings. There was a claim made to control investigation and restrain its freedom; this claim was partly founded upon the medieval supremacy of theology, and partly upon the increased rigidity of control caused by the Tridentine reforms. A reconsideration of the relations between theology and other sciences, a wiser limitation of the Church's sphere, might have lessened this special difficulty; but the very hardening and purification of the late reforms made the Church claim with greater insistence, and in fear of results, this wide control of thought. Then too there was the special machinery through which these principles of thought had worked. It was hardly to be looked for that the Roman Church, working through the Index and the Inquisition, should admit a freedom on the part of science which it would not grant generally. The Index and the Inquisition might plead definite reasons for their existence and might serve some useful ends, but even so much depended upon the spirit that inspired them. Large institutions are called into existence for some definite end; they soon come to consider their working more important than their end and forget their limitations; their action then becomes hurtful. It was so here. The treatment of Galileo forced men of science either to conceal their views or to treat as a tentative hypothesis what they knew to be a truth. Either course led to unreality and to an assumed antagonism between religion and science. After two centuries this position was quietly given up by the Roman authorities. The details of the case, although much discussed, are less important than the principles involved; the latter may have some additional interest as part of the great debate upon papal infallibility, but the advocates of this condemn the judges of Galileo for having treated as definitely closed a theological decision which admitted of reconsideration. But the claim for freedom of thought and investigation raised a wider question than that of infallibility. Theologians erred, as they have often erred, and this weakened their advocacy of the truths they had to guard. The great problem of the Church was how to train, control,

and utilise new currents of thought. In many ways she failed
to solve the problem. The Council of Trent had wrought
many reforms, but it had taken up an attitude which made the
correct handling of scientific questions more unlikely than
before and less free than in the Middle Ages. The temper of the
Roman Church further made it difficult to abandon this attitude
when once it had been taken up, and there was at hand
machinery for rapidly and firmly carrying out a decision once
taken. The decision thus became of an importance almost
critical.

A comprehensive view of the whole period (1503–1648)
shows how much depended upon the Popes and their action.
Men in high position, most of all those in high
spiritual position, cannot escape moral judgment Summary.
for the use of their responsibilities. The Popes have often
enough fared strangely in this respect. If we regard the Reformation as a movement either hostile to the Papacy or
springing up wholly apart from it, it is hard to see how the
Popes, differing as they did among themselves, can be blamed
for agreement in opposing it. If the great aim of the Reformation as a whole was to overthrow the catholic conception of the
Church it was the duty of all who valued that conception to
oppose it. But that is surely a narrow and unhistorical view of
the Reformation itself. A wide and deep movement in favour
of change, seeking to carry out higher ideals and to cast out
evils, to read a fuller meaning into old forms of life and to
enter into the many-sided heritage of a world that was growing
new, this is the movement with which our period began. It
was a movement that was general and most of all was found
within the Church itself. That in some ways it became
hostile to the Church, departed from its unity and created
bodies opposed to it, was partly due to errors on the side of
those who became leaders of the movement, partly to political
causes that intensified division and used it for ignoble ends, but
partly at any rate to the leaders of the Church, and to the Popes
or their advisers above all. They failed (as it is so easy for
leaders of the Church to fail) to place themselves at the head
of a great movement, to direct forces that under wise guidance

might have saved the world, but which, wrongly directed, only intensified its evils. The Popes of the Renaissance hardly took life, or even religion, seriously, and it was long before the currents of reform rose to the papal throne. The delayed reform at Trent was the too tardy answer to the call for wise leadership in a Church revived and eager for its work. Historical criticism in these days has risen above the vulgar view which condemns a Pope as such, or for fulfilling the ordinary duties of his position. But it leads us in most cases to a condemnation of a different order. With some exceptions the Popes of the period are condemned not as bad men or faithless priests (for such they were not), but as those who did not rise to the height of their responsibilities, or who fastened their eyes upon an unessential or minor attribute of their office when they should have pursued the great aim placed before them—the deepest, widest spiritual welfare and working efficiency of the Church of Christ. From many charges and imputations impartial criticism may free the Papacy as an institution and the Popes as men. But a higher test remains unsatisfied. It is something to avoid the negation of evil, but that alone is not enough: there must be the highest fulfilment of all possible activities for good.

And the same has to be said of the Church at large. Here again historic criticism casts aside the mere enumeration of abuses as if they were all that existed. We have to recognise the existence of great improvements, to trace out movements for education, reform, and the cultivation of piety; we meet great social movements and individual types of excellence. The existence in these movements and along with them of serious defects must not blind us to the good they contain. However sad the union may be, we see even in our own days the combination of fanaticism with piety, of intolerance with a high morality; we too mourn separations from the Church and divisions within it. The Church has often had much to learn from those outside her pale, or from those she has been unable to keep to herself, and she can never escape responsibility for those who have left her fold. Combining these considerations, we shall probably form an estimate of the Church during the

Reformation very different from that which is popular and current. But even with this estimate we have to admit with sorrow that the Church failed to meet as it should have done all the needs of the age; that it failed to control and guide forces that were capable of mighty good, and which because of their force stood specially in need of guidance. The history of many of those movements which drifted away from the Church, their excellencies and their defects, their possibilities even with their fundamental errors, is the best commentary upon what they missed in not receiving such guidance and upon the failure of the Church in not giving it. The Church must always be judged not only by what it did, but also by what it left undone. It must be measured by its ideal as well as by its deeds. It is a hard judgment, but it is the only possible one to pass upon the Church. The nations should walk in the light of it, and therefore its light should not be dim. The kings of the earth should bring their glory into it, and therefore its spirit should be purer than theirs. But that was not always the case. It is a heavy responsibility for an age to bear when it has to face the charge of creating separations wider and more fundamental than that between the Eastern and Western Churches—wider because not purely local, more fundamental because of the questions they raised. And yet there seemed something almost accidental in the way in which they were raised; political influences made use of their existence and prolonged it into permanency. Situations badly handled led to estrangements of temper; tempers wrongly indulged were regarded as principles. It is sad to see how politics and policies could eat away the Church's life and sap her strength. To those who see in her mission the salvation of the world it is painful to see errors and evils within her, piety and excellence severed from her or even fighting against her; to see a new division within the Catholic Church, and bodies of men sincerely religious estranged from her. But although the age of the Reformation has its own great sins and short-comings to answer for, it has its own special difficulties to plead, its own ideals to hold forth. There are currents within the great stream of the Church's life that tend in varied ways.

There are tendencies in the lives of men that make for ends that are not their own. Within the Church, and without the Church the paradox is true, both of her life and the lives of men, testing them in their parts as well as in their whole—" *Qui non est mecum; contra me est.*" " *Qui enim non est adversum vos, pro vobis est.*"

NOTE ON JUSTIFICATION BY FAITH

As the medieval doctrine is often misunderstood, and as the different views then taken make it misleading to speak (as is often done) of one consistent medieval view, it needs discussion. Whatever interpretation be given to S. Augustine's teaching, and perhaps it is not always consistent, he laid unique stress upon (*a*) God's sovereignty and free grace; (*b*) a change of life in man. Justification deals with the relation between God and man; hence it is fundamentally connected with the Incarnation of Christ, with its effects (if one can so speak reverently) upon God Himself, and its effects upon the sinner. Here is room for two opposite kinds of treatment. The same relation is also closely connected with Regeneration, which places man in a new corporate relation to God, and with Sanctification, by which he grows nearer to God in thought and deed. A difference of view would also arise according as each of these terms is held to imply one definite act or (more rightly) a process. Salvation, again, may be regarded as a definite end or as a process. Here again there is much room for divergency. It may be said at once that the medieval theologians connected Justification with Regeneration—the entrance into the divine society with all its attendant duties and privileges. Luther, on the other hand, rather regarded Sanctification as a state of holiness than as a continued process. The medieval Catholic view laid stress upon life in the Church with its sacramental life and its growth in grace—salvation, or " the being saved " ("a state of salvation"), as a process. Luther, on the other hand, regarded salvation as a gift given once for all, conferred with Justification.

The history of the doctrine may be given shortly as follows: St. Anselm's *Cur Deus Homo?* brought in a new conception of the sinner's reconciliation with God by Christ's death, spiritualising the conception and discarding once for all the theory of a ransom paid to the devil. The idea of a vicarious sacrifice he modifies, by holding Christ's death to be the inevitable result of his stand for righteousness against sin. The solidarity of mankind underlies his view but it is tinged by the legal conceptions of his day. From this work one leading line of opinion was derived. Abelard was the founder of another school; he made the reconciliation of the sinner with God depend upon the moral disposition towards each other of the two parties in the reconciliation. His conception was mainly ethical, while that of St. Anselm was partly legal; but Abelard's conception easily lent itself to abuse through its possibly lower view of God's grace. According to Abelard, God's condescension to man by the sending of Christ, and Christ's surrender of Himself to death, awaken in man a bond of love towards God, and this is the ground for the forgiveness of man's sin. St. Anselm's theory, which was far from being so dominant in the Middle Ages as is often supposed, applied to all mankind, while Abelard's applied only to the elect. Abelard's was also subjective. He made the purpose of the Incarnation the illumination of the world by Christ's wisdom and the stimulation of it by His love.

In these views two conceptions are to be distinguished: Christ's merit which passes on to man, and His satisfaction rendered to God. Peter Lombard (followed by later medieval writers) developed the idea of Christ's merit and rather suppressed that of His satisfaction. He further developed the legal conception, but he also enlarges the idea of redemption from the power of the devil, which comes about by Christ's death awakening in us a love of Him which extinguishes sin. Upon this side he follows Abelard. The view of St. Thomas Aquinas is more important, and if perhaps incomplete in itself, yet recognises all these factors, and also that of satisfaction. But he too lays most stress upon the idea of Christ's merit, although he also speaks of the love of Christ awakening love in us. Thus in his teaching the two ideas of (*a*) Christ's satisfaction rendered to God and (*b*) the merit of Christ's sacrifice are insisted upon. But his whole conception starts with the grace of God working in us. And the grace works in the sphere of

Christ's Church. It is not going too far to say that the reformers, on the other hand, started with the idea of a moral external law which has to be satisfied, and was satisfied by Christ.

The conception of Duns Scotus, differing in some elements, yet came to much the same result as that of Aquinas. But Duns made the Incarnation of Christ only of use to the elect, and also independent of the fall of man and not intended (as in the debased Puritan conception popularised by Milton) merely as an after-thought to the fall. So he did not consider the sufficiency of Christ's death (which extended to all the world) to exceed its efficiency (which only covered the elect); he made the two equivalent, both affecting the elect only. Aquinas made Christ's sufferings be borne by Him as the Head of the Church; Duns rather regarded them as being borne by Him as an individual. The many and varied elements in the medieval doctrine can thus be seen, and a varying stress might be laid upon any one element. But it cannot be too strongly insisted upon that its statement always involved the idea of God's grace, that it recognised the facts of life, and above all the existence of Christ's body upon the earth. The doctrine is apt to become colourless and to lose its vast significance in relation to the corporate life, if the living union of the believer with Christ is made a purely individual concern apart from life in the Church. Justification in the medieval view means that God by His grace makes righteous the unrighteous man. God's grace and man's activity are united. According to Aquinas, the habitual grace implanted in man by God's gracious act is Justification. To a sinner this is wrought through forgiveness of sin, and involves it. With Duns, on the other hand, the forgiveness of sins is treated as being less important; he lays more stress upon the idea of man's activity.

A further complication was brought in by the Nominalists, who made merit *de congruo* have a value in itself towards gaining *gratium primam*; or the first gift of grace. With their mere purely human view of everything the Nominalists asserted the efficacy of human merit. Hence came endless discussions which had this in common, that they exalted man's power at the expense of God's grace. Thus they obscured the idea of God's grace, they lessened the significance of sin, and in both ways departed from the medieval Catholic position.

It has been shown most clearly by Denifle that Luther's interpretation of the "righteousness" or "justice of God" (Rom. i, 17) was not novel. Luther depicts himself as depressed by understanding "the justice" here to mean "the formal or active justice" by which God punishes sinners, this being, as he says, the current interpretation. Then it came into his mind that it meant rather the "passive" justice by which God communicates His own righteousness to man, and he became happy ("the just shall live by faith"). A series of citations given by Denifle show, however, (1) that Luther's predecessors from St. Augustine had taken this view, which he describes as novel, and (2) that he himself in his commentary upon Romans had made the fullest use of their works and shared their view before this supposed change in his opinions. Intentional untruth on Luther's part might be supposed, but a preferable explanation is defective memory and the difficulty of correctly describing one's past and one's development over a distance of changing years.

Ritschl, in the work mentioned on p. 171–2 (which is largely used in this note), protests vigorously against describing any theologian, who happens to lay stress upon the grace of God or the need of faith upon the part of man, as a " Reformer before the Reformation." He is, I think, hardly fair to the German mystics, with whom the school of Ritschl and Harnack have little sympathy, but this protest is undoubtedly right (see Ritschl, pp. 99–120).

The doctrine of Justification before the Reformation was not so simple, certainly not so corrupt and foolish, as it is sometimes stated or assumed to be. Scholastics and Reformers had a different basis: medieval theologians assumed the Church, the corporate life; the Reformers, on the other hand, were much more individualistic, if not purely so. What was excellent in the teaching of the Reformers was the stress laid upon God's grace and man's sinfulness; here they reaffirmed the best elements of the medieval teaching—elements which the Nominalist teaching and the abuses of indulgence had overlaid.

What was defective in the Reformers' teaching was the neglect of the corporate life and the separation of faith from life itself. The Tridentine Decree endeavours to recognise, if not adequately, yet in some degree, all these elements. The Reformation shifted the point of view, as may be seen not only in Lutheranism and Calvinism, but in the Anglican Article XI; in discussing any view—St. Paul's, the medieval, the Tridentine, the Anglican, or the Reformer's—both the point of view and the balance of the details, should be considered. Nothing but harm is done by the isolation of parts of a statement from the whole. In doctrine so much depends upon the point of view and the context of an assertion. Luther, for instance, enlarged St. Paul's "justification by faith" into "justification by faith *alone*": taken along with the dangerous assertion that man's salvation depended upon his own conviction of its truth this expression became mischievous. But taken by itself as a reaction against the importance assigned to works it might be merely a strong assertion of the supremacy of God's grace as against works, and further, it rightly lifted the whole process from the sphere of man's activity into that of spirituality. But, like the assertion of salvation by works, it was too likely to limit its view to man and man's own view of his position, for it made man's feelings the central point, hence in the end it shut out the conception of God and His grace which it was originally meant to emphasise; this result was hastened by the disregard of life within the Church; united to individualism the phrase became licentious, and, as a party badge under other conditions when it was not necessary to insist upon the subordination of works, the phrase lost all value. The Anglican Article XI adopts the Lutheran phrase, but uses it in the proper sense stated above, viz. that of an emphatic contradiction of salvation by works, upon which Article XII enlarges. The Anglican Articles start from the Reformation point of view, and assert the primitive doctrine in the light of Reformation controversies. Their caution is seen in their brevity and in their omission of all but essential points; they leave aside medieval speculation and Protestant theories. The Tridentine Decree, on the other hand, is cautious in its fulness of balanced statement and in its attempt to express all that was true in medieval theology while condemning Protestant novelties. But to reach this end and yet to satisfy all parties in the Council was very hard. I have used the term "the mediating theologians" to describe the school of Pflug and Gropper. Their view, however, was not really formed by a combination of that of the Reformers and of the medieval Catholic Church, but by a reassertion of elements found in the medieval view itself; these elements—broadly the assertion of God's grace and the sinfulness of man—they asserted with limitations and conditions disregarded by the German Reformers. The Jesuit view, which emphasised a side of the doctrine forgotten by the Reformers—the need of righteousness on man's part and the existence of his free will—might be derived either from the Catholic medieval view or from the Nominalist statements. But here again the truth it embodied was liable to exaggeration, and could easily suffer from the non-presentation of other elements along with it.

Man was absolutely evil; the best of his deeds, the whole of his goodness was evil in itself, and the more Luther drew nearer **Luther's** to God and the more he felt the horror of sin, the **Problem.** more troubled his conscience became. This was his great trouble: the gulf between his conscience and what he wished to be became deeper as he grew. He tried to bridge it by his doctrine of imputed righteousness, and this imputed righteousness was to be realised by man's conviction of his salvation. A quickened conscience meant the intensification of the internal struggle which the Catholic doctrine quieted by its assertion of God's grace and Christ's pervading love. Luther found it in man's conviction of his salvation. The solution of his enigma, the attainment of the long-sought peace, he found by combining imputed righteousness with his assurance of his own salvation. Unlike the medieval theologians he almost forgot in the sight of Christ's death the rest of His work; unlike them, again, he made no attempt to reconcile reason with religion. And his solution of his enigma, indeed, removed his doctrine from the sphere of reason. It became something almost unreal and remote from actual life or simple piety, but it was capable of being taught in sermons and in writing with force and power. So it became the platform of the Lutheran Reformation, the foundation of the latter "Protestant Scholasticism." Later generations looked on it as the foundation of theology and of the inner Christian life, but it was not, to begin with, the motive power of the Lutheran movement.

INDEX

INDEX

The references are to pages throughout. Saints are entered under the initial letter of their names.